# Solving Social Dilemmas

# Solving Social Dilemmas

## Ethics, Politics, and Prosperity

Roger D. Congleton

OXFORD
UNIVERSITY PRESS

# OXFORD
## UNIVERSITY PRESS

Oxford University Press is a department of the University of Oxford. It furthers
the University's objective of excellence in research, scholarship, and education
by publishing worldwide. Oxford is a registered trade mark of Oxford University
Press in the UK and certain other countries.

Published in the United States of America by Oxford University Press
198 Madison Avenue, New York, NY 10016, United States of America.

© Oxford University Press 2022

Library of Congress Cataloging-in-Publication Data
Names: Congleton, Roger D., author.
Title: Solving social dilemmas : ethics, politics, and prosperity / Roger D. Congleton.
Description: New York, NY : Oxford University Press, [2022] |
Includes bibliographical references and index.
Identifiers: LCCN 2021058982 (print) | LCCN 2021058983 (ebook) |
ISBN 9780197642788 (hardback) | ISBN 9780197642801 (epub) | ISBN 9780197642818
Subjects: LCSH: Social choice—Moral and ethical aspects. | Social ethics. | Civil society.
Classification: LCC HB846.8 .C657 2022 (print) | LCC HB846.8 (ebook) |
DDC 302/.13—dc23/eng/20220304
LC record available at https://lccn.loc.gov/2021058982
LC ebook record available at https://lccn.loc.gov/2021058983

DOI: 10.1093/oso/9780197642788.001.0001

1 3 5 7 9 8 6 4 2

Printed by Integrated Books International, United States of America

This exchange society and the guidance of the coordination of a far-ranging division of labor by variable market prices was made possible by the spreading of certain gradually evolved moral beliefs which, after they had spread, most men in the Western world learned to accept. These rules were inevitably learned by all the members of a population consisting chiefly of independent farmers, artisans, and merchants and their servants and apprentices who shared the daily experiences of their masters.

They held an ethos that esteemed the prudent man, the good husbandman and provider who looked after the future of his family and his business by building up capital, guided less by the desire to be able to consume much than by the wish to be regarded as successful by his fellows who pursued similar aims.

—Hayek ([1979] 2011, pp. 164–165)

# Contents

# Contents

# Preface

Hayek's explanation for the emergence of extensive networks of exchange has been accepted by a subset of economists and historians, but it is by no means the most common explanation for economic development. This may be because no scholar has taken the time to analyze the ways in which rules of conduct can directly and indirectly affect the extent of commerce. This book undertakes that task.

It is an important project for several reasons. First, it fills an important lacuna in economic, political, and social theory by explaining how ethical dispositions tend to affect the scope of market activities. Second, it helps to explain the variety of "market outcomes" witnessed through time within and among societies. Market networks can be extraordinarily productive systems for satisfying material wants and generating the free time necessary to pursue other interests, but not all markets are equally productive—a variation that requires an explanation. Third, the analysis suggests that other explanations such as scientific advance, urbanization, and capital accumulation are secondary rather than primary causes of development. Fourth, a better understanding of the root causes of prosperity can improve our current policies—for example, avoiding laws and regulations that tend to undermine the ethical dispositions that have contributed to and continue to support our prosperity.

Prosperity and progress are surprisingly recent phenomena, and the continuation of our past two centuries of exceptional economic history is by no means guaranteed. If some ethical dispositions facilitate economic development, others must have long impeded it. To fully understand the roles that ethical dispositions play in economic development requires exploring both dispositions that support extensive trading networks, specialization, and innovation, and those that do not. It also requires explaining how such dispositions can emerge and be sustained. It is not ethical behavior per se that generates economic growth, but rather a small subset of principles and rules of conduct deemed ethical that do so.

This book suggests that solving critical social, economic, and political dilemmas is the key to prosperity, and it turns out that many of the rules that we consider ethical or moral tend to solve or ameliorate those dilemmas. A subset of the most critical dilemmas have long been solved or ameliorated, as necessary for the emergence of attractive sustainable communities. However, overcoming the dilemmas most critical for economic growth was achieved far more recently—most likely through changes in norms that produced quite different notions of the "good life" and "good society" in the past few hundred years.

As a consequence, general prosperity emerged for the first time in human history, and commerce became more central to the lives of more people than it had been at any previous time in human history. The commercial society had emerged.

## The Commercial Society

Contemporary adult lives in much of the world are centered on the "workday" and "workweek," which are the periods in which one "hires oneself out for wages" and accepts the duties associated with such an exchange. Most food and clothing are purchased from large economic organizations, rather than homegrown, homespun, or homemade. We keep our savings at banks or at brokerage firms, rather than under the mattress or buried in the backyard. "Vacations" are special times when we can leave our jobs and focus on activities other than ones we are paid to do. When on holiday, we take our cash and credit cards to a destination of interest and rent or purchase the necessities of life—the roofs over our head, meals, transport, and perhaps a few more frills than usual. Leisure has come to mean the absence of job duties rather than a time of rest, recuperation, and reflection. Indeed, those who pursue active forms of leisure while on vacation often engage in greater physical efforts while on holiday than when at work. They may climb a mountain, take long walks through city streets, undertake a bit of remodeling, or catch up on yard work at home.

The pattern of life associated with the commercial society has greatly increased the material comfort and longevity of most persons participating in the complex networks of voluntary transactions that make up the world's great networks of exchange, production, and innovation. Those highly productive networks emerged in the past three centuries—which is a long period in terms of a human life, but a short one in human history.

Commerce itself is not new. A small subset of humanity has traded and consumed products from all over the world for several thousand years. Goods from ancient China are found, for example, in the tombs of Egyptian kings. Trading families and centers of trade have existed even longer than international trade, but relatively few people outside capital cities and seaports devoted much of their lives to producing goods for sale. Markets existed, but for the most part, they were elite phenomena in which only a relatively small number of urban artisans and shippers participated. The vast majority of persons during human history were hunter-gatherers, farmers, or farmworkers. Their cycle of life was tied to the seasons rather than to a workweek determined by commercial organizations. Farmworkers and servants were paid mostly in kind with "room and board" rather than money. And most farm communities were largely self-sufficient, producing most of the necessities of life for their owners, employees, and renters.

Subsistence farmers and their associated communities were not truly parts of a commercial society, even in cases in which they sold a bit of their produce and occasionally purchased spices from the Far East, olive oil from Italy, or a few pieces of hardware or jewelry from urban artisans. Most of the goods traded were produced by nearby small family enterprises: village potters, spinners, millers, carpenters, smiths, and farmers. Village tradesmen were often participants in local commercial societies, in that they used their barter and money receipts to acquire most of their necessities of life, rather than producing them themselves; but village networks of exchange tended to be local for the most part, rather than regional, national, or global. And relatively few people were primarily engaged in such activities. Indeed, rather than trust to market networks, the largest farms often included such artisans among their employees.

Even in relatively commerce-oriented regions of the world, most people lived in the countryside, and most of their "productive hours" were devoted to agriculture and household production, rather than market-oriented activities undertaken at the behest of large commercial organizations.

## The Recentness of Progress

That ancient seasonal agricultural-based pattern of life largely disappeared in the West during the past two centuries, as urbanization increased and as farming became more market oriented. Rather than the long-standing 90:10 (or more) ratio of farmers to persons employed by commercial enterprises, the new division of labor generated a ratio of 10:90 (or less) during the twentieth century, with fewer and fewer farmers. The vast supermajority of persons began "hiring themselves out for wages" to both large and small organizations devoted to producing things and services with the aim of selling them to others at a profit, rather than consuming them.

By historical standards, this was a relatively swift and radical change, far faster than the emergence of agricultural communities 8,000 to 12,000 years ago, or regional governance and writing, which took place over many centuries in the period after agriculture emerged. In just a few centuries, extended markets and specialization replaced self-reliance at the level of farms and farm villages as the main source of food, clothing, and shelter—first in what came to be known as "the West," and then in much of the rest of the world.

That great extension of trading networks and specialization was generated by a series of increases in the net benefits that could be realized from market activities. Many of these were associated with technological innovations such as improvements in agriculture and shipping. Others were, arguably, generated by changes in organizational and institutional innovations. A third causal element involved changes in culture—in particular, changes in the ethos of persons living in the communities where commercial societies emerged.

The ethical explanation for the rise of commerce is the main focus of this book. The first two parts of the book demonstrate how internalized rules of conduct can increase the efficiency of market networks both directly through effects on the behavior of market participants and indirectly through effects on the rate of innovation and the nature of government policies. Social dilemmas are commonplace, and without solutions to them, progress is blocked—or at least greatly slowed down—and it turns out that changes in internalized rules of conduct are the most likely explanation for such solutions. Part III of the book provides evidence that changes in internalized norms did in fact provide greater support for trade and production in the period leading up to the great acceleration of commerce in the nineteenth century. Other shifts in norms helped induce public policies that encouraged or at least did not greatly impede the process of commercialization. And it turns out that much of the observed change in norms occurred at the period just before the acceleration of economic development occurred.

Normative dispositions were not the only factor that induced shifts from agrarian lives to commerce-based ones, but they were arguably the most important factor. Indeed, they were often prerequisites for the others. Subtle changes in ideas about character, life, and society played central roles in all the processes through which commercial societies emerged. Solutions to social dilemmas reduced what economists refer to as transactions costs, increased rates of capital accumulation and innovation, and induced changes in public policies that had long impeded economic development.

## Problems with Other Explanations

There are, of course, other possible explanations, but this book suggests that the other contributing factors were themselves consequences of changes in norms, rather than root causes of economic development. Advances in agriculture and mechanical, metallurgical, chemical, electrical, and aeronautical engineering all had obvious and tangible effects on possible modes of production, transportation, and lifestyles, which increased specialization and allowed many new products to be brought profitably to market. The steam engine, electricity, telephone, automobile, airplane, radio, computer, and Internet all had significant effects on the productivity of resources that could be focused on innovation, production, and exchange. However, it is clear that commerce did not expand solely because of technological advances.

Technology is, in principle, completely portable and can be applied anywhere in the world, but it was not widely used to extend commerce outside the West when it first emerged. Most of the world failed to take advantage of developments in engineering and large-scale organization during the nineteenth century, and so failed to commercialize during the nineteenth and early twentieth centuries. This was true of even relatively advanced and sophisticated societies such as Turkey and China. The mere invention of a "better mouse trap" was not sufficient to induce the world to beat a path to the Western door.

Nor is the cultural explanation for economic development intended to deny the importance of urbanization. Great cities are all at least partly dependent on food imports for their existence because urban residents lack sufficient space to grow enough food to sustain themselves. Trade, however, is not the only method for bringing food to towns and cities. The political elites of ancient towns and cities often controlled the surrounding lands and those farming them, and simply took what they needed as tribute, rents, payments for protection, or tax collection. It was only when food and other necessities were *purchased* from farmers in surrounding territories and from farmers in distant trading posts that significant trading networks emerged. And this change from extractive sources of wealth to more productive ones required norms, customs, and laws that supported voluntary exchange.

The relative importance of extraction versus exchange as a source of prosperity for the most famous capital cities can be assessed by comparing the size and wealth of those cities with nearby port cities. Such secondary, but still relatively prosperous places were normally far smaller and far less lavishly decorated with monumental buildings and palaces than capital cities. This observation implies that trade, per se, was less important than taxation and other methods of expropriation as an explanation for the prosperity of major cities that emerged around the home bases of regional, national, and imperial governments.

Urbanization is nonetheless an important event in the history of commerce. Many persons in cities were full-time participants in commerce, even in capital cities that were largely supported by tax revenues, tribute, and slavery. Thus, many of the norms, organizational patterns, technologies, and laws that support commerce emerged first in urban areas. Several ancient capital cities have survived and remain significant commercial centers today—Athens, Baghdad, Beijing, Byzantium, Cairo, Kyoto, Madurai, Multan, and Rome are examples. However, none of these ancient cities played a central role in the great expansion and acceleration of commerce that occurred during the nineteenth century. Urbanization alone was not sufficient to generate the prosperity associated with truly commercial societies.[1]

## Overview

This book provides a behavioral explanation for the rise of commercial societies. All communities confront an endless series of social, economic, and political dilemmas that have to be solved or ameliorated for social and economic progress to be sustained. Solutions require systematic changes in behavior. Without such changes, problematic equilibria continue, and progress is blocked or is far slower than possible. Hobbes ([1651] 2009) and Ostrom (1990) suggest that formal and informal rule-bound organizations (institutions) often emerge to address social dilemmas. This book is similar in spirit to those classic books, but focuses on a solution that is arguably prior to formal institutions, namely the internalization of principles and rules of conduct that directly affect individual behavior and thereby group outcomes.

Parts I and II demonstrate that a subset of such internalized rules—rules that are largely regarded to be ethical or moral rules—can directly and indirectly solve or ameliorate social, economic, and political dilemmas. They do so by altering the manner in which alternatives are evaluated. Ethical dispositions, for example, can ameliorate the critical problem of excessive conflict noted by Hobbes ([1651] 2009) and the communal resource management problem noted by Ostrom (1990) and Diamond (2005). They can also solve or ameliorate most of the other economic and political dilemmas analyzed by economists and public choice scholars.

The central claim of the book is not that commercial networks result from ethical as opposed to unethical behavior, but that some ethical systems

<hr>

[1] The association between governance, religion, and market cities suggests that tax and religious revenues provided the demand that supported relatively large cities, in effect subsidizing urbanization. These "capital" cities were larger than their commerce alone would have supported. Their exports (sales to others outside the cities) were smaller than their imports (purchases from surrounding farms and businesses). The other non-market revenues paid for the rest.

include rules that broadly support the development of extended market networks, specialization, and innovation. Others provide weaker support, solve a smaller subset of critical problems, or oppose economic development. Moreover, many norms have consequences that are context specific, and thus conditional in subtle ways. For example, a work ethic may facilitate productive activity in markets or support diligent efforts by government officials to expropriate all the social surplus generated. To be productive, a work ethic requires choice settings in which productive lives tend to be more rewarding than extractive ones.

This approach suggests that the extent and efficiency of commercial networks are not simply consequences of the considerations focused on in economic textbooks: production technology and tastes for goods and services—holding all other factors constant. Rather, it is largely the result of the factors being "held constant" for the purposes of simplifying the analysis undertaken in such textbooks. A good deal of statistical and historical evidence suggests that social and political support for or opposition to commerce has had major direct and indirect effects on the course and rate of economic development.

Although the scope of the book is ambitious, the analysis is undertaken with the simplest mathematical tools that are sufficient to demonstrate the logic of the argument. Parts I and II of this book use elementary game theory to demonstrate how ethical dispositions can overcome social dilemmas associated with life in communities, with economic dilemmas associated with voluntary exchange, team production, and innovation, and dilemmas that tend to make governments extractive rather than productive. An implication of Part I is that the ethical dispositions that ameliorate social dilemmas at least partially determine every community's customary law—the rules that all "good" people in a community follow. Part II demonstrates that ethical dispositions also largely determine how customary and other laws are enforced and the manner in which new laws are adopted. Honest, conscientious law enforcement can "top up" existing norms and thereby reinforce informal solutions to social dilemmas. New laws can also speed up the process of social evolution by addressing social dilemmas that remain unaddressed by a community's ethos.

However, governments are not "naturally" productive in either sense. In the absence of internalized norms and institutional arrangements that induce officials to advance the shared interests of citizens, the temptations to adopt extractive policies are too great. As a consequence, historically, most governments have been extractive enterprises. Such governments impede rather than facilitate economic development.

Part III provides evidence that ethical dispositions in the West became more supportive of markets and economic development in the period leading up to the great acceleration of commerce in the West. It does so using intellectual history—a history that, perhaps surprisingly, is partly empirical in nature, although this is neglected by most intellectual historians. Most ethical theories in the period of interest were grounded in a scholar's assessment of what the persons around them regarded to be ethical. And to persuade others that a new explanation or principle can account for ethical rules and sentiments required illustrations that readers would have found convincing. Thus, all but the most abstruse contributions to ethical theory between 1600 and 1900 are partly exercises in what would later be called social science. This empirical grounding of widely read philosophical work allows it to be used as a source of evidence about the mainstream ideas of a "good" life and "good" society in a scholar's time and place.

The authors who are reviewed were all widely read during their times (and thus taken seriously by their contemporaries). Most are still read today. Their conclusions and illustrating examples provide evidence that ethical support for lives devoted to commerce, material comforts, representative forms of government, and the rule of law generally increased in the period before the great acceleration in commerce of the nineteenth and early twentieth centuries. The stigma associated with careers in markets declined. And gainful employment, material comforts, and innovation gradually became indicators of the quality of one's life and character, rather than evidence of weakness, decadence, or other failings. The analysis of Part III parallels that developed by McCloskey (2006), although it uses philosophical, political, and economic texts as windows into cultural developments, rather than popular literature.

Among the many philosophical developments associated with commercialization, perhaps the most remarkable is that during the twentieth century, the extent of a society's commercialization (its gross national product or gross national product per capita) became the most widely used measure of the quality of life across continents, nation-states, regions, cities, and individuals. Prosperity had become not only part of a good life and good society, but its primary measure.

# 1
# Grounding Ideas and a Short Overview

## Introduction: How to Read This Book

The Preface provides the gist of the argument and reasoning undertaken in this project. This first chapter provides its foundational ideas. The book is organized logically from fundamentals to theories and from theories to supporting evidence. The choice settings are ordered into an analytical narrative and supporting evidence is provided in footnotes and toward the end of the book. Although there is an overarching narrative, the individual parts are all written to enable readers to "thumb through" the book to find the parts that they find of greatest interest.

Unfortunately, there is no single best order for all imagined readers. For readers who want to fully understand the foundations and reasoning of this book, Chapter 1 is the place to begin reading. It also provides a more detailed outline of the book than that developed in the Preface. Readers who are more interested in results than grounding assumptions may want to skip on to Chapter 2. For those who want to know how the argument fits into the existing literature before tackling the main text, the first appendix to Chapter 13 might be the place to start. Readers who want a bit of statistical evidence before digging into the theory might want to begin with the material surrounding Table 8.3 (in Chapter 8) and Figure 13.1 (in Chapter 13). For economists who are most interested in its direct economic implications, Chapter 3 is the place to start. Finally, when I use this book in class, I normally start with Part III, because few economic students have a sufficient background in ethical theories to appreciate what is meant by internalized rules of conduct without that material. That many different ethical theories can be used to assess the role of commerce in a good life and good society is not always obvious even to those familiar with mainstream Western philosophy.

## On the Use of Analytical Narratives

This book relies heavily on what are sometimes referred to as analytical histories. Analytical histories use sequences of real and imagined choice settings

*Solving Social Dilemmas*. Roger D. Congleton, Oxford University Press. © Oxford University Press 2022.
DOI: 10.1093/oso/9780197642788.003.0001

to provide a coherent outline of how we got from some point the distant past to another some years or centuries later. That approach is implicitly used in all historical accounts in order to condense and organize what must be related to readers in a manner that is likely to make sense to readers. However, the abstract nature of most historical narratives is likely to be less obvious to readers than the ones undertaken herein.[1]

Some simplification and abstraction are always necessary to reduce history down to book-length narratives. A complete diary of an individual person living an ordinary life takes many volumes to write down and would not provide much of interest to readers. As a consequence, the history of even single persons is normally told as a sequence of discrete events connected with short transitions. Most broader histories employ similar techniques. Many world histories emphasize periods of technological development: the Stone Age, the Agricultural or Bronze Age, the Iron Age, the Industrial Revolution, and the Modern or Information Age. Such technological narratives mark off various periods by major innovations in tools and materials that are presumed to have triggered a series of developments in social organization. They rarely use mathematical models, but it is clear that they nonetheless use abstraction to simplify and rationalize their historical accounts. The Iron Age did not appear overnight in one great leap forward.

Other historical narratives use political events, rather than technological ones, to identify periods or phenomena of interest. Many refer to the great empires of history and mark periods by the beginnings, reach, and ends of relatively large empires or societies. Others study a single territory and mark off its various periods by changes in its form of government or ruling elite. In most Western histories, there is the Egyptian Period, the Phoenician Period, the Greek Period, the Roman Period, the Byzantine Period, the Islamic Empires, the Carolingian Period, the French and British Empires, and so forth. These narratives are organized around political developments and associated innovations in law, religion, and military power that often are discussed only briefly. Great battles are often emphasized only when they have significant effects on rule makers in the top echelons of power within subsequent governments. But again, a single battle or change in leadership rarely truly triggers the next step in governance or empire (although occasionally they do).

---

[1] The Preface provides the gist of the main argument and approach of the book. This chapter provides its structure, its foundational ideas, and a more detailed outline of the book. Some readers who want to get on with the main argument or who are more interested in results than assumptions may want to skip on to Chapter 2. Although Chapter 1 may seem to be a digression—and it is to some extent—it logically belongs at the beginning rather than at the end of the book.

Alternatively, the rise and fall of urban centers and literacy might be used to develop a narrative for the social and economic development in a given place or region. We know that written language and numbers are not "natural" aspects of life in society for humans but were invented after settled communities and agriculture emerged. Prior to that, humankind was illiterate and evidently roamed in relatively small groups, fishing, hunting, and gathering their necessities from the forests, plains, lakes, rivers, and seas near which they lived. There was evidently little if any social life or commerce beyond the family, band, and tribe in that period—although a bit of trade did exist.

After agriculture and settled communities emerged, a region might have various "golden periods" of prosperity, literacy, and urbanization followed by "dark periods" in which literacy fell and urban centers and trade diminished. Like iron tools, urban centers, literacy, trade, and the arts are in a sense "unnatural"; they are artifacts—inventions—of humankind. They were not always present everywhere and, thus, are interesting features of social development, although relatively recent ones given humanity's roughly quarter-of-a-million-year history prior to the emergence of agriculture and written laws and histories.

This book focuses on another series of artifacts—ones that are far less tangible than a stone hammer, government, or great city—namely, rules of conduct that influence behavior. This requires even more speculation than other attempted histories of the period(s) before the emergence of writing. The relevant behavior is also unnatural or artifactual because it was no longer entirely guided by biological impulses. Changes in dispositions to behave one way rather than another are important because human development confronts thousands of social dilemmas associated with life in communities. Unless the most critical dilemmas are overcome, attractive human communities are unlikely to emerge—a point convincingly made by Hobbes ([1651] 2009).

Without settled communities, prosperity is unlikely, because opportunities for specialization and capital accumulation tend to be far more limited in small migratory groups than in larger stationary communities. Migratory patterns of life require that all capital goods be portable and robust. Innovations occur and knowledge accumulates, but it is focused on a relatively narrow domain of puzzles and dilemmas. Far less specialization takes place and far smaller trading networks—if any—are developed.

It was not one step from Africa to Athens, or from Athens to Amsterdam, or two steps from Plymouth Rock to Pittsburgh and Silicon Valley. A long series of "social traps" that impede social, political, and economic development had to be overcome for attractive communities and prosperous societies to emerge and sustain themselves.

Two sorts of analytical histories are used to support this conclusion. The first characterizes a sequence of social dilemmas that tend to impede social development. Parts I and II of this book analyze simple game-theoretic characterizations of choice settings in which (1) outcomes are jointly determined by the decisions of many persons and (2) what might be called the "natural" outcomes are less good or attractive than others that are possible. These two features are the defining characteristics of social dilemmas. (3) In each case, it is demonstrated that a variety of internalized rules of conduct can overcome the dilemma of interest by changing the relative attractiveness of the alternatives available to the individuals in the choice settings of interest. The internalization of ethical principles and civic norms causes behavior (strategies) considered to be moral to rise in value and those considered immoral to fall in value.

The dilemmas analyzed are highly simplified instances of thousands of more complex but fundamentally similar dilemmas that all communities, all commercial networks, and all democratic governments have to overcome to achieve good results—which is to say, results that are consistent with their residents' most common conceptions of a "good" life and "good" society. The order in which the dilemmas are analyzed is intended to provide an analytical history of the emergence of a commercial society. It is not rooted in historical observations, although it is informed by research in anthropology, history, economics, and political science. Each element in the sequence analyzes choice settings in which a roadblock to development exists and demonstrates how internalized norms can overcome the trap confronted. This allows the manner in which ethical dispositions contribute to economic development to be demonstrated.

Any sequence of the same or similar dilemmas would work nearly as well, in the sense that it would have similar implications. The one developed should strike most readers as plausible, but other orders may be equally or more so. The sequence shows that many social dilemmas exist and that each would impede social and economic development. In most cases, the emergence of norms to ameliorate the problems confronted is the only plausible solution. Other less direct political solutions generally require moral support for reasons developed in Part II.

Without solutions, both communities and markets tend to be far smaller and far less efficient as institutions for advancing human aspirations. Lives are subject to greater uncertainty, and are materially poorer, more conflicted, shorter, and generally less attractive, as they have been in most places for most of human history. Lives may not be quite as unattractive as Hobbes postulates for a state of anarchy—"brutish, nasty and short"—but few would opt for the short uncomfortable lives of the past over their more comfortable, healthier, and longer counterparts of today's commercial societies.

Elementary game theory allows the nature of social dilemmas to be demonstrated quickly, because it focuses on the essential behavioral features of problematic choice settings and ignores all extraneous details—a process of abstraction that was difficult for persons to undertake when facing real dilemmas before game theoretic concepts and models were developed. The abstraction and simplification of the models used tend to make solutions more obvious than they would be to persons experiencing the unpleasant outcomes of real-world dilemmas in which their essential features are entangled with many others that are less important. This is, of course, a benefit to readers because it makes both the behavioral aspects of the problems and their solutions crystal clear.

A second type of analytical history is developed in Part III. It reviews a series of theories and conclusions developed by scholars with interests in both ethics and economics. It provides evidence of changes in the intangible norms of persons throughout northwestern Europe and the United States in the period before the great economic acceleration of the nineteenth century. The evidence consists of the observations of widely read scholars from several time periods and countries during the period of greatest interest. All the philosophers and economists surveyed provide illustrating examples of how their theories explain ethical conduct, and naturally the examples employed are ones that the authors expect to be "obvious" to their anticipated readers. Their illustrating examples and conclusions thereby provide evidence of their community's ethos. The series of works reviewed reveals a general trend in ethical theories during the period from 1600 through 1920. Reservations about commerce generally diminish, and support for commerce generally tends to increase. For example, the concern that commerce tends to undermine ethical dispositions nearly disappears in the late nineteenth century. By the 1920s, the extent of prosperity (national income) was increasingly used as an indicator or index of the "goodness" of societies.

Western authors are focused on for several reasons: partly for space considerations, partly because I am more familiar with them than with writers from other parts of the world, and partly because fully commercial societies emerged first in the West. It would also be possible to explore the most commonplace norms in other periods and places in which commerce flourished in a particular city or region and to contrast them with ones from times and places in which commerce was less commonplace. These other possibilities are left for future research in order to keep the book to a reasonable length.[2]

## *Homo Constitutionalus*: Rule-Bound but Not Fully Rule-Determined Choice

Behind the analytical narratives of this book is a conception of human nature that I have termed *homo constitutionalus* (Congleton 2019).[3] This model provides a logical basis for concluding that rules affect behavior and, with additional assumptions, that the effects of "rule internalization" can be characterized using rational-choice models similar to those routinely applied in game theory, economics, and rational choice–based sociology and political science.

The homo constitutionalus model begins with the observation that individuals are born into the world knowing very little. Newborns know nothing of their family, their home, their native language, the community in which they will live, their future friends and career choices, nor very much about how their actions may affect all those things. They are "naturally ignorant," although they are not blank slates. Humanity has many shared genetically transmitted dispositions—because members of the species have repeatedly confronted similar choice settings during its long migratory period and a subset of genetic variations solved the problems of survival in that context better than others. As a consequence, we all cry to attract parental assistance as we enter the world—or shortly thereafter. We all have similar data provided by our sense organs, and we all have propensities to interpret the data provided in similarly useful ways using our "untrained" brains.

However, left to our own innate propensities, individuals would neither survive nor flourish. Parental support and lessons taught by them and others are necessary. This fact demonstrates that the ability to learn from and to teach others are among our most important inherited facilities.

---

[2] For example, Japan experienced a shift from a mercantilist ruler to a more market-oriented one in the shift from the Tokugawa Shogunate to Emperor Meiji in Japan in the late nineteenth century. China experienced a shift from a communist ruler to a more market-oriented one with Mao Zedong's replacement by Deng Xiaoping in the late twentieth century. Both these shifts accelerated the commercialization of the territories ruled. Again, it is shifts in norms or values that drive change, but in those cases the most important ones were among those who determined their nation's public policies. Many social dilemmas had already been solved by the norms internalized by their respective citizenries in what might be called their earlier and medieval periods, well prior to those shifts of leadership.

[3] Two colleagues have noted that proper Latin would require the term to be *homo constitutionalis* rather than *homo constitutionalus*—but I decided to hold on to my original spelling because for most readers it will establish the intended link to homo economicus, a term familiar to economists.

Before knowledge can be passed on, however, it has to be invented or worked out. Thus, an equally important facility is our ability to "make sense" of the world, by which it is meant the ability to use various sensory data to postulate a variety of "if-then" regularities—not all of which are correct—beginning with, if we cry, then mother or father will come. Over the course of life, we discern a huge number of such relationships from our experience tasting, listening, watching, and thinking about what we've tasted, heard, and seen. The ability to invent new if-then relationships is logically prior to our ability to learn from and to teach others, but without the other two capacities it would be far less useful.

Together these three abilities allow us to understand the world far better than any lone individual could ever hope to, because knowledge can be accumulated from a myriad of experiences and conclusions about possible if-then relationships examined by a variety of persons with different experiences. When if-then positive and normative rules are developed that seem to "work," they are likely to be passed on to others. As such rules are gradually generalized, relatively more abstract if-then relationships are passed on to others. All such rules are grounded in the experience of dozens or thousands of individuals acting in a variety of specific circumstances. Some of the posited if-then relationships prove to be broadly useful, and these are the ideas most likely to survive because they continue to be taught to and accepted by others.

As a consequence of the accumulation of such rules, a person with a "trained" brain lives a somewhat longer and healthier life than he or she would have without the lessons learned from others. And thus, these three capacities have genetic support and also support social evolution and progress.

## Rules as If-Then Relationships

In this book the term *rules* is used as a synonym for if-then regularities and relationships. There are three broad categories of such rules. One subset is used to understand the world as it is. For example, if an object is red, originally from a tree with a particular kind of bark, edible, and has a particular taste, then it is an apple. A second category is used to understand how our actions can affect the future. If we place an apple in our mouth, chew it up, and swallow it, it will reduce our hunger. Moreover, if one eats apples, one may live a bit longer than if one does not. A third class of such rules helps us to make decisions. Such if-then rules help us determine which actions are "best" in various choice settings. If one want wants to live longer, then one should eat apples.

The three types of if-then relationships can be described as scientific, technological, and ranking rules. These three categories of rules also include if-then relationships that describe life in society. If a group includes an adult man and woman and children, then it is likely to be a family. If one offers the members of a family apples and they like apples, then they are likely to regard such an offer as pleasant. If instead of offering apples to the family, one throws apples at them in a manner that causes pain, then the recipients may be hurt by such a use of apples—though apples are freely presented. Thus, if one wants to befriend a family or be deemed praiseworthy by them, one should gently offer apples to them, rather than throw apples at them.

Systems of rules can be internalized. This is a special form of learning through which new rules are incorporated into a person's own system for recognizing a choice setting, the actions that might be undertaken to alter the future, and selecting the "best" action in the circumstances in which one finds oneself. In normal circumstances, internalized rules are used reflexively (without much thought) to identify the situation, the associated alternatives, and make choices. Adam sees Eve pick up an apple and throw it at him, he realizes that he can catch it before it bumps into his nose, concludes that that is a good idea, catches it and takes a bite of the apple and smiles at Eve—all without much conscious thought. In such cases, throwing an apple could be a good strategy for Eve if she wants to befriend Adam even though it violates the logic worked out above. It turns out that there are exceptions to most rules. Exceptions do not, as some say, "make the rule," but they do make our systems of internalized rules more complex, conditional, and less certain.

Internalized rules are an important component of oneself. In computerese, they are our "software," and they generate dispositions to reach various conclusions about the world, our possibilities within it, and the relative merits of alternative actions—just as our genetic endowments do, what might be called our "firmware" in computerese.[4] The existence of the latter implies that our "software" does not generate dispositions that are entirely independent of our nature. Acquired dispositions must in a sense be compatible with our

---

[4] When our "ranking rules" are (locally) internally consistent, their implications for behavior can be characterized with what utilitarians, economists, and game theorists call a utility function—which allows every alternative to be mapped into real numbers with higher numbers being associated with higher ranked alternatives. A global utility function covers the entire domain of alternatives, a local utility function covers only subsets of that domain (as it is understood). A relatively tractable version of such a model is used below. It assumes that individuals rank alternatives by associating costs and benefits with the alternatives that attract the most attention. The chooser is modeled as a net-benefit maximizer in the choice settings

genetically transmitted "firmware" or the ideas would be unlearnable or instinctively rejected.

Although both our firmware (genetic dispositions) and our software (learned dispositions) jointly determine much of our character, it is the latter that is focused on in this book.

Our software is the part of our character that we can be said to have some control over because learning rules from others, refining what is learned, and creating new rules is always an active process. Observing others and listening to stories and other lessons always requires interpretation. As a consequence, we are all "self-programmed at the margin," rather than fully determined by our genes and culture. And because our software is accumulated during a lifetime, it can change far more rapidly than our DNA.

A fourth capacity that arguably is a consequence of our capacity to invent new rules and refine old ones is that we have the ability to revise and ignore both rules that we have learned from others and also a subset of our genetically transmitted dispositions. For example, we may overrule our biological dispositions by taking vows of celibacy, sacrificing our lives for a cause, or committing suicide. Similarly, we may rebel against the norms learned from others by behaving in ways most persons in our community would disapprove of or by inventing new, controversial theories of nature—as Copernicus and Galileo did.

Had we all been fully determined by our genes or culture, we would have remained "cave men and women" and the modern world would never have emerged.[5]

## Ethical Rules as a Subset of Ranking Rules

Among the evaluative or ranking rules that we internalize are what might be termed "practical" and "normative" rules. Practical or pragmatic rules tend to promote our biological interests in survival, reproduction, health, and comfort directly or indirectly. Such rules create dispositions to learn about the world and, given the results, use them to avoid danger, to find mates, and

---

characterized. Such a person will make consistent (transitive) choices, but only insofar as particular costs and benefits are stable. The use of net benefits allows significant elements of many choice settings to be discussed in plain language that yields intuitive results without the need for a lot of explicit assumptions about the shapes or continuity of utility functions.

[5] For a longer discussion of the "homo constitutionalus" model of man and its relevance for contemporary economic and political theory see Congleton (2018a, 2020b, 2020c). That model is not a precondition for the analysis undertaken in this book; rather, it is one possible foundation for the analysis undertaken in this book.

acquire status. Subordinate rules may encourage the accumulation of wealth, insofar as reserves make one more likely to survive, more attractive to prospective mates (who recognize that wealth implies that food and shelter will be available for their children), and may be associated with respect or deference within a particular community.

Normative ranking rules do not directly affect one's likelihood of survival or reproduction (although they may do so indirectly). Instead, they tend to generate self-esteem and approval by fellow members of a person's community.[6] Normative ranking rules include a variety of "ought to" and "ought not to" relationships and principles that can be used for guidance in specific choice settings. Ethical rules, in turn, are a subset of normative rules. They characterize "dutiful" conduct that tends to produce "good" choices, "good" character, a "good" life, or a "good" society, where the meanings of "dutiful" and "good" vary with the ethical rules systems internalized. Most economic and game-theoretic analysis implicitly assumes that individuals are pragmatists, although psychology suggests that persons who are uninfluenced by socially transmitted normative rules are rare.[7]

Examples of general rules of conduct include the Jewish Halakha (the way to behave), the five virtues of the Confucian Way, the five precepts of Buddhism, the ten commandments of Judeo-Christian Old Testament, and the five pillars of Islam. General secular ethical principles include Aristotle's virtue-based theory of moral excellence, Adam Smith's pursuit of praiseworthiness, Immanuel Kant's categorical imperative, and Jeromy Bentham's utility principle.

Ethical rules affect behavior insofar as they are internalized and relevant for a given choice setting. For example, imagine two identical twins, one with and one without a particular ethical disposition. As a consequence of differences in predispositions, each twin would tend to behave differently in ethically relevant choice settings, because they will reach different conclusions about the relative merits of the alternatives before them. The pragmatic twin will be indifferent to considerations that may be considered very important to the ethical or idealistic twin. The pragmatist may steal bread from his or neighbor to reduce his or her hunger, whereas the

---

[6] Such rules may also indirectly contribute to one's survival and reproductive opportunities but needn't do so. Indeed, some normative rules may reduce both possibilities, as with duties to defend a community against invaders, dietary rules that rule out perfectly edible foods from one's diet, and rules that encourage chastity.

[7] Such persons suffer from what psychologists term *psychopathy* or *sociopathy*. See Pinker (2012, Ch. 8) for an overview of how such traits may generate "antisocial" behavior—for example, amoral behavior. See Edens and Cox (2012) for a discussion of how assessments of such traits play roles in criminal trials, especially those involving murder.

moralist may endure considerable hunger rather than violate his or her ethical prohibitions against theft.

It is the subset of ethical and other normative rules that affect behavior in social settings that is of greatest interest for the purposes of this book, because such rules may solve social dilemmas. These include rules that explicitly encourage particular forms of behavior in social settings, such as the golden rule and tit-for-tat, and others that are self-oriented such as the principles associated with virtue ethics that induce tendencies to behave in particular ways whether one's behavior directly affects others or not. A brave or honest person is brave and honest when acting alone or in groups.

## Fuzzy Boundary between Ethics and other Norms

It should be acknowledged that the boundary between ethics and other norms is no sharper than the boundary between a fast walk and slow run or the colors blue and purple. For example, failure to spell correctly is normally regarded to be an intellectual rather than a moral failing. Failure to use the "right" fork or spoon at a formal dinner is regarded to be a breach of etiquette, rather than unethical conduct. Dressing in the wrong way for a given occasion may violate a community's complex norms for context-specific fashion but generally would not be regarded to be immoral. Such mistakes or nonconforming choices violate norms outside the domain of ethics.

Some norms are simply conventions that people follow because they help make life in society easier or more attractive. For example, following a convention like "always drive on the right" does not yield better results than following the convention of "always drive on the left." The use of 110 volts in one's electrical systems is not more ethical than using 12 or 220 volts. The use of one alphabet or character set to communicate an idea or conclusion is not more ethical than another. There is no right or wrong among such rules, only alternatives that "work," in the sense that they facilitate a desired outcome or avoid undesirable ones. One does not sin when one moves from the United States where they drive on the right to Australia where they drive on the left. There is no "right" or "wrong" or "better" or "worse" side of the road, only practical advantages associated with uniformity.

However, there are also norms that are "nearly ethical." For example, performing the duties associated with membership in a community may be regarded as evidence of good character or propensities to engage in ethical conduct. A dutiful community member pays his or her taxes, although it is not usually regarded to be immoral if one pays the lowest amount allowed by law. Crossing an empty street on a rainy night when the stop or crossing light is red may be illegal but may or may not be improper according to local norms. However, if individuals are deemed to have a moral duty to follow all of a community's laws, crossing the street in such cases reveals one's lack of moral character—at least with respect to that community's prevailing ethos—even though it affects no one else. Similarly, driving on the left in a right-hand society may be deemed evidence that a person is reckless, dangerous, and unethical—although the convention itself may be acknowledged to be ethically neutral.

Reasonable people may disagree about whether a particular principle, rule, or choice setting is part of the domain of ethics or not, or is a useful convention or not. That such disagreements exist affirms one of the assumptions that underlie the theoretical parts of this book: namely, that ethical ideas and conventions vary among individuals and societies. Such disagreements would not exist if there were a single universal ethical propensity that was hardwired into human nature, or if we were all destined to converge to a single ethical system through some Bayesian or evolutionary process, or if we were all pragmatists with essentially the same genes and information about our circumstances.

It is differences among ethical dispositions, rather than the precise meaning of the term *ethics*, that are most important for the current research project, because such differences can generate different behavior with respect to social dilemmas.

## "Rationality," Ethical Dispositions, and Social Dilemmas

When an individual's system of ranking rules—both pragmatic and normative—generates choices that are (locally) consistent, one can use numerical representations of interests to characterize choices. More highly ranked alternatives are assigned higher numbers, and less highly ranked ones are assigned lower numbers. These numbers in turn can be used to characterize how choices are made in circumstances in which only a few choices are possible. This property is used to ground and simplify the analysis undertaken in Parts I and II of the book. Such numbers do not truly characterize how decisions are made, but characterize the results of an individual's deliberative process. It the process of decision-making that determines expectations about how one's actions may alter the course of events. The rank order of the alternative actions and their likely consequences is determined by that speculative and evaluative process.

Choices that can be characterized with such numbers—sometimes referred to as utility levels or preference rankings—are said to be "rational," because they are internally consistent. Both pragmatic and normative rules and various combinations of the two can be "locally rational" in this sense, even in cases in which they are not internally consistent across all possible choice settings. Thus, the internalization of ethical rules does not necessarily generate "irrationality," although the rules may induce behavior that is not entirely consistent with biological dispositions or pragmatic interests.

Such numerical characterizations of preferences are used throughout this book to illustrate an important subset of the huge variety of social dilemmas that exist in communities. Such numerical characterizations of the outcomes of choice also serve as the points of departure for most economic models and the rational choice strands of political science, sociology, and anthropology. The appendix to Chapter 2 provides a short overview of elementary game theory for those unfamiliar with its grounding ideas and models. In most cases, the prose associated with the game matrices will be clear enough that readers will not have to look at the game matrices if they do not wish to, but the matrices provide the logical foundations for the prose and much of this book.

A social dilemma occurs when an outcome is determined by the independent choices of two or more individuals (or two or more groups of individuals), and the outcome is one that is disadvantageous for all the persons or groups involved, despite each person or group's intention to achieve the best possible result for themselves (as determined by their internalized ranking rules). Table 1.1 illustrates such a dilemma.

In the choice setting characterized, player Y is better off choosing strategy B regardless of what player Z does ($4 > 3$ and $2 > 1$) and player Z is also better off choosing strategy B regardless of what player Y does ($4 > 3$ and $2 > 1$). The outcome is jointly determined by their choices, which in this case is the lower right-hand cell where both players have chosen to adopt strategy B. This outcome is associated with "payoffs" of 2 for both Y and Z.

**Table 1.1** A Simple Social Dilemma

|  | Player Z Chooses Strategy A | Player Z Chooses Strategy B |
|---|---|---|
| Player Y Chooses Strategy A | (Y, Z)<br>3, 3 | (Y, Z)<br>1, 4 |
| Player Y Chooses Strategy B | 4, 1 | 2, 2 |

Unfortunately for both Y and Z, this outcome is less desirable than other possibilities. Indeed, there is one possibility that would make both better off than they are in the lower right-hand cell. Had each chosen A instead of B, the outcome would have been in the upper left-hand cell, and both would have regarded the outcome to be better than the one realized (3 > 2). This is the defining feature of all social dilemmas. Individuals independently choose with their own best interests in mind and yet the result is bad for each—not because of mistaken calculations, but because of the incentives (payoffs) associated with the choice setting confronted.

## Beneficial Effects from Internalized Norms

Internalized ranking rules generate the assessments that ground the numerical characterization of an individual's choices. Thus, any change in those rules can alter the ranking of alternatives and thereby the numbers associated with the various outcomes of a social dilemma. The models used to characterize the effects of relevant changes is the simplest possible which captures the tension that may exist between ethical and pragmatic ranking rules and also allows some of the trade-offs between them to be clearly illustrated. Most of these effects can be captured by additive forms of what economists and utilitarians regard as utility functions.

In effect, ordinary idealists rank their alternatives both pragmatically and ethically, and the result is represented by adding the pragmatic and moral assessments together to create utility numbers that characterize their overall ranking of the alternatives. This method also allows the relative strengths of the two ranking systems to be characterized. The stronger the normative ranking rules are internalized, the larger the utility supplements or decrements associated with those rules tends to be.

If pragmatic interests are regarded to be innate—e.g., consequences of genetic predispositions and ethical interests are regarded to be learned, then culturally transmitted moral principles and maxims can be said to alter human behavior. For example, suppose that according to some ethical theory, strategy A comes to be regarded as more ethical or moral than strategy B. Persons who have internalized that idea retain pragmatic interests but also now gain what might be called a "virtue" or "righteousness" supplement from choosing A over B. Strategy B, in turn, might now be associated with a "guilt" or "wrongness" decrement. Together these effects make A relatively more desirable than it would have been had such rules not been internalized. And if the virtue supplement and guilt decrement are large enough, they may alter the choices of persons confronting the choice setting of Table 1.1.

**Table 1.2** A Simple Social Dilemma with Ethical Players

|  | Player Z Chooses Strategy A | Player Z Chooses Strategy B |
| --- | --- | --- |
| Player Y Chooses Strategy A | (Y, Z) $3 + v, 3 + v$ | (Y, Z) $1 + v, 4 - g$ |
| Player Y Chooses Strategy B | $4 - g, 1 + v$ | $2 - g, 2 - g$ |

Table 1.2 shows how the effects of internalized normative rules can be modeled and how they may beneficially change perceptions of the relative merits of two strategies—even if the underlying nature of the dilemma is unchanged and unrecognized. The virtue supplement is characterized by "v" and the guilt decrement is characterized by "g." If the ethical beliefs are strongly held by both Y and Z (where strongly in this case means $v + g > 1$) their ethically informed choices will generate a different outcome, namely that of the upper left-hand cell. (The Nash equilibrium is again denoted with italics.) In this manner, internalized ethical rules and principles can solve social dilemmas. They do so, not by eliminating practical interests, but by modifying them.

Together, Tables 1.1 and 1.2 demonstrate that ethical innovations may, in principle, solve preexisting social dilemmas when they are internalized sufficiently by most members of a community. Moreover, insofar as important social dilemmas are generated by the natural (genetically transmitted) predispositions of humanity, in the absence of such innovations, social dilemmas would have remained unsolved until biological evolution changed those dispositions. Rule innovation and social evolution take far less time and so provide a quicker escape, which provides evolutionary support for the three rule-related human capacities mentioned above.[8]

Rules that ameliorate humanity's primeval dilemmas give the persons and groups that have internalized such rules a survival advantage. By increasing their material payoffs, they make such groups more likely to survive, and thus it is such rules that are the most likely to be taught to successive generations. Groups that have internalized such rules that tend to flourish relative

---

[8] That biological evolution has not solved all the social dilemmas confronted by humanity suggests that such problematic choice settings are relatively uncommon in a state of nature, that new ones emerge as biological evolution alters human predisposition to solve the most common or important dilemmas, or (most likely) that advances in human knowledge of nature and technology produce new dilemmas. The latter may, for example, be generated by improvements in human understanding of nature. For examples, hunters with better (but incomplete) understandings of nature and technology may over-harvest animals by employing techniques that were formerly impossible. Once the source of the problem is recognized, the hunters may subsequently invent new norms for employing those techniques that solve the dilemma.

to others. This is not to say that social dilemmas are never caused by rule innovations (some are, as discussed in Parts I and II), but rather to suggest that the first dilemmas confronted were consequences of our innate interests, rather than counterproductive innovations in rules.

## The Temptations of Ordinary Idealists

Table 1.2 also provides a systematic way of thinking about the degree to which rules have been internalized. The more strongly a normative rule has been internalized, the larger are its associated virtue supplements and/or guilt decrements, and the more likely it is that a person will follow that rule when assessing the relative merits of choices in which moral rules are relevant. Contrariwise, the weaker the internalization and greater the reward associated with violating a moral principle, the more likely it is that a person's pragmatic interests will ultimately determine their choices.[9]

The degree of moral conduct—which is to say, conduct consistent with one's internalized ethical maxims and principles—is thus a continuum rather than a yes/no assessment. One is not moral or not, but is more or less moral according to the strength of his or her predisposition to follow the rules (the $v$ increment) and his or her aversion to violating the rules or principles internalized (the $g$ decrement). Strongly internalized rules largely determine a person's choices in morally relevant circumstances. They are not followed to obtain practical advantages; rather, they partially determine what self-interest is in morally relevant circumstances. Weakly internalized rules also influence behavior but are more easily overwhelmed by pragmatic interests. Ordinary idealists are not angels, saints, or true believers. They make trade-offs between practical and moral interests.

The ethical men and women who populate this book are not persons whose lives are entirely or mainly driven by their ethical ideas. Rather, they are persons whose choices are generated by complex systems of internalized

---

[9] I sometimes divide individuals into three rough categories. Pragmatists only follow rules when they advance practical interests. Ordinary idealists follow them because they influence, but do not fully determine, their assessment of "their interests." True believers regard some maxims or more principles to be "supreme duties" that fully determine their highest interests, because a subset of a true believer's moral duties is ranked lexicographically higher than all of their biological interests. Pragmatists and true believers thus provide the endpoints to a spectrum of moral conduct. Pragmatists never behave "immorally" because their supreme duties trump all other interests. Ordinary idealists occupy the middle ground between the two, which characterizes a continuum of ethical dispositions.

Some political implications of true believers are explored in Congleton (2020b). The importance of ordinary idealists for good governance are developed in Part II of this book, a subset of which appears in Congleton (2020a).

principles and rules of conduct that they have accumulated, internalized, and revised during their lifetimes. The rules internalized include ethical as well as practical principles, and circumstances exist in which ethical rules affect an individual's behavior sufficiently to be relevant for social science and history.

## The Inertia of Socially Transmitted Rules

That people are good at learning, inventing, and internalizing rules may lead some to conclude that people can be easily transformed by others or by themselves, which is to say that people are in a sense "plastic" quick studies. However, most of us are not. Many of the rule systems that we learn from others take decades to absorb, make sense of, and internalize. Formal classroom studies can take 12, 16, or 20 years, and most are incomplete. Other systems of ideas take even more of a lifetime to master. Contemporary scholars, for example, often spend most of their adult lives studying one relatively narrow area of knowledge—mathematics, physics, history, ethics, religion, medicine, economics, and so on. Such examples suggest that we are neither quick studies nor particularly plastic.[10]

This is at least partly because our systems of if-then rules are intricate and interconnected. Thus, our grounding rules cannot be revised without simultaneously revising many others. Such revisions are possible, but they are difficult, time consuming, and in some cases painful. Minor revisions are easier because they are less central to our worldview and less tied to other rules. For example, we may change our mind about whether butter, margarine, or olive oil is best for cooking a given food without adopting a new code of ethics or modifying many of our dietary routines. Changes in grounding beliefs are more difficult because their implications support a wide array of complementary rules that we find useful and intuitive. Giving up a mechanically causal view of the universe for a statistical one (or vice versa) requires most of our ideas about the world to be adjusted, including our understanding not only of nature, but also of our possibilities and the best ways to evaluate them.[11]

---

[10] Normative training takes place in a similar and lengthy fashion. Most "good" students in "good" schools sit in their assigned places, listen courteously to their teachers, ask appropriate questions, and conscientiously turn in their papers and exams on time. The rules that generate such behavior are not genetically transmitted, are largely unwritten, and were internalized by most students over many years. Such simple rules also take many years to be internalized, as any elementary or high school teacher would be happy to affirm.

[11] Examples of rule inertia or rigidities are easily observed. For example, most immigrants speak their second language with a bit of "foreign" accent, something most cannot really hear themselves, because of their original training in another language. Irregularities in their new second language remain mysteries for even very smart and active students of languages learned late in life, that many, but not all, native-speaking young adults understand without much conscious effort. Similar conundrums exist regarding

As a consequence of what might be termed "software inertia," we may meet an old friend after many years and find that he or she is essentially the same person that we knew long ago. He or she has the same dispositions not because of physiological continuities, but because his or her internalized systems of rules have not changed very much. They have retained their worldview, likes and dislikes, ethical ideas (or lack of them), manner of speaking, and sense of humor.

Less benign instances of rule inertia also occur, as with what psychologists refer to as cognitive dissonance. A "fact" may disconfirm one or more internalized rules, yet the rules go on being used, rather than being revised to take account of the new facts. For many persons, it is just too hard to reorganize their systems of rules to take account of such "outliers." The individual may subsequently attempt to avoid confronting such conflicting facts in order to maintain his or her reflective equilibrium.

Time and attention are scarce resources, and that scarcity makes our internalized systems of rules more stable than they would have been if we could costlessly adjust all of our rule systems to reflect the world as it is, or to induce behavior that more ideally advances one's own long-term interests as they are understood by the individual him- or herself. However, cognitive dissonance may be "fully rational" given the difficulties (psychic and other costs) associated with major changes in one's internalized systems of rules.[12]

The same "software" inertia affects the systems of rules passed on from one generation to the next. If relatively few new major lessons are learned in the period before parenthood, then relatively few new major lessons will be passed on from parents to children. This is not to say that a community's ethos is static, but it is to suggest that it changes slowly, because major revisions

the etiquette and ethos of their new communities. This is not to say that they cannot function well in their new communities, but it is to say that immigrants remain, in a sense, noticeably foreign because they have not fully internalized the most commonplace rule systems of their new homes. Similar internalization challenges are often associated with changes in location within a country, with movements up or down a country's classes (both of which may require learning and speaking a different dialect of the same language and mastering different rules of etiquette and "common sense"). Other internalization challenges are associated with major transformations imposed on a society, as when the Iron Curtain fell. Persons who had grown up in the Soviet system faced the challenges of learning how to function in a market-based system. This inertia is not produced by genetic rigidities, but rather is generated by grounding lessons learned early in life.

[12] This an example of the "belief disconfirmation" aspect of cognitive dissonance theory. See Festinger (1962) for an overview of early research in that area, and Harmon-Jones and Mills (2019) for an overview·of subsequent research. Much of that research affirms rule system inertia with respect to core beliefs and ranking rules, while also indicating that modest revisions of rule systems take place in what might be considered marginal areas of rule systems. For example, there is a particular tendency to adjust one's ranking rules to favor something that one has over something that one does not. For example, after learning that one of two more or less equally valuable gifts must be returned, the gift kept is commonly reassessed and comes to be regarded as more valuable than the one that must be returned. Applied to theories and lifestyles, such marginal adjustments tend to make one more content with one's core beliefs about the world and the good life.

are difficult to conceive, difficult to persuade others to adopt, and sometimes painful to implement because so many previously internalized rules
and routines need to be revised or unlearned to do so. Modest incremental
changes are more likely to be internalized and passed along to others.

## The Rarity of Major Innovations as Evidence of Inertia

That major innovations are rare is indicated by the paucity of innovators
mentioned in historical accounts that are not themselves narrowly focused
on such people. The dearth of such innovators in general histories is partly
due to the fact that the process of disseminating new ideas and internalizing
them takes time, and so the original innovators are often forgotten long before
the import of their contributions come to be widely recognized. Thus, many
innovators are unsung and forgotten, as with the inventors of the wheel and
wedge or the concept of duty.

That major innovations do occasionally take place is indicated by the fact
that a few innovators are mentioned in general histories. Newton and Darwin
are often mentioned because of their contributions to our understanding of
nature. A handful of major religious figures such as Buddha, Mohammed,
Luther, and Calvin are routinely mentioned as instances of theological
innovators. And, a sprinkling of philosophers and social scientists such as
Aristotle, Montesquieu, Smith, Kant, and Marx may be mentioned in passing.
Those who are mentioned are usually associated with innovations that are
regarded to be breakthroughs that affected the course of history, rather than
mere refinements of earlier theories. Yet, the refinements are often as important as the original breakthroughs because without subsequent refinements,
breakthroughs are less likely to be widely studied, disseminated, internalized,
or put into practice.[13]

---

[13] Many original ideas were lost until rediscovered by others, because they were not studied and refined
by successive generation of scholars. Ideas that were given serious attention by others were more broadly
disseminated and internalized, at least among intellectuals. For example, a heliocentric model of the relationship between the earth and the sun had been worked out by the Greek astronomer Aristarchus of
Samos around 250 BCE, but it did not succeed in replacing the older, more intuitive geocentric theory. The
success of Copernicus's theory was likely aided by subsequent refinements and extensions, such as Kepler's
theory of planetary motion and Newton's theories of motion and gravity. These complementary theories
provided a general framework in which Copernicus's characterization of the solar system fit into a more general system of rules. The telescope helped support the predictions of the new model of planetary motion,
although its predictions were not often significantly more precise than Ptolemy's geocentric theory. Inertia
is evident in that the shift to the heliocentric view did not appear overnight, but took more than a century
to become the dominant conception of our solar system among educated persons. Inertia, nonetheless, remains evident in the expressions that English-speaking persons use to discuss dawn—as "sun rise" rather
than sun approach, and "sun set" rather than shadow approach, which would be more apt descriptions of

Other major innovations are scarcely mentioned. An example of a notable but neglected innovation is the Roman alphabet—a significant innovation in writing originating in approximately 600 BCE that transformed earlier alphabetic scripts. Modest refinements in the shapes of Roman letters and Arabic numbers—Garamond, Times Roman, Bookerly, and the like—took place as mass printing replaced hand-copied manuscripts, but these refinements were largely unrecognized outside of printing factories, until the word-processing software associated with the computer age made every writer into a typesetter. It has been used throughout Europe, essentially without change, for more than 2,000 years. Similarly, Roman numerals were also in use for many centuries. The displacement of Roman numerals by Western Arabic numerals in Europe occurred approximately five hundred years ago during the fifteenth and sixteenth centuries—although Roman numerals did not disappear entirely. Once adopted, the "new" numbering convention has remained in place for five centuries. Such innovations are few and far between.[14]

Cultural histories such as Fischer (1989) and Sowell (2009) demonstrate that a variety of less easily observed ideas and practices have also been internalized and passed on for centuries. For example, immigrants to North America brought their internalized systems of rules with them and passed them on to their children, and they on to theirs, and so on. Thus, many naming conventions, holidays, and many other rules of conduct in North America have European roots and have been stable for centuries, even though the social and natural context of the "new world" differed significantly from the European one in which they emerged.

Subsequent emigration from throughout the world to North America created a great stew of cultural varieties, reflecting rule systems worked out in different places and passed on from one generation to the next—albeit with some evolution at the edges as ideas and many rules from the dominant culture were adopted and internalized while others from outside Europe were taken into the prevailing culture. Adaptations to the dominant language (English) are clearly evident, but regional accents are often distinguishable for

___

our spin from the shadow to the direct light of the sun as dawn occurs each morning and our return to shadow in the evening.

[14] Of course, Arabic numerals did not catch on all at once. Europeans had been introduced to the 10-digit way of representing numbers by Arabic speakers several hundred years earlier. It also bears noting that the numeral characters adopted throughout Europe by the sixteenth century (and much of the rest of the world) differed somewhat from earlier Arabic numerals and gradually emerged during the half millennium in which they gradually displaced Roman numerals. Evidently, the movable-type printing press largely ended the evolution of Europe's numeric characters.

a couple of generations before the mainstream idioms and enunciations are fully internalized.[15]

Long periods of stability are also associated with religion and their associated rules of conduct. Particular religions often dominate particular regions of the world for centuries at a time. Indeed, even the buildings in which religious services are held are often many centuries old, as with the great cathedrals of Europe, mosques of the Levant, and temples of Asian Buddhism. Many secular philosophical theories of the good life and good society are similarly stable. Aristotle's list of virtues still forms the core of most such lists today.

Yet some nontrivial refinements to theology and virtue theories are evident, as developed in Part III of this book. As it turned out, many of those refinements supported the development of extensive networks of exchange, specialized production in large economic enterprises, and greater rates of productive innovation—and, thereby, the emergence of commercial societies.

## The Main Hypothesis and Conclusion: Ethical Foundations of Commercial Societies

The rule-based model of decision-making sketched out above provides a behavioral basis for thinking about ethical dispositions from the perspective of social science. Ethics are a subset of the rules that are internalized and used for ranking alternative actions that can be undertaken in a given choice setting. They affect behavior and thereby affect social outcomes both directly and indirectly. Direct effects are evident when particular types of actions that are deemed immoral, such as murder or theft, cease to be commonplace. When strongly internalized, internalized norms can reduce rates of murder and theft even in settings where murder and theft would advance practical interests. These reductions, in turn, make life in communities more attractive, increase rates of urbanization, and extend opportunities for voluntary exchange.

---

[15] The difficulty of adopting "foreign" ideas can be illustrated with the rules of the road. That an individual has internalized his or her community's "rules of the road" becomes obvious when a person accustomed to driving on the right has to drive a car in a society where the rule is to drive on the left side of the road. Although many other rules of driving remain the same, one's "driving reflexes" (one's driving dispositions) are no longer automatic. One has to consciously attempt to drive on the correct side of the road and look in the "right" direction to observe traffic signs or oncoming traffic. One may also have to relearn how to decipher signs. This requires consciously overriding many driving habits, which is to say the breaking and revising of a number of internalized positive and normative rules. It can be done, but it takes some time and can be unsettling, stressful, and dangerous during the transition. Modifying even such "non-core" rules is not easy—and can be dangerous, which doubtless accounts for much of our personal rule-system inertia.

Once internalized, a duty or moral principle is as real as genetic dispositions and may conflict with biological impulses. For example, a sect of Quakers called the Shakers internalized norms of celibacy and pacifism for all of its members. To continue, they had to continuously recruit outsiders, but as recruitment fell, the group gradually disappeared for quite natural reasons, leaving behind ideas for a spare style of living and furniture that many still find attractive—if not the requirement for celibacy. To be passed on across generations, the norms invented and internalized have to be in some sense compatible with survival or—like the Shakers—they would gradually disappear.[16]

Although considerable freedom to adopt norms exists, the ones that are most likely to survive and spread are consistent with biological necessities. Although such concerns may not be explicitly among the ranking rules associated with every moral code that can be imagined or internalized, they must be implicitly associated with them if the individuals and communities following the rules are to be able to sustain themselves.

Just as the wedge, wheel, steam engine, and internet are inventions, so are socially transmitted rules. As is true of other inventions, rules are invented because they are expected to improve human life. The if-then rules worked out to account for nature (science) may broaden our understanding of the universe, and rules that describe how nature's course may be altered by human action (technology) expand our domain of possibilities. Ethical and other ranking rules provide systematic ways to select among those possibilities. Improvements produce outcomes judged better by the persons using those rules than those generated by other rules. A subset of those rules may also advance practical interests by solving social dilemmas and thereby further expand the domain of human possibilities.

Given what might be termed the practical advantages associated with a subset of ethical principles, the term *moral progress* takes on a specific meaning. It is the gradual development and internalization of systems of principles and maxims that solve an increasingly broad array of social dilemmas that would otherwise impede human development. The more commonplace and consequential the ameliorated dilemmas are, the more important the solutions provided by internalized rules and principles of conduct are.

To demonstrate that moral progress and human development are connected, it is sufficient to focus on any non-moral area of progress. The one focused on in this book is economic development. This may seem a surprising choice, given that the founder of modern economics, Adam Smith

---

[16] To be fair, the Shakers have not entirely disappeared. According to Wikipedia in 2021, there were two left.

(1776, 6), once wrote, "It is not from the benevolence of the butcher, the brewer, or the baker, that we expect our dinner, but from their regard to their own interest." In that famous quote, Smith explicitly suggests that ethical dispositions are irrelevant for understanding market transactions—a claim that must have surprised those who had been favorably impressed by his previous book, *The Theory of Moral Sentiments* (1759). That book had argued that much of human life was motivated by moral sentiments and that both individual lives and societies were better because of them. Similarly, James Buchanan's (1984) claim that public choice analysis takes the "romance" out of politics suggests that ethical ideas also have little or no effect on large-scale political systems.

This book suggests that the opposite is true in both cases. Communities with an ethos that tends to support market transactions, team production, specialization, innovation, and public policies that do not impede economic development benefit from more extensive and productive commercial networks. As a consequence, the citizens of those communities live longer, more comfortable, and more interesting lives; and their societies prosper.

## The Organization of the Book

Parts I and II of the book are organized as an analytical history, for reasons already discussed. They analyze a series of social dilemmas roughly in order of their relative importance, which is likely to resemble the order in which communities confronted and solved them in the past. Chapter 2 characterizes problems that have to be overcome to escape from the Hobbesian jungle. It examines problems of unproductive conflict, commons problems, externality and public goods problems, conventions, and free-riding on teams. Chapter 3 focuses on dilemmas associated with the emergence of commerce; it addresses problems with trade itself, fraud, team production, and the effects of productive ethical dispositions on markets for both final goods and labor. It also discusses the long-term effects of labor markets on the most commonplace ethical dispositions in a community. Chapter 4 is the most traditionally economic of the chapters. It shows how ethical dispositions can be brought into conventional neoclassical models of price determination and how such extended models can be used to characterize a socioeconomic equilibrium. Chapter 5 examines the effects of ethics on capital accumulation and innovation, and thereby on economic development.

Part II takes up the dilemmas associated with good governance, which is to say governments that advance the broadly shared interests of their residents, rather than maximizing the benefits of government officials through expropriations from "their" subjects. Chapter 6 shows that a customary law-enforcing agency can contribute to the attractiveness of a community, by reinforcing moral and other normative solutions to social dilemmas. It can do so by supplementing informal penalties for violating norms with additional penalties. However, the analysis also reveals that this is unlikely to be the case, unless law enforcers have internalized appropriate ethical dispositions. Without such dispositions, extractive rather than productive law-enforcing agencies tend to emerge. Chapter 7 explores the roles that ethical dispositions play in majority-rule-based governance. Such norms can reduce cycling problems, curtail excessive redistribution, and provide support for policies that broadly support economic development. Chapter 8 examines the role of ethics in constitutional or system-wide choices and provides some empirical evidence that constitutional democracies tend to be more prosperous when supportive norms are present than when they are not.

Parts I and II shed light on the emergence of ethical dispositions and norms from the dawn of history to the present. However, their main purpose is not to provide a rational-choice–based anthropology, but to demonstrate that a wide range of social dilemmas exist, that ethical dispositions and other internalized norms can ameliorate them, and thus ethical innovation is likely to play an important role in human progress. Ethical dispositions are likely to have causal roles in the emergence of well-functioning communities with markets, legal systems, and governing organizations. The main implication of Parts I and II is that all flourishing communities have norms that at least partially ameliorate their most critical social dilemmas. Without such solutions, attractive communities cannot exist.[17]

Another implication is that many of the dilemmas of past periods may be so well-solved by internalized norms that they have disappeared and been long forgotten. Thus, some readers might well conclude that the pragmatic behavior that initially generated the social dilemmas is "unrealistic," because "that is not how real people behave." Of course, such a critique is actually supportive of the analysis undertaken. The internalized ethical dispositions of most readers would have induced them to behave differently than pragmatists in the choice settings examined—which is, of course, the main point of Parts I and II.

---

[17] This is not to say that social dilemmas were entirely neglected before game theory was worked out, but without game theory, problematic choice settings were more difficult to analyze and understand. I have often noted in my class that Plato's *Republic* and Hobbes's *Leviathan* could have been much shorter books if they had had a few principles from game theory at their disposal.

For some readers, the logic of the analysis and its correspondence with the logic of social evolution may be sufficient to cause the analyses of Parts I and II to be accepted. Others will expect additional evidence, which is provided in Part III.

Part III provides evidence that the conclusion reached in Parts I and II can account for the great acceleration of commerce in what came to be called "the West" during the nineteenth century. It provides evidence that ethical dispositions in the West shifted in a manner that reduced opposition to and increased support for economic development in the centuries immediately prior to the great acceleration, as would be required if a subset of ethical innovations provides the foundations for a commercial society.

Part III uses a novel source of evidence for the ethical dispositions of persons in Western society during the period from 1500 until 1920, namely the observation of philosophers and other scholars who wrote about both ethics and economics during that period. Many of their theories of virtue and duty were not products of deduction, but products of observation and pattern recognition. They were empirically grounded in the norms within the communities with which the scholars were familiar. And, to get their ideas across, they used examples of conduct in their communities that their readers would be familiar with. These helped to demonstrate the merits of their new or revised theories of virtue, good character, and the good society.

It is this empirical foundation that allows the writings of widely read scholars and other intellectuals to be used as evidence of existing norms in their communities. This, in turn, allows a series of such authors to be used as evidence of ethical trends in the same communities. All the scholars reviewed were widely read during their lifetimes and most still are highly regarded.

Chapter 9 is devoted to Aristotle partly because of his empirically based approach to understanding the role of ethics in a good life, partly because essentially all the other scholars reviewed would have been familiar with his work, and partly because it provides a window into the ethos of an early commercial center. Chapter 10 jumps forward to the late Middle Ages and the beginning of the Enlightenment. It begins with reviews of two influential anti-market Catholic authors, Erasmus and More, both of whom are still read today. These late medieval scholars are used as a point of departure for the rest. They are followed by reviews of two subsequent pro-market Dutch thinkers, Grotius and La Court; two English theologians, Baxter and Barclay; and the English philosopher John Locke. Chapter 11 reviews influential philosophers from the period of classical liberalism. It provides brief overviews of the theories and conclusions reached by Montesquieu, Franklin, Smith, Kant, and Bastiat. Chapter 12 provides overviews of four utilitarian philosopher-economists: Bentham, Mill, Spencer, and Pigou. It also includes a short appendix on contemporary contractarians. The theories are presented for the most part with paragraph-long excerpts from the authors and works reviewed.

Their scholarship provides evidence that reservations about commerce declined in the period leading up to the great acceleration and support for it tended to increase. Subtle shifts in ethics and related norms in Western Europe gradually accorded commercial activities a more central role in both private lives and society. Industriousness was added to lists of virtues and became a sign of good character, and material comfort became associated with theories of a good life and good society. A good society was increasingly seen as a prosperous society, rather than a religious or militarily powerful one. That most of this shift occurred before industrialization and the emergence of relatively open markets suggests a possible causal link between ethical and industrial developments in light of the results developed in Parts I and II.

Part III does not provide a complete history of Western ethical theory, but rather focuses on a subset that has empirical roots and addresses both ethical and economic issues. It focuses exclusively on Western ethics partly because of space considerations, but also because it is in the West that commercial societies—as opposed to commercial centers—first emerged.[18] It differs from most histories of philosophical thought in that it is at least as interested in the examples and illustrations used by the authors as in their theories, and because it focuses more attention on the economic implications of the theories reviewed than a typical intellectual history would.

Chapter 13 concludes the book. It summarizes the main line of argument developed and provides additional evidence in support of its main hypotheses. Two appendices summarize the book's contributions to the literature and describe how this author came to invest so many years in the project.

---

[18] Commercial centers were often larger in East Asia and the Middle East than in Europe. The great urban centers of China, Japan, and Turkey were several times larger than the largest cities in Europe in the millennium before 1600. However, their associated societies were not commercial ones in the sense used in this book. Outside urban centers, the rhythm of life was largely determined by the seasons and the demands of agriculture, rather than generalized market forces and the routines of mass production.

# Appendix to Chapter 1: A Few Quotations in Support of the Main Hypothesis of This Book

The opportunities for knavery are certainly more numerous than they were; but there is no reason for thinking that people avail themselves of a larger proportion of such opportunities than they used to do. **On the contrary, modern methods of trade imply habits of trustfulness on the one side and a power of resisting temptation to dishonesty on the other,** which do not exist among a backward people. Instances of simple truth and personal fidelity are met with under all social conditions: **but those who have tried to establish a business of modern type in a backward country find that they can scarcely ever depend on the native population for filling posts of trust.** (Marshall *Principles of Economics*, [1890] 2012, p. 7)[19]

This has not only been the normal attitude of all ethical teachings, but, what is more important, also that expressed in the practical action of the average man of pre-capitalistic times, pre-capitalistic in the sense that the rational utilization of capital in a permanent enterprise and the rational capitalistic organization of labor had not yet become dominant forces in the determination of economic activity. . . . Now **just this attitude was one of the strongest inner obstacles** which the adaptation of men to the conditions of an ordered bourgeois-capitalistic economy has encountered everywhere. **The most important opponent** with which the **spirit of capitalism, in the sense of a definite standard of life claiming ethical sanction, has had to struggle, was that type of attitude and reaction to new situations which we may designate as traditionalism.** (Weber [1905] 1958)

This exchange society and the guidance of the coordination of a far-ranging division of labor by variable market prices was made possible by the spreading of certain gradually evolved moral beliefs which, **after they had spread, most men in the Western world learned to accept.** These rules were inevitably learned by all the members of a population consisting chiefly of independent farmers, artisans and merchants and their servants and apprentices who shared the daily experiences of their masters. . . . They held **an ethos that esteemed the prudent man,** the good husbandman and provider **who looked after the future of his family and his business** by building up capital, **guided less by the desire to be able to consume much**

---

[19] In this appendix and throughout the rest of the book, bolding has been added to draw the readers attention to parts of the quote that are most important for the book. In a few cases, wording has been slightly modernized, in which case the words that have been substituted for the original are bracketed.

than by the wish to be regarded as successful by his fellows who pursued similar aims. (Hayek [1979] 2011, pp. 164–165)

**Virtually every commercial transaction has within itself an element of trust, certainly any transaction conducted over a period of time.** It can be plausibly argued that much of the economic backwardness in the world can be explained by the lack of mutual confidence. (Arrow, "Gifts and Exchanges," 1972, p. 372)

There is a general failure to recognize that the very behavior that is observed in the exchange processes of the market, whether these be simple or complex, reflects the presence of predispositions on the part of participants, without which the whole structure would not function. **The person who enters into a voluntary exchange with another is predisposed to accept that the goods on offer are not fraudulent, that promises will be kept, that contracts will be honored.** (Buchanan, *Why I Too Am Not a Conservative*, 2005, p. 105)

Is not man capable of surmounting the generalized public goods dilemma of modern politics by moral-ethical principles that will serve to constrain his proclivities toward aggrandizement of his narrowly defined self-interest? (Buchanan, "Markets, States, and the Extent of Morals," 1978, p. 366)

So, for all the flaws in human nature, it contains the seeds of its own improvement, as long as it comes up with norms and institutions that channel parochial interests into universal benefits. Among those norms are free speech, nonviolence, cooperation, cosmopolitanism, human rights, and an acknowledgment of human fallibility, and among the institutions are science, education, media, democratic government, international organizations, and markets. Not coincidentally, these were the major brainchildren of the Enlightenment. (Pinker, *Enlightenment Now: The Case for Reason, Science, Humanism, and Progress*, 2018, p. 28)

# PART I
# SOCIAL DILEMMAS, ETHICS, AND
# THE ORIGINS OF COMMUNITIES
# AND COMMERCE

## Introduction

Part I focuses on fundamental issues in social science. How do communities emerge? What patterns of life do they support? What roles are accorded to market activities? It attempts to answer these and other questions through the lens of elementary game theory. It examines a series of choice settings in which natural pragmatic propensities tend to generate dilemmas of various kinds. The first series of dilemmas analyzed are ones that reduce the attractiveness of life in communities. The next series of dilemmas analyzed are those associated with economic activities. Internalized rules of conduct can improve life by ameliorating or overcoming such dilemmas—dilemmas that confront all communities. A subset of the rules that make life in community relatively attractive also support behavior that can produce extensive networks of trade and production. Such rules increase the prosperity of communities by encouraging specialization, capital accumulation, and innovation. A third series of dilemmas associated with governments is examined in Part II. These problems tend to impede social and economic development through corruption and extractive public policies.

The choice settings analyzed are highly simplified ones that demonstrate why the outcomes generated by independent, rational, decision-making may be less than the best possible, according to the participants' own assessments. Not all choice settings have this property, but the problems generated by such dilemmas can be severe, and they are sufficiently commonplace to be important. Social dilemmas can block or impede the emergence of both attractive communities and extended markets. Thus, understanding how social dilemmas can be overcome is central to the main purpose of this book.

These roadblocks to social development are not the result of individual stupidity, biases, or other sources of systematic error, although these too can create social dilemmas. Rather, in problematic choice settings, each individual's evaluative processes lead to choices that produce less than the best outcome possible when judged from the perspective of each individual's own perceived interests. Every individual adopts strategies that are the best for him- or herself, but the joint result is problematic in various ways—some obvious and some not.

Chapter 2 uses elementary game theory to analyze how internalized ethical dispositions can solve or reduce the severity of commonplace social dilemmas confronted by all communities. It is arguably such dispositions that make communities possible. Thus, all communities have rules that enable them to survive and flourish, although not identical ones. Given reasonably peaceful and attractive communities, Chapters 3, 4, and 5 analyze dilemmas that have to be overcome for commerce to emerge and flourish.

Although some familiarity with elementary tools from game theory and economics is assumed throughout Part I, the arguments and conclusions are developed in a manner that should be clear to those without much knowledge of either. Game theory is used in the text, because it makes many problems clear, sheds light on possible solutions, and does so with far fewer words and unmentioned assumptions than would be possible without it.[1] Although elementary game theory was not available to philosophers or social scientists writing before World War II, many philosophers and economists had employed arguments that implicitly relied on game theoretic reasoning. However, without the aid of game matrices, it took many pages of prose to make a point that could have been illustrated with a single game matrix.

The analysis of Part I uses modest extensions of standard rational choice models from game theory and economics. The extended models are grounded in the theory of rule-bound choice sketched out in Chapter 1. From that perspective, it is the ability to create and internalize rules that ultimately allows normative innovations to alter behavior and improve life in communities. Other perspectives can also produce the required changes in behavior, and thus readers do not have to fully embrace the *homo constitutionalus* model in order to accept or understand the analysis of Part I, but it provides a useful foundation for all that follows herein.

---

[1] The classic texts for game theory are von Neumann and Morgenstern (1944) and Luce and Raiffa (1957). The appendix at the end of Chapter 2 provides a short introduction to elementary game theory for interested readers.

That informal norms can solve a variety of problems associated with conflict, commons problems, public goods, and externalities is evident in "pickup" games of soccer, basketball, football, and ultimate frisbee, which are played throughout the world without referees. Most players follow very similar rules, have internalized those rules, and are embarrassed or feel guilty if they violate the rules. Violators are informally punished (e.g., chided) by their fellow players. While moderating some forms of conflict, the same rules also generate intense coordinated efforts to "win" the game—a pure public good for each team. The rules also support notions of fairness and duty, both with respect to the rules of each sport and with respect to the division of tasks. And it is often the case that such informal games are as "clean" as games played with formal referees and penalties—albeit partly because the stakes are usually lower.

A central theme of this book is that internalized norms and principles inform behavior in other parts of life as well. A huge number of rules have been internalized, and such rules affect behavior because they are either internalized or informally enforced by fellow members of the relevant community. Indeed, it is arguably humanity's ability to informally develop and internalize rules that explains why humans are the only mammals on Earth that routinely live in large communities that make significant use of specialization and extended networks of voluntary exchange.

Although governments are often assumed to be necessary for peaceful relations within communities, the analysis of Part I suggests that this assumption exaggerates the extent to which governments are necessary to solve social dilemmas. Part II takes up the manner in which governments may make communities even more attractive. However, it turns out that supportive ethical dispositions are necessary to avoid extractive behavior by even the simplest rule-enforcing organizations.

# 2
# Ethics and the Quality of Life in Communities

## The State of Nature, the Hobbesian Dilemma, and the Origins of Community

Most people live in communities, although it is not completely obvious why they do so. There are numerous problems that arise when living in groups, and these can largely be avoided by living alone. That most people live in communities implies that there are additional benefits from living in groups that are greater than the problems and associated costs for each member of any community that is based on voluntary association. Otherwise, communities would simply disintegrate as its members left for more attractive alternatives.

There are significant disadvantages—as with violent conflict, overuse of local resources, free-riding, coordination problems, and negative externalities. And there are also numerous potential benefits associated with life in a family, tribe, or village—as with advantages associated with pooling knowledge, friendship, children, specialization, team production, and social insurance. Nonetheless, the costs can easily exceed the potential benefits of life in communities.[2] This chapter suggests that the emergence of ethical dispositions that solve or at least ameliorate the worst problems helps explain the emergence of both stable groups and settled communities. They reduce the costs and increase the benefits of life in communities.

Among the greatest of the problems that have to be overcome is the problem of conflict noted by Thomas Hobbes ([1651] 2009). He argued that intense conflict tends to emerge among narrowly self-interested persons in all settings where resources are scarce and in high demand. In the absence of rules of conduct—whether internally or externally enforced—he argued that communities would be very unattractive—indeed impossible. Individuals would tend to fight over control over scarce resources, and that conflict would

---

[2] It bears noting that many other mammals do live solitary lives as true of orangutans, bears, leopards, skunks, and porcupines, among many others. This suggests that even biological propensities to live in groups need an explanation. It is likely that both food types and behavioral norms (possibly genetically transmitted) similar to those developed in this section partly account for the differences among species.

*Solving Social Dilemmas*. Roger D. Congleton, Oxford University Press. © Oxford University Press 2022.
DOI: 10.1093/oso/9780197642788.003.0002

tend to escalate to "a war of every man against every other." As a consequence, individuals in what Hobbes termed the "natural state" have relatively short and miserable lives—an endless war of every person or every family or every tribe against every other.

> Whatsoever therefore is consequent to a time of War, where every man is Enemy to every man; **the same is consequent to the time, wherein men live without other security, than what their own strength**, and their own invention shall furnish them withal. **In such condition, there is no place for Industry; because the fruit thereof is uncertain; and consequently no Culture of the Earth; no Navigation, nor use of the commodities that may be imported by Sea; no commodious Building; no Instruments of moving, and removing such things as require much force; no Knowledge of the face of the Earth; no account of Time; no Arts; no Letters; no Society;** and which is worst of all, continual Fear, and danger of violent death; **And the life of man, solitary, poor, nasty, brutish, and short.** (Hobbes *Leviathan*, [1651] 2009, pp. 70–71)

Hobbes proposed a political solution that would later be called the *contractarian solution*. He argued that people would recognize their dilemma, imagine possible solutions, and agree to create a strong central government—a Leviathan or commonwealth—to enforce rules that would limit losses from conflict. Such a government, might, for example, create and enforce laws that protected life and property. By changing the rewards associated with war and theft, Hobbes argued, such a government would improve life for all—even if the government itself could not be easily restrained.

Hobbes was not the first to link prosperity to law and order; but his clear statement of the dilemma generated by narrow self-interest in settings where resources are scarce and persons are uninhibited by internally or externally enforced rules of conduct and his proposed solution to unrestrained conflict were both new. Both had significant influence on political theory, both during and after the Enlightenment.[3] What is most relevant for the purposes of Part I of the present book is Hobbes's claim that human interests are not inherently harmonious, rather than his proposed solution.

Subsequent Enlightenment scholars did not all agree with Hobbes's bleak assessment of the "natural state," nor about the impossibility of constraining governments once created; nonetheless, most regarded the

---

[3] The Leviathan was written by Hobbes in the relative security of Paris during the English Civil War, a war that may have inspired his idea of the war of every man against every other. The details of Hobbes's social contract and its associated theory of legitimate state action are beyond the scope of this book, although the contractarian approach to social ethics is taken up in Part III.

problem characterized by Hobbes to be serious and fundamental.[4] Writing nearly 40 years later, John Locke ([1690] 2009) also used a natural state and social contract to explain the emergence of legitimate government, although he regarded the natural state to be more pleasant than Hobbes did. Locke's more pleasant original state exists because individuals have internalized ethical ideas (termed "natural laws" in Locke's writings) that reduce the problems confronted in the absence of government.

**The state of nature has a law of nature to govern it,** which obliges everyone, and reason, which is that law, **teaches all mankind,** who will but consult it, that being all equal and independent, **no one ought to harm another in his life, health, liberty, or possessions.** (Locke *Two Treatises on Government*, [1690] 2009, KL: 3286)

Locke assumed that such rules had divine origin, but his analysis also goes through if such internalized rules are products of biological or social evolution. The important new factor in Locke's account of the natural state is the existence of widely internalized norms that reduce conflict.[5] Locke suggests that most persons in a state without governments would have ethical dispositions that induce them to avoid taking another's life, health, liberty, and possessions. Locke, nonetheless, suggests that some persons will violate natural law and, therefore, an external law-enforcing organization—a government—can improve life in a community.[6]

This chapter and the rest of Part I can be read as a theory of the transition from conditions analogous to the Hobbesian natural state to ones that are analogous to the Lockean natural state. The net benefits realized from community life, after an appropriate set of norms are internalized, provide

---

[4] Contemporary archaeologists have found that the Hobbesian jungle was a reasonably accurate depiction of society from the dawn of agriculture through the Iron Age. Although the warfare was not literally man against every man, but band against every band or tribe against every tribe, life was poor, nasty, and short. Considerable resources were devoted to attack and defense. See, for example, Keeley's (1997) book-length overview of that evidence. Pinker (2011) has provided an overview of the general decline in violence from prehistoric to contemporary societies.

[5] Hobbes (1651) also suggested a dozen or so norms that could reduce conflict within a community. Hobbes termed these "natural laws." The first three are: "[T]he first, and Fundamental Law of Nature; which is, 'To seek Peace, and follow it.' The Second, the sum of the Right of Nature; which is, 'By all means we can, to defend ourselves.' [And,] from that law of Nature, by which we are obliged to transfer to another, such Rights, as being retained, hinder the peace of Mankind, there followeth a Third; which is this, 'That Men Perform Their Covenants' . . . " (1651, pp. 73–80). Individuals have a duty to pursue peace, defend themselves when necessary, and keep their promises. Together these (and others mentioned) tend to help maintain peace in communities.

[6] All persons, according to Locke, have a common understanding of natural law, evidently more or less, as in Grotius's ([1609] 2004) theory of natural rights and duties. More or less the same rules may also emerge from social evolution, as demonstrated in this chapter. Whether biological and social evolution are set in motion by divine causes or not is a topic beyond the scope of this book and would not significantly affect its argument or implications.

both an explanation for life in communities and evolutionary support for the human capacity to invent and internalize useful rules. The role of ethics in governments that advance a community's broadly shared interests are taken up in Part II.

Readers who are skeptical of pre-governmental characterizations of the natural state can read Part I as a series of *ceteris paribus* analyses undertaken in settings in which government enforcement activities are imperfect and are held constant for purposes of analyzing the many roles that ethical dispositions may play in such circumstances.

## The Hobbesian Dilemma as the Nash Equilibrium of a Non-Cooperative Game

Game theory was not available to Hobbes and Locke, but their analyses of human behavior in the natural state are entirely consistent with elementary non-cooperative game theory. Elementary game theory implies that conflict among narrowly self-interested individuals living in close proximity to one another can be expected to produce lives that are "poor, nasty, brutish, and short." Elementary game theory also implies that the Lockean natural state would be less problematic than the Hobbesian natural state because a subset of internalized norms can reduce natural tendencies for violent conflict. After such norms or ethical principles have been internalized, life in communities would be far more attractive than it would have been in the Hobbesian environment. (A short introduction to non-cooperative game theory is provided in the appendix to this chapter.)

## The Hobbesian War of Every Man against Every Other

The historical narrative begins with the Hobbesian dilemma, which is to say, in a world of scarcity without ethics or governments. Essential features of this choice setting can be characterized by a two-person, two-strategy struggle over holdings of some man-made resource. The two persons are assumed to have equal abilities and resources and to be unconstrained by internalized ethics or external legal sanctions. In effect, what the two-person version of the Hobbesian natural state does is factor a community down to its component bilateral relationships. One cannot simultaneously attack every other person in the region in which one lives, but one might decide whether to attack or steal from a neighbor.

**Table 2.1** The Hobbesian Dilemma

|  |  | Thomas | |
|---|---|---|---|
|  |  | Produce | Attack |
| John | Produce | (J, T) | (J, T) |
|  |  | (12, 12) | (0, 14) |
|  | Attack | (14, 0) | (2, 2) |

Each person is assumed initially to control their own labor and a small stock of useful items such as food, clothing, water, and firewood. Labor (time) can be used to produce more of those goods from a natural resource freely available in the area, or it can be used to attack the other person and attempt to capture their stocks of goods. Such attacks take time and other resources away from productive activities. In this context, steal, attack, and defend are equivalent strategies. They all require an individual to divert his or her efforts from productive activities in order to increase his or her control over other resources that already exist. The alternative strategy (produce) employs one's time and other resources to create useful resources for oneself and one's families, rather than taking them from others, or fending off attacks.[7]

The numbers in Table 2.1 are the payoffs for John and Thomas in terms of control over physical resources, where higher numbers indicate more resources under one or the other's control. They may both produce rather than attack, which produces the "payoffs" of the upper left-hand cell. They may both attack, which produces the payoffs of the lower right-hand cell. Or, one may attack and the other one may not, which generates the lower left-hand and upper right-hand outcomes. The outcome that emerges is jointly determined by the choices of both persons.

If the person attacked is not fully engaged in defense (or attack), he or she loses everything, their initial reserve (2) plus that which was produced (10). Surprise attacks on poorly defended neighbors thus are rewarding for the victor (14 > 12), who does not produce anything, but adds that produced by the neighbor and the neighbor's reserves to his or her own reserves (10 + 2 + 2 = 14). However, if both individuals (or families) are fully engaged in conflict, no new production takes place and the result is a standoff, in which their

---

[7] One could analyze how such an individual would divide up their time between both activities, but by focusing on a binary choice, the essential nature of the problem is revealed without the necessity of more advanced mathematical tools.

reserves are defended, but nothing new is produced. In that case, both are poorer than if they had both chosen to produce rather than attack (2 < 12), although this outcome is still better than being the undefended victim of a surprise attack (2 > 0).

Consider the thought process that such individuals would undertake if they make their decisions independently of one another and both try to maximize their control over real resources. If, on the one hand, Thomas believes that John will not attack, then he can also not attack, in which case he engages in peaceful production and gets a payoff of 12; however, if John is engaged in peaceful production, Thomas could attack John and get a payoff of 14, which is a better result for him. If, on the other hand, Thomas believes that John will attack, then if he engages in peaceful production Thomas will lose everything and get a payoff of 0, whereas if he also attacks (or strenuously defends) he gets a payoff of 2. In this choice setting, Thomas is better off attacking John (or engaging in strenuous self-defense) regardless of what John does (14 > 12 and 2 > 0). He has a dominant strategy. So, logically, he will always attack and produce little.

Because both persons are in similar circumstances and undertake similar pragmatic assessments of the alternatives, they both reach the same conclusion; thus, both persons attack and the result is the outcome in the bottom right-hand cell. This outcome characterizes the Hobbesian state of nature, a war of every man and woman against every other. That combination of strategies is said to be a Nash equilibrium, because no person can increase his or her own payoff by changing his or her strategy, given the strategy chosen by the other(s).[8]

Note, however, that—although neither can do better by changing their own strategy, given what the other player is doing—both would be better off if neither adopted the attack strategy. The upper left-hand result is better for each than the lower right-hand result (12 > 2). There are mutual advantages that can be realized through a social contract between John and Thomas, as argued by Hobbes. Unfortunately, a simple agreement will not suffice because by assumption, both persons are uninhibited by ethical ideas, such as keeping one's promises. Since each can benefit from secretly reneging on the agreement and

---

[8] Only the rank order of the payoffs matter for this and most of the other game matrices used in this and the following chapter. The numbers are used to illustrate various problems, temptations, and possible solutions. One-shot games are used to characterize the Hobbesian choice setting, because they are simpler to characterize and easier for readers to process. However, the matrices can also be considered to represent strategy choice in finite repeated games, in which the payoffs represent present-discounted values associated with a finite sequence of play. Repeated contest settings have the same equilibrium, unless the temptations are relatively small and the discount rates are also relatively small. For more general analyses with similar results, see Bush and Mayer (1974); Skaperdas (1992); or Garfinkel and Skaperdas (2008).

launching a surprise attack on the other, the conflict resumes.[9] The upper left-hand corner is not a stable outcome, unless the payoffs change in some way.

Hobbes argued that escape from the dilemma generated by conflict over scarce resources can be achieved by creating a permanent law-enforcement regime. A governing organization can alter the payoffs of the game by punishing persons for attacking or stealing from others. Such an organization may be costly to operate and may cause other problems, but as long as rules against attacking others are well enforced and the overall cost of government is less than 10 units for each, both John and Thomas would be better off with such an organization than without it.[10]

If an agreement to create and maintain such a rule-enforcing organization is reached, it can be said that the government is both productive and legitimate. However, it does not imply that such organizations are the only possible solution to the Hobbesian dilemma, nor that productive law-enforcing organizations are easily created, as noted in Part II.

Moreover, in the circumstances that Hobbes imagines, rules, peaceful communities, and responsible governments have never been experienced, and they are unlikely to be imagined by persons constantly at war, living poor miserable lives of fear. It would take a great stroke of genius by all the persons involved to imagine a more peaceful prosperous society that might be created by a social contract. None living had ever experienced such a society, observed a contract, or been subject to productive good governance.

## Civil Ethics and Moderation of the Hobbesian Dilemma

Locke's characterization of the natural state points toward a more plausible escape from the Hobbesian "jungle." If people are inhibited by internalized rules of conduct—whether divinely conferred or products of social evolution—they may refrain from attacking their neighbors. The process of internalizing such rules changes the subjective payoffs associated with the two strategies. And it is the payoffs from the strategies that ultimately motivate behavior. Such persons, in effect, have two systems of ranking rules that are jointly used to assess their strategies. They have the pragmatic rules presumed by Hobbes

---

[9] That this property is not immediately obvious to readers who are not familiar with game theory is evidence that you (the reader) have probably internalized a "keep your promises" ethic or norm. Such norms can produce self-enforcing agreements to move from (2, 2) to (12, 12) for reasons characterized by Table 2.2.

[10] Not all governments would achieve better results. For a good introductory analysis of the effects of alternative government regimes on losses from conflict, see Congleton (1980).

under which more control over more resources is always good. And they have internalized normative rules that assess the manner in which the resources are obtained. Some methods of obtaining control over resources are deemed proper, ethical, or fair, and others not. This alters the payoffs associated with particular strategic choices.

The knowledge that a surprise attack is difficult to launch at a wary neighbor may lead both to engage in defensive investments. A wall may be built around the family abode or tribal compound. After a period of time, such defensive behavior may become routinized—followed without much thought—and violations of it—attacking the other—may come to be considered "wrong" or "immoral." At that point neighbors may be said to have internalized a non-attack norm and also believe that their neighbor has as well. Alternatively, such normative ideas and rules may emerge from conversations and agreements among neighbors to modestly reduce their defensive efforts. Such agreements are grounded in easily observed reciprocity. Again, as such behavior comes to be routinized, violating such agreements and engaging in attacks may be taken to be wrong or immoral.

The effects of such routinized rules of conduct can be modeled in several ways. They can be represented as (i) taking some strategies off the schedule of life's possibilities; (ii) reductions in the perceived payoffs associated with the "attack" choices (because of guilty feelings associated with immoral choices, the dereliction of civic duties, or anticipated disapprobation from others); (iii) increases in the perceived payoffs of the "virtuous choices" (because of increased self-esteem, the satisfaction of doing one's duty, or anticipated praise from others); or (iv) various combinations of all three. This book assumes that internalized ethical rules alter rankings of alternatives (the payoffs) rather than eliminating undesirable strategies. To truly eliminate strategies from consideration requires stronger blinders than plausible for rational individuals—although there may well be cases in which such "blinders" exist and solve problems.

If one accepts the homo constitutionalus model of humanity proposed in Chapter 1, the internalization of such normative rules would naturally alter their assessments of alternatives in all morally relevant choice settings. It is, after all, internalized rules—both pragmatic and normative rules—that generate the assessments being characterized with the matrix payoffs. Other things being equal, "ordinary idealists" feel better off (virtuous) when they follow their normative rules of conduct and worse off (guilty) whenever they violate those rules. However, they retain pragmatic interests. If the ethical supplements and decrements are large enough, some or all persons will refrain from attacking or stealing from their neighbors. If not, they will not.

The effects of relevant internalized ethical rules of conduct are incorporated into the ameliorated Hobbesian dilemma characterized by Table 2.2. The dilemma is solved whenever the "ethical decrement" (G) associated with violating the internalized norm is greater than 2 for both persons. In that case, $14 - G < 12$ and $2 - G < 0$, which makes the productive strategy better for both John and Thomas. Consequently, both choose the "don't attack" strategy, and the outcome is the upper left-hand cell of the game matrix, rather than the lower right-hand one. That equilibrium characterizes a relatively benign Lockean natural state and is stable as long as neither the ethical dispositions nor the choice setting and its associated practical payoffs change.

Thus, it is possible that ethical dispositions can solve or at least ameliorate the Hobbesian dilemma, and it bears noting that this solution requires a more plausible level of insight on the part of the players than that required for the formation of a productive government. A group of individuals that knows no rules or laws and have never seen a civil society or a government that protects property rights is unlikely to imagine that a social contract which creates a productive government will generate a civil society. Neighbors, however, might agree to refrain from attacking each other. Such an agreement may initially be based on defensive strategies, credible promises to retaliate if attacked by the other. As the associated strategy choices or evaluative processes become habitual, the equilibrium of Table 2.2 would tend to emerge and be stable.

Table 2.2 also demonstrates that the nature and strength of the internalized ethical rule(s), as well as the magnitude of the practical advantages obtained by violating them, matter. Finite feelings of guilt reduce the (subjective) payoff of the improper, immoral, or unfair strategy by amount G. The magnitude of the guilt decrement would vary both with the internalized rules that characterize moral action and the strength of one's disposition to avoid immoral or improper actions. Modest guilt ($G < 2$) does not solve this dilemma, although it would solve less-tempting dilemmas and thereby reduce that frequency of conflict in a group that faces similar dilemmas of varying magnitudes. The

**Table 2.2** Solving the Hobbesian Dilemma with Ethical Dispositions

|  |  | Thomas | |
|---|---|---|---|
|  |  | Don't | Attack/Steal |
| John | Don't | (J, T) *(12, 12)* | (J, T) (0, 14 – G) |
|  | Attack/Steal | (14 – G, 0) | (2 – G, 2 – G) |

greater is the temptation, the stronger the feeling of virtue or guilt required to overcome it.

As a consequence, the widespread internalization of rules that reduce conflict—a community ethos—is not necessarily sufficient to solve all such dilemmas. For example, if the strength of ethical dispositions generated guilt decrements that were uniformly distributed between 1 and 6, about 20% of the village would engage in violent conduct in the circumstances of Table 2.2.

Examples of ethical maxims and principles that can solve the Hobbesian dilemma include various reciprocity-based rules such as the peaceful version of "tit-for-tat"—engaging in peaceful conduct first and continuing to do so as long as the other does also, nonaggression principles such as "self-defense is honorable, but never attack first," various sharing rules, and what might be called private property rules that call for accepting each other's holdings and production as properly "yours" and "mine." There is no unique solution.

Such rules may be facilitated by other rules that tend to make agreements binding, such as "promise-keeping" norms. In those cases, subsequent agreements to follow particular rules might be negotiated at informal meetings among neighbors, as posited by Hobbes.

Although every viable community must have internalized rules to avoid the Hobbesian dilemma, there is no uniquely "best" norm for escaping it. A wide variety of rules of conduct and ideas about fairness, right, and wrong can alter the subjective payoffs of the Hobbesian dilemma in a manner that makes the "attack" strategy less personally rewarding or the "don't attack" strategy more personally rewarding. Such rules may be regarded as more or less universal by community members. They may apply only to one's neighbors, only to one's village, only to one's tribe, only to one's society, or to the world at large.[11]

It also bears keeping in mind that it is not simply the internalization of rules of conduct that solves the Hobbesian dilemma. Although there are many rules of conduct that can solve or ameliorate the Hobbesian dilemma, not all rules do so. Some rules increase the probability and intensity of conflict. For example, both military asceticism and power-based norms such as "to the victor go the spoils" tend to increase the subjective payoffs from attacking and to reduce those associated with productive work. Such normative theories tend to perpetuate the Hobbesian dilemma, rather than curtail it. Variations of

---

[11] Montesquieu (1748) argues that communities and states would emerge as methods for escaping from Hobbes's war of every man against every other, and that the rules for group members would differ from those of outsiders. Intercommunity relations would remain problematic unless other informal rules emerged that tended to reduce conflict among communities. Keeler (1997) summarizes archaeological evidence that implies that preliterate tribal norms solved a variety of problems within their communities but also supported raids and warfare between communities.

such rules (attack outsiders but protect fellow community members) can contribute to solving a village's free-rider problems with respect to self-defense, a topic taken up later in this chapter. Such rules are conditional rather than universal because outsiders and insiders are treated differently. Variations of such rules can create new larger-scale social dilemmas after relatively peaceful communities have emerged.

Locke (1690/2009) and many others suggest that ethical dispositions are not generally strong enough to eliminate all risks to life and property, and so government is necessary. However, Spencer (1851, Ch. 4), among others, argues that the evolution of norms can potentially solve all the problems associated with life in a community without the need for government and its associated police and court systems. This book regards the present state of social evolution to be closer to Locke's natural state than to Spencer's utopian one, although it does not totally reject Spencer's argument with respect to the very long run.[12]

## Managing Shared Resources: Commons Problems

From this point forward, it is assumed that rules of conduct have been sufficiently internalized that the most serious Hobbesian problems within communities are solved. Solutions to the Hobbesian dilemma allow people to live in groups, more or less in peace, which is a necessary first step for the emergence of viable communities.

For the purposes of the next section, it is assumed that sharing rules have been internalized for at least a subset of the resources in the community of interest. Sharing rules reduce conflict by making private holdings of some types of property improper and thus resources are not used to block the access of others entitled to share such resources. Such things are common property resources for members of the community. It may, for example, be regarded to be improper for an individual or family to own the only source of potable water in a community that resides in a desert, or improper to prevent fellow community members from hunting and gathering in the forest surrounding a temporary village site. Common property or sharing rules are relatively simple to imagine and provide a solution to a subset of possible Hobbesian dilemmas, although they might not have been adopted for that purpose.

[12] For a simulation analysis of how evolutionary pressures affect a community's rules of conduct, see Vanberg and Congleton (1992) or Congleton and Vanberg (2001).

Community sharing rules may, for example, have emerged because they were natural extensions of norms used within families.

In such communities, sharing "rights" are applied to at least a subset of potentially excludable resources such as pastures, natural orchards, woodlots, springs, streams, and lakes. Other resources in the same community may be subject to "mine and thine" rules. These may include homemade tools, articles of clothing, dwellings, and, as agriculture emerges, ownership of particular animals and gardens. "Privateness" for such goods tends to increase efforts to produce and take care of them. Most communities have a variety of particularized solutions to the many Hobbesian choice settings confronted.

Equal-access or sharing norms reduce conflict over resources by forbidding any user from excluding others and also produce benefits by generating a sense of collegiality among those sharing access rights to common resources. However, in the absence of rules governing usage, equal-access rules may generate other problems.

An important social dilemma associated with open and equal-access rules was noted by Garrett Hardin (1968). As a shared or common resource is used by more and more people, its productivity eventually tends to fall, and this effect can be catastrophic.

> The tragedy of the commons develops in this way. Picture a pasture open to all. It is to be expected that each herdsman will try to keep as many cattle as possible on the commons. Such an arrangement may work reasonably satisfactorily for centuries because tribal wars, poaching, and disease keep the numbers of both man and beast well below the carrying capacity of the land. Finally, however, comes the day of reckoning, that is, the day when the long-desired goal of social stability becomes a reality. At this point, the inherent logic of the commons remorselessly generates tragedy. (Hardin, 1968, p. 1245)

Table 2.3 illustrates the tragedy of the commons for two persons, which, as in the previous Hobbesian cases, can easily be generalized to a group or community of any size and to finitely repeated versions of the same game. In the choice setting characterized by Table 2.3, grazing one's herd on the commons reduces the amount of grass left for the animals of other herd owners and therefore may reduce the average weight gain of the animals using it. In small groups with small herds, this effect is often trivial, but it is important for small commons areas and it increases in importance as a large commons is used more and more intensively. The result in either case may be a rather barren communal pasture, as implied by Hardin's parable, or simply a pasture that produces less agricultural output than it could have.

**Table 2.3** The Tragedy of the Commons

|        | Garrett | | |
|--------|----------|----------|------------|
|        | One head | Two head | Three head |
| Elinor | (A, B)   | (A, B)   | (A, B)     |
| One head | 5, 5   | 4, 9     | 2, 12      |
| Two head | 9, 4   | 7, 7     | 4, 8       |
| Three head | 12, 2 | 8, 4    | 5, 5       |

Game matrix 2.3 illustrates the case in which the output of the resource in question is maximized with moderate usage. The payoff numbers in the cells are based on useful output from the commons—pounds of food or fur generated. As in the previous matrices, it is the relative magnitudes of the payoffs that are important, rather than their absolute magnitudes. There are, however, some restrictions on the cell payoff totals that have to do with the nature of the problem. For example, unless there is an obvious difference among the cattle or flocks, the output totals have to be the same whenever the same total number of animals (heads) are on the commons. In the case illustrated, the output or net benefit from the commons is maximized when a total of 4 heads are on the commons. This generates 14 units of useful weight gain for a given period of time such as a month or season. (The commons modeled is a relatively small one. Larger ones could be modeled in much the same way by interpreting the herd sizes as dozens or hundreds rather than single heads.)

As in the Hobbesian dilemma, there are pure dominant strategies for each player. Each herdsman's own net benefits are maximized if he or she places 3 heads of cattle on the pasture. The result is that a total of 6 head of cattle are on the pasture at the Nash equilibrium, and a total output of 10 rather than 14 is realized from the commons.

The commons is overused, although not tragically so in the case modeled, because its output is well above zero. (Hardin's tragic result might emerge if we added another row and column or two.) The productivity of the pasture is not entirely exhausted in the illustration; it is simply less than it could be. Nonetheless, for communities that live near the edge of survival, realizing 40% less food than possible is a serious problem.[13] As is true of the Hobbesian dilemma, the nature of a commons problem may be obvious to the participants (overgrazing) and so may the nature of the solution: each user should curtail

[13] Diamond (2005) analyzes several cases in which communities disappeared because of failures to solve commons problems that emerged as they began to thrive or as weather changes altered the nature of commons problems previously overcome. One need not completely accept his analysis of particular cases to

their use of the commons. However, for large common pastures used by many herdsmen and shepherds, neither the problem nor the solution may be clear. Is overall output maximized or not? If not, is it caused by overgrazing, bad weather, insects, excess manure, a grass disease, or divine intervention?

## Normative Solutions

In small groups, one can imagine a variety of informal solutions once the nature of the overuse problem is recognized. The simplest is that the group may simply move on to another site with an unused pasture and take up life there. This migratory solution was evidently used by early Homo sapiens for tens of thousands of years before stationary communities emerged. The migratory solution to both the Hardin and Hobbesian problems is easy to implement as long as unclaimed fertile empty places exist that are not too far away. Such a solution does not require an understanding of either the Hobbesian or Hardin problems. When fertility declines and the hunting, grazing, or gathering becomes difficult, it is "obviously" time to move on.

However, as the number of persons or tribes increases, the migratory solution becomes more difficult. The migratory solution, for example, may cease to be easy if other tribes have adopted non-migratory solutions, and have organized to defend "their" territory from migratory tribes. When simply moving ceases to be easy, a tribe has to find a new solution to the Hardin problem if it is to sustain itself. Indeed, a large-scale commons problems among tribes may emerge in which even relatively large territories are overgrazed, overhunted, and over-gathered.

Once the nature of the commons problem of Table 2.3 is understood, the users of the common may agree to reduce their use of the commons. In the illustration, the two herders may agree to place two head of cattle, at most, on the commons, which will solve the problem if the agreement is supported by other promise-keeping norms. Other norms that may solve the commons dilemma include conditional norms of "fair use" that are adjusted so that pasture output is maximized and property-types of norms under which herdsmen keep their cattle in particular non-overlapping subsets of the common. If a strong promise-keeping norm has been internalized, agreements to follow such usufruct rules would be sufficient to solve the problem; otherwise such

accept his general line of argument, that failures to solve commons problems can be catastrophic for communities. He also discusses a few success stories in which relatively complex systems of rules were able to solve such ecological dilemmas in places, such as South Pacific Islands where many resources were very scarce.

rules have to become routinized and internalized to solve or ameliorate the Hardin problem.[14]

An agreement among pure pragmatists would not be kept, because each herdsman continues to benefit from grazing more than two head of cattle on the commons and thus has a good reason to cheat on the agreement. The middle cell is not a Nash equilibrium for pragmatists and so is not stable unless supported by internalized norms or diligent external law enforcement. Each pragmatist would simply ignore his or her agreement and put additional cattle on the commons—while hoping that the others would adhere to the agreement. As with the Hobbesian dilemma, the necessary strength of the ethical disposition varies with the extent of the commons problem. For the problem illustrated, norms do not have to be very strong to avoid the problem. The central [7, 7] cell can be sustained with a guilt level greater than 1 for herds larger than two head.

## More or Less General or Generalizable Solutions

The Hobbes- and Hardin dilemmas also illustrate another important difference among rules of conduct that may be internalized. Rules differ in their ability to solve multiple social dilemmas. Some principles or rules of conduct solve or help to solve only a particular problem. Others solve or help support solutions to many social dilemmas. For example, both a promise-keeping norm and a "partitioning" or "mine/thine property" norm can solve both the Hobbes and Hardin problems if the norms are sufficiently internalized, and the resource is sufficiently divisible that proper claims are easily recognized. Property norms when strongly internalized tend to reduce conflict and also eliminate incentives to overuse a resource. Open access norms, in contrast, may solve the problem of conflict but tend to generate commons problems. Other norms may not directly solve problems but may facilitate their solutions. Promise-keeping norms do not directly solve any social dilemmas but can support and sustain a variety of agreements that ameliorate them.

Communities that have internalized ethical principles or norms that reduce a variety of problems are more likely to flourish than ones that have a different norm or ethical maxim for every problem that emerges. General rules can overcome more social dilemmas and can do so without requiring that

---

[14] Agreements among tribes to divide up a very large commons area generates tribal territories—although not necessarily settled communities if the territories are large. Such territorial agreements are arguably easier to negotiate than a general solution because it allows each tribe to follow its own customs (rules) within their territories, rather than agreements about universal rules that are to be followed by all tribes.

each dilemma be recognized and a solution agreed to. Generalizable rules can make newly recognized social dilemmas easier to solve, because such rules suggest or support "obvious" solutions to new problems. Such general and generalizable rules (principles) also tend to be easier to teach to successive generations of children than a catalog of particularized solutions.

Of course, such advantages do not imply that general or generalizable principles of conduct are easier to develop than particularized ones. For example, property norms can solve both the Hobbesian and Hardin problems, but they are somewhat more complex than sharing norms. They require the internalization of systems of rules, rather than following one or two rules. Persons deemed to be "owners" are conceded the "right" to do more or less as they please with "their" property, and each "owner" has the "right" to exclude others from using his or her property. Non-owners, in turn, have the "duty" not to "trespass" on another's property. This requires the notions of "owner," "right," "duty," and "trespass" to emerge, and these are not entirely obvious ideas. Moreover, as mentioned above, the property solution is not always possible, because some resources are difficult to partition, and others are arguably too important for exclusion to work well (as with a rare natural spring or well in a desert). Moreover, property norms may conflict with other sharing norms and notions of fair or just deserts previously internalized by the persons involved.[15]

With respect to the emergence of markets, a topic taken up in the next chapter, some solutions to the Hobbesian and Hardin dilemmas create circumstances in which commerce is more likely to emerge than others. Ownership rights over personal herds, flocks, tools, clothing, jewelry, gardens, and pasture lands create numerous exchange possibilities that are absent under generalized sharing rules. When claims to particular things can be transferred to others, trade will tend to emerge because of mutual gains associated with differences in skills, interests, and opportunities. For example, one person's chickens may be exchanged for another's carrots or homemade tools.

The first markets for goods—albeit limited and local ones—are likely to have emerged within the subset of communities that adopted informal ownership rights as solutions to at least a subset of their Hobbesian and Hardin problems.

---

[15] Note that partitioning land can undermine the "sharing" solution to the Hobbesian problem. If some regard such exclusion to be to be unjust or unfair, they may violate their neighbor's property, which can renew conflict over resources and regenerate the Hobbesian problem. Thus, some norms may solve one problem but reduce prospects for solving other problems that emerge later.

# Ethics and the Provision of Public Services in Stationary Communities

After the Hobbesian and Hardin problems have been ameliorated, stationary communities can emerge and be self-sustaining. However, these are not the only dilemmas that have to be overcome for stationary communities to flourish. Success often creates new dilemmas to be overcome. For example, as communities prosper, they become attractive targets for organized groups of roving bandits and conquerors. As population grows, passageways through a village or territory tend to become more congested and communal resources become more likely to be overused. Assuring potable water and the disposal of waste products becomes more difficult and more important. Thus, village defense, various infrastructure projects, and management of communal resources become increasingly important as a community flourishes.

Let us now assume that the Hobbesian and Hardin problems have been ameliorated or solved, and a settled community has emerged, most likely in a location that is especially good for hunting, fishing, or farming. Insofar as the Hobbesian and Hardin problems have been ameliorated, the community is relatively peaceful and self-sustaining. As the population grows and a village or town emerges, some of the previously solved dilemmas may reappear in new forms. The temptations for theft and extortion increase as more goods are manufactured (clubs, arrows, tools, bowls, jewelry, fishing nets, boats, huts, farm fields, houses, and the like). Some commons problems also become more severe as usage of shared resources intensify. Overcoming these may require stronger internalization of old norms or new norms that address the new problems, but let us assume for now that generalizations of the previously internalized norms are sufficient to ameliorate such problems.

## Free-Riding and the Public Goods Dilemma

A stationary community also confronts problems and opportunities that migratory groups do not, and it is likely that several new problems had to be overcome simultaneously for settled communities to be viable, which would partly account for the slow emergence of communities with permanent locations. Rule-based solutions initially would tend to emerge haphazardly as a sequence of innovative solutions to problems in particular settings, and it is possible that only a small subset of communities developed an ethos that could generalize to life in settled communities. As attractive villages emerged and solved their problems, their solutions and ethos might have been copied by a subset of others.

We next consider services that might make life in a hunting, fishing, or farming village more attractive and robust. There are many services that might make everyone in a stationary community better off, such as village defense and passageways, and also rules that can potentially reduce health problems associated with life in stationary communities, such as rules for waste disposal. Many of these are what economists call *pure public goods*, goods whose provision benefits everyone in the community. Other services may not be "public" in that sense but are produced through methods that exhibit what economists call *economies of scale*. Their average costs fall as more of a service is provided or as it is provided to more people. In a fishing village, these include village docks, storage facilities, and meeting places. They may also include networks of cart paths through the village to facilitate the comings and goings of folks from their huts, places of work and worship, and markets, if any arise.

Many of the public-goods problems associated with life in settled communities differ from those associated with migratory patterns of life. For example, a settlement tends to be a more attractive target for roving bandits than migratory tribes, because stationary tribes tend to accumulate more wealth and reserves than migratory tribes, partly because they do not have to carry everything along with them. A subset of that wealth is portable and profitable for raiders to take, such as food stocks, animals, jewelry, and relatively sophisticated portable tools. Other assets cannot be taken by raiders because they are too large to carry off; however, the threat to destroy the fixed assets such as farm fields, granaries, and housing can be used to extort tribute from a stationary community. In contrast, migratory tribes are at somewhat lower risk from such raids because they have smaller stocks of tangible wealth and so can simply gather up most of their assets and flee to safety. Village defense is thus likely to be a greater concern for stationary communities than migratory ones.[16]

Table 2.4 characterizes the free-rider dilemma associated with producing community-wide services (what economists refer to as *local public goods*). The individuals represented decide whether to contribute to the production

---

[16] This problem is analogous to the Hobbesian one, but it differs in that it involves conflict among groups of persons rather than individuals or families. Such groups may have basically peaceful relationships within them, while engaging in raids of conquests of other groups. Solutions to such conflicts are evidently more difficult to devise and internalize, because they remain unsolved (although ameliorated) through to the present. Instances include gang warfare, civil war, and international conflict.

Table 2.4  The Public Goods Dilemma

|        |            | Paul | |
| --- | --- | --- | --- |
|        |            | Contribute | Free-ride |
| Alfred | Contribute | (A, P)<br>(3, 3) | (A, P)<br>(−2, 8) |
|        | Free-ride  | (8, −2) | (0, 0) |

of community-wide services or not. For purposes of illustration, it is assumed that the service can be produced by a single individual (or subgroup) living in the village, albeit at a high cost for that individual or subgroup. The others obtain benefits from those services at no or little cost. Or, the service can be produced by essentially all members of the community, who in that case share equally in both the cost and benefits of its production. A two-person game is again used to illustrate problems that are likely to be more severe in larger groups. Paul and Alfred may turn out to defend the village or not, spend time servicing the local transport network or not, serve on a posse or not, contribute to a community insurance fund or not, and so on.

Production of the service is assumed to consume scarce time and energy (labor) of the person or persons engaged in producing the service. The cost of such efforts is simply the value of alternative uses of that time and energy. Instead of contributing to the production of the public service, an individual's time and energy might have been used for attending to one's family, garden, cattle, fishing nets, dwelling, etc. The payoffs are individual net benefits from the service for various combinations of efforts or contributions to produce the community service. Such net benefits may be calculated in terms of local money goods if money has emerged or in terms of net gains in calories or satisfaction (utility) if they have not.

The illustration assumes that the public service can be produced with resources that would otherwise have been used to produce 10 units of benefits if used in an alternative activity. Producing the public service can thus be said to have an opportunity cost of 10 units of benefits whether measured in money, calories, or utility. If the public service is produced, it provides 8 units of benefits for each person in the community. If one person provides the public service, he or she pays the full cost and realizes net benefits of −2, $(8 − 10 = −2)$. If two people contribute, each bears half the required cost and realizes a net benefit of 3, $(8 − 10/2 = 3)$. If the good or service is not produced, no new net benefits are generated, and the payoff for each is 0.

Note that free-riding is the dominant strategy for both Paul and Alfred. If Alfred believes that Paul will contribute, then he is better off free-riding (8 > 3). If Alfred believes that Paul will free-ride, Alfred is again better off free-riding (0 > -2). No matter what Paul does, free-riding is Alfred's best choice. The same logic applies to Paul's decision. Consequently, the Nash equilibrium is the (0, 0) outcome. Both persons free-ride and the public service is not produced.[17]

The result is a social dilemma for the same reason as the previous two types of dilemmas and could be critical for the survival of settled communities. Independent decision-making by two or more parties produces an outcome that is less attractive than others that are feasible. At least one of them is preferred by all the persons whose choices generated the relatively unattractive outcome. All community members would be better off if the services were provided, and the costs shared (3 > 0). Nonetheless, the practical interests of each individual leads each to free-ride in a community without internalized rules that inhibit free-riding (and externally enforced rules that do so).

Note that this tends to be true even if residents of the community have internalized norms that have solved the Hobbesian and Hardin problems, and so are not true pragmatists. The rules required to solve the free-rider problems are quite different from most rules that solve the problems of excessive conflict and over use of shared resources. Moreover, solving critical public services such as community defense, potable water, and law enforcement, the free-rider outcome can be as important to solve as the problems of unproductive conflict and overuse of common resources. A community may not be viable unless it is able to defend itself from roving bandits, resist the annexation efforts of neighboring communities, assure drinkable water, dispose of waste products safely, and maintain an adequate system of village passageways.

Whenever free-rider problems exist, both Alfred and Paul would favor low-cost steps to move from the (0, 0) cell to the (3, 3) cell, where the service is provided, and the cost is shared among all members of the community. However, a "solution" that costs more than 6 units would not be agreed to because such a solution would cost more than it produces in total benefits (3 + 3).

---

[17] As in the Hobbesian game, this game can also be represented in continuous and infinitely repeated forms. In the former case, some of the public services will be provided, but far less than maximizes member welfare. In the latter cases, the relative payoffs in the matrix should be considered present discounted values of the pure strategy choices, and the equilibrium depicted as a subgame perfect Nash equilibrium. (The payoffs are normalized so that, if the service under consideration is not produced, the payoffs for both Paul and Alfred are zero.)

## Civic Duties as Solutions to Public Goods Problems

Table 2.5 modifies Table 2.4 to illustrate the effects of internalized codes of conduct that reduce propensities to free-ride. As in the Hobbesian and Hardin illustrations, the effects of internalized civic duties can be represented as a subjective loss associated with not performing one's duty (G) or as a subjective benefit from feelings of virtue associated with performing one's civic duty (V). Table 2.5 illustrates the case in which contributing to the community service of interest is regarded to be a virtuous civic duty. In the case illustrated, the benefits from free-riding are relatively small, so the virtue supplement does not have to be very large to solve the problem. A virtue supplement greater than the loss associated with producing the service by oneself (V > 2) is sufficient to assure that the public service is provided. However, it is not sufficient to assure that the costs are shared, which in this case requires a far stronger ethical disposition, V > 5.

Several points emerge from the game matrix and minor extensions of it. First, the choice setting characterized demonstrates that the extent to which norms can be relied upon to solve a public good problem varies with the strength of the norms, the cost of the service, and the size of the community. If the strength of civic duty is modest (e.g., V = 2), public services costing up to 10 can be overcome via civic ethics in the 2-person case illustrated, but not ones costing more than 10—other things being equal. Second, it demonstrates that internalized ethical dispositions need not be universally held by all members of a community to solve public good problems. In the case in which V = 3 for either Alfred or Paul, the public goods problem (lack of provision) is solved, although there may still be free-riders. For example, if V = 3 for Alfred but V = 0 for Paul, Alfred provides the service and Paul free-rides.

The logic of the above free-rider problem can be easily extended to communities with large numbers of members in which internalized codes of conduct vary among members. For example, if the assumptions of Table 2.4 are

**Table 2.5** Solving the Public Goods Dilemma through Internalized Civic Duties

|  |  | Paul | |
|---|---|---|---|
|  |  | Contribute | Free-ride |
| Alfred | Contribute | (A, P) <br> (3 + V, 3 + V) | (A, P) <br> (−2 + V, 8) |
|  | Free-ride | (8, −2 + V) | (0, 0) |

retained, the net benefits of sharing production costs increase as the number of persons contributing increases. The payoffs of the upper left-hand cell become (8 − 10/N), which rises toward 8 as the number of persons (N) in the community increases. This reduces the virtue payoff required to induce everyone to contribute to the production of the public goods of interest. A virtue supplement greater than 5 was required to induce everyone to contribute in the 2-person case, but a virtue payoff greater than 1 will solve the 10-persons version of the same problem.

Large communities are also likely to have a wider distribution of values for "G" and "V" among their residents than small communities. The strongest norms in larger communities tend to be stronger and the weakest weaker. This increase in variation, perhaps surprisingly, tends to reduce public goods problems in large communities. In the above example, it is sufficient for at least one person to have a virtue payoff greater than 2 for the public good or service to be provided, which is more likely when there are more residents of the community of interest. For example, if the strength of ethical dispositions in a given society typically has a normal distribution, the probability that at least one person in a community has a virtue benefit greater than 2 increases with population, even if the average person has no civic virtue.[18] Individuals with higher-than-average civic virtue and propensities to resist free-riding are likely to team up to provide public services, even if all others free-ride.[19]

## The Teaching of Productive Rules of Conduct as a Public Good

Among the most important free-rider problems confronted by communities is the one associated with the transmission of norms that solve Hobbesian, commons, and free-rider problems. In communities without formal systems of education, such norms are transmitted informally by families, friends, and

---

[18] This is a property of sample size for normal distributions. It assumes that a community's distribution of persons with norms of various strengths is randomly drawn from a normal distribution of norm strengths. If the distribution sampled has a maximum value, as in a uniform distribution, there are limits to this sampling effect.

[19] For services that increase in average cost as community size increases, larger communities will not necessarily provide more public services than smaller ones. Whether such services are provided or not depends on the rate of increase in average cost and in the number of especially virtuous persons. With favorable distributional characteristics, a large community will have a sufficiently large number of persons with relatively strong civic virtue to contribute to public services. For example, in large communities, charitable contributions have often funded churches, town meeting halls, residences for the poor, public education, libraries, museums, opera halls, medical research, and many other community services. However, there are certainly cases in which average costs rise faster than the required increase in especially virtuous residents, in which cases smaller communities are more likely to provide them than larger ones.

village wise men and women. Encouraging successive generations (and other new arrivals) to internalize productive rules involves a variety of costly activities in which the private benefits are often much smaller for the "teachers" than are realized by both the "students" and other members of their communities.

This is not to assert that every rule is equally productive or equally challenging to teach. In every community's system of rules there are bound to be at least some unproductive rules that have not yet been winnowed out. There may be rules, for example, that contributed to a community's success in the past but are unproductive or counterproductive in the present circumstances. Nor is it to suggest that all acts of teaching have public goods problems associated with them. For example, some ethical training directly benefits parents, such as rules that encourage children to engage in household production, follow parental instructions, avoid dangerous activities, take care of fellow family members, and the like. Such norms would be transmitted because of a parent's practical interests.

However, insofar as a subset of normative rules makes life in a community more attractive by solving social dilemmas or increasing the community's ability to sustain itself, teaching them is a public good for members of the community, and free-rider problems exist. Activities that support normative training include the teaching of norms and also the encouragement of "good" behavior through approbation, deference, and other rewards. It also includes efforts to discourage violations of such norms with chiding, disapprobation, shaming, and other informal punishments. These are all costly activities, many of which provide only very small direct benefits to the individuals supporting the development of virtuous dispositions in their communities.

To solve these free-rider problems, other "higher order" norms emerge that support the teaching and encouragement of ethical dispositions. These include chiding and disapprobation of parents for failures to teach their children appropriate norms or providing "inadequate" support for the norms taught, and for failing to chide others for violating their community's most common and important norms. It also includes expressions of outrage when such norms are violated by others and of admiration for those who undertake to encourage valuable norms in especially challenging circumstances. The importance of rule transmission across generations is so great that parents arguably inherit biological disposition to teach their children well. Those who do not do so will have fewer of their genes transmitted to subsequent generations.[20]

---

[20] Evidence of the heritability of a parental teaching instinct has been observed in great apes as well as humans. See, for example, Whiten (1999) and Barnett (1968).

Together, the internal and external rewards for encouraging virtuous behavior induce families to engage in moral training and friends and families to support more or less the same norms through praise, stories, and by providing helpful explanations of the good life, dutiful conduct, and praiseworthy behavior. These behaviors help induce ethical rules to be internalized, which in turn induces successive generations of community members to undertake their civic duties. They may grab their bows and arrows or guns and rush to the defense of their community at a moment's notice, volunteer to take a bucket and help put out a fire, or induce folks to sort through their trash and separate recyclables into designated bins.

Communities that provide less support for the teaching of norms to successive generations may still be viable—as long as the most important rules are taught, but their communities tend to be less attractive than those that encourage a broader array of productive rules to be internalized.[21]

## A Digression on the Advantages of Ethical Solutions to Public Goods Problems

From a utilitarian perspective, informal solutions are generally superior to formal tax-financed solutions, because collecting tax revenues and organizing the provision of public services takes resources from other net-benefit generating activities—and often more than is required to sustain an informal system of norm-following encouragements. Those who have internalized an ethical principle know when they have violated or followed it, and their internalization assures that they will be self-punished or self-rewarded accordingly. A formal system requires costly inquiries into whether a particular person has violated a law or not, a formal process for determining and meting out penalties (or rewards). All these are resource-intensive activities. Moreover, coercive aspects of taxation are a further cost of the tax system that reduces the net benefits of community life.[22]

It also bears keeping in mind that normative theories are not always taught with solving a particular dilemma in mind. For example, if bravery, per se, is regarded to be a praiseworthy aspect of a person's character, that virtue may be

---

[21] The process of encouraging the internalization of ethical and other rules of conduct can, of course, also be overdone. This is most likely to occur when the usefulness of particular norms is overestimated. The norms that are most important to transmit are those that solve social dilemmas. Unfortunately, the rule-creating and internalization capabilities of humans are not limited to what might be termed socially productive rules.

[22] See Martinez-Vazquez and Winer (2014) for a recent analysis of the welfare effects of coercion within utilitarian and contractarian frameworks.

developed for private rather than civic reasons. Aristotle, for example, argued that bravery enables one to live a more satisfying, less fearful life. That bravery also helps solve the problem of village defense would be a beneficial and praiseworthy effect, but it may not be the original motivation for encouraging or accumulating courageous dispositions. Norms that generalize across many choice settings may solve other dilemmas so well that they are never noticed.

In cases in which ethical dispositions are not strong enough to solve a particular free-rider problem, governments can potentially improve upon informal solutions, as is also true of informal solutions to the Hobbesian and Hardin problems. However, even in those cases, internalized ethical dispositions tend to reduce the overall cost of governmental solutions. For example, in Table 2.5, the higher the virtue supplement, the smaller external subsidies need be to induce the provision of the service of interest, and the smaller the tax payments required to fund those subsidies. Thus, a community with relatively strong civic virtues requires a less burdensome government than one with weaker ethical dispositions against free-riding, other things being equal.[23]

Moreover, as noted before and developed in Part II, the fact that governments can potentially ameliorate social dilemmas does not imply that they necessarily do so.[24]

## Conventional Behavior: Internalized Norms as Solutions to Coordination Problems

Beyond peace and security, managing access to natural resources, and the provision of public services, a variety of other problems can be ameliorated to make life in a community easier, more pleasant, and productive. Among the most important of these are conventions that reduce various coordination problems. Examples include language, alphabets, measures and weights, and calendars. Other less important conventions include day-to-day customs, including rules for using public passageways such as always pass on the right (or left), naming conventions for boys and girls, and greetings based on time of day and occasion.

---

[23] It bears noting that relatively low expected penalties are sufficient to induce very high levels of tax compliance in the United States and in much of Western Europe. Although the penalties are not trivial, the probability of being punished is very low. That trustworthiness plays a role in tax payments has been demonstrated by Feld and Frey (2002) and by Feld and Tyran (2002). We return to these and other related issues in Part III.

[24] Most public economics textbooks, for example, suggest that many public-goods problems remain unsolved—even in relatively well-governed places—rather than use public-goods problems as an explanation for particular government activities.

Useful conventions are solutions to coordination games. Coordination games have the property that all participants are better off when everyone chooses the same strategy, although no particular strategy is inherently better than another. The equilibria of many coordination games are both desirable and stable, in contrast to the other social dilemmas that we've examined. Internalized norms thus contribute less to generating and stabilizing such outcomes than the other dilemmas, but they may still be useful.

Table 2.6 illustrates the payoff structure of a coordination game for the case of passing people on the left or right on a path or sidewalk. Note that in this case, a pattern of community behavior is likely to emerge that is stable and requires neither ethical nor legal support. Narrow self-interest (pragmatism) is sufficient to sustain either equilibrium when one emerges. Neither player has a sufficient reason to violate the convention after it has emerged. Persons in a given community consequently tend to routinely pass on the right when driving, walking, horseback riding, sailing, and so on. Random choices would slow traffic and increase accidents.

The same matrix can be used to think about a wide variety of coordination problems. Similar advantages are associated with a common language and "ordinary" usage of words from that language. Persons in a given community normally learn their "home" language, and users of a language tend to converge on a few uniform greetings, such as "good morning" or "good day," when meeting another. Internalized norms can support conventions in several ways. Conventions that generalize can speed the emergence of a new equilibrium when new circumstances emerge from technological advance, pandemics, or other innovations and emergencies.

When rules for solving a coordination problem become internalized, one of the strategies increases in value relative to the other. It becomes the "right or natural thing to do" and the other(s) become the "wrong or unnatural thing to do." In a society where there is an internalized disposition to drive on the right, driving on the left is uncomfortable, feels wrong, and is disorienting for its drivers. Similarly, a native speaker might feel

**Table 2.6** Coordination Problems: Walking on Community Pathways

|  |  | Harold | |
|---|---|---|---|
|  |  | Pass on left | Pass on right |
|  |  | (D, H) | (D, H) |
| Duncan | Pass on left | (1, 1) | (−1, −1) |
|  | Pass on right | (−1, −1) | (1, 1) |

**Table 2.7** Internalized Convention for Walking on Community Paths and Sidewalks

|  |  | Harold | |
| --- | --- | --- | --- |
|  |  | Pass on left | Pass on right |
| Duncan | Pass on left | (D, H) | (D, H) |
|  |  | (1 + V, 1 + V) | (−1 + V, −1 − G) |
|  | Pass on right | (−1 − G, −1 + V) | (1 − G, 1 − G) |

uncomfortable with violations of his or her community's rules for greetings, pronunciation, grammar, and expression. Not only would they be unwilling to use slang, pronunciation, or spellings from another region or dialect, they may be uncomfortable when such pronunciations and phrases are used by others. An unconventional speaker may be dismissed as incoherent, an idiot, or a barbarian.

As norms and habits of thought and behavior emerge, one of the possible equilibria associated with new coordination games becomes more likely and more stable than others, because it is reinforced with either a virtue supplement or guilt decrement or both, as well as praise or disparagement. Table 2.7 illustrates the effects of such internalized conventions.

Convention-supporting dispositions shorten or eliminate the period of disequilibrium by reducing incentives to "be unconventional." Even a small nudge provided by an internalized normative principle can be sufficient to induce the "right" strategy choice in unfamiliar circumstances within a given community. The combination of "pull" toward a community's conventions (civic virtue, V) and aversion to deviation (sense of guilt from failure to behave conventionally, G) only have to be sufficient to exceed the temptations to adopt the unconventional strategy, as with $(V + G) > 2$. As conventions emerge and are generalized, the unfavorable off-diagonal results occur with less frequency.[25]

Although violations of conventions are often discouraged by strong feelings of guilt or embarrassment, conventions themselves are not usually regarded to be matters of morality or ethics. This is because most conventions are entirely arbitrary. However, some conventions have morally relevant consequences and can be analyzed with ethical principles. For example, conventions of

---

[25] That frequency tends to be larger in large communities than in small ones, other things being equal, because of mistakes made by their more numerous visitors (who may use different conventions at home) and because of the intentional choices of their more numerous nonconformists.

the variety illustrated in Tables 2.5 and 2.6 satisfy the Kantian imperative. The results of either strategy are good if everyone follows them, and so following such rules can be regarded as possible moral duties under Kant's categorical imperative. Similarly, because following conventions benefits all members of a community and so increases aggregate utility, either strategy can be moral from the utilitarian perspective. However, neither Kantian nor utilitarian theory provides guidance about which of the two strategies should be followed, because the results are identical in terms of universality and contributions to aggregate utility. (Overviews of these theories are provided in Part III.)

Nonetheless, internalized conventions often elicit the same sort of psychological and social reactions as those associated with unethical acts. Violating conventions, as with poor spelling, generates guilty reactions by the misspeller and disapprobation from fellow community members in much the same manner as actions regarded to be unethical. It is this sense of guilt or virtue that allows the effects of internalized conventions to be represented in the same manner previously used for ethical decisions. Once established, following community norms may be supported by other higher-level virtues that are unrelated to specific conventions such as prudence or a duty to follow community laws.[26]

The point of this subsection is that conventions tend to become internalized, often advance the interests of members of a community, and are supported in much the same manner as ethical conduct, although relatively few conventions are regarded to be subjects of ethics.[27] Conventions enrich a community's life by increasing the likelihood that one of the more rewarding equilibria emerges and is sustained, which tends to reduce accidents, conflict, and transactions costs.[28]

---

[26] There are conventions that individuals may violate in a manner that yields private benefits while imposing losses on others, as with cheating on weights and measures. Merchants, for example, might be tempted to label an item that weighs 15 ounces as a full pound, or 950 grams as a full kilo. Such temptations can undermine the usefulness associated with both the English or metric conventions for weights and measures—although which system of weights a community uses is itself of little consequence. Such violations are often considered to be unethical.

[27] See Brennan and Pettit (2004) for an analysis of markets for esteem.

[28] It bears noting that there are usually more social conventions and uniformity norms than there are coordination problems to be solved. Examples from ancient and more recent history include dress codes, dietary restrictions, and state-sanctioned religious beliefs. In these cases, the benefits from eliminating uniformity norms and formal penalties for violating them were evidently larger than their long-run costs, because they were not solutions to coordination problems. They were unproductive restrictions on choice and occasionally generated Hobbesian conflict about which convention should be imposed. Tolerance for a bit of nonconformity may help weed out conventions that do not address coordination or free-rider problems.

# A Generalization: Social Dilemmas as Externality Problems

Thousands of problematic choice settings fall into one of the four subcategories of social dilemmas reviewed to this point—unproductive conflict, overuse of a shared resource, free-riding, and coordination problems. Therefore, possibilities for further generalization may be regarded as unnecessary. However, all four subcategories share a common characteristic.

All the social dilemmas discussed above are instances of what economists refer to as *negative externality* problems. They are choice settings in which a person's pragmatic interests lead to actions that reduce the net benefits realized by others. In the Hobbesian dilemma, the attack strategy reduced the net benefits of the person being attacked. In the Hardin dilemma, the overuse of a common resource reduced the productivity of the commons for other users. In the free-rider dilemma, decisions to free-ride reduce the extent of public services available to others within the community. In coordination games, the welfare of others is diminished when people adopt nonconformist strategies.

As a consequence, total net benefits, whether measured in terms of physical output, money, or subjective appraisals (utility), were not maximized. Other choices could have produced outcomes considered superior to the one realized by every person whose choice partly determined the outcome. Solutions to externality problems also share properties; they induce behavior that explicitly or implicitly takes account of the external harm (or benefits) imposed on others. Although particular instances of externality problems have been recognized from humanity's earliest days, the recognition that most social dilemmas are instances of externality problems only emerged in the past century and a half.

Many externality problems are more difficult to recognize and to solve than the two-by-two game matrices suggest. Such social dilemmas can be illustrated by examining choice settings in which more strategies are possible and in which the outcomes deemed most useful, advantageous, or moral are intermediate ones rather than extreme ones.[29]

Table 2.8 illustrates a typical reciprocal externality problem. The choice setting illustrated is one that might emerge as settled communities and husbandry emerge, although it is also one that some towns and cities are

[29] The concept of "externality" is a mid- to late-nineteenth-century invention that is often attributed to Alfred Marshall. It was further elaborated by Arthur Pigou and many others working in the subfields of welfare economics and public economics during the nineteenth century. The extent to which this concept is recognized outside of economics remains surprisingly limited (except as special cases). Fitzgerald et al. (2016) demonstrate that relatively few individuals have internalized the concept of externalities.

**Table 2.8** An Externality Problem

|  |  | James | | |
|---|---|---|---|---|
|  |  | 1 chicken | 10 chickens | 50 chickens |
| Craig | 1 chicken | (C, J)<br>(4, 4) | (C, J)<br>(3, 6) | (C, J)<br>(1, 8) |
|  | 10 chickens | (6, 3) | (5, 5) | (2, 6) |
|  | 50 chickens | (8, 1) | (6, 2) | (3, 3) |

concerned about today. Suppose that raising chickens in a village creates "external costs" such as noise, smells, and pests. Urban farming is beneficial for the persons undertaking it or it would not be undertaken. However, each farmer's quality of life is diminished by the noises and smells associated with their neighbor's fowl farms.

Three farm sizes are used below to illustrate the case in which an externality problem is not of the all-or-nothing variety. In the case illustrated, the Nash equilibrium is one with relatively large household poultry farms throughout the village. These provide benefits to the chicken owners but impose significant "external" costs on their neighbors. A social dilemma exists because there is another outcome that is feasible and generates additional net benefits for each poultry farmer, namely the outcome associated with smaller flocks (5 > 3).

In this case, the best outcome in terms of aggregate net benefits is an intermediate outcome, rather than a simple yes/no or right/wrong outcome. (This was also the case for the commons problem of Table 2.3.) Urban chicken farming is not usually regarded to be morally wrong or right, but some levels of activities may be regarded as "more proper" within a village or town than others. As in Aristotle's theory of ethics, moral behavior is a mean between two extremes, in the case illustrated, the ideal is an intermediate level of urban chicken farming.

Generating the "right" level of such activities, however, is not easy because it requires individuals to "internalize externalities," an activity that is explicitly required for utilitarian theory but no others. Instead of simple "always do X" or "avoid doing Y" solutions, the best solution to an externality problem varies with circumstances. Agreements may be reached about the proper use of the village for a specific type of fowl farming, but that level may not be the best for some other. The villagers may agree that urban farms in this village should have 10 or fewer chickens, and their agreement may be supported by other norms such as promise-keeping norms or a sense of civic duty—but

Ethics and the Quality of Life in Communities 63

**Table 2.9** Solving the Externality Problem

| | | James | | |
|---|---|---|---|---|
| | | 1 chicken | 10 chickens | 50 chickens |
| Craig | 1 chicken | (C, J) (4, 4) | (C, J) $(3, 6-G_{10})$ | (C, J) $(1, 8-G_{50})$ |
| | 10 chickens | $(6-G_{10}, 3)$ | $(5-G_{10}, 5-G_{10})$ | $(2-G_{10}, 6-G_{50})$ |
| | 50 chickens | $(8-G_{50}, 1)$ | $(6-G_{50}, 2-G_{10})$ | $(3-G_{50}, 3-G_{50})$ |

without implying that other similar enterprises—as with raising geese or ducks—should be subject to identical rules, or that the same rules would work as well when the community grows.

A more general solution would rely upon a graduated guilt (or virtue) function that rises with the external costs that one's activities impose on others. Such a guilt function is said to "internalize" the externality. Table 2.9 illustrates how a graduated association of guilt with the imposition of negative externalities operates. Guilt rises as the external costs generated by the externality-generating activity increase $(G_{50} > G_{10} > 0)$. Table 2.9 demonstrates that internalized norms that associate guilt with activities that generate external costs (negative externalities) can potentially ameliorate a wide variety of externality problems. Such a normative system would generalize in that it would generate different behavior according to the extent of the externality generated.

The rule of conduct required is not simply a "right or wrong" norm, but "righter" and "wronger" norm—a rank ordering of the morality or appropriateness of the strategy choices—here the size of each person's chicken farm. If the externality is perfectly internalized, the guilt associated with a flock size would be equal to the external costs (reduced payoffs) imposed on all others in the community. Such a normative principle tends to produce the utilitarian ideal outcome, which maximizes the sum of the payoffs (profits or satisfaction) generated within the relevant community, and such outcomes tend to be Pareto efficient, in that no other outcome can improve the results for one person without reducing them for another.[30]

---

[30] Readers familiar with public economics might find it of interest that an ideal utilitarian ethical disposition, with its associated feelings of virtue and guilt, serves as a subjective Pigovian tax for externality-generating activities, which perfectly internalizes the externality. In discrete choice settings, perfect internalization is not necessary to achieve the best result. For example, a graduated guilt schedule that only approximately links guilt to external costs, such as $G_{50} > 2$ and $G_{10} < 1$, generates the middle cell as an equilibrium.

The difficulty of utilitarian solutions to externality problems is that they require external costs to be known or accurately estimated, and it also requires an ideal schedule of guilt decrements or virtue increments that is well suited for the externality problem of interest. These vary with each problem because external costs vary among choice settings. With respect to urban farming, the external costs vary with community size, density, and the types of animals involved.

Thus, the existence of a principle for solving externality problems does not imply that a unique "guilt schedule" can solve all such problems. Each guilt schedule has to be calibrated to the external costs associated with a particular externality in a particular community. The dearth of fully generalizable norms is thus not entirely a consequence of the fact that the common features of social dilemmas are unknown to community members.[31]

Social dilemmas are often subtle and complex and therefore difficult to recognize. And, once recognized, the same tends to be true of both general solutions and the subset of those solutions that are compatible with the systems of norms already internalized by a community's residents.

Recall that the choice settings reviewed in this chapter all look quite different from one another. Some involved violent conflict, others the peaceful use of shared resources, others jointly produced services for the community, and others somewhat arbitrary rules that tend to make life in a community more attractive. Their associated problematic equilibria also look different, as with injured bodies, desolate pastureland, missing useful services, and increases in accident rates or transactions costs. They do not look like the same problems, nor are their solutions obviously cut from the same cloth.

It is only after they are placed in a game theoretic framework that their common features are evident. Once that commonality is discerned, one may be on the lookout for "spillover" costs and benefits from private activities and then check to see if the outcomes are ones for which additional benefits may be gleaned by internalizing new rules of conduct. Most externality-generating activities have both properties. A more general understanding of social dilemmas allows them to be more easily identified, although it does not necessarily make their resolution much easier.[32]

---

[31] That contemporary governments tend to address externality problems with specific, direct regulations rather than with graduated Pigovian taxes is consistent with this proposition.

[32] It should be noted that the external approach to identifying social dilemmas has its limits. Buchanan and Stubblebine (1962), for example, show that one can have external costs without generating social dilemmas if there are no external costs "at the margin." It should also be noted that when governments are tasked with solving externality problems, they often fail to do so, for reasons taken up in Part II.

# Conclusions: Ethics and Life in Communities

From an evolutionary perspective, the capacity to develop and internalize rules improves survival prospects for individuals and groups of individuals. It does so by allowing knowledge to accumulate in the form of "if-then" rules about (1) what is real and what is not, (2) whether a particular aspect of the universe can be changed through human action or not, and (3) how to choose among the possibilities for doing so when it is possible. Such knowledge allows both risks and alternatives to be better assessed and better choices to be made—choices that on average increase a person's and community's prospects for survival. Ethical dispositions are a subset of the rules used to assess the relative merits of alternative courses of action. They contribute to survival (both of the persons that have internalized such beliefs and the beliefs themselves) insofar as they solve or ameliorate critical personal and social dilemmas.

This chapter has analyzed a series of problematic choice settings that illustrates the many contributions that internalized rules of conduct can play in the emergence of relatively peaceful, viable, stationary communities in the period before significant economic development took place. Ethical and similar normative dispositions can reduce conflict, mitigate commons problems, help assure that critical community services are provided, solve coordination problems, and reduce other externality problems. If the choice settings explored are interpreted as a pre-history, they imply that every community has an ethos—a system of normative rules that ameliorates the most important social dilemmas confronted in the location and environment in which its members reside. Without such rules, conflict would be endemic and many resources would be poorly used.

The illustrations also indirectly demonstrate that ethical principles and maxims need not be internalized completely to provide the foundations for a flourishing community. Not all social dilemmas have to be solved for viable relatively attractive communities to emerge. It is sufficient that enough persons have internalized productive systems of rules that ameliorate social dilemmas.

In addition, the analysis suggests that survivorship and rule innovation imply that a community's positive and normative systems of rules tend to improve through time—although the rate of improvement is likely to vary among communities. Although social evolution is normally much faster than biological evolution, it is sufficiently slow and haphazard that it can take place for thousands of years without reaching a perfect understanding of the universe or an ideal system of ethical dispositions. Some known problems remain unsolved. Many others remain unrecognized or yet to be confronted. Thus, as roadblocks to social development are confronted, there may be long pauses in social evolution of the punctuated variety similar to those associated with biological evolution, rather than a continuous series of improvements.[33]

If so, what we observe is more akin to Locke's original state in which various internalized rules of conduct (moral maxims, principles, and their associated duties) have been internalized to varying degrees by persons within a community and problematic choice settings have been ameliorated rather than fully solved as they would be at Spencer's ideal.[34] Locke's conception of the natural state was, of course, not entirely hypothetical. It was partly based on the experience of English colonists in the Atlantic colonies of North America, where governance was often weak. Yet, informal communities emerged, and life in a subset of those communities was sufficiently attractive that their residents stayed where they were, rather than moving on. Through time, many such communities flourished as new immigrants arrived and joined the most attractive communities and colonies that they were aware of.

With respect to the main focus of this book, ethical solutions to the problems of life in stationary communities can be considered prerequisites for economic development, because towns and cities are the places where commerce is most evident, and commerce is the surest route to prosperity, for reasons taken up in the next few chapters. As Hobbes pointed out more than 350 years ago, without some security of life and property, industry, the arts, and commerce are unlikely to emerge.

## Appendix to Chapter 2: A Brief Introduction to Non-Cooperative Game Theory

The use of game theory to study politics began in the eighteenth century, and in economics in the nineteenth century. Condorct and Borda used rational choice models to analyze the effects of different voting rules in the period just before the French Revolution, and Cournot developed his well-studied duopoly model in the mid-nineteenth century. Cournot's model provides an example of a what would later be termed a Nash equilibrium of a

[33] See Eldredge and Gould (1972) or Bak and Sneppen (1993) for overviews and models of punctuated equilibrium. See Congleton and Vanberg (1992, 2001) or Boyd and Richardson (1988, 2002) for evolutionary models of the emergence of norms.

[34] Remarks in Spencer's autobiography ([1904] 2014) suggest that at some point after 1851, he changed his mind about the feasibility of an evolutionary cultural equilibria, probably because he came to believe that society and human nature change more slowly than new problems emerge.

non-cooperative game in the mid- to late twentieth century. Other game-theoretic representations of the outcomes associated with markets that were less than perfectly competitive were developed in the 1930s, as with the Stackelberg duopoly model and Chamberlin's model of monopolistic competition.

It was not until shortly after World War II that game theory emerged as a separate field of study. The book that first brought that field to the attention of persons outside a small group of applied mathematicians is *Theory of Games and Economic Behavior* by von Neumann and Morgenstern (1944). A second, more accessible, classic work was published a decade later, *Games and Decisions* by Luce and Raiffa (1957).

Game theory can be used to model a wide variety of human behavior in small-number and large-number economic, political, and social settings. The choice settings in which economists most frequently apply game theory, however, are small-number settings, because these are sufficient to illustrate the various types of outcomes that may emerge when they are determined jointly by the decisions of independent decision-makers. In non-cooperative game theory, individuals are usually assumed to maximize their own payoffs (utility) without taking account of the effects of their choices on other persons in the game. The game players are usually assumed to be pragmatists without internalized ethical dispositions. The outcomes of non-cooperative games are jointly determined by the strategies independently chosen by all players in the game. Consequently, each person's welfare depends, in part, on the decisions of other individuals "in the game."

For example, in a **Cournot duopoly**, two firms compete in a single market, and each firm's profits depends upon its own output decision and that of the other firm in the market. In a setting where pure public goods are consumed, one's own consumption of the public good depends partly on one's own production level of the good and partly on that of all others. After a snowfall, the amount of snow on neighborhood sidewalks depends partly on one's own efforts at shoveling and partly that of all others in the neighborhood. In an election, each candidate's share of the votes depends partly on his or her own policy positions and those taken by the other candidate(s).

The simplest games that can be used to model social interdependence are games with two persons, each of whom can independently choose between two strategies, $S_1$ and $S_2$. There are four possible outcomes in such games:

(1) Both players may choose $S_1$;
(2) Both may choose $S_2$;
(3) Player A may choose $S_1$ and player B may choose $S_2$; or
(4) Player A may choose $S_2$ and player B may choose $S_1$.

The combination of strategies chosen determines which outcome emerges, and the outcome determines the rewards or losses (payoffs or utilities) realized by the two decision-makers.

Such games allow a variety of interdependencies to be analyzed systematically. They also shed light on more complex settings involving many strategies and many players, as well as settings in which the same choice settings are confronted (repeated) a finite number of times. Such extended models, perhaps surprisingly, normally generate very similar behavior and outcomes.

A game is said to have a **Nash equilibrium** when a strategy combination is "stable" in the sense that no player can independently change his or her strategy and increase his or her own payoff by doing so. Some games have more than one Nash equilibrium, others have only one, and some have no simple (pure strategy) equilibria. For example, coordination games have two equilibria. In equilibrium, no relevant decision-maker (player) can become better off by changing their strategy (alone) given that of the other player(s) in the game.

A state of the world or game outcome is said to be **Pareto optimal**, or Pareto efficient, if it is impossible to reach another state where at least one person is better off and no one is worse off. It is said to be Pareto suboptimal if another feasible outcome would make at least one person better off and no one worse off.

The **Prisoner's Dilemma (PD) game** is probably the most widely used game in social science. PD games represent cases in which the so-called "cooperate, cooperate" solution is preferred by each player to the "defect, defect" equilibrium, $[v(S_1), v(S_1)] > [v(S_2), v(S_2)]$. The noncooperative equilibrium of a PD game also requires that the value generated by defecting to be greater than that associated with cooperating regardless of whether the other player cooperates or not. Often the payoffs are represented ordinally with (3, 3) for the mutual cooperative solution and (2, 2) for the mutual defection result. The other payoffs are then (1, 4) and (4, 1) with the defector receiving 4 and the cooperator 1.

However, the PD payoffs can be represented numerically or algebraically with (abstract) payoffs. For example, (C, C) and (D, D) can stand for the payoffs of the mutual cooperation and mutual defection outcomes. In addition (S, T) and (T, S) can stand for the "temptation" and "sucker's" payoffs when one person defects and the other is "played for a sucker." In a PD game, $T > C > D > S$. Many PD games have nothing to do with prisoners—indeed the ones that do are among the least interesting of PD choice settings.

The PD game's main limitations as a model of social dilemmas are its assumptions about the number of players (2), the number of strategies (2), the period of play (a 1-shot game), and the interests of the players (self-centered).

However, in most cases, most of these assumptions can be dropped without changing the basic conclusions of the analysis. Essentially, the same conclusions follow for N-person games in which the players have an infinite number of strategies (along a continuum) and play for any *finite* number of rounds.

However, if the players have internalized ethical dispositions, many of the settings thought to have payoffs consistent with prisoner's dilemmas (as many lab experiments in which players have small objective money-based payoffs) will not actually have a PD payoff structure in subjective utility terms, as demonstrated in this chapter.

The **mathematical requirements for completely specifying a game** are met in the PD game. The possible strategies are completely enumerated. The payoffs for each player are completely described for all possible combinations of strategies. The information set is (implicitly) characterized. (A player is said to have perfect information if he knows all details of the game. A perfectly informed player knows the payoffs for each party, the range of strategies possible, and whether the other players are fully informed or not.)

The use of game theory to analyze social dilemmas continues to be among the most fruitful areas of applied game theory in economics, political science, sociology, philosophy, and biology. A quick look at any economics or political science journal published in the past half century and many philosophy journals published in the past three decades will reveal a large number of articles that use elementary game theory to analyze behavior in settings where independent choices jointly determine outcomes. Most contemporary work on the self-enforcing properties of contracts, credible commitments, renegotiation, the private production of public goods, externalities, and political and social competition use game theoretic models as their engines of analysis.

# 3
# Ethics, Exchange, and Production

If I have two journeymen, **one naturally industrious**, the other idle,
but both perform a day's work equally good, ought I to give the latter
the most wages? Indeed, lazy workmen are commonly observed to be
more extravagant in their demands than the industrious; for, if they
have not more for their work, they cannot live as well. But though it be
true to a proverb that lazy folks take the most pains, does it follow that
they deserve the most money?

If you were to employ servants in affairs of trust, would you not bid
more for one you knew was naturally honest than for one naturally ro-
guish, but who has lately acted honestly?

—Benjamin Franklin "Self-denial Is Not the Essence
of Virtue" ([1734] 2012), Kindle locations 414–419

## Introduction: Specialization and Exchange

Many of the advantages of life in communities are associated with specialization. Some persons devote more time to the production of subsets of various
goods and services than others. Many such specializations are sufficiently old
that the persons engaging in them have been given names, such as hunters,
farmers, carpenters, potterers, and masons. "Specialists" tend to be more productive at their specialties than the average person because, as the saying goes,
"practice makes perfect." One's understanding of possibilities and the ability
to take advantage of them tend to improve with repetition, and more practice
is possible for a narrow set of activities than a broad one. Persons who specialize may also make or acquire tools of various kinds (capital goods) that
further increase their efficiency at producing their specialties. By increasing
the extent to which hours of work yield useful goods and services, specialization tends to increase the extent of a community's material resources and
its knowledge base. As a consequence, a community that takes advantage of
specialization tends to be wealthier and to have a greater ability to survive
life's many unpredictable hazards. In this manner, rules that facilitate and

*Solving Social Dilemmas.* Roger D. Congleton, Oxford University Press. © Oxford University Press 2022.
DOI: 10.1093/oso/9780197642788.003.0003

encourage specialization tend to contribute to both a community's durability and its prosperity.

Some specialization is likely to occur simply because of variation in the genetic endowments of community members. Individuals naturally vary in their height, strength, flexibility, speed, eyesight, hearing, health, and in their ability to internalize, invent, and revise rules. Such heritable differences would tend to induce variations in the types of activities that individual group members are inclined to undertake—which is to say, within any group, there is likely to be some degree of natural specialization simply because individuals differ from one another.

These natural dispositions to specialize may be reinforced or countered by socially transmitted norms internalized over the course of a lifetime and also by rewards associated with the various specialties that might be undertaken. In a society without many resources, rewards include praise, deference, and gifts, as well as opportunities for romance and marriage. Communities in which it is possible to trade goods and services for others provide additional pecuniary rewards for a subset of specialties, which makes some forms of specialization more profitable than others. Tradability and trade thus encourage persons or families to specialize in producing goods that others are willing to pay for and which may not directly contribute to their sustenance, but that do so indirectly through that which is received in trade. Among the ancient specialties, gatherers, hunters, and farmers can survive by consuming only the products of their efforts. In contrast, potters, basket weavers, carpenters, masons, and blacksmiths make useful things, but their products are not edible, and so such specialties cannot directly sustain the lives of persons that specialize in these activities.

Sophisticated sharing rules that support specialization or rules that support exchange are thus prerequisites for many forms of specialization. Without such rules, there would be far less specialization, and communities would tend to be less prosperous, other things being equal. Neither voluntary exchange nor specialization is as natural, easy, or automatic as economic textbooks make them appear to be. There are a variety of dilemmas that impede the development of markets and extended trading networks. Unless these are overcome, it is unlikely that significant commerce will emerge or that a community will benefit much from specialization.

Were trade and specialization as automatic as assumed in most economic textbooks, most animals—not just humans—would live in cities, engage in voluntary exchange, and take advantage of specialized production.[1]

---

[1] Ecologists might insist that we do see a lot of specialization and complementarities in nature. However, this specialization is not a product of exchange but of the evolution of natural proclivities. Specialization

Chapter 3 continues our analysis of communities without government or a formal law-enforcing organization. Again, the purpose of neglecting formal governance is to focus on the evolution of norms that ameliorate social dilemmas and to simplify the narrative. Chapter 2 demonstrated that informal communities can be sustained by internalized norms that reduce unproductive conflict, regulate the use of common resources, reduce coordination problems, assure the provision of critical public services, and ameliorate other significant externality problems. Chapter 3 shows that there are other dilemmas associated with exchange and team production that must be overcome for markets and prosperous communities to emerge. Social dilemmas associated with governance are taken up in Part II. (For readers uncomfortable with the informal community perspective, the illustrating examples can be interpreted as cases in which informal solutions emerge for problems not yet resolved by a community's legal system.)

This chapter focuses on dilemmas associated with voluntary exchange and production, and it largely ignores complex sharing rules and coercive systems that might also promote specialization. It does so because history suggests that commercial societies are more likely to generate extensive prosperity than other forms of social organization, largely because of the greater productivity of the specialization and diligence encouraged by such systems. A good deal of the specialization and diligence observed in commercial societies is arguably the result of the personal, social, and pecuniary rewards associated with trade. For example, Smith (1776), Stigler (1951), and Buchanan and Yoon (1994b) all argue that the extent of specialization is limited by the extent of trading networks. However, this chapter demonstrates that pecuniary rewards alone are unlikely to fully account for either the specialization or diligence associated with commercial societies.

The economic dilemmas examined in this chapter tend to reduce the size of market networks and thereby also tend to reduce specialization and prosperity. Many of these dilemmas are most plausibly ameliorated by internalized norms, just as the social dilemmas of Chapter 2 were.

Ethical dispositions can be said to facilitate trade and specialization by reducing what economists refer to as *transactions costs*—a catch-all term for a variety of informational and incentive problems associated with trade,

---

by species occurs, rather than specialization within species. To the extent that there are complementarities and biological networks, these reflect opportunities to specialize rather than gains from trade. That more life and more variety of life are supported through the emergence of specialized species thus illustrates the enormous advantages of specialization even when it is not generated by voluntary exchange. The primary orders of insects that live in colonies—ants, bees, and wasps (Hymenoptera) and termites (Isoptera)—however, make only very limited use of specialization (Wilson 2014).

production, and innovation. However, the term *transactions cost* does not do justice to the dilemmas analyzed in this chapter. Problematic choice settings are not mere surcharges on individual transactions, but prevent some types of market activities from taking place.[2]

## Realizing Gains to Trade without Transactions Costs among Honest Trading Partners

That shifting resources between two persons can make both parties better off is counterintuitive to many students of economics, which implies that some innovation in understanding about possibilities is necessary for trade in goods—as opposed to trade in favors—to emerge. This may reflect the fact that the realization of mutual gains from trade and advantages of specialization is rarely easy. The difficulties include the one pointed out by Hobbes. An individual or group that wants what another party initially controls may simply try to use force to take over that control, as two children may fight over a toy, or dogs may fight over a bone or carcass. The result of such efforts, along with the defensive ones of others, may escalate to a war of every human against every other if similar choices are made by most persons in the region of interest and everyone has roughly the same ability to organize and produce force.

After the Hobbesian dilemma is resolved, trade, specialization, and capital accumulation may or may not be possible. Whether they are or not depends partly on the nature of the solutions worked out.

Chapter 2 mentions partitioning as one of the possible ways that communities can solve the Hobbesian and commons problems. Such solutions reduce conflict by making some claims of control over resources uncontroversial and thereby legitimate, just, or fair. In some cases, partitioning rules include the ability to shift control over a resource from the original "user" to another person or group. A user-owner in such cases may give part or all of such resources to his or her children, to other family members, or to friends. Transferability also makes voluntary exchange or trade possible. An individual or family may agree to transfer control over a subset of their

---

[2] Douglas North (1981, 1990) was among the first to stress that gradual reductions in transactions costs account for much of the gradual extension of trading networks. The main hypothesis of this book is compatible with North's analysis, but it focuses on internalized dispositions rather than innovations in organizational rules. North (1992) explicitly includes rules of conduct among what he terms "informal institutions," although he does not analyze how ethical or normative dispositions reduce transactions costs by solving a variety of economic dilemmas.

transferable resources to another person or group in exchange for a transfer of some of the resources controlled by the other person or group.

In contrast, communities that solve their most serious Hobbesian and Hardin problems with various non-transferable sharing rights are less likely to see trade emerge. Even the possibility of exchange may go unrecognized in such communities, because the concepts of "ownership" and "transferability" are unfamiliar to them or are deemed immoral.[3] Such communities are likely to have less specialization, because the rewards associated with specialization are smaller in such communities than in communities whose norms support voluntary exchange. Moreover, the more of a community's outputs that are shared, the greater are the free-rider problems that have to be overcome to produce them. Thus, other things being equal, a lower standard of life in terms of goods and services is likely to emerge in communities that rely exclusively on sharing rules to solve their most critical social dilemmas than in ones that rely at least in part on partitioning rules. This is not to say that such sharing-based communities are necessarily less attractive to their members than ones in which trade is possible, but it is to say that they tend to be materially less comfortable, other things being equal.[4]

For trade to be commonplace, the peaceful transfer of control (ownership) of particular things from one person to another must be possible, deemed morally permissible by the traders, and believed to yield benefits for each.

Communities that use a mixture of privatization and sharing rules—as most do today—will see trade emerge for many of the goods and services that are potentially tradable, although not for goods and services in the shared or untradable categories. The broader the potentially tradable category is, the more extensive exchange and specialization tend to be. However, simply allowing transferable ownership rights for a subset of the resources in

[3] This is not to say that trade is impossible in such communities. The shares themselves may be tradable, although that requires a sophisticated means of adjusting shares and tracking share ownership and also norms that support such transactions. For example, shares in corporations are commonly traded. However, such share trading is not very common for common forms of communal property. No one, for example, trades part of their right to use a sidewalk for part of someone else's right to use a roadway or bicycle path. Such partitionable tradable shares simply do not exist for most commonly owned goods.

[4] A contemporary example of communities grounded in sharing rules and supportive norms is the Israeli kibbutz. The kibbutzim began as communal or cooperative farming communities in the early nineteenth century. During the second half of the twentieth century, most gradually "privatized" their reward systems, allowed for employment outside the kibbutz, and engaged in trade with persons outside their communities. In this manner, over the course of a century, initially (largely) self-sufficient communal communities gradually became more focused on exchange with the outside world, used reward systems that incentivized work on communal projects, and provided more extensive partitioning (ownership) within the kibbutz. This experience demonstrates both the continuum of common versus private ownership and tendencies in contemporary society to support greater partitioning and privatization as external markets become more extensive and efficient. About 1.2% of Israelis live in kibbutzim today, and very few remain as communal as most were at their founding.

a community does not necessarily produce significant markets in those goods and services or significant specialization. There are additional problems that must be solved for this to occur.

## A Game Theoretic Representation of Textbook Voluntary Exchange

Every trade involves making and accepting offers. A seller makes an offer (e.g., displays goods for sale) and potential buyers decide whether to accept the offer or not. In the easy textbook cases, the goods or services to be exchanged are well understood by both parties, and the "price" is known to produce mutual advantages for both buyers and sellers. Yet, even in this simple setting, trade is not entirely automatic. Offers still have to be made and accepted.[5]

Table 3.1 characterizes a choice setting in which trade is likely to emerge. It is the trading setting of most economics textbooks, but expressed as a game in normal form. Note that in three of the four cells, no trade takes place, because a voluntary exchange requires both a willing buyer and a willing seller.

Perhaps surprisingly, this "exchange game" has two potential Nash equilibria. The trade equilibrium postulated by economics textbooks occurs in the upper left-hand corner. The trade outcome is stable in that neither trader can improve his own payoff by changing his strategy (3 > 0). Note, however, that this is also true of the lower right-hand "no-trade" outcome. Neither Adam nor Friedrich can improve his payoff by changing his strategy from "do not"

**Table 3.1** An Exchange Game without Transactions Costs

|  |  | Friedrich (seller) | |
| --- | --- | --- | --- |
|  |  | Make offer | Do not |
| Adam (buyer) | Accept offer | (A, F) (3, 3) | (A, F) (0, 0) |
|  | Do not | (0, 0) | (0, 0) |

---

[5] See Vernon Smith (1962) for an experimental demonstration that a process of offers and acceptance can generate equilibria similar to those of competitive markets. Experiments based on his induced preference methodology are often used in classroom demonstrations of how market prices emerge from decentralized decision-making (Holt 1999). Nozick ([1974] 2013) uses the offer and acceptance vocabulary to develop implications of voluntary relationships in communities with well-defined property rights of the Lockean variety.

to his alternative strategy $(0 = 0)$. Trade is possible, but is not the only possible stable outcome.

It can be argued that the trade equilibrium dominates the no-trade equilibrium because players in the lower right-hand cell can change their strategies from their "do not" to their "do" strategies without cost and without risk. Thus, it can be argued that making, soliciting, and accepting offers are (weakly) dominant strategies for each potential trader in this setting. They yield results that are at least as good for each potential trader as the alternative strategy, regardless of what the other does. Adam is at least as well off accepting or seeking an offer than not accepting or seeking offers, no matter what Friedrich does. Similarly, Friedrich is at least as well off making the offer as not making it, regardless of what Adam does. This implies that the textbook result of the upper left-hand corner is the most likely outcome of this choice setting, although this conclusion involves a subtler understanding of the rewards from exchange than that used to characterize the individual incentives in the choice settings explored in Chapter 2.

Note that very strong assumptions are made to assure this outcome. Offers must be costless to make and accept, the evaluation of offers must always be correct, and it must never be possible to simply take what is wanted. Neither ethics nor law can improve market outcomes in such cases, except insofar as these are necessary to define ownership and the proper manner for shifting control over the goods from one party to another.[6]

## Gains to Trade with Transactions Costs among Honest Trading Partners

Let us now modify the choice setting by assuming that making, seeking, and accepting offers takes time, attention, and energy that could have been used for other purposes. Assume that both making and accepting offers requires sacrificing 1 unit of benefit from other activities. (Economists refer to such sacrifices as the *opportunity cost* of an activity, here attempting to engage in a specific trade.) The seller may have to travel to a particular location, create a sign or shout out his or her price, or move an item to an easily seen place that implies that it is for sale. The buyer may also have to make a special trip to

---

[6] As in the previous chapter, the matrices can be interpreted either as one-shot games or as repeated games in which the payoffs are present discounted values (net benefits) for the pure strategies. The equilibria in the latter cases are subgame perfect equilibria in pure strategies.

**Table 3.2** Exchange Game with Transactions Costs

|  |  | Ronald (seller) | |
|---|---|---|---|
|  |  | Make offer | Do not |
| Douglas (buyer) | Accept offer | (D, R) (2, 2) | (D, R) (−1, 0) |
|  | Do not | (0, −1) | (0, 0) |

observe what is for sale, make sure that he or she has a means of payment, and evaluate the offer of goods for sale.

Traders are again assumed to be well informed about the details of the offers made. There is neither fraud nor any misunderstanding of the terms of trade. This choice setting is characterized in Table 3.2. Transactions costs affect the net gains to trade that are ultimately realized and also the off-diagonal payoffs that occur when offers are made but ignored, or sought but not discovered.

The existence of transactions costs transforms the exchange game into what is called an *assurance game*. Assurance games are similar to the coordination games used to analyze the value added by conventions in Chapter 2 in that there are two or more possible Nash equilibria. However, in an assurance game, one equilibrium is regarded by all the participants to be better than the other. Nonetheless, either equilibria may plausibly emerge from independent decision-making.[7]

There are no dominant strategies in this game, because the best choice depends entirely on what the other(s) do. Douglas will not look for an offer to accept if he anticipates that Ronald will not make an offer, because Douglas would bear the transactions cost of doing so without realizing any gains to trade. Similarly, Ronald should not bother to make an offer if he anticipates that Douglas will not look for or accept his offer. Gains to trade may exist but are not necessarily realized, because making and accepting offers is costly.

Contemporary examples of such unrealized gains to trade include all of the "treasure" that lies buried in today's basements, attics, and closets that could have been sold, but hasn't, on one of the Internet-selling services. Some is sold

---

[7] See Skyrms (2001) for an overview of assurance games in settings where there are advantages to coordinating in a productive activity (the stag hunt). See Brosnan et al. (2011) for an examination of how humans and other primates participate in such games and their tendency to find the higher payoff equilibrium in small-number settings. They found both similarities and systematic differences among the five species examined; humans and chimpanzees behave the most similarly in the choice setting examined, and were the most likely to converge on the higher reward Nash equilibrium.

(as at the top-left cell), but much is not even offered for sale or looked for, as at the bottom-right cell.

In the beginning, before the notion and routines of trade emerge, the lower left-hand corner would surely have been the more common equilibrium.

## Culture and the Emergence of Markets

Adam Smith's classic text, the *Wealth of Nations* (1776), suggests that trade takes place because people have a "propensity to truck, barter, and exchange one thing for another." In such cases, transactions costs may be offset by the joy of trading. A similar propensity would be associated with normative dispositions that regard trade to be an inherently virtuous activity because, for example, it tends to increase aggregate utility, as argued by nineteenth- and twentieth-century utilitarians.

Table 3.3 represents such internalized predispositions to trade as V, a benefit associated with trading itself that is independent of whether a trade actually takes place or not. If the trading propensity is sufficiently strong, making offers and accepting them becomes the dominant strategy for each player and all of the potential gains to trade are realized. In Table 3.3, $V > 1$ is sufficient to assure that the potential gains to trade are realized.

Moral and other cultural support for trade causes more gains from trade to be realized. And as trade increases, additional specialization is supported, markets expand, and the relevant community becomes more prosperous because more desired things are made using relatively fewer resources. Specialized producer-sellers are more efficient than unspecialized producer-sellers (e.g., can sell more at a lower cost) and the community's material welfare tends to increase.

The opposite occurs when there are predispositions against trade. For example, in Thomas More's *Utopia* ([1516] 1901) trade is discouraged, and guilt

**Table 3.3** Gains from Trade with Transactions Costs in a Trade-Supporting Culture

|  |  | Friedrich (seller) | |
|---|---|---|---|
|  |  | Make offer | Do not |
| Adam (buyer) | Accept offer | (A, F) (2 + V, 2 + V) | (A, F) (−1 + V, 0) |
|  | Do not | (0, −1 + V) | (0, 0) |

rather than virtue tends to be associated with market activities. This would cause a guilt decrement (G) to be subtracted from the make-offer and accept-offer strategies, rather than a virtue supplement added to them. Such normative systems reduce the potential gains to trade, which reinforces the no-trade equilibrium of Table 3.2. In a community in which such anti-trade norms are common, only transactions that would have generated relatively large gains from trade (in the absence of such norms) will ever be realized. This tends to reduce specialization and reduce a community's prosperity. (In More's idealized society, there is little or no specialization and only necessities are produced.) In the case illustrated, trade in the goods or services represented will not take place at all if $G > 2$.

Thus, for a given distribution of practical or economic gains to trade and transactions costs, the greater a community's normative support for exchange, the broader markets tend to be, other things being equal. A general increase in the extent of trade tends to increase the rewards associated with specialization, which increases the rewards of innovation and capital accumulation, and these effects (better and more tools) tend to further reduce the average cost of producing goods for sale, and thereby increases a community's material welfare through increases in productivity. Conversely, the more a community's ethical dispositions tend to discourage trade, the fewer trades occur, and the less specialization, innovation, and capital accumulation occur, and the lower the average material quality of life tends to be.[8]

## The Problem of Fraud and Market Support for Ethical Sellers

Transactions costs themselves are not always simply a matter of the resources consumed making offers, looking for offers, or moving goods and services from one place to another. There are a variety of other informational costs and risks that have to be overcome as well. The true terms of trade are not always known or obvious. Many, indeed most, potential trades have net losses rather than benefits associated with them. Far more things are available for sale than an individual or family actually purchases. To determine what is on offer and what gives the best value for money, buyers devote significant time and

[8] New goods and services may be introduced and new modes of selling may reduce transactions costs, such as standardized selling hours and posted prices. Such innovations also tend to increase the extent of commerce. These are neglected here to focus on the effects of normative dispositions. It bears noting that the rate of technological advance is similarly affected by ethical dispositions toward and ideas about the possibility of progress, a topic taken up towards the end of Part I.

attention to assessing the quality of the goods on offer and their prices. Sellers, similarly, undertake many steps to assure that they will profit from the goods produced and sold, and that consumers will find their offerings pleasing.

These uncertainties imply that mistakes can be made among honest buyers and sellers, which is to say that either a buyer or seller may regret having participated in a particular exchange.

However, not all sellers or all buyers are completely honest. A buyer might be intentionally misled by a seller into purchasing a product or service that is not as good as claimed, or a buyer may promise to pay a seller but pay less than promised. Shoplifters, for example, simply take goods on offer rather than pay for them. However, for the purposes of this chapter, it is assumed that theft does not take place or takes place infrequently enough that it can be ignored, and that the main problem is fraudulent offers. (Analytically, these are similar problems, and moral solutions exist for the problem of theft as well as the problem of fraud.)

The risk of fraud can make it difficult to realize many potential gains from trade. Indeed, in markets in which fraudulent offers are commonplace, the risk of fraud tends to rule out markets for many kinds of goods and services.

## Pragmatic Sellers

An honest offer accurately describes the product and terms of sale, as in the illustrations above. A fraudulent offer is one for which the true quality of a product or service offered for sale is less—often far less—than that which the seller claims. Fraud-based profits are possible whenever lower-quality goods or services are less costly to produce than higher-quality ones, and differences between high- and low-quality goods are not immediately obvious to most or all potential purchasers. The gains from trade for the buyer are much lower when a fraudulent offer is accepted than when an honest offer is; indeed, the net gains from such trades are often negative rather than positive for the purchaser.[9]

The effects of fraud on the extent of trade can be analyzed by adding a new row to the game characterized in Table 3.2. The new row of Table 3.4 characterizes a seller's profits from making and a buyer's losses from accepting fraudulent offers.

[9] For the purposes of the illustration, the possibility that fraudulent offers produce subjective benefits for the buyer are ignored. A buyer might, for example, benefit subjectively from the idea that he or she has an original Picasso until it is identified as a copy. Such cases are acknowledged to exist but are clearly less common and worrisome than the one(s) illustrated.

**Table 3.4** The Dilemma of Fraud

|  |  | Gordon (buyer) | |
| --- | --- | --- | --- |
|  |  | Accept or solicit offer | Ignore all offers |
| Richard (seller) | Fraudulent offer | (R,G) (3, –3) | (R, G) (–1, 0) |
|  | Honest offer | (2, 2) | (–1, 0) |
|  | Do not make offers | (0, –1) | (0, 0) |

This choice setting—when it is recognized by buyers—has only a single equilibrium. If Richard expects Gordon to accept his offer, then he should make a fraudulent one (3 > 2 > 0). If Richard expects Gordon to refuse or ignore the offer, then he should not bother making either type of offer (0 > –1), because making offers is costly. Gordon will only accept an offer if he anticipates an honest one, but given Richard's incentives, this is not likely.

In this setting, there is just one Nash equilibrium, which is to say one stable outcome rather than two: the no-trade cell in which offers are neither made nor accepted. The potential profits of fraudulent offers *can eliminate markets* for products whose quality is not immediately apparent to potential buyers.[10] Thus, in choice settings in which buyers are aware that they cannot distinguish fraudulent offers from honest ones, many markets will not emerge because offers will not be made or accepted.

The no-trade equilibrium is problematic because there is a feasible outcome that could make both parties better off without making anyone else worse off. The honest-trade cell makes both traders better off than the no-trade equilibrium. The no-trade equilibrium is also problematic from a utilitarian perspective because it fails to maximize aggregate utility, here the sum of the payoffs in each cell (2 + 2 = 4 > 0). The outcome is also problematic from the perspective of community survival insofar as trade promotes specialization, which increases a community's material reserves for addressing and weathering crises that tend to emerge in all communities from time to time.

[10] This market is a special case of the market for lemons developed by Akerlof (1970). Repeated dealings may also affect the payoffs associated with honest and fraudulent offers, although there are clearly cases in which the present discounted value of a long series of transactions have payoffs with relative magnitudes similar to those of Table 3.4.

In certain special cases, it is possible for prices to convey (signal) useful information about product quality. Several of these are discussed below. However, pure price-signaling solutions are neglected herein because terms of trade are assumed to be known in this chapter, and neglected in the next because such solutions require more than a plausible amount of sophistication on the part of buyers and sellers. See Baye and Harbaugh (2021) for a nice overview of those possibilities.

If Erasmus's (1532) characterization of medieval merchants was accurate—in which sellers routinely cozen and cheat their customers—one would anticipate relatively small trading networks in Europe's medieval period. Only easily assessed goods and services would be routinely purchased by prudent buyers. And, as predicted, medieval markets were far less extensive than those associated with today's commercial societies.

## Ethical Sellers

The likelihood of fraud can be reduced in a number of ways. In principle, it can be reduced by posting bonds and other warrantees by sellers (such as a money-back guarantees). However, claims about bonds and warrantees resemble the goods characterized in Table 3.4; their true quality is difficult to assess at the point of sale, and fraudulent guarantees are likely to be more profitable than honest ones. The likelihood of fraud can also be reduced by formal laws against making false claims. However, court cases against fraud are costly, which make well-enforced anti-fraud laws an effective deterrent only for frauds involving relatively large losses that can be profitably recovered through lawsuits. Moreover, it is not always the case that law enforcement is free from corruption or favoritism.

The likelihood of fraud can also be reduced by the ethical dispositions of sellers. A variety of internalized norms can reduce a seller's propensity for making fraudulent offers. For example, both an internalized norm against telling lies and a narrower norm with respect to misleading one's customers would inhibit sellers by associating guilt with making fraudulent offers. Alternatively, feelings of virtue or pride may be associated with truth telling or with making only fair and honest offers or selling only high-quality products. Such internalized norms change the perceived rewards associated with fraudulent or honest offers.

Table 3.5 characterizes the effect of guilt associated with making fraudulent offers. It demonstrates that internalized ethical or normative beliefs that make fraudulent offers less attractive for sellers can ameliorate or solve the dilemma of fraud. Associating a sufficiently strong guilty reaction with making fraudulent offers can cause the honest trading cell, (2, 2), to emerge as a possible equilibrium, as occurs when $G > 1$.

To benefit from the offers of honest sellers, at least some buyers must be able to distinguish honest from dishonest sellers. Which is to say, a subset of buyers must be able to accurately appraise a seller's character. Can the seller's claims about the product and price be trusted or not? The ability to assess the

**Table 3.5** Markets with Fraud and Guilt from Fraudulent Behavior

| | | Gordon (buyer) | |
|---|---|---|---|
| | | Accept or solicit offer | Ignore all offers |
| Richard (seller) | Fraudulent offer | (R,G) (3.– G, –3) | (R, G) (–1 – G, 0) |
| | Honest offer | (2, 2) | (–1, 0) |
| | Do not make offers | (0, –1) | (0, 0) |

character of others is arguably a skill that most persons acquire through time, although it is rarely perfectly accurate.[11]

As experience with honest and dishonest sellers accumulates, honest sellers will acquire reputations for forthright dealings with their buyers and dishonest ones with reputations for making false claims. Buyers naturally favor sellers who routinely give good value for money over those who do not; thus, honest sellers will thrive and dishonest ones will gradually disappear. Reductions in information costs and in the risk of mistaken purchases provide buyers with good reasons to frequent honest sellers. These additional net gains from trade imply that buyers are willing to pay a premium to purchase goods from sellers known to be honest. Honest merchants provide a higher quality or more reliable service than other sellers of similar products. This reputational premium is likely to be shared between buyers and sellers, which tends to further increase the profits of sellers that are well known to be trustworthy.

In order to retain their customers, pragmatists have to adopt—or at least appear to adopt—rules similar to those followed by honest sellers. Only by doing so are they likely to attract and retain a significant customer base. Moreover, by diligently following such rules, such practices may become habitual; in which case, pragmatists are transformed into honest merchants. In other words, competition among sellers for customers tends to increase the extent to which honesty—at least with respect to making offers—is commonplace in the community of interest. In this manner, market competition tends to improve the ethos of the community at the same time that it increases the scope of trade and specialization, as noted by La Court and Barkley in the late seventeenth century regarding commerce in the Netherlands (see Chapter 10).

[11] Frank (1988), for example, suggests that this ability is aided by various genetically supported signals that a dishonest person tends to exhibit, such as facial expressions, blushing, posture, and nervousness.

It should be noted that aversion to making fraudulent offers alone is not sufficient to assure that all gains from exchange are in fact realized. There are again two possible equilibria associated with the ethical dispositions characterized by Table 3.5. Additional support is needed to realize all potential gains to trade, as developed above. Note, however, that an ethical disposition that associates feelings of virtue with honest dealing, rather than guilt with dishonest ones, produces different results. If a sufficient virtue supplement is associated with making honest offers ($V > 1$), a single unique Nash equilibrium emerges, namely, the one previously illustrated in Table 3.3, in which only honest offers are made and these are accepted.

Thus, even very similar ethical dispositions can have different effects on the extent of commerce. "Minor" differences in internalized norms can have nontrivial effects on the course of economic development.

## Moral Consumers Who Have Peculiar Market Demands

When a seller attempts to answer such questions as—How can I improve my products for my customers? How can I make shopping a more pleasant or efficient process for them?—the seller must imagine buyer interests and attempt to advance them. Such sellers are not usually altruists, but the required thought process and the types of answers developed are ones that are similar to those that would be undertaken by altruists. As a consequence, the question most often heard when one walks into a service-oriented store is "Can I help you?" rather than "How can I profit from you?" even though a pragmatic owner/manager is more interested in the latter than in the former. What buyers want is a complex combination of attributes when they purchase products, rather than a single-dimensional one. The courtesy and trustworthiness of a merchant's employees is part of the service they seek and expect from sellers.

In addition to rewarding trustworthy sellers with greater sales and profits, buyers may also reward sellers who directly advance their moral interests, which is to say, their interest in being a "good" person, living a "good" life, or contributing to the "good" society, as those are understood by particular subsets of buyers. Many theories of "the good" have implications for the types of sellers that ethical buyers have a duty to frequent and the types of goods and services that they should attempt to purchase. That such "moral" goods are produced for sale demonstrates that moral buyers exist and that sellers respond to their special needs when there is sufficient demand for their particular "moral" goods and services. Examples include products used in religious observances and for religious holidays, among many others.

Consumers may also have ethical dispositions that imply that some kinds of services and some kinds of goods are "better" than others. In such cases, ethical dispositions directly affect a consumer's demand for goods and services. Such customers may be willing to pay a higher price for the services produced by persons they deem virtuous, good, honorable, praiseworthy, deserving, or who share their ideas about duties associated with the "good life" or "good society." In contemporary markets, we observe buyers who are willing to pay a premium for "fair trade" products and for "organic" goods produced with minimal or no use of chemical pesticides. Many members of religious groups also have demands for goods produced in particular ways— as with kosher foods—and for products that complement activities required by their internalized beliefs—as with Christmas trees, crosses, menorahs, and prayer rugs.

When relatively small numbers of such consumers exist, a subset of merchants may specialize in providing the desired "moral" services, as with sellers that provide goods and services for orthodox members of various religious and ideological groups. As the numbers of such "ethical consumers" increase, larger retailers may start to espouse normative positions consistent with idealistic consumers in mind, because complete indifference to the ethical concerns of large groups of consumers would tend to reduce their customer base and profits. They may decorate their stores in a manner consistent with particular holidays, play appropriate music, and stock special merchandise for celebrations even if they have not internalized the same moral, ideological, or religious beliefs.

Similarly, conventions about lifestyles that "good" people should follow tend to affect the design of houses, clothing, the composition of food products, and the type of music readily available from builders, haberdasheries, grocery stores, and music vendors. Even such nearly universal goods as footwear, eating utensils, toilets, and windows vary significantly among contemporary societies. Not all such goods have designs that are informed by ethical considerations—although many do—but insofar as being "normal" or "conventional" is thought to be evidence of good character or required by it, the extent of the market for "normal" goods and the nature of such goods and services are influenced by ethical dispositions. Conventional lifestyles, in turn, allow economies of scale in production to be realized on a wider variety of goods than would otherwise have been possible. And, by reducing the prices of such goods, economies of scale provide economic support for a community's conventional lifestyles.

This is another way in which normative dispositions affect the nature, extent, and scope of commerce. Normative dispositions partially determine what "goods" and "services" are, as well as how they can be profitably produced and sold.

## Specialized Commercial Organizations: Rule-Bound Production by Teams

As trade and specialization expand, it is often useful for manufacturers of products to organize teams of specialists, because team production can lower costs and increase profits and sales. In many cases, organized groups of craftsmen (teams) can more efficiently produce products for sale than a group of independent solo craftsmen producing the same products. There are several reasons for this. Some tasks can only be undertaken by teams, as with moving a large rock or log with manpower or undertaking a complex surgical operation in a modern hospital. Many products can be produced more efficiently by teams of specialists than by individual specialists, as, for example, Adam Smith (1776) pointed out regarding the manufacturing of pins during the mid-eighteenth century. Smith noted that a single craftsman could produce on the order of 20 pins a day, whereas a well-organized group of 10 persons could produce 48,000 pins per day, some 240 times as many as 10 individuals each making pins entirely by him- or herself.

Such increases in productivity are partly consequences of practice, and partly consequences of specialized tools that can be profitably used to increase the output of specialized teams—as was the case for the pin factory described by Adam Smith in the first pages of his most famous book.[12] Increases in productivity are also products of the rules that govern behavior at each stage of production within an organization. It is such rules—when they are followed— that transform a group into a team. Indeed, to organize is simply an expression for intentionally inducing rule-bound behavior.

Historically, specialized production teams were normally small and often largely based on families. Family businesses are still commonplace in today's commercial societies.

However, the great expansion of commerce in the nineteenth century was associated with much larger commercial enterprises. Larger commercial

---

[12] A good deal of contemporary research reaches the same conclusion. Other classics in this research program include Coase (1937) and Alchian and Demsetz (1972). More mathematical characterizations of the shirking problem and the manner in which internalized norms or chiding by other workers may ameliorate such problems are in Congleton (1991a) and Buchanan and Yoon (1994).

enterprises confront a variety of recruiting, retention, incentivizing, and monitoring problems—referred to as *agency problems* by economists. These largely consist of various social dilemmas associated with team production. Many, like fraud, can be regarded as problems associated with asymmetric information, but such an interpretation tends to obscure the essential problem. The output of teams is a joint product of efforts by all the members of the team, and it is difficult to fully incentivize such efforts.

## A Digression on the Nature of Commercial Organizations

Commercial organizations are voluntary organizations in which their team members are free to leave and seek other employment. This limits the demands that entrepreneurs can make of their team members and also the types of punishments for nonperformance of duties that can be meted out. Because of their voluntary nature, commercial enterprises are self-sustaining only if they benefit all members of the organization. If an organization fails to do so, it tends to disintegrate as members leave for other firms or self-employment, or its formeteurs disband their association (as often induced by bankruptcy). The possibility of exit is a feature of commercial organizations that distinguishes them from many other organized groups, such as those that produce military power and rely upon slavery, where exit is not permitted (although it is often difficult to block entirely.) Exit from such forms of team production is illegal and may be severely punished.

The aim of commercial formeteurs is the profitable production of goods and services for sale to persons outside their organization.[13] Commercial organizations may be formed by a single person (a proprietor) or small group of formeteurs (partners) who believe there are advantages (normally profits) that can be realized by organizing a team to produce and sell particular goods and services.

To create organizations, the formeteurs adopt a variety of rules that tend to increase output and reduce costs. There are, for example, complex rules for assigning and undertaking tasks, encouraging working rather than shirking, and for sharing the profits or outputs produced by the team. Initially, those rules ordinarily are largely based on rules used by other teams that the

---

[13] Other organizations, such as tribes and villages, are likely to have emerged well before commercial enterprises, and these and other organizations confronted many of the same problems as commercial organizations. Thus, the analysis undertaken in this section, although focused on commercial organizations, also has implications for many other organizations that contribute to a community's viability and attractiveness. Indeed, Chapter 2 has already analyzed several relevant problems.

formeteurs of new organizations are familiar with. These may subsequently be unilaterally revised by formeteurs or altered as a consequence of bargaining between the formeteurs and their team members after the team is up and running.

Team members are encouraged to undertake their assigned tasks through organizational sanctions of various sorts. In the voluntary organizations of interest here, these include chiding, financial rewards and penalties, promotions, and expulsion from the organization. The rules are often complex, subtle, and largely unwritten, and following the rules is "part of the job," which is to say a duty associated with being a team member or employed by the organization. However, following "the rules" is not always in the immediate interest of the individual members of the team.

Through time, following the rules becomes "routine" and so gradually the rules become internalized by many, perhaps most, team members in much the same manner as ethical dispositions are. Naturally, an organization's rules are most likely to be followed when team members are familiar with them and are predisposed to dutifully follow them. It is partly for this reason that experienced team members are generally more highly valued and rewarded than beginners.

Most rule-making and governance issues are neglected here in order to focus on what economists refer to as *agency problems*. (A subset of organizational governance issues is indirectly addressed in Part II and more fully discussed in Congleton, 2011).

## The Shirking Dilemma and Team Production

Although production by teams can be highly efficient, there is a sense in which team production is unnatural. Every person on every team has private incentives to underprovide services to the team. Each member's effort increases the productivity of other team members, but these effects can be ignored by a person who decides to goof off a bit rather than fully devote him- or herself to team production as characterized by the team's rules. They are inclined to "shirk" rather than "work."

To illustrate this dilemma, suppose that a team is organized as a "natural cooperative." Team members undertake similar tasks and share their joint output produced equally. Each person participates in the team's activities for eight hours. For purposes of illustration, the team's output is assumed to be two times the total effort invested in production (work effort). Suppose, however, that an individual's effort is unobservable to others—such as when a

**Table 3.6**  The Shirking Dilemma of Team Production in Natural Cooperatives (hours of effort)

|  |  | Harold | | |
|---|---|---|---|---|
|  |  | 8 hours | 6 hours | 4 hours |
| Armen | 8 hours | (A, H)<br>16, 16 | (A, H)<br>14, 17 | (A, H)<br>12, 18 |
|  | 6 hours | 17, 14 | 15, 15 | 13, 16 |
|  | 4 hours | 18, 12 | 16, 13 | 14, 14 |

group tries to lift or carry a heavy object, separately searches for fruit to harvest and share, or jointly develops a complex computer or phone app. The benefits of leisure in contrast to work effort (the absence of productive effort) are realized only by the person(s) shirking.

Table 3.6 illustrates the "shirking" dilemma for a two-member team, which is the smallest possible team. (The shirking dilemma tends to be larger for larger teams, because there are more persons to monitor and incentivize.) The payoffs in the game matrix are net benefits measured in output units. They are the sum of each team member's share of the team's output plus the value of each player's own leisure. The value of an hour of shirking to the individual benefiting from it is assumed to be equivalent to 1.5 units of the team's output. This choice setting has a single Nash equilibrium at the lower right-hand corner of Table 3.6. A good deal of shirking takes place in equilibrium.

That a problem exists is implied by several normative theories, as for the other dilemmas already reviewed. There are other feasible outcomes that would make all team members better off. For example, both Armen and Harold would benefit if they both diligently worked eight hours each day instead of four. To the extent that shared output or shared profits are correlated with utility levels, aggregate utility is not maximized. And, to the extent that the output of the team contributes to a village's survival by increasing its material reserves, the shirking dilemma diminishes its likelihood of survival in the long run.

## The Economic Value of a Work Ethic

The shirking problem is an ancient problem, and so are various ways of reducing it. In communities with governments, laws could be passed against

**Table 3.7** How a Work Ethic Reduces the Shirking Dilemma (hours of effort)

|  |  | Harold | | |
|---|---|---|---|---|
|  |  | 8 hours | 6 hours | 4 hours |
| Armen | 8 hours | (A, H)<br>16, 16 | (A, H)<br>14, 17 – G | (A, H)<br>12, 18 – 2G |
|  | 6 hours | 17 – G, 14 | 15 – G,15 – G | 13 – G, 16 – 2G |
|  | 4 hours | 18 – 2G, 12 | 16 – 2g, 13–G | 14 – 2G, 14 – 2G |

shirking (idleness), as was done in some periods in ancient Athens and in the early English Puritan colonies of Massachusetts during the seventeenth century. In productive organizations with their own governing rules, the rules governing compensation may be adjusted to encourage work over shirking, as with piece rates and wages conditioned on effort, although these solutions are limited to cases in which output or effort can be observed and in which the rules governing wage conditionally are honestly followed.

Alternatively, dispositions that reduce problems associated with shirking may emerge, and persons with such dispositions may be recruited as team members. Formeteurs may, for example, hire only persons with a good "work ethic" or attempt to induce all their team members to develop such dispositions. Indeed, all readers who regard the term "shirking" to have a negative connotation have themselves internalized work-supporting norms.

Norms that reduce propensities to shirk can take many forms. The simplest is an internalized duty to work diligently—a work ethic—that brings forth feelings of virtue when one diligently performs all one's duties while at work and guilt when one does not. The "guilt" variety of a work ethic is incorporated into Table 3.7. In the case illustrated, guilt-avoidance indirectly increases happiness (and income) by increasing team output and team member rewards. The practical reward may be a share of a commercial organization's output or higher wage or piece rates when money goods emerge. Table 3.7 demonstrates that a team composed of persons with sufficiently strong work ethics can solve the shirking problem. A work ethic that associates a guilt penalty greater than one unit of the practical reward, $G > 1$, is sufficient to do so. Note that the result is increased utility or net benefits for all ($16 > 14$).[14]

---

[14] Although not important for the purposes of this illustration, some readers may be interested to know that the individual cell payoffs for Armen are $1.5 (8 - E_A) + 2(E_A + E_H)/2$ where $E_A$ is the number of hours in which Armen devotes his energies to team production, rather than shirking. The payoffs for Harold

Other norms, such as promise-keeping and reciprocity norms, can achieve similar results by inducing team members to abide by commitments made as conditions for acceptance on the team or to try to exceed the efforts of others. Notions of "fair" or "reasonable" efforts may induce fellow team members to chide, embarrass, or evict members who shirk their duties. Partially internalizing the benefits realized by others on the team—as devout utilitarians tend to— would also reduce an individual's subjective gains from shirking.

The point here, as in the other illustrations of this chapter, is that a variety of internalized norms can ameliorate dilemmas associated with team production, and that communities that have such norms will tend to have more and more efficient commercial organizations and thereby achieve broader, more effective markets than those that do not. Again, the illustrations are the simplest ones that illustrate the essential problem, which often are more subtle and complex than the two-person varieties make them look.[15]

It bears noting that there are also normative dispositions that tend to undermine the productivity of teams. For example, a subset of team members may believe that shirking (sometimes called soldiering) advances norms such as solidarity or justice. Shirking may be praised as evidence of cleverness or "beating the system." Such norms tend to produce leisure for the relevant team members, but they reduce team output and thereby the extent to which teams can be used to realize advantages of coordination and specialization in production by reducing their efficiency. In communities where such norms are commonplace, the shirking dilemma may be marketwide rather than specific to a particular economic organization. Output diminishes, and average material comforts in such communities tend to be below that of other more industrious communities.

Norms that undermine team production may account for the fact that commercial organizations that employ large teams of free laborers (as opposed to slaves) were rare until a century or two ago.[16]

and Armen are $1.5 (8 - E_H) + 2(E_A + E_H)/2$. ($E_A = 4$, $E_H = 4$) is the Nash equilibrium of the continuous version of this game. The joint optimum is assumed to be an 8-hour day for each, although much longer workdays were commonplace in the late nineteenth and early twentieth centuries and are still common among "overachievers" today.

[15] The dilemma in the case illustrated emerges from the sharing rule rather than through effects on the marginal products of other workers. See Congleton (1991a) for a mathematical illustration in which paying each worker exactly their marginal revenue produce is not sufficient to solve all shirking problems. In cases in which monitoring is not sufficiently accurate to incentivize work, conditional reward systems tend to be less effective than hiring persons with strong work ethics, as most readers will acknowledge from their own experience.

[16] That ethics can increase the productivity of teams has been studied by relatively few economists. See, for example, Congleton (1991a), Buchanan and Yoon (1994b), and Rodgers (2009) for general analytical

## Tendency to Under-Specialize

There are two types of team production, as noted in passing above. First, there is team production in which all team members do essentially the same thing. A group may jointly pick up a large rock or log, jointly pull a boat or large fish to shore on a rope, gather apples in an orchard, rake off a large field, and so forth. The other type of teams takes advantage of specialization. A large rock may be relocated using various combinations of wedges, levers, ropes, animals, and so forth, with different team members undertaking quite different tasks, none of which is sufficient to move the rock alone, but which jointly may be sufficient to do so. A song may be sung with harmony rather than in unison, with different notes being sung by different subgroups of singers. In more elaborate specialized production processes, there may be dozens or hundreds of specialized co-producers as in contemporary hospitals, universities, or chip foundries.

One reason that teams of specialists are used, rather than trusting to the spontaneous order or market incentives to generate and coordinate the various specializations, is that specialization tends to be risky and may not be undertaken by individuals without either strong encouragement from market prices or instruction (rules) by a team's manager(s). Table 3.8 illustrates what might be called the under-specialization dilemma.

In the choice setting characterized, Armen and Harold may choose to specialize in either activity A or activity B and then trade their outputs to secure

**Table 3.8** The Under-Specialization Dilemma

|  |  | Harold | | |
|---|---|---|---|---|
|  |  | Specialize in A | Half A and Half B | Specialize in B |
| Armen | Specialize in A | (A, H) 4, 4 | (A, H) 5, 7 | (A, H) 6.5, 8 |
|  | Half A and Half B | 7, 5 | 5.5, 5.5 | 7, 5 |
|  | Specialize in B | 8, 6.5 | 5, 7 | 3, 3 |

assessments. Although Weber's ([1909] 2012) famous short book on the Protestant ethic seems to imply that the work ethic was first associated with Protestantism in Europe, this is not likely to be the case, although it is possible that Protestantism increased its relative importance. Several academic pieces, for example, have been written on the Islamic work ethic. See, for example, Murtaza et al. (2016). Based on the above illustration and the discussion in the next section, work ethics and other norms that moderate shirking problems are likely to have emerged in most communities, although with somewhat different intensities and internalized duties.

the other good, or they may "generalize" and spend half of their time on each activity, in which case they are each self-sufficient, but do not benefit from specialization. The payoffs are in utility levels, and the demands for different outputs of the two activities are assumed to be somewhat inelastic. So, if the supply of one increases a lot, its price falls a lot. Thus, when one person is a generalist and the other is a specialist, the generalist is better off because the value of the good produced by the specialist falls, while that not produced by the specialist increases. As a consequence, the center cell is a Nash equilibrium in this choice setting—both are generalists and miss out on the gains from specialization (14.5 > 11).

Internalized norms can solve the problem, as when a craftsman is proud of their specialty and so receives a virtue payoff from their ability to produce more or higher quality outputs. In cases in which both specialists receive such a virtue supplement, the upper and lower corners may be transformed into stable Nash equilibria and the benefits for specialization are realized. Aristotle, for example, notes that specialists often appear to realize such virtue or happiness supplements. An informal team may achieve similar effects by praising the specialized skills of its team members insofar as team members all enjoy being praised, as argued by Adam Smith. Similarly, a commercial organization may encourage specialization by changing the "natural" constellation of rewards (e.g., paying each laborer their marginal revenue product) and encouraging greater specialization than is in the natural interests of the individuals on the team.

However, insofar as persons in a community are encouraged to behave like others in the community, such specialization may be discouraged by a community's ethos, and even less specialization may occur. Many anthropologists suggest that self-sufficiency or well-roundedness was the norm rather than the exception in pre-agricultural societies, which suggests that solutions to the under-specialization dilemma, although fairly straightforward, were not widely adopted.

Agriculture arguably increased the gains from specialization and thus generated more choice settings without that problem. Notice that if the two off-diagonal payoffs of 6.5 were 7.5, the dilemma would disappear, and the upper right-hand cell and the lower left-hand cells would both become Nash equilibria. Pretty much anything—internalized norms, praise, wage premiums, profits—that increases the rewards from specialization tends to mitigate the dilemma. Contrariwise, anything that reduces the rewards from specialization—norms favoring self-reliance or increases in conflict associated with differences in income—tends to reduce specialization and prosperity.

## Market Support for Persons with Productive Ethical Dispositions

Insofar as the productivity of every organization depends in large part on the rule-following propensities of its members, organizations will attempt to recruit members who are likely to act in accordance with their rules. Thus, a potential member's normative disposition will be one of the considerations when an organization recruits or accepts a new member, because these dispositions have significant effects on a new member's productivity. This is not to say that only mild-mannered, rule-following individuals will be admitted into organizations, but it is to claim that whether a person can be expected to follow the organization's rules or not is a nontrivial consideration in hiring decisions. Some rule-breaking behavior must be acceptable if an organization is to evolve or innovate, but it cannot be the norm. An organization would cease being organized if all of its rules were routinely ignored by its team members.

Of course, normative dispositions are not the only consideration. There are skills that potential team members have accumulated that also contribute to their productivity. An ideal team member is a highly skilled person with the disposition to work hard and diligently at his or her assigned tasks. Such team members are clearly preferred to lesser skilled persons who are inclined to shirk rather than work, other things being equal (such as wage rates and availability).

When a sufficient number of ideal team members are not available, formeteurs and their recruiters have to make trade-offs among productive normative dispositions and other task-related skills. Whether a firm would hire a highly skilled but untrustworthy individual over a less skilled but trustworthy individual depends upon a variety of factors, including the difficulty of monitoring particular tasks, difference in potential output from high- and low-skill workers, and differences, if any, in their market wage rates.

Table 3.9 illustrates the trade-off confronted by a commercial organization's owners or managers when assembling a team from persons who would join the organization if asked. The numbers characterize their anticipated marginal products, which is to say the additional output likely to be produced by the various combinations of skills and ethical dispositions of potential employees. An asterisk is placed after the five most highly ranked potential team members to illustrate how such trade-offs would affect a firm's first five hiring decisions.

If all nine types of potential employees are willing to work for the same wage or share of the firm's output, the firm will first hire the high-skill and high-ethics worker. The second person hired is the one with moderate skills

**Table 3.9** Menu of Potential Team Members and Their Anticipated Marginal Revenue Products

|  | High Skill | Moderate Skill | Low Skill |
|---|---|---|---|
| High Ethics | 10* | 8* | 6* |
| Moderate Ethics | 7* | 6* | 4 |
| Low Ethics | 5 | 4 | 3 |

* Five most highly ranked potential team members.

but high ethics. That person works hard or honestly enough to offset his or her lower skills. The third person hired is the person with high skills and a modest work ethic, and so forth, until the new team is staffed out or departing members are replaced. The last to be hired are unskilled, unmotivated folks who would require both constant monitoring and much training to be productive in the positions to be filled.

The same table can be used to illustrate the demand for ethical dispositions that increase an employee's marginal product. Ethical dispositions have a larger effect on expected marginal products for tasks that are difficult to monitor than for ones that are relatively easy to monitor and incentivize, so there are also cases in which ethical disposition would play a relatively larger or smaller role in hiring decisions. Low ethics in this context does not necessarily imply criminal behavior—although it may—but rather a vector of dispositions that tend to increase one's propensity to shirk in the position being filled. The virtues sought are, in general, those that tend to make an employee more worthy of trust. It is such considerations that Franklin was contemplating in the quotation at the beginning of the chapter.

Given the productivity differences implied by the illustration, it is likely that in the long run, high-skill employees will earn more than low-skill employees, and those with productivity-enhancing virtues will earn more than those without them. This variation in wage rates would alter the hiring sequence because formeteurs and recruiters will consider the cost of employees, as well as their skills and ethical dispositions. They cannot afford to pay more for an employee than he or she contributes to the firm.

Ethical premia may be required to hire honest persons because they are relatively scarce in the community of interest, and such premia would be paid only in cases in which honesty significantly increases an individual's marginal product. The same is true of other skill premiums. Skill will determine hiring decisions only in cases in which a skilled employee's output is substantially greater than an unskilled person's and is easily observed.

Such differences would affect patterns of employment if they are correlated with other aspects of the persons seeking employment. For example, if women are on average more honest or rule-following than men, as some have argued, more women than men will be hired as cashiers and for other positions where trustworthiness is highly productive. If more men than women have invested in the training to become plumbers, because they are generally stronger or less averse to getting dirty, then more men than women will be hired as plumbers.

## The Difficulty of Assessing Skills and Ethical Dispositions

Unfortunately, a person's skillset and trustworthiness cannot be perfectly assessed when a team member is recruited and hired. Nonetheless, estimating a potential team member's true marginal revenue product is sufficiently important that firms devote a good deal of time and energy attempting to do so in recruiting efforts. Interviews are conducted to assess character and skills. Various objective measures that are correlated with skills and ethical dispositions are collected, such as college degrees, criminal records, and letters of recommendation. These are used to estimate both the skills and ethical predispositions of potential employees, along with an interviewer's assessments of a potential team member's talents, skills, and character.

Both interviews and trial periods would be less commonplace and shorter if objective measures were completely reliable or if only easily observable skill-related differences were most important.

That both skills and virtues are subsequently revealed by performance on the job partly explains why wage rates and salaries typically increase in the years after a person joins a team. That trade-offs between skill and ethical disposition vary among firms and industries is indicated by surveys that indicate that some industries and professions are considered more trustworthy than others, as well as by statistical evidence that wage rates for similar tasks vary by industry and firm.[17]

---

[17] All of the above examples assume a Ricardian rather than Marshallian market structure in both the short and long run. In such cases, every firm is a bit different from others in its industry. They employ somewhat different production processes, their organizational rules differ, as do their personnel, location, customers, and so forth. These differences affect the types of team members that are "the best fit" within a firm (e.g., most productive in particular positions) and a firm's willingness to pay premiums for particular skills and ethical dispositions. Such variation in wage rates is evident in contemporary studies of the variation in salaries among firms and industries within a given country. The same worker will have a different marginal revenue product when employed by different firms. See, for example, Card, Heining, and Kline (2013) or Levy and Murnane (1992).

# Firm Reputations and the Ethical Dispositions of Employees

It is sometimes argued by economists that trustworthiness is not required, only a "good" reputation. But this is just a word game—a good reputation implies trustworthiness. Firms that cannot be trusted to treat their customers well will lose their customers to firms that can, as noted earlier in this chapter.

The formeteurs need not be honest, themselves, but able to recognize the profits associated with a "good reputation." In such cases, the firm's internal rules of conduct clearly matter insofar as they substantially determine how customers will be treated. The hiring of ethical employees—in the sense used in this section—is clearly one the most effective ways to generate both rule-following behavior and a good reputation. Persons who have industrious dispositions do not require as much training or monitoring as those who do not. Persons who are diligent and honest are less likely to neglect or make fraudulent offers to customers or steal from the firm than persons who are not. Moreover, the routine adherence to such rules tends to induce a gradual internalization of those rules by both a firm's management and its employees.

As this takes place, rules that induce the conduct desired by consumers and consistent with firm profits tend to induce behavior that is increasingly generated by internalized norms. "Good reputation" is thus simply a neutral-sounding phrase that means predictably diligent, trustworthy, fair, or ethical conduct.

# The Effects of Market Rewards on a Community's Distribution of Ethical Dispositions

All the above observations imply that markets tend to support subsets of ethical dispositions that increase mutual gains from trade. Markets tend to support any ethical disposition that increases productivity or makes a firm's products more attractive to consumers. Conversely, markets tend to discourage ethical dispositions that decrease productivity or make a firm's products and services less attractive to consumers. Ethical dispositions without such effects are neither encouraged nor discouraged. They are irrelevant to a firm's hiring or promotion calculus. Firms that do not take ethical dispositions into account when hiring persons or assigning persons to particular tasks tend to have goods and services that are more expensive to produce and of lower average quality than firms that do. As a consequence, such firms tend to disappear in the long run as consumers discover the firms offering more reliable and less expensive goods and services.

This section explores how market rewards affect the distribution of ethical dispositions in a community. Markets arguably have only small effects on a community's ethos in the short run, but may have significant effects on them in the long run. For example, if parents care about their children's future material comfort or income, they will encourage particular virtues more than others. As children grow up, they may also come to realize that exhibiting some virtues tends to be rewarded with praise and income and so devote more effort to further developing such dispositions in themselves and their children. Franklin, among many others, argues that developing particular dispositions tends to advance one's economic and social interests, and that those effects are sufficient reasons for investing in them.

Financial rewards are not the only reason that persons acquire ethical dispositions, but such rewards affect the investments that individuals and families make in developing such dispositions at various margins.

## Investing in Virtuous Dispositions

Table 3.10 illustrates how rewards associated with the various virtues affect a person's allocation of time among five activities, three of which contribute to the development of virtuous dispositions: honesty, prudence, and bravery. The numbers in the cells represent marginal utilities or marginal net benefits associated with successive hours of investment in the five activities, including

**Table 3.10** Ben's Allocation of Time and Effort (Cell Entries Are Marginal Utility, 16 Hours Allocated)

|  | Leisure | Work | Acquisition of Virtue | | |
|---|---|---|---|---|---|
|  |  |  | Honesty | Prudence | Bravery |
| 1 hour | 20 | 30 + s | 11 + s | 12 + s | 11 |
| 2 hours | 16 | 24 + s | 9 + s* | 11 + s | 10 |
| 3 hours | 12 | 18 + s | 7 + s | 10 + s* | 9* |
| 4 hours | 9* | 12 + s* | 6 + s | 8 + s | 8 |
| 5 hours | 6 | 8 + s | 5 + s | 6 + s | 6 |
| 6 hours | 3 | 4 + s | 4 + s | 4 + s | 4 |
| 7 hours | 4 | 2 + s | 6 + s | 2 + s | 1 |
| 8 hours | 2 | 1 + s | 4 + s | 1 + s | 0 |

investments in three virtues. With respect to virtues, individuals may practice them because they produce self-satisfaction or self-esteem, because they are praised by fellow members of their community, and/or because they are financially rewarding. All the activities are assumed to exhibit diminishing marginal returns, as normally assumed by economists about other methods and factors of production.

For purposes of illustration, it is also assumed that Ben can only work at one activity at a time and that the marginal utilities of the five activities are independent of one another. This simplification allows a discrete allocation of time to be represented in a single table, which is useful for purposes of illustrating how time might be allocated among activities and is not entirely unrealistic. The cells with asterisks in Table 3.10 represent Ben's initial allocation of 16 hours among the five activities. The initial decision may characterize a pre-market setting or preexisting market setting that later changes. The initial allocation maximizes Ben's lifetime utility or net benefits from these activities in the original circumstances. The letter "s" represents changes in the marginal net rewards from work and a subset of virtues associated with a change in economic development. The underlined payoffs characterize Ben's new allocation of time after the new pattern of rewards is recognized. Expanding commerce is assumed to increase the returns to work, honesty, and industry, which all increase by two utils or two units of net benefits (s = 2) because of increased rewards (such as increases in salary and praise) associated with the new economic circumstances.

Given the new pattern of rewards, Ben's utility-maximizing or net-benefit-maximizing allocation of his waking hours changes a bit at the margin. The new rewards induce Ben to shift an hour from leisure to work and to shift an hour of time previously spent perfecting bravery to perfecting prudence, because prudence is now relatively more rewarding. This reallocation of time gradually weakens dispositions to be brave and strengthens dispositions to be prudent.

Table 3.10 thus illustrates a tension between commerce and a subset of virtues, a tension that has been stressed by many critics of commerce. Whether ethical conduct has increased or fallen as a consequence of the effects of commerce depends on the relative value that an observer places on virtues such as prudence, work, and bravery. If prudence is regarded to be a more important virtue than bravery—as believed by post-Enlightenment scholars such as Benjamin Franklin, Adam Smith, and Frédéric Bastiat—average virtue has been increased by the expansion of commerce, rather than decreased. If bravery is regarded to be more important than prudence, ethical conduct can be said to have declined within the community of interest.

Table 3.10 can also be used to illustrates how a shift from one community to another may affect an individual's ethical dispositions in the long run. When a person emigrates from a relatively less commercial society to a more commercial one, the rewards associated with various ethical dispositions tend to change, which will induce behavioral changes at the margin. Conscious efforts may be undertaken to acquire a reputation for the dispositions valued in the new circumstances. And as those virtues are practiced more frequently, they become routinized, which is to say they become more strongly internalized. Again, whether such persons have been "corrupted" or "improved" by the new environment depends on the relative importance that an observer places on the dispositions affected.

Herbert Spencer and John Stewart Mill, among many others writing in the late nineteenth century, observed that predispositions to cooperate with fellow employees became more commonplace during the second half of the nineteenth century in northwestern Europe. This, they argued, tended to greatly increase the productivity of commercial enterprises in this region of the world relative to most others. Writing a few decades later, Max Weber argued that ideas about the good life had also gradually changed in the West as commercial societies replaced preindustrial societies. Older ideas about a good life, in which leisure was very highly valued, were gradually replaced with the notion that a good life is an active, productive, and materially comfortable life. Table 3.10 illustrates why such changes could be induced by the expansion of commerce.

Weber attributes the original impulse for this shift in normative beliefs to various changes in doctrine associated with the Protestant Reformation of the sixteenth century. Nonetheless, he concludes that by the early twentieth century, hard work had become a "calling" in its own right and no longer required theological support. New norms had emerged and had been internalized, although in Weber's view, they had taken two or three centuries to do so.[18]

A man does not "by nature" wish to earn more and more money, but simply to live as he is accustomed to live and to earn as much as is necessary for that purpose. **Wherever modern capitalism has begun its work of increasing the productivity of human labor by increasing its intensity, it has encountered the immensely**

---

[18] Such shifts in dispositions may also have partly been consequences of increased support for mass (public) education throughout the West during the nineteenth century. A "good" student in a classroom follows the rules. He or she does not disrupt the class, properly interprets his or her assignments, turns them in on time, and undertakes them diligently. In this manner, even if ethics per se are not taught, students tend to develop virtues that are useful within commercial and other organizations—virtues that tend to make cooperation on large teams easier to generate.

**stubborn resistance** of this leading trait of pre-capitalistic labor. And **today it encounters it the more, the more backward (from a capitalistic point of view) the laboring forces are with which it has to deal. . . .**

[In a commercial society,] labor must, on the contrary, be performed as if it were an absolute end in itself, **a calling.** But such an attitude is by no means a product of nature. It cannot be evoked by low wages or high ones alone but can only be the product of a long and arduous process of education. (Weber [1905] 2012, KL: 271–315)

## Conclusions: On Ethics and Prosperity

Together, Chapters 2 and 3 characterize the ethical prerequisites for early market networks. Without solutions to the most important social dilemmas of life in communities, villages, towns, and cities are unlikely to emerge, be sustainable, or occupy a place rather than a migratory circuit. Without a stable place, significant trade and specialization are unlikely to emerge. Without significant partitioning and transferability of user rights, trade in things would be impossible. Without some disposition to engage in trade beyond pragmatic advantage, trading networks and specialization tend to be smaller than with them. Without solutions to the problem of fraud, trade in many goods and services would be unlikely to emerge or be sustained. Without solutions to problems associated with team production, the efficiencies associated with sequential specialized procedures for production would be less apt to be realized.

Many such dilemmas have to be overcome for market networks to become dense and extended. They are prerequisites for the emergence of a commercial society.

The game matrices of this chapter and the previous one demonstrate why social dilemmas are likely to be significant impediments to the emergence of settled communities and significant commercial networks. The small-number settings used to illustrate the essential features of particular classes of dilemmas tend to make the problems appear to be obvious—which is, of course, advantageous to readers—but real-world dilemmas are rarely as obvious as the game matrices make them appear. There are dozens and dozens of particular dilemmas that share the general features of the dilemmas illustrated, but which are not obviously examples of the same dilemmas. The most complex, larger-scale social dilemmas may never be fully understood and so would not consciously be solved, although they may be incidentally solved by rules adopted to address other problems. Fortunately, rules developed for small-number dilemmas often generalize to larger settings, and some of those rules ameliorate problems that bear little resemblance to the ones they were originally developed to solve.

With respect to commerce, this chapter has shown that trade and production are no more "natural" or "automatic" than life in communities. There are numerous preconditions that must exist for markets to emerge and flourish. For example, ownership rights have to exist, and it must be possible to shift ownership rights from one person or group to another. Ownership rights, however, are unlikely to have emerged because they facilitate trade and specialization, but because they are among the solutions to the dilemmas discussed in Chapter 2. Norms that support "partitioning" or "legitimate control" over various subsets of resources ameliorate both the Hobbesian dilemma and local commons problems. If "legitimate control" can be shifted from one person or family to another, or from one generation to another, then the time horizon of resource management increases and trade becomes conceptually possible.

Without such "legitimate" shifts of control from one person to another, the only manner in which resources can be shifted from one person or tribe to another is by forcibly taking what one wants, as many animals do (including household pets of the same species). Readers may have noticed that there are no obvious exchange relationships between cats and dogs or other animals.

Economic history suggests that specialization emerged gradually as various productivity gains from dividing tasks were discovered, as trading networks for particular goods emerged and spread, and as rules of conduct necessary to support informal exchange and contracting emerged and became commonplace. The emergence of various money goods subsequently extended the variety of trades that were possible by eliminating the necessity for the coincidence of wants that barter requires. Money goods have been found in archaeological digs as old as 10,000 BCE, which is roughly the same time that settled communities and agriculture emerged.[19] That money and local trading networks emerged at roughly the same time as settled communities suggests that many of the rules of conduct that allow reasonably peaceful and comfortable communities to emerge also facilitated commerce, albeit not everywhere and not perfectly.

---

[19] See Aristotle's *Politics* or Menger (1892) for early evolutionary theories of the emergence of money. See Davies (2010) for an overview of contemporary theories of the emergence, use, and importance of primitive monies. Einzig (2014) provides a useful overview of anthropological research on the uses of primitive money. See Stigler (1951) for a penetrating discussion of why the extent of markets ultimately determines the extent of specialization.

By supporting transferable ownerships rights, and reducing problems associated with fraud and agency problems, innovation in rules and principles of conduct can increase the scope of markets and help sustain extended trading networks. And, as noted in a classic paper by Nobel laureate George Stigler (1951), the benefits of specialization increase with the extent of markets. The advantages of specialization are greater when a group of specialists can profitably make hundreds of the same goods to sell, rather than just a few dozen. Productive skills increase through repetition, error correction, and focused innovation. It is equally true that the extent of markets tends to increase because of economies associated with specialization. As specialization increases, new mutually advantageous trading opportunities tend to emerge, because specialization increases productivity (prices tend to fall) and specialized producers can produce more types of goods for sale, increasing both gains from trade and real income.

Insofar as the scope of markets increases as social dilemmas are solved and ethical dispositions contribute to those solutions, prosperity can be said to have ethical foundations.

# Appendix to Chapter 3: Contractual Solutions to Team Production Problems, Economizing on Ethical Dispositions

This chapter has emphasized what might be called the recruiting solution to team production problems. Most economists, in contrast, emphasize contractual and organizational solutions. This appendix illustrates how reward systems can be adjusted by the firm to elicit better outcomes from team members.

A variety of conditional reward systems can ameliorate team production problems. Such contractual solutions, of course, also have ethical roots. They rely upon formeteurs and managers to diligently and fairly apply the rules that incentivize its team members.

The game matrix (Table 3.11) below illustrates a pecuniary solution to the shirking or team production dilemma. Team production is again assumed to be worthwhile, which implies that the productivity of each member is increased by the efforts of the others. In the teams analyzed in the main body of the chapter, the group's output was shared equally, which created a shirking dilemma or agency problem. In the game below, the same production process is assumed to be used, but a formeteur has created a formal reward structure for his or her team. Each team member receives a reward (R) for work

**Table 3.11** Contractual Solutions to the Shirking Dilemma of Team Production (hours of effort)

|        |         | Harold |         |         |
|--------|---------|--------|---------|---------|
|        |         | 8 hours | 6 hours | 4 hours |
| Armen  | 8 hours | (A, H) | (A, H) | (A, H) |
|        |         | R, R | 14, 17 – G | 12, 18 – 2P |
|        | 6 hours | 17 – P, 14 | 15 – P, 15 – P | 13 – P, 16 – 2P |
|        | 4 hours | 18 – 2P, 12 | 16 – 2g, 13 – G | 14 – 2G, 14 – 2G |

and a penalty (P) for shirking that is independent of the efforts of other team members.

Notice that when $R > 17 - P$ and $18 - 2P$, the shirking problem is solved. Note also that the difference between 2R and the total output produces a profit for the formeteurs. This organizational profit creates an economic incentive for formeteurs to create commercial organizations.

For conditional rewards and punishments to be as effective as internalized norms, the monitoring and penalty-imposing processes have to be accurate, and the required penalties have to be nontrivial but not too harsh. If they were too harsh, persons would leave the organization and seek another with better rule enforcement or simply produce as individuals rather than in teams. Moreover, rewards cannot be higher than an individual's contribution to the firm's output without bankrupting the firm. Thus, exit possibilities and economic viability constrain the domain of rewards and penalties that can be used to incentivize employees.

It bears noting that relatively modest incentive and monitoring schemes are sufficient to solve the shirking problem when most employees have a work ethic. This allows a broader range of agency problems to be overcome when such employees can be identified and recruited—even if the strength of the work ethic internalized cannot be directly observed by those recruiting team members.

# 4
# Ethics and Neoclassical Price Theory

> [M]odern methods of **trade imply habits of trustfulness on the one
> side and a power of resisting temptation to dishonesty on the other,**
> which do not exist among a backward people.
> —**Alfred Marshall,** *Principles of Economics* ([1920] 2012),
> **8th ed., digireads.com, Kindle edition, p. 16**

## Introduction

The previous two chapters have shown how ethics can solve social and economic dilemmas and thereby make life in communities more attractive
and market networks more likely to emerge because they both become more
fruitful. This chapter shifts the focus of analysis from mutual gains to trade
and team production to prices and sales. In Chapter 3, prices were largely
ignored. This is partly because goods for sale do not always have fixed prices.
In many marketplaces, the terms of trade are worked out between individual
sellers and buyers, more or less one at a time. In such cases, the terms of trade
or price are partly determined by the bargaining routines of the sellers and
buyers, given other offers thought to be available in the community of interest. Such personalized pricing is commonplace when there are relatively
few buyers and sellers. It is still common in many small communities and in
international markets in which a handful of firms dominate production and
purchases. However, as the number of buyers and sellers increases, uniform
"take or leave" offers and "posted" prices become more commonplace. This is
the setting focused on in this chapter.

The buyer-seller choice settings analyzed in Chapter 3 took place after the
terms of trade had been worked out and the choice was to accept the offer to
sell or not, or the offer to purchase or not. In this chapter, the effects of internalized rules of conduct on market prices and sales are examined.

The foundations of contemporary price theory were worked out in the
West during the late nineteenth and early twentieth centuries, after commercial activities were extensive and price competition was common for many
products and services. Prices in such settings were less often determined by

*Solving Social Dilemmas*. Roger D. Congleton, Oxford University Press. © Oxford University Press 2022.
DOI: 10.1093/oso/9780197642788.003.0004

bargaining between individual purchasers and sellers, although bargaining, of course, continued to take place in many markets. The price theory developed by neoclassical economists of that period concluded that the terms of trade in competitive markets are largely determined by market-wide conditions "at the margin" and tend to converge on prices that set market supply (the amounts on sale from all sellers) equal to market demand (the amounts purchased by all buyers). Thus, according to that theory, the prices observed in competitive markets are "market-clearing" prices that equate supply with demand and in which each consumer's marginal benefit equals each supplier's marginal cost of producing the goods for sale. This model of price determination is still taught in contemporary principles of economics classes, and generalized versions are still taught in upper-level and graduate classes in microeconomic theory.

Neoclassical price theory provides a general explanation for prevailing prices whenever there are "large" numbers of buyers and sellers. It also provides useful qualitative predictions about the price and sales adjustments that occur when, for example, average income increases, input prices change, or when new regulations or taxes are imposed on a market. Generalized models show how prices and sales throughout trade and production networks change as a consequence of both temporary and permanent changes in market conditions. This chapter shows how changes in the most common-place ethical dispositions in a community affect prices and sales in that community, and also how the prices that emerge affect the distribution of ethical dispositions in a given community.

The price theory taught in most undergraduate and graduate textbooks implicitly assumes that all the problems reviewed in Chapters 2 and 3 have been solved—except in the chapter on commons and externality problems if one is included. For example, consumers are assumed to completely understand the characteristics of all the goods available in their local and Internet markets—which of course, would not be the case unless the problem of fraud has been solved. Firms are assumed to use the best technology of their day to minimize the cost of producing every good and service, which of course, they would be unable to do unless every firm had solved its agency problems. All relevant goods and services are assumed to be tradable and shifted from one owner to another only through binding contracts, which would not be the case unless the problems of transferability, theft, and violent conflict had been solved.

As a consequence of all of these implicit assumptions, there is no risk of theft or violent takings of the variety reviewed in Chapter 2, and a sufficient domain of partitioned goods with transferable ownership rights exists that trade in many goods and services can take place. Such characterizations of circumstances were plausible for the West in 1900 when price theory emerged after more than a century of research on economic systems, although they would not have been reasonable assumptions a century or two before.

The usual assumptions, in effect, take for granted the existence of internalized ethical dispositions that solve the most critical social dilemmas within and among communities and within commercial organizations. The quote from Marshall at the beginning of this chapter demonstrates that this was well understood when neoclassical economics was first being worked out, although it has largely been forgotten. This chapter shows how such dispositions affect the extent and scope of markets and specialization through effects on the quality of products, the marginal product of labor, and the feasibility (profitability) of alternative methods of production.

The first sections of Chapter 4 explore settings in which productive ethical dispositions exist, but their productive effects are ignored by both firm owners and employees. It shows that even in such cases, the internalized ethics of employees in an industry can affect the sales of and prices paid for an industry's output, as long as differences in the quality of a firm's output can be recognized by a subset of consumers. Such effects, once recognized, create incentives for firm owners to take productive disposition into account and this will have effects on wage premiums associated with those dispositions.

This chapter is somewhat less self-contained than the other chapters in this book, in that it assumes that readers are familiar with the geometric economic models taught in elementary economics courses. The most important basic concepts and geometric representations are briefly reviewed in the chapter. Readers who are unfamiliar with or uninterested in such "tools" may prefer to skip forward to Chapter 5. Geometric illustrations rather than calculus are used, because these are likely to be familiar to most readers, and diagrams require less time and attention to understand than calculus-based presentations. An illustrating mathematical model of a social equilibrium and its associated "evenly rotating" economy is provided in the appendix to this chapter.

## Quality Control, Diligence, and the Sale of Products with Uncertain Characteristics

Virtually all products, from automobiles to zucchini, have properties that cannot be perfectly assessed by consumers at the point of sale. Much of this uncertainty is not a consequence of fraudulent claims but of variation in quality that can be attributed to nature, human error, and the cost of quality control in manufacturing processes. A given edible plant may receive more or less sunshine, rain, and grow on more or less fertile ground. Machines benefit from a variety of adjustments as they are used and wear out. And without such adjustments the average quality of their output tends to diminish. Workers can be more or less attentive to their assigned tasks in the sequence of productive activities that generate products for sale. Products are occasionally damaged when transported to shops, put on display, and sold. The designers of production processes and the persons engaged in overseeing the quality of the output can be more or less diligent in their oversight and planning. As a consequence, the quality of most products tends to be randomly distributed at the point of sale.

## A Model of the Demand for Products of Uncertain Quality

Consider a consumer's decision to purchase products when the probability of a defect is known (or can be estimated). A consumer's willingness to pay for a product can be characterized with his or her total benefit curve for that product. The highest price that a consumer is willing to knowingly pay for Q units of a good is a just bit less than the total benefit generated by that good (his or her reservation price), measured in the currency used in his or her country—dollar, euro, yen, etc.—or in units of satisfaction or pleasure—utility. Successive units of goods and services normally produce additional benefits, and so total benefits tend to rise with the number of units obtained. The additional benefit generated by one additional unit of a good or service is called its marginal benefit and can be interpreted as the highest price that a person will knowingly pay for the Q-th unit of a good. Economists normally assume that marginal benefits fall with quantity, so marginal benefit curves tend to slope downward, and total benefit curves thus tend to rise more slowly as the quantity acquired increases. The first unit of a good is used for its highest valued purpose, and the second, to its second most valuable use, and so forth.

When the quality of a product varies, the marginal benefit received from a given unit cannot be known with certainty unless defects are obvious at the point of sale. To simplify the narrative, it will be assumed that only two degrees of quality exist: perfect and defective. Successive units of goods or services have one marginal benefit associated with them when they are perfect and another when they are defective. The marginal benefit curve associated with defective units lies below that of perfect units. To further simplify, it is assumed that consumers are risk neutral—which means that consumers use statistical averages when determining the "expected value" of a particular unit of a particular good. If probability of a "perfect" unit of a good is p and a "defective" unit of the good is $1 - p$, the expected or average marginal benefit (MB) from a particular unit of the good is $p*MB(Q)^+ + (1-p)MB(Q)^-$ where $MB(Q)^+$ is the marginal benefit of the Q-th unit of the good when it is perfect and $MB(Q)^-$ is its marginal benefit when defective. This implies that the expected marginal benefit curve lies between the marginal benefit curve of perfect units and that of defective units.

Figure 4.1 illustrates a consumer's decision about the number of units of a good to purchase when its per unit price (marginal cost) is P. If the probability of a perfect unit is one half, $P = 0.5$, then the expected MB is exactly halfway between the $MB^+$ and $MB^-$ curves. As the probability of perfect units increases, the $MB^e$ curve moves closer and closer to the $MB^+$ curve.

The consumer purchases all of the units the good for which the expected marginal benefits are greater than their marginal cost(s), which implies that $Q^*$ units of the good are purchased by the consumer illustrated. Economists refer to the difference between the total benefit received from Q units of a good and the total cost of Q units of a good as its *net benefit* or *consumer surplus*. The expected consumer surplus is $CS^e(Q^*) = TB^e(Q^*) - TC(Q^*)$, with superscript "e" denoting expected values. The expected total benefits of Q units of the good is the area under the $MB^e$ curve from 0 to Q, and the total cost of

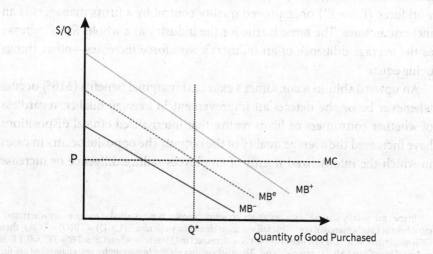

**Figure 4.1.** Maximizing expected consumer surplus.

Q units is the area under the marginal cost (MC) curve from 0 to Q. Thus, the consumer surplus realized by purchasing $Q^*$ units of the good is the triangular area between the $MB^e$ and MC curves from 0 and $Q^*$. The area of this triangle is a measure of a consumer's net gains from trade and is one interpretation of the payoffs that consumers realize in the various game matrices of Chapter 3. The quantity characterized by the intersection of the $MB^e$ and MC curves, $Q^*$, is the quantity of the good that maximizes this buyer's expected consumer surplus.[1]

## Ethical Dispositions and Quality Control

Although some of the variation in quality of a good or service is unavoidable, much of it reflects the diligence of the persons who design and produce the product being sold. The ethical dispositions of those persons—along with their skills—affect the probability that a particular worker creates a defective unit of the good or service. The more skill and diligence applied, the lower is the probability of a defective unit.

Figure 4.2 illustrates the effect of an increase in the average strength of internalized ethical dispositions that increase diligence. Such dispositions increase the average quality of the products sold and thereby increase the expected marginal benefit realized by each consumer. (As the probability of a defect falls, the $MB^e$ curve shifts toward the $MB^+$ curve.) As a consequence, our representative consumer and other similar consumers purchase more units of the good and realize higher average consumer surplus. The result of more diligent workforce ($E'' > E'$) or improved quality control by a firm's managers is an increase in sales. The same is true for the industry as a whole. Sales increase as the average diligence of an industry's workforce increases—other things being equal.

An upward shift in a consumer's expected marginal benefits ($MB^e$) occurs whenever he or she detects an improvement in average quality, regardless of whether consumers or firms realize that internalized ethical dispositions have increased the average quality of the output. The opposite occurs in cases in which the internalized norms of employees reduce diligence or increase

---

[1] In the case usually assumed by economists, consumer surplus is maximized at the quantity where marginal benefit equals marginal cost. This follows from elementary calculus. If $CS(Q) = TB(Q) - TC(Q)$ then CS is maximized when the first derivative of CS with respect to Q is zero or when $CS' = TB' - TC' = 0$. $TB'$ is marginal benefit and $MC'$ is marginal cost. The mathematics are not important for this chapter but are the simplest way to explain why finding the quantity that sets $MB = MC$ maximizes consumer surplus—the net gains from trade for a consumer.

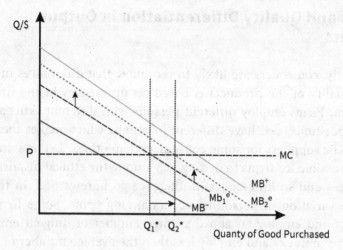

**Figure 4.2.** Effect of an increase in productive ethical dispositions on a typical individual's demand.

shirking—other things being equal. The more haphazard the production and assembly of products and services, the higher the probability of defects and the lower the expected marginal benefits and the quantities purchased by typical consumers at a given price.

Max Weber ([1905] 1958) argues that the Protestant Reformation of the seventeenth century tended to expand commerce by providing new theological support for diligence, working long hours, and saving within Protestant communities. Figure 4.2 demonstrates that such an effect is plausible. If the Protestant Reformation increased the average diligence of employees and employers, it would have increased the average quality of products sold and expanded commerce. If increased saving increased the funds available to purchase better or more tools for working people (capital), it would have further increased the average quality of goods and services produced for sale in markets.

Thus, Weber's explanation for the greater economic development of northern Europe after the Protestant Reformation is consistent with neoclassical economics when the effects of ethical dispositions on quality and on the supply of labor are taken into account, even when those dispositions are not directly taken into account by firms or consumers.[2]

---

[2] Figure 4.2 can be used to represent markets as well as consumer choices, if one assumes constant returns to scale in production with respect to both defective and perfect units and identical consumers. Note that the market expands as defective units of goods and services diminish.

# Ethics and Quality Differentiation in Output Markets

Eventually, consumers are likely to recognize that differences in the average quality of the products is based on differences in the firms that sell them. Firms employ different persons with different skills and ethical dispositions, and have different locations, which makes them more likely to be suppliers for some consumers than others. Let us assume that it is impossible for firms to distinguish among the ethical dispositions of employees and so differences in diligence go unrewarded. In this case, random variation in personnel occurs among firms. Some firms are a bit lucky and employ an above average number of diligent employees. Others are unlucky and employ less than the average number of diligent employees.

Such differences can produce detectable differences in the average quality of output among firms. If at least a few consumers can distinguish between the highest- and lowest-quality firms, the highest-quality (lowest-defect) firms will have higher sales and profits than the lowest-quality (highest-defect) firms. If a sufficient number of consumers can do so, the market may separate into two or three submarkets—high-quality, average, and low-quality firms—even if the products themselves remain superficially indistinguishable from one another.

## Price Premiums for Differences in Average Quality

When some firms become known for producing relatively more of the "good" version of the product and fewer of the "bad" version, such firms may come to be referred to as the "good" firms. Good firms produce good products. In this case, the term "good" reflects the unintentional higher average virtue of the firm's employees. If the "good" firms cannot satisfy the demand for their more consistently "good" products at the preexisting market prices, they may raise prices without losing their customers, because of the lower risk of defects. In this way, prices at "good," "average," and "bad" stores may come to differ—as necessary for a separating equilibrium—even though the products themselves are indistinguishable from one another at the point of sale. A premium will be paid for high-quality "brands" and a discount for defect-prone "brands."

## Social Networks, Expert Opinion, and Prices as Signals of Quality

There are relatively few products that a single consumer will purchase enough of to be able to distinguish between high- and low-quality firms. Thus, some method of aggregating the experiences of buyers across firms is usually necessary for systematic quality variations to become known. This aggregation of information can take place in several ways. For example, consumers may chat with one another about their experiences among firms, and their discussions may reveal systematic differences in the products provided by individual firms. To the extent that the information that informs such informal recommendations is unbiased, the average or median estimate of such social network assessments will be more accurate than that of a typical member of the network, because it takes more information into account—which is to say that conclusions (average quality estimates) are based on larger samples.[3]

Another method of identifying high-quality firms and products is the use of expert opinion. There are economies of scale in sampling and testing. Thus, an honest "recommendation organization" can test products from several venders or survey dozens of customers and use the results to produce more precise assessments of product quality than can be gathered from a consumer's own direct experience or from a modest network of friends and neighbors. Unfortunately, "expert assessments" are also products that cannot easily be appraised by consumers at the point of sale. "Expert" assessments are only as good as the skill, honesty, and diligence of the persons undertaking the assessments. Pragmatic experts may simply sell some or all of their recommendations to the highest bidders. To "validate" their opinions, they might organize contests in which the products associated with the largest bribes always win "first" or "second" place.[4]

When a sufficient number of consumers have good reason to believe that particular quality-assessing organizations tend to be staffed by honest

---

[3] See Paula Fitzgerald (1995) for evidence that word-of-mouth accounts of quality influence consumer decisions. With the profits generated by informal favorable assessments in mind, many contemporary Internet vendors include consumer comments and ranking information on their websites. It bears noting, however, that fraudulent assessments at such sites are commonplace, because it is possible for vendors to hire people to post "favorable" recommendations for products they have neither purchased nor used (see, for example, J. Swearingen [Dec. 7, 2017] *Intelligencer*).

[4] Nelson (1974) suggests that the size of an advertising campaign can itself be used as a proxy for quality, in that it makes the most economic sense to spend one's advertising dollars on products most likely to sell in the long run.

evaluators who use reliable methods for assessing the quality of products and firms, such experts or groups of experts will attract more attention for the same reason that the most reliable producers of ordinary goods and services do. In this manner, advice-giving organizations with relatively more diligent personnel tend to acquire favorable reputations and supplant those with lesser reputations, other things being equal. They will tend to flourish relative to others by providing useful dependable information.[5]

When either of these two information-aggregating methods work, assessments of the quality of the products sold by different firms will be accurate and the price differences among producers of similar products will be correlated with quality. The higher-priced ones will be among those that produce the most reliably high-quality units.

This allows uninformed buyers to use price as a proxy for quality, because hundreds or thousands of other consumers—many of whom are well-informed—have assessed the quality of the products on offer by polling their friends and reading honest expert opinions and have accurately concluded that particular firms are providing "premium" products that are "worth" the extra money.

## The Market Demand for and Distribution of Ethical Employees

In markets where sellers use different methods of production and different inputs, relatively high profits are often realized by firms with relatively high sales and high-quality personnel. Rival firms will attempt to determine the source of those profits. Insofar as it is average quality that drives profits in

---

[5] In the United States, the magazine *Consumer Reports* has a very good reputation for objective reviews of all sorts of products. Their nonprofit nature implies that firms cannot bribe them to overrate their merchandise.

For-profit magazines and websites also undertake product assessments, but somewhat less reliably because they are open to influence by their advertisers. However, they can only bias their assessments within limits without losing their readership and thereby their advertisers. The signal of quality from such sources is thus somewhat unreliable but can still be useful. Objective information may be honestly produced and provided, as when car magazines provide evidence of noise levels in decibels, standardized acceleration rates, top speeds, gas mileage, etc. Other subjective characteristics may be shaded to favor their advertisers as with style or ease of use assessments. Nonetheless, a reputation for honest, diligent, assessments clearly increases readership and advertising revenues from the most honest firms, albeit at the cost of lower revenues from less honest firms.

When the latter spend more on advertising than the former, such private sources of information tend to be unreliable and the magazines remain in business for reasons other than their quality assessments, such as the quality of their prose and photos. Insofar as magazine subscribers can distinguish between informative and noninformative magazines, a spectrum of more or less informative magazines may be supported by markets.

the market of interest, rivals will investigate each other's production methods and may come to realize that teams are more productive when particular ethical dispositions are common among their members. As a consequence, they will take steps to identify and recruit appropriately ethical team members or employees. If, for example, differences in diligence is the primary driver of quality and profits, the quest for profits will induce employers to attempt to search for diligent employees. And it will induce firm owners and managers to determine where best to deploy employees with particular ethical dispositions. Not every virtue on a philosopher's list is likely to increase production, reduce defect rates, improve service, or otherwise increase the quality of a firm's products, but those that do would be sought out and deployed in the most profitable manner.

As efforts to recruit diligent employees takes place, such persons dispositions will be paid a premium when such persons are scarce and have higher marginal revenue products. Prices—here wage rates—rise for the relatively "high-quality" employees relative to the "lower-quality" ones, which in this case is mainly attributed to differences in productive ethical dispositions. Such persons require less direction and monitoring than their more pragmatic substitutes, and so they would be most valuable in difficult-to-monitor positions and in positions in which shirking poses the greatest risk of losses to firm owners.[6]

## On the Distribution of Ethical Persons Within an Economic Organization

Figure 4.3 illustrates hiring decisions of a firm for two different positions within the firm. Type A employees are assumed to be relatively ethical in the sense of being relatively more honest and diligent when not closely monitored. Type B employees are assumed to require more monitoring and more complex contracts to achieve similar results in the less easily monitored and motivated position 1, but are perfect substitutes for one another in the other, position 2. The employer's demand for the two types of individuals is based on their expected marginal revenue product in the two positions—which is

---

[6] In cases in which a separating equilibrium arises and separate markets for high-, average-, and low-quality versions of the same product are sustained, differences in recruiting would be observed, with the producers of low-quality (cheaper) being somewhat less interested in more ethical and more skilled employees, because they are more costly to employ. Nonetheless, as quality standards increase for their products, even such producers are induced to hire employees with productive internalized norms for positions in which such ethical dispositions are especially valuable.

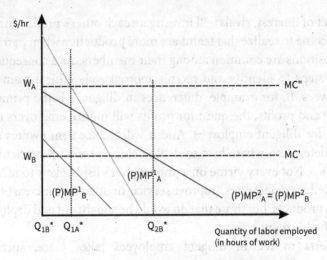

**Figure 4.3.** Hiring more (A) or less (B) ethical persons for two different positions (1 or 2).

simply the firm's output price, P, times the typical marginal products of the two types of employees within the two positions, $MP^A$ and $MP^B$ (the extra revenue produced by an additional hour of work from a type A or type B employee in the two positions).

The lower marginal revenue product curve represents the demand for positions in which monitoring is relatively easy and so the marginal product of honesty in that position is relatively low. The higher marginal revenue product curve represents the demand for type A employees in positions in which monitoring is difficult or honesty especially important, and the lowest line is the demand for type B employees in the same positions. The marginal product of more diligent and honest employees is higher in one role and the same in the other. Because the wage rates needed to attract the two types of employees differ for reasons already discussed, the honest-diligent types (A) tend to be hired for the difficult-to-monitor position (1) and the type B employees for the easy-to-monitor and -motivate positions (2). Note that in the case illustrated, more type B employees are hired than type A employees, although this is not always the case.[7]

When wage-rate differences among the groups change, firms will adjust the mix of persons they hire for the two positions. In the separating equilibrium illustrated, each of the two types of labor is hired for particular types of

---

[7] For example, Frederick Taylor (1913, 44–47) tells a story about picking out an especially diligent and hard-working day laborer (referred to as Schmidt in the text). With some additional training, his productivity became triple that of other workers (at loading pig iron in a Bethlehem foundry), for which Schmidt received a 60% premium on his daily wages. Taylor is regarded by many to be the inventor of scientific management.

positions. In other cases, a mixture of employee types might be hired for one or both positions, although the mix may vary with their marginal productivities at the positions of interest.[8]

## On the Distribution of Ethical Persons among Industries and Firms

Figure 4.3 can also be used to characterize the demand for employees with different ethical dispositions but the similar skill levels in different industries and markets. Interpreted in this way, the logic of labor markets implies that a subset of industries may outbid the others for most persons with particular internalized norms. The higher salaries of what might be called the market for especially diligent, honest, or hard-working employees would attract most such persons to those positions (and, of course, some persons pretending to have such ethical dispositions, who would have to be weeded out). The same sorting, of course, tends to be true for other productivity-enhancing human capital as well. Ditch diggers are unlikely to be hired from among the graduates of medical schools, and surgeons are unlikely to be hired from among high-school dropouts (even if we ignore medical licensing requirements). The services of skilled doctors are worth more to consumers desiring medical services than are the services of ditch diggers, so doctors tend to be paid more for their services.

As is true of output markets, the segmentation of labor markets requires reliable indicators of differences among potential team members. Diligence, for example, might be revealed by past employment experience, reference letters from former employers, their course of study and grades at university, and reference letters from college professors. Other evidence might be garnered from criminal records, club memberships, and church attendance, as with Weber's Protestantism hypothesis. That persons involved in scandals and ex-cons are widely reported to have a difficult time finding jobs is, of course, an implication of ethics-based hiring—and it is a difference that is hard to explain without taking the productivity of ethical dispositions into account.[9]

---

[8] The marginal revenue product curves assume the production function is linear in these two kinds of labor, more or less of the form $Q = h(L') + g(L'')$ where labor of type (') is most productive in process $h$, and labor of type ('') is most productive in process $g$. The same diagram can also be used for more general types of production functions, but in such cases, the marginal products would each reflect the number of other types of labor already hired; so the diagram would reflect the final pattern of hiring, rather than the independent decisions to hire each type of labor.

[9] Of course, this is not entirely caused by the ethical propensities implied by arrest and conviction. Convicts have often invested less in other forms of human capital as well. An accessible overview of the issues and evidence on the effect of a criminal record appears at: https://www.prisonlegalnews.org/news/2011/dec/15/study-shows-ex-offenders-have-greatly-reduced-employment-rates.

## The Supply of Persons with Market-Supporting Ethical Dispositions

The wage premiums paid to persons with productive ethical dispositions will also affect the distribution of ethical dispositions within every community, although they are unlikely to fully determine those distributions. The ethical theories reviewed in Part III suggest that individuals have several separate reasons to invest in ethical dispositions. Aristotle suggests that virtuous dispositions tend to increase lifetime happiness and contentment. Immanuel Kant argues that performance of one's ethical duties can be a source of sublime satisfaction. Theology-based theories of ethics argue that internalizing particular rules of conduct increases one's probability for an afterlife or indicates divine favor. Adam Smith suggests that virtue tends to attract praise and approbation from members of one's community. Utilitarians such as Jeromy Bentham and John Stuart Mill suggest that ethics can be a source of long-run pleasure, which increases social utility as long as it does no harm to others. Benjamin Franklin and Claude-Frédéric Bastiat argue that a subset of virtues tends to be associated with higher income and wealth.

Ethics are a means rather than an ultimate end in all of these theories: a means to personal contentment in the present or in an afterlife, to praise, to wealth, and/or to an improved society. Yet, there are costs as well as benefits associated with developing such dispositions. Time and energy are consumed in the process of learning about and internalizing ethical principles and moral maxims, and there are often conflicts between one's long-term ethical interests and one's immediate pragmatic inclinations. Immoral and blameworthy conduct is often pleasurable or profitable, at least in the short run. The acquisition of virtuous dispositions often requires such immediate pleasures and advantages to be willingly sacrificed.

## Private, Social, and Economic Determinants of Virtuous Dispositions

As individuals reach the age of maturity, their investments in moral dispositions are undertaken more self-consciously, although their moral interests reflect past training that affects their understanding of the nature of morality and expectations of the rewards associated with various virtues. A typical adult's decision to exercise or further develop a virtue is illustrated

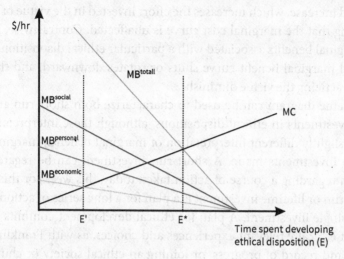

**Figure 4.4.** Investing in an ethical disposition for social, personal, and economic reasons.

in Figure 4.4. The virtue of interest is assumed to advance all three of the earthly categories of personal benefits mentioned by the authors reviewed in Part III: personal (increased self-esteem and contentment), social (increased praise, respect, and status), and economic (increased income and wealth). The individual's overall marginal benefit from exercising such virtues is the vertical sum of the marginal benefits anticipated from personal, social, and economic rewards associated with the virtues of interest. The diagram makes the usual economic assumption about the marginal opportunity cost of time devoted to developing the virtue illustrated. Time redirected from other activities to the development of virtue sacrifices larger and larger alternative sources of benefits. (The diagram has been simplified a bit by assuming that the additional praise, self-esteem, and income all reach zero at the same point, which makes the task of adding the three contributing MB curves to obtain the total MB curve easier to undertake and interpret.) The forward-looking person depicted in Figure 4.4 invests E* hours exercising and strengthening the virtuous disposition illustrated.

Note that a change in any of the various marginal reward schedules for an ethical disposition induces the individual to adjust his or her efforts devoted to developing the virtuous disposition of interest, which affects the time available for other activities, including efforts to exercise other virtues. As any of the marginal benefits increase (MB curves shift or rotate upward), the overall marginal benefits associated with investments in the virtuous disposition depicted increase, which increases the effort invested in the virtue of interest, assuming that the marginal cost curve is unaffected. Contrariwise, if any of the marginal benefits associated with a particular ethical disposition decline, the total marginal benefit curve shifts or rotates downward, and the hours spent practicing the virtue diminish.

The same diagram can be used to characterize both short-run and long-term investments in ethical dispositions, although these interpretations require a slightly different interpretation of marginal benefits, marginal costs, and the investments made. A short-run investment can be regarded as a decision regarding a course of action taken today, this week, or this month. A long-run or lifetime investment is a plan for a long series of actions, rather than a single investment. A plan for ethical development commits one to a series of ethically relevant experiences and choices, as with Franklin's list of virtues and record of progress, or joining an ethical society or church. It is the rules of conduct followed over many years that determine one's character, again holding other things equal.[10]

If we accept the usual rational choice models of personal investments, differences in the marginal benefits and costs among the possible virtues one might pursue elicit different patterns of investments and therefore different collections and degrees of virtue among persons from the same families and communities. Differences among families are likely to be larger than those within families, and differences among communities are likely to be larger than differences within communities because there is likely to be greater variety in the perceived rewards of ethical dispositions and efforts made to develop or inculcate virtues among families than within families, and among communities than within a community.[11]

The same logic implies that differences in market settings affect investments in virtue at the margin through effects on the marginal economic benefits associated with various ethical dispositions. For example, suppose that the private

[10] Figure 4.4 assumes that the virtues are entirely separate, as suggested by the virtue lists of Aristotle and Smith and many others, so investments in one do not necessarily directly affect others. However, there are cases in which some choices or experiences affect more than one virtuous disposition simultaneously, and in such cases, the joint effects would be taken into account. One way to do this geometrically for a particular virtue is to assume that a fourth contributory marginal benefit curve exists that includes the net marginal beneficial side effects of practicing the virtue of interest (diagrammed) on other virtues. This fourth curve would be added to the other three to determine the overall marginal benefit of investments in the virtue of interest.

[11] From the perspective of neoclassical economics, parental, educative, and religious efforts to inculcate particular values can be regarded as subsidies that encourage children to invest in particular dispositions. Rational choice models imply that the greater the family and community subsidies (social rewards for particular ethics), the greater is the increase in the ethical dispositions subsidized. That the results differ within families and communities suggests that other private interests and natural inclinations and abilities vary enough to affect the consequences of social pressures.

and social rewards of two virtues are identical, but that one of these virtues is economically rewarding and the other is not. The duties of one type of employment, for example, may frequently place one in choice settings where particular ethical dispositions are relevant, whereas other dispositions may not be.

When particular virtues are rewarded by their employer or employment, individuals have additional reasons to devote more time to developing such virtues and also have a lower marginal cost for doing so, insofar as opportunities for developing the requisite habits of thought and action are provided by their employment. If similar rewards and opportunities are provided by most employers in the community, the typical member of the community will exhibit more of the economically rewarding virtues and (relatively) less of the economically neutral or counterproductive ones, other things being equal.

However, as mentioned previously and indicated by the philosophers surveyed in Part III, market rewards are only one of the reasons why rational individuals invest in ethics. Indeed, only Franklin and Bastiat among the authors reviewed in Part III stress the financial advantages of ethical dispositions. Figure 4.4 demonstrates that a person who invests in acquiring an ethical disposition for pecuniary reasons alone tends to invest less than others who also receive the other two sources of benefits as well. As a consequence, such persons will receive a smaller ethical wage premium, other things being equal, than those who invest in the same virtue(s) for personal and social reasons as well as economic rewards ($E'' < E^*$). (In Figure 4.4, such economically motivated investments are represented as the least important of all the influences, although they needn't be.)

Together, all three types of rewards jointly determine the distribution of ethical dispositions within a person and within a given community in the long run. However, if economic rewards change more frequently or vary more than social or personal support for ethical dispositions, changes in the economic rewards associated with particular ethical dispositions will have a more obvious, if small, effect on the extent to which particular virtues are accumulated within and among communities.

## The Supply of Productive Virtues and Economic Development

The variance and average of a community's distribution of ethical dispositions are relevant for economic analysis because they affect both the supply of and demand for goods and services. If persons with unusually productive (or unproductive) ethical dispositions can be identified, then employers will seek out the high outliers and attempt to avoid the low outliers when choosing the persons to employ for positions in which ethical dispositions are most productive.

When individual propensities cannot be easily determined, then the average level for the pool of job candidates provides a useful estimate of the likely propensities of employees. That estimate, in turn, partly determines advantages from alternative methods of organizing production. In such cases, average propensities partly determine the gains from specialization and thereby the extent of market networks. As noted above, market-supporting norms have effects on the extent of markets, whether they are recognized and rewarded or not.

When they are recognized, productivity-increasing virtues tend to be rewarded by markets, and this, in turn, affects the distribution of ethical dispositions within the community from which employees are hired. Figure 4.5 holds the other sources of support for the virtue of interest constant and illustrates the long-run effect of an increase in demand for economically productive virtues such as diligence or industry. Such increases in demand may be generated, for example, by better recognition of the quality of products by consumers, reductions in transportation costs that broaden the reach of firms, or by technological advances that can be realized only by large organizations in which many tasks are difficult to monitor. The effect is analogous to the long-run effects on supply generated by increases in the demand for ordinary economic goods and services.

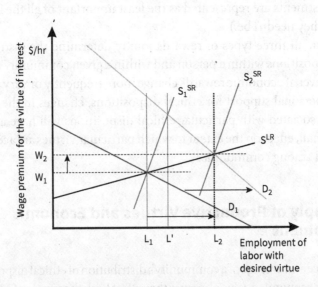

**Figure 4.5.** Effect of increasing demand for ethical employees in the long run, generated by effects on investments in the sought-after ethical disposition.

In the (very) long run, wage increases induce increases in the supply of persons with the economically productive virtue from $L_1$ to $L_2$, whereas the short-run effect on supply is much smaller (the increase to $L'$), although the short-run wage effect is much larger (the increase to $W'$). The long-term effect reflects the cumulative investments made by many families and individuals over decades.

As productive ethical dispositions become more commonplace, markets expand, and economic organizations increase in size and complexity—other things being equal—because such dispositions make economic organizations more efficient. Specialization also tends to increase within and among firms, further increasing the efficiency with which goods and services are produced and sold.

## Ethical Innovations and the Cost of Goods and Services

Ethical innovations that increase the average productivity of labor, by reducing monitoring costs and creating new possibilities for organization, tend to increase output in all markets. Contrariwise, ethical innovations that increase monitoring costs and reduce organizational possibilities tend to reduce purchases of the goods sold, which may make some markets and some organizational forms disappear. Figure 4.6 illustrates the effect of ethical innovations that induce a general increase in productive ethical dispositions. Such ethical

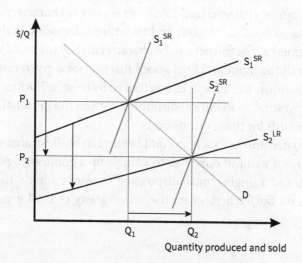

**Figure 4.6.** Effect on the output of final goods and services induced by an increased supply of employees with productive ethical dispositions in the long run.

developments reduce production costs, which induces an increase in both short-run and long-run supply, both of which tend to reduce prices and increase the quantity of goods sold in output markets. Prices fall in the long run, while output increases.

Insofar as similar effects occur for a broad cross section of industries and markets, increases in the supply of persons with productive ethical dispositions promote economic development, as argued by Weber.

## The Co-determination of Ethics and the Extent of Markets

Aristotle, Smith, and Kant argued that personal and social returns from virtue, rather than economic ones, determined individual investments in virtuous dispositions and actions. Nonetheless, as suggested by Bastiat, Franklin, and the analysis in this and the previous chapter, market rewards for virtuous conduct create additional incentives for family and personal investments in such dispositions. Thus, when ethical propensities create new market opportunities and markets reward such propensities, market and ethical systems are co-determined in the long run—at least at the margin.

This section shows how one can use the geometry of neoclassical economics to model this interdependence and to characterize a socioeconomic steady state. (A lean mathematical model of such an equilibrium is developed in the appendix to this chapter, for those interested in more detail about how such an equilibrium can be characterized.) A stable society is characterized by long-run equilibria in both its markets and the ethical dispositions that are relevant for commerce. The former can be characterized by the usual neoclassical equilibria in all the input and final goods markets for a given distribution of ethical dispositions. The latter is characterized by the equilibrium of personal and family investments in ethical dispositions given the personal, social, and economic rewards for those dispositions.

The essential features of such an equilibrium can be illustrated with the last three diagrams if we limit ourselves to a single final good, a single input (virtuous labor), and a single ethical disposition (a work ethic).[12] This approach may seem a bit far-fetched, given the wide variety of final goods, types of

---

[12] Diligence is not on any of the lists of virtues discussed in Part III, but combines various aspects of self-discipline (Aristotle), prudence (Smith), and dutiful behavior (Kant). It is also consistent with Franklin's discussion of conduct in his discussion of the way to wealth.

labor, ethical dispositions, and inputs actually present in a commercial society, but such simplifications are often used in economics to illustrate key relationships. Figure 4.7 depicts such an equilibrium.

The demand for final goods is affected by ethical dispositions because average product quality increases and the quantity demanded is affected by changes in price associated with increases in quality and labor productivity. The supply of final goods is affected because production costs are reduced by the increased productivity of labor. The supply of ethical labor increases as the income and satisfaction associated with work increases with the strength of a typical employee's work ethic. The strength of the ethical dispositions of the persons seeking employment, in turn, is determined by the (marginal) private, social, and economic rewards associated with those dispositions and their opportunity costs. The economic rewards realized by persons with ethical dispositions depend on their effects on production costs and the premiums paid for persons with particular dispositions.

In equilibrium, all three types of "markets" simultaneously "clear," in the sense that firm owners, employees, and persons making ethical investments are completely satisfied with their own choices, given prevailing prices and

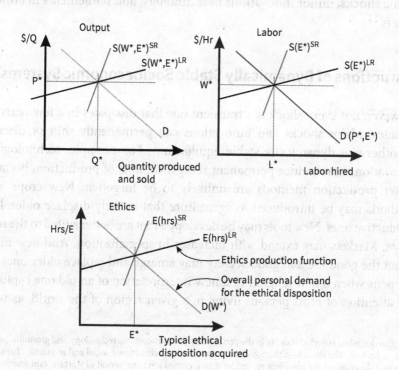

**Figure 4.7.** Social and economic equilibrium.

other factors such as technology, social support, and preferences determine the shape of the three sets of demand-and-supply curves, and the ethical production function, which characterizes how time spent practicing the ethical conduct of interest internalizes and strengthens propensities for virtuous conduct.

The existence of such socioeconomic equilibria provides an explanation for the long-term economic and cultural stability typical of many pre-commercial societies. Many systems of ethical beliefs and their associated markets were stable for centuries at a time. Gordon (2016), for example, reports that before 1800 long-term economic growth rates throughout the world were generally less than 1% per year. Such stable or "evenly rotating societies" may be disrupted by political and military shocks (such as invasions), climate changes, and pandemics, but if the equilibrium is dynamically stable, the basic pattern of life re-emerges after the shock and communities return to the preexisting equilibrium.

It is only a slight exaggeration to assert that during the five hundred years prior to the emergence of commercial societies in the eighteenth and nineteenth centuries, stable patterns of life were sustained in most regions of the world in spite of many and varied political, environmental, and pandemic shocks, minor innovations in technology, and refinements in ethical beliefs.[13]

## Disruptions of Dynamically Stable Socioeconomic Systems

However, not every shock is a transient one that dissipates in a few years or decades. Major shocks and innovations can permanently shift or disrupt an otherwise dynamically stable equilibrium. For example, technological innovations may induce permanent reorganizations of production, because better production methods are unlikely to be forgotten. New crops and methods may be introduced to agriculture that entirely displace older, less productive ones. New tools may be developed that are better suited to the new crops. Markets may extend with increases in specialization. And new ideas about the good life and good society may emerge and replace older ones, as happens when a new religion or a new interpretation of an old one captures the attention of most persons living in a given region of the world, as with

---

[13] This doubtless reflected stability in the various factors of production, technology, and grounding ethos of those periods. The shocks—although often severe—did not affect those social and economic characteristics that determined the equilibrium, and so it re-emerged after the period of warfare, odd weather, or plague was over.

the spread of Confucianism, Buddhism, Christianity, Islam, Protestantism, Contractarianism, and Utilitarianism. As noted in the previous chapters, innovations in a community's ethos alter behavior in ways that may improve or reduce the viability of communities. Not all changes are for the better, but many are. And, as indicated by the analysis in this and the previous chapters, such changes can affect the manner in which market networks and production are organized.

Such shocks permanently alter parameters of their social systems, rather than temporarily modifying them, as when a war or pandemic ends. After such transformative shocks, a society shifts to a new equilibrium.

The effects of such transformative disruptions can also be analyzed using the diagrams included in Figure 4.7. For example, suppose that the new philosophy increases a typical individual's demand for a productive disposition (in the bottom diagram). This change affects both the supply and demand curves in the labor market. The productivity of labor with productive ethical dispositions increases. The greater productivity of the labor employed increases the supply curve for the final good, and any improvement in quality increases consumer demand. The real wage premium realized by relatively ethical employees may increase or decrease, but in either case, a productivity-enhancing ethical innovation increases total economic output and thereby increases prosperity.

In this manner, an increase in social support for a productivity-increasing disposition, such as that suggested by Weber ([1905] 1958), or an increase in general support for commerce as noted by McCloskey (2006), can simultaneously increase the extent of commerce and real wage rates. In Chapter 5, it will be argued that such market-supporting innovations can also increase the rates of technological innovation and capital accumulation, which tend to disrupt social steady states and accelerate economic development.

Similarly, a technological innovation may increase the long-run demand for particular ethical dispositions. After assembly lines are introduced, a single shirker can affect the performance of the entire line, which implies that timeliness and a predisposition to work hard—a work ethic—become more important. Adam Smith argues that the division of labor within a firm tends to encourage a work ethic simply because workmen no longer have to move from one task to another. "The habit of sauntering, and of indolent careless application, which is naturally, or rather necessarily, acquired by every country workman who is obliged to change his work and his tools every half hour, and to apply his hand in twenty different ways almost every day of his life, renders him almost always slothful and lazy" (Smith, 1776, p. 4). This may account for the wage premium paid by Henry Ford as his assembly line production of automobiles was introduced. Aguiar and Hurst (2007) report that leisure has increased more for low-wage than for high-wage persons during the past 50 years, which may reflect a contemporary premium for educated persons with a strong work ethic. Higher premiums for workers with productive ethical dispositions will increase the supply of persons with such dispositions in the long run.

Of course, other types of ethical and technological innovations are also possible. Ethical innovations can also reduce the productivity of labor. Ethical principles that favor leisure over work, dishonesty over honesty, spontaneity over predictability, and so forth, tend to reduce the productivity of a community's workforce by reducing a firm's ability to use complex, roundabout methods of production. Reduced realization of advantages associated with team production, such as greater intra-team specialization and associated economies of scale, tend to reduce income and average material comforts. A technological innovation that reduces the marginal revenue product of labor with ethical dispositions relative to those of pragmatists reduces the wage premiums associated with ethical dispositions, which reduces subsequent investments in those dispositions, reducing somewhat the gains realized through such technological advances.

The first cases demonstrate that progress is always possible. The latter cases demonstrate that, nonetheless, progress is not inevitable.

## Conclusions: Ethics, Prices, and the Extent of Markets

This chapter has explored the effects of ethical dispositions on market prices and output levels by integrating ethics into neoclassical models of price determination in competitive markets. Such an extension does not require abandoning the textbook economic models, although it does require broadening the usual scope of analysis. Such expansions of the scope of analysis have occurred many times in the past, as when the effects of taxes and regulations were first incorporated into economic models. Similar expansions occurred when legal, political, and economic interdependencies were analyzed. In all those cases, expanding the scope of analysis led to a more complete understanding of the manner in which economic systems operate.

The power of the neoclassical approach is that its relatively simple and clear models reveal general interdependencies that at least partially account for (and predict) the more complex phenomena of the real world. The same is true of many extensions of the core models. This chapter has shown how the inclusion of ethical dispositions can also deepen our understanding of economic systems and socio-economic systems. In terms of the previous literature, ethical dispositions can be regarded as a particular form of human capital, a subset of which increases the productivity of labor. Evidence that human capital affects productivity is both obvious and widely affirmed in statistical analyses (Crook, Todd, et al., 2011).

The analysis of this chapter and Chapter 3 demonstrates that internalized norms are likely to have a variety of effects on the extent of markets for both final goods and inputs. The extent and kind of ethical dispositions affect labor markets, the organization of production, and the quality of the goods and services produced. Norms that characterize "the orthodox" or "the good life" or "the good society" affect the demand for specific goods and services that are believed to advance such ends. And they also partly determine the attributes that characterize "good" products and "good" services.

Differences in ideas about the good life are obvious as one travels about the world, although countries are more homogeneous than they were a century ago. Every upscale department store in Tokyo seems to have a kimono shop, but not those in New York or Paris. An eating utensil store in Berlin or Stockholm will have a wide variety of artistically designed forks, spoons, and knives, but in Beijing, Seoul, or Kyoto a similar shop would have dozens of types of designer chopsticks instead. The windows of most homes in northern Europe open in and out rather than sliding up and down as is most common in the United States. Foods on offer in grocery stores vary as well. Although markets for fruit, vegetables, fish, and meat have become increasingly globalized, "ordinary" food still has a regional character.

It can be argued that little is lost by neglecting the effects of different ideas about the good life and good society in settings in which they are stable, as in short-run analyses of a single community or region. However, as the period of interest expands or if regional variations in relevant ethical and aesthetic dispositions exist, ignoring the effects of those dispositions can lead to significant errors, both in modeling causation and interdependencies and in estimating the determinants of market outputs, prices, wage rates, and industrial concentration. Relevant causal factors will have been left out.

Moral communities do not provide firms with an endless supply of trustworthy hardworking "angels" to employ, but some induce more productive dispositions than others. Such dispositions make some types of markets and some forms of organization possible that otherwise would not be.

## Economic Effects on Ethical Dispositions

The above discussion suggests that the extent of markets is at least partly determined by a community's ethos—its most commonplace internalized rules of conduct—in particular, the subset of those rules that ameliorate or solve social dilemmas associated with life in communities, market transactions, and productive activities on teams. In addition, the analysis suggests that the types of products sold in the markets that emerge are also significantly affected by the most commonplace ideas about a good life and good society in the community of interest.

However, as developed toward the end of this chapter and the previous one, causal links do not run unidirectionally from ethics to markets in the long run. In the short and medium run, ethical dispositions are less responsive to markets than markets are to ethical dispositions. In this sense, a community's non-economic support for ethical dispositions can be said to determine or, perhaps more accurately, to anchor the extent and rate of a community's economic development. In the long run, however, there is feedback between markets and the distribution of a community's ethical dispositions. Thus, a long-run social equilibrium—an evenly rotating society—requires prices and responses to prices to be those that are associated with stability in labor and output markets and support for a community's ethos.

The next and final chapter of Part I explores the effects that ethical dispositions have in the rate of economic development that takes place in a society. The evenly rotating economies and societies of classical and neoclassical economics do not truly characterize a contemporary commercial society. Such societies are endlessly changing. In commercial societies, progress rather than stability is taken for granted. Real wage rates are expected to increase every year, and new and better products are expected every year or so.

Commercial societies have been able to move beyond the Malthusian wage trap that caused most people in prior times to live at the edge of subsistence. The great acceleration that took off during the nineteenth century and continued through the twentieth century allowed wages and salaries well above subsistence levels to become typical rather than the rare exception. Technology is often said to be the main driver of that period, but supportive ethical dispositions were, perhaps, even more important, because they were prerequisites for technological advance.

## Appendix to Chapter 4: A Simple Mathematical Characterization of a Socioeconomic Equilibrium

This appendix develops a simple mathematical representation of a steady-state society. It provides an example of the mathematics behind Figure 4.7. To simplify the analysis and keep it reasonably accessible to readers who are not model builders, it is assumes that relevant utility and production functions are exponential functions, of which the widely used Cobb-Douglas function is a special case.

Suppose that the virtue of interest contributes to both human happiness and productivity. Let the typical individual's utility function be $U = aY^b V^c$. The production of the universal good $Y$ can be modeled as $Y = dW^e V^f$ where $d = gT^h K^i$. $W$ is the time spent working, $V$ is the worker's virtue, and $d$, $e$, $f$, $g$, $h$, and $i$ are constants for the period of interest. Constant $d$ characterizes the effects of other inputs, such as capital ($K$) and technology ($T$), which are taken to be constant for the period of analysis. Virtue is also produced with labor, so $V = mM^j$ where $m$ and $j$ are constants and $M$ is the time devoted to moral training. The individual divides his time, $T$, between moral training, $M$, and productive effort, $W$. Unproductive leisure is left out of the model to simplify the mathematics and discussion, though it would be relatively easy to include. In production, shirking is assumed to be the opposite of the effect of $V$: it falls as $V$ increases. As it is determined by $V$, it need not be included in the model.

The individual maximizes utility by dividing his/her productive time between moral training and the production of the universal good $Y$. He/she maximizes:

$$U = aY^b V^c \tag{4.1}$$

subject to

$$Y = dW^e V^f \tag{4.2}$$

$$V = mM^j \tag{4.3}$$

and

$$T = W + M \tag{4.4}$$

Note that one can use a bit of substitution to account for the three constraints and reduce the two-dimensional time allocation problem to a single-dimensional maximization problem. The following equation embeds the various constraints in the utility function in a manner that characterizes utility as a function of investments in the moral disposition. (In effect, this is Aristotle's characterization of the production of happiness, holding intellectual excellence constant.)

$$U = a\left\{d[T-M]^e[mM^j]^f\right\}^b\{mM^j\}^c$$
$$= a\left\{d^b[T-M]^{be}[m^{bf}M^{fbj}]\right\}\{m^cM^{cj}\}$$
$$= ad^bm^{bf+c}[T-M]^{be}[M]^{fbj+cj}$$

Differentiating with respect to $M$ yields a first-order condition describing the ideal investment in ethical dispositions:

$$ad^bm^{bf+c}\left\{-be[T-M]^{be-1}M^{fbj+cj} + (fbj+cj)[T-M]^{be}[M]^{fbj+cj-1}\right\}=0 \qquad (4.5)$$

which implies that:

$$be[T-M]^{be-1}M^{fbj+cj} = (fbj+cj)[T-M]^{be}[M]^{fbj+cj-1}$$

Dividing both sides by $[T-M]^{be-1}$ and $[M]^{fbj+cj-1}$ yields:

$$beM = (fbj+cj)(T-M)$$

or

$$(be+fbj+cj)M = (fbj+cj)(T),$$

which implies that the ideal investment in moral training, $M^*$, for ethical disposition $V$ is:

$$M^* = \left[(fbj+cj)/(be+fbj+cj)\right](T) \qquad (4.6)$$

Given that result, the level of virtue and work effort are:

$$V^* = m[M^*]^j \tag{4.7}$$

$$W^* = T - M^* \tag{4.8}$$

which implies an average output per worker in equilibrium of:

$$Y^* = d[W^*]^e [V^*]^f \tag{4.9}$$

In a perfectly competitive market, this equilibrium would be induced through adjustments in wage rates. Wages tend to reflect the typical worker's marginal product, $de[W^*]^{e-1} [V^*]^f$, which rises as the virtue of interest increases.

Note that a technological shock that increases $e$ without affecting any of the other model parameters tends to decrease investments in moral training, because $e$ appears in the denominator of equation 4.6, but not in the numerator. More time, however, is consequently devoted to work; the increase in income generated (and implied increase in the consumption of the universal good) is sufficient to increase utility, even given somewhat lower productivity and satisfaction from virtue.

The effect of increased cultural support for an ethical disposition can be represented in several ways. First, it can be regarded as a change in $m$, which has no effect on the individual allocation of time between moral training and work. Second, it can be regarded as an increase in exponent $j$, which makes virtue less costly for individuals to obtain, or in exponent $c$, which makes acquiring virtue more personally satisfying. These last two changes affect both the numerator and denominator of equation 4.6. However, because the denominator is larger than the numerator, the effect on the numerator is relatively greater than that on the denominator, so an increase in $c$ or $j$ tends to increase investments in moral training.

Average income may rise or fall depending on whether the reduction in output generated by working fewer hours is more than offset by increases in productivity generated by the increased virtue, which varies with the relative size of the two exponents in the production function. If the productivity effect of the virtue of interest is relatively large, income will rise as well as virtue. In other cases, income may fall, although utility nonetheless increases.

This model can be generalized in a number of ways; other virtues can be added by regarding $M$ and $V$ to be vectors of moral training and dispositions.

In that case, the mathematics above is that associated with individual elements of those vectors, holding the other virtues constant. Leisure could also be added to the model as another term in the individual's utility function. Intertemporal relations and trade-offs could be explicitly modeled. As long as the exponential functional form is retained, results very similar to those developed in this model would still follow, although some terms would be more complex. A forward-looking individual's allocation of time would still reflect the time constraint $T$ and ratios of the various exponents in the production and utility functions.

# 5
# Ethics and Economic Progress

> These revolutions periodically reshape the existing structure of industry by introducing new methods of production—the mechanized factory, the electrified factory, chemical synthesis and the like; new commodities, such as railroad service, motorcars, electrical appliances; new forms of organization—the merger movement....
>
> Every piece of business strategy acquires its true significance only against the background of that process and within the situation created by it. It must be seen in its role in the **perennial gale of creative destruction**; it cannot be understood irrespective of it or, in fact, on the hypothesis that there is a perennial lull.
>
> —J. A. Schumpeter, *Capitalism, Socialism, and Democracy* ([1942] 2012), KL: 1519–1521 and 1844–1847

## Introduction: On the Possibility of Progress

The previous three chapters provide a possible explanation for the emergence of attractive stable communities with markets in ancient times. Stable patterns of life tend to emerge as a long sequence of social dilemmas are overcome and others are left unsolved. In most cases, the first solutions were likely to be informal decentralized ones. Rules of conduct are worked out by individuals, families, and neighbors. A subset of these is internalized, and serviceable ones are passed on from one neighbor or family to another and from one generation to the next. The rules that produce attractive communities tend to survive, and those that do not do so tend to be weeded out.

Socially productive rules include ones that produce more or less peaceful relationships among community residents and more or less self-sustaining use of local resources. Markets tend to emerge when the rules imply that there is a subset of "things" over which individuals or families can properly exercise control and that authority to control some such things may be voluntarily transferred from one person to another. Transferability allows markets to

*Solving Social Dilemmas*. Roger D. Congleton, Oxford University Press. © Oxford University Press 2022.
DOI: 10.1093/oso/9780197642788.003.0005

emerge. After the problems of fraud and shirking have been ameliorated, the extent of trade expands. Specialization and team production increase in efficiency, which induces such practiced to be adopted, which further expands trade and production within and among communities.

At this point, some village and urban tradesmen and merchants may be said to reside in commercial societies because, as specialists, they rely upon market transactions for most of their necessities. A blacksmith might sell his creations for money and use that money to buy his food from local farmers, his cloth from local weavers, and his raw materials from local miners. Organizations—mostly family based at first—may be created to undertake specific market activities such as transport of goods among communities, mining, construction, textile production, and large-scale farming. As specialization increases, connected networks of communities emerge (societies).

All this initially took place while most persons remained hunter-gatherers, subsistence farmers, crop sharers, or farm employees. Market networks were frequently used, but mostly were used by a minority of individuals in those societies. Most of those societies reached equilibria of various sorts as various combinations of internalized norms and rewards induced stable patterns of life that largely were repeated for dozens of generations. Such societies reside in one of many punctuated equilibria, reflecting their community ethos, technology, and local environment, as in the models of evenly rotating societies developed toward the ends of Chapters 3 and 4.

Such stable patterns of community life have been commonplace in world history. For example, patterns of life were evidently stable for several thousand years in the prehistorical period before settled communities based on farming emerged some ten or twelve thousand years ago. After the agricultural revolution, life in the countryside remained remarkably stable—although not perfectly so—in the period that followed until around 1500 AD. More or less the same crops and animals were grown in more or less similar manners. Life was tied to the seasons, and most of the agriculture was for subsistence rather than commerce.[1] Life in large towns and cities experienced greater changes, but in most places and times, a city dweller would not find life radically different in the same town or city a hundred years later—as is clearly indicated

---

[1] Subsistence farming remained the norm for independent farms, as opposed to noble land grants, until well into the seventeenth century by many accounts. See, for example, Fagan (2017, Ch. 6, KL1152) for an account that links farming and farm output to climatic changes in northern Europe. He notes, for example, "Surprisingly few archaeologists and historians have had a chance to observe subsistence farming at firsthand, which is a pity, for they sometimes fail to appreciate just how devastating a cycle of drought or heavy rainfall, or unusual cold or warmth can be. Like medieval farmers, many of today's subsistence agriculturalists in Africa and elsewhere have virtually no cushion against hunger. They live with constant, often unspoken environmental stress. The same was true in Europe at the end of the 16th century, where well over 80 percent of the population was engaged in subsistence agriculture, by definition living barely

by the numerous medieval town and city centers that remain in contemporary Europe.

During the fifteenth and sixteenth centuries, things began to change in Europe. Systems of rules that described the nature of the universe, the part of it that could be altered by human action, and rules concerning how to properly evaluate and rank the latter had been relatively stable for centuries. These medieval rule systems were disrupted by new facts, new theories, and new practices. New lands were discovered by Columbus. A new heliocentric view of the solar system began to replace the ancient geocentric one. Religious dogma throughout Europe was being "protested" by groups of influential theologians, who came to be called Protestants. A new government was founded in the Netherlands that departed from the medieval pattern for Europe in that it lacked a proper king and official church but nonetheless prospered. A century later, the enclosure movement reduced the extent of communal lands and increased the extent and marketability of land that was privately held.

These and other changes helped induce the so-called Western Enlightenment, sometimes referred to as the Age of Reason. Rates of discovery and innovation in fields as diverse as geography, theology, ethics, politics, biology, and metallurgy all increased. Changes in norms, technology, and governance caused the extent of commerce throughout the West to gradually expand. It would accelerate a bit in the late seventeenth century and again in the early nineteenth century as the great acceleration took place.

Figure 5.1 illustrates the course of per capita real GNP for England using data from the Maddison project. Note the three-century-long flat period in which average income remained stable, from approximately 1375 through 1675. Note also the slight, but obvious, growth in average material well-being for the next 150 years, and the great acceleration that takes off around 1825.[2]

The date at which the great acceleration of economic development began in what came to be known as "the West" can be debated, but not that the sustained rate of economic development was far faster in the West during the nineteenth and twentieth centuries than it had ever been before. By the late nineteenth century, average income had quadrupled, and the modern commercial society had emerged and had begun to spread around the world.

above subsistence level and at the complete mercy of short-term climatic shifts." Such lives at the edge of survival were partly generated by Malthusian population pressures. Families would tend to expand during decades of plentiful harvests and contract (via starvation) during lean ones.

[2] National account data for real gross national product (GNP) per capita are, of course, unavailable for most of the period plotted. The data points are those estimated by the Maddison project and included in their 2018 data set. United Kingdom data are used for the period after 1871. Adam Smith (1776) makes use of that stability in his analysis of long-term trends in wages, family size, profits, rents, and inflation.

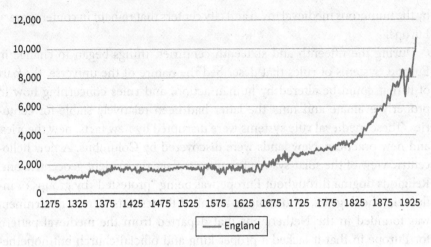

Figure 5.1  English real per capita GNP, 1275–1940.

The continuing increase in average wage rates provided an escape from the Malthusian trap in which most families had long lived. Modest increases in income ceased being routinely offset by modest increases in family size (population). Instead, improvements in agriculture, sanitation, and diet contributed to longer, materially more comfortable lives. A much smaller fraction of the persons living in England in 1900 lived at the edge of subsistence than in 1600.

As innovations in agriculture and production took place, the centrality of farming in most people's lives gradually diminished and largely disappeared in the twentieth century as commerce and urbanization increased. Subsistence farming largely disappeared, and fewer and fewer people worked on the commercial farms that remained. Most lives became governed by their conventional workdays and workweeks, rather than the seasons. Both material comforts and reserves for emergencies increased as commerce expanded.

It is clear that much of that which changed appears to be technological in nature. Improvements in agriculture allowed fewer persons to be employed on farms without reducing national food supplies. New products and mechanical marvels were invented and refined: the steam engine, railroads, telegraph, telephone, phonograph, central heating, toilets, electric lights, automobiles, airplanes, and so on. Innovations in sanitation, lighting, and transport made urban lives more attractive.

By 1900 farmers, their employees, and associated suppliers of agricultural services had become a minority of the producers in Western societies, rather than a supermajority, as they had been since farming took hold in the West.

Populations expanded but less rapidly than the availability of food and material comforts, for the first time since agricultural and other settled communities became commonplace after several thousand years of global warming ended the last ice age and made such lives feasible in northern Europe. The average length and quality of life for commoners rapidly increased and improved—although, of course, that did not imply that lives were always easy or without risks.

## The Social Conservatism of Former Times

That the "new" could in some sense be "better" than the "old" was a radical idea that would not have been obvious or supported in earlier times. The old ways, after all, had stood many tests and had been deemed worthy of transmission to the next generation, albeit with many small adjustments across the centuries. They were products of hundreds or thousands of years of puzzle solving and lessons learned. Chapters 2 and 3 demonstrate that such beliefs can be defended and were likely to be substantially true. Stable, reasonably comfortable societies emerged because of systems of complex and subtle internalized rules of conduct that solved a wide variety of social dilemmas. In periods when most persons lived at the edge of survival, most prudent members of stable communities would naturally regard deviations from the norm and experiments as frivolous uses of resources or as risky enterprises that might endanger their communities.

Moreover, many innovations would tend to violate "do-no-harm" norms and maxims. In communities where markets had emerged, innovations that significantly reduced the cost of producing a good or service tended to harm rival producers by reducing their profits. As sales diminished, those working at such enterprises would have to search for new jobs, their families would suffer, and many formerly collegial relationships between those firms, employees, and their customers would disappear. Many of these effects are similar to those associated with arson, and those harmed would naturally disapprove of such innovations, much as they would disapprove of arson or thievery, and attempt to block both. Moreover, the intense rivalry of innovators and those opposed to their innovations might return their communities to the Hobbesian jungle or undermine their sustainable methods of providing food and other necessities.

For all these reasons and others, disruptive forms of economic development of the variety that Schumpeter referred to as "creative destruction" were resisted and often deemed immoral in earlier times. The Amish, for example, do not regard the past century or two of innovations to be improvements.[3]

## Progress as an Ethical Assessment

Determining whether "progress" has occurred or not is often a normative rather than a technological assessment. Whether a particular innovation is good or better than what preceded it requires judging whether one's life and society have been improved by a change or not. That is to say, to argue that some changes constitute progress is to argue that those changes on balance improve our character, our lives, our communities, or our society. The metrics by which "improvements" are assessed are largely ethical in nature. Is deprivation good for the soul, or should it be avoided? Are material comfort and longevity proper aims of a good life, or evidence of decadence, weakness, and a lack of character?

Conclusions about such matters largely determine the moral merits of the four main drivers of economic development: two of which have already been examined—solutions to social dilemmas and specialization. The other two are examined in this chapter: capital accumulation and innovation. Assessments of moral merits of capital accumulation and innovation will, of course, also influence the decisions of most of the persons who might undertake them.[4]

---

[3] J. B. Bury ([1921] 2011) provides an intellectual history of the idea of general progress written at about the same time that Weber, Schumpeter, and Knight were analyzing economic development. Bury notes that two broad conceptions of progress were present in the West during the nineteenth century (Ch. 12). "Theories of progress are thus differentiating into two distinct types, corresponding to two radically opposed political theories and appealing to two antagonistic temperaments. The one type is that of constructive idealists and socialists, who can name all the streets and towers of 'the city of gold,' which they imagine as situated just round a promontory. The development of man is a closed system; its term is known and is within reach. The other type is that of those who, surveying the gradual ascent of man, believe that by the same interplay of forces which have conducted him so far and by a further development of the liberty which he has fought to win, he will move slowly towards conditions of increasing harmony and happiness. Here the development is indefinite; its term is unknown, and lies in the remote future. Individual liberty is the motive force, and the corresponding political theory is liberalism" (p. 236). Bury's book is available online from the Gutenberg project: www.gutenberg.org/files/4557/4557-h/4557-h.htm#link2HCH0011.

[4] For example, one might be tempted to argue on technological grounds that a new machine is better than an older machine if it can do everything that its predecessors could and "more." However, "more" must be desirable or morally acceptable. A new production method that produced as much or more than earlier machines but harmed many more operators than previous machines would not be regarded as progress unless other benefits more than compensated for this new feature. Similarly, self-driving cars may be considered an instance of progress or not. They make transportation easier and safer; however, critics argue that such vehicles are instances of retrogression, because they undermine the character of drivers by simultaneously removing their responsibility for actions on the road and reducing their competence at the various skills required to drive their vehicles. If, in the end, self-driving cars dominate the highways, those who have internalized the first conception of the good life would conclude that progress has occurred. Those who have internalized the second would disagree, even if they themselves use self-driving cars. The normative theories used to evaluate the merits of a given innovation largely determine the conclusions reached.

# A Digression on Equilibrium as Stability

The term *equilibrium* is sometimes used as an ideal and sometimes as a descriptor. It can be regarded as a reasonable description of a life of contentment and also a variety of systems that are stable in the sense that repetitive patterns are evident, as in the orbits of the planets, the pattern of life in a stable ecosystem, the process of lawmaking in a stable system of government, the pattern of production and exchange in a market with little innovation, and so forth. Some changes take place within such stable systems, but the main characteristics of such systems are stable in that they are constant, repetitive, or cyclic—as when one generation of residents replaces the previous one and engages in essentially similar behavior throughout their lives. The term *stable* is sufficiently elastic that it includes cases in which "unimportant" shocks temporarily disrupt or slightly change the patterns of interest, but which can be ignored without loss for most purposes of discussion, analysis, and planning during the period of interest. The orbits of the planets change a bit every year, but such changes can be ignored without loss for many pedagogical and astronomical purposes.

Within human social systems, equilibrium is an apt description of patterns of life that largely repeat themselves. Such repetition has long been evident for the seasonal patterns of life of subsistence farmers, the biological cycle of a human life, and more recently, the seasonal inventory cycles of contemporary grocery stores and other retail businesses. This is not to say that there are no changes in those stable cycles of life. Gradual improvements in plants, plows, and plantings occurred in the period after settled agricultural communities emerged. Yet such improvements did not significantly alter the basic patterns of rural life. This was partly because of the Malthusian dilemma, the tendency of family size to increase in periods of prosperity, which intensifies competition for resources and jobs in future decades, reducing most family incomes back to their long-run average—e.g., subsistence plus or minus a bit. Even mechanization did not disrupt the perennial cycles of life at first. There were annual seasons for planting, growing, and harvesting. Similar cycles were also associated with town centers, where there were shops with more or less regular hours during which purchases were possible, and many of the shops were clustered together on shopping streets.

Historians and anthropologists refer to stable periods with terms such as *age*, *era*, and *epoch*. Stable patterns of life allow historians and anthropologists to describe various periods and states of development with short useful phrases such as the Stone Age, the Bronze Age, the Iron Age, the medieval period, classical Greece, the modern period, and so forth. Shifts from one "age" to another are often referred to as "revolutions"—as with the shift from the Paleolithic to the Neolithic period, from the Stone Age to the Bronze Age, and from the Bronze to the Iron Age. Particular shifts in technology are often used to characterize when they begin and end, but other markers could also be used.

Equilibrium and stability concepts are also commonplace in ethical and theological dispositions. A philosopher or theologian reaches a *reflective equilibrium* when he or she remains satisfied with his or her conclusions about a phenomenon, author, or philosophical issue. Ethical principles are often regarded to be timeless, because they are thought to be true and unalterable, even in cases in which a new conception is proposed. For example, the word *progress* does not appear in Rawl's ([1971] 2009) highly regarded *Theory of Justice*. The word *innovation* appears just a single time. However, such reflective equilibria may be disrupted by new insights and new circumstances, and thus ethical and other forms of progress are possible—as Rawls clearly regarded his new theory of a just society.

It was the mistaken finality and timelessness of the claims made by most philosophers that induced Spencer to develop his evolutionary theory of ethics in the mid- to late nineteenth century. It was the failure of equilibrium-based economic theories to account for the acceleration of commerce during the late nineteenth and early twentieth centuries that induced Schumpeter (1912, 1934) to suggest a new, more dynamic model of economic progress. However, it is clear that neither was able to disrupt their respective fields' reflective equilibria significantly at the time that they first expressed proposed their theories. The reflective equilibria of most philosophers and economists of their times were locally stable.[5]

## Replacing the Ideal of Stability with the Ideal of Progress

Part of the appeal of the concept of a "social equilibrium" is that, after critical social dilemmas are ameliorated, the patterns of lives that emerge are often predictable, relatively safe, sustainable, and comfortable. All of these properties are widely regarded to be features of attractive lives and societies. In

---

[5] Critiques of the equilibrium view of markets continued through the twentieth century. See Schackle (1961); Kirzner (1973); Cowen and Fink (1985); Grossman and Helpman (1991); and Hanusch and Pyke (2007). It should be acknowledged, however, that these critiques and modeling extensions were minority views in economics for most of the twentieth century. Growth was acknowledged to be possible and commonplace, but a tendency toward equilibrium growth paths was nearly always assumed.

contrast, even today, the concepts of perturbation, deviation, disequilibrium, and crisis all sound unsettling and dangerous—events to be avoided rather than embraced. A crisis might cause a social collapse for reasons noted by Hobbes and Hardin. A perturbation may disrupt a fragile social equilibrium. Thus, after a crisis or major perturbation, a return to preexisting patterns of life—a return to normalcy—tends to be regarded as good or desirable. Why give up on what worked well or at least reasonably well in the recent past?

When "equilibrium" is believed to be the proper aim of a good life and good society, innovations are naturally discouraged. Innovations are mistakes to be avoided, rather than potential improvements that might create new desirable possibilities or results. Such conservatism is associated even with quite advanced societies. For example, several Chinese innovations were underappreciated because of such dispositions, including at least two innovations that subsequently changed the world: steam propulsion and gunpowder.[6] Europe's medieval period was also characterized by social conservatism.

> The idea of the universe which prevailed throughout the Middle Ages, and the **general orientation of men's thoughts were incompatible with some of the fundamental assumptions which are required by the idea of Progress**. . . . Again, the medieval doctrine apprehends history not as a natural development but as a series of events ordered by divine intervention and revelations. If humanity had been left to go its own way it would have drifted to a highly undesirable port, and **all men would have incurred the fate of everlasting misery.** (Bury *The Idea of Progress*, [1921] 2011, KL: 321–332)

Bury ([1921] 2011) argues that such beliefs began to change during the eighteenth and nineteenth centuries. A wide variety of innovations were introduced in this period, and many were found to be improvements on the old ways. In most cases, the individual innovations induced small changes in the manner in which people lived, rather than major disruptions, as the Franklin stove resembled a fireplace, but used less wood to produce more heat, or as the toilet subsequently replaced chamber pots. Other more significant changes also tended to be almost invisible, as shifts in the techniques for production tend to be, or took place slowly enough that adjustments to successive innovations were easy to accommodate. For example, the use of early steam engines to pump water out of mines was nearly invisible to all

---

[6] Note that the term *underappreciated* is normative and for most persons in the West a plausible interpretation of these Chinese "mistakes." This perspective itself reveals an appreciative perspective on scientific and economic development, that is to say, it incorporates the idea of progress. A true conservative would regard the Chinese behavior as appropriate and unexceptional.

except the miners working at the places where such machines were used. After the first useful steam engines were developed, refinements of such engines could be used to power sawmills and textile mills at locations where water-power was not feasible, or to transport materials out of mines on tracks more easily or quickly than animals could. The same ideas led to railroads and to steam-powered ships. As refinements were introduced over the course of several decades, they become increasingly visible, but also increasingly were perceived as being useful and interesting.

It is not mere innovation that tends to be supported by commerce, but innovations that are useful in that they lower costs, increase quality, or attract the interest and purchases of consumers. The filters of markets screen out unprofitable innovations and reward profitable ones. The profits and praise realized by successful commercial inventers, in turn, encourage further innovation, but also discourage innovation that does not produce profits or praise. Markets thus mainly reward innovations that are useful, entertaining, and not obviously disruptive.[7]

One of the earliest defenses of commercial innovation was penned by Jeremy Bentham in the late eighteenth century, one of the founders of modern utilitarianism.

> So soon as a new die, more brilliant or more economical than the old ones, a new machine, or a new practice in agriculture—has been discovered, a thousand dyers, ten thousand mechanicians, a hundred thousand agriculturists, may reap the benefit: and then—though the original authors of the invention have been ruined in the bringing the discovery to perfection—as it respects the national wealth, of what consequence is this, when considered as the price of so much gain? (Bentham, *A Manual of Political Economy*, [1843] 2011, KL 1015)

That utilitarian assessment implied that commercial innovation is a moral activity because it tends to make many more people better off than worse off. Schumpeter termed this process "creative destruction" (*Schöpferische Zerstörung*), because major innovations create new patterns of life that are much different than earlier ones, as with indoor plumbing, steam engines, factories, electric motors, telephones, lights, washing machines, and automobiles. This process continued through the twentieth century with

---

[7] Isaac Newton is known for his characterization of scientific progress: "If I see further it is only by standing on the shoulders of giants," written in a letter to Robert Hooke in 1676. The possibility of continual progress, in effect, requires Newton's giants to multiply and grow taller through time—or at least that successive innovators be strong enough for others to stand on their shoulders.

radios, jetliners, televisions, microwave ovens, computers, the Internet, and smart phones.[8]

However, the shift from the ideal of equilibrium to the ideal of progress most likely took place, not because of major innovations, but because each of the long sequence of gradual improvements through which Schumpeter's process of "creative destruction" normally operates tend to be far less disruptive than the sequence as a whole. Indeed, major disruptions that take place over several decades may not be obvious to those who live through such transformative periods unless they take the time to look back at the changes that have transpired.

One's conclusions about whether a sequence of changes constitutes progress or needlessly undermines and disrupts life ultimately depend on one's views concerning the nature of a good life and good society—and also one's experience with innovations. Indeed, Smith's, Bentham's, and Bury's analyses suggest that experience with innovations gradually induced a re-evaluation of old norms. A good life and a good society became active creative enterprises substantially devoted to self-improvement and economic and social progress—rather than stable ones with relatively simple predictable patterns of life.

## Economic Growth (1): Capital Accumulation and Community Norms

Given that notions of progress have normative foundations and that some ethical theories—albeit not all such theories—imply that a steady increase in material comforts and longevity is evidence of progress, we next focus on two of the main drivers of economic development. We have already discussed how solutions to social dilemmas and specialization can generate increasingly attractive societies, and now turn to two other factors: the rates of capital accumulation and innovation, which also require overcoming social dilemmas and also are affected by normative innovation. The least disruptive of these—capital accumulation—was the one first incorporated into neoclassical economic models and is the first analyzed.

Although the importance of capital equipment has long been recognized—a person can move more dirt with a shovel than one's hands, with a wheelbarrow than with a shovel alone, with a mule and cart than a wheelbarrow,

[8] Although a long time coming, Schumpeterian growth models are by now commonplace. See, for example, Mueller (2005) or Van den Berg and Lewer (2007) for short overviews and Bento (2014) for a nice synthesis of microeconomic and macroeconomic Schumpeterian approaches.

with a dump truck than a mule and cart, and so on—the first mathematical models of economic development based on capital accumulation were worked out after World War II. The first neoclassical growth models assumed that there was just one homogenous type of capital, which was usually imagined to be a general universal form of physical equipment. This reduced mathematical complications. Human capital (knowledge, training, experience, and organization) was added to the second generation of neoclassical growth models. As human and physical capital accumulate, economic output increases, because both forms of capital increase the productivity of each individual's time spent producing goods and services. (Ethical dispositions, of course, can be regarded as a form of human capital, although little, if any, attention was directed to them by neoclassical growth theory.) As a consequence of increased productivity, more can be produced with a given amount of labor. This in turn implies that the average consumer obtains more of the many products that can be efficiently produced with capital- or skill-intensive methods.[9]

For a given stock of capital, market prices operate in the usual manner and equate demand with supply in all markets and cause rates of return on alternative investments to equalize risk-adjusted marginal rates of return. Thus, as argued by Adam Smith and Max Weber, among many others, an increase in propensities to save and invest tends to increase capital accumulation and promote economic development.

Contrariwise, in the absence of moral and political support for saving and investments, less of each would take place and the beneficial effects of capital accumulation would be reduced. In a steady state, the existing stock of capital is essentially stable. Existing capital is replaced as it wears out (depreciates) rather than augmented with additional new equipment.

## Technological Externalities among Capital Investments

There are often direct and indirect complementarities in the equipment used in production, and as the scale of production increases, a variety of externalities tend to be associated with industrialization. As a consequence, there are a variety of social dilemmas associated with capital accumulation and industrialization. A subset of the externalities associated with large-scale production such as air and water pollution are fundamentally similar

[9] For an overview of early growth theory grounded in capital accumulation, see Solow (1970). For an early model of economic development that includes human capital accumulation, see Romer (1990).

to the ones reviewed in Chapter 2 and will not be repeated in this chapter. Technological externalities, however, differ from those associated with waste products, and they are the main focus of the rest of the section on capital accumulation.

When decisions to acquire physical and human capital are made independently of one another and have complementary effects on productivity, capital may be underinvested in because those purchasing the relevant equipment or training fail to take account of the productivity effects of their investments on other producers.

Table 5.1 illustrates choices to make capital investments in cases in which such "technological" externalities exist, and a community's norms are initially neutral with respect to capital accumulation. Productivity externalities imply that each enterprise or contractor can in a sense free-ride on the other's capital accumulation, because the capital accumulation of the other(s) increases their own productivity—which is to say, the extent to which their own efforts contribute to final outputs and profits. The payoffs of Table 5.1 are indices of each commercial organization's profits or net revenues. In the choice setting illustrated, the equilibrium investments are below those that maximize their joint profits.

Note that the capital accumulation problem is analogous to the shirking problem developed in Chapter 3. Underinvestment in capital equipment is in effect a form of shirking on the joint enterprise (providing inputs for final products sold to consumers). As was true of that case, there are also several possible solutions to the underinvestment dilemma, including mergers and complex contracts among relevant firms. However, when the number of interdependent firms producing different but necessary intermediate goods is large, such solutions are difficult to implement. In such cases, generalized cultural support for capital accumulation may be the only plausible manner in which the problem can be ameliorated.

**Table 5.1** Technological Externalities and the Accumulation of Capital

|  |  | Robert (Investments in Capital) | | | |
|---|---|---|---|---|---|
|  |  | 8 units | 6 units | 4 units | 2 units |
| Paul | 8 units | (P, R) 6, 6 | (P, R) 4, 7 | (P, R) 2, 8 | (P,R) 1, 7 |
| Investments in Capital | 6 units | 7, 4 | 5, 5 | 3, 6 | 2, 5 |
| Capital | 4 units | 8, 2 | 6, 3 | 4, 4 | 3, 3 |
|  | 2 units | 7, 1 | 5, 2 | 3, 3 | 2, 2 |

**Table 5.2** Technological Externalities, Social Norms, and the Accumulation of Capital

|  |  | Robert (Investments in Capital) | | | |
|---|---|---|---|---|---|
|  |  | 8 units | 6 units | 4 units | 2 units |
| Paul (Investments in Capital) | 8 units | (P, R)<br>6+ V, 6 + V | (P, R)<br>4 + V, 7 + V | (P, R)<br>2 + V, 8 + V | (P,R)<br>1 + V, 7 |
|  | 6 units | 7 + V, 4 + V | 5 + V, 5 + V | 3 + V, 6 + V | 2 + V, 5 |
|  | 4 units | 8 + V, 2+V | 6 + V, 3 + V | 4 + V, 4 + V | 3 + V, 3 |
|  | 2 units | 7, 1 + V | 5, 2 + V | 3, 3 + V | 2, 2 |

Cultural support for producing and accumulating capital goods is most likely in societies whose norms also support long-term material comfort, industriousness, and the accumulation of wealth. Residents of such communities may regard an entrepreneur's purchase of new equipment for their labor force to be associated with praiseworthy traits such as generosity, foresight, prudence, and industriousness. In contrast, residents of communities that generally believe that a good life is an ascetic one in which leisure and contemplation are maximized would tend to be less supportive of capital accumulation and its associated roundabout methods of production, and less of it would occur. Table 5.2 illustrates the effects of a community whose norms that generally support capital accumulation.

In such communities, feelings of virtue and praise from others in the community would be associated with capital investments and more would be accumulated than in those without those supplemental rewards. For example, if V > 1, the new equilibrium is the upper right-hand cell (6 + V, 6 + V).

When the accumulation of capital is deemed both virtuous and praiseworthy—as Max Weber argues was a consequence of the Protestant Reformation, and as is strongly suggested by La Court's comments on industriousness, reviewed in Chapter 10—then capital accumulation would be larger than in the original case. More technological economies in production would be realized, more output would be produced, and more material comforts would be available during nonwork hours.[10]

Changes in the degree of support or opposition to capital accumulation causes the virtue payoff to change through time. As cultural support waxes or wanes for capital-intensive projects, rates of capital accumulation and

[10] Buchanan and Yoon (1994b) explore the possibility of increasing returns that may be generated by technological externalities and increased specialization. Buchanan's introductory chapter provides an overview of the issues and possible roles that ethical dispositions play in the Marshallian and Solow approaches to economic development.

economic development would also tend to wax and wane—other things being equal. Similarly, as support for the accumulation of productivity increasing human capital varies, so would the extent and growth of economic output. In periods of support, more of the complementarities among types of human capital are realized and economic development accelerates. In periods of opposition to materialism and productive skills, fewer complementarities are realized and rates of economic development decrease.

Other variations in norms may also affect the extent to which capital is accumulated. For example, there might be decades in which "market towns" take pride in the size of their markets, "mill towns" in the number and variety of their mills, "steel towns" in the size of their steel mills, "rail towns" in the extent of their rail networks, "electrified towns" in the extent of electrification, and "digital towns" in the extent and speed of their Internet or cell-network service companies. Periods of support might be interspersed among decades of indifference or opposition to capital-intensive methods of production because of ethical concerns about mass production itself (making work less satisfying or praiseworthy) or externalities associated with industrial production—such as traffic congestion and waste products. The latter may become common as prosperity increases. Such changes in norms clearly affect the extent, kind, and rate of a community's economic development through effects on capital accumulation.

Similar normative effects and potential variation in growth rates are, of course, also associated with cycles in forms of moral education and training that tend to increase team productivity or support the accumulation of other forms of productive human capital.

## Economic Growth (2): Innovation and the Innovation Commons

The Solow family of neoclassical growth models assumes that production becomes more efficient as more physical and human capital are used in the production of final goods and services (those desired by consumers). Preexisting products are produced more efficiently, and the equilibrium mix of those products may change as the products that benefit from more capital-intensive forms of production tend to increase in supply relative to others.

However, increasing the production of familiar products through increasingly capital-intensive methods is only one of the changes associated with economic growth, and not the most important one in contemporary commercial societies. Most of the economic development associated with a commercial society occurs through *improvements* in capital and final goods and as *entirely new* capital goods and consumer services are brought to market. These new machines and products, in turn, may cause production and productive organization to be reorganized and new lifestyles to be adopted by willing suppliers and consumers.

Although canoes, rowboats, sailboats, steamers, and container ships all provide "transportation services" on water, they are produced with quite different methods, provide substantially different services, and support more or less extensive networks of trade and specialization. Similarly, semaphore, smoke signals, mail services, telegraphs, radio, and fiber-optic networks all provide communication and data delivery services, but they use completely different technologies and provide conversations and other information services at vastly different speeds. Moreover, within each category of service-generating capital goods, many refinements have been adopted through time. For example, there are hundreds of obvious differences between the automobiles of 1920 and 2020, although both provide transportation services over roads.[11]

Joseph Schumpeter (1883–1950) was among the first to recognize and analyze the innovation-induced growth that characterizes commercial societies. Writing in the first half of the twentieth century, Schumpeter argued that innovation and its associated disruptions were essential features of economic development:

> The fundamental impulse that sets and keeps the capitalist engine in motion comes from the new consumers' goods, the new methods of production or transportation, the new markets, the new forms of industrial organization that capitalist enterprise creates. (Schumpeter, *Capitalism, Socialism, and Democracy*, [1947] 2012, KL: 1823–1825)

Economic innovation is generated by unusually creative and ambitious men and women who assemble teams of researchers that refine old production methods and products or who invent entirely new products and methods of production.

Innovations, even in competitive circumstances, often create opportunities to realize extraordinary returns from investments. Some inventions are simply more productive, more entertaining, or simply more satisfying than previous methods and products. Entrepreneurs who create such inventions

---

[11] Oddly enough, jet-setters have a nostalgic fondness for old-fashioned modes of transport such as sailboats and horses.

temporarily realize extraordinary returns on their investments in product development—until rivals create similar or better methods and products. These above-normal profits reward both innovators and their investors, which encourages additional efforts to innovate. In this manner, the Schumpeterian impulse for growth tends to supplement that associated with what might be termed "ordinary" capital accumulation.

Innovations combined with capital investments have often facilitated the creation of major new economic enterprises. Examples include such American firms as Alcoa, AT&T, General Electric, Ford, Transworld Airlines, Boeing, IBM, Intel, Microsoft, Apple, Google, Amazon, and Facebook. Other large innovative firms emerged during the same period or somewhat later in Europe, Japan, Korea, and more recently, China. Not all of these innovative firms continued to prosper, but a surprising number have done so for more than a century.

Innovation, like many other aspects of mass production, is enhanced by specialization, and the firms that emerge from innovation often continue to invest heavily in product development to stay ahead of their rivals. When they are successful at doing so, which requires a bit of luck along with investment, insight, and planning, such firms may continue to realize extraordinary returns for decades. However, there are problems associated with innovation that are similar to those associated with capital accumulation, but which tend to be more difficult to solve because innovations are rarely entirely the product of a single person or team of innovators.[12]

## Technological Externalities among Innovators

A recent book by Jason Potts (2019) reminds us that there are positive technological externalities among innovators. Transformative innovations very rarely occur in single revolutionary leaps of imagination; rather, innovations stimulate other new ideas, which stimulate still others, and so forth. Some new combinations of ideas, materials, and machinery are more lucrative and transformative than others, and which ones are so is rarely initially obvious. Thus, the more innovative ideas and results that are available in what Potts

---

[12] That innovation produces uncertainty is self-evident within microeconomics. That it generates macroeconomic uncertainty is nearly self-evident, as developed in Schumpeter's research on business cycles. Toward the end of the nineteenth century, a new school of macroeconomics emerged that argues that many, if not all, business cycles are generated by "productivity shocks," which is simply another name for innovations that affect manufacturing methods. See, for example, Greenwood, Hercowitz, and Hoffman (1988) or McCallum (1988).

terms the "innovation commons," the more subsequent useful innovation takes place. As the innovation commons expands, rates of innovation tend to accelerate. However, such expansions do not always occur.

Normative opposition or support for innovation has effects similar to those analyzed above for capital accumulation in Table 5.2. Table 5.3 illustrates how conditional norms that favor evenly rotating societies over more dynamic ones tend to reduce innovation rates and thereby slow or block economic development by reducing complementary efforts to develop new or improved materials, devices, procedures, or theories.

The initial equilibrium in the slow-slow cell can be regarded as the rate that would have occurred without normative opposition to innovation, which may occur for reasons discussed in the next section of this chapter. Normative opposition to innovation (here $G > 1$) would reduce the rate to the minimal level that typified most of the period after agricultural methods and supporting rules were worked out approximately nine to ten thousand years ago. The most common equilibrium was minimal-minimal in most communities.

Such opposition was and is not uncommon. Even in England, as the great acceleration began to take off, there were several instances of organized opposition to the production of familiar things by new, more capital-intensive methods. New machines had created new, more capital-intensive methods of production that required fewer skilled workers than in the past. The so-called Luddites of the late eighteenth century opposed the new more capital-intensive methods of producing textiles. A few decades later, the Swing Riots of 1830 in England protested the mechanization of agriculture with new threshing machines. In both cases, new machines created new more capital-based methods of production that reduced the demand for and thus the salaries of particular types of workers.

**Table 5.3** Technological Externalities With Social Opposition to the Innovation Commons

| | | Robert (Rate of Innovation) | | | |
|---|---|---|---|---|---|
| | | Rapid | Moderate | Slow | Minimal |
| Joseph (Rate of Innovation) | Rapid | (J, R)<br>$6 - G, 6 - G$ | (J, R)<br>$4 - G, 7 - G$ | (J, R)<br>$2 - G, 8 - G$ | (J,R)<br>$1 - G, 7$ |
| | Moderate | $7 - G, 4 - G$ | $5 - G, 5 - G$ | $3 - G, 6 - G$ | $2 - G, 5$ |
| | Slow | $8 - G, 2 - G$ | $6 - G, 3 - G$ | $4 - G, 4 - G$ | $3 - G, 3$ |
| | Minimal | $7, 1 - G$ | $5, 2 - G$ | $3, 3 - G$ | $2, 2$ |

**Table 5.4** Technological Externalities: With Social Support for the Innovation Commons

| | | Robert (Rate of Innovation) | | | |
|---|---|---|---|---|---|
| | | Rapid | Moderate | Slow | Minimal |
| Joseph (Rate of Innovation) | Rapid | (P, R)<br>$6+V, 6+V$ | (P, R)<br>$4+V, 7+V$ | (P, R)<br>$2+V, 8+V$ | (P,R)<br>$1+V, 7$ |
| | Moderate | $7+V, 4+V$ | $5+V, 5+V$ | $3+V, 6+V$ | $2+V, 5$ |
| | Slow | $8+V, 2+V$ | $6+V, 3+V$ | $4+V, 4+V$ | $3+V, 3$ |
| | Minimal | $7, 1+V$ | $5, 2+V$ | $3, 3+V$ | $2, 2$ |

However, at that time, there were no laws against innovation and so the profit motive and other support for innovation dominated the resistance—in part because, as Bentham noted, there are usually far more winners than losers from economic innovations. Together such ethical and economic support may explain why innovation proceeded apace in England, rather than diminishing in the face of violent opposition.

Table 5.4 illustrates the opposite case in which normative support for innovation accelerates growth rates by encouraging creative individuals and teams to refine old rules, old production methods, and old products, or to replace them with new ones that are facilitated by a better understanding of the possibilities for improvement. If the virtue/praise supplement is sufficient (here $V > 1$), the rapid innovation equilibrium emerges and, insofar as the innovations prove profitable for producers and beneficial for consumers, economic development accelerates.

Moral support for innovation increases rates of innovation by increasing both the efforts of individual innovators and the size of the innovation commons. As knowledge accumulates, the creative leaps required to imagine the next steps tend to become smaller and easier to discern. In this manner, an expanding innovation commons tends to increase rates of innovation, and insofar as useful ideas occur at roughly the same (or an increasing) proportion as before, economic development tends to accelerate. Societies that generally encourage the accumulation of capital and innovation thereby tend to prosper relative to those that do not.

## The Complex Ethics of Innovation and Economic Development

Of course, not all significant innovations are motivated by increases in gains to trade, nor are they limited to market-relevant ones. Innovations can take place in each of the three categories of rules mentioned in Chapter 1.

New and refined rules and principles can be developed that improve our understanding of the universe (science), how the natural course of the universe can be changed through human action (what economists refer to as technology), and how best to assess the merits of the changes that may be pursued—as with philosophical innovations in understandings of a good act, a good character, a good life, attractive community, or good society. Innovations in fields having little to do with commerce often make new economic possibilities easier to imagine and less costly and controversial to implement, although the reverse is also possible. Research that led to the Internet, for example, was initially funded by the US Department of Defense (DARPA) because of its potential for robust communication during warfare. Many such innovations indirectly increase the rate of economic innovation by modifying the knowledge base that individual innovators and teams of innovators draw on to create improvements in products and lifestyles and the values that partially determine the extent of both theoretical and applied research and the nature of better lifestyles.

However, few innovations truly benefit everyone in society. New theories and new products necessarily compete with older ones for support and sales. Successful new theories often reduce the value of previous investments in human capital among rival scientists whose research becomes less valued and less supported. Successful products affect the equilibrium price vector toward which market prices tend to gravitate and thereby the pattern of income, consumption, and employment associated with those prices. Some products and firms lose market share and others gain. Because wages are simply another name for the prices of various kinds of specialized labor, they are among the prices affected by innovation. As a consequence, some incomes increase and others fall. Similar effects occur on the rates of return on specialized capital goods and related assets.

Significant economic innovations thus harm many others, whose income and wealth decrease as consumers abandon old products for the new. Indeed, when new products or production methods are far better than previous ones, some old products and sources of income may essentially disappear as, for example, buggy whip manufacturers and downtown feed stores largely disappeared after widespread adoption of automobiles. Iceboxes essentially disappeared as refrigerators were developed and fell in price. Slide rules disappeared after the introduction of digital calculators and computers. And rotary dial telephones disappeared in the age of digital dialing and cell phones. Many of the persons who made their living by developing, manufacturing, and selling such products were induced to pursue other often less-rewarding opportunities than the ones they had previously profited from.

Innovations in production methods often have similar effects. New, more efficient production methods such the Bessemer and Hall smelting processes, assembly lines, and computer-aided manufacturing reduced the cost of a subset of existing products and bankrupted many of their less-efficient rivals and induced others to make major new investments in plant and equipment to remain competitive. The negative effects of innovation clearly violate Mill's "do no harm principle." Such disruptive effects are what Schumpeter had in mind when he referred to "the gale of creative destruction" in the quote at the beginning of the chapter.

## The Risk and Uncertainty Associated with Innovative Societies

Rather than the evenly rotating society that typified pre-commercial societies, commercial societies are constantly being altered by innovations of various kinds. The evenly rotating society is replaced with an ever-changing spiral as a few aspects of life are changed every year or decade. Subsequent innovations often tend to reduce such risks but do not eliminate them. For example, markets tend to screen out both unproductive and unattractive innovations. Producers have no interest in the former, and consumers have no interest in the latter. Markets also tend to shift risks away from the most risk averse toward those most willing to accept risks, as noted by Frank Knight ([1921] 2009), who was writing at about the same time as Schumpeter. Insurance products of various kinds emerge and may be purchased by risk-averse investors and consumers. Knight argued that markets can adapt to shocks that have a statistical pattern (risks) and that, in those cases, markets tend to shift risks to those individuals and organizations that are most risk tolerant and away from individuals who are most risk averse.

Other shocks lack a clear statistical pattern, and so these risks cannot be as easily shifted. Knight termed these unpredictable events as "uncertainty" and argued that uncertainty is the ultimate source of significant profits and losses for entrepreneurs. Innovation necessarily increases uncertainty, because one never knows what new idea or product will emerge next, or their consequences for one's own specialties and lifestyle. Losses from uncertainty, nonetheless, may be reduced to some extent through knowledge, specialization, and confidence. In Knight's words:

Uncertainty thus exerts a fourfold tendency to select men and specialize functions: (1) an adaptation of men to occupations on the basis of kind of knowledge and judgment; (2) a similar selection on the basis of degree of foresight, for some lines of activity call for this endowment in a very different degree from others; (3) a specialization within productive groups, the individuals with superior managerial ability (foresight and capacity of ruling others) being placed in control of the group and the others working under their direction; and (4) those with confidence in their judgment and disposition to "back it up" in action specialize in risk-taking. (Knight, *Risk, Uncertainty, and Profit*, [1921] 2009, KL: 3154–3159)

According to Knight, uncertainty accounts for both the extraordinary profits and losses realized from market activities.

Extraordinary profits, for example, are realized by individuals and organizations that own or purchase the "right" asset at the right time—where both "right" and "wrong" times are essentially unknowable matters of luck at the time of purchase. Here contemporary readers might recall that Amazon stock sold for around $2 a share in the early 2000s when it was not certain that the company would survive. At present, it is among the world's largest firms and its stock sells for more than $3,000 a share, a more than 40% annual rate of return for those who bought AZM at the "right" time. These lucky investors may have had plausible reasons to believe that the firm would survive and prosper, but they had no way to predict that a thousand-dollar investment in a two-dollar stock would be worth more than a million and a half dollars two decades later.

Although market innovations and public policies sometimes reduce risks and uncertainty associated with high rates of innovation, they cannot eliminate them. Innovation thus may be opposed not just by the losers from a particular innovation, but because they increase both known risks and unknowable uncertainty. To accept innovation as a useful process, one has to adopt a perspective similar to that of Bentham and conclude that on average, in spite of the risks and uncertainties, the overall result is beneficial for most persons—which is to say that it produces progress rather than unpleasant disorder.

## New Social Dilemmas Produced by the Commercial Society

As mentioned previously, solutions to social dilemmas improve life, but nonetheless often produce circumstances in which new social dilemmas become significant or even critical. For example, solutions to dilemmas that allowed commercial societies to emerge tended to make intensive and mechanized methods of production more profitable, which increased their use and also increased the use of air and water systems as methods of disposing of waste products. Eventually, the scale of such uses made water in some rivers less safely drinkable and air inside and outside of factories less safely breathable. Urbanization also increased the problems associated with the waste products of ordinary life. As automobile replaced horses, one source of pollution (horse manure and so forth) was replaced with others, and new sources of congestion were added to roads, along with new kinds of noises and accidents.

These new dilemmas were addressed through various combinations of refinements of old rules, new informal rules, and new formal regulations adopted by city, state, and national governments. For example, new applications of informal "rules of the road" emerged regarding speeds and the importance of staying to the right (or left). As automobiles and trucks became more powerful and faster, such rules became more important than they had been for the various forms of the muscle-powered traffic that had preceded them. When those norms were not sufficient to reduce the dangers associated with the new forms of transportation, governments were asked (or felt it necessary) to intervene by creating new formal rules of the road and enforcing them.

In this manner, new social dilemmas tend to stimulate both the evolution of ethical maximums ("keep to the right"), principles ("drive defensively"), and new formal rules and regulations enforced by rule-enforcing organizations such as governments. The new rules increased the productivity of road networks by improving traffic flow and reducing accidents. Road deaths fell (as a fraction of the population) while road usage increased during the entire course of the twentieth century.[13]

## Ethical Innovation and the Great Acceleration

General ideas about an attractive community and society also changed both before and during the period in which new problems arose. On the one hand, a good society was increasingly regarded to be a prosperous society, and dispositions that increased one's contribution to prosperity (thriftiness, industriousness, and creativeness) tended to be added to older lists of virtues. On the other, it was also increasingly acknowledged that uncertainties associated with life in commercial societies implied that some persons failed

---

[13] See Pinker (2018) for a compilation of statistics on the declines in highway deaths and accidents in the United States in the period after automobiles and trucks were introduced.

through no fault of their own. Bad luck was clearly possible, as well as good, in a dynamic setting. Progress took place, but problems were also associated with changes widely regarded to be on average beneficial.

The analysis of the previous two chapters implies that ethical and economic development are co-determined in what economists term the *long run*. Ethical dispositions affect markets, and markets affect ethical dispositions. Although ethical dispositions tend to respond more slowly to changes in circumstances than market prices, they also are affected by market rewards, albeit slowly. This co-determination implies that innovations in ethical theories may affect the extent of specialization and market networks and the rate of innovation. The effects of relative price changes and innovations in other domains, in turn, affect the distribution and strength of ethical disposition in a given community. New maxims may emerge as new social dilemmas and coordination problems are confronted, which in turn may induce changes in the ethical theories of philosophers as new norms and maxims are taken into account by their theories.

New circumstances, thus, often induce ethical innovation. They do so by disrupting the reflective equilibria of thoughtful men and women with sufficient time and interest in grappling with ethical and other philosophical ideas to work out better principle-based explanations for the moral sentiments of the persons with whom they are familiar. For example, changes in the nature of lives widely judged to be "good" or societies widely regarded to be "good" may induce those with scientific or philosophical interests to devise principles that better account for such lives and attractive societies. Such principles, insofar as they are persuasive, may also induce changes in ideas about "the good" among their readers. The changes in behavior induced by such innovation may thereby affect behavior in markets. In this way, ethical innovations can affect the extent and growth rates of commerce. Shifts in ideas about the good life and good society were noted, for example, in J. B. Bury's ([1921] 2011) analysis of the history of ideas about progress.

Positive experience with innovations may, for example, catalyze developments in ethical assessments of innovators and philosophical speculations about the proper role of innovation in a good society. As noted in Chapter 3, Adam Smith's (1776, Ch. 1) favorable analysis of pin factories provides one such instance. He realized that specialization, in combination with innovative equipment and organization, increased the productivity of labor used to produce pins by a factor of approximately 250. (A productive team of pin makers could make 48,000 pins, in contrast to the 200 produced by 10 independent artisan pin makers.) His widely read book would have affected his readers' opinions about factory-level specialization. Similarly, Jeremy Bentham's assessment of the process of technological innovation a few decades later (cited above)—acknowledges both its failures and successes—but reaches a favorable conclusion about the consequences of innovation—at least for ones that are filtered by markets. His analysis would have influenced his readers to accept disruptive innovations that were becoming common at the time of his writing, because on average they increased aggregate utility. Those who were advantaged by innovation gained more than those who were disadvantaged lost.

As such arguments were internalized, the rate of innovation tends to increase, for reasons discussed in this chapter. Innovation becomes a moral, praiseworthy activity instead of a useless or disruptive waste of time and resources. Potential innovators are encouraged by feelings of virtue, praise from their friends and families, and increases in their incomes. More persons choose such careers and those already engaged in innovation are more likely to devote more time and attention to innovative efforts than before. Indeed, innovation may be added to lists of virtues. "Invention," for example, is listed as a praiseworthy activity—a virtue—in Adam Smith's (1759) *The Theory of Moral Sentiments*.

Increased moral support for innovation, thus, provides a behavioral explanation for an expanding innovation commons and thereby for the increased rates at which new products and methods of production are developed. Insofar as such moral support became commonplace toward the end of the eighteenth century and the beginning of the nineteenth, such changes also account for the timing of the great acceleration of commercialization that occurred in the nineteenth and twentieth centuries, which generated and sustained our contemporary commercial societies.

## Some Conclusions from Part I: Ethics, Progress, and Prosperity

Part I has argued that a huge number of social dilemmas have to be solved to generate attractive communities. Additional ones need to be solved to promote the trade, specialization, capital accumulation, and productive innovations associated with prosperous societies. The analytic illustrations of Chapter 2 demonstrate that a subset of ethical dispositions can ameliorate or solve many critical social dilemmas. Those of Chapters 3–5 demonstrate that a subset of the rules that do so also tends to promote voluntary exchange, specialization, capital accumulation, and innovation. In this manner, a subset of the ethical solutions to commonplace social dilemmas facilitate the emergence of prosperous commercial societies.

Some of these dispositions are sufficiently important that they may be supported by biologically transmitted tendencies. As features of human nature, such tendencies would tend to ground other norms that are subsequently created by individuals and families. Although such propensities evidently exist, it should be acknowledged that few genetically induced tendencies cannot be overturned by humanity's ability to ignore and refine internalized rules. For example, sons and daughters may kill their parents (and vice versa); individuals may take a vow of chastity or commit suicide by starving themselves to death—all of which runs counter to genetic survival. The focus of Part I has thus been on social rather than biological evolution.

Social evolution proceeds in a manner analogous to biological evolution insofar as the rules that are passed on from one generation to the next are in a sense "fit"; they make the individuals that internalize them more likely to survive and their communities to flourish. Ethical innovations, in turn, occur through processes analogous to those of science and markets. New ideas and refinements of older ideas about proper behavior, virtue, a good life, or good society tend to be catalyzed by changes in circumstances that disrupt an individual's reflective equilibrium and produce new individual insights. New maxims, principles, and rule systems are "field tested" as they are internalized by a few individuals, and when the results turn out to be attractive, others may adopt the same or similar rules. When new rules produce results that are ultimately not attractive, early adopters may lose their lives or simply abandon the new rules or principles of conduct and return to the old. Thus, through a process of creativity, trial, refinement, and adoption, the systems of rules internalized by members of a community tend to become more fruitful in the choice settings most commonly encountered.

The internalization required for norms to affect behavior implies that this process is slower than one's day-to-day choices. They are the rules that guide such choices. Many of these rules and choices have little or nothing to do with commerce per se, but a subset of such rules has implications that affect the extent of trade, specialization, and innovation. Changes in norms may affect either or both the products and services consumed and manner in which they are produced. They do so both directly by affecting an individual's ranking of alternatives and indirectly by facilitating the development of scientific and technological knowledge.

Although progress is possible, it is by no means inevitable or necessarily rapid, because a huge variety of social dilemmas tend to impede or block social and economic development. A variety of social equilibria (and dead ends) are associated with unresolved dilemmas. The illustrative game matrices demonstrate why this is so for several general categories of dilemmas, most of which exist in thousands of particular forms among dozens or hundreds of persons whose decisions jointly determine the various outcomes associated with lives in communities.

Stable equilibria may occur at all levels of economic development. The illustrative game matrices demonstrate that ethical innovation provides a possible mechanism for moving from one equilibrium to another. Innovations in ethical ideas may disrupt a community's current equilibria by solving new dilemmas or undoing solutions to problems that had long been forgotten. In the first case, progress occurs. In the second, retrogression occurs.

That life in communities is not inherently safe or pleasant, for reasons described by Hobbes and Hardin, implies that all societies have solved or ameliorated at least a subset of their most critical social dilemmas. Otherwise, communities and connections among them would tend to disintegrate because of escalating conflict or the overuse of local natural resources. That societies face similar problems also implies that the norms internalized have much in common. However, the ethos of one community is unlikely to be identical to that of another because of both minor and major differences in circumstances and in the insights of the persons whose ideas solved or ameliorated the problems confronted. Normative systems are path dependent although not path determined.

Only a subset of the rules that solve the most important social dilemmas tends to support markets and trade-based networks. Markets require norms that support personal property—norms that imply that a single person or small group may control the use of particular things with little or no obligation to share the things or decisions about them with the community at large. Such ideas about legitimate control also have to be transferable in order for gift-giving or trade to be possible. Other sharing rules can also ameliorate the most problematic Hobbesian and Hardin problems, and such rules seem to have been commonplace among migratory tribal societies. In such societies, markets tend to be very limited, if they exist at all.

Given the existence of personal or private property, a variety of trades make take place. Trade in turn creates additional advantages for specialization. In some cases, specialization may produce lifestyles that are in a sense fully commercial in that some persons produce goods that cannot be used to sustain life unless they are traded for goods that do so. For example, at least a few individuals and families living in early villages, towns, and cities lived lives that depended on commerce—that is to say, they purchased most of their necessities of life from income generated by selling various things and services. Such small urban commercial communities have been common in most, but not all, societies. It also bears keeping in mind that many of the artisans living in towns and cities in earlier times were supported by extractive governments rather than commerce per se.

Nonetheless, most persons in most societies during what some refer to as premodern periods were hunter-gatherers or subsistence farmers who were largely self-sufficient at the level of families, tribes, or villages. Such persons lived lives that were largely determined by nature's annual cycles rather than by market incentives. Many, perhaps most, persons in the countryside and in towns lived just beyond the threshold of subsistence, partly for reasons noted by classical economists such as Smith and Malthus.

To move beyond what may be termed *medieval societies* with their stable family-based hierarchies and modest trading networks requires additional social dilemmas to be addressed. The norms that do so tend to support industry over leisure, the use of capital in production rather than in fortification and ornate architecture, and innovation in products and production methods, rather than deference to the old ways. The transition from a society with no or modest growth to one that grows endlessly ultimately requires moral support for innovation and tolerance for the many problems associated with a dynamic society. Mokyr (2016), for example, argues that a culture of growth emerged in England in the period just before the great acceleration began. Part III of this book provides additional evidence of shifts in norms that tended to provide increasingly unreserved support for market activities throughout western Europe in the centuries immediately prior to the great acceleration.

However, before turning to that evidence, the role of governments in this process needs to be examined. Rule-creating and enforcing organizations can potentially solve social dilemmas in a manner similar to that generated by ethical dispositions: by providing incentives for individuals to avoid behaviors that contribute to social dilemmas. However, governments do not always act in a manner that tends to make life more attractive for the average citizen. Historically, governments that extract social surplus from their residents are far more common than those that add to it.

The next part of the book, Part II, explores political dilemmas that must be overcome for "good" governments to emerge, where "good" in this case means ones that encourage rather than impede the emergence of attractive, prosperous societies. Readers will not be surprised to find that internalized norms are the most plausible mechanism through which good governments and policies emerge and are sustained.

# Appendix to Chapter 5: Reducing Uncertainty: On the Superficial Appeal of Central Planning

Mid-twentieth-century utilitarians moved beyond Pigou's welfare economics to argue that an economy could, at least in principle, be directed by a utilitarian central planner who would improve the average quality of life by eliminating uncertainty while increasing aggregate utility, much as More's magistrates did in his imagined *Utopia* ([1516] 1901). It was argued that such a planner could increase aggregate utility by improving the distribution of income, eliminating externality problems, and reducing both risks and uncertainty. Such conclusions were consistent with mainstream economic models of the twentieth century, which implied that a perfectly informed, all-powerful, utilitarian ruler analogous to Plato's philosopher king could improve on the commercial society by replacing it entirely or by administering a broad subsection of it. Indeed, many scholars maintained that such a system was successfully being implemented in northern Asia.[14]

This was a radical challenge to mainstream utilitarianism, which had long favored commercial societies as developed in Chapter 12. This debate involved many technical economic issues; so it is unsurprising that the central planning debate took place chiefly among economists. What might be surprising is that much of the debate over central planning relied upon utilitarian reasoning—which is to say that it ultimately rested on a particular normative theory.[15]

Those who challenged the analysis of the proponents of central planning used several lines of attack. First, critics argued that using neoclassical models as the foundation of their analysis generated several misleading conclusions. The commercial society was far more innovative and dynamic than those models implied. Second, the implicit informational assumptions of neoclassical models implied that planners and market participants had far more information at their disposal than they were likely to have in reality. Thus, the "first best" outcomes of utilitarian planning were not feasible.

[14] Note that such a society, without markets but with ideal production and distribution, resembles Thomas More's *Utopia* ([1516] 1901) with its sharing of labor and distribution squares. It seems clear that such a society could not exist without ethical foundations, in that shirking rather than working tends to be more prevalent when work is unrelated to salary than when it is. The ethical foundations for such a society are beyond the scope of the present volume.

[15] A useful collection of essays on the original central planning debate was assembled by Hayek (1935), which has been reprinted several times. Interest in somewhat more limited forms of central planning continued after World War II, as in Tinbergen (1964). The arguments were not often conducted in terms of utility per se but, with respect to economic output and growth, more or less in the manner pioneered by Pigou, a subset of whose insights is reviewed in Chapter 12. Late twentieth-century commentary and critiques of central planning include Lavoie (1985) and Boettke (2002).

Planners would not be able to produce an innovative society, nor would they have sufficient information to replicate the equilibrium allocation of resources generated by markets in the short term. Third, it was argued that the persons who become central planners were not likely to be utilitarians. Thus, the outcomes associated with even perfectly informed planning were not likely to maximize aggregate utility or even attempt to do so. As a consequence of all three factors, the result of central planning would have far lower aggregate utility (as proxied by economic output) than that generated by a dynamic commercial society.

Regarding the second line of attack, Friedrich Hayek (1899–1992) reminded proponents of central planning that information is not freely available at a central depository, but remains disaggregated in the minds of individuals. This, in combination with the heterogeneity of the knowledge that we each possess (and our ignorance) implies that planners would not know all that was necessary to coordinate the behavior of market participants as well as market prices do.

> It is useful to recall at this point that all economic decisions are made necessary by unanticipated changes, and that **the justification for using the price mechanism is solely that it shows individuals that what they have previously done, or can do now, has become more or less important,** for reasons with which they have nothing to do. (Hayek, "Competition as a Discovery Process," [1968] 2002, p. 9)

Hayek also argues that markets take account of far more information than a real benevolent central planner or team of such planners could.

> [T]he **two advantages of a spontaneous market order** or catallaxy: **it can use the knowledge of all participants, and the objectives it serves are the particular objectives of all its participants in all their diversity and polarity.** The fact that catallaxy serves no uniform system of objectives gives rise to all the familiar difficulties that disturb not only socialists, but all economists endeavoring to evaluate the performance of the market order. (Hayek, "Competition as a Discovery Process," [1968] 2002, p. 23)

In Hayek's view, this ignorance extends to the common understanding of markets themselves.

> Even today the **overwhelming majority of people,** including, I am afraid, a good many supposed economists, **do not yet understand that this extensive social division of labor, based on widely dispersed information, has been made possible**

**entirely by the use of those impersonal signals** which emerge from the market process and tell people what to do in order to adapt their activities to events of which they have no direct knowledge. (Hayek [1979] 2011, p. 162)

That in an economic order involving a far-ranging division of labor it can no longer be the pursuit of perceived common ends but only **abstract rules of conduct**—and the **whole relationship between such rules of individual conduct and the formation of an order** which I have tried to make clear in earlier volumes of this work. (Hayek [1979] 2011, p. 162)

Another crucial issue was whether the central planner would tend to be benevolent or not (utilitarian or not), an issue that goes back at least as far as Plato's and Aristotle's analyses of ideal governments. Postwar public choice analysis suggests that the persons most likely to rise to positions of authority are unlikely to be utilitarians or altruists.

The rapidly accumulating developments in the theory of public choice, ranging from sophisticated analyses of schemes for amalgamating individual preferences into consistent collective outcomes, through the many **models that demonstrate with convincing logic how political rules and institutions fail to work as their idealizations might promise**, and finally to the array of empirical studies that corroborate the basic economic model of politics—these have all been influential in modifying the way that modern man views government and political process. (J. M. Buchanan, 1984, p. 20)

**The romance is gone,** perhaps never to be regained. The socialist paradise is lost. **Politicians and bureaucrats are seen as ordinary persons much like the rest of us, and politics is viewed as a set of arrangements, a game if you will, in which many players with quite disparate objectives interact** so as to generate a set of outcomes that may not be either internally consistent or efficient by any standards (J. M. Buchanan, 1984, p. 20)

What Hayek, Buchanan, and many other economists suggest is that feasibility cannot always be deduced from economic models, because the models necessarily abstract from many details in order to facilitate theoretical developments. Unfortunately, those details cannot always be ignored in practice. The disintegration of the Soviet Union in 1992 affirmed most of the critics' conclusions. It revealed that Soviet planners could not or would not replicate the production efficiency or the material comforts of Western commercial societies after more than a half century of active central management. The Soviet economy generated very few innovations and it seemed obvious that the central planners were not utilitarians (nor communalists).

In the centralization debate, differences in normative theories were arguably less important than differences in the expected implications of central planning, because the debate was largely among utilitarians or persons who had accepted the neo-utilitarian approach of Pigou.

Nonetheless, assumptions about the ethical dispositions of persons in the societies to be centrally managed were also central to the argument. A central planner who had internalized utilitarian theory would do better at maximizing aggregate utility—to the extent this can be discerned—than a pragmatist interested in maximizing his own income and authority. Moreover, economic incentives matter less if all persons have internalized a strong work ethic and a rule-following norm.[16] The arguments in favor of central planning thus implicitly assumed a very supportive normative foundation for their ideal society—much as Thomas More had done. Without that ethical foundation, it was behaviorally infeasible, regardless of whether it was economically feasible or not.

[16] It is interesting to note that markets tend to reward these core ethical beliefs insofar as they tend to increase firm profits, individual incomes, and consumer satisfaction. Without such market rewards, it is clear that the distribution of internalized norms in centrally planned societies would be different than those of market-based societies. Market rewards for a work ethic and for rule-following behavior tend to cause such ethical dispositions to be more commonplace and strongly internalized, as demonstrated in Part II.

# PART II
# ETHICS AND THE POLITICAL ECONOMY
# OF PROSPERITY

> Had this [praise of virtue] been the universal strain, had you sought to
> persuade us of this from our youth upwards, we should not have been
> on the watch to keep one another from doing wrong, but **everyone
> would have been his own watchman**, because afraid, if he did wrong,
> of harboring in himself the greatest of evils.
>
> —Plato, *The Republic*, p. 30, Kindle edition

## Introduction

Part II analyzes the contributions that governments can potentially add to the processes through which social dilemmas are solved or ameliorated and the extent to which government policies are likely to promote rather than inhibit commerce. The aspect of governments that is given most attention is their "governing" activities, that is, their development and enforcement of rules. In principle, as argued in many public economics textbooks, governments can adopt and enforce rules that address all the dilemmas examined in Part I. Moreover, they can potentially do so faster than social or biological evolution can, and can thereby speed the process of developing attractive communities. By systematically imposing appropriate penalties on behavior that generates social dilemmas, a good government can induce good behavior even in communities populated by pragmatists, as argued long ago by Hobbes (1651/2009), among many others.

However, whether that potential is realized is not as obvious or natural as suggested by Hobbes and the implicit assumptions of most public economic textbooks. Good governance requires a variety of political dilemmas to be solved. History suggests that governments that adopt laws that broadly improve life for most residents of the territories governed are rare. Far more common are governing organizations analogous to what Mancur Olson (1993) termed "stationary bandits" who extract resources from the populace governed in order to improve the lifestyles of rulers and members of small influential groups whose acquiescence or cooperation are required to maintain their positions of authority. Those benefiting are often termed "political elites" in the political science and sociology literatures, but they are simply persons able to provide the necessary military, cultural, and economic support for the current rule-makers to retain power. Until very recently, extractive rulers with narrow interests and support among elites were far more common than governments that promote the interests of a broad cross section of their residents, and they are still not uncommon.

Part II does not spend very much time examining the policies or organization of extractive regimes; instead it focuses most of its attention on the ethical prerequisites of "good" or "productive" governments that generally advance the shared interests of those governed. It is not presumed that such governments do so perfectly or that extractions fall to zero, but rather that most of their policies benefit non-elites—the persons outside government and not among its most influential supporters. A secondary focus of Part II is the extent to which a government tends to support or impede the emergence of commercial societies. For many scholars, these two issues are one and the same because average income (per capita real gross national product or real gross domestic product) is considered to be a very useful index of the quality of life within and among countries. Under that metric, the more commerce there is, the higher the average income, and the better the average quality of life. However, promoting commerce is not taken to be the only measure of good governance herein.

Nonetheless the assertion that good governments always promote commerce is of historical interest, because in contemporary life it is regarded to be "obvious" that such a link exists; although from the perspective of this book, the extent of commercial development should be regarded as simply one of many possible indices of the "goodness" of a society. That it was widely used in the twentieth and early twenty-first centuries as an index of the quality of both life and governance is significant, in part, because it was not the main yardstick for "betterness" used in former times.

The analysis begins with the simplest possible state, one analogous to that posited by Locke, where a community decides to establish a rule-enforcing organization to reinforce its customary laws. It notes dilemmas associated with even such simple governments. It then analyzes dilemmas associated with more powerful governments that use majority rule to directly or indirectly select the rules to be enforced and a bureaucracy to implement those laws and produce its services. It concludes by analyzing the policy choices of still more powerful democratic governments that may attempt to create specific social systems within the territory governed. Extractive regimes require little support from ethical dispositions, as argued long ago by Montesquieu (1748), and they are given little attention except as the type of regime that tends to emerge when various political dilemmas are not solved or ameliorated.

Productive governments are sometimes referred to in the text as "good" governments, but in doing so the term "good" is being used in a narrower manner than in the rest of the book—namely as a synonym for consensus-based governance or governments that broadly enhance the quality of life for the persons governed. It bears keeping in mind that the words "ideal" or "optimal" when applied to public policies are just scientific-sounding ways to describe the policies of a "good" society, where "good" is open to a variety of interpretations. Ideal policies are often implications of particular normative, ethical, political, or religious theories, given human, technological, and resource possibilities. Most public economic textbooks, for example, implicitly adopt the utilitarian perspective. However, what is "optimal" for a single person in one society is not necessarily optimal for others with different conceptions of the "good," because each person's conclusions about the "ideal" changes as his or her notions of the good life and good society change. Views of "the good" within a society tend to be more similar than those among societies, but are not completely uniform.

Montesquieu (1748) argued that ethical dispositions are more important to sustain democratic regimes than monarchies or oligarchies. The analysis of Part II supports that contention, although that is not its main focus. However, if ethical dispositions are required for productive governance, then it cannot be argued that governmental policies and ethical disposition are truly substitutes for one another—as has been suggested for more than three centuries. Instead, they are complements; preexisting internalized ethical dispositions are prerequisites for productive governments. After a productive government is up and running, such governments may subsequently have beneficial effects on unsolved social dilemmas and on the distribution of a community's ethical dispositions. However, without some initially supportive dispositions, their laws would not advance the shared interests of those governed nor be uniformly enforced.

Chapter 6 focuses on the simplest possible notion of a good government, as an organization that buttresses preexisting norms in the community of interest—a conception of government first developed by John Locke in 1690 in his counterpoint to Hobbes's *Leviathan*. It focuses on fundamental political dilemmas associated with rule-enforcing regimes that must be overcome for such organizations to be productive rather than extractive governments. Chapter 7 analyzes political dilemmas associated with majority-rule-based governance. Democracies are not inherently productive in the sense used here, but only if a series of political dilemmas are resolved. Solutions to those dilemmas are likely to require various combinations of constitutional rules and complementary ethical dispositions. Chapter 8 concludes Part II with an analysis of the extent to which the framing institutions and policies chosen by voters are likely to directly or indirectly be supportive of commercial development.

# 6

# Ethics, Customary Law, and Law Enforcement

[T]he community comes to be umpire, by settled standing rules, indifferent, and the same to all parties; and by men having authority
from the community, for the execution of those rules, decides all the
differences that may happen between any members of that society
concerning any matter of right; and punishes those offences which
any member hath committed against the society, with such penalties as the law has established: whereby it is easy to discern, who are,
and who are not, in political society together. Those who are united
into one body, and have a common established law and judicature to
appeal to, with authority to decide controversies between them, and
punish offenders, are in civil society one with another.

—Locke, *Two Treatises* ([1690] 2009), p. 30

## Ethics and Customary Law

Part I can be said to provide a theory of customary law—a theory of the emergence of productive informal rules that influence behavior in communities
that lack written laws or formal law-enforcing institutions. Such rules are a
subset of those promulgated by parents, friends, and village wise men and
women. Most are internalized to varying degrees; thus, most members of a
community follow those rules whether they are being watched by others or
not, unless the temptations to violate them are too great. Such internalized
rules and their associated feelings of virtue and guilt are part of the "self"
and thus part of the perceived self-interest that guides individual choices and
behavior. In today's world, we observe such rules in most of our day-to-day
dealings with others, only a small subset of which are reinforced by laws formally adopted and enforced by governments.

Chapter 6 explores why a law-enforcing organization might be adopted by
a community that has customary laws, and also the ethical dispositions that
are necessary for such organizations to be "productive" in the sense that they

*Solving Social Dilemmas*. Roger D. Congleton, Oxford University Press. © Oxford University Press 2022.
DOI: 10.1093/oso/9780197642788.003.0006

contribute to the attractiveness of a community, rather than undermining it through extraction. A number of dilemmas have to be overcome for productive rule-enforcing organizations to emerge. Many of these are similar to those required for team production to be effective. Groups of men and women within governing organizations have to be induced to behave as teams—which is to say, to effectively advance the interests of their organization. However, the aim of a good government, as that term is used in this book, is to advance the shared interests of the persons governed, rather than those of the organization (the government) itself.

## A Lockean Point of Departure: The Simplest Form of Government

We begin our analysis of governing organizations in a community that has already emerged, which implies that informal rules have been internalized that address the most pressing problems of life with fellow humans. The development and internalization of such rules are not instantaneous, but the product of decades or centuries of experimentation. Their internalization is largely the product of the encouragement that persons in the community provide to children and immigrants to abide by the most commonplace rules of their community. The rules are followed year in and year out, and they become habitual and part of their systems for ranking alternatives.

Many, but not all, parts of the systems of rules passed along have survived for decades, if not centuries. A subset of the rules passed along has evolutionary support in that they made both communities and members of those communities more likely to survive in the environments in which they found themselves. Many have solved or ameliorated critical social dilemmas and made life in communities more attractive. However, although rule bound, individuals are not rule determined, the rules internalized must be interpreted, and rule innovation is possible at many margins of the rule systems that have been internalized.

As part of transmission of a community's most common rule systems, members of the community provide a variety of informal rewards for following the rules (praise and prizes) and punishments for violating the rules (chiding and cuffing). Those violating community norms may be disparaged, may be excluded from other activities of direct individual value, may be shunned, or in extreme cases may be expelled from the community. As the severity of punishments increase, punishments generally become more costly for individuals to impose on their own. This creates a free-rider problem regarding norm reinforcement, as illustrated in Table 6.1.

**Table 6.1** The Private Law-Enforcement Dilemma

|  |  | Richard | | |
| --- | --- | --- | --- | --- |
|  |  | Always enforce rule | Enforce half the time | Never enforce |
| Gordon | Always enforce rule | (G, R) 5, 5 | (G, R) 3, 6 | (G, R) 1, 7 |
|  | Enforce half the time | 6, 3 | 4, 4 | 2, 5 |
|  | Never enforce | 7, 1 | 5, 2 | 3, 3 |

In the setting illustrated, there is a single equilibrium with respect to rules that are costly to informally enforce, namely one in which all free-ride, in which case, the rules are only weakly encouraged, and thus they are less likely to be strongly internalized.

This "enforcement dilemma" is normally ameliorated by higher-level norms that create duties to encourage adherence to the rules and to mete out punishment to those who violate the rule of interest. Indeed, duties to reinforce such rules may be sufficiently important that parents have genetic predispositions to teach their children the "facts of life" in their community. However, parental teaching and encouragement may be less than that required to fully inculcate their children with the most common and important rules in their community, and the other socially transmitted norms may be too weak to fully top up parental dispositions. The more costly punishment is, the less likely it is that rules will be strongly internalized and the less likely it is that the rules internalized will solve all significant social dilemmas.

Such communities are in the Lockean state of nature. They have customary laws that essentially everyone is familiar with, but the laws are not always routinely followed by all members of the community. Rules that tend to discourage violence, theft, and excessive use of common resources are followed by most, but are occasionally violated. The undesirable consequences and causes of such rule violations tend to be obvious, and the rule-following members of a community may agree that life in their community could be made more attractive by creating a customary law-enforcing organization. Such an organization may further encourage adherence to the community's most important rules by supplementing the informal punishments with additional penalties for violating the rules.

A customary law-enforcing official or organization is arguably the simplest form of government possible. Such an organization does not develop new laws, provide new public goods, or concern itself with public finance beyond that required to pay the salaries (if any) of the law enforcers. In small communities, it may be sufficient for a single man or woman to be granted authority to reinforce community norms with stronger external punishments. A customary law enforcer would initially serve at the pleasure of the community, but the free-rider problem implies that it would not always be easy to remove such an official or group when he or she or they fail to execute their duties tolerably well.

## The Productivity of Ethical Dispositions in Law-Enforcing Organizations

Unfortunately, it is no small task to assure that a community's enforcement agent(s) dutifully enforce its common laws. The enforcement dilemma can be illustrated with the enforcement of any customary law. An example that is linked to a community's prosperity is the enforcement of a community's anti-fraud norms. Chapter 3 demonstrated that norms that discourage fraudulent offers increase the scope of trade, facilitate specialization, and thereby increase economic development. Thus, diligent reinforcement of those norms by law enforcers would increase the prosperity of a community whenever anti-fraud norms are too weakly internalized by merchants to solve important fraud problems.

Table 6.2 illustrates the effect of a fine on ordinary sellers who would otherwise be inclined to make fraudulent offers. The guilt decrement ($g$) associated with making fraudulent offers and the virtue supplement ($v$) associated with making honest offers are assumed to be too small to solve the problem ($v + g < 1$). Thus, fraudulent offers for the product of interest are commonplace, and markets for that product tend to disappear for reasons discussed in Chapter 3. Let $F$ be the expected fine to be imposed on a merchant who routinely makes fraudulent offers. If the anticipated fine, $F$, is sufficient, sellers will no longer be tempted to mislead buyers and will make only honest offers. The stronger

Table 6.2  Effect of Well-Enforced Laws against Fraud

|  |  | Richard (R; buyer) | |
|---|---|---|---|
|  |  | Accept or solicit offer | Ignore all offers |
| Gary (G; seller) | Fraudulent offer | (G, R) $(3 - g - F, -3)$ | (G, R) $(-g - 1 - F, 0)$ |
|  | Honest offer | $(2 + v, 2)$ | $(-1 + v, 0)$ |
|  | Do not make offers | $(0, -1)$ | $(0, 0)$ |

is the internalized normative system, the smaller the expected fine has to be to achieve this result.

In the illustration, an expected fine that is greater than 1 is sufficient to do so in the case when merchants are pragmatists (with $v = g = 0$). An expected fine of ½ is sufficient when merchants have weakly internalized the norms against fraudulent offers (as when, $v = g = ¼$). The first case is the law and economics solution to crime as developed by Becker, the second, with the less onerous fines, is the setting imagined by Locke.[1]

Both law-enforcement solutions to the problem of fraud assume that law enforcers are themselves honest and diligent. However, in the environment developed by Hobbes (1651/2009) and routinely assumed in the law and economics literature, individuals are all pragmatists without internalized norms. Such law enforcers are unlikely to uniformly enforce a community's customary laws or its legal code. They are not bound by ethical or other normative anti-corruption norms, and as law enforcers, they have discretion to choose whether to punish a fraudulent seller or not. Given that discretion, pragmatic sellers might offer to share their profits with the law enforcers if they will ignore the sellers' crimes, and pragmatic law enforcers will be willing to do so.

There are gains from trade that can be realized by fraudsters and pragmatic law enforcers, although those defrauded are made worse off by such agreements. A pragmatic seller can offer an amount up to the total profits associated with fraudulent sales to the person(s) tasked with law enforcement (here, up to $3 - 2 = 1$, when $v = g = 0$). The law enforcer would naturally bargain with the merchant and attempt to maximize his or her benefits from the exchange. However, this does not imply that the equilibrium rate of bribery is 1 or that the probability of imposing a fine will normally be zero.

The profits of fraudsters and the bribes received by law enforcers are both affected by the probability of enforcement of anti-fraud laws and the magnitude of the profit sharing required to avoid enforcement. Profits fall to zero when anti-fraud laws are perfectly enforced (a probability of $F > 1$ of 100%). They also fall to zero when they are not enforced at all (a probability of 0%) because of the disappearance of markets in which fraudulent offers are commonplace. Similarly, bribe receipts fall to zero when the profit sharing required

---

[1] Becker (1968), Tullock (1971), and Posner (1972) initiated the law and economics literature and provided useful introductions to the issues raised by rational choice models of law enforcement and criminal behavior. The expected fine reflects a seller's assessment of the probability of being caught and convicted, $P$, and the normal penalty, $F^A$, with $F = PF^A$.

to reduce enforcement approaches either 100% or 0% of merchant profits. In between is a probability and sharing rule that maximizes the bribes received by enforcers. The customary laws are partially enforced by bribe maximizing anti-fraud agents, but the result is a smaller economy than would have been the case if anti-fraud laws were fully enforced.[2]

The mere creation of anti-fraud laws with significant fines and an organization tasked with enforcing those laws is not sufficient to solve the problem of fraud or violations of other customary laws when law enforcers are pragmatists. The laws must be well enforced to do so.

## Anti-Corruption Laws, Pragmatism, and the Extent of Corruption

The law and economics solution to the problem of bribery is the creation of anti-corruption laws and an anti-corruption organization (or unit) to enforce those laws. Communities that adopt such a solution would create a two-tiered system of law enforcement in which the higher-level law enforcers (the anti-corruption unit) monitor the lower-level law enforcers that police the community. Anti-corruption laws, in combination with appropriate fines, could significantly reduce corruption in the anti-fraud enforcers and thereby increase the extent to which other laws were properly enforced. However, a moment's thought reveals that this is not likely to be the case if the new higher level of law enforcement is also staffed by pragmatists. Pragmatic anti-corruption law enforcers would be inclined to "turn a blind eye" to bribery in exchange for some fraction of the profits realized by the anti-fraud police.

Table 6.3 illustrates a choice setting in which each law enforcer is paid salary $S$ and the bribes are equally shared between the anti-fraud enforcer and

---

[2] The bribery-maximizing profit-sharing rule (bribery rate) and probability of imposing a fine require knowing how consumers respond to random fraudulent offers as opposed to deterministic ones, a problem that cannot easily be reduced to a game matrix. An increase in rates of fraud is analogous to an increase in the defect rate analyzed in Chapter 4. It reduces the average marginal benefits of the product of interest. Holding price constant, the demand for the good of interest can be characterized as $Q = q(f)$, where $f$ is the probability or frequency of fraudulent offers (here, an intentional defect). The quantity purchased falls as $f$ increases, holding price constant. If $\pi$ is the profit associated with a fraudulent offer, then $B = s\pi f^*Q$ is the bribe revenue, where $s$ is the share of the merchant's profits paid as bribes. The rate of fraud $f^*$ is a function of the profit-sharing rate ($s$), the probability of being fined ($P$), and the fine ($F$). The first-order conditions for the combination of $s$, $P$, and $F$ that maximize bribe revenue from a given merchant are: $B_s = \pi f^*Q + s\pi f_s^*Q + s\pi f^*Q_f f_s^* = 0$, $B_P = s\pi f^*Q_f f_P^* = 0$, and $B_F = s\pi f^*Q_f f_F^* = 0$. A bribe-maximizing law enforcer takes account of the rate of fraudulent offers, the size of the fraudster's market, and the effects of his enforcement and profit-sharing routines on the rate of fraud and purchases of fraudulent (defective) products by consumers.

**Table 6.3** The Enforcement Dilemma: Enforcing Laws against Fraud
and Bribery

|  |  | Gordon (G; enforces anti-corruption law) | |
|  |  | Enforce law | Accept bribe |
| Andrei | Enforces law | (A, G) | (A, G) |
| (A; enforces |  | S, S | S, S |
| anti-fraud law) | Accepts bribe | S + B − F, S | S + B/2, S + B/2 |

the anti-corruption enforcer. The person (Andrei) charged with enforcing the anti-fraud law can receive a bribe of amount $B$, but he would pay a fine of amount $F$ if he does so and the anti-bribery law is enforced. Anti-corruption laws will bind Andrei if the expected fine is greater than his or her bribe income, $F > B$.

Unfortunately for the community, the enforcer of the anti-corruption laws (Gordon) may also be a pragmatist. By sharing the bribe revenues, both pragmatic enforcers are enriched and neither law is well enforced.

There are two Nash equilibria to this game, but one clearly dominates the other for the two enforcement agents. They are both better off under the bribe-sharing arrangement than they are under the enforcement equilibrium, and presumably would take steps to assure that this equilibrium is the one that emerges, which is stable once it does emerge. The assumption that the bribes are equally shared is used for illustration. (Other sharing rules with shares between 0 and 1 would yield similar results.) Gordon would adjust his share to maximize his income from bribery (as characterized in footnote 2), which would be greater than zero to benefit from additional income, and it must be less than 1 or Andrei would not engage in efforts to collect bribes from fraudulent merchants.[3]

In contrast to the previous social dilemmas, there is no incentive for the persons involved to propose or develop solutions to the problem of corruption and poor enforcement of customary laws, because the corruption

[3] Hillman and Katz (1987) show that bribe-sharing arrangements tend to generate competition to obtain the positions that receive such supplementary sources of income. Contests for such positions consume scarce resources (at least the time and energy of the officials) and so may dissipate the net gains from those jobs. In highly competitive environments, the rents are entirely dissipated, which means that the total cost of acquiring jobs with bribe income equals the average extra revenue obtained. Those at the top ranks of authority, as residual claimants, have incentives to adopt standing rules to reduce the associated reduction in their revenue flows—as with efficiency-based rules for promotion and fixed sharing rules of the sort used in the illustration.

dilemma is external to the enforcement organization. The losses from their derelictions of duties are not borne by the law enforcers, who are enriched by corruption, but by those who would have benefited from diligent law enforcement: consumers and honest firms. Moreover, this enforcement dilemma cannot be solved by adding a third level of law and law enforcement. Pragmatists only enforce the laws when doing so increases their effective salaries or otherwise advances their narrow interests. Diligently enforcing the law is not likely when bribery, favoritism, or other forms of extraction are profitable for law enforcers.[4]

Other possible sources of revenue for law enforcers are often even more problematic. For example, an enforcer may threaten honest merchants with fines if they do not "kick in" with payments as "other" merchants do. This "tax" on honest merchants tends to undermine the emergence of well-functioning markets by reducing or eliminating the profits of honest merchants. If there are more honest merchants than pragmatic ones, extortion may generate more income for enforcers than bribery. Unlike bribery, which generates modest law enforcement, and therefore modest benefits for the community, extortion can make members of a community worse off than they would have been without their customary law-enforcing agency by extracting most of the net benefits associated with commerce (or more generally, life) in the community thus afflicted.

## Ethical Dispositions as Prerequisites for Effective Law Enforcement

Under the Hobbesian conditions analyzed at the start of Part I, only pragmatists would exist, and corruption and extortion would be rampant in any government created. Such regimes would be extractive rather than productive organizations. Some improvement might take place over that associated with anarchy as posited by Hobbes, although this is by no means guaranteed. The enforcement of productive laws undertaken may be better than no enforcement; but the extraction undertaken via extortion could easily generate losses greater than the benefits realized by such law enforcement.

---

[4] Becker and Stigler (1974) suggest that the enforcement dilemma can be solved by efficiency wages, that is, by paying law enforcers somewhat more than the difference between their opportunity cost wage and their expected bribe revenue. They argue that the fear of being dismissed would induce such overpaid officials to diligently enforce the law. However, notice that the game represented above implies that the same partial enforcement of the laws tends to occur regardless of the salaries earned if punishment (here dismissal) is unlikely.

**Table 6.4** An Ethical Solution to the Enforcement Dilemma: Enforcing Laws against Fraud and Bribery

|  |  | Gordon (G; enforces anti-bribery law) | |
| --- | --- | --- | --- |
|  |  | Enforce law | Accept bribe |
| Andrei (A; enforces anti-fraud law) | Enforce law | (A, G)<br>$S, S + V$ | (A, G)<br>$S, S$ |
|  | Accept bribe | $S + B - F, S + V$ | $S + B/2, S + B/2$ |

Life would continue to be poor, nasty, brutish, and short—although it would no longer be solitary.[5]

In the Lockean natural setting currently being explored, however, most persons in the community are not pragmatists. They have internalized rules that create predispositions to abide by their community's customary laws when temptations to do otherwise are not "too great." Insofar as internalization varies, some would resist more temptations than others would. Law enforcement in such cases can be improved by recruiting enforcers from among the most law-abiding individuals in the community. Such ethical law enforcers would resist taking bribes because they regard such action to be immoral or to violate their oaths of office and thereby induce guilty feelings.

When only a few such very dutiful law enforcers are available, they should be employed in the anti-corruption agency rather than in the anti-fraud agency, because the enforcement of anti-corruption laws encourages pragmatists in the anti-fraud agency to resist taking bribes. Table 6.4 illustrates this case.

In the case in which the anti-bribery enforcers regard the rewards of virtue to be greater than the temptation to share in the bribery, the anti-bribery laws would be enforced, which in turn induces the enforcement of anti-fraud laws. Even the simplest government requires moral behavior on the part of some government officials. In Table 6.4, avoiding the enforcement dilemma requires, $V > B/2$ and $F > B$.

[5] For those familiar with Olson's (1993) theory of stationary banditry, this claim may be counterintuitive. However, Olson assumes that stationary bandits use relatively simple uniform tax systems to collect revenues from those governed, rather than lump sum taxes and threats of death to transfer resources from those governed to the rulers. The upper bound of transfers from those governed to those in government is the full surplus above subsistence in such cases. Somewhat less than this amount might be taken as a means of encouraging greater work from those governed, but it need not be very much. Free-rider problems on the part of those governed and security measures by those governing tend to reduce the ability of commoners to overthrow such extractive regimes.

Strongly internalized norms are most important for the officials with the most authority. In the case in which the lower-level enforcer is dutiful and the upper-level enforcer is a pragmatist, the anti-bribery laws may be enforced, but the upper-level enforcer will be unhappy with the dutiful behavior of the anti-bribery enforcer. He would rather have a bit of extra income than have the anti-bribery laws perfectly enforced. Consequently, upper-level pragmatists would make life difficult for the honest anti-fraud enforcer. He or she might, for example, file unflattering reports or falsely accuse such agents of corruption. Insofar as the anti-corruption bureau plays a role in hiring, pragmatists will prefer to staff the anti-fraud agency with fellow pragmatists to profit from their "flexibility."

Of course, it would be best to have dutiful enforcers at all levels of the law-enforcing agency, because bribery is difficult to monitor and anti-corruption laws are consequently difficult to perfectly enforce, even if all anti-corruption officials are virtuous and hardworking. In the absence of such dispositions at the most important nodes of government, extractive rather than productive enforcement of the laws is likely to characterize governance.

The lack of suitably strong norms may be a reason why many bands and tribes typically have a judge rather than a law enforcer and leave enforcement to the individuals and families themselves (Fukuyama 2011, Ch. 4; Emsley 2021, Ch. 1, Broman and Vanberg, 2021). Alternatively, when judges or mediators are adopted before police, it may imply that informal enforcement of customary law is working fairly well, except in cases when disagreements about the nature of customary laws exist, at which point honest judges who understand and respect the nuances of the community's laws become an important part of a customary law system.[6]

It bears noting that a variety of internalized ethical theories—although not all—can induce law enforcers to dutifully enforce customary laws. Agents may have strongly internalized the norms that produced the customary laws, as discussed previously. Agents that have promised to enforce "the law" when

---

[6] Although policing is associated with all attractive societies, the evidence suggests that through most of recorded history, policing was substantially an informal activity undertaken by volunteers, although informal enforcement was often topped up by government officials of one kind or another, as with the regional sheriffs of medieval England and similar officials elsewhere. Formal police departments that specialized in law enforcement did not emerge until the eighteenth and nineteenth centuries in Europe in the period in which urban centers were growing rapidly and decentralized and informal methods of enforcement would have functioned less effectively. Corruption was often a problem in both the sheriff and the departmental systems of law enforcement (Emsley 2021, Chs. 1–4). On the other hand, it is interesting that as bureaucracies became more effective through a combination of changes in norms and organization, policing agencies became more effective and on average less corrupt. Weber (1947, p. 338) suggests that the rise of large commercial organizations played a role in both processes.

they accepted their jobs and have taken oaths of office may feel duty-bound to abide by their oaths because they have internalized a duty for keeping promises. Enforcers may also regard their community's customary law to be very special or of divine origin and thus deemed worthy of support simply because it is "the law of the land" or "god's law." Others may have internalized general normative theories, such as those associated with some forms of utilitarianism and contractarianism in which law enforcement is regarded to be the foundation of civil society, as argued, for example, by both Hobbes and Mill.[7]

## Corruption and Agency Problems Increase as Governing Responsibilities Grow

The logic of the preceding model suggests that an extractive state may be accidentally created by failing to account for the kinds of moral conduct necessary to assure that even simple governments are productive rather than extractive. Similar extractive methods may also be used by intentionally extractive governing organizations that conquer a territory and attempt to maximize the net advantages of rule. Such governments would also modify or overturn preexisting laws to increase their revenues and reduce the probability of uprisings. Extractive regimes are less dependent on the internalized norms of their team members than productive governments, because the ruler's practical interest in better lifestyles induces them to organize extraction in the manner that solves team production problems and assures a steady flow of revenues to their coffers and deference to those with the most authority. Such extractive regimes are commonplace in world history.

Productive governments, in contrast, are rarer, possibly because they are more dependent on the normative dispositions of those enforcing laws and also, as analyzed in the next chapter, on the internalized norms of their rule-makers. This is not to say that productive governments need to be staffed by angels, only that the moral dispositions of government officials are important. And they are more critical at some positions than at others. It is arguable that

---

[7] See Congleton and Vanberg (2001) for evidence that such "enforcer" dispositions may emerge and be viable in settings in which multi-person prisoner-dilemma-like settings exist and individuals are free to exit from dysfunctional small groups. They demonstrate that persons with the ability to target punishments at persons who engage in uncooperative behavior tend to improve team performance enough that such dispositions are evolutionarily supported even if there are nontrivial costs associated with imposing penalties on "shirkers."

the larger and more complex the tasks undertaken, the greater is the risk that bribery and extortion will reduce the efficiency of the organization and transform a productive state into an extractive one.

The challenge of avoiding accidental and intentionally extractive regimes is nontrivial and important for the purposes of this book because such regimes are unlikely to promote prosperity for those outside of government. Their aim is to transfer as much as possible from those outside government (those ruled) to those inside government (the rulers), and this tends to reduce or eliminate both the ability and incentive for commoners to invest in physical and human capital or to innovate. The elite may do so, to some extent, and thus prosper from both their investments and extraction from commoners, but widespread prosperity would not be produced in such societies.

The problem of corruption is not unique to governing organizations. Similar logic applies to all large organizations. Every organization's internal rules need to be followed for it to be effective. It is such rules, after all, that transform a group of individuals into a team. Nonetheless, the rules are never perfect or perfectly enforced. All large organizations confront a variety of agency problems that have to be overcome if they are to advance organizational aims effectively, whether the aim is extraction, profits, votes, public service, or the welfare of the organization's most powerful officials. Temptations for individual employees to use their authority within an organization to promote their own interests rather than those of the organization or its formeteurs exist in every organization. Such temptations tend to increase with the size of an organization because more people have to be incentivized and monitored.

Nonetheless, agency problems tend to be more severe for governments than for other organizations. First, the productivity of government employees and agencies is often more difficult to determine than that of employees in private organizations. Individual contributions to money profits and sales can be estimated within most economic organizations—albeit not always as precisely as economic textbooks imply. In contrast, there are few obvious indices that can be used to assess the productivity of government employees in productive as opposed to extractive regimes. The extent to which a government employee advances the shared goals of members of a community is difficult to quantify. Private-sector agency problems thus tend to be somewhat smaller, more objective, and so more manageable than those of productive governments, although such assessments are rarely completely accurate within private organizations. Second, the agency problems of governments tend to have greater effects on persons who are not employees of government. The policy decisions of commercial organizations tend to affect only their employees, suppliers, and customers. The effects of malfeasance by senior government officials tend to affect people throughout the community governed.[8] Third, the latter effect implies that persons and organizations outside government have stronger incentives to attempt to bribe or otherwise persuade government officials to use their authority in a manner that narrowly benefits particular outsiders than the same persons and groups have to bribe or otherwise subvert persons working within private organizations.[9]

Fourth, abuse of authority within economic organizations may affect the nature of the output produced, how and where it is produced, and through such decisions, the average cost of its products and services. In private firms, corrupt "buyers" may purchase inputs from friends and family members or favor suppliers who provide "kickbacks" of various kinds, rather than purchasing from high-quality or low-cost providers. Such abuses tend to increase production costs and reduce owner profits and, through effects on prices, reduce consumer surplus. As a consequence, firms that are most riddled by agency problems tend to shrink and disappear, reducing the impact of its corruption on consumers. Similar abuses of authority in governments often involve larger contracts and so have larger effects on the distribution of profits among firms and income levels of their employees. However, a government's "consumers" cannot easily take their business to less corrupt or more efficient suppliers of government services. Taxes and fines will be collected whether one approves of one's government's services or not.

The temptation to misuse authority tends to increase as the extent of the laws to be enforced and the services provided by governments increase. As the scope of governance increases, its effects on persons outside government increases, which encourages more efforts to affect government policies. This implies that ever more tantalizing offers and persuasive arguments from groups outside the government of interest have to be resisted by government employees. Consequently, the usefulness of personnel with appropriate moral dispositions tends to increase as government responsibilities expand.

[8] There are, of course, exceptions to this generalization. The temptations faced by senior managers of international corporations clearly exceed those of junior managers and teachers employed by state and local governments and may rival those of officials from national governments. Nonetheless, within most territories and at most times, the most important source of rules, the largest employer, and the organizations spending the most money are national governments. For example, Google employs about 72,000 persons, whereas the State of California has more than 500,000 employees. Denmark, a relatively small nation-state, has around 750,000 public-sector employees, about 10 times the number of Google employees. Google's annual revenues are less than $80 billion per year, whereas the tax revenue of California is more than $100 billion and that of Denmark is more than $150 billion per year.

[9] There is a large game theoretic literature on contests that shows how the "prizes" at stake affect investment in efforts to influence those with the authority to hand out the prize. See Garfinkel and Skaperdas (2008) or Konrad (2009) for overviews of contest theory. See Congleton and Hillman (2015) or Congleton, Hillman, and Konrad (2008) for overviews of the rent-seeking and rent-extraction literatures and analysis of how such contests are generated by and affect government policies.

Of course, encouraging employees to resist such temptations is not entirely left to moral dispositions. Organizations all have their equivalents of the anti-fraud and anti-corruption agencies modeled in the previous sections. The preceding analysis implies that the normative dispositions of the persons charged with such tasks—supervisors and managers—affect the effectiveness with which such internal enforcement is undertaken. Attempting to recruit persons likely to be "good team members" also remains important. The more strongly the organization's rules are internalized by their employees, the less monitoring and penalties are required to solve their agency problems. This is especially true of hard-to-monitor agency problems such as those associated with corruption, extortion, and other abuses of authority.[10]

Keep in mind that it is not ethical conduct per se that ameliorates these problems, but a subset of the behavior induced by rules and principles of conduct regarded to be ethical. Some maxims and ethical principles have no implications for behavior within organizations. Some norms may reinforce rather than counter such problems as corruption and shirking. It is only the subset of ethical dispositions that increase an organization's efficiency that are relevant for the organization, and these vary to some degree with the positions that persons are recruited for, as discussed in Chapter 3.

With respect to enforcing a community's or an organization's own rules, persons with ethical dispositions that incline them to be diligent rule enforcers may be identified and rewarded with employment opportunities, higher salaries, and greater authority.[11] By diligently enforcing "the law," such persons tend to make their governments more productive and their communities more attractive by reducing a wide variety of social, economic, and political dilemmas.[12]

## Law Enforcement Encourages Stronger Internalization of the Rules Enforced

After the agency problems for customary law enforcement have been solved, enforcement rates increase, which increases adherence to a community's customary laws. At this point, formal law enforcement may be said to "top up" the

[10] See Aidt (2003, 2009) for surveys of the economic theories of the effects of corruption on economic development. See Congleton (1982) for models of bureaucratic inertia and bias. See Congleton (2015) for various institutional methods for reducing rent-seeking and other forms of conflict within organization.

[11] For example, the honesty of accountants, purchasers, and senior managers tends to be an important qualification for those positions, and the persons occupying those positions are often very well paid.

[12] Congleton and Vanberg (2001) demonstrate that a propensity to punish need not be a universal trait for it to be supported by survivorship. When punishment can be undertaken at a modest cost, persons who freely do so can enhance group productivity enough to compensate for their additional costs.

informal law enforcement provided by internalized normative dispositions and informal community sanctions. It is only in such cases that formal law enforcement and internalized ethical dispositions can be regarded as substitutes for each other. In those cases, internalized norms, informal community sanctions, and law enforcement advance the same ends and induce the same kinds of behavior.

Such law enforcement tends to further encourage the internalization of a community's ethos for reasons similar to those discussed regarding commercial rewards in Chapters 3 and 4. Government employment of persons with productive ethical dispositions increases the demand for and salaries of persons with what might be called "rule-following and rule-enforcing" dispositions. Such dutiful enforcers allow even very simple forms of government to avoid becoming extractive regimes. In addition, the penalties imposed for violations of customary laws encourage investments in the relevant dispositions by families and individuals. As a consequence, the routines associated with avoiding legal penalties tend to become more habitualized, and so more strongly internalized by persons in the community who were not formerly rule followers. The less perfect informal and informal enforcement are, the smaller these virtue effects tend to be.

Effective customary law enforcement tends to further stabilize patterns of life associated with a community's ethos, but also slows the process of social evolution by reducing opportunities for experimentation with alternative rules.[13]

## Customary Law Enforcement and the Emergence of Common Law

When creating a customary law-enforcing organization, communities may direct their law enforcers to focus most of their efforts on violations of particular customary laws, rather than all of their customs. Not all customs solve social dilemmas or solve coordination problems, and solutions to some social dilemmas are more important than others. Such practical decisions are partly

---

[13] See Pinker (2012, Ch. 3) for a discussion of how changes in internalized rules reinforced by governments tended to reduce violence in Europe and also for overviews of the anthropological literature on violence in days before written histories are available. Emsley (2021), however, notes that a good deal of the actual enforcement of laws was undertaken by families and volunteers, rather than by organized police forces until the nineteenth century, when police forces were organized by many cities. Community enforcement began with judges rather than organized law enforcement, with family enforcement and possies, rather than law-enforcing specialists. Readers of this chapter will not be surprised that both sheriff-based systems and the first police departments often suffered from problems of corruption.

matters of ethics—which rules are most important—and partly matters of economics—how much time and energy should be devoted to law enforcement? Should formal law enforcement be a part-time or full-time job of one or more persons, and should there be one or more levels of law—laws for the community and laws for the law enforcers?

Those choices, in turn, are influenced by the extent to which important customary laws are being violated—which, in turn, is determined by the strength of the weakest ethical dispositions in the community. If few or no important violations occur, formal law enforcement may not be helpful. If important violations are commonplace, then the advantages of formal law enforcement are substantial if agency problems can be overcome.

A consensus for creating and funding an enforcement agency requires agreement that significant problems exist, that particular laws should be enforced, that particular resources should be used to fund the agency, and that better enforcement will significantly increase law-abiding behavior and thereby make life in the community more attractive. If formal law enforcement is expected to have little effect on behavior, then it is worthwhile only if it is very inexpensive. The more law enforcement reduces nonconformity with community norms, the greater are the expenditures on law enforcement that can be justified. Such agreements are complex and not automatic, but were, for example, commonplace in the early European communities of North America.

Table 6.5 illustrates the kind of enforcement trade-offs associated with the Lockean natural state. Locke suggests that the internalized norms will include: "no one ought to harm another in his life, health, liberty, or possessions." Table 6.5 translates Locke's short list into contemporary categories of crime and includes another law (or fashion) with respect to language usage in public. Several of the rules to be enforced are ones that ameliorate the conflict and common problems analyzed in Chapter 2.

**Table 6.5** The Net Marginal Benefits of Law Enforcement and the Scope of Formal Law

| Murder | Enslavement | Assault | Theft | Destruction | Grammar |
|--------|-------------|---------|-------|-------------|---------|
| 30     | 28          | 26      | 23    | 21          | 6       |
| 29     | 27*         | 24      | 22*   | 19*         | 4       |
| 25*    | 18          | 20*     | 13    | 14          | 3       |
| 17     | 16          | 15      | 9     | 7           | 2       |
| 12     | 11          | 10      | 8     | 5           | 1       |

To simplify the discussion, the numbers are assumed to characterize a consensus about how an additional unit of enforcement contributes to the attractiveness of the community. They combine assessments of the effectiveness of efforts (how much a particular transgression is diminished by additional policing effort) and the normative and practical importance of such reductions (how morally and economically significant are the reductions in crime generated). The illustration also assumes that rule-following law enforcers have been found and employed by the community's law-enforcing agency, so that agency problems are minimal.

The cells with asterisks indicate how members of this particular tribe, village, or town would allocate the first 12 units of law enforcement effort (hours of enforcement, the number of enforcers, and so on). The numbers are intended to illustrate the nature of the trade-offs that jointly determine both the scope of law and the intensity of law enforcement. Other communities might reach different conclusions—for example, religiously based communities might place higher value on the regulation of speech. In the illustration, more of law-enforcement effort is devoted to reducing murder and assault than to the other crimes considered. This focus is partly determined by the damages associated with such crimes and partly by expectations concerning the effects of law enforcement on crime rates. Fewer resources are invested in preventing enslavement because it is easier to detect and enforcement is more effective at discouraging it than other crimes. In the case illustrated, a subset of customary laws is beyond the scope of the enforcement organizations' assignment. No resources are devoted to the enforcement of language rules.

The community may also acknowledge that the rules that should be enforced may change from time to time because deference to a community's norms may change as it increases in size or new circumstances emerge. The ideal pattern of customary law enforcement thus tends to be less stable than community norms. Similar changes may be called for if the most commonplace internalized norms change through time. Both sorts of changes may induce the community to alter the duties of their customary rule-enforcing organization.

In this manner, an agency initially created to improve conformity with long-standing customary laws may gradually become a common law system with standing procedures such as juries or village meetings that periodically adjust the rules the law enforcers are tasked with adjudicating and enforcing. In such common-law systems, the evolution of law tends to track the evolution of community norms, which in the Lockean setting would be revealed by changes in the consensus about the laws that should be enforced. The laws of such communities exhibit substantial stability for the same reason that personal normative systems do, but they are not chiseled into stone.

## Conclusions: Some Common Features of Simple Productive Governments

The analysis of this chapter has provided an analytical history for the emergence of customary law–based governments. It is broadly consistent with the available evidence on the origins of simple family-based and tribal governments developed by anthropological and archaeological research.[14] It has several implications about the nature of the earliest productive governments. First, governments (rule-enforcing organizations) that emerge from community consensus tend to have duties that are grounded in the normative theories and maxims of the communities in which rules are to be enforced. Such customary laws differ somewhat from community to community because solutions to critical social dilemmas vary to some extent, although commonalities in the problems confronted imply that many similarities and overlaps in customary laws exist. Such variations and commonalities have long been noted by travelers, anthropologists, and historians.

Second, the extent to which laws are well enforced is largely a consequence of the preexisting ethical dispositions of the person or persons granted law-enforcing and law interpreting authority. The extent to which such persons, termed *government officials* or *magistrates* here, perform their duties is substantially determined by their sense of obligation to do so. Dutiful conduct is most important at the upper levels of law enforcement—as in the courts and anti-corruption agencies—and tends to increase in importance as law-enforcing organizations (governments) increase in size and complexity. In the absence of such internalized duties, the laws will be unequally and corruptly applied. Rule enforcement by pragmatists tends to be extractive, and law-enforcing authority will be used to benefit members of government and their families, rather than the shared interests of the community governed.

Third, when customary laws are well enforced, the result tends to be a more virtuous community, because well-enforced customary laws provide additional reasons for persons to follow and internalize the community's ethos. Abiding by their community's customary laws reduces self-imposed guilt, socially imposed disapproval, and also avoids new formal punishments imposed by the law-enforcing system. Formal enforcement efforts thereby reinforce the habits of thought and action that produce dispositions to routinely make lawful decisions rather than ones that violate their community's ethos.

[14] A concise overview of this literature is provided by Fukuyama (2011, Chs. 3–4). See Emsley (2021, Chs. 1–3) for an overview of commonplace law-enforcing systems in the period before tax-financed police forces and judicial systems were organized.

Fourth, a community's customary laws are durable but not unchanging, and thus in the long run some systematic way of revising the laws enforced by a community's law-enforcing system is required. A community's ideal enforcement agency should not endlessly enforce the same rules as if they were chiseled into stone, but should enforce rules that are customary at the time of enforcement. To do so, standing procedures for adjusting the scope of governance may be adopted. In governments grounded on consensus, such procedures may take various forms: the advice of a wise leader or a council of elders, decisions reached at village meetings, the use of juries, and so forth.

The productive governments examined in this chapter are the simplest forms of government. Such systems or organizations make communities more attractive by reinforcing preexisting norms that ameliorate social dilemmas and coordination problems, rather than by creating new laws or providing services beyond those required to enforce existing customary laws. Governments grounded on custom and consensus may be quite simple—a single widely respected person may be empowered to determine whether a customary law has been violated and, if so, the appropriate punishment. Or, they may be more complex, involving large numbers of enforcers organized into a hierarchical bureaucracy with village oversight. But their productivity—the extent to which they make a community more attractive or not—is ultimately caused by the internalized norms of those tasked with law enforcement. Without norms that support the diligent application of the community's customary laws, even simple governments tend to become extractive rather than productive organizations.

Other forms of government—extractive governments—tend to be less productive because their aim is to advance the interests of those inside the governing organization, rather than those outside. Simple extractive governments may somewhat advance community interests by improving law enforcement; however, pragmatic rule enforcers tend to make a community less attractive for those outside government by extorting payments from law-abiding members of "their" community as well fines as from commoners that violate "their" community's laws.

Chapters 7 and 8 examine the importance of ethical dispositions in more complex and powerful governments.

# 7
# Ethics and Democratic Governance

> The essence of Government is power; and power, lodged as it must be
> in human hands, will ever be liable to abuse.
> —James Madison's 1829 "Speech at the Virginia
> Constitutional Convention," in Hunt (1910), p. 361

## Introduction: On the Ethical Foundations of Democratic Governance

To this point, the analytical narrative has explained how ethical dispositions contribute to the emergence of reasonably attractive viable communities with a bit of commerce and relatively simple law-enforcing organizations that could be considered governments. This chapter examines the roles of norms in the governance of larger, more complex societies. Its focus is again on productive or relatively good governance as opposed to extractive governments. In particular, it focuses on dilemmas associated with governance grounded in elections and majority-rule decision-making processes.

Majoritarian rules may be used to select government leaders or to directly make policy decisions for a community, as with town or village meetings. Such governments are not common historically, although autocracies are, which suggests that democracies are not naturally superior to autocracy as a method of governance. This chapter provides a possible explanation for the scarcity of democracies during most of recorded history and, indirectly, for the emergence of states grounded on elections as a viable alternative to various forms of autocracy and oligarchy in the nineteenth and twentieth centuries. (The latter was the focus of Congleton, 2011.)

The purpose of this chapter is not to explain the emergence of liberal democracy—a topic tackled in a previous book—but to explain why democratic governance tends to be problematic when it is not supported by normative dispositions within both the citizenry and the roster of government officials. This is not to say that voters and government officials have to internalize norms that are in some sense "democratic," although such norms do help

*Solving Social Dilemmas.* Roger D. Congleton, Oxford University Press. © Oxford University Press 2022.
DOI: 10.1093/oso/9780197642788.003.0007

with some of the problems confronted. Rather, it is to suggest that a subset of norms that emerge to solve other social dilemmas also provide support for democratic governance. To establish this conclusion, a series of democratic dilemmas are examined, and various normative solutions to them are discussed and illustrated.[1]

The focus of this chapter is on democratic governance is not intended to suggest that authoritarian regimes are unimportant phenomena or that they never benefit their communities. A community that forms an organization that extracts tribute from its neighbors may enrich itself through a variety of extractive enterprises. Empire builders are given substantial attention in most political histories in large part because well-organized extraction provides the resources to create glorious capital cities with impressive fortresses, monuments, and palaces. They also provide the resources to support court historians. Moreover, as Olson (2000) points out, stable extractive regimes have good reasons to ameliorate social dilemmas associated with conflict, commons problems, and trade within the domain ruled, because solutions to those problems increase possibilities for taxation and other forms of extraction. Such policies advance the pragmatic interests of rulers by providing additional resources for living luxurious lives (living like kings), eliciting deference within the communities ruled, and helping them to maintain their authority by providing resources for cementing alliances, suppressing rebellions, and obtaining tribute from nervous neighbors. Many persons in large extractive states thus benefit from their extractive governments.

However, that manner of increasing the prosperity of a community clearly has limits, because its success ultimately depends on the productive efforts of those subjected to its taxation, demands for tribute, and other forms of extraction. All forms of extraction reduce incentives to work, invest, and innovate and also tend to undermine the norms that would otherwise encourage such activities. Moreover, the rules enforced by authoritarian states tend to reward conformity and deference to authority, which tends to discourage creativity and reduce productive experimentation in areas other than those that help buttress the government's authority. Entrepreneurship and innovation are further diminished by the threats of confiscation and destruction

---

[1] An address prepared for the end of my term as president of the Public Choice Society drew upon the arguments of this chapter and was subsequently published in *Public Choice* (Congleton 2020a). Chapter 7 is thus the chapter that most overlaps with my previously published work, although the prose, tables, and figures differ from those in that address.

used to maintain control over both the home community and those subjugated. All these effects tend to reduce rates of commercial development and prosperity.

Such effects may be moderated when the rulers of extractive states internalize normative theories and cease being pure pragmatists. A subset of internalized norms may induce the powerful to moderate their rates of extraction or enhance the services provided, as with so-called enlightened despots and theories of noblesse oblige. The result can be a less extractive government and a more productive and prosperous society. In other cases, however, new internalized norms can lead to death and destruction. The most disastrous example of ideological rule in the twentieth century was probably Pol Pot's Cambodian government (1976–1979), which killed about 20% of its citizenry in pursuit of the normative goals of its leadership.

It should also be acknowledged that most contemporary liberal democracies passed through long periods of autocratic rule. Outside of North America, there are few if any records of productive town governments merging with others to create productive state governments, which merged with other states to create productive national governments. The more common path to democracy is the one explored in *Perfecting Parliament* (Congleton 2011) in which shifts in norms—in particular those associated with liberalism and technological innovation—emerged, spread, and created bargaining possibilities for (largely) peaceful constitutional reforms that gradually produced increasingly democratic and prosperous societies.

The focus of this chapter is on the democratic dilemmas that must be solved one way or another for democratic governance to be viable and to support attractive societies. For this purpose, it matters little whether election-based governance gradually emerges from autocracy through constitutional reforms or from social compacts within and among communities. The narrative, however, is most straightforward if the analysis is framed as a product of community-level agreements and experimentation, and that is the line of analysis adopted. It is also the most natural extension of the narrative developed to this point in this book.

Although democracy is often touted as having almost magical properties to generate "good" policies by its proponents, it turns out that achieving "good" outcomes from election-based governance is unlikely unless a variety of supportive normative dispositions are commonplace among voters and government officials. Majority rule is not a magical elixir for all the problems of governance. It may ameliorate some problems, but has its own problems that first must be overcome for it to be a useful method for choosing rule-makers or community policies.

## Majority Rule, the Median Voter, and Ethical Aspects of Democratic Public Policy

At this point in our analytical history of rule-based governance, we turn our focus to societies with relatively powerful democratic governments, leaving the distant past behind, as we did with respect to markets in our analysis of commercial development in Chapters 4 and 5. Let us assume that the problems associated with customary governance have been solved and that law enforcement is done diligently and honestly, which is to say, mostly in accord with a community's prevailing normative dispositions. Having established an effective rule-reinforcing agency, the community may come to recognize advantages that can be realized by delegating other authorities to government. With that in mind, a community may extend its customary law-enforcing agency's authority to enforce laws and implement policies that do more than reinforce the community's ethos.

Rather than also delegating rule-making authority to the law-enforcing organization, a separate procedure for selecting new laws is likely to be created. Such a division reduces the extractive temptations of both the law enforcers and lawmakers, although it does not eliminate them. The rule-making process is likely to be based on preexisting routines for making decisions in various subgroups of the community that undertake productive or amusing activities together, as in hunting coteries or story-swapping groups. With such "clubs" in mind, a rule-making council or community meeting may be adopted to revise old rules and create new ones, using consensus or majority-based decision rules. For example, new laws may be adopted that reduce previously neglected or new externality problems, prescribe methods through which resources are made available to the government and the manner in which government services are to be produced and distributed.

The new government is, in effect, divided into a legislative branch that makes laws and an executive branch that implements the laws adopted, which is an instance of the template for divided governance referred to as the "king and council" template in *Perfecting Parliament* and in other research. The legislature may have authority beyond making new laws; for example, it may be able to appoint and/or remove the top "executive" from his or her position of authority for malfeasance, and the executive branch may also have additional authority, including partial or full veto power over the proposals made by the legislative branch.[2]

---

[2] There are many advantages associated with such divided forms of government (Congleton 2010, 2013), but these are beyond the scope of this chapter.

The focus of this chapter is on the legislature rather than relationships between the executive and the legislature, which were analyzed at length in *Perfecting Parliament*. It is assumed that sufficiently ethical persons have been recruited for the executive branch and incentivized so that the decisions of the legislature are faithfully implemented by that branch of government. Of course, this is not likely to be perfectly done, but residual agency problems in the executive are ignored in the analysis that follows. Even with a completely responsive and honest bureaucracy, communities that count votes to select policies or representatives confront new problems that have to be overcome for the legislative branch to be a productive part of government, rather than an extractive or dysfunctional one.

To begin with, a legislature has to make decisions, and both consensus and majoritarian decision rules have their problems. The use of consensus for adopting new rules minimizes extractive temptations, because those at risk of being extracted from can veto the policies that would do so. However, the problem of holdouts reduces the number of useful rules that may be adopted because a single person or small group can block rules favored by a large supermajority. This problem is often addressed with what might be called "anti-hold-out norms," which imply that one should not hold out unless it is believed that many others in the group agree with one's opposition to a new policy or that the issue is "really" important. (Such norms are commonplace in faculty meetings, in my experience, where disagreements with the main opinion or the administrator's opinion are often greeted with chiding or are simply ignored.)

Majority rule is by now a commonplace procedure and is assumed to be the choice system used by the rule-making branch of the new more powerful community government. Majority rule may emerge as a procedure for allowing a fuller discourse to take place, to reduce the authority of subgroups of the community that are especially good at chiding; or because the jury-theorem properties of majority rule tend to produce better decisions.[3] It would be impossible to count votes before arithmetic and counting emerged; so doubtless, this method of group decision-making emerged long after consensus or supermajority rules were used.[4]

[3] For those unfamiliar with Condorcet's jury theorem, see Grofman et al. (1983) or Congleton (2007) for useful introductions and overview of its main implications. In cases in which the strong version of the median voter theorem holds (as developed later in this section), the median voter's assessments of the relative merits of a policy tends to be a robust and accurate estimate of his or her net benefits from public policy, even if he or she is not especially well-informed, as long as most voters are able to make an unbiased estimate of their benefits and costs from the policies or candidates being voted on.

[4] Congleton (2020c) provides evidence that agreement-based governments are likely to rely upon consensus or supermajority rules. Majority rule is used in the examples that follow, because it is so widely regarded to be the best rule for collective action—where "best" is used in its normative sense. Such majoritarian norms are likely to play a role in solving the last majoritarian dilemma examined in this paper.

# A Digression on the Weak and Strong Forms of the Median Voter Theorem

To illustrate how majority rule affects policy choices and why the ethics of moderate voters tend to be most important determinants of majoritarian decisions, consider a choice among candidates for one of the positions in a community's rule-making body. The first column of Table 7.1 lists pairs of candidates (represented by their letter indexes) who are running for office; the next three columns list the votes cast by three voters (or three types of voters); and the last column lists the outcome of the contest between the two candidates in the first column. Al's ideal candidate is L, Bernie's is N, and Cathy's is R. Unfortunately, their ideal candidates may not choose to run for office or may have been eliminated by earlier rounds of voting.

The letter-based index is assumed to characterize each candidate's combination of skill, trustworthiness, and policy preferences. For the purposes of illustration, the three voters (or types of voters) are assumed to reach the same conclusion about the index values of the various candidates running for office. They are also assumed to use what might be called "alphabetic distance" from their own hypothetical ideal candidate to rank the candidates running in a given electoral contest. The closer an alternative candidate comes to matching a voter's ideal letter, the higher he or she is ranked. (All three voters in Table 7.1 are thus "spatial voters" in the terminology of rational voter models.)

A series of hypothetical elections is modeled in Table 7.1 by posing alternative slates of candidates and using each voter's and candidate's index letters to assess their relative merits for each voter. Each voter casts his or her vote for the candidates on the ballot that are closest to his or her ideal candidate. The first four elections illustrate that a variety of outcomes are possible, depending

**Table 7.1** Votes and Outcomes

| Alternatives | Al (L) | Bernie (N) | Cathy (R) | Majority Outcome |
|---|---|---|---|---|
| L vs. O | L | O | O | O |
| M vs. R | M | M | R | M |
| R vs. Q | Q | Q | R | Q |
| O vs. N | N | N | O | N |
| N vs. L | L | N | N | N |
| N vs. M | M | N | N | N |
| N vs. R | N | N | R | N |

on the alternatives. However, note that Bernie always votes in favor of the outcome that is selected by the majority. His column of votes is the same as the outcome column.

The votes for the first three ballots illustrate what has been called the weak form of the median voter theorem. In pairwise elections, the median voter always votes with the majority. The median voter is the voter whose ideal point is the median of the distribution of voter ideals, which in this case is Bernie. Although, the right-hand column is the same as Bernie's votes, Bernie is not a dictator, he is simply "pivotal" in all elections. The weak form of the median voter theorem allows many possible outcomes, but the winner is always the policy or candidate preferred by the median voter, given the alternatives available.

The votes for the last four ballots illustrate the strong form of the median voter theorem. In those cases, one candidate dominates all the others, namely Bernie's ideal candidate (N). If the median voter's ideal candidate is one of the two options voted on, he or she will always win. The median voter's ideal may emerge from the voting process if, for example, the winner of the previous round is always one of the two candidates running for office. Once the median voter's ideal candidate is on the ballot, he or she will win all future elections unless the median voter changes his or her beliefs about the nature of an ideal candidate or the characteristics of a candidate on the ballot.[5]

Another electoral system in which convergence to the median voter's ideal often takes place is one in which two candidates actively compete for votes by adjusting their policy positions, while holding skill and character constant (neither of which is easily manipulated in the short run). As the two candidates adjust their policy positions, it turns out that candidates tend to converge on the policies favored by the median voter, because the candidate that is closest to the median voter's position always wins.

The desire to be re-elected induces candidates to behave in a manner that is consistent with both the ethical and practical interests of the voters they need to win over to remain in office, which is to say, with the ethos of their marginal supporters. Thus, each candidate's practical interests in returning to high office may be sufficient to induce them to behave in the manner that moderate voters want (at least in public).

---

[5] See, for example, Holcombe (1989) or Congleton and Bose (2010) for statistical evidence that a median voter model can account for the trajectory of both minor and major government programs in the West. See Fiorina and Plott (1978) or Palfrey (2016) for experimental evidence that moderate policies tend to emerge from majoritarian politics, albeit not always the median voter's ideal predicted by the Downsian (1957) model developed in Table 7.1. See Congleton (2004) for an overview of strong and weak versions of the median voter theorem.

Of course, that candidates behave morally in public does not always assure that they always do so in private, even when they are basically trustworthy men and women. Even candidates who are generally trustworthy may cheat in private (disavow their promises) when the temptations are sufficiently high. Candidates who undermine their reputations for trustworthiness, however, tend to lose to otherwise similar candidates whose behavior and platforms are more consistent with the norms of middle-of-the-road, moderate voters (or at least appear to be so).

Electoral competition of this sort thus implies that successful politicians share various characteristics: they will come across as trustworthy individuals and favor policy positions that advance the median voter's practical and ethical (ideological) interests. This is not to say they are clones, but rather that they are cut from the same cloth (or at least, are able to convincingly pretend to be so).[6]

## The Possible Dominance of Ethical Considerations in Mass Elections

The above discussion assumes that voters cast their votes in a sincere manner, which is to say, in a manner that accurately reflects their true evaluation of the relative merits of the candidates running for office, including both ethical and pragmatic considerations. There are several theories of strategic voting that imply that voters will not cast their votes in a sincere way, especially when a sequence of votes will determine the policy or candidate chosen. For example, given a choice among three candidates, strategic voters may vote in favor of their second choice when they believe their second choice has a far greater chance of winning than their true favorite. Alternatively, one might vote in favor of a weaker candidate in a primary election, because, if that person wins the primary, the strategic voter's preferred candidate will have an easier time winning the final round. However, in a mass election, one's vote has such a small effect on the outcome that there is little reason to vote dishonestly with such effects in mind, although some voters may do so.[7]

---

[6] Anthony Downs (1957) noted that there is a tendency for pragmatic candidates for high office to claim that their ideal policies are more or less the same as those of the median voter of the electorate of interest. In such cases, pragmatists tend to win elections but have promised to advance median voter interests. Whether they keep those promises or not depends partly on the institutions that shape their practical interests. If the median voter tends to vote against candidates who break their promises, this encourages even pragmatists to keep their promises—at least in public, much as pragmatic shopkeepers in Chapter 3 kept their promises—because most will wish to hold on to their elective offices.

[7] See Farquharson (1969) for the introduction of the strategic voting concept and speculations about its implications. Analyzing the implications of strategic voting has generated a very large literature on strategic voting and various tests of its propositions. For early experimental results on the existence of strategic

There is another type of strategic voting of greater interest for the purposes of this book called *expressive voting*. The idea behind expressive voting is that a single voter has relatively weak incentives to vote in a manner that gives his or her practical interests much weight, because he or she is unlikely to affect the final outcome in elections with large numbers of voters. However, an individual's vote will definitely affect what has been termed his or her "expressive" interests—his or her personal interest in affiliating oneself with policy positions that are deemed virtuous either for oneself or for the group to which one belongs or seeks membership. Virtuous feelings can be assured by simply casting one's vote based entirely on one's moral interests, if that vote is unlikely to affect the outcome.

The certain benefits of voting morally versus the uncertain (and very unlikely) chance that such a vote will ultimately affect the outcome in a manner that undermines one's practical interests gives voters in mass elections a good reason to ignore their practical interests and vote in a manner that makes them feel virtuous or appear virtuous to their friends and associates. Such voters cast their votes as if they are moral or ideological zealots—even when this is not the actually the case (Brennan and Hamlin 1998).

The expressive voting literature often argues that such moralistic voting tends to generate outcomes that conflict with practical interests and so electoral outcomes that may be worse in terms of overall net benefits when they are determined by expressive voting than when determined by the sincere voting assumed in Table 7.1. However, the fact that individuals behave more virtuously in voting booths than in their daily lives implies that electoral outcomes are more driven by moral considerations and thus are closer to the "good" as conceived by moderate voters than policies would otherwise be.

This may not be a "bad" outcome, unless the vision of the "good society" that lays behind such voting is unrealistic in ways that ultimately undermine its true "goodness." The "over" emphasis of moral considerations may be problematic, for example, if one's ethical dispositions are ill suited to broad public policies, even though they solve social dilemmas in one's day-to-day life. Dispositions that work well when all other actors share the same or a similar ethos may produce conflict and other policy mistakes in settings where that assumption is false. If, however, a voter or community's ethos generalizes to the broader issues of public policy, the results would generally be better—would generate a better society—than that generated by voting one's genuine

voting, see Eckel and Holt (1989). See Kliemt (1986) for a rationale for sincere voting, given what he terms the "veil of insignificance."

interests (which include practical goals, some of which are deemed immoral or incompatible with one's ideas about a good life or good society).

In either case, the personal advantages associated with expressive voting imply that analytical results based on the assumption of sincere voting should be regarded as the lower bound of the influence of ethical principles on the policies that emerge from democratic procedures.

## Majoritarian Dilemmas (1): Indecisiveness

Although the median voter model serves as a useful first approximation for many real-world elections and provides quite accurate predictions about the paths of policy in democracies, there are many choice settings in which no median voter exists. When no median voter exists, majority-rule decision-making lacks a stable equilibrium. The resultant disequilibria are sometimes termed *majoritarian cycling or indecisiveness.*

Indecisiveness is a problem that has been known about and studied since the rational choice literature on elections emerged after World War II with Black's (1948) and Arrow's (1951) path-breaking analyses of voting by rational self-interested individuals. And, unfortunately, such choice settings are sufficiently commonplace with respect to public policy that they tend to reduce the usefulness of majority rule as a decision-making process.[8]

This may surprise most readers who are unfamiliar with rational-choice-based voting models, because majority-based decision-making is so widely used in contemporary commercial societies. However, as was the case for our escape from other social dilemmas, it is likely that the cycling problem has been solved through normative dispositions present in the communities, legislatures, and committees that successfully make use of majoritarian procedures. Such norms can induce distributions of voter preferences with a (more or less) stable median where there would otherwise not be one.

## The Majoritarian Cycling Problem

The cycling problem is usually presented as an odd possibility associated with unlikely preferences, rather than a problem that is central to democratic

---

[8] See Mueller (2003) or Part II of Congleton, Grofman, and Voigt (2018) for overviews of the voting literature that is grounded in rational-choice models.

governance. However, when governments have the authority to purchase, finance, and distribute public services, they necessarily also have the ability to distribute the costs and benefits of those programs more or less as they please. In such cases, it turns out that there is no median voter if all voters are pragmatists. The same is true for policies that redistribute existing income or wealth and others that affect the paths of wealth accumulation by individuals and families. Because many public policies have distributional effects, there are many cases in which majority rule tends to be indecisive if voters are all pragmatists.

Avoiding such cycles can be critical to a community's survival. To illustrate why this is so, imagine a village located in a territory where roving bandits exist. The community unanimously agrees that a defensive wall would solve problems associated with the raiders and agrees to construct such a wall. Suppose that the wall can be constructed with 1,200 hours of labor and that the issue is how to divide the burden of constructing the wall. The burden is to be divided among three equally sized groups in the village— shepherds, masons, and merchants. The division is to be chosen using majority rule at a village assembly where proposals about how to divide the burden of constructing the wall are made and then voted on until a final decision is reached.

One proposal might be simply to divide the costs equally among the three groups. Such an apportionment may be plausibly justified by the common interests advanced by the wall. The distribution of the tax burden or cost shares can be written as $(T_{shepherd}, T_{mason}, T_{merchant})$, which in this case is (400, 400, 400). A second proposal for undertaking the wall's construction might be based on comparative advantage. Perhaps, the wall should be provided by those best able to provide the needed services, which in this case would be the masons, who are already skilled at wall construction. Some might argue that the middle-class masons should be public spirited and undertake most of the work of constructing the wall for the city, while the other groups contribute toward the materials (200, 800, 200). A third proposal might be developed based on differences in the ability of the townspeople to pay for the wall. Proponents of that view might argue that labor for constructing the wall might be hired from neighboring communities, rather than provided by the villagers themselves. Taxes would be collected to pay for hours of labor, rather than labor directly provided. In this case, it might be suggested that the community should take account of wealth differences among citizens. A very progressive tax schedule might be suggested that implies burdens of (100, 400, 700), with merchants paying the lion's share. Proponents of a fourth proposal might argue that the shepherds could benefit from learning the craft of masonry and, moreover, have more free time available for undertaking the required work. The shepherds arguably have the most to gain (new skills and higher future incomes) and the least to lose by undertaking most of the work. Indeed, it might be argued that the merchants are already carrying the burden of expanding the town's cathedral (600, 500, 100). All four burden-sharing systems are sufficient to assure that the wall is built and all are Pareto efficient in that it is impossible to reallocate the burden among the groups in a manner that makes one group better off without making another worse off.[9]

Note also that majority rule fails to settle on any of these proposed divisions of costs. Pragmatists all favor the option with the lowest cost share for themselves and will vote with that in mind. Given that, the first proposal loses to the second by a vote of two to one. The second similarly loses to the third by a vote of two to one, the third to the fourth, and the fourth to the first. There is a majoritarian cycle that continues ad infinitum and so no final decision is ever reached.

As a consequence, the defensive wall is not built, and the town continues to be ravaged by the roving bandits, or it may be annexed by a neighboring extractive regime.[10]

## Normative Solutions to the Cycling Problem

The majority cycling or indecision problem is another social dilemma that can be ameliorated through shared ethical dispositions. Internalized norms can eliminate the cycle by inducing a stable majority to favor one of the alternatives, despite their pecuniary interests.

Recall that all of four proposals had normative justifications. If two of the groups have internalized normative theories that imply that only one of the proposed distributions is fair or distributionally just, voting in favor of that distribution of cost shares would be deemed virtuous, and those voting to

---

[9] A Pareto-efficient tax system has the property that any reduction in the financial obligations of one group necessarily reduces the welfare of other taxpayers, holding revenues and planned expenditures constant.

[10] The four-step cycle is contrived for purposes of illustration. Such cycles are associated with every "dividing a pie" decision among pragmatists under majority rule. If each voter wants a larger slice of the pie (or smaller part of the tax burden to pay for a desired service), there is always another division of the pie that can achieve majority support. The four divisions of tax burden used are simply one of an infinite number of possible cycles.

adopt it would benefit from a virtue supplement—and additional subjective reward from voting morally (v)—that reduces the subjective net burden of that allocation of burden. The virtue supplement there by increases voter support for the morally favored option. For example, if two of the three groups had internalized a norm favoring equal burdens, the subjective burdens of the equal-share rule change from (400, 400, 400) to (400 − v, 400 − v, 400).

The more strongly the norm is internalized, the less costly is the normatively preferred apportionment. If $v$ is large enough, suggestions to shift away from the equal burden distribution would be unsuccessful, and the wall would be built—although the virtue supplement (or guilt decrement) would have to be fairly large in the series illustrated to completely stabilize the outcome. A widely shared norm concerning fair or just taxation tends to narrow the scope for cycling and can generate a unique stable division of net benefits when it is strongly held.[11]

Other types of norms can also stabilize or contribute to majoritarian stability. These include, for example, procedural norms. Minor refinements may be rejected for normative reasons such as "do not let the perfect be the enemy of the good" or "compromise makes the best policy." It may also be widely regarded as improper, unfair, or unsportsmanlike to reintroduce cost-sharing schemes that have already been rejected. Or, it might be the custom that the last vote at a town or village meeting is binding and the meeting times are determined by other durable customs.[12]

In all these ways, internalized norms with respect to distributive justice and proper procedures can increase the decisiveness of day-to-day democratic politics by increasing consensus and reducing the domain of policy deliberations. Without such stabilizing norms, majority rule would be a far less fruitful method of making collective decisions, and democratic governance would be both less viable and less attractive.

---

[11] In large-scale elections, the effects of moral expressive voting when commonplace make the virtue supplement even more important, because ethical ideas fully determine how such voters cast their votes. In such cases, norms would not have to be strongly internalized to be decisive.

[12] Usher (1981) demonstrates that tax systems that preserve the pre-tax rank order of income tend to be more stable under majority rule than those that do not. Such a rule tends to increase stability by limiting proposals within a relatively narrow range of tax systems. However, such a rule is not sufficient to generate a stable outcome unless ideas about distributive justice are sufficient to anchor the tax system.

Shepsle and Weingast (1981) suggest a variety of institutional provisions that could reduce the likelihood of such cycles, but such rules are unlikely to be adopted or followed without anchoring normative dispositions.

Most median voter models of public policy determination assume that the tax system used to finance the policy will not be changed by the policy of interest. The existence of a preexisting customary form of taxation would also solve the problem, but it again is ultimately grounded in normative dispositions that support the "old" over the "new," although such norms may have little to do with ideas about distributional justice.

# Majoritarian Dilemma (2): Redistribution and the Democratic Poverty Trap

Given a customary or ethically based ethos sufficient to assure that majority rule generates unique choices for most distributions of tax costs and service benefits, the next major problem involves whether the choices reached are ones that tend to produce attractive societies or not. Not every norm-constrained majoritarian choice does so. For example, concerns about excess redistribution and spending associated with democratic governance have long been expressed. Both Aristotle and Montesquieu, among many others, mention problems associated with the budgets and redistributive programs of democracies.

The redistributive dilemma can be illustrated with a few equations and a diagram based on the influential Meltzer and Richard (1981) model. Consider, for example, votes over policies with respect to a "demogrant" or universal income program of redistribution. Suppose that the demogrant is to be financed with an earmarked proportional tax on everyone's total income of $t$ percent. The tax revenues are used to provide equal lump-sum payments (demogrants) to all persons in society. Voter "i" would have an after-demogrant income of $X_i = (1 - t)Y_i + G$, where $Y_i$ is voter i's pretax income, t is the tax rate, and G is the demogrant received. Because the demogrant is paid for with an earmarked proportional tax on income, total expenditures on the demogrants equals the total tax revenue generated by the tax, $NG = \Sigma tYi$. This implies that the demogrant paid out is simply total tax revenue divided by the number of residents (N), which implies that the grant received (G) is simply t times average income, $G = tY^A$, where $Y^A$ is average income. The demogrant is ultimately determined by the tax rate selected and average income in the community of interest given that tax rate.

## The Majoritarian Poverty Trap

If individuals are pragmatic income maximizers, they will favor the tax-grant combination that maximizes their own after-tax income, which is the program that sets their marginal benefit from the demogrant equal to its marginal tax cost for the voter of interest, which occurs when $\left[ Y^A + t\dfrac{dY^A}{dt} \right] - \left[ Y_i - (1-t)\dfrac{dY_i}{dt} \right] = 0$. The first bracketed term can be interpreted as taxpayer i's marginal benefit from the program and the second as his or her marginal cost. However, this equality, perhaps surprisingly, may never occur.[13]

---

[13] This demogrant program is a slightly simplified version of that used in Meltzer and Richards (1981). Meltzer and Richards, however, failed to point out the possible corner solutions to a demogrant program

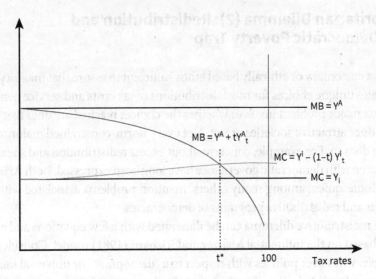

**Figure 7.1.** The majoritarian poverty trap.

Figure 7.1 illustrates two choice settings. In the first case, voters do not expect taxes to affect work effort or average income. In that case, the marginal benefit from the tax is $Y^A$ and its marginal cost is simply the voter's own income, $Y_i$. Thus, if a voter has below-average income, $Y_i < Y^A$, the marginal benefit of the demogrant exceeds its marginal cost over the entire 0%–100% range of possible taxes. As a consequence, their preferred tax rate is 100%, the upper bound of this tax and transfer program. (This is the case illustrated with the dark lines at the top and middle that characterize marginal benefits and marginal costs for persons with below-average income.) If a voter has above-average income, the reverse holds and his or her preferred tax rate is 0%. The distribution of pragmatic voter preferences is bimodal in this case. The median voter is determined by median income. If the median voter has below-average income, as is usually the case, the tax chosen will be 100% and the demogrant program will assure that every voter's income is the same and equal to the average income in the community of interest.[14]

when voters cast votes entirely based on their pecuniary interests. (Meltzer and Richards focus on case 2 below, in which the tax base is expected to fall as taxes increase.) Majoritarian stability and a median voter outcome emerge from the assumed structure of the transfer program: equal grants financed by a proportional tax, which implies a single control parameter (either the tax rate or demogrant size). The existence of other taxes and services are neglected here in order to focus on the redistributive choice.

[14] The analysis implicitly assumes that voters are either perfectly informed or that the information problems confronted by voters are indirectly solved through aggregation. The Condorcet Jury Theorem implies that if a sufficient number of voters are diligent policy analysts and have gathered enough information to cast reasonably intelligent votes (e.g., ones that are likely to advance their pragmatic and moral interests), then competitive electoral outcomes provide unbiased estimates of the policies that most advance the interests of the median voter (Congleton 2007).

In the second case illustrated in Figure 7.1, voters expect work, investment, and innovation to be reduced by taxation, and the marginal benefits and marginal costs are no longer horizontal straight lines. The demogrant system reduces each individual's own work effort so his/her marginal cost (reduction in after-tax personal income) rises with the tax rate. It has a similar effect on others in the economy and thus the marginal benefit (average income) falls as the tax rate increases. The downward-sloping MB line characterizes the new marginal benefit curve ($MBi = Y^A + tY^A_t$ with $Y^A_t < 0$). The upward-sloping MC line characterizes a below average income voter's marginal cost for the program, including his/her own reduction in work effort and income ($MCi = Y_i - (1 + t) Y_{it}$). These incentive effects tend to reduce the voter's ideal tax rate ($t^* < 100\%$), although it may still be quite high if the voter's income is well below average.

When the incentive effects are taken into account by voters, moderate voters prefer intermediate levels of taxation and transfers. This is the case focused on in Meltzer and Richard's classic paper on majoritarian redistribution (1981). The poorer the median voter is and the smaller the incentive effects are expected to be, the higher taxes and transfers tend to be. If the median voter is very poor, taxes can approach 100%, even if average personal income levels decline toward subsistence levels as a consequence of the tax and incentive effects. The result of a demogrant program in such communities is a population of more or less equally poor persons engaging in a good deal of leisure.

This is the democratic poverty trap. Such communities undertake more redistribution than would maximize aggregate income or utility.[15] An example of such policies is that of early twenty-first-century Venezuela, whose voters supported redistributive policies that transformed a relatively prosperous society with significant income inequality into a poor one with a more uniform distribution of income and much lower average income.

## Avoiding the Majoritarian Poverty Trap

A variety of internalized ethical dispositions and other norms can reduce a community's tendency to fall into the democratic poverty trap—although not all normative theories do so. For example, it may be widely believed that

---

[15] In Aristotle's *The Politics*, he recounts an instance in Magara, where redistribution led to the end of democracy. The popular leaders, in order to please their relatively poor supporters, expelled the wealthiest families, which allowed them to confiscate their wealth under Megara's property laws and use it to fund public services. This continued until they had created many exiles. The exiles organized and returned to reclaim their properties, defeated the people in battle, and established an oligarchy. He also suggests that similar redistributive ends to democracy occurred in Heraclea and Cyme (*The Politics*, 2nd edition, University of Chicago Press, 1992 p. 139).

market rewards reflect "just deserts," or that transfers undermine the virtue of recipients, or that private property is sacred and involuntary tax and transfer programs are tantamount to theft. Tax and transfer systems also tend to be reined in by utilitarian and a subset of contractarian norms. These support modest redistribution, but tend to oppose redistributive programs that reduce the average well-being of persons in a community. Other norms may limit the types of transfers deemed acceptable. For example, tax-financed insurance services may be regarded as useful risk-sharing, rather than redistribution, and redistribution per se may be regarded to be immoral except in extraordinary circumstances.

Violating norms that tend to rein in redistribution would induce feelings of wrongness or guilt. Thus, if the median voter has internalized redistribution-inhibiting norms, his or her marginal cost function of redistribution tends to be higher than that of an otherwise similar pragmatist. Figure 7.2 illustrates how the marginal cost-increasing effects of such internalized norms affect a demogrant program. A voter's marginal subjective burden from taxation used to finance transfer programs is increased—here by amount $g(t)$—which represents the marginal guilt or loss of self-esteem associated with inappropriate types and levels of taxation or transfers (the blue line). The greater the guilt or loss of self-esteem associated with redistribution is at the margin, the smaller is the ideal demogrant program for persons with below-average income. The new ideal tax rate is characterized by tax rate $t^{**}$ in the diagram.

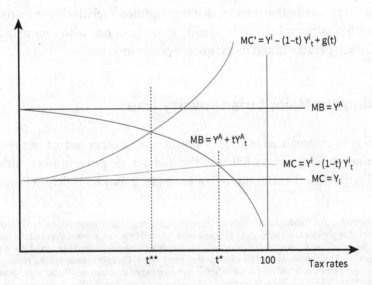

Figure 7.2. Escape from the majoritarian poverty trap.

The ideal demogrant program of such voters tends to be smaller—possibly much smaller—than ones based on economic interests alone, $t^{**} < t^* < 100$. As a consequence, the incentive effects of the tax and redistribution system are smaller, and the society is more prosperous.

Evidence that norms inhibited redistribution in the West during the nineteenth and early twentieth centuries is apparent in the types of transfer programs adopted during that period. This was the period in which the first "safety net" programs were adopted by national governments, and these typically provided benefits only to persons experiencing unusual bad luck (unemployment or ill health), rather than to all those earning below-average income. Other norms, such as egalitarianism and Rawls's ([1971] 2009) maximin characterization of distributive justice tend to encourage rather than limit redistribution. Such norms make the democratic poverty trap more, rather than less, likely.

## A Digression on Ethics and Ongoing Electoral Politics in Well-Functioning Democracies

In well-functioning representative democracies, candidates compete in elections every few years, and voters choose which candidates will be given their votes. Voter decisions are partly based on a candidate's stated policy positions, as developed by Downs, but also based on competence and character assessments that help voters determine whether they can trust a candidate or party to implement (or at least try to implement) their promised policies. Character and competence assessment also help voters to imagine the kinds of policies a candidate for office is likely to adopt behind closed doors, where few if any voters will ever know of the decisions reached.

To illustrate the effect of character, suppose that several candidates are running in an intra-party or primary election, and being from the same party, they adopt similar positions on most issues. In this case, voters can only distinguish among candidates by assessing differences among their skills as policy analysts and their character. Does a candidate have the talent and experience to choose effective policies? Would his or her understanding of "good" policies be the one that advantages the voter economically or by advancing his/her norms regarding a "good" society? Can the candidate of interest be trusted to do the "right" thing, even when I am not watching?

Table 7.2 characterizes a series of imaginary candidates with various combinations of skills and trustworthiness. The ideal candidate is one that is both skilled and trustworthy. However, the candidates actually running for office

**Table 7.2** Voter Rankings of Candidates Making Similar Promises, but with Different Ethical Dispositions and Skills as a Policy Analyst or Supervisor of Such Analysts

|                        | High Skill | Moderate Skill | Low Skill |
| ---------------------- | ---------- | -------------- | --------- |
| Very trustworthy       | 10         | 8              | 6         |
| Moderately trustworthy | 7          | 6              | 5         |
| Not trustworthy        | 5          | 4              | 3         |

are often less than ideal. In a choice between a highly skilled but untrustworthy candidate and a less skilled but trustworthy one, a typical voter (at least the one characterized by Table 7.2) may vote for the less skilled but more trustworthy candidate, because he or she is anticipated to be a better agent for that voter, in spite of his or her lack of skill as a policy analyst.

If this is a reasonable characterization of how voters rank candidates, we would expect to see many advertisements during campaigns for high office that focus on character, perhaps even more frequently than advertisements that provide detailed information about a candidate's policy positions. Such advertisements might, for example, tout a candidate's own character and trustworthiness while denigrating that of their opponent's. Without having spent a lot of time watching and tabulating such advertisements, it is certainly my impression that candidate ads rarely mention specific policy positions and very often mention a candidate's own "outstanding" character and the "defects" of their rival's character.

Insofar as voters accurately assess candidate character, the candidates elected would tend to be among those perceived to be most trustworthy, although not necessarily very good policy analysts. This in turn provides a selection mechanism through which relatively ethical agents tend to occupy the highest posts in government, as required to address the problems discussed in this chapter and the previous one. This is not to say that the persons elected to high office are all angels or idealistic zealots, only that they tend to be relatively ethical, trustworthy, and predictable. Such electoral outcomes are consistent with the theory developed herein but are not consistent with an entirely pragmatic view of voters and politicians, whose campaigns would tend to be more policy oriented, although their post-election behavior would be less trustworthy and predictable.

The latter would be especially true of pragmatic officeholders at the end of their terms because re-election aims would fail to constrain their behavior. That most candidates do not shift their positions radically in their last term of office suggests that their behavior is more grounded in character and promises made in the past than a pragmatist's would have been.[16]

## Majoritarian Dilemma (3): Why Hold the Next Election?

Although government officials "make and formalize rules," the rule-makers of constitutional democracies are not themselves above the law. They are constrained by ordinary laws and customs and by duties that are specific to their positions of authority. Elected government officials and coalitions of such government officials (political parties) also are supposed to abide by constitutional laws and norms that characterize proper procedures for making new laws and the types of laws (and other policies) that can be lawfully adopted.

Among the most important rules for governing officials in a democracy is the requirement that open and fair elections for their offices be held every few years. Periodic elections tend to align the interests of government officials with those of moderate voters and also provide a peaceful systematic way for voters to replace incompetent, untrustworthy, and corrupt officials with others expected to be better. What is of interest for the purposes of this section is the extent to which ethical theories and their associated dispositions affect the likelihood that such rules are actually followed. (The selection and modification of the formal procedural rules and constraints that are supposed to govern the behavior of elected officials are taken up in Chapter 8.)

### Incumbent Disinterest in Holding the Next Election

For those living in well-functioning democracies, it may be a surprise that it is not usually in the interest of pragmatic officeholders or their supporters to hold the next election. Holding the next election can only make current officeholders and those supporting them worse off. If current officeholders lose that election, they return to careers that they find less attractive than their current offices. If they win, they are no better off than they currently are. They continue to hold their offices of authority. The same is true for their supporters. They are worse off if their preferred incumbents lose, because of policy changes anticipated by their successors. If their preferred incumbents

---

[16] Lott and Bronars (1993), for example, find little or no evidence of significant policy or voting changes in a candidate's last term of office.

win, the same policies or trajectory of policies remain in place and they are no better off. This disinterest in holding future elections tends to be true for both pragmatic and many moral voters in the coalition that elected the current incumbents. As long as incumbents are considered trustworthy and reasonably competent, and their supporters care more about government policy than constitutionality or democracy, per se, why bother holding the next election?[17]

## Normative Support for Elections

Of course, not all voters are indifferent to constitutional procedures. Voters who believe that democratic procedures are an important feature of a good society will support holding the next election, even if it puts their preferred policies at risk. In addition, pragmatic voters whose preferred party lost the last election all favor holding the next election so that their preferred party might win the election and its associated policies adopted. Thus, a coalition of "constitutionalists" from the incumbent party(s) and pragmatists favoring other candidates and parties might be sufficient to guarantee that the next election is held. Whether this is so depends on the distribution and strength of the constitutional norms that have been internalized by the "constitutionalists" in the persons and parties holding office.

Let us suppose that the legislature has the authority to postpone elections and alter election laws. It might, for example, have the power to postpone elections or modify election laws during "emergencies." In this case, continuing elections ultimately depends on the strength of the internalized constitutional norms of the persons holding seats in the legislature. In particular, it depends on the norms of members of the current majority coalition. Table 7.3 illustrates a plausible rank order of informal and formal constitutional reforms by legislators. Pragmatic legislators in the current majority coalition would all favor changes in rules that reduce electoral competition. Members of the current majority coalition who are weak constitutionalists might favor disenfranchising some members of the party that lost the previous election but oppose endlessly postponing the next election or canceling all future elections ($g_1 < 2$ and $g_2 > 3$). Legislators who are strong constitutionalists

---

[17] The word "trustworthy" is an important caveat. If there is a significant risk that those elected to high office would cease promoting the interests they promised to support during their campaigns, holding regular elections would reduce losses from official malfeasance. In cases in which incumbents are not deemed sufficiently trustworthy, even pragmatists will support elections, although they would prefer elections in which opposition interests are underrepresented or undercounted.

**Table 7.3** Majority Coalition Member Support for Holding Next Election or Not, with and without Moral Support for Democracy

|  | Pragmatist | Weak Constitutionalist | Strong Constitutionalist |
|---|---|---|---|
| Hold next election | 6 | 6 | 6 |
| Disenfranchise some opposition party voters | 8 | $8 - g_1$ | $8 - G_1$ |
| Cancel next election | 9 | $9 - g_2$ | $9 - G_2$ |

Note: If strong constitutionalists are pivotal, voting rights and elections will be sustained when $G_2 > 3$ and $G_1 > 2$.

would oppose all reforms that reduce the openness and fairness of elections ($G_2 > g_2 > 3$ and $G_1 > g_1 > 2$).

The pragmatists of the party out of power would all favor holding the next election, as would their constitutionalists. Thus, if there are a sufficient number of constitutionalists among the members of the ruling coalition, a coalition of legislators from the party out of power and the constitutionalists of the party in power would have veto power over major procedural reforms. Reforms that end future elections would be blocked if a sufficient number of members of the ruling party are weak or strong constitutionalists. Reforms that favor the present majority over the minority would be blocked if a sufficient number of the ruling party are strong constitutionalists.

It is important to note that continuing support for elections does not require that a majority of legislators be constitutionalists, but it does require a substantial minority of the legislators in all significant parties to be constitutionalists, rather than pragmatists or idealists who are indifferent to constitutional procedures. The greater the differences in the anticipated policies of the parties in and out of power, the stronger the requisite normative support by incumbent constitutionalists has to be for antidemocraticreforms to be blocked.[18]

The temptation for incumbent constitutionalists to accept electoral reforms that favor their own party in future elections is increased when it is expected that the next majority coalition may have fewer "constitutionalists" among

---

[18] Here, it bears noting that reforms that protect the positions of all incumbents may well be adopted if they do not confer a permanent advantage on a particular coalition or party. In the United States, for example, most representatives to the House of Representatives are elected from "safe" districts in which supporters of the current legislator (or his or her party) are far more common than those of his or her opposition.

its members and so be more inclined to selectively disenfranchise voters or cancel future elections. In such cases, constitutionalists of the current majority who anticipate being permanently in the minority in the future may be inclined to "lock in" their advantages, rather than take a chance on the constitutional norms of future majorities that are expected to adopt electoral reforms favoring their own party in future elections. Such expectations produce a game format referred to as a centipede game. They increase the net benefits of reforms that effectively end democracy and may do so sufficiently that they induce such "reforms" after the first competitive election is held—as happened in most African countries after independence in the 1950s and 1960s.

In initially open and fair electoral systems, it is voters that ultimately determine the mix of candidate types elected to the legislature. The analysis of the previous sections implies that the legislators holding office have been judged to be reasonably trustworthy and hold ideas about "the good society" that are similar to those of pivotal voters. Unfortunately, such ideas and their associated norms do not always include support for open and fair elections or other constitutional procedures. But if they do, open and competitive elections may continue to be held.

## Majoritarian Dilemma (4): Voter Ignorance and the Impacts of Interest Groups

Having ameliorated problems associated with law enforcement, indecision, poverty-inducing redistribution, and ongoing elections through various internalized norms—sometimes referred to as political culture—our relatively good democratic government is now up and running—more or less as posited in classic books by Downs (1957) and Buchanan and Tullock (1962), but with ethical support that solves problems neglected in those books. The government that has emerged is relatively "good" in that it advances ideas about the good life and good society held by moderate voters and its core procedures are regarded to be fair and effective enough to be acceptable to most non-moderate voters. Such governments are "good" partly because of institutional design—elections tend to focus attention on issues of broad interest, and divided government tends to reduce temptations for extractive policies—but also because of ethical dispositions that support diligent rule-bound governance and policies that tend to produce good attractive results.

We now turn to another source of problems associated with majoritarian governance, namely losses associated with corruption and other efforts to obtain preferential public policies that advance narrow rather than broadly shared interests. In well-functioning democracies, such problems are ultimately consequences of voter ignorance, which is doubtless lower today than it was in the past, but it is still substantial. With the scale of governance today it is impossible for any single individual to fully master the nuances of all public policies—although some theories allow their general properties to be reasonably well understood, as with the median voter theorem and public economics. The median voter theorem implies that moderate voter interests tend to determine the broad outlines of policies that voters are familiar with—but it does not have clear implications about the details of policies that voters are unlikely to ever know about.

We are born into the world knowing very little and gradually learn about our local environment, possibilities for changing it, and methods for evaluating those possibilities. Although voters have all learned much by the time they reach voting age, they all remain more than a bit ignorant about many things that would be useful to know. Much of what has been learned has been conveyed to them by others and thus, insofar as their remaining ignorance is recognized, voters continue to remain interested in information provided by others in their communities.

Consequently, information provided by others remains to be an important source of knowledge about alternative public policies and their relative merits. Through that information, we may learn about yet unsolved social dilemmas, possible solutions to those problems, and be able to determine which solution is likely to be most effective; alternatively, we may be misled into believing things that are not true about the extent of problems confronted and their possible solutions. Although voters do not blindly accept all that they are told, they simply do not have the time or information-gathering and -processing capacity to master all the nuances of day-to-day life or public policy on their own. As a consequence, in policy areas where voter ignorance prevails, opportunities for policymaking mischief abound.

Knowing that individuals are open to learning from others and hence persuadable, some members of the community will attempt to influence the opinions of others. Firms do so through advertising to increase consumer purchases, office seekers through advertising and public appearances expected to increase their vote shares, and interest groups (rent seekers) undertake persuasive campaigns to increase support for public policies that they expect to profit from. The groups that undertake such persuasive campaigns tend to be relatively small ones with relatively intense interests, because it is such groups that are most likely to overcome their problems of free-riding (Olson 1965).

Persuasion is not usually easy, because we are all aware that efforts to win our approval through false claims are commonplace; thus, we "filter" the messages sent our way to adjust for the perceived biases in what we see, hear, and read. However, it is not possible to do so perfectly, and consequently both pragmatists and moralists more than occasionally succeed in persuading us to favor policies that advance their own interests without benefiting most of the rest.

Persuasive campaigns can induce mistaken choices by voters, and government officials, for much the same reason that merchants occasionally profit from fraudulent offers (Congleton 1986, 2001). In areas in which public policies are complex, voters and government officials often lack the information necessary to fully understand the consequences of the policies being touted.

Such efforts generate two problems for systems of governance grounded in elections. First, to the extent that they are successful, such efforts generate policies that tend to make a society less, rather than more, attractive—at least for moderate voters. Second, to the extent that the efforts of rival groups largely offset each other or are otherwise ineffective, considerable time and energy are wasted in persuasive contests. The public choice literature refers to such losses as rent-seeking losses.[19]

## Rent-Seeking and Rent-Seeking Losses

The policies favored by pragmatic groups are often—although not always—narrow ones that confer net benefits on a group's members (often higher profits) and net costs on persons outside the interest group (often in the form of higher prices or taxes). The disadvantages of such policies are obvious. All such lobbying efforts can be considered wasteful in that they reduce rather than increase aggregate utility, or shift policies away from ones deemed "good" by moderate voters. Such costs can be significant because the persuasive efforts used to induce such policies may divert considerable resources from productive to unproductive or extractive purposes.

---

[19] To an economist, a "rent" is unearned income, rather than an amount paid to use a room or house. Mancur Olson (1965) developed analytical models that explained why relatively few interest groups attempt to advance general interests. Gordon Tullock (1967, 1980) more fully accounted for the losses associated with such efforts by taking account of the losses associated with the process of lobbying and similar activities, which came to be called *rent-seeking*, a term coined by Anne Krueger (1974) in her research on losses from the monopoly policies of India and Turkey. The academic literature on rent-seeking is too large and complex to summarize here. For overviews of the literature and illustrative applications, see Congleton, Hillman, and Konrad (2008) and Congleton and Hillman (2015).

**Table 7.4** A Rent-Seeking Contest and the Dissipation of Profits

|  |  | Lobbyists Employed by Group A | | |
| --- | --- | --- | --- | --- |
|  |  | 1<br>(G, A) | 10<br>(G, A) | 20<br>(G, A) |
| Lobbyists Employed<br>by Group G | 1 | (6, 6) | (4, 7) | (1, 8) |
|  | 10 | (7, 4) | (5, 5) | (2, 6) |
|  | 20 | (8, 1) | (6, 2) | (3, 3) |

Table 7.4 illustrates the escalating tendency of persuasive campaigns undertaken by lobbyists and the effects that competition has on the net returns realized by the groups participating in such political contests. The Nash equilibrium implies that a relatively high degree of lobbying efforts and relatively low average profits are typical features of such contests. Although winners do relatively well, the losers do not. In evenly matched contests of the sort illustrated, each of the rival organizations would benefit if all would limit the extent to which their resources are invested in this process. However, agreements that do so are not credible, because the rivals individually would each benefit from greater investments than agreed to, regardless of whether they expect others to adhere to the agreement or not.

As a consequence, political conflict within reasonably well-functioning democracies tends to be peaceful, but nonetheless often exhibits escalating properties that are not entirely dissimilar to Hobbes's war of every man against every other.[20]

When economic interest groups succeed in their persuasive campaigns to obtain trade advantages, those outside the contest are normally made worse off. Commercial groups, for example, often lobby for entry barriers of various kinds that shield their members from competition and thereby generate higher prices for consumers, which imply that fewer goods and services are sold, but higher profits are realized by the merchants benefiting from reduced competition. The public policies sought include tax preferences (loopholes), protective tariffs, import quotas, regulations with grandfather clauses (which impose higher costs on new entrants), narrowly targeted subsidies, and explicit grants of monopoly privilege. Suppliers of government services also routinely attempt to secure better contract terms than possible in competitive

[20] Some models of rent-seeking imply that all the profits generated by persuasive contests are "dissipated" by rent-seeking efforts. See Tullock (1967) or Hillman and Samet (1987). Other models suggest that less than full dissipation occurs, as in game matrix 7.3 (Congleton 1980). See Wärneryd (2019) for an overview of such models. Mathematical analyses of rent-seeking contests began with Tullock (1980).

markets, which tends to make public services more costly and taxes higher than necessary.

In the illustrating game, the cost of lobbying is indicated by changes in total profits as one moves down the diagonal, which may be presumed to generate the same expected profits, an equal division of rents, between the two equally effective interest groups. Half of the potential profits $[(6 + 6) - (3 + 3) = 6]$ are consumed in the two-group lobbying contest illustrated.

The "crony capitalism" that emerges from societies in which rent-seeking is commonplace also tends to increase social, political, and economic inequality. The consequent higher prices, lower quality, more limited choices, and higher taxes also tend to reduce the extent and scope of commerce. Together these effects also tend to increase tensions and conflict between the organized groups that benefit (sometimes referred to as "the elite") and the unorganized groups that do not. All these effects tend to reduce a community's prosperity.

## Ethical Interest Groups

Fortunately, not all interest groups are organized in the pursuit of narrow interests. Many groups are organized to pursue broad interests or at least interests that their members regard to be broad. For example, the utilitarian advocacy groups of the nineteenth century often organized to promote policies that they believed would increase average welfare in their societies, such as suffrage expansion, public education, emancipation, and free trade.[21] The efforts of such groups may counter the efforts of rent-seeking groups by lobbying against barriers to voluntary exchange and against favoritism and corruption in governance. In cases in which there are truly general interests being advocated, the results may be significant improvements in public policy (from the perspective of the community's shared ethos and/or that of moderate voters). Such groups may lobby, for example, for the passage of laws that reduce rent-seeking and for constitutional reforms that reduce the ability of governments to pass legislation that narrowly benefits particular interests or regions of the territory governed.

When groups are believed to have ethical, rather than pragmatic, motives, their advice is more likely to be listened to, because such groups are regarded to be less likely to be trying to fool voters into believing things that are not

---

[21] For somewhat unflattering overviews of utilitarian arguments regarding British colonial policies during the nineteenth century, which included many of the above policy aims, see Schultz and Varouxakis (2005). Bentham, perhaps surprisingly, turns out to be the most sophisticated utilitarian analyst of such policies.

entirely true. That such groups tend to be more influential (even if fewer in number) than groups attempting to advance narrow economic or political interests is evident in that the latter often cloak their arguments in "general" interest terms, with the hope of being more persuasive—even when their main aim is higher profits or narrowly favorable government policies.

Groups advocating narrow interests would not bother to do so unless normative arguments were generally more persuasive than narrowly self-interested ones. Very few groups openly argue that specific policies are desirable only because they increase an interest group's profits or political power—although lobbying activities are often rooted in such practical aims.

When ethical groups are successful (and their ideas are not entirely wrong or infeasible), they avoid one of the two sources of losses associated with interest group politics. Polices become more likely to advance shared interests, rather than less so. Resources, however, are still consumed in persuasive contests. Insofar as general benefits are obtained, such costs may be regarded as useful investments rather than a drag on social progress as long as the policies advocated actually do advance shared interests.

Unfortunately, when groups with different visions of the good society compete against each other and all favor quite different policies, the results are similar to those illustrated in Table 7.4. The efforts of opposing ideological groups largely offset each other's, tend to escalate, and produce nontrivial losses as resources are diverted from more generally beneficial uses (Congleton 1991b). Indeed, ideological contests to influence or control government policy sometimes produce civil wars.

Evidence that ethically motivated interest groups on balance have been productive in the West for most of the past century or two, rather than destructive, is provided by the fact that the most attractive contemporary societies provide broad rights to assemble and petition government, rather than rules that forbid or discourage such activities.[22]

## Not All Normative Systems of Rules Generalize to Democratic Politics

In the very long run, social evolution favors the emergence of normative systems that support economic and political systems that generate the most

---

[22] To the extent that trust increases with the degree that policies advance moral rather than pragmatic ends, such "reformed" governments are likely to be more trusted than ones that lack "proper" incentives or are staffed by persons without widely accepted values.

attractive communities. Emigration patterns, for example, are nearly all from societies with less commercial activity to those that have more, and away from countries where corruption is commonplace to countries where it is less so. However, large-scale non-extractive governance and commercial societies are relatively new, and thus the norms that support such systems cannot have emerged through trial and error within such social systems over centuries of experimentation. Rather, it is likely that such systems emerged from innovations and experimentation with normative theories worked out within earlier political-economic systems where they resolved other older dilemmas and incidentally provided useful support for both liberal democracy and commercial societies. That such systems are extraordinarily rare in human history and that extractive governments and mercantilism are historically commonplace suggests that the norms required to support the new more open systems are also historically rare.

Innovations that played roles in the emergence of contemporary democratic and market systems included both positive and normative theories. New positive theories that implied that markets networks are largely self-regulating and tend to produce prosperity were developed in the eighteenth and early nineteenth centuries, most obviously in Adam Smith's (1776) *Wealth of Nations*. The manner in which election-based governments operate was carefully analyzed at about the same time by Montesquieu (1748) and in the *Federalist Papers*, the latter of which were originally published as editorials in New York newspapers in the late 1770s. These theories, together with experience that was largely consistent with those theories, changed the minds of many persons who had previously expected quite different outcomes from open competitive commercial and political systems. Further support was provided by normative theories that concluded that lives and societies in which commerce played large roles can be "good" gradually replaced those that implied that such lives and societies were necessarily "bad," and by theories that suggested that a "good" government is grounded in the consent of the governed, rather than divine approval for governing elites.

Both types of new theories, insofar as they were believed, would have reduced resistance to reforms that tended to support commercial careers and societies. Other normative theories that provided support for governments grounded on popular sovereignty and equal protection of the law also tended to support broad suffrage, which became more commonplace during roughly the same period in which the commercial society emerged. Together, these normative trends reduced opposition to political reforms that tended to broaden suffrage and reduce regulations that limited entry into careers and markets.

After a century or two of subsequent theoretical innovations that were largely in accord with the works of Smith, Montesquieu, and Madison, the collection of positive and normative theories associated with neoclassical economics and political liberalism provided more integrated support for the ideas and reforms that helped produce what some term *democratic capitalism*—social systems that include liberal democratic constitutions, mass education, extensive specialization, and extended commercial networks. (Evidence of such trends is provided in Part III of this book.)

Of course, not all of the norms that support the expansion of markets also support effective good governance. For example, norms that tend to improve commercial systems have the opposite effect on political transactions. Agreements to terms of trade in markets tend to make the directly affected parties better off, and no one (or very few) persons worse off. In contrast, agreements to terms of trade between interest groups and government officials tend to make the direct participants better off, while making most others in the community worse off. Competition among sellers for the favors of buyers in private markets tends to reduce prices and increase quality, which tends to benefit most members of the community and increase the extent to which goods and services are produced and sold. Competition among interest groups for the favors of politicians, bureaucrats, and voters often worsen public policies while consuming more and more resources in unproductive conflict over those policies.

Norms that support voluntary exchange and competition in markets tend to make communities more attractive by increasing the net benefits associated with commerce. Norms that support the same activities in political systems tend to make communities less attractive, by reducing the net benefits of governance. When exactly the same ethical principles are applied to commerce and rent-seeking, they tend to have opposite effects on the attractiveness of a community!

Although norms that support honesty, diligence, and promise keeping are useful in most social systems, few other norms generalize to both democratic politics and commercial systems.

## Conclusions: Ethics and Democratic Governance

This chapter has accepted the widely held contemporary constitutional norms that "good" governments are grounded in the consent of the governed and that the persons selected for positions of the greatest authority in governments should be chosen through open, competitive elections. The governments characterized by these two features are democratic, although as demon-strated, they are not necessarily very effective or good. A series of democratic dilemmas have to be overcome for majoritarian-based governance to advance broadly shared interests, rather than be extractive. The chapter provided an overview of several of the most important democratic dilemmas, which, like the dilemmas reviewed in previous chapters, exist in many forms within representative governments grounded in elections.

Policymaking via majority rule may be indecisive, the policies chosen may impoverish a nation, elections may be canceled or unfairly conducted, bribery and corruption may be commonplace, and interest groups may be able to secure policies that favor themselves and harm almost everyone else. In sum, democratic governments can be corrupt and extractive, rather than produc-tive. Nor does a short series of elections assure that a democracy will be self-sustaining. The interests of incumbents and many of their supporters tend to favor unfair elections in which their votes count for more than those whose candidates lost the previous election.

In order for democratic governance to produce "good" results—meaning in this case results that broadly advance the electorate's shared practical and eth-ical goals—the voters have to have normative dispositions that induce them to be somewhat informed about policies and candidates for office. They must be interested in the ethics or character of the persons they vote for, generally opposed to favoritism, and generally supportive of ongoing routine and open elections—even in cases in which the latter conflict to some degree with their practical or ideological interests. For democracies to produce "good" results, in the sense of advancing broadly shared interests, these and many other conditions to be met.

Such liberal predilections can be reinforced with institutional designs. For example, a formal constitution may support equality before the law, specify or support open and competitive elections, and include a constitutional court with the authority to make sure that constitutional provisions are followed, which is staffed by persons committed to that end and whose judgments will be found persuasive by most voters and most officials in government. They may also specify formal procedures for amendment that allow governance to adapt to new circumstances, but which block informal amendments that tend to undermine procedures thought to be fair and supportive of non-extractive rule.

However, such institutions are unlikely to be in place unless a superma-jority of the electorate and officeholders believe that they are necessary for "good" government—as the term "good" is generally understood by most residents (or at least moderate voters) of the territory of interest. And, even when in place, such constitutional provisions are unlikely to be followed if most officeholders are pragmatists rather than persons with supportive ethical dispositions.

With respect to economic development, the analyses undertaken suggest that the policies of well-functioning democracies may reinforce or impede commercialization according to the prevailing ethos of the electorate of interest. If commerce is widely regarded to be a good or praiseworthy activity, public policies will tend to support it; if not, public policies will impede, rather than support, economic development. Neither good governance nor prosperity are necessary features of societies with election-based governance.

The next chapter takes up what might be called the selection of a society's constitution or grounding institutions. One can imagine democratic governance and commercial societies emerging by various combinations of accident and intent, but once they have done so, would they be sustained by subsequent constitutional choices or the broadest of public policies? As readers might anticipate, whether they do or do not depends in large part on the most commonplace ethical dispositions of voters and politicians.[23]

---

[23] Evidence in support of the variety of democratically chosen economic policies can be found the work of De Haan and Sturm (2003), who found only a weak correlation between democratic governance and economic freedom. Previously, Gwartney, Lawson, and Holcombe (1999) had found a strong correlation between a vector of policies that they regard to be market supporting (summarized as an economic freedom index) and income and growth rates. With respect to other aspects of a community's ethos or political culture, Mauro (1995) provided evidence that corruption reduces investment and economic growth rates. Aidt (2016) discussed connections between rent-seeking and corruption, which are not always equivalent activities.

# 8

# Choosing a Good Society

> There is a limit to the legitimate interference of collective opinion
> with individual independence; and to find that limit, and maintain
> it against encroachment, is as indispensable to a good condition of
> human affairs, as protection against political despotism.
>
> —John Stuart Mill, *On Liberty*
> (Walter Scott Publishing, 1901, KL 262)

> Just as the regimen of the healthy is not suited to the sick, one must
> not try to govern a corrupt people by the same laws as those that suit
> a good people. Nothing proves these maxims better than the long life
> of the Republic of Venice, which still retains a simulacrum of existence,
> solely because its laws are suited only to wicked men.
>
> —Jean-Jacque Rousseau, *The Social Contract*
> (Gourevitch, 1997, p. 135)

## Introduction

This chapter continues the analytical narrative. It focuses on constitutional
choices among types of governments and types of political economy systems that may be confronted as possibilities for major reforms are proposed.
Such choices might occur at a constitutional convention, or might motivate
reformers to press for a long series of small reforms that gradually transforms
their existing society into one widely regarded to be superior to the old.
Historically such major reforms are rare, but this perspective allows us to imagine how individuals might vote if consulted about major reforms of their
existing social systems, and also why thoughtful individuals might reject such
reforms and continue to support their existing institutional arrangements.

The analysis begins by discussing three templates for "good" government
and why one might be favored over the others for practical as well as ethical reasons. It notes the roles that normative dispositions play inside those
governments and how voter expectations about such norms affect decisions
to favor one institutional form over the others. It also suggests that even the

*Solving Social Dilemmas.* Roger D. Congleton, Oxford University Press. © Oxford University Press 2022.
DOI: 10.1093/oso/9780197642788.003.0008

"best" institutions tend to be riddled with political dilemmas. As a consequence, as noted in Chapters 6 and 7, even governmental designs motivated by clear ideas about the "good" society may lead to extractive governments rather than productive ones. Once this is acknowledged, practical considerations (and risk aversion) tend to support divided forms of governance with constitutional bounds.

The arguments developed in this chapter draw on the results of the previous chapters, so no new game matrices or social dilemmas are introduced. Rather, additional applications and implications of results worked out earlier are drawn on to reach conclusions about the nature of the "best" constitutional designs when "best" is characterized by both the ethical and practical interests of those who will be subject to them. Evidence of the significance of ethical dispositions for the productivity of democratic governments is provided toward the end of the chapter.

## Ideal Forms of Government (1): Philosopher Kings and Authoritarian Governance

For many individuals, the best imaginable government is an all-powerful organization whose aims are perfectly aligned with their own. Such a government would use its authority for rule adoption and enforcement to create a "good" or "perfect" society as the individual imagines it (filling in the details as necessary). Such an idealized government would be fully staffed by true believers (of the right sort) and the laws would ideally all be implemented in accord with one's own conception of the good, regardless of whether it is based on religious, philosophical, or pragmatic premises, and regardless of whether the particular notion of the good implemented is uniformly believed by all others or not. This is the form of government preferred, for example, by Plato in his hypothetical idealized republic governed by philosopher kings with ideas similar to his own. It is also routinely used by contemporary economists who make use of "benevolent" social planner models to characterize ideal societies. It is a very common fancy of nearly everyone who has a clear conception of a "good" or "ideal" society.[1]

Unfortunately, such regimes cannot be as ideal as imagined without overcoming many significant problems. The first of these is that "ideal" policies are always incomplete for reasons already discussed. The social systems that

---

[1] I sometimes call this the magic wand theory of governance: hand me an all-powerful magic wand and I will make everything perfect, or at least a lot better than it is now.

produce attractive viable communities are complex, and no single individual is likely to fully understand all the dilemmas confronted, nor how best to solve or ameliorate those dilemmas. No system of rules works perfectly in every circumstance, at least none that has been developed to this point in human history.

An individual's conception of the "ideal" is more like a slice of Swiss cheese than a finely cut diamond: a bit soft with numerous gaps, a bit smelly, although tasty to those with similar ideas of the good. "Ideal" solutions may make a society more attractive, but they may also make them worse. Oversimplification and lacunas are always greater for efforts to adjust society-wide rules than for narrower efforts that address specific problems, because there are many more interdependencies that have to be taken into account, not all of which are known or understood. As a consequence, new systems often cause problems unimagined by their proponents—as with the English Civil War and the French Revolution.

Second, it is difficult in practice to select an all-knowing perfect ruler because those competing for the imagined all-powerful high office would pretend to have the "right" beliefs and knowledge even if they do not. The ruler chosen may turn out to be a wolf in sheep's disguise, and once in power, he or she might use his or her unbounded authority to maximize extraction rather than to promote the good society imagined. Third, even if we ignore the knowledge problems associated with radically new ideal systems and the selection problems associated with staffing out its leadership, it is unlikely that a sufficient number of "true believers" or "devout idealists" exist to implement all the rules required to fully enact the ideal policies imagined.

Such systems tend to be authoritarian, because there is almost never a consensus about "ideal" policies in a large group. The imagined perfect rules have to be imposed by force. Even adult clones would disagree about some things because of minor differences in experience and conclusions reached about a good life and a good society. Thus, there would be disagreements about the nature of the ideal philosopher king and his or her ideal policies. Many would resist the rules imposed by another's philosopher king, and in some cases, resistance would escalate to civil war. In this manner, the mere prospect of major reforms may create a new Hobbesian dilemma, which in this case is caused by a clash of ideals and rulings rather than the scarcity of natural resources.

Ignoring the problems associated with disagreements—as most proponents of such systems tend to—the above discussion implies that the philosopher-king conception of good or perfect governance is extremely reliant on the internalized norms and essentially complete knowledge of both the king and government officials. Without nearly perfect and strong internalized norms, the temptations associated with unbounded authority would be impossible to resist. The problem of ignorance implies that mistakes will be made and that with unbounded authority, such mistakes can have dire consequences for the persons ruled.

As a consequence, it is unsurprising that attempts to create such systems end in failures. Notable failures of societies based on philosopher kings and idealistic juntas include Cromwell's Republic in the period after the English civil war, the reign of terror during the French Revolution, and the short rule of Cambodia by Pol Pot in the twentieth century. Cromwell's Puritan republic was sufficiently unsatisfactory that a consensus (at least among elites) for restoring the old royal system emerged and a restoration took place shortly after Cromwell's death. The Jacobin reign of terror led by idealists ended with the pragmatic authoritarian rule of Napoleon, and Pol Pot's bloody ideological regime was overthrown within a few years after millions of his subjects had been killed. Few non-compatriots would regard such regimes to be major improvements over the ones they replaced.

The problems associated with a philosopher king—even assuming that such persons could be identified—are sufficiently great that more complex systems of governments have to be taken into consideration. How do we replace persons of authority when they turn out to be less idealistic or competent than initially believed? How are the agency problems and other social dilemmas associated with all levels of governmental decision-making resolved if "ideal" persons cannot be found to staff out all positions of authority? How can compromises be worked out if the persons ruled disagree about the nature of the good society? How do we adjust policies and the persons in authority when significant innovations in theories of the good society or unanticipated problems with current theories occur?

## Ideal Government (2): Divided Governance: The King and Council

The problems of ignorance and the temptations of unbounded authority can be reduced to some degree by adopting a somewhat more complex policymaking process. An organizational form that historically has been widely used divides governing responsibilities between a chief executive or king and a committee or parliament. It is a template that I have termed the "king and council" template for policymaking and governance (Congleton 2001, 2011). Authority can be divided between the king and council in a variety of ways, and the individuals holding positions in both parts of government can be selected in a variety of ways. Together, these variations in implementation allow the template to be nearly infinitely variable and so it can be adjusted incrementally to adapt to changing circumstances and understandings of the good society.

One extreme among the distributions of authority is the case in which the council is simply advisory and helps the king overcome his or her informational problems. At the other extreme is the case in which the council makes policy, and the king simply implements it. In between are various divisions of authority and procedures under which policymaking is a joint activity. In those cases, the policies chosen tend to be between the ideals of the king and those of the pivotal member(s) of the council or assembly. These intermediate divisions of authority tend to moderate policy choices and make major mistakes less likely to occur.

The selection of the persons to be kings and members of councils can also be characterized in many ways. For example, the council may be elected and choose the "king," as in prime-ministerial forms of government. Or both the council (parliament or legislature) and the king (president) may be independently elected, as in contemporary presidential system of governance. Or the office of king and membership in the council might be family property passed on to the oldest child in each family, as with a hereditary monarch and council of nobles. Or the council may be entirely or largely selected by the king from a subset of the kingdom's nobles, as was commonplace during the absolutist periods of European governance (and elsewhere). The first two are more likely to advance the shared interests of a region's residents than the last two, because elections tend to align the interests of those in government with those of the electorate for reasons discussed in Chapter 7. Hereditary rule-makers have their own personal interests and are unlikely to be philosopher kings of the sort imagined by Plato—although pretending that they are would be useful for court philosophers and advisors.

The rule-making and rule-enforcing tasks of governance may be divided in many ways between the king (prime minister or president) and council (parliament or legislature) in many ways. One possible division of authority is that suggested at the beginning of Chapter 6, in which new laws are chosen by the council (legislature) and the king (president or prime minister) enforces (or executes) the laws adopted. Another possibility is that an elected council might have veto authority over the budget proposals of the king and his or her major executive decisions, such as declarations of war, while leaving the rest to the king's discretion. The latter somewhat mitigates risks associated with executive discretion, because those serving on the council or in parliament would be better informed and more actively engaged in monitoring executive behavior than ordinary voters tend to be. Thus, they would be better able to recognize major errors and intervene between elections.

When major officeholders in the parliament and executive are all elected, significant misalignments between moderate voter interests and the average or median interests of a group of legislators are less likely than those between voters and elected presidents, because mistaken judgments about the character and ability of a single official are more likely than mistakes about a group of such officials elected independently of one another.

In electorally grounded versions of the king and council template, the rules adopted tend to reflect the most common ethical dispositions and pragmatic interests of moderate voters in the electorate, as developed in Chapter 7. Insofar as elections are considered to be a "good" way to select representatives, disagreements among voters would tend not to escalate to violence, although many voters will be dissatisfied with the candidates elected and the policies adopted. From the perspective of moderate voters, their community's public policies and laws would tend to have a moral character, because they are partly grounded in the ethical dispositions of those voters—as they should be, according to Aristotle, Locke, Bentham, and Kant, among many others.

Together with the analysis of Chapter 7, this implies that, in the long run, election-grounded forms of the king and council template tend to enforce rules that have ethical foundations and address social dilemmas, although other counterproductive rules may also be adopted because of lobbying by special interest groups, the pragmatic interests of voters, and errors caused by voter and official ignorance (Olson 1965; Congleton 2001). In the very long run, both the informal and formal laws of representative democratic versions of the king and council template would be subject to evolutionary pressures of the variety that Spencer and Hayek discuss. The laws would change through time, and many of those changes—perhaps most—would be improvements from the perspective of the evolving internalized norms of moderate voters.[2]

---

[2] Locke and Kant argue that even in cases in which governance is grounded in a social compact or universal law, many laws would (and should) lack a foundation in ethics. Laws, for example, may be adopted simply to solve problems of life in a community, such as conventions for walking or driving on the right, as discussed in Chapter 2. In other cases, the laws adopted may conflict with ethical theories because they advance only narrow interests or are mistakes—as evidenced by ex post regrets. Bentham argues that there are also ethical rules that should not be codified in law because the benefits of doing so would be smaller than the costs.

# Ideal Government (3): Constitutionally Constraining the King and Council

Electorally grounded king and council governments have a distribution of authority that is generated by bargaining between the two parts of government and electoral pressures. As a consequence, shifts in both the division and scope of authority tend to take place through time. When such governments are characterized by written constitutions, these adjustments tend to be more difficult to make, which tends to anchor them near their original divisions and scope of authority. Bargaining between the king and council may still affect the division and scope of authority between them, but that bargaining is constrained by the procedures and constraints specified in constitutional documents. Formal amendment procedures allow revisions to the core procedures and constraints of governance, but amendments are more difficult to adopt than ordinary laws and so occur less frequently than that which would have emerged through bargaining among the branches of government.

Rule-bound governance is most likely to emerge when a government's most important procedures emerge as a product of custom and internalized norms among those entitled to participate in governance—voters and elected officials in contemporary democracies. Informal constitutions may be transformed into formal constitutions for the same reason that customary laws are often written up as legal codes or digests of the law. They make the rules more precise and therefore more likely to be binding, because violation of them will be more obvious—although juridical judgment remains necessary because no body of law can be complete or unambiguous. Constitutional review reduces the scope for ignoring constitutional procedures and the bounds of authority.

The separation between law creation, law execution, and constitutional oversight is similar to that associated with ordinary laws, where law writing, law enforcement, and the determination of guilt or innocence with respect to following a community's laws are normally undertaken by independent government agencies. That separation somewhat reduces opportunities for extractive behavior, by assuring that most laws are uniformly enforced and applied. Although, as noted in Chapter 6, opportunities for corruption exist at each stage in this process, and thus restraining the extractive temptations of government agents ultimately rests on the ethical dispositions of agents, especially those with the greatest authority. Without ethical inhibitions and adherence to oaths of office, agreements to share the bribes and other extractions would likely emerge, albeit with ongoing conflict over how the illicit revenues should be divided.

Another institutional method of reducing the extractive temptations of government officials is to bound their authority. This reduces the scope of policy and thereby reduces the scope for potentially extractive policies as well. This can be done at the constitutional level by assigning specific areas of policymaking authority to its legislature, executive, and judicial branches of government. The bounds can be made somewhat tighter by also ruling out particular kinds of lawmaking, such as those that discriminate among groups, open discussion of policies, and laws reducing political competition (such as ending elections).

The normative dispositions of those selected for constitutional review committees and courts are especially important for much the same reason that normative dispositions of the anticorruption law enforcers mattered most in Chapter 6. Their decisions bind all the rest. The decisions of the persons on the constitutional court (or review committees) determine the constitution in place through their interpretations of constitutional language and precedents. Thus, they must be able to overcome the temptation to do more than the courts are supposed to do according to the constitution. Otherwise, a court becomes a new higher level of rule-making, rather than a dutiful juridical agency. In effect, such a court would be an unintended ruling junta, rather than a source of juridical interpretations of constitutional law.

A secondary effect of curtailing informal refinements of constitutions through informal bargaining rather than formal amendments is that it tends to further stabilize the political system by reinforcing institutional conservatism and deference to custom. This is not to suggest that a constitution should never change, but a formal process for constitutional amendment allows new circumstances and ideas to be explicitly taken into account, rather than informally without much discussion and analysis. This somewhat protects minority interests by placing a more robust lower bound on their rights and benefits—namely those associated with the preexisting procedures and constraints of governance.

It bears noting that the liberal democracies associated with the emergence of prosperous commercial societies in the late nineteenth and early twentieth centuries were all variations of this last form of idealized government. Such bounded systems of election-based governance remain reliant upon the ethical dispositions of persons in all three parts of government, but less so than the other ideal types, insofar as the constitutional limits of authority are partly determined by institutionalized divisions and incentives. Insofar as citizens are aware of the potential abuse of authority by government officials and are risk averse, such provisions tend to increase the breadth of support associated with constitutional governance relative to other less rule-bound systems of government.

## A Digression on Extractive Regimes and Their Economic Limits

The difficulty of establishing "good" governance is suggested by world history. Extractive authoritarian governments are historically far more commonplace than direct or representative democracies. This in turn suggests that extractive regimes are relatively easier to create and tend to be more stable forms of governance once they are in place. Extractive regimes are simpler to organize because they need not ameliorate all of the dilemmas associated with election-based governance discussed in Chapter 7 and so are less dependent on ethical dispositions to achieve their intended results. A pragmatic ruler or ruling junta of a durable government attempts to maximize long-term extractions, rather than minimize them.

Such governments are free to use draconian penalties to motivate compliance with their organizing rules. These might, for example, include death penalties for corruption (e.g., taking part of tribute or bribes that "belong" to the ruler) or failing in one's duty to maximize the sustainable harvest of such revenues. Fear induced by severe penalties can solve a great many team production problems. On the other hand, it should be acknowledged that extractive regimes also benefit from ethical support. Insofar as some norms induce deference to authority, diligence, and hard work, such norms would tend to increase the productivity of extractive regimes for reasons developed in Chapter 3. Such normative dispositions reduce monitoring costs and free-riding.[3]

Although maximizing extraction is a simpler task than attempting to create and sustain a "good" society, it is not an easy or trivial task. It requires acknowledging the limits of one's information and the resource cost of "harvesting" social surplus from those ruled. Moreover, there are issues associated with the timing of extractions. Maximizing lifetime or dynastic extraction normally requires extracting less in the short run so that more can be extracted in the long run.

---

[3] Montesquieu ([1748] 2008, Kindle locations 543–565), for example, argues that "Virtue is not the Principle of a Monarchical Government," although he also concedes that in monarchies "honour ... supplies the place of the political virtue of which I have been speaking. . . ." Nonetheless, "perpetual ridicule cast upon virtue, are, I think, the characteristics by which most courtiers in all ages and countries have been constantly distinguished."

# The Limits of Extraction

In the absence of monitoring and enforcement costs, pragmatic rule-makers would be inclined to reduce all others in the community to slavery or serfdom in order to extract the entire social surplus—the value of all services less subsistence for the slaves and serfs. Thus, it is not surprising that slavery has been commonplace in societies with authoritarian governments. Slavery is found in the early large-scale governments of the Middle East, Egypt, and China. Greece and Rome also used slaves. Land-bound serfdom remained commonplace in northern Europe, China, and Japan until a few centuries ago. It may be more surprising that slavery is also found in societies that had elected governments or partially elected governments (with restricted suffrage that excluded slaves and others), as in ancient Greece, the Roman Republic, England, and in the southern states of the United States during most of its first century. (Slavery had been phased out or eliminated from the northern United States during its first few decades.)

However, enslavement is less rewarding than the rulers might initially have expensed for several reasons. First, production entirely by slaves requires central planning and management. In societies with relatively simple production processes, central planning would be feasible, but management would require managers (slave drivers), who are able to exercise some discretion over what their teams do, and thus are not themselves entirely enslaved. The more slave managers are necessary, the smaller is the fraction of a populace that is fully enslaved. Second, as more complex tasks are undertaken, such as the construction of public works that require designing, engineering, and organization, other persons would also be granted at least given some discretion (and training) and also would not be entirely enslaved. Similar reasoning applies to the planners of military campaigns, to the designers of military equipment, and to those managing the use of force to maintain order and passivity among those enslaved. Even in relatively simple agrarian economies, enslavement of the entire population outside government is not possible if the aim is to maximize sustainable extractions.

Third, in more complex economies, the central management of all goods and services tends to produce less output than that generated by independent teams of slaves managed by non-slaves (freemen) and coordinated through markets and competition. Such mixed systems have a significant number of slave owners who are not themselves members of government, as indicated by, for example, the legal code of Hammurabi (1750 BCE) in its section on laws governing slavery. Fourth, in cases in which a government's territory is assembled by conquering other relatively free communities, it is often more profitable to demand substantial tribute than to enslave and centrally manage all the persons in the territories conquered. The production of force and threats of force requires scarce resources that can often be more profitably used to expand the territory governed rather than to extract more revenues from those already subject to its rule—where the term *profit* includes both money and non-money goods of interest to the rulers.[4]

When slavery is not possible or is obviously less profitable to the rulers than systems that are more open or mixed systems, forward-looking rulers may adopt laws that promote economic development, because such laws increase the social surplus enough to provide them with greater wealth and power (Tullock 1972; Olson 2000) even if rates of extraction are below those of slave societies. Thus, as the complexity of a society's goods and services increases, even pragmatic autocratic rulers have what Olson (1965, 2000) terms an "encompassing interest" in the economic development of their societies. Laws that promote economic development increase the stock and flow of goods and services potentially realizable by freemen, and these, in turn, increase the long-term expected revenues collected by the government in the form of taxation, bribes, rent extraction, and extortion.

A forward-looking ruler would not simply immediately take all that is produced by the freemen of his or her society, but would extract it at rates that maximize his or her long-run revenues. Such limited taxation and the provision of public services are undertaken for the same reasons that a gardener fertilizes his or her crops and waits for them to mature before harvesting them: because such steps increase the harvest. A ruler might, for example, attempt to improve transport networks and adherence to civil and criminal law because these tend to increase the extent of the wealth produced and available for harvest. Such laws and services reduce transaction costs, encourage specialization, and thereby increase the fruits of governance.

Nonetheless, one rarely observes well-functioning markets in dictatorships. This is partly because the tenure of most dictators is highly uncertain, which tends to induce rulers to live for today rather than plan for and invest in the future.[5] It is also partly because the support necessary to hold on to power is

---

[4] Two quotes attributed to Genghis Khan illustrate what the "profits" of conquest consist of and the difficulty of ruling territories conquered: (1) "The greatest happiness is to vanquish your enemies, to chase them before you, to rob them of their wealth, to see those dear to them bathed in tears, to clasp to your bosom their wives and daughters." (2) "Conquering the world on horseback is easy; it is dismounting and governing that is hard." These quotes are taken from https://www.goodreads.com/author/quotes/5272 307.Genghis_Khan#:~:text=Genghis%20Khan%20quotes%20Showing%201,punishment%20like%20 me%20upon%20you.%E2%80%9D&text=%E2%80%9CIf%20you're%20afraid%20%2D,don't%20be%20 afraid!%E2%80%9D&text=%E2%80%9CCan%20action%20comitted%20in%20anger,an%20action%20 doomed%20to%20failure.%E2%80%9D.

[5] See Bienen and van de Walle (1989) for evidence of high turnover among dictators in the nineteenth century.

often produced through grants of special privileges to persons, families, and towns whose support is most valuable or most easily obtained through such grants. Contrariwise, special penalties and restrictions are often imposed on those deemed most likely to oppose the ruling group.

The persons, organizations, and towns so privileged are well aware that their privileges require supporting the rulers and so (within limits) will support the central government and defend both its rules and authority. Those punished for their tendency toward insurrection will lack the resources and organization(s) required to challenge the ruling group because they are impoverished by the rules to which they are subject.[6] Both kinds of policies tend to undermine economic development, although they tend to make authoritarian governments more durable and robust.

## Promoting Normative Disposition as a Means of Increasing Extraction

Although extractive regimes are less dependent on ethical disposition than a productive government, they too benefit from internalized rules of conduct. For example, a ruler's net extraction increases if those ruled have a strong work ethic and so are inclined to work hard and diligently even when rates of extraction (taxation, regulation, etc.) are high. Similarly, deference to authority tends to reduce the likelihood of revolt, which allows the ruling group to spend fewer resources trying to uncover conspiracies and punish co-conspirators.

As a consequence, even pragmatic rulers have good reasons to promote the internalization of supportive norms of various sorts. Pragmatic interests tend to be advanced by hierarchical deference, loyalty, and obedience. Such norms tend to extend the ruler's period of rule by reducing internal conflict and improving coordination. If those in the lower levels of government and those ruled can be induced to aspire to be productive while living simple ascetic lives, more of their community's output is available for the ruler's projects and entertainment. Extractive rulers thus have good reasons to support norms that encourage ascetic, stoic, and "rule-following" dispositions within their territories.

Some normative dispositions are more useful in some positions than in others. For example, the parts of extractive organizations that produce coercion tend to be more effective if their members have internalized virtues such

---

[6] See Tullock (1972) for a short exposition on this idea, or Mesquita, Smith, Siverson, and Morrow (2003) for a more thorough development.

as toughness, courage, and deference to authority. Military units that lacked such internalized norms would be less effective than those that do and so would be less likely to emerge victorious in military contests (for given levels of technology). Unit members who lacked such virtues would tend to give in to their natural fear of death and injury and "free-riding" would be endemic. Thus, such Spartan dispositions are often encouraged through praise, esteem, medals, status, rank, and conditional shares in an extractive regime's bounty. And their opposites are discouraged through severe punishment.

The rulers also benefit from distributive justice principles that accord leaders a "just claim" on a large fraction of the resources produced by their societies. Their power and lifestyles, they may argue, are obvious products of divine intent and therefore inherently proper and just. Similarly, elitist theories of distributive justice may be encouraged because they tend to imply that leaders should be rewarded well because of their unusual cleverness, strength, and bravery—all virtues that might be claimed to be extraordinarily strong within an extractive regime's leadership. They may also support theories of distributive justice, including such ideas as "to the victor go the spoils" and "might makes right," which would induce even pragmatists to defer to persons in powerful positions within government.

## Extractive Regimes and Inequality before the Law

The rule-enforcement abilities of all governments imply that government agents can undertake activities that would be illegal if attempted by ordinary citizens. They may, in some cases, kill, injure, extort, and take control of property owned by others—all acts that would be deemed improper, immoral, and illegal if undertaken by persons not in government. Thus, some asymmetries in the "rights" of government officials and those ruled exist in all governing regimes, whether they are extractive or not. The laws that apply to government agents differ from those of citizens, and they must be if the formal rule-enforcing power is vested in a governing organization.[7]

---

[7] There is some evidence that democracy tends to reduce the asymmetry between the powers of government officials and citizens outside government. For example, prior to the electoral reforms of 1832 in Great Britain, there were 220 crimes for which the death penalty was called for, including poaching and pickpocketing. As support for equality before the law increased in the eighteenth and nineteenth centuries, the number of crimes that could be punished with execution gradually diminished. The largest reduction in Great Britain occurred in the same year as the first major suffrage reform. The Punishment of Death Act of 1832 reduced the number of capital crimes in Great Britain by two-thirds. Subsequently, public executions were ended, and the death penalty was gradually eliminated as a possible penalty for many other

Such asymmetries tend to be greater in extractive regimes than in productive ones because threats of violence are used to extract resources from those governed, as well as to enforce the law. Other asymmetries are also more common. Favored groups will receive more lenient treatment under rules that apply to all groups, and many rules may apply only to subsets of the population. Disfavored groups will receive less lenient treatment under rules that apply to all groups and find themselves subject to rules that apply to no others—as with the slavery rules in the Code of Hammurabi. In some cases, such discriminatory laws are used to reward supporters and punish opponents. In others, legal privileges may, in effect, be sold off to the highest bidder, in which case asymmetries reflect past efforts at rent-seeking.[8]

## Changes in Ethical Dispositions and Transitions to Democracy

Extractive regimes are chiefly of interest for the purposes of this book because they help explain the absence of true commercial societies. The widespread use of slaves and serfs for production tends to reduce investments in human capital and thereby productivity. The confiscatory powers of such regimes tend to make both civil liberties and property rights more uncertain, which reduces incentives for and abilities to accumulate capital and to innovate. This is not to say that all persons in such regimes are poor. For extraction to be profitable, at least some economic activity has to take place either in the home territory or in the surrounding territories—otherwise extraction would not be possible. The profits of extraction, in turn, tend to support commercial enterprises that advance the aims of the rulers, including grandiose architecture and amusements. Those that profit directly or indirectly from extraction, naturally, tend to support such forms of governance. However, extraction tends to reduce economic development by broadly undermining incentives to engage in many of the activities that generate a commercial society.

crimes during the next century. Use of the death penalty was formally ended in the United Kingdom in 1965 through legislation.

[8] Democratic regimes may also exhibit some asymmetries in law, but tend to be more constrained by "equal protection of the law" norms, because without such norms, majority-rule-based governments tend to be less stable and decisive (Congleton 1997).

Extractive regimes are also of interest because transitions to both democratic and commercial societies often emerge from extractive regimes. The corruption and conquest pathways to extractive regimes are not always one way.

Such transitions are at least partially generated by changes in the rules and principles of conduct internalized among political elites; which is to say the ethical dispositions of the persons in positions of authority and others who can directly or indirectly influence their policy decisions. For example, changes in ideology provided the most plausible explanation for the emergence of Western democracy in the nineteenth and early twentieth centuries, as developed at length in *Perfecting Parliament* (Congleton 2011). Such transitions are relevant for the present chapter, although less central to the aims of the present book. Commercial systems are also products of decades or centuries of experiments as new trading relationships and organizations are formed to take account of shifts in consumer demands and innovations in products, manufacturing, transport, and norms.

Many of the changes in ideas about the good life and good society that helped motivate the emergence of commercial societies also tended to support the reforms that gradually produced democracy in western Europe. Moreover, to the extent that democracies were less extractive than the authoritarian regimes that they replaced, prosperity tended to increase as the electoral foundation of governance increased in places where democratic dilemmas of Chapter 7 were ameliorated by the same or complimentary norms.

Political economy systems are complex systems of formal and informal rules and relationships. In the countries where election-based governments emerged in the nineteenth and early twentieth centuries, liberal democracy was normally a product of a series of formal and informal reforms, rather than a single constitutional convention. Political parties gradually emerged and became central participants in policy formation, suffrage laws were gradually expanded to include all adults, and the influence of elected parts of government steadily gained in authority.

The next subsections provide a very short overview of the manner in which changes in ethical ideas can induce changes in the nature of governments. Changes in ideas about the good life and good society can generate a series of constitutional bargains that gradually produce governments grounded in electoral processes. The analysis begins with a few examples of the use of ethical ideas to evaluate governments and governing systems. (The comments included are all from authors reviewed in Part III of the book.)

## On the Use of Personal Ethics for Assessing Officials, Policies, and Institutions

Most ethical codes of conduct can be used to assess both one's own behavior and that of others. In this respect, all personal ethical systems are generalizable. Thus, theories of character and virtue can be used to assess policymakers and their policy choices. There is nothing new about this, although the freedom to write down one's opinions about government officials without fear of retribution is a relatively recent phenomenon and is still far from universal.

For example, the Dutch businessman and author Pieter de la Court ([1662] 1776) regarded the nobility of the Netherlands to be less than praiseworthy. They could not generally be trusted to pay their debts, deal courteously with women, or exercise self-discipline with respect to drinking or public policy:

> **Inferior lords** usually and **without scruple** take possession of their paternal estates without paying any debts; and all young and healthy lords are violently inclined to women. . . . and indeed two of these having either never married at all, or not 'till they arrived to a considerable age, could not have been **guilty of so great a crime** if they had been engaged in marriage.
>
> As to the **profusion and excess of drinking** used in their court, to the great diminution of its revenues, 'tis a thing so universally practiced, especially in the Northern parts, that none of these princes ought to be so much blamed for it. . . . [In contrast] prince Maurice **deserves to be commended for the frugality and sobriety of his family.** (La Court, *The True Interest and Political Maxims*, [1662] 1776, p. xxi)

La Court was simply applying the Calvinist norms held by many persons in the Netherlands in his critique of noble character and behavior. Government officials should behave just like the rest of us, with prudence and frugality.[9]

Public policies can be assessed in more or less the same manner. Both day-to-day and quasi-constitutional policy choices may be considered unethical because they violate norms associated with life in a community or

---

[9] It is interesting to note that the terms "noble" and "ignoble" were often used to describe both family lineage and personal character. Whether Dutch nobles were unusually ignoble in their behavior or not is beyond the scope of this chapter. It bears noting that the Netherlands was at this point in its history a republic and a relatively liberal one in which there was greater freedom to express one's views in print than elsewhere in Europe. Its most powerful position, however, was informally a hereditary one held by a family that held a title from France, the Prince of Orange. Willem the Second would have held that title at the time that La Court wrote, but more important, also held the position of "stadthouder" in the Netherlands. A century and a half later, the same family, after interventions by Napoleon and Great Britain, came to hold the monarchy of the new Kingdom of the Netherlands.

with virtuous conduct in general. Again, quotes from La Court serve as an illustration:

> [T]he **governours** of the United Provinces, who seemed **willing to give up the liberty of their country**; and in all respects to be able, willing and necessitated to bear an universal slavery, **by granting and promising to a child the future succession of all his father's offices**; and whether the said prince, **Willem** the second, **who was continually conversant with foreigners,** and other slavish courtiers, had any better education or conversation with men than other ordinary monarchs use to have. (La Court *The True Interest and Political Maxims*, [1662] 1746, pp. xxvii–xxix)

> **To grant authority to a child without knowing how he will grow up is the height of imprudence,** risking both incompetent leadership and worse. (La Court, *The True Interest and Political Maxims*, [1662] 1776, p. 13)

In this case, Dutch policymakers are being criticized for taking risks that a prudent man would not, that is, for letting emotion and tradition, rather than reason, determine their choices.

By the mid-nineteenth century, the French politician and economist Frédéric Bastiat was able to use other commerce-supporting norms in his critique of tax policies in France:

> But when John Q. Citizen **gives a hundred sous to a Government officer, and receives nothing** for them unless it be annoyances, he **might as well give them to a thief.** It is nonsense to say that the Government officer will spend these hundred sous to the great profit of national labor; the thief would do the same; and so would John Q. Citizen, if he had **not been stopped on the road by the extra-legal parasite, nor by the lawful sponger.** (Bastiat, "That Which Is Seen, and That Which Is Not Seen," [1850] 2007, p. 9)

The rhetoric of contemporary political and lobbying campaigns continues to draw heavily on the internalized personal ethics of voters to critique and support alternative candidates and public policies.

Conclusions about political officeholders and policies may in turn be used to assess political institutions. Institutions that tend to select and retain virtuous officials are regarded to be moral or proper, but not those that tend to select and retain the nonvirtuous. In this manner, personal ethics and various generalizations of them can serve as a foundation for assessing the merits of entire systems of governance and entire political economy systems. In the quotes above, La Court is defending the Dutch republican form of government of his time and criticizing the tendency of some policymakers to adopt reforms that would make the Netherlands more of a kingdom than a republic.

## Ethics and Constitutional Bargaining

Constitutional bargaining resembles the problem of exchange developed in Chapter 3. There are honest and fraudulent offers and the possibility of realizing mutual advantages from exchange. In Europe constitutional bargains were often of the form of additional parliamentary authority in exchange for additional or emergency funding for the king. The specific nature of the exchange is not initially of interest here, but what is of interest is that ideas about the good society or virtue associated with a proposed reform can influence whether or not a trade takes place by altering the perceived benefits or costs associated with a particular reform.

Table 8.1 illustrates a case in which the status quo ante distribution of authority generates net benefits of $A_K$ for the king and $A_L$ for the pivotal member of the parliament or legislature. A specific proposal may be made (here by assumption by the king) which has practical net benefits of $B_K$ for the king and $B_L$ for the pivotal member of the legislature. In addition, the proposal has virtue payoffs $V_K$ and $V_L$ associated with reforms that move the government closer to its "ideal" form ($v_i > 0$) or away from its ideal form ($v_i < 0$). The bargaining illustrated takes place entirely among political elites—which is to say by persons occupying relatively powerful positions in government. However, if either or both relevant participants in the bargaining are elected, then the interests of ordinary citizens tend to be represented in the bargaining, for reasons developed in Chapter 7. Elected officials have to please a majority of voters to continue in office. Here, it is assumed that single-member district elections determine representation in parliament, in order to simplify discussion. (Pivotal members of legislatures selected via proportional representation

**Table 8.1** Ethics and Constitutional Exchange

|  |  | Pivotal Member of Legislature | |
|---|---|---|---|
|  |  | Accept constitutional reform | Reject proposal |
| King | Propose constitutional reform | (K, L)<br>$B_K + V_K, B_L + V_L$ | (K, L)<br>$A_{K+} + V_K, A_L$ |
|  | Make no offer | $A_K, A_L + V_L$ | $A_K, A_L$ |

are normally members of the most influential party in the governing coalition, which is often the party preferred by the median voter.)

The proposal made by the king is accepted only if there are mutual advantages from the reform, as in ordinary market transactions, which requires $B_K + V_K > A_K$ and $B_L + V_L > A_L$. In a kingdom with a stable balance of authority, such mutually advantageous offers rarely exist, very few are made, and most that are made are rejected. Offers rejected may have a virtue payoff for the person making or seeking the offer, as assumed, but this simply encourages bargaining rather than necessarily generating a reform.

In late-medieval European kingdoms, constitutional reforms required ascent by both parts of government. This was largely a matter of political custom and constitutional law, but in former times, it also reflected the military power of the nobles represented in parliament. As gains from constitutional exchange were generated by emergencies and shifts in norms, constitutional bargains were consummated, and the relative authority of kings and parliaments adjusted at various margins. There were periods in which policymaking, taxing, and military authority generally shifted from the parliament to the king and others in which the reverse occurred. This depended on the king's need for emergency funds, which varied by circumstance. It was also affected by the king's talent as a ruler and negotiator relative to that of pivotal players in parliament. In addition, constitutional bargaining was affected by shifts in the notion of a good government and good society. Such views included royalist periods and anti-royalist periods, and reforms often paralleled shifts in those ideas.

In terms of the Table 8.1, this suggests that $V_K$ and $V_L$ were often important factors in the reforms adopted. Parliaments would sometimes cede authority to the king for little or nothing in return when loyalty to the royal family was strongest. During periods in which the king was simply another part of government, parliamentary leaders would often demand and obtain more authority for themselves. This was especially true when the king faced an unusual emergency or was himself sympathetic to the idea that divided government was an important feature of a flourishing nation-state.

The processes that generate shifts in B's and V's are complex, and so the particular values associated with specific reform proposals can be thought of as more or less random, with the mean value of the sum of the parliament's and king's B's somewhat below those of the A's, and with the mean value of the V's roughly equal to zero. In such cases, the status quo ante would generally be stable. The few reforms that shifted authority from the king to the parliament or the parliament to the king would resemble a random walk, driven largely by changes in norms, including those that promote feelings of loyalty, religiosity, and nationalism, or by other unusual circumstances.

The parliaments of medieval Europe were normally multi-cameral, with as many as four separate chambers, each representing a different relatively wealthy group. In a four-chamber system, one represented the nobility, one represented the state-sponsored church, one represented wealthy commoners from towns, and one represented wealthy commoners in the countryside. In the British two-chamber system, the noble and church chambers were combined into a House of Lords, and the town and country chambers were combined into a House of Commons. Members of the House of Commons were elected by quite restricted suffrage, and many elections for seats in Commons were uncontested in the period before the electoral reform of 1832. That basic architecture for English governance emerged in the fourteenth century and remains in use today, although suffrage and the competitiveness of elections expanded dramatically in the century following the 1832 reforms.

In spite of its architectural stability, there were many reforms of the relationships between the English kings and parliament and between the chambers of parliament after the fourteenth century. However, those of the eighteenth and nineteenth centuries are of greatest interest for the purposes of this chapter. During that period, there was broadly increasing moral support for equality before the law and representative governance. These produced a series of election reforms that gradually expanded suffrage for the House of Commons (often with the support of the king) and that gradually diminished the authority of both the House of Lords and the king.

In terms of the simple model above, the V's associated with democratic reforms exhibited a trend and increased sufficiently, so that even if the B's associated with reforms were generally a bit lower than the A's for the chamber or office losing authority, the moral force of the arguments favoring "democracy" were sufficient to induce passage of modest reforms by both parliament and the king. By 1920, the government in Britain was transformed into one where elections, rather than privileged birthrights, determined authority. It was accomplished without a revolution—and through a series of "small" reforms rather than a single revolutionary reform. (The largest increase in suffrage was the extension of suffrage to most adult women in 1918.)

Trends in support for equality before the law, elections, suffrage for all "responsible" citizens, and for elections as a determinant of national interests, had reversed the ancient balance of power in which the king and the House of Lords were the two most important determinants of public policy. By 1930, the House of Commons was elected by universal adult suffrage and dominated policymaking through its selection of prime ministers, who became the new "kings" in the democratic era of governance in England, while the royal family retired from policymaking and politics, for the most part, to their royal estates and important social occasions.

Similar bargaining paths were evident in Sweden, the Netherlands, Belgium, Norway, and Denmark, and similar trends were evident in Germany and Japan—although representative democracy was not generated through bargaining alone in those countries. The French and United States cases were different. Constitutional bargaining favoring election-based governance in the United States began in its colonial period. The French had a true democratic revolution at the end of the eighteenth century, but the king was restored to office in 1814, and constitutional bargaining arguably determined the course of democratization after the restoration.

The collection of ideas associated with democratization in the nineteenth century, often termed *liberalism*, also tended to favor commerce and industrialization. Together with the increasing influence of voters, this moral and positive support for market activities eliminated the remaining medieval constraints on trade (which had long been fading) and helped to encourage economic development through infrastructure investments and policies that tended to open borders up to international trade—both of which increased the extent of the markets that could be serviced by a single firm, which increased the advantages of economies of scale.

All this is not to suggest that politically relevant values and arguments simply percolated through societies. Many were propelled by organized interest groups that published editorials and books or funded lobbyists to press for liberal reforms. Coalitions of idealists and pragmatists with similar reform and policy aims were commonplace. But it is to say that changes in ideas about the nature of a good society were important and provided necessary moral support for trends in suffrage, the influence of the elected chamber(s) of government relative to the others, and for shifts in authority that favored parliaments over royal and noble families.

A long series of such reforms gradually replaced the king-dominated systems of the West's medieval period with parliamentary-dominated systems grounded in broad suffrage. These political reforms also also led to a shift in economic regulation from extractive systems based on favoritism and privilege to more open market systems, partly because there were shifts in norms that made material comfort and market activities more central elements in the most commonly held theories of the good life and good society, and partly because there were new economic theories that suggested that such reforms advanced national interests. All of these changes tended to accelerate rates of commercial development in what came to be known as the West—but not elsewhere, where older ideas and theories continued to dominate political decision-making.

# Grand Social Aspirations: Ethics and Support for Particular Political Economy Systems

Until the second half of the eighteenth century, it could be argued that a region's political-economic system was largely a product of initial circumstances, chance, and gradual social evolution. Where and to whom one was born largely determined the resources at one's disposal and the environment one confronted during life. Most knowledge of nature and norms were learned from fellow members of one's family and its social network. These included rules that characterized nature, what could be changed by human efforts, and how to evaluate those possibilities. The rules that were taught were mostly old rules that their teachers believed "worked," in that they were "truths" that produced relatively attractive results. A subset of the most commonplace normative rules determined the community's customary laws, and various combinations of its normative assessments and experience largely determined the community's formal organizations, including both firms and governments. Occasionally, a few useful-appearing innovations occurred, and a subset of the new understandings were passed along—but the cycle of life and the distribution of wealth and political influence were quite stable.

By the eighteenth century, however, the idea that individuals could design entirely new social, political, and economic systems had started to become commonplace among intellectuals and, during the next two centuries, common among non-intellectuals as well. The perceived scope of human possibilities had expanded, and the possibility of progress in all things, including socio-politico-economic systems, had come to be taken for granted.

## Choosing a Good Society

Of course, the idea that one can design a social system is not the same as the ability to do so. Such assertions normally assume that knowledge of social systems is more complete and accurate than it actually is, and often assume that culture and humanity are more malleable than history suggests they are. As a consequence, many large-scale social experiments fail to work as expected and disappear. For example, two major innovations in authoritarian governance—national socialism (fascism) and communism—failed to survive the twentieth century. Other more modest nineteenth-century experiments in democratic governance survived. Twentieth-century innovations such as women's suffrage and the great expansion of social insurance and government services also have survived into the twenty-first century. The polities that adopted these reforms not only survived; they flourished, especially in the second half of the twentieth century. All these experiments suggest that a contemporary society can engage in innovations at a larger scale than typical in history—although they are not always successful.

Within democracies, such innovations reflect conclusions about what this book has termed "the good society." Minor amendments will be broadly supported when they are widely believed to advance a shared conception of a good society and/or shared pragmatic interests. Major reforms will be broadly supported when existing institutions are widely believed to be failing—e.g., retrogressing rather than progressing. After the nineteenth century, choices among major reforms were no longer flights of fancy, but became subjects of ongoing policy debate and governmental choices. Mistakes may well be made because of incomplete knowledge and mistaken beliefs, but such grand policies may nonetheless be consciously undertaken by the rule-makers of contemporary governments.

Parts I and II suggest that ethical dispositions play several roles in such policy choices. First, they often provide a stable customary foundation from which such choices are to be considered. Second, they provide metrics for judging the relative merits of both ordinary policies and grand reforms of the preexisting society. The nature of "good results" and the meaning of the term "good governance" vary according to ideas about the good society and the good life. For a liberal democracy, the aim of a "good government" is to advance general or at least a majority's interests. For advocates of a commercial society, the aim of a "good" society is to produce interesting, materially comfortable lives and to encourage the virtues and skills associated with producing such lives. For advocates of a Spartan society, a good government produces military power: the ability to defend against invaders and dominate others in the region of interest, which is believed to require lives devoted to mastering military virtues and skills. For a religious society, a good government produces devout lifestyles and great devout works that are pleasing to its conception of "the" divinity. Such societies encourage lives devoted to acquiring religious virtues and dispositions, rather than material comforts. Other normative theories may not include a particular view of the good society or good life, but nonetheless indicate that a good society pursues particular goals—such as the utilitarian's interest in maximizing aggregate utility.

Third, the ethos of a society partly determines what is feasible, because the ethical dispositions of the persons elected to high offices and government employees affect both their trustworthiness and efficiency. The informal routines of governance are influenced by the ethical dispositions of policymakers and bureaucrats, as developed in Chapters 6 and

7. A community's political culture thus affects the types of policies adopted and manner in which they are implemented. This includes more or less ordinary services such as infrastructure as well as others that affect the normative dispositions of a society, such as the core curricula of public education systems. Fourth, within constitutional democracies, the internalized norms of voters and elected officials also jointly determine the extent to which the informal routines of governance are in accord with the written constitution.

Once the many roles that ethical dispositions play in governance and society are recognized, assessments of those dispositions will also affect choices regarding reforms of governments and social systems, because they determine many of the consequences of such choices. If most moderate voters regard their existing institutions to be "ideal" or "nearly ideal," given the ethos of their society, there will be few reforms. If moderate voters regard the existing institutions to be less than ideal, given the ethos of their society, and agree about the direction or types of reforms that would generate improvements, both minor and major reforms may be adopted. It turns out that such reforms may encourage or discourage prosperity.

## An Illustration: Utilitarian Choices among Political-Economy Systems

To illustrate how perceptions of a community's ethos affect conclusion about the "ideal" scope of governmental authority, it is useful to focus on a few broad categories of governmental authority and their associated political-economy systems. A government may have unbounded authority (or nearly so), or it may have authority that is bounded but nontrivial, or it may have very limited authority. For purposes of illustration, the delegation of broad authority to an elected government is termed *social democracy*, intermediate delegations of authority are termed *mixed political economic system*, and delegations of very limited authority are termed a *laissez-faire society*. Obviously, there is a continuum of authority and outcomes that is being illustrated, and these descriptions of governance and outcomes may be less than the best possible. The use of three categories simplifies and sharpens the conclusions and the discussion. In all three cases it is assumed that democratic procedures are themselves open and competitive and that the bounds of authority are respected by government officials because of various combinations of electoral incentives, internalized norms, and divided authority.[10]

[10] At the level of system choices, there is an irreducible element of uncertainty because the necessary

Table 8.2 Trustworthiness and the Ideal Political Economy System

|  |  | Moral Character of Governmental Policymakers | | |
|---|---|---|---|---|
|  |  | Excellent | Mediocre | Poor |
| Moral Character of Market Participants | Excellent | Laissez-faire | Laissez-faire | Laissez-faire |
|  | Mediocre | Mixed | Laissez-faire | Laissez-faire |
|  | Poor | Social democracy | Mixed | Laissez-faire |

The illustration also assumes that a normative theory similar to utilitarianism has been internalized by the persons undertaking the evaluation. Such a theory does not start with a particular notion of the good society or good life, but rather provides a consistent basis for choosing among proposals. According to utilitarian theory, a good government maximizes or generally increases aggregate utility. A good life is simply one that maximizes average lifetime utility: the average person's satisfaction, contentment, or happiness as imagined by the voter or voters, or government official or officials of interest. Such ethical theories are likely to be among the most widely known to readers of this book. (A chapter-length overview of nineteenth-century utilitarianism is provided in Chapter 12.)

The conclusions characterized by Table 8.2 are intended to be illustrative, rather than logically necessary. They are consistent with the analysis above and are in the spirit of arguments by Ludwig Von Mises and John Rawls, who both argue that good governance is more dependent on ethical dispositions than effective markets are.[11] Thus, when ethical men and woman are equally influential in political and economic systems, fewer government interventions in the private economy are useful or desirable. For example, the more ethical private actors are, the fewer externalities and the lower crime rates tend to be. In addition, products tend to be of generally higher quality and charity more generous and well organized. Thus, there are fewer reasons for governments to intervene. (Those skeptical of these conclusions might want to replace "laissez

information and science required for a complete and detailed description is beyond the ability of any single analyst or small group of analysts, whether political philosophers or social engineers. Agreement among pivotal voters or government officials about general rules or constitutional principles may be possible, but not specific details. In such cases, the coarse categories of governmental authority analyzed Table 8.2 may be a reasonable characterization of the alternatives considered and decisions reached.

[11] Von Mises ([1927] 2002) and Rawls (2009) can be used to characterize the domain of contemporary liberalism, as the term is used in this book, with Von Mises characterizing "right of center," or *laissez-faire* liberalism, and Rawls characterizing "left of center," or progressive liberalism of social democracy. All of the choices in Table 8.2 can be regarded as constitutionally liberal. Constitutionally liberal governments assure equality before the law, broad spheres in which individuals are free to choose, election-based governance, relatively open and competitive markets, support for innovation, and usually also support for mass education and various forms of social insurance.

faire" with "mixed" in the middle diagonal cells of Table 8.2.) In cases in which the typical government official is more ethical than the typical market participant, governments can often improve on market outcomes by ameliorating neglected social dilemmas. In such cases, a clear utilitarian case for more extensive government interventions exists.

In cases in which market outcomes are always poor because market participants are not particularly ethical (large externalities, a good deal of fraud, or extensive monopoly power) and government officials are generally more ethical and so their policies usually are regarded to be improvements, broader authority should be delegated to government. In cases in which market outcomes are poor but government policies are imperfect, less authority should be delegated. In cases in which public policies are generally poor—whether because of random errors, ignorance, or moral depravity—a watchman state is likely to do the least damage. In general, the more virtuous the character of government agents are relative to market participants, the broader the scope of governance should be.[12]

Analysis from a contractarian perspective tends to reach similar conclusions. (See the appendix to Chapter 12 for a short overview of contractarian analysis.) If citizens generally expect government policies to increase their own net benefits, which in most cases are correlated with social net benefits, they will be disposed to delegate more authority to their community's government. If significant agency problems exist, or voter ignorance is anticipated to be extensive, governments would be granted authority only in policy areas in which gains appear to be largest and most likely. In areas in which few or no personal net benefits are anticipated, authority would be withheld. Redistribution might, for example, be limited to various community insurance programs that are likely to advance the interests of all subscribers, rather than demogrant or universal income programs.

Other ethical systems might reach somewhat different conclusions regarding the optimal delegation of authority to intervene in markets or lifestyles. Many egalitarians, for example, would support far greater community control and far less personal autonomy in order to force equality in opportunities and outcomes, as in More's utopia. Not all ethical systems are supportive of discretion in private lives or supportive of the policies that enable a commercial society to emerge.

---

[12] If, for example, the opinions of Erasmus and More were mainstream in 1500 and Smith and Bentham in 1800, one would predict more government interventions in the sixteenth century than in the nineteenth century, which was in fact the case. See Part III for an overview of the analyses and conclusions of Erasmus, More, Smith, and Bentham.

In the long run, conclusions about the proper extent of governmental authority are conditional and subject to revision. Thus, constitutional and quasi-constitutional provisions may be amended from time to time as new problems emerge and the perceived relative trustworthiness of government officials and market participants changes. Such changes may, for example, be induced by improved constitutional and administrative designs that reduce the risk of governmental malfeasance or increase its effectiveness. Many ethical systems support the conclusion that the ideal domain of authority tends to expand as governments become more trustworthy and effective.[13] Similarly, the more ethical and effective market participants are—entrepreneurs, employees, and consumers—the smaller are the problems associated with commerce, and the narrower the optimal degree of regulatory authority tends to be, other things being equal.[14]

Such refinements in the scope of governance would tend to have moral legitimacy from both the utilitarian and contractarian perspectives insofar as the process of amendment is believed to advance the shared interests of essentially all community members.

## Some Evidence of the Importance of Ethical Dispositions in Democracies

One of the difficulties with major social reforms is that the absence of supportive internalized ethical dispositions tends to reduce the attractiveness of even those reforms that generally are regarded as improving the preexisting systems. For example, the political dilemmas analyzed in Part II imply that the effectiveness of democratic reforms is substantially determined by the ethical disposition of voters and government officials. Constitutional bargaining that produces democratic rule will thus achieve different results according to the most commonplace ethical ideas of voters, elected officials, and government employees, because democracy itself does not include solutions for all the dilemmas associated with election-based governance. As a consequence, one should observe differences among even relatively well-functioning democratic governments,

[13] Evidence that voters take account of these trade-offs is provided in the political science and political economy of trust literatures. See, for example, Miller (1974) and Blanco and Ruiz (2013). Examples of governments that roughly follow the path of the analytical narrative developed to this point include Switzerland, the United States, and the Dutch Republic, short overviews and addition historical references for which are provided in Congleton (2018b and 2020c).

[14] Montesquieu (1748) argues that political ethics were more important in democracies and aristocracies than in autocracies but acknowledges that ideas of "honor" tend to play the role of ethics in unrestrained monarchies.

**Table 8.3** On the Variety of Democratic Outcomes

| | 13 Poorest Democracies (Polity 8, 9, 10) | | | | 13 Richest Democracies (Polity 8, 9, 10) | | |
|---|---|---|---|---|---|---|---|
| | Trust WVS+ | RGNPpp WDI | Corrupt TI | | Trust WVS+ | RGNPpp WDI | Corrupt TI |
| Liberia | 17.37 | 1,161 | 28 | Norway | 68.18 | 65,389 | 84 |
| Sierra Leone | 22.67 | 1,421 | 33 | Switzerland | 49.56 | 68,060 | 85 |
| Solomon Islands | NA | 2,149 | 42 | United States | 40.57 | 55,719 | 69 |
| Nepal | 22 | 2,741 | 34 | Netherlands | 56.94 | 49,787 | 82 |
| Kenya | 9.49 | 3,076 | 28 | Denmark | 69.24 | 48,419 | 87 |
| Kyrgyzstan | 27.37 | 3,446 | 30 | Sweden | 64.34 | 47,717 | 85 |
| Nigeria | 21.01 | 5,315 | 26 | Austria | 39.59 | 46,260 | 77 |
| Myanmar | 19.1 | 5,922 | 29 | Germany | 39.53 | 45,393 | 80 |
| Moldova | 16.75 | 6,452 | 32 | Australia | 48.01 | 45,377 | 77 |
| Cape Verde | 5.42 | 6,614 | 41 | Canada | 47.73 | 44,078 | 77 |
| India | 30.62 | 6,888 | 41 | Belgium | 31.9 | 43,582 | 75 |
| El Salvador | 13.12 | 7,393 | 34 | Finland | 60.59 | 42,060 | 86 |
| Guatemala | 21.5 | 7,508 | 26 | United Kingdom | 37.06 | 40,522 | 77 |
| Average | 18.87 | 4,622 | 32.62 | Average | 50.25 | 49,412.54 | 80.08 |
| Standard Deviation | 6.80 | 2,350.20 | 5.43 | Standard Deviation | 12.02 | 8,586.25 | 5.09 |

because of differences in ethical dispositions that affect the behavior of government officials and bureaucrats, as well as voter demands for public policies.

Evidence of such differences is provided in Table 8.3. It lists the 13 poorest and 13 richest democracies, using the most recent Polity Index for Democracy (Polity IV, 2018, categories 8, 9, and 10), to determine which countries are democracies and the most recent World Development Indicators data (March 2020) for real per capita gross national product (using the PPI method of calculated inflation and cost of living adjusted GNP) to determine their average incomes. Polity's index tends to focus the constraints on a nation's most powerful government official (its prime minister, president, dictator, etc.), rather than on a government's internal institutions, but is adequate for the purposes of this section and remains among the most widely used indices of democracy in empirical research.[15]

[15] Table 8.3 and some of the discussion are largely taken from Congleton (2020a), which in turn was based on an earlier version of this chapter.

Table 8.3 also includes two indicators of ethical dispositions or political culture: perceived corruption (from Transparency International's Corruption Perception Index 2019) and generalized trust (from Bjørnskov and Méon 2013). Higher scores on the corruption index denote lower levels of perceived corruption.[16]

Table 8.3 demonstrates that democracies are not all the same and suggests that ethical dispositions are a determining factor. The poorest democracies have much lower generalized trust and higher corruption than the wealthiest ones. If generalized trust can be used as a proxy for the ethical and related normative dispositions that are most commonplace within a country—as argued by Bjørnskov and Méon (2013), among many others—and if supportive ethical dispositions are necessary to solve the various dilemmas associated with both markets and democracy, as argued in Parts I and II of this book, then the data tabulated in Table 8.3 provide indirect evidence of both resolved and unresolved social dilemmas.

If, for example, the political culture of a country has failed to solve the rule of law problem (e.g., the corruption problems analyzed in Chapters 3 and 6), corruption would be higher, markets would be less developed, and relatively lower average incomes would be the predicted consequence. Such differences are evident in the data presented. Note that the data sets do not overlap. The averages of the rich and poor democracies for the three variables tabulated are more than 2 standard deviations apart from one another in all three cases. In two of the three cases, the difference in means is more than 3 standard deviations. Insofar as culture changes more slowly than economic development and public policies, the causality tends to run from culture to the other two variables, rather than in the opposite direction, although some degree of long-run feedback from consequences to a nation's ethos is likely to play a role in the evolution of the most commonplace ethical dispositions in a given territory or region of the world.[17]

Chapters 6 and 7 have argued that democratic institutions work better when supportive ethical dispositions are commonplace. The data provided by Table 8.3 suggest that this is in fact the case. The lower is trustworthiness, the

[16] Table 8.2 omits one even higher-income state (Luxembourg) regarded as a democracy because its PPP per capita RGDPs were implausibly high. Including it would not have changed the basic results.

[17] Bjørnskov and Méon (2013) provide persuasive econometric support for the generalized trust causality explanation. Insofar as generalized trust characterizes trustworthiness and trustworthiness is generated by a community's most commonplace ethical dispositions, the main body of this chapter can be regarded as providing one plausible theoretical explanation for their results. See, for example, Paldam and Gundlach (2008, 2018) for evidence that changes in economic circumstances can also generate such changes.

higher is corruption, and the lower average income tends to be. Political culture matters as well as institutions.[18]

## A Short Recapitulation of the Logic and Implication of Parts I and II

### Knowledge as Systems of Rules

The analysis of Parts I and II rests on two grounding ideas: social dilemmas and internalized rules. Social dilemmas are choice settings in which the outcomes generated by self-interested behavior tend to be less than the best possible, where "best" is judged by the persons whose choices generated the outcomes. These are not the only choice settings faced by humans, but they are sufficiently commonplace and problematic to be important to solve. A general conception of rules is used throughout the book. Rules are if-then relationships. Some rules characterize nature—some aspects of which are permanent, while others can be changed by human action. Other if-then rules provide systematic ways for determining the relative merits of the actions that can be taken and their effects upon the world. Individuals internalize all three types of rules, which together characterize an individual's perceptions of possibilities and interests—his or her worldview or ideology. Individuals have the capacity to invent, refine, ignore, and internalize rules and thus are rule bound but not fully rule determined.

The rules passed on from one generation to the next are not static. Innovations occur, and a subset of the rules invented or revised are believed to be improvements and subsequently passed on to or copied by others. Such changes in internalized rules induce changes in behavior because new possibilities are recognized or new conclusions about the relative merits of old possibilities are reached. Some changes in behavior improve survival prospects and others worsen them. Rules that enhance survival prospects or produce more attractive lives and societies naturally tend to be passed on more often than those that do not. Thus, rules that solve or ameliorate social dilemmas tend to be passed on, even in cases in which the nature of the social dilemmas solved are not fully understood or recognized.

---

[18] Notice that "vintage" is not necessarily decisive. India's and Germany's democracies are of approximately equal age and in force long enough to have influenced the political culture of their politicians and parties, but are still very different in terms of their effects on average income and perceived corruption. However, it also bears noting that India exhibits the highest generalized trust of the poor democracies and Germany has among the lowest generalized trust of the rich democracies.

The result of such rule innovations and survivorship is progress: a general tendency for longer and better lives and more robust and attractive societies to emerge because of improvements in the rules internalized by most of a community's members. Nature and possibilities for adapting it to human purposes become better understood and more social dilemmas are solved or ameliorated. As rule systems become more complex, they naturally take longer to transmit to others. They also tend to include rules that, if they do not undermine survival, may not directly increase survivorship or produce more attractive lives and societies—although they may help systematize or increase the teachability or adherence to the rule systems they are part of. Many aspects of religious beliefs seem to have this character. Although social evolution tends to be faster than biological evolution, it is still a relatively slow process.

## Internalized Ethical Rules as Solutions to Social Dilemmas

Part I discussed possible social equilibria that might emerge in societies without government (or with relatively small and unimportant ones). Such models are useful for thinking about life in small communities before agriculture emerged. Anthropological research suggests that governments in the sense of formal law-creating and -enforcing organizations did not exist in that period. That context was analyzed because it is useful for thinking about life in societies in which governments do not play an active role in solving social dilemmas or creating new ones. The absence of a governing organization does not mean that such communities were lawless. A sustainable community has customary rules for mitigating the Hobbesian and Hardin problems. All attractive communities have solved their most critical public goods, coordination, and externality problems. Relatively prosperous communities also have norms that support and encourage voluntary exchange, specialization, and team production.

A community that is at a social equilibrium has a stable knowledge base describing human possibilities (nature and technology) and a stable body of normative principles and maxims used to assess the alternatives available to individuals, families, and groups. It has solved or ameliorated a variety of social dilemmas, but others exist that limit or block progress. Such equilibria describe much of humanity's history. This is not to say that there was no progress—many minor innovations in hunting, gathering, tools, farming, and home construction took place—nor that governments were entirely irrelevant throughout most of human history. But early human communities tended to be small and to have stable patterns of life grounded in customs, and commerce was a relatively small part of ordinary lives. Governance of rural communities remained for the most part local affairs even after settled communities and agriculture emerged (except perhaps in China).

Part II took up the analysis of governments: rule-enforcing organizations that all contemporary societies have and most urban centers in earlier times also had. For that purpose, two general categories of governments were discussed, productive ones and extractive ones. Productive governments are created by a community to advance its common purposes. Extractive governments may also be created by a community but are intended to extract resources from a community or its neighbors. Extractive governments may also be accidently created when a productive government lacks sufficient ethical inhibitions to resist the many extractive temptations of governance. The latter implies that productive governance requires ethical foundations.

The main focus of Part II was on dilemmas that must be overcome to sustain a productive or "good" government from the perspective of those governed. In order to be productive, a government has to improve life in the community governed. It may do so by further solving or ameliorating social dilemmas. Chapter 6 noted that improved customary law enforcement could make a community more attractive by increasing adherence to productive community norms and ethical principles. Chapter 7 noted that democratic government tends to advance moderate voter interests, but to do so it must solve or ameliorate a variety of democratic dilemmas. Without solutions to these and other political dilemmas, ruling organizations tend to be extractive rather than productive governments. Most of the most plausible solutions are products of ethical support.

## Prosperity

Not all sustainable communities are attractive. And not all attractive communities are prosperous. What distinguishes a prosperous community from others is either its ability to extract from others in the surrounding territory or its ability to trade with others. Extraction requires the organization of force sufficient to take or extort resources from the surrounding area. Trade requires ownership or usufruct rights that are transferable. Gains from trade emerge when there is sufficient comparative advantage that others want to trade their own stuff for that produced by others. Specialization emerges when a person or group can more effectively produce a narrow range of services or products than a broad one. Trade allows such specialists to survive and flourish. Specialization tends to require both capital (specialized equipment) and innovations (new ideas about products and production methods). The accumulation of capital requires defense from raiders and from the extractive temptations of one's own government. Innovation requires freedom to experiment and bring new products to market.

As this short list demonstrates, there are more prerequisites for commerce than there are for extraction. Thus, commercial centers are more difficult to establish and sustain than are centers of extraction.

Prosperity tends to increase as critical social dilemmas are solved, as rules that facilitate voluntary exchange and specialization emerge, as particular kinds of innovations are supported or at least tolerated, as team production becomes more efficient, and as market networks expand and transactions costs diminish.

Internalized norms and external rules created by economic organizations and governments play roles in these processes. Governments may contribute to prosperity by reinforcing customary solutions to social dilemmas and by solving dilemmas not previously addressed. They may adopt policies that reinforce the norms that encourage trade, specialization, and innovation, and that provide services such as road networks and civil law that reduce transactions costs and risk. They may also encourage capital accumulation and public education, which tends to further increase the productivity of labor and its associated organizations and market networks.

Whether a government promotes prosperity or not is a choice ultimately made by its rule-makers. In democratic governments, many, perhaps most, public policies are grounded in the internalized norms of persons eligible to vote. Voters may favor market activities and innovation or disfavor them. The norms that tend to support commercial systems are often very similar to those that encourage personal commercial activities, as with a work ethic, promise-keeping norms, and a theory of "just deserts" that links proper rewards to productive effort and skills. Such normative theories imply that a good life is an active, creative, productive life, rather than one focused on leisure, spirituality, or military conquest.

Overall, the theories worked out in Parts I and II imply that only a subset of the rules that may be internalized support both progress and prosperity. Only a subset of the norms that may be internalized contribute to solving social, economic, and political dilemmas, and also governments and policies that tend to encourage innovation and commercial activities.

## Further Evidence

For readers familiar with rational choice models and who believe that they are generally useful and true, the theoretical analysis of Parts I and II may be all that is required to persuade them that ethical dispositions play a critical role in social and economic development. For others, some additional factual support may be required to make the analysis persuasive. Numerous footnotes have demonstrated that the logic of the analysis produces conclusions that are largely consistent with the anthropological and historical record. This chapter has provided a bit of statistical evidence that economic performance is affected by normative disposition through effects on governance and public policy.

Part III provides additional evidence. It demonstrates that ethical theories often have implications for commerce and political design. And it provides evidence that overlapping and reinforcing shifts in ethical ideas occurred in the decades immediately before the great acceleration of economic activity occurred in western Europe. Together, the theory and the evidence provided in Part III thus account for the timing of what might be considered the most important event in human history since settled agriculture emerged, the increased rate of economic development in the West that lifted a supermajority of its residents out of poverty in the twentieth century and created the commercial society.

The associated new forms of commerce and political organization subsequently increased prosperity in other parts of the world where they were adopted, and thus economic progress continues apace into the twenty-first century.

# PART III

# A SHORT HISTORY OF ETHICAL ASSESSMENTS OF COMMERCE

## Introduction

The previous two parts of the book provide the logic behind the main hypothesis of the book and a bit of historical support for the theory developed. If social dilemmas are commonplace, they must be solved for social, economic, and political progress to take place. The evolution of normative systems of rules provides a possible means through which a long (and likely endless) series of such dilemmas may be ameliorated or solved. It is likely that only a subset of the normative rules internalized by individuals ameliorate or solve social dilemmas, but these are critically important for human progress, which explains why every community has an ethos, whether grounded in custom, myth, theology, or reason.

The dilemmas examined in the first parts of the book are abstract idealized ones, rather than specific historical examples. They are archetypes that characterize the essential features of millions of choice settings in which problematic outcomes tend to arise. The choice settings are cases in which no individual's decisions are truly decisive, and thus each person's, family's, or organization's choices affect the welfare of others. Although the choice settings share common analytical properties, they are not obviously similar. Social dilemmas associated with conflict, commons problems, free-riding, trade, and majority rule tend to be externality problems and are often generated by the practical interests of the persons whose choices jointly determine the outcomes. However, the specific settings that generate such problems tend to look quite different from one another. Many are complex and go unrecognized, and therefore continue to impede economic, political, and social development. For example, Cox, North, and Weingast (2012) argue that variations of the Hobbesian dilemma continue to impede economic development in the twenty-first century. And Ostrom ([1990] 2015) and most contemporary environmentalists continue to analyze and stress ongoing problems associated with various Hardin's dilemmas.

Although the illustrations make the properties of problematic choice settings clear, real dilemmas are rarely as easily recognized because each instance of a dilemma appears to be unique to those confronting it. For example, water and air pollution involve different effluents, arise from different specific forms of behavior, are affected by different kinds of meteorological phenomenon, and generate spillover costs in different ways. They are all instances of commons problems, although they have no obvious connections to communal pasture lands or forests. The free-riding problems confronted when constructing a house or assembling a cell phone look quite different from those associated with transmitting ethical dispositions on to the next generation or creating an innovation commons. They also look quite different from the free-riding problems associated with putting out a fire in the village or defending a nation or region from attack. Thus, quite different norms may contribute to solving each of these problems, although they are species of the same genus of social dilemmas.

It is this specificity that makes solving social dilemmas challenging and social development such a slow process. A dilemma may or may not be recognized or deemed potentially solvable. And even when it is recognized and deemed potentially solvable, new applications of old rules or minor extensions of them may not solve the problems uncovered. Major innovations may be necessary. And not all of the new rules proposed will actually ameliorate the problem of interest, nor would such rules be instantly internalized by most persons in a community. Ameliorating social dilemmas does not always require internalization of the same rules by all the relevant individuals, but they often require a significant fraction of the community's members to do so before a problem can be ameliorated.

Without solutions, social dilemmas block or impede social, political, and economic progress as assessed by those confronting particular dilemmas. Some solutions may emerge from intent—as when a rule of conduct is proposed at a village meeting and agreed to—or they may be generated by felicitous luck, as when a rule developed for another purpose inadvertently solves other problems. The latter implies that social evolution can produce solutions that are unrecognized by the persons whose normative systems do so. Indeed, in the long run, even the problems solved may be long forgotten.

Of course, to demonstrate that a subset of internalized principles and rules of conduct can solve crucial social dilemmas does not prove that they do or did so. Such dispositions are a sufficient, rather than necessary, condition for human progress.

Part III provides evidence that ethical dispositions change through time—albeit slowly—and that changes in the seventeenth and eighteenth centuries were in the direction that would tend to accelerate economic development in what came to be referred to as "the West," largely because of subsequent similarities in the economic and political trajectories of western European countries. Such changes did not occur as a single quantum leap, but as a series of innovations in ethical theories that reached somewhat similar conclusions about the merits of commerce and tended to reinforce one another. For example, secular theories of mutual gains to trade and market efficiency tended to reinforce earlier theological analyses that concluded that prosperity was a divine blessing, rather than a curse or distraction from more important activities.

To provide evidence of such changes, Part III provides overviews of a small sample of widely read books and pamphlets written between 1500 and 1925. Widely read books "talk" to their readers in the sense that their arguments and conclusions must seem plausible to their readers. Readers of such books may subsequently alter their behavior, but that is not the reason that these books are reviewed herein. The main interest in the works reviewed is not the persuasive ability of the authors, but rather that the theories developed were grounded in widely shared observations about the societies in which the authors and readers lived. Widely read philosophical books on ethics in this period systematized commonplace ethical ideas and used numerous examples that were consistent with the beliefs already in the minds of their readers.

Adam Smith's *Moral Sentiments* is the most obvious instance of this, but all the work reviewed in Part III were written by authors with a nuanced understanding of the most commonplace norms in their communities. Their theories of ethics and markets would not have attracted significant attention unless their conclusions were generally compatible with the preexisting beliefs of their readers, even in cases in which new ideas and relationships were successfully communicated to those readers.

Contemporary readers of such books, of course, have different ideas in their minds than their first readers, and so we tend to react somewhat differently than the first and second generations of readers would have. What seems clear and interesting to us may be quite different from that which captivated early fans of the authors reviewed here. However, when the authors use concrete, real-world examples to illustrate their proposed ethical theories, we are in a better position to appreciate both what the authors intended their readers to understand and also the types of behavioral rules that their readers took for granted. Such illustrations have to be "obvious" to an author's expected readers to serve their intended purpose. They must be ethically uncontroversial.

The norms revealed by a widely read author's illustrations and conclusions thus provide evidence about the commonplace norms of their readership at the time and in the place in which their books or pamphlets were written. Insofar as newer analyses were largely compatible with the older ones, successive innovations in theories of the "good" life and "good" society deepened and reinforced earlier arguments without necessarily replacing them.

Together the pieces reviewed in Part III provide evidence of a steady increase in the breadth and depth of support for commerce in a good life and good society, as theologically based analyzes are later buttressed and supplanted by secular ones. In the West, such innovations provided additional moral support for careers in commerce and for government policies that tended to increase prosperity. At the beginning of the period focused on, 1500, commerce and careers in commerce were deemed morally suspect. Reservations about commerce gradually disappear during the next four centuries, while supportive arguments multiply. By 1900, reservations have largely disappeared— at least among typical (but not all) members of Western communities.

Indeed, authors in the nineteenth century are generally more concerned about public policies that discourage commerce or slow economic development than they are about whether commerce should play a central role in a good life or good society. Even theorists such as Pigou, who were somewhat skeptical about markets, suggest that gross national product (the extent of commerce) can be used as a proxy for aggregate utility. According to Pigou and other authors that were more supportive of commerce, the extent of economic prosperity is one of the best indices of "the goodness" of both societies and individual lives.

A secondary purpose of Part III is to induce readers who have not dipped into classic works in ethical, economic, and political theory to become familiar with the main differences among highly regarded ethical theories and their conclusions about commerce. Ethical assessments are not (and should not be) simply a matter of "gut reactions" any more than counting inventory or assessing one's bank balance are or should be. One's understanding of ethical issues can be deepened, just as one's understanding of arithmetic and statistical relationships can. Moreover, it is possible to systematically draw conclusions regarding the role of commerce in a good life and good society, given an internally consistent ethical theory.

Readers who have not read much ethical theory are likely to have absorbed a "moral sense" or "intuitionalist" theory of ethics that regards morality to be grounded in an individual's own intuitions about right and wrong, good character, the good life, and the good society. According to this theory, people "instinctively" know what is wrong and right. However, in most cases, as argued in Chapter 1, those "intuitions" emerge from rules learned from others during one's childhood, rather than as consequences of the human genome. The religious doctrines that people internalize, for example, are largely regionally and family dependent. Other non-religious norms that people internalize are similarly influenced by the culture in which they grow to adulthood. Such learnings may produce an intuition that is important to one's sense of self and society, but they are substantially products of past innovation, learning, and reflection, rather than aspects of human nature—although the ability to develop and internalize such rules are features of human nature.

Productive ethical ideas or systems of rules are no more "intuitive" or "obvious" than the laws of nature, mathematics, or language. They are products of innovation and social evolution and often are more sophisticated and nuanced than their users appreciate. And—as is true of the laws of nature, mathematics, and language—moral sentiments or intuitions are sufficiently complex that both past and present "experts" often spend much of their lifetimes trying to more completely understand them.

The works covered in Part III focus on scholar-experts who wrote about both economics and ethics and devoted significant attention to each. Many of the theories are explicitly empirically grounded and so may be regarded as scientific theories of ethics, a field of study that is clearly part of social science as well as philosophy. All are closely reasoned, draw on practical illustrations from their societies to illustrate propositions, and are well written by the standards of their day. Scientific ethical theories attempt to identify commonalities among the moral maxims of their time and place through a combination of observation, reflection, and generalization. The aim of such ethicists is to understand as much as possible about their area(s) of study—as true of the participants in other scientific enterprises. The end product is normally a few general principles that both characterize and extend the ethos of their communities and, through that distillation, provide a more encompassing guidance for subsequent ethical conduct.

In period before most contemporary academic specializations emerged, ethicists were often social scientists. They would use their knowledge of local customs and ideas from previous scholars as data from which they attempted to provide coherent explanations for and theories of ethical conduct. Several of the ethical theorists reviewed in Part III conclude that a single principle can explain a broad subset of moral intuitions and serve as a useful guide for conduct in both familiar and unfamiliar circumstances. Others argue that more than one principle is required to characterize and clarify the essential features of morality and moral conduct. Utilitarianism is an example of the former, and virtue ethics is an example of the latter.

Such works contrast with what might be called "folk ethics," which normally consists of a long series of rules (maxims) that "all good people" have or should have internalized to some degree: "be brave," "be truthful," "be generous," "learn from your mistakes," "be careful," "be kind to others," and other behavior that they should avoid: "don't fight with others," "don't steal from others," "don't mislead your friends," and so forth. What most ethicists attempted to do (at least before 1900) was to identify principles that could be used to explain such maxims and provide insights relevant for other choice settings that a person might confront. Their proposed theories identified shared properties of a community's maxims and shed light on moral dilemmas that earlier theories could not, while at the same time simplifying the reasoning necessary to reach normative conclusions.

However, it is their use of what might be termed "folk ethics" for illustrations that is of greatest relevance for this book. It is such illustrations that most clearly connect their work with the ethos of their communities.

The main aim of Part III is to provide evidence that reservations against commerce and lives devoted to commerce diminished, and that support for it increased and deepened in the West during the period just before and during the period in which the great acceleration of commerce occurred (roughly from 1600 to 1925). The individual ethical theories and maxims reviewed are incremental and reinforcing steps in this process. According to the analysis of Parts I and II of the book, such changes in ideas about the "good" life and "good" society would have induced more "good" persons to participate in commerce, reducing problems of fraud and team production, and also provided support for public policies that contributed to the emergence of more productive, extensive, and innovative trading networks. Such changes in behavior would tend to accelerate economic development. And it turns out that major innovations in arguments that supported commerce did occur shortly before instances of acceleration, as developed in Chapter 13.

Part III focuses mostly on the period after 1500, but it begins with Aristotle because his work was familiar to most persons writing in the period of interest, and his work was often implicitly used as a point of departure for the later works reviewed in this part of the book. Aristotle's arguments and conclusion are also of interest because they provide one of the best examples of an empirically based theory of ethical conduct and because he wrote in an early commercial society. Athens was a major commercial center during the Aristotle's lifetime.

After Aristotle's foundational conclusions about a good life, good society, and commerce are reviewed, the focus shifts to the period between 1500 and 1925. The astute reader will notice many echoes of Aristotle's ideas in that body of work, echoes that suggest that most of the authors had read Aristotle or had read authors who were influenced by him, and also that the ethical systems that produce commercial societies share many conclusions about the nature of a good life and ethical conduct. Aristotle, himself, is less supportive of commerce than many writers in the nineteenth century were, but more supportive of commerce than many Catholic authors were during the Middle Ages.

Although I spent a good deal of time on the authors and works reviewed, I am by no means an expert, and their words are obviously more authoritative than my or any other interpretation of them can be. Thus, paragraph-length quotes are used throughout to illustrate their main lines of reasoning and conclusions. In many cases, several translations were available, and I generally chose relatively early translations that would be closer to the period of greatest interest for Part III.

# 9

# A Beginning

## Aristotle on Ethics, Markets, and Politics

### Aristotle and Scientific Ethics

The scientific or rational approach to ethics was pioneered by a brilliant Greek philosopher named Aristotle in approximately 330 BCE. His conclusions about the aims of ethics and nature of virtuous dispositions, together with the reasoning used to support those conclusions, had profound effects on the work of future theologians, philosophers, and social scientists. As a consequence, Aristotle's influence on subsequent ethical theories, economics, and political science is broad, subtle, and underappreciated. Wikipedia, for example, notes the following:

> In metaphysics, Aristotelians profoundly influenced Judeo-Islamic philosophical and theological thought during the Middle Ages and continues to influence Christian theology, especially the scholastic tradition of the Catholic Church. Aristotle was also well known among medieval Muslim intellectuals and revered as "The First Teacher." ("Western canon," *Wikipedia*, 2021)

Several hundred years later, his research on ethics, economics, and politics were studied by Adam Smith and Charles Montesquieu, the founders of contemporary economics and political science. His work is only one of many influential Western scholars covered in Part III of the book, but it clearly affected most of the others.

For much of the past 500 years, educated persons in the West were familiar with Aristotle's approach to ethics, logic, physics, and politics because his work was required reading in the core curricula of high schools and colleges. For much of this period, Greek was routinely taught in high schools so that students could read Greek works in their original language. This continued to be the case in many places well into the twentieth century. However, as specialization increased and the teaching of classical languages and literature declined, knowledge of his work became less widespread, translations rather than the original words were read, and hence the need for the review

*Solving Social Dilemmas*. Roger D. Congleton, Oxford University Press. © Oxford University Press 2022.
DOI: 10.1093/oso/9780197642788.003.0009

undertaken in Chapter 9 before launching into our analysis of economically relevant ethical developments from the late Middle Ages forward.[1]

Aristotle benefited from a relatively open, tolerant society in which secular education and scholarship were valued. The city in which Aristotle taught, Athens, was a rare instance of a relatively liberal and open democratic society. Many private schools existed in Athens during its classical era, and Aristotle was sent there from his native Macedonia because those schools were held in high regard. He was a student and colleague of Plato for nearly two decades. After Plato's death, he returned to Macedonia to serve as a teacher of Alexander the Great. He subsequently returned to Athens and founded a new school, the Lyceum. His writings while head of the Lyceum helped launch several research programs in philosophy, science, and social science.

Aristotle's approach to knowledge begins with a review of what others have argued. To these he adds his own observations and conclusions about the field of study being worked on. He attempts to determine essential categories and relationships among the phenomena that define field of study that he is thinking and writing about, and in doing so, he takes both data (observations) and logic seriously. His work on logic, physics, biology, ethics, politics, and economics all apply that very rational, empirically grounded approach to knowledge.[2]

That so many of his conclusions about ethics and politics remain relevant today might suggest to readers that knowledge and intuitions about the good life and good society have not changed very much in the past 2,500 years. However, it is more accurate to say that ideas about the good life and good society in western Europe gradually returned to ones similar to those present in the classical period of Athens after many detours. It is this return to somewhat similar circumstances and beliefs that mostly accounts for the fact

[1] Translators attempt to precisely interpret both his ideas and reasoning as they shift from Greek into the world's other languages, although this is difficult to do exactly, because a bit of interpolation is often required to do so. There are thus subtle variations in the translations available. For the purposes of this volume, I use a mid-nineteenth-century translation of the *Nicomachean Ethics* by D. P. Chase (Aristotle 1897). This translation is used because it was widely read in the nineteenth century and accorded significant praise by the next generation of translators. The Chase translation was largely replaced by the Ross (1925) in the twentieth century, whose translation was widely used in philosophy classes during the twentieth century. It also served as a point of departure for subsequent translations. Two recent translations are also noteworthy, Irwin (1999) for its precision and Crisp (2014) for its clear prose. Appendix I of this chapter provides a sample of translations from several scholars of two critical passages so that readers can see examples of the subtle variations in translation.

[2] Aristotle's methodology differs from that of the modern physical sciences in that he rarely, if ever, conducts experiments or statistical tests of his theories. (Statistics was not developed for nearly 2,000 years.) Nonetheless, his deductive and synthetic approach continues to be the main one used by theorists in the social sciences, history, and philosophy.

that he is still widely read in the West today, if not as much as in the past few centuries.[3]

Aristotle's genius includes his breadth, creativity, and depth. He wrote on an extensive number of subjects during his period as a teacher in Athens and provided new insights and general theories in most of them. His aim was not simply a better "synthesis" of existing ideas but a deeper, more general, and more coherent understanding of the world and life in it. He did all this amazingly well, which is why his work is still of interest nearly 2,500 years after it was first written. His work is not perfect. Many of his theories are no longer thought to be useful, but even among critics, he is admired for his breadth and depth and for his many original insights.

For the purposes of this book, insights from Aristotle's two "practical" books are most relevant: *Nicomachean Ethics* and the *Politics*. We begin with a review of some of the main arguments developed in *Nicomachean Ethics*. In this work, Aristotle attempts to determine whether anything general can be said about a good or praiseworthy human life. Is there an ultimate aim for human action? If there is an ultimate end, are there general methods for effectively advancing that end? He answers yes to both questions.[4]

## A Brief Overview of Aristotle's Theory of Ethics: Virtue Contributes to Human Happiness (*Eudaimonia*)

*Nicomachean Ethics* begins by observing that most goals are simply means to other ends. Most are thought to contribute to an individual's happiness. Happiness differs from other goals because it is not sought as a means to advance some other end. Thus, Aristotle concludes that happiness (*eudaimonia*) is a final end rather than a secondary goal.[5] Given that ultimate end, Aristotle attempts to determine whether there are any general principles for living that tend to produce human happiness. He notes that

---

[3] It bears noting that many of his other conclusions with respect to logic, causality, and science also held up quite well for the next 2,000 years, although many of his scientific claims were revised or disproved in the nineteenth century.

[4] Among his many insights and arguments, Aristotle suggests that a young person "is not a fit student of Moral Philosophy, for he has no experience in the actions of life" (*Nicomachean Ethics*, p. 26, Kindle edition). There is some truth in this as in the rest of his arguments and conclusions, but young readers should ignore his conclusion on this point as they read through Part III.

[5] Aristotle does not mention women in his analysis in large part because women were usually not very important in Greek society, although there were Greek goddesses, and the famous Oracles of Delphi were women. The status of women in the West did not improve much until the eighteenth and nineteenth centuries.

many people are happy because they enjoy their work and suggests that the best forms of work tend to perfect one's soul or spirit. Human character, he argues, consists largely of two parts, a moral part and an intellectual part. He argues that humans tend to be happiest or most content when their choices tend to perfect both their intellectual and moral selves (souls or character). Moral excellence, for example, is generated by virtuous choices. Figure 9.1 in Appendix II of this chapter provides a flow diagram of Aristotle's theory of the how virtuous and other choices tend to yield happiness or contentment.

Aristotle's conception of happiness differs from that implied by the rational choice models used in economics and game theory. Rational choice models generally assume that everyone knows how best to increase their own happiness, which is characterized as "utility," "net benefits," or "welfare." Aristotle assumes that the best way of achieving happiness is not obvious and needs to be taught. The process of developing dispositions consistent with happiness or contentment is not automatic or instantaneous, but takes place through time as one makes deliberate choices, especially moral choices. Without training, practice, and experience, most people make systematic mistakes and so achieve less satisfying lives than they could have. Stated in economic terms, Aristotle argues that happiness requires investments in particular types of human capital, what might be called moral and intellectual capital.[6]

This implies that the nature of a person is not entirely "static," as implicitly assumed in most rational choice models. Instead, at least according to Aristotle, a person's character or essence emerges gradually through time. This is partly a matter of one's nature at birth (what we would call a genetic endowment), but it is largely produced by training, choices, and experience. A person's character is both a subject of choice and a consequence of choice, rather than permanent or predetermined.

With this brief overview, we are now in position to review Aristotle's theory of ethics in more detail. This chapter relies on the 1897 D. P. Chase translation of the *Nicomachean Ethics* (Aristotle 1897), which is among the older translations in modern English. The choice of translation was not an easy one. Chase's translation is used for a variety of reasons, but mainly because it was developed before industrialization, before the emergence of the welfare state, and before Darwin's work on evolution transformed ideas about the nature of man and the good life among educated persons in the

---

[6] Stated in this way, Aristotle's view of ethics is analogous to Stigler and Becker's (1977) discussion of the effects of human capital on the enjoyment of music.

West. Chase's translation is thus likely to give us a better sense about how the scholars surveyed in Part III would have interpreted Aristotle than later translations would. Appendix I to this chapter includes short samples from several other translations so that readers can see for themselves how subtly varied they tend to be.[7]

## The Pursuit of Happiness

Aristotle begins by arguing that the chief good and the main aim of a good life is happiness, although he concedes that there is much disagreement about what happiness (*eudaimonia*) means. Happiness unlike other aims of human action, is desired for its own sake.

> **So far as the name goes, there is a pretty general agreement**: for happiness both the multitude and the refined few call it, and "living well" and "doing well" they **conceive to be the same with "being happy"**; but about the nature of this happiness, men dispute, and the multitude do not in their account of it agree with the wise. (Aristotle 1897, p. 26)

> Happiness is manifestly something final and self-sufficient, being the end of all things which are and may be done. (Aristotle 1897, p. 34)

> As for the life of money-making, it is one of constraint, and **wealth manifestly is not the good we are seeking, because it is for use, that is, for the sake of something further.** (Aristotle 1897, p. 29)

> Happiness is . . . [pursued] always for its own sake, and never with a view to anything further: whereas honor, pleasure, intellect, in fact every excellence we choose for their own sakes, it is true (because we would choose each of these even if no result were to follow), but we choose them also with a view to happiness. (Aristotle 1897, pp. 33–34)

---

[7] The D. P. Chase (1897) translation is freely available at Google Books and in a slightly edited form in the Kindle format and in hard copy from Public Domain Books (without translation notes, but with an introduction written much later by J. A. Smith). Other noteworthy options included the highly regarded W. D. Ross translation (1912), the recent Irwin translation (1999) with its copious translation notes, and the well-written, recently revised Crisp translation (2014). Some of the quotes taken from the Chase translation are lightly edited to improve readability. For example, contemporary rules for capitalization and punctuation were applied and some sentences slightly shortened without altering his meaning. Words and letters that were added in this process are framed in brackets. Bolding has been added to draw the reader's attention to key phrases.

Given that happiness is the chief good or ultimate human end, is there anything general that can be said about the most effective means of achieving it? It turns out that "work" or purposeful activity is one of the ways to achieve happiness, especially efforts to perfect one's human capacities for excellence.[8]

> This object [happiness] may be easily attained, when we have discovered **what is the work of man**; for as in the case of flute-player, statuary, or artisan of any kind, or, more generally, all who have any work or course of action, **their chief good and excellence is thought to reside in their work.** (Aristotle 1897, p. 34)

> **So, it would seem to be with man, if there is any work belonging to him.** (Aristotle 1897, p. 34)

> **What then can this be? not mere life**, because that plainly is shared with him even by vegetables, and we want what is peculiar to him. We must separate off then the life of mere nourishment and growth, and next will come the life of sensation: but this again manifestly is common to horses, oxen, and every animal. (Aristotle 1897, p. 34)

> There remains then a kind of **life of the rational nature** apt to act: and of this nature there are **two parts** denominated rational, the one as being obedient to reason, the other as having and exerting it. (Aristotle 1897, p. 34)

> The **good of man** comes to be "a **working of the soul in the way of excellence,**" or, if excellence admits of degrees, in the way of the best and most perfect excellence. And we must add, **in a complete life; for as it is not one swallow or one fine day that makes a spring**, so it is not one day or a short time that makes a man blessed and happy. Let this then be taken **for a rough sketch of the chief good,** since it is probably the right way to give first the outline and fill it in afterwards. (Aristotle 1897, p. 35)

There are two general areas in which deliberate activities can improve one's soul or character: the moral and the intellectual. Both can be further subdivided.

> **Human excellence** is of two kinds, intellectual and moral. The intellectual springs originally, and is increased subsequently, from teaching (for the most part, that is),

---

[8] Later translations would use the word "function" instead of "work." The term "work" captures the idea of deliberate purposeful activity, whereas function captures the idea of a specific task or purpose that can done more or less effectively. Evidently, the Greek term includes elements of each. See Appendix I to this chapter for variations in the translations of three of the key passages in Book I of *Nicomachean Ethics*.

and needs therefore experience and time; whereas the moral comes from custom [routines, habits, or dispositions]. (Aristotle 1897, p. 49)

In speaking of a man's moral character, we do not say he is a scientific or intelligent but a meek man, or one of perfected self-mastery: and we praise the man of science in light of his mental state; and of these such as are praiseworthy we call excellences. (Aristotle 1897, p. 48)

Moral character is "meek," but in a different sense than that word is used in contemporary English. Later translators often use the word "temperate" or "prudent" rather than meek, although neither seems to fully capture what Aristotle has in mind, namely self-mastery.

[T]he notion represented by the term meek man is being imperturbable, and not being led away by passion, but being angry in that manner, and at those things, and for that length of time, which reason may direct. (Aristotle 1897, p. 114)[9]

## Moral Choice Requires Reason and Freedom of Action

How does one "work the soul" to develop excellence in moral character? One does so by developing virtuous dispositions. Such dispositions emerge from a lifetime of deliberate actions that are undertaken partly to develop such dispositions. Virtuous dispositions are not natural according to Aristotle because nature is unchanging and permanent, whereas one's dispositions can be altered through training, choices, actions, and experience. Both virtue and vice are produced by a person's past decisions.

So too then is it with the virtues: for by acting in the various relations in which we are thrown with our fellow men, we come to be, some just, some unjust: and by acting in dangerous positions and being habituated to feel fear or confidence, we come to be, some brave, others cowards. Similarly is it also with respect to the occasions of lust and anger: for some men come to be perfected

[9] The above translation was written about two centuries after the King James (1611) version of the New Testament's "Blessed are the meek, for they shall inherit the earth" (Matthew 5.5). It is possible that the same meaning of the word "meek" was intended when this translation of the New Testament was undertaken, rather than the more modern one, which implies being a timid person, rather than a person that is temperate or has achieved self-mastery.

> in self-mastery and mild, others destitute of all self-control and passionate. (Aristotle 1897, p. 50)

> From this fact, it is plain that *not one* of the moral virtues comes to be in us merely by nature: because of such things as exist by nature, none can be changed by custom. (Aristotle 1897, p. 49)

A morally relevant action is one that can be deliberately and voluntarily chosen. To be voluntary, the aim of the action must be feasible, and the consequences of the action must be those intended. To be a moral or ethical choice, the consequences must include effects on one's own character.

> **Involuntary actions** then are thought to be of **two kinds**, being done either on **compulsion**, or by reason of **ignorance**. An action is, properly speaking, compulsory, when the origination is external to the agent, being such that in it the agent (perhaps we may more properly say the patient) contributes nothing; as if a wind were to convey you anywhere, or men having power over your person. (Aristotle 1897, p. 67)

> If this be so, **no other animal but man, and not even children, can be said to act voluntarily.** (Aristotle 1897, p. 71)

> But **not all voluntary action is an object of moral choice.** (Aristotle 1897, p. 74)

> Now since that which is the object of moral choice is something in our own power, which is the object of deliberation and the grasping of the will, **moral choice must be a grasping after something in our own power consequent upon deliberation: because after having deliberated we decide, and then grasp by our will in accordance with the result of our deliberation.** (Aristotle 1897, p. 77)

Not all choices are moral choices. This distinction among choice settings is not always included in subsequent moral theories, but it is central to Aristotle's theory of moral development. Moral choices are ones that tend to promote or reveal character development. They are virtuous choices through which moral excellence is gradually accumulated.

> Furthermore, it is wholly irrelevant to say that the man who acts unjustly or dissolutely does not wish to attain the habits of these vices: for **if a man wittingly does those things whereby he must become unjust he is to all intents and purposes unjust voluntarily.** (Aristotle 1897, p. 80)

Both virtue and vice are acquired dispositions, reflecting our past choices. Even in cases in which the ends of action are not chosen, the means often are, and those choices may also have effects on one's character.

Whether then we suppose that **the end impresses each man's mind with certain notions not merely by nature, but . . . is somewhat also dependent on himself; or that the end is given by nature, and yet virtue is voluntary because the good man does all the rest voluntarily.** (Aristotle 1897, p. 82)

Even in cases in which ends are parts of one's character that are induced by nature, the actions undertaken are chosen by the individual himself. If the actions chosen induce virtuous habits of the mind, then the individual controls his moral development. Virtue is increased or diminished by every moral choice made during one's lifetime.

In economic terms, the process of deliberation, the choices made, and actions taken all affect our stock of moral capital. Our preexisting accumulation of moral capital affects our desires, our wishes, and also our will. Exercising those dispositions tends to increase or diminish them according to the decisions made and actions taken. Both moral and immoral dispositions are produced by morally relevant choices and are among the intended consequences of those choices.

## On the Nature of Virtue: Moderation and the "Golden Mean"

If happiness requires moral excellence, and moral excellence requires virtuous dispositions, the next question is whether anything general can be said about the nature of virtuous dispositions. Aristotle argues that virtues have common properties, although they describe different dispositions and address different choice settings. He argues that nearly all virtues are midpoints between extremes that are widely regarded to be vices. To prove this point, he reviews widely acknowledged virtues and attempts to show that a common pattern exists: they nearly all lie between two widely acknowledged vices.

First, then, of **courage. Now that it is a mean state with respect of fear and boldness**, has been already discussed. The objects of our fears are obviously things fearful or, in a general way of statement, evils; which accounts for the common definition of fear, viz. "expectation of evil." **Of course we fear evils of all kinds: disgrace,** for instance, poverty, disease, desolateness, death; but not all these seem to be the object-matter of the brave man, **because there are things which to fear is right and noble, and not to fear is base.** (Aristotle 1897, p. 83)

One can improperly ignore risks as well as overreact to them. A brave person is not foolhardy but, rather, is fearful only for good reasons.

He then analyzes the virtue of self-mastery, which is arguably the most important virtue in Aristotle's theory, because it is a prerequisite for excelling at all the others.

Next let us speak of perfected **self-mastery,** which seems to claim the next place to courage, since these **two are the excellences of the irrational part of the soul.** It is **a mean state,** having for its object-matter pleasures . . . **a man destitute of self-control is such because he is pained more than he ought to be at not obtaining things which are pleasant** (and thus his pleasure produces pain to him). **The man of perfected self-mastery is such in virtue of not being pained by their absence,** that is, by having to abstain from what is pleasant. (Aristotle 1897, pp. 90–94)

Aristotle goes on to analyze several other virtues, among which liberality and meekness are among the most relevant virtues for the purposes of this chapter.

We will next speak of **liberality.** Now this is a **mean state having for its object-matter wealth.** The liberal man is praised not in the circumstances of war, nor in those which constitute the character of perfected self-mastery, nor again in judicial decisions, but in respect of giving and receiving wealth, chiefly the former. By the term wealth I mean all those things whose worth is measured by money . . . **the Liberal man will give from a motive of honor, and will give rightly;** I mean, **to proper persons, in right proportion, at right times,** and whatever is included in the term "right giving" and this too with positive pleasure, or at least **without pain.** . . . The man who gives to improper people, or not from a motive of honor but from some other cause, shall be called **not liberal** but something else. (Aristotle 1897, pp. 97–99)

Here **each of the extremes involves really an excess and defect** contrary to each other: I mean, the prodigal gives out too much and takes in too little, while the stingy man takes in too much and gives out too little. (Aristotle 1897, pp. 60–61)

With respect to meekness (often translated as "temperance" or "prudence" in later translations), Aristotle regards it to be a virtue with respect to anger and other passions. It is an end toward which reason might direct or constrain one's irrational character.

> We call the virtuous character meek, we will call the mean state meekness, and of the extremes, let the man who is excessive be denominated passionate, and the faulty state passionateness, and him who is excessive angry, and the defect angerlessness. (Aristotle 1897, p. 62)
>
> With respect of **pleasures and pains** (but not all, and perhaps fewer pains than pleasures), the **mean state is perfected self-mastery**, the defect total absence of self-control.
>
> There is a character that takes **less pleasure than he ought** in bodily enjoyments. Such persons also **fail to abide by the conclusions of reason.** The man of self-control is the mean between him and the man of imperfect self-control—that is to say, the latter fails to abide by them because of somewhat **too much**, the former because of somewhat **too little**.
>
> The man of self-control and the man of perfected self-mastery have this in common, that they do nothing against right reason on the impulse of bodily pleasures, but then the former has bad desires, the latter not. The latter is so constituted as not even to feel pleasure contrary to his reason, the former feels but does not yield to it. (Aristotle 1897, p. 193)

Aristotle concludes that a very broad range of virtues are means between extremes that are widely regarded to be vices, and that the virtues are all highly regarded, praiseworthy aspects of human character.[10] The vices are condemned or shamed.[11] His analysis of virtue can be regarded as an exercise in social science insofar as it is based on observations of Athenian assessments of various dispositions regarded to be virtues and vices.

However, he acknowledges that not all virtues have this property. Two virtues that seem to lack this property are truthfulness and justice.

> Now **since falsehood is in itself low and blamable**, while **truth is noble and praiseworthy**, it follows that the **truthful man** (who is also in the mean) is **praiseworthy**.
>
> I call him truthful, because we are **not** now meaning the man who is true in his agreements **nor** in such matters as amount to justice or injustice (this would come within the province of a different virtue), but, in such as do not involve any

---

[10] Praise and praiseworthiness move to center stage in Adam Smith's theory of moral sentiments, written about 2,000 years later.

[11] It is interesting to note that his arguments do not conflict very much with contemporary assessments of virtuous conduct, suggesting that opinions about praiseworthy behavior tends to be similar in commercial societies.

> such serious difference as this, **the man we are describing is true in life and word simply because he is in a certain moral state.**
>
> And he that is such must be judged to be a **good man: for he that has a love for truth as such** ... he will have a dread of falsehood as base, since he shunned it even in itself: and **he that is of such a character is praiseworthy.** (Aristotle 1897, p. 119)

Aristotle argues that justice has several meanings, some of which—but not all—are consistent with his theory of virtue.

> We see then that all men mean by the term justice a moral state such that in consequence of it men have the capacity of doing what is just, and actually do it, and wish it. (Aristotle 1897, p. 124)

> **Justice, it must be observed, is not a mean state in the same manner as the forementioned virtues,** but because it **aims at producing the mean,** while injustice occupies both the extremes. (Aristotle 1897, p. 137)

The notion of justice that attracts most of Aristotle's attention is with respect to that which might be called fairness or just deserts. Just relations between men and women are those that are fair in the sense that rewards are proportionate, which is not usually the same thing as being equal.

> The **just, then, is a certain proportionable thing.** For proportion does not apply merely to number in the abstract, but to number generally, since it is **equality of ratios.** (Aristotle 1897, p. 131)

He goes on to use economic relationships to illustrate what he means by proportionate justice. In doing so, he provides several pioneering insights into what would later be termed *price theory*.

## Market Exchange as an Instance of Just Relations between Men

Aristotle argues that proportionate justice is the basis of both economic exchange and community.

> In **dealings of exchange** such a principle of justice as this **reciprocation forms the bond of union,** but then **it must be reciprocation according to proportion and not exact equality,** because **by proportionate reciprocity of action the social community is held together.** (Aristotle 1897, p. 134)

In markets, the appropriate reciprocity is not determined by equality in weight or numbers, but by market prices. Justice in exchange involves equality of value as determined by money prices.

> The builder is to receive from the shoemaker of his ware, and to give him of his own. **If there is proportionate equality, the reciprocation [exchange] takes place, [and] there will be the just result of which we are speaking.** If not, there is not the equal, nor will the connection stand.... And this is so also in the other arts, for they would have been destroyed entirely if there were not a correspondence in point of quantity and quality between the producer and the consumer. (Aristotle 1897, p. 135)

Relative prices imply that exchange can be objectively "equal" in that the total values of goods exchanged are equal, and thus just, according to Aristotle's theory of proportionate justice. Note that this equality of market value rules out speculative profits, which is also the case in neoclassical models of competitive equilibrium. If A purchases $100 of goods from B, A cannot resell those goods to C for $150, because this would violate proportionate reciprocity. Such trades could not be sustained in what contemporary economists would refer to as being "in equilibrium," which Aristotle refers to as "standing connections."

Aristotle observes that money and money prices allow goods and services to be compared with one another. This facilitates exchange. Without money, only barter would be possible, and without money prices, proportionate justice would be far more difficult to achieve.[12]

> All things **which can be exchanged should be capable of comparison. For this purpose, money has come in, and comes to be a kind of medium. It measures all things** and so likewise the excess and defect. [It determines] for instance, **how many shoes are equal to a house or a given quantity of food.**
>
> As then the builder to the shoemaker, so many shoes must be to the house (or food if instead of a builder an agriculturist is the exchanging party); for unless there is this proportion there cannot be exchange or dealing, and this proportion cannot be [acceptable] unless the terms are *in some way* equal. (Aristotle 1897, pp. 135–136)

[12] From 1920 to 1950, there was a centralization debate among economists regarding the feasibility and merits of centralized command and control economies like the one to which the Soviet Union aspired. Those defending markets argued that, without money prices, rational investment decisions are impossible because one cannot compare alternatives. See Pareto (1927), Mises (1927), and Hayek (1935) for key contributions; or Murrell (1983), Lavoie (1985), and Boettke (2000) for summaries and overviews. It is clear that this property of money prices was recognized by Aristotle, whose analysis arguably forms the foundation of the much later one.

Let A represent an agriculturist, C food, B a shoemaker, D his wares equalized with A's. Then **the proportion will be correct, A:B::C:D; now reciprocation will be practicable,** if it were not, there would have been no dealing. (Aristotle 1897, p. 136)

In the space of a couple of pages, Aristotle sketches out a theory of equilibrium money prices and uses it to illustrate his principle of proportionate justice. Contemporary economics would interpret Aristotle's characterization of price ratios as those associated with markets in competitive long-run equilibrium.

He goes on to sketch out a theory of money's role as a medium of exchange and store of value.

Now that what connects men in such transactions is demand. [This] is shown by the fact that, **when either one does not want the other or neither want one another, they do not exchange** at all, whereas **they do when one wants what the other man has, wine for instance, giving in return corn for exportation.**

And further, **money is a kind of security to us in respect of exchange at some future time** (supposing that one wants nothing now that we shall have it when we do): the theory of money being that whenever one brings it one can receive commodities in exchange: of course, this too is liable to depreciation, for **its purchasing power is not always the same, but still it is of a more permanent nature than the commodities it represents.** (Aristotle 1897, p. 137)

Let B represent ten minæ, A a house worth five minæ, or in other words half B, C a bed worth 1/10th of B: it is clear then how many beds are equal to one house, namely, five. **It is obvious also that exchange was thus conducted before the existence of money: for it makes no difference whether you give for a house five beds or the price of five beds.** (Aristotle 1897, p. 137)

Aristotle notes that holding money is not without risk, because of possible changes in the value of money (what present-day economists would call the risk of inflation). Nonetheless, Aristotle argues that holding money is less risky than holding most other assets. He also notes that the same trades and trading ratios could have been achieved without money.

In this short section, Aristotle invents or at least discusses several important ideas in economics. Aristotle is among the first to argue that money allows comparisons among disparate goods. Such comparisons are necessary for his theory of proportionate justice in exchange. Evidently, prices in Athens exhibited this property well enough for trade to serve as a useful illustration of his theory.

This equality is a property of what would later be referred to as just prices— that the money value of the goods traded should be the same across all markets. In contemporary economic theory, this is often called the no-speculation condition of competitive equilibrium. In equilibrium, there are gains to trade but no speculative gains because all prices satisfy Aristotle's transitivity of value ratios.

Aristotle's economic theory is not central to his analysis or interests. Rather, it is worked out simply in order to illustrate an important part of his theory of justice.

## Aristotle's Conclusions about Profits, Interest, and Occupations

Proportionate reciprocity plays a central role in Aristotle's theory of justice, markets, and society. In the *Politics*, which characterizes his theory of the good society, Aristotle discusses both positive and negative features of market activities. For example, Aristotle makes an ethical case in support of private property and for some types of production and exchange. On the one hand, he favors household management (what we would call farming) because it is productive and provides many opportunities for intellectual and moral development. On the other hand, he criticizes trade in preexisting goods (what Kirzner [1973] would much later call entrepreneurship) because it tends to generate an excessive focus and regard for money profits. The same tends to be true of the exchange of money for interest (usury).

Aristotle is not opposed to maximizing profit, per se, but to an excessive focus on profits. For example, he suggests that farmers (and implicitly other producers) should know the rate of return from alternative investments.

> The useful parts of wealth-getting [for farmers] **are, first, the knowledge of the livestock which are most profitable,** ..., for example, what sort of horses or sheep or oxen or any other animals are most likely to give a return. **A man ought to know which of these pay better than others, and which pay best in particular places,** for some do better in one place and some in another. Secondly, husbandry, which may be either tillage or planting, and the keeping of bees and of fish, or fowl, or of any animals which may be useful to man. **These are the true or proper arts of wealth-getting** and come first. (Aristotle, 1885, KL: 282)

However, he disapproves of trade in preexisting goods and finance because they are overly focused on money profits and provide fewer opportunities to develop virtuous dispositions. In between farming and finance are careers devoted to harvesting nature's bounty, as with timbering, fishing, and mining.

There are **two sorts of wealth-getting: one is a part of household management, the other is retail trade. The former is necessary and honorable,** while that which consists in exchange is justly censured; for it is unnatural, and a mode by which men gain from one another.

**The most hated sort, and with the greatest reason, is usury, which makes a gain out of money itself, and not from the natural object of it.** For money was intended to be used in exchange, but not to increase at interest. And this term interest, which means the birth of money from money, is applied to the breeding of money because the offspring resembles the parent. **Of all the modes of getting wealth this is the most unnatural.** (Jowett, *Politics*, 1885, KL: 275)

A third sort of wealth getting . . . is also concerned with exchange, viz., the industries that make their profit from the earth, and from things growing from the earth which, although **they bear no fruit,** are nevertheless profitable; for example, the cutting of timber and all mining. (Jowett, *Politics*, 1885, KL: 285) Those occupations are most truly arts in which there is the least element of chance; **they are the meanest in which the body is most deteriorated, the most servile** in which there is the greatest use of the body, and **the most illiberal in which there is the least need of excellence.** (Jowett, *Politics*, 1885, KL: 295–296)

It is doubtful that this rough ranking of the merits of commercial professions was original with Aristotle, but his work was read for many centuries afterward and so his remarks on this subject are important. They doubtless influenced the assessments of many of his later readers.

His ranking of the relative merits of occupations is largely based on the extent to which an occupation contributes to one's moral and intellectual development, but also on what would later be termed their *value added*. Farming requires more choices and tends to add more value than extractive occupations—at least according to Aristotle's assessment. Extractive occupations, in turn, add more value than organizing trades of existing goods. Moreover, the latter tends to overemphasize money profits and possessions.[13]

It is not clear where his own occupation fits into this hierarchy: teaching and running a college, where knowledge is traded for money. He most likely regarded it as a form of production (household management) in which skill was important and opportunities for intellectual and moral development were plentiful.

It is interesting (and important) to note that normative conclusions similar to Aristotle's about the relative merits of farming, mining, commerce, banking, and finance were widely codified in laws and other public policies

---

[13] In the *Politics*, Aristotle makes this explicit: "External things, like any instrument, have a limit: everything useful belongs among those things an excess of which must necessarily be either harmful or not beneficial to those who have them" (Aristotle 1992, p. 188).

during the next 2,000 years. Loaning money for interest was widely illegal in both medieval Europe and in the Islamic domains to the southeast of Europe for much of the next 2,000 years. Farming remained a highly regarded activity, indeed a noble one, for most of that period as well.

## Limits of General Principles in Virtue and Law

In the *Nicomachean Ethics*, Aristotle focuses for the most part on virtue's role in a good life. The *Politics* analyzes the manner in which a society is organized—its legal system and political institutions—and how those institutions contribute to the development of intellectual and moral excellence through effects on the skills and dispositions that tend to produce lifelong happiness.[14]

Aristotle's analysis of what might be called the rules for a good society begins with his discussion of justice. Among the concepts of justice reviewed are ones grounded in formal rules or laws, what might be termed *formal* or *legal justice*. A law is just in this sense if it has been lawfully adopted, which is to say, adopted through the procedures specified in a community's constitution. Good laws advance common interests, including moral development, which is to say they generally increase happiness (*eudaimonia*) in the community. Note that laws can be legally just without necessarily being good laws.

All **lawful things are in a manner just, because by lawful we understand what has been defined by the legislative power** and each of these we say is just.

The laws too give directions on all points, **aiming either at the common good of all, or that of the best, or that of those in power** (taking for the standard real goodness or adopting some other estimate). **In one way we mean by just, those things which are apt to produce and preserve happiness** and its ingredients for the social community. (Aristotle 1897, p. 126)

---

[14] As in the case of *Nicomachean Ethics*, there are numerous translations of *Politics*. My first preference was for a translation of about the same vintage as used for the *Nicomachean Ethics*, but I was unable to find one that was sufficiently readable for the purposes of this chapter. In the end, I decided to use the 1885 Jowett translation, which is widely available on various classic websites, from Google books (in the original, with a very long introduction) and also in Kindle format from *Penguin Classics* (without the introduction or translator notes). The latter is the version used here and is adopted partly because of its time of translation. The Kindle version of Jowett's 1885 translation unfortunately includes only Kindle location numbers, rather than page numbers; these are listed as "KL:" followed by the location number(s) in the text. Second choices included the Tayler translation (1811), the very readable translations by Carnes Lord (2013) and the C. D. C. Reeve translation (1998), which includes relatively detailed translator notes. I was especially tempted to use the Tayler translation because it antedated Bekker's 1837 compilation of Aristotle's writings in Greek and the major developments of the nineteenth century, but it seemed to be less complete and well-organized than subsequent translations (possibly because it pre-dated Bekker's careful research). I have lightly edited the quotes from Jowett to improve their readability. For the most part, this involved updating his punctuation. In a few cases, I untangled his phrasing, but only if this could be done without changing his meaning.

> [T]he law commands the doing of deeds not only of the brave man (as with not leaving the ranks, nor flying, nor throwing away one's arms), but those also of the perfectly self-mastering man, as abstinence from adultery and wantonness; and those of the meek man, as refraining from striking others or using abusive language, and in like manner in respect of the other virtues and vices commanding some things and forbidding others, rightly if it is a good law. (Aristotle 1897, p. 126)

The idea that virtue can be compelled by law appears to conflict with his earlier analysis, which argued that freedom of action is necessary for moral choices. However, the law may be regarded as encouraging rather than necessitating particular types of actions. One may choose to follow or disregard the law. If so, a law that discourages vice can be said to promote the common good and happiness by encouraging the formation of virtuous dispositions.

In his discussion of justice and the law, Aristotle considers both universal laws—laws that should apply everywhere—and local variations in law that may be regarded as just because they have been adopted by legitimate governments. The latter will differ among polities.

> A parallel may be drawn between the just which depend upon convention and expedience, and measures; for wine and corn measures are not equal in all places, but where men buy they are large, and where these same sell again they are smaller.
>
> In like manner, the justs which are not natural, but of human invention, are not everywhere the same, for not even the forms of government are, and yet there is one only which by nature would be best in all places. (Aristotle 1897, p. 141)

He also notes that the impossibility of creating a complete guide for ethical behavior—which is why practical wisdom is required—implies that developing a perfect, universal set of laws is also impossible. The law, however, needs to be general, but it cannot therefore always be correct.[15]

> Where then there is a necessity for general statement, while a general statement cannot apply rightly to all cases.

---

[15] Early in Book I of *Nicomachean Ethics*, Aristotle warns the reader about the limited precision that is possible in ethical analysis: "We must be content then, in speaking of such things and from such data, to set forth the truth roughly and in outline; in other words, since we are speaking of general matter and from general data, to draw also conclusions merely general. And in the same spirit should each person receive what we say: for the man of education will seek exactness [only] so far in each subject as the nature of the thing admits" (*Nicomachean Ethics*, p. 26).

The law takes the generality of cases, **being fully aware of the error thus involved**; and rightly too notwithstanding, because **the fault is not in the law,** or in the framer of the law, but is **inherent in the nature of the thing,** because the matter of all action is necessarily such.

When then the law has spoken in general terms, and there [are always] **exceptions** to the general rule, **it is proper—insofar as the lawgiver omits the case and by reason of his universality of statement is wrong—to set right the omission by ruling it as the lawgiver himself would rule were he there present.** (Aristotle 1897, p. 149)

## Aristotle on the Merits of Private Property

Among the laws most relevant for economic activity are those with respect to private property, contract, and exchange. Aristotle provides a clear defense of private property in the *Politics*. Aristotle's famous teachers (Socrates and Plato) had advocated relatively broad common ownership. Aristotle disagrees with their analysis and notes practical problems associated with communal property and advantages of private property.[16] Moreover, he also argues that an "ideal" that is not possible cannot really be ideal.

The members of a state must either have (1) all things or (2) nothing in common, or (3) some things in common and some not.

That they should have **nothing in common is clearly impossible,** for the community must at any rate have a common place—one city will be in one place, and **the citizens are those who share in that one city.** (*Politics*, KL: 371–373)

**In framing an ideal we may assume what we wish, but should avoid impossibilities.** (*Politics*, KL: 528)

He argues that, as a rule, property should be private because there will be fewer disputes and property will be used more productively when it is privately held or owned.

**Property should be in a certain sense common, but, as a general rule, private**; for when everyone has a distinct interest, men will not complain of one another, and

---

[16] Aristotle and fellow scholars at his school collected and analyzed a large number of constitutions from the many city-states in the region that modern-day Greece now encompasses. The results of that project are summarized in *Politics*, which arguably launched the field of political science, as distinct from political theory. His analysis of political systems thus tends to be empirically based, although his assessment of their relative merits returns to ideas developed in the *Nicomachean Ethics*. The *Politics* also analyzes policy issues of his time, such as public education (which he supports) and slavery (which he did not condemn but argued that more persons were slaves than should be).

**they will make more progress,** because everyone will be attending to his own business. (*Politics*, KL: 458–460)

Besides the practical advantages of private ownership, Aristotle also notes that ownership can be a source of pleasure and, moreover, is necessary to develop some virtues.

How immeasurably greater is the pleasure, when a man feels a thing to be his own; for surely the love of self is a feeling implanted by nature and not given in vain. Although selfishness is rightly censured; this is not the mere love of self, but the love of self **in excess,** like the miser's love of money; for all, or almost all, men love money and other such objects in a measure.

And further, **there is the greatest pleasure in doing a kindness or service to friends or guests or companions, which can only be rendered when a man has private property.** These advantages are lost by excessive unification of the state.

The exhibition of two virtues, besides, is visibly annihilated in [without private property]: first, temperance towards women (for it is an honorable action to abstain from another's wife for temperance' sake); secondly, liberality in the matter of property. **No one, when men have all things in common, will any longer set an example of liberality or do any liberal action; for liberality consists in the use which is made of property.** (*Politics*, KL: 465–473)

Aristotle also suggests that many of the problems that opponents of private property point to are not caused by that mode of ownership but by aspects of human nature.

Such legislation [placing everything in common] may have a specious appearance of benevolence; men readily listen to it, and are easily induced to believe that in some wonderful manner everybody will become everybody's friend, especially when someone is heard denouncing **the evils now existing in states, suits about contracts, convictions for perjury, flatteries of rich men and the like,** which are said to arise out of the possession of private property.

**These evils, however, are due to a very different cause—the wickedness of human nature.**

Indeed, we see that there **is much more quarreling among those who have all things in common,** though there are not many of them when compared with the vast numbers who have private property. Again, we ought to reckon, not only the evils from which the citizens will be saved, but also the advantages which they will lose. (*Politics*, KL: 470–478)

Overall, Aristotle's case for private property rests on a variety of practical advantages associated with it. There are benefits and costs, but he argues that the benefits are generally far greater than the costs. Communal ownership is impractical, because of what economists would later refer to as free-rider and commons problems. It also undermines two important virtues and eliminates a significant source of pleasure. Private property is thus generally the better form of ownership. Private property (generally) increases the lifetime happiness of people living in a community relative to that associated with communal property.

That it does so without necessarily increasing moral or intellectual excellence implies that there are other sources of happiness than the two given most attention in *Nicomachean Ethics*.

## Political Institutions and the Good Society

Aristotle's *Politics* also explores a variety of issues associated with governments, why they exist, and what form is most likely to produce a good society. Active governments are necessary because of the imprecision of law and the dynamic environment of human life. Laws at least occasionally need to be refined to accommodate changes in circumstances. The best governments do this with the happiness or contentment of their citizenry in mind. Indeed, communities emerge because they enhance prospects for a good life.

> EVERY STATE is a community of some kind, and every community is established with a view to some good; for mankind always act in order to obtain that which they think good
>
> **The state or political community which is the highest of all**, and which embraces all the rest, **aims at good to a greater degree than any other, and at the highest good.** (*Politics*, KL: 26–35)
>
> When several villages are united in a single complete community, large enough to be nearly or quite self-sufficing, the state comes into existence, **originating in the bare needs of life, and continuing in existence for the sake of a good life.** (*Politics*, KL: 63)

The state increases the survival prospects of individuals and can increase their virtue and happiness. Government is thus in one sense a major innovation, but its universality implies that it is a feature of nature rather than custom.[17]

---

[17] Such mutual benefits of ceding authority to governments would much later be used to provide the foundation for contractarian theories of the state, as with Hobbes (1651).

The proof that the state is a creation of nature and prior to the individual is that the individual, when isolated, is not self-sufficing; **and therefore he is like a part in relation to the whole.** . . . A social instinct is implanted in all men by nature, and yet he who first founded the state was the greatest of benefactors. (*Politics*, KL: 80–82)

Although governments are necessary and productive, some forms of government are better than others. One of the aims of the Politics is to characterize the best form of government. To do so, he extends the approach used in *Nicomachean Ethics* to assess the relative merits of governments. As the best character is that which produces a life of happiness or contentment, the best constitution is that which produces good lives for its citizens and is sufficiently robust to do so for a long period of time.[18]

What is politically possible is partly an empirical question, and Aristotle and his colleagues examined the constitutions, successes, and failures of the wide variety of governments in the territories in and around the Aegean Sea that is often referred to as "Classical Greece." After that study, which is summarized in the *Politics*, he attempts to characterize the best constitution.

**We have now to inquire what is the best constitution for most states, and the best life for most men,** neither assuming a standard of virtue which is above ordinary persons, nor an education which is exceptionally favored by nature and circumstances, nor yet an ideal state which is an aspiration only, but having regard to the life in which the majority are able to share, and to the form of government which states in general can attain. (*Politics*, KL: 1641)

He suggests that the relative merits of governments can be analyzed in much the same manner as ethics. He begins by looking at existing governments and attempting to discern universal principles from those examples. He argues that the lawgivers can exhibit virtue and vice just as ordinary men can. A good government increases the level of virtue and thereby happiness of individuals in the communities governed.

In the end, he supports representative democracy, which he regards to be a mixed or intermediate form of government. However, the best form of government depends partly on the income distribution in the communities to be governed.

---

[18] Note that these assertions differ from those of Hobbes in that he argues that people do not have an instinctive social nature, but one that tends toward endless conflict. Parts I and II of this book suggest that such social instincts are products of social evolution and are taught, rather than genetically transmitted aspects of human nature.

[T]he **best political community is formed by citizens of the middle class,** and that those states are likely to be well-administered in which the middle class is large, and stronger if possible than both the other classes, or at any rate than either singly; for the addition of the middle class turns the scale, and prevents either of the extremes from being dominant....

**The mean condition of states is clearly best,** for no other is free from faction; and where the middle class is large, there are least likely to be factions and dissensions. For a similar reason, large states are less liable to faction than small ones, because in them the middle class is large. (*Politics*, KL: 1679–1687)

Regarding the best form of government, Aristotle argues that the best form of governments takes account of the interest of all the economic classes within the polity. Such governments combine elements of direct democracy with representative (aristocratic or oligarchic) elements.

**It is also a good plan that those who deliberate should be elected by vote or by lot in equal numbers out of the different classes**; and that if the people greatly exceed in number those who have political training, pay should not be given to all, but only to as many as would balance the number of the notables....

Again, in oligarchies either the people ought to accept the measures of the government, or not to pass anything contrary to them; or, if all are allowed to share in counsel, the decision should rest with the magistrates. The opposite of what is done in constitutional governments should be the rule in oligarchies; the veto of the majority should be final, their assent not final, but the proposal should be referred back to the magistrates. **Whereas in constitutional governments they take the contrary course; the few have the negative, not the affirmative power; the affirmation of everything rests with the multitude.** (*Politics*, KL: 1786–1796)

However, Aristotle is less concerned with the exact form of the ideal government than with the general characteristics of good governments. In direct democracies, policies are selected in open public meetings subject to the vetoes of elected officials (possibly for constitutional reasons), or a representative body should propose policies that are subject to the veto of the citizenry in public meetings. The specific characteristics of the populace, time, and place will affect which policies are best for a given populace. What is most general about good governments is the aim of the government formed and the means for advancing it.

[T]he form of government is best in which every man, whoever he is, can act best and live happily. (*Politics*, KL: 2718)

Since the end of individuals and of states is the same, **the end of the best man and of the best constitution must also be the same**; it is therefore evident that there ought to exist in both of them the **virtues of leisure**; for peace, as has been often repeated, is the end of war, and leisure of toil. **But leisure and cultivation may be promoted, not only by those virtues which are practiced in leisure, but also by some of those which are useful to business. For many necessaries of life have to be supplied before we can have leisure.** (*Politics*, KL: 3069–3073)

Although the virtues are developed one person at time through a long series of moral choices, Aristotle believes that governments can encourage the formation of virtue through laws, as discussed above, and also through public education. He therefore is among the earliest supporters of public education.[19]

[T]he legislator should **direct his attention above all to the education of youth**; for the neglect of education does harm to the constitution. The citizen should be molded to suit the form of government under which he lives. For each government has a peculiar character which originally formed and which continues to preserve it. The character of democracy creates democracy, and the character of oligarchy creates oligarchy; and always **the better the character, the better the government.**

And since the whole city has one end [the encourage of virtues necessary for happiness and survival], **it is manifest that education should be one and the same for all, and that it should be public, and not private.** (*Politics*, KL: 3172–3178)

**The good citizen** ought to be capable of both; he **should know how to govern like a freeman, and how to obey like a freeman.** These are the virtues of a citizen. And, although the **temperance and justice** of a ruler are distinct from those of a subject, the virtue of a good man will include both; for the virtue of the good man who is free and also a subject, e.g., **his justice, will not be one but will comprise distinct kinds, the one qualifying him to rule, the other to obey.** (*Politics*, KL: 990–993)

We must remember that good laws, if they are not obeyed, do not constitute good government. Hence, there are **two parts of good government**; one is the actual

---

[19] Although many of Aristotle's arguments are accepted by Enlightenment scholars and nineteenth-century liberals, not all accepted his argument concerning public education. Liberals such as Adam Smith and Herbert Spencer argued that public education is unnecessary. Adam Smith's ethics are discussed in Chapter 11 and Herbert Spencer's in Chapter 12. Aristotle's suggestion that the virtues that should be taught in public schools vary with the type of government is, however, accepted by Montesquieu.

obedience of citizens to the laws, the other part is the goodness of the laws which they obey. (*Politics*, KL: 1607–1608)

## Lessons from Aristotle Regarding Ethics and Commerce

Perhaps the most important lesson from Aristotle for the purposes of this book is his methodology, his approach to learning. He listens and observes widely and then attempts to distill general categories of phenomena and logically consistent, useful relationships among them from that body of knowledge. This approach enabled him to create coherent theories of great importance for ethics, economics, political science, biology, physics, and logic—to name just a few of the fields in which he is regarded as either a pioneer or a founder.

With respect to the aim of this chapter, it is his conclusions about ethics, commerce, and politics that are most important. He believed that virtue is the foundation of both a good life and good society. Happiness it the ultimate end for each, and virtue is the surest route to happiness. *Eudaimonia* is most reliably obtained through character development and institutions that support it, rather than the extent of one's wealth, battles won, or extravagant feasts enjoyed.

> Some think that a very moderate amount of virtue is enough, but set no limit to their desires of wealth, property, power, reputation, and the like. **To whom we reply by an appeal to facts, which easily prove that mankind does not acquire or preserve virtue by the help of external goods, but external goods by the help of virtue,** and that happiness, whether consisting in pleasure or virtue, or both, is more often found with those who are **most highly cultivated in their mind and in their character,** and have only a moderate share of external goods, than among those who possess external goods to a useless extent but are deficient in higher qualities. (*Politics*, KL: 2688–2693)

Virtuous dispositions are feasible for most educated persons, in part, because virtue is a "mean," rather than an extreme form of behavior. Vice, in contrast, occurs at the extremes.

It bears noting that Aristotle does not assert that virtuous dispositions by themselves guarantee happiness, nor that virtue is the only source of happiness. The development of moral and intellectual excellence are simply the most reliable sources of long-run happiness. Aristotle also emphasizes that the mere understanding of what virtue is does not imply that one is virtuous. Moral conduct requires both practical wisdom (an understanding of context and consequences) and sufficient experience that practical wisdom and virtuous habits—e.g., ethical dispositions—are accumulated. The good life is not a passive one, but an active one in which choices are made, actions are undertaken, and experiences are accumulated.

His analysis of the ideal state stresses the importance of legal and political institutions. Political institutions and laws should increase prosperity, reduce conflict among citizens, and provide for community defense. There are institutional and material prerequisites for a good society. However, ultimately, good laws promote virtuous living and community happiness.

The latter does not imply that the material comforts generated by commerce are unimportant. A tolerable level of material comfort is a prerequisite for the development of most virtues, and it is production and exchange (at just prices) that tend to provide those comforts. Such necessities imply that commerce has a role, if not a central one, in both a good life and good society.

With respect to economics, Aristotle argues that trade can be an instance of just relationships among individuals. Sustained trading relationships require proportionate reciprocity, which thus exemplify proportionate justice. Money facilitates exchange and helps assure that trade is properly reciprocal. With respect to property, he suggests that property systems that are largely private tend to produce better results than common property systems. Private property reduces conflict, encourages good management, and facilitates the development of several virtues, including liberality and prudence. Ownership can also be a direct source of pleasure for those who own something.

With respect to economic activities themselves, he regards directly productive ones (e.g., farming and construction) to be the most praiseworthy, followed by occupations that harvest the fruits of nature (as with mining and timbering), followed by traders of merchandise (merchants and speculators) and, last, those who deal in money alone (banking and finance). This rank order of careers is implicitly a rank order of the tendencies toward virtue that he associates with each type of occupation. The most virtuous occupations promote moderation and excellence, the least promote excessive concern for money and unjust (nonreciprocal) forms of behavior.

Although not stressed by Aristotle, for the purposes of this book, it bears noting that many of the virtues and excellences analyzed are market supporting.

Athens was a center of commerce during its golden age, and it is clear that many of the virtues listed by Aristotle would have helped contribute to that prosperity. The virtue of honesty tends to facilitate commerce by reducing fraud and simplifying contract enforcement. The virtues of prudence (meekness and self-mastery) and bravery tend to encourage both saving and reasonable risk-taking. The same virtues also contribute to solving social dilemmas with respect to conflict and commons problems. His defenses of private property and many—but not all—commercial careers and activities would encourage virtuous persons to include such activities in their own lives, to regard them as praiseworthy when undertaken by others, and to favor them within their communities—albeit within limits.[20]

> Workings in accordance with [excellence] are proper to man. I mean, we do actions of justice, courage, and the other virtues, towards one another, in contracts, services of different kinds, and in all kinds of actions and feelings too, by observing what is befitting for each: and all these plainly are proper to man. (Aristotle 1897, p. 274)

It is the prevalence of such ethical dispositions, system of education, and relatively open democratic institutions, that likely accounted for Athen's success as a center of commerce and scholarship. However, it also bears noting that Aristotle had significant reservations about commerce—it could reduce virtuous propensities by producing lifestyles in which virtuous dispositions were unlikely to be developed (as in mining) and also by encouraging extreme forms of behavior (as in banking and finance) that conflict with virtue and thereby reduce an individual's lifetime happiness or satisfaction.

---

[20] Aristotle's work is still studied in large part because so many of his conclusions accord well with contemporary ideas about science, reason, the good life, the good society, and good government. (Indeed, many of those ideas are doubtless grounded in his analyses more than two thousand years ago.) Nonetheless, it should be acknowledged that a subset of Aristotle's work is less appealing to modern sensibilities, although many of these also stood the test of time quite well. His ideas about physics remained relevant into the seventeenth century when Newton's revolution in physics took place. His ideas concerning biology remained relevant until Darwin's revolution in biology in the late nineteenth century. His illiberal positions on women's rights and slavery would have been regarded as moderate ones in Western society until the mid- to late eighteenth century. Some of his ideas about education, property, and common meals also seem strange, but it should be kept in mind that Greece was a pre-industrial society, based on trade and agriculture, and cities were much smaller then—often towns with fewer than 5,000 full citizens. His support for public education would have seemed relatively extreme until the mid- to late nineteenth century, although today it seems obvious and uncontroversial—if some of his specific recommendations seem less than apt.

# Appendix I to Chapter 9: Some Illustrative Variations among Translations of Aristotle's Nicomachean Ethics

| Translation | First Sentence | On Man's Work/Function |
|---|---|---|
| Gillies, J. (1797) Aristotle's *Ethics and Politics*. London: Cadell and Davies [1813 edition]. | Since every art and every kind of knowledge, as well as all the actions and the deliberations of men constantly aim at something which they call good; good, in general may be justly defined, "that which all desire" (p. 240). | The proper good of man consists then in virtuous energies, that is, in the exercise of virtue continued through life; for one swallow makes not a summer; neither does one day, or a short time, constitute happiness (p. 253). |
| Chase, D. P. (Aristotle 1861) *The Nicomachean Ethics*. Translated by D. P. Chase. London: MacMillan. | Every art, and every science reduced to a teachable form, and in like manner every action and moral choice, aims, it is thought, at some good: for which reason a common and by no means a bad description of the Chief Good is, "that which all things aim at" (p. 1). | If all this is so, the Good of Man comes to be a working of the Soul in the way of Excellence, or, if Excellence admits of degrees, in the way of the best and most perfect Excellence. And we must add; for as it is not one swallow or fine day that makes spring, so it is not one day or a short time that makes a man blessed and happy (p. 20). |
| William, R. (1876) *Nicomachean Ethics of Aristotle*, Newly Translated into English (2nd edition). London: Green. | All Moral Action, that is to say all purpose, no less than all art and all science, would seem to aim at some good result. Hence has come a not inapt definition of the chief good as that one end at which all human actions aim (p. 1). | If all this be so, we shall find that the chief good of man consists in an activity of the soul in accordance with its own excellence (or, in other words, such that the essential conditions of excellence are fulfilled), and, if there be many such excellencies or virtues, then in accordance with the best among them. And we must further add the condition of a complete life; for a single day or even a short period of happiness, no more makes a blessed and happy man than one sunny day or one swallow makes a spring (p. 14) |
| Welldon, J. E. C. (1892) *The Nicomachean Ethics of Aristotle*. London: Macmillan. | Every art and every scientific inquiry, and similarly every action and purpose, may be said to aim at some good. Hence the good has been well defined as that at which all things aim (p. 1). | It follows that the good of Man is an activity of soul in accordance with virtue or, if there are more virtues than one, in accordance with the best and most complete virtue. But it is necessary to add the words "in a complete life." For as one swallow or one day does not make a spring, so one day or a short time does not make a fortunate or happy man (p. 16). |

| Translation | First Sentence | On Man's Work/Function |
|---|---|---|
| Ross, W. D. (1925) Ethica Nicomachea. Oxford: Clarendon Press. (Quotations taken from the MIT classics website.) | Every art and every inquiry, and similarly every action and pursuit, is thought to aim at some good; and for this reason the good has rightly been declared to be that at which all things aim. | If this is the case, human good turns out to be activity of soul in accordance with virtue, and if there are more than one virtue, in accordance with the best and most complete. But we must add "in a complete life." For one swallow does not make a summer, nor does one day; and so too one day, or a short time, does not make a man blessed and happy. |
| Irwin, T. (1999) Aristotle, Nicomachean Ethics. (Second Edition) Indianapolis: Hackett. | Every craft and every line of inquiry, and likewise every action and decision, seems to seek some good; that is why some people were right to describe the good as what everything seeks (p. 1). | And so the human good proves to be activity of the soul in accord with virtue, and indeed with the best and most complete virtue, if there are more virtues than one. Moreover, in a complete life. For one swallow does not make a spring, nor does one day; nor, similarly, does one day or a short time make us blessed and happy (p. 9). |
| Crisp, R. (2014) Aristotle, Nicomachean Ethics. Cambridge: Cambridge University Press. | Every skill and every inquiry, and similarly every action and rational choice, is thought to aim at some good; and so the good has been aptly described as that at which everything aims (p. 3). | If this is so, the human good turns out to be activity of the soul in accordance with virtue, and if there are several virtues, in accordance with the best and most complete. Again, this must be over a complete life. For one swallow does not make a summer, nor one day. Neither does one day or a short time make someone blessed and happy (p.12) |

# Appendix II to Chapter 9: A Schematic of Aristotelian Ethics

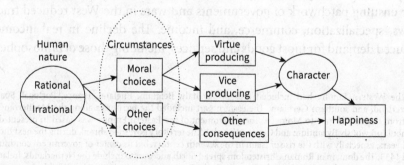

**Figure 9.1.** Schemata of Aristotle's theory of moral choice and happiness.

# 10

# From Renaissance
# to Early Enlightenment

## Setting the Stage: A Short History of the Loss and Recovery of Greek Philosophy

Athens during the time of Aristotle was an unusually tolerant, creative, and prosperous place. It was a major center of commerce with trading posts scattered around the Mediterranean Sea. It was also a significant regional naval power during that period. It lost its independence late in Aristotle's life when Macedonia conquered Greece. A century and a half later, the Romans conquered Macedonia, and Greece became part of the Roman Empire. Athens remained a center of learning for much of that period, and many Roman leaders sent their children to Athenian schools. Aristotle's own school, the Lyceum, survived for nearly two centuries.

Aristotle's writings were initially housed in the Lyceum's library and subsequently parts and copies were shifted to other libraries in Rome and Egypt. After the Christianization of the Roman Empire and the disintegration of the western part of the empire in the fifth century, interest in the writings of Greek and Roman scholars largely disappeared from western Europe. Although handwritten copies of their works remained in many medieval libraries, they were rarely studied in Europe for the next 800 years.[1]

There were several reasons for this. The collapse of the Western Roman Empire ended a large relatively free trade zone with a common legal system. The ensuing patchwork of governments and wars in the West reduced trade flows, specialization, commerce, and income. The decline in real incomes reduced demand for most goods and services, including those of philosophers

---

[1] The Western Empire had included present-day Italy, Belgium, England, France, Portugal, Spain, Switzerland, and southern Germany. The eastern part included the territories along the Mediterranean Sea from the east of Italy to Morocco. The government of the Eastern Empire was based in present-day Istanbul (previously Byzantium and Constantinople). The territory governed shrank during the next thousand years, especially with the rise of Islam in the seventh century, but its center of government continued until 1453. The domain of Roman Christendom spread north and west to include the Netherlands, Ireland, the rest of Germany, Scandinavia, and subsequently the European colonies in the New World.

*Solving Social Dilemmas.* Roger D. Congleton, Oxford University Press. © Oxford University Press 2022.
DOI: 10.1093/oso/9780197642788.003.0010

and educators, who were largely regarded as luxury goods in that period. Christian theology during this time tended to focus on the afterlife, spiritual development, and faith, rather than human development, reason, and life on earth. Catholic normative theory stressed prayer, miracles, and good works for the Church, and its emphasis on the afterlife tended to redirect time and energy away from market and other secular activities toward religious activities, both among devout believers and those wishing to appear devout. Christian scholarship focused on textual interpretation, rituals, and prayer, about which little could be learned from Greek and Roman secular writings. Ethical and economic practices were grounded in divine texts, rather than reason, although interpretation and application continued to occupy both scholars and Catholic courts in the period after the Western Roman Empire disintegrated, where facts and arguments, as well as faith and intra-Catholic politics, mattered.[2]

The result was a lower standard of living for most in the period that some later scholars referred to as the Dark Ages, which was "dark" because so little was written this period. Such economic and literacy effects would not have concerned those advocating a religious life, however, because their aim was salvation, rather than a satisfying or fruitful life on earth.[3]

Western copies of classical Greek and Roman manuscripts were not destroyed but retired to little used archives of monastic libraries in western Europe. Indeed, the spread of monasteries throughout Europe, the Middle East, and northern Africa provided a robust form of "knowledge storage" that could be tapped when interests expanded to include natural laws and other laws that might be assumed to have divine origins. Classical Greek and Roman scholarship continued to be of interest in the Eastern Roman Empire (sometimes called the Byzantine Empire) and subsequently in the Islamic empires of the Middle East, northern Africa, and southwestern Europe, where trade continued much as before the disintegration of the Western Roman Empire.

Religious ideas and culture proved to be more robust than state authority in this period of western European history. Rome lost its secular authority, but remained the capital of western Europe's new religion. Latin remained the main language of literate persons and scholars in the West, as well as the language of formal church rituals.

---

[2] For an accessible overview of medieval Christian philosophy and the classics, see http://plato.stanford.edu/entries/medieval-philosophy.

[3] Maddison's (2007) estimates of per capita GDP in Europe for the years 1 and 1000 AD show a 25% decline in average income—from 576 to 427.

# Renewed Interest in the Classics and the Rediscovery of Aristotle

Around 1200, the West began to rediscover the ancient scholars, partly because of the Crusades, which brought western Europe in closer contact with what remained of classical Roman and Greek culture in the Eastern Empire. Translations into Latin were undertaken from Greek sources in Constantinople and also from Islamic sources in Toledo, Spain, which at the time was an important center of Islamic and classical study. Many scholars subsequently relocated to Italy, which became a center for innovation in architecture, art, and philosophy.[4] That Latin was still the language of educated persons in Europe allowed the renewed interest in Greek and Roman ideas to influence the relatively few literate persons in western Europe, and interest in secular ideas gradually increased.

Sustained interest in the works of Aristotle and other Greek scholars occurred at about the same time that new universities were founded throughout Europe in the period referred to as the Renaissance—the rebirth. Universities were established in Bologna, Italy, in about 1088; Paris, France, and Oxford, England, in about 1170; Cambridge, England, in about 1200; Heidelberg, Germany [Palatinate], in about 1386; and in several other less famous places during the same period. The new universities were places of scholarship and teaching, focused for the most part on educating priests and lawyers. The latter caused secular interests to be revisited by Catholic scholars and teachers.

A subset of university scholars (who were normally Catholic monks or priests during this period) had a relatively broad interest in all forms of knowledge that could shed light on the nature of divine will, even if it did not necessarily increase prospects for salvation, produce better legal analysis, or improve military strategies. A subset of the new scholarship attempted to enrich medieval theories of ethics and law by taking account of the work of ancient scholars. This process in turn focused on its own puzzles and lacunae, and led to significant extensions of Catholic ethical, economic, political, and astronomical theories. There was much about divine will that

---

[4] The territory of the Eastern Roman Empire (and subsequent Arab empires) extended from somewhat west of present-day Turkey and along the southern Mediterranean coast through Spain. Between the seventh and tenth centuries, most of this territory was conquered by Islamic armies, and Islam consequently replaced Catholicism as the dominant religion in that region. (Some Jews and Christians continued living in these territories but paid a special tax.) Spanish kings gradually pushed Muslims out of present-day Spain, ruling all of it by about 1492. The territory's new rulers adopted laws that forced conversion to Catholicism or emigration by Jews and Muslims. Rather than convert, Jewish scholars often migrated to Italy and Byzantium, taking many of their books and notes with them.

could be learned through a deeper understanding of ethical and scientific principles.

The rediscovery of Aristotle was especially important. He was the most studied secular scholar in this period because of his breadth and depth, although universities were still mainly focused on Christian theology and legal training. Thomas Aquinas (1225–1274), an influential Catholic scholar from that period, referred to Aristotle as "the philosopher." Others referred to him as "the teacher," as had been the case among Islamic scholars. Aristotle's work on logic, science, and ethics was carefully studied and discussed. This was evident in both classroom curricula and new scholarship.[5]

The effect of the Renaissance can be easily observed in museum art collections. If one walks through a major European or North American art museum with collections that reach back into the twelfth century, one can see that statues and paintings of men and women in non-religious settings become increasingly commonplace as one walks through exhibits from 1200 to 1600. Before 1400, there is essentially only "flat" religious art. After 1400, "flat" religious art gradually becomes less commonplace and "three-dimensional" paintings of aristocrats and persons in ordinary life become more common—at least among paintings and sculptures considered to be of museum quality.

That shift suggests that those purchasing art and perhaps the artists themselves had become relatively more concerned with life on earth and somewhat less focused on religion or pleasing the Church, although the latter clearly remained important, indeed central to life. Tolerance had evidently somewhat increased, and a wider range of art, arguments, and methods for disseminating them became legal or at least less actively prosecuted throughout much of Europe.

Toward the end of this period, movable type printing was introduced to Europe by Gutenberg (around 1450), which greatly facilitated the dissemination of Aristotle and other authors by reducing copying costs. Subsequent improvements in printing, paper, and binding technologies further reduced book and pamphlet printing costs. Although the Bible was the first book printed with the Gutenberg's innovation, movable type allowed all sorts of new ideas to be disseminated at far lower cost than had been possible in previous times.

---

[5] In some places, as at the University of Paris, some parts of Aristotle's work were banned from university lecture halls because they conflicted with Catholic doctrines of that time, although that censorship lasted only a half century or so. See "The Twelfth Century and the Rise of Universities" (Chapter 5) in http://plato.stanford.edu/entries/medieval-philosophy.

## Four Great Shocks between 1500 and 1600 Undermine the Medieval Worldview

The medieval order in Europe, with its dominant Catholic church, its relatively small "duchies" and city-states ruled by hereditary nobles and kings, and its associated views of miracles, class, ethics, and the afterlife, stood for nearly a thousand years. However, in the sixteenth century, it was subjected to several major shocks that undermined its intellectual foundations.

### Discovery of a New World

In 1492 Columbus discovered formerly unknown lands and peoples. His voyage and the dozens that followed implied that medieval geography and its associated history of mankind were incorrect. Both the earth and human society were larger than previously believed. Subsequent exploration in the sixteenth century demonstrated that new places, peoples, plants, and animals had to be added to Europe's knowledge base. Long-standing theories and histories had to be adjusted to take account of new facts.

Acknowledging these great geographical and historical lacunae undermined the meditative and scholastic approaches to knowledge. All that could be known was not already known. There were clearly many new things to be learned, and these could not simply be dug out from the works of previous generations of brilliant scholars. What might be called the sophisticated armchair approach to understanding the physical world had proved to be inadequate. Exploration and other data-generating procedures could reveal important facts that were previously unknown to even the most thoughtful and widely read ancient scholars and mapmakers.

The subsequent conquest and settlement of South and Central America by Spain and Portugal also changed the balance of wealth and power in Europe as New World gold and silver were expropriated and exported to Portugal and Spain.

### The Protestant Reformation

At roughly the same time, an increasing number of religious scholars began criticizing a subset of the theological rituals and doctrines of the Catholic Church. Martin Luther (1483–1546) and John Calvin (1509–1564) were the most influential of the Church's many critics in this period. Their protests launched a great reform movement among Catholics in the sixteenth century that ultimately produced new denominations and churches, rather than substantial reforms of the old one.

It was not simply discussions about Christian theology and rituals that produced the Protestant Reformation. The reformers were supported by many local rulers in Germany and Switzerland, who were interested in controversies about religious doctrines (as many persons would be at this time); however, they also likely understood that the Protestant movement had political implications. In the territories of the Holy Roman Empire (northern and central continental Europe), rulers would anticipate that a more decentralized church would indirectly advance their efforts to resist centralization by the Habsburg government (centered in present-day Austria) and by the Church itself.[6] Together, the persuasiveness of Calvinist and Lutheran arguments and northern political and military support produced a new geopolitical and religious map for northern Europe.[7]

Several new Lutheran- and Calvinist-based religious organizations were founded that were independent of the Church of Rome. The new Protestant theologies were based on a narrower reading of the Bible and placed greater emphasis on predestination and rebirth than Catholic doctrine had. Among the new religious societies were the precursors to the contemporary Baptist, Congregational, Lutheran, Methodist, Presbyterian, Episcopalian, and Reformed churches. No longer was there a single unified religious organization and theology whose claims of universality and accuracy could been taken for granted as they had been for centuries by most western European Christians.

Max Weber, writing three and half centuries later, argued that several elements of Protestant theology encouraged new outlooks on life and work that made it possible for capitalism and the commercial society to emerge. These included new ideas about divine duties and the proper role of commerce in a good life and good society, as developed in this chapter.[8]

[6] The emperor of the Holy Roman Empire was an office of relatively little authority at that time, but substantial influence. It had been held by leaders of the Habsburg family for many years, who were the most important family in the German-speaking territories, and arguably the most important in Europe in the sixteenth century, during which time the family ruled Spain and its territories, as well as Austria and many other duchies in Europe. They had often attempted to reduce the autonomy of other noble families, and they had not been entirely unsuccessful. (The German-speaking territories of the Holy Roman Empire are sometimes referred to as the "first Reich.)

[7] Several wars were fought between Catholic and Protestant armies during the sixteenth century. These were finally ended by a series of Europe-wide treaties negotiated at or near Westphalia in 1648. The Peace of Westphalia formally ended several military conflicts and formally granted ruling nobles and kings the authority to determine the religion of their territories.

[8] See Weber ([1905] 1958), *The Protestant Ethic and the Spirit of Capitalism*. Several of the authors used in this and the next chapters were used by Weber to demonstrate that shifts in norms generated by Protestantism tended to favor commerce. Weber argues that Protestant emphasis on predestination tends

## The Copernican Revolution

At about the same time that the Protestant Reformation was gaining ground, innovative theories about man's place in the physical universe were being worked out and read by other scholars. In 1543, Copernicus published a book in which he proposed a new astronomy in which the earth circled the sun, rather than the sun and stars circling the earth, as had long been believed. The new theory provided a simpler explanation for the motions of stars, planets, and the sun than alternative theories available at that time. His book, *The Revolutions*, was initially little read but gradually rose to prominence during the next half century, after which it was banned by the Catholic Church (in 1616), as were many other books, including some parts of Aristotle's work.

Thomas Kuhn (1957, 1962) argues that the heliocentric astronomy introduced by Copernicus helped launch a series of paradigm shifts that are referred to as the Scientific Revolution. Supporting data were provided by Galileo's (1609) astronomical research, and the orbits themselves were explained by Newton's (1687) theory of gravity, momentum, and physical interaction.[9] The gradual increase in the precision of astronomical measurements and the accuracy of the predictions associated with the new theory and its subsequent refinements increased the aspirations and norms for precision in other fields of study as well. The universe may be simpler than previously believed, because it can be explained by fewer "if-then" principles than were previously thought necessary.

## The Dutch Revolt

Later in the sixteenth century, and not entirely independent of the Protestant Reformation and discovery of the New World, a war of secession took place in the Rhine river's delta. The provinces and cities of the northern delta won their war of independence against the powerful Habsburg dynasty (the leader of which resided in Spain at that time). The northern provinces joined forces

to make people more career oriented than Catholicism did. Under Calvinist predestination doctrine, it was not good works for the Church that mattered, but God's long-standing decisions about a person's salvation, which one could not influence by personal behavior. Whether one was "elected" or not, however, could be deduced by how people behaved and their success in life. Success in one's earthly career provided evidence of God's favor and the likelihood of having been chosen for elevation (for an afterlife). This naturally encouraged people to work hard in their daily lives and to adopt prudent lifestyles.

[9] Aristotle was an early proponent of the geocentric universe. As the heliocentric theory replaced the long-standing geocentric one, a substantial part of Aristotle's physics was also overturned.

to form a new national government, the United Provinces of the Netherlands. Their government had a decentralized federal structure with seven sovereign provinces, but without a national monarch.[10] This new form of government and its associated more open and commercial life undermined medieval theories of both politics and economics.

Rather than imposing a single religion, the Netherlands was a relatively tolerant place in which there was considerable freedom of religious conscience, although not always freedom of public worship. It was also a place that was more tolerant of new secular ideas than other European countries. The Netherlands thus attracted religious, economic, and intellectual emigrants from throughout Europe. Rival Protestant churches existed side by side in the Netherlands, and intellectuals from other countries in Europe often published their books there to avoid censorship in their home countries. Its relatively open markets and hard-working residents allowed the Netherlands to become the wealthiest country in Europe (based on per capita income) within a few decades. In many respects, the Netherlands of the seventeenth century could be thought of as the new Athens.

Its economic and political success, in turn, demonstrated that countries could succeed economically and politically without the traditional medieval template for governance, religion, or economic regulation. The success of the Netherlands demonstrated that other systems could work as well or better than the medieval political-economic system. Hierarchical systems based on royal and noble families with a monopoly church and heavily regulated markets were evidently not the only systems of governance and life that could obtain divine blessings.

## Long-Term Consequences

Together, these four great shocks of the sixteenth centuries had undermined the medieval order, although this was not entirely obvious at the time. Medieval doctrines and patterns of life did not instantly disappear. Instead, the shocks induced gradual transformations of ideas and institutions throughout western Europe and its colonies, which gradually replaced the medieval order with the modern one. Interest in natural laws led to new scientific innovations such as Newton's three laws of motion. A greater focus on

---

[10] The republican form of government was adopted partly by accident. Leaders of the revolt solicited the protection of several kings, but none was willing to challenge the Hapsburg dynasty for authority over the northern half of the Rhine's delta. See Congleton (2011, Ch. 15) for additional details and references.

life on earth and increase in tolerance induced economic, political, and intellectual innovations. What came to be called "the Enlightenment" had begun.

Of particular relevance for this book is that ethical theories were gradually revised in a manner that generated more favorable conclusions about commerce itself and careers in commerce. These in turn tended to encourage private behavior and public policies that made broad trading networks and more roundabout methods of production easier to organize and less risky for those who chose to initiate or participate in such enterprises. The emergence of the commercial society of the course of three centuries is arguably one of the long-term consequences of the shocks of the sixteenth century.

Progress was not entirely caused by the emergence of more open societies or the scientific and technological revolutions, as is sometimes argued. Shifts in norms and institution that made such innovations acceptable and possible were also necessary.

The remainder of this chapter provides evidence that shifts in norms and conceptions of commerce were associated with what came to be called the "Enlightenment." These shifts tended to make trade, specialization, and innovation more morally acceptable, and thus more appropriate in a good life and good society.

## Two Late Renaissance Catholic Perspectives on Work, Property, and Commerce

### Desiderius Erasmus (1466–1536)

Late medieval skepticism about commerce can be illustrated with a few quotes from two widely read books from the early 1500s, Desiderius Erasmus's *Praise of Folly* and Thomas More's *Utopia* ([1516] 1901). Both authors were politically well-connected Catholic scholars during the early sixteenth century.[11] Erasmus was a full-time scholar with contacts throughout western Europe, including Pope Leo X and several kings.[12] Sir Thomas More was a lawyer by

---

[11] During Europe's dark ages and early medieval periods, Constantinople, Alexandria, Cordoba, and cities in Asia such as Beijing and Tokyo were clearly more important and innovative places than any city in western Europe. Nonetheless, the commercial society that emerged in the late nineteenth and early twentieth centuries was grounded in European ethical theories, science, and institutions, rather than those associated with such places. It is for this reason that this chapter and the rest of Part III in general focuses on western European developments, rather than ones in the Muslim world or in Asia.

[12] The *Praise of Folly* was widely read and elicited significant acclaim from many, but not all, church authorities because of its criticisms of medieval scholasticism, church wealth, and some of its ceremonies. Erasmus maintained good relations with many prominent Catholic scholars and officials. He opposed the reformation and many of Luther and Calvin's ideas. Nonetheless, the author of the Erasmus entry in the *Catholic (New Advent) Encyclopedia* (1914) considered the *Praise of Folly* to be "a cold-blooded, deliberate

training and subsequently a member of Parliament, diplomat, and advisor to Henry VIII.[13]

What is relevant for the purposes of this book is not these scholars' distinguished career paths, class, or genius, but that a subset of their writings was widely read throughout western Europe in the period after they were published. Their books thus provide evidence of common beliefs concerning economic activities, wealth, and property among literate persons in the late medieval period. Both criticized mainstream institutions and behaviors that they regarded to be immoral or wasteful. Their views were not uncontroversial, but both authors were regarded to be among the more informed and thoughtful of that period. (Indeed, they are still widely read for the same reason.) Their books would not have been read unless their ideas resonated with those already in the minds of their readers.

Both writers are highly critical of commerce for reasons similar to those developed by Aristotle—because commerce promotes an excessive interest in money and attracts unethical people.[14]

> But **the most foolish and basest of all others are our merchants**, to wit **such as venture** on everything be it never so dishonest, and manage it no better; who though **they lie by no allowance, swear and forswear, steal, cozen, and cheat, yet shuffle themselves into the first rank**, and all because they have gold rings on their fingers. Nor are they without their flattering friars that admire them **and give them openly the title of honorable, in hopes, no doubt, to get some small snip of it themselves.** (Erasmus, *The Praise of Folly*, 1532/1993, KL: 733–37)

This quote from Erasmus's *The Praise of Folly* suggests that the upward mobility and wealth sought by merchants are "foolish and base" and that the deference that churchmen provide wealthy merchants is inappropriate. The quote suggests that a life devoted to market activities is improper because of the means through which wealth is acquired ("steal, cozen, and cheat") and

attempt to discredit the Church, and its satire and stinging comment on ecclesiastical conditions are not intended as a healing medicine but a deadly poison."

[13] Thomas More's service to Henry VIII famously ended with his resignation in 1533 and beheading in 1535 for a charge of treason. More had opposed the English separation from the Catholic Church, refused to accept Henry as the leader of the new church, and ultimately refused to take Henry's demanding oath of loyalty. For his opposition to the English church, writings, and sacrifice, he was beatified by the Catholic Church some three hundred fifty years later (1886, canonized in 1935), and thus contemporary Catholics refer to him as Saint Sir Thomas More.

[14] Excerpts are from the 1993 Radice translation of the 1532 version: *Praise of Folly and Letter to Maarten Van Dorp 1515*. A digitized version (2012) is available from Amazon and is the version used here. *The Praise of Folly* was originally written in 1509, it is said, to amuse his good friend Thomas More after a trip to Rome. "KL" refers to kindle locations and bolding has again been added to direct readers to key parts of the quote.

because trade itself is in some sense improper because it is motivated by the pursuit of wealth and status.

## Thomas More (1478-1535)

A few years later, Thomas More ([1516] 1901) characterized an ideal or good society, one which bears a closer relationship to that described in Plato's *Republic* than to the one characterized in Aristotle's *Politics*, although there are also echoes of Aristotle's reasoning. More goes beyond both these philosophers in his support for an egalitarian society without markets or private property. Happiness remains the chief good, but it is achieved through contemplation rather than an active life.[15]

His characterization of the ideal society implies that leisure is to be maximized and that common property is better than private. Similar ideas about utopia are still common among those advocated by contemporary communitarians and other idealists of "the left."[16]

The magistrates never engage the people in unnecessary labor, since the chief end of the constitution is to regulate labor by the necessities of the public, and **to allow the people as much time as is necessary for the improvement of their minds, in which they think the happiness of life consists.** (More, *Utopia*, [1516] 1901, p. 50)

Every city is divided into four equal parts, and in the middle of each there is a **marketplace. What is brought thither, and manufactured by the several families, is carried from thence to houses appointed for that purpose, in which all things of a sort are laid by themselves; and thither every father goes** and **takes whatsoever he or his family stand in need of, without either paying for it or leaving anything in exchange.** (More, *Utopia*, [1516] 1901, p. 52)

There is no market-based exchange of money for goods in *Utopia*. Necessities are produced in relatively short six-hour days and distributed according to needs, which are presumed to be simple, basic, and limited. In effect, More's ideal community is a well-governed self-sufficient monastery or university.

---

[15] Excerpts are from a digitized version of the 1901 edition of Thomas More's *Utopia* (1651/1901) published by Cassell, which is available from Amazon.com.

[16] Before 1900, such persons were regarded as communalists or communists. The meaning of the word *communism* changed after the rise of the Soviet Union, after which it was routinely used to describe its very centralized and regimented social system with geopolitical aspirations.

It is important to recognize that More's utopian society requires persons with particular internalized norms to function well. Individuals have to be willing to work hard without obvious return (no wages were paid). They have to have only limited desires for material comforts and none for decoration, ostentation, or status. They have to seek contemplative self-improvement—whether spiritual or secular is unclear, but likely both. The residents also have to be willing to defer to the authority of elders and leaders of their communities, who determine much about their daily lives, more or less as the head of a monastery would organize the lives of resident novices and monks.

Utopia is essentially self-sufficient and trades little with the outside world. In many respects, it is similar to Plato's ideal self-sufficient republic ruled by philosopher kings, which was much criticized by Aristotle for its impracticality. There would be many free-rider problems to be addressed in such a society. The internalized ethical dispositions of the leadership and the community's residents would have to be strong enough to overcome most such problems. The magistrates would have to be clever and devoted enough to ameliorate any social dilemmas that remained unsolved, while resisting the many extractive temptations of authority. As imagined, utopia was a comfortable world with benevolent leadership and regulation of life, with production for necessities, rather than exchange or hedonistic impulses. (The same vision of utopia remains commonplace among many university scholars today.)

It is evident that both Erasmus and More believe that hard work, honesty, and integrity are important virtues. Their own hard work is evident in their distinguished careers and in their writings. They were both extraordinarily active men. However, neither thought that participation in commerce could be a genuinely useful or noble activity. In this they shared Aristotle's concern that commerce was a dishonorable occupation. Farming and other productive activities were necessary, but they were "ennobling" only to a very limited extent. Intellectual and spiritual development were far more important.[17]

---

[17] Toward the end of the *Nicomachean Ethics*, Aristotle makes an argument that contemplation may be the best manner to achieve happiness. "And, in proportion as people have the act of contemplation, so far have they also the being happy, not incidentally, but in the way of Contemplative Speculation because it is in itself precious" (*Nicomachean Ethics*, p. 277). He goes on to suggest that a contemplative life has the most potential for happiness. However, he does not thereby renounce his argument that physical resources and life experiences are necessary to develop most virtues. The most consistent interpretation is that a good life includes substantial time for contemplation, although contemplation alone is insufficient to produce such a life.

If Erasmus' and More's assessment of the ethics of commerce were widely held among educated persons at the time they wrote (and their readership suggests that they were), trade would tend to be a relatively risky and unrewarding activity. When only the relatively unethical participate in markets, every trade and trading network tend to be prone to fraud for both buyers and sellers. Promises would not be routinely kept, broken or misleading contracts would be commonplace, and markets would be relatively inefficient institutions. Only the largest and most obvious gains from comparative advantage and specialization would be realized in such a society.

This, of course, would not be a concern to those who regard ascetic communal lives of religious and intellectual contemplation to be the only "good life," as a monk or university professor from this period might have. However, for persons who regard material comfort and an active life to be parts of a good life, life in More's utopia would be less than ideal. For them, his utopia would be far less than the best society possible.

## The Early Enlightenment Perspective on Work, Property, and Markets

Erasmus was a Dutchman writing in the early sixteenth century, a half century or so before the Dutch Republic was formed. More was an Englishman writing in the same period, somewhat before the English Reformation occurred. We now turn to two late seventeenth-century Dutchmen writing after the republic was formed and the Protestant Reformation was well underway, Hugo Grotius and Pieter De La Court. This is followed by short overviews of books by two English theologians and one philosopher: William Baxter, Robert Barclay, and Thomas Locke.

The seventeenth century is a period often referred to as the "Enlightenment." It accelerated trends already present in the Renaissance. It was a period of many innovations in theology, ethics, epistemology, political theory, physics, and navigation. Scholarly books continued to be written in Latin during the first half of the seventeenth century. Publishing in the natural languages of Europe—Dutch, English, French, German, Italian, and Spanish—had become commonplace by its end.

What is most relevant for this book are the conclusions that philosophers and theologians reached about good character, a good life and a good society. A small sample of remarks from serious, widely read works by influential persons is again used to provide evidence of ideas that captured the attention and imagination of literate persons in the Dutch and English societies of this period.

# Hugo Grotius (1583–1645)

Hugo Grotius was trained as a lawyer and scholar and wrote his first book at the age of sixteen. He was successful within the Dutch politics of his day, becoming an important legal official in Holland, mayor of Rotterdam, and subsequently Swedish ambassador to France. His books were less widely read than those of Erasmus and More, but they were also influential during his time (and after), especially his *Mare Liberum* (1609; the *Free Sea*). International law is the field in which Grotius's work is best known.[18]

*Mare Liberum* was written in large part to support the claim that Dutch merchants should have free access to all the potential trading partners that could be reached by sailing ships. It develops very general arguments in support of that claim. These include theories of natural law, private and common property, and their relevance for international relations and commerce. Grotius concludes that the sea is and should be common property, and the use of it should be open to everyone.

His theory of natural law is grounded in a combination of moral intuition and reason, rather than religious texts, although he provides a supernatural basis for moral intuition. His interest is the law rather than ethics per se, but his arguments include several religious and moral justifications for commerce. He argues that natural law applies equally to all and that commerce is ultimately a blessed activity.[19]

> And to this house or city built by him [god] that great prince and householder **had written certain laws** of his, not in brass or tables, but **in the minds and senses of everyone**, where they shall offer themselves to be read of the unwilling and such as refuse. By **these laws both high and low are bound.** It is no more lawful for kings to transgress these than for the common people. (Grotius, *The Free Sea*, [1609] 2004, p. 15)

> But as in man himself **there are some things which are common with all, and other some whereby everyone is to be distinguished from other,** so of those things which nature had brought forth for the use of man she would that some of them

---

[18] Grotius also participated in several of the religious debates of his time, but more as a legal, than religious, scholar and official. He suggested, for example, that different views about predestination could coexist, as with Luther and Erasmus. He was persecuted not only for those views and the view that the government should play a role in enforcing tolerance, but also for being associated with Oldenbarnevelt, who had opposed the *stadthouder* of that time (Willem II) on important matters of policy. Grotius is famous for escaping from prison in a large book chest and fleeing to Paris in 1621. It was in France where he completed his most famous works.

[19] Excerpts are from the English translation from Latin by Richard Hakluyt (circa 1615) as edited by David Armitage ([1609] 2004). The manuscript is available in hard copy and various digitized forms from Liberty Fund and in Kindle format from Amazon ([Evergreen Review] without introductory notes).

should remain common and others through every one's labor and industry to become proper [private]. But **laws were set down for both,** that all surely might use
common things without the damage of all and, for the rest, every man contented
with his portion should abstain from another's. **No one can be ignorant of these
things, unless he cease to be a man.** (Grotius, *The Free Sea,* [1609] 2004, p. 15)

The sea therefore is in the number of those things which are not in merchandise
and trading, that is to say, which cannot be made proper [private]. Whence it
follows, if we speak properly, no part of the sea can be incorporated in the territory
of any people. Which thing Placentius seems to have meant when he said, "That
the sea was so common, that it may be in the dominion of none but God alone,"
and Johannes Faber, "When the sea shall depart, left in his ancient right and being,
wherein all things were common." (Grotius, *The Free Sea,* [1609] 2004, p. 31)

. . . that **it is lawful for any nation to go to any other and to trade with it.** God himself speaks of this in nature, seeing he will not have all those things, whereof the
life of man stands in need, to be sufficiently ministered by nature in all places and
also granted some nations to excel others in arts. **To what end are these things
but that he would maintain human friendship by their mutual wants and
plenty.** . . . (Grotius, *The Free Sea,* [1609] 2004, p. 19)

Eight steps in Grotius's reasoning are revealed by these excerpts: (1) Knowledge
of natural law (essential rights and rules of conduct) is an essential feature
of human nature—written in the minds everyone. (2) Natural laws apply to
all, to rulers as well as to the people ruled. (3) Natural law specifies that some
things should be held in common and others private. (4) The sea, for example,
is common to all, because it cannot be possessed. (5) Free passage over the seas
and international trade is lawful (ethical) under natural law. Indeed, (6) that
trade is intended by the divine is implied by the uneven distribution of raw
materials and talent in and among societies. (7) Moreover, trade is a source of
amity among men. (8) Thus, no nation should interfere with it.

Note the sharp contrast between More's utopia and Grotius's theories with
respect to commerce. Grotius argues that free trade is a God-given or natural
right. It is implied by natural law and the distribution of goods and services
around the world. It is necessary to satisfy human wants and helps to assure
extended networks of human friendship. There is no conflict between economic activity and ethical behavior. Moreover, because all human beings
should follow natural law, it is immoral and should be illegal to interfere with
or try to prevent free trade. The importance of trade in human affairs stands
in sharp contrast with the perspective of Thomas More, who argued a century

earlier that trade is at best a necessary inconvenience that distracts one from the important activities of life.

In Grotius, as in Aristotle, there is a clear connection between private and civil ethics; what is right for individuals is also right for kings and other government leaders. However, in contrast to Aristotle, Grotius suggests that natural law is universal and relatively easy to discern, because it is written in everyone's mind. Grotius does not try to find secular foundations for natural laws; rather, he argues that they are God-given and obvious. Thus, everyone can and should follow them.

## Pieter De La Court (1618–1685)

Pieter De La Court wrote *The Interests of Holland* ([1662] 1776) a half century after *Mare Liberum* was written. During that half century, the Netherlands had risen to prominence as a major center of international commerce and had attracted the emigration of Protestant entrepreneurs from around Europe. La Court was a second-generation immigrant to the Netherlands from present-day Belgium. His family ran a successful cloth-manufacturing business.[20] He was educated at Leiden University (which now has a building named after him) and was politically active in the Dutch Republic for much of his adult life, writing books and pamphlets in support of the republican form of government, free trade, and religious tolerance. The Netherlands was arguably the freest and most open country on earth during his lifetime. The blessings associated with nearly a century of independence, federalism, republican governance, and relatively open markets were by La Court's time self-evident.

*The True Interest and Political Maxims of the Republic of Holland* is not a book on ethics per se, but about economics and public policy. However, it indirectly sheds light on how private codes of conduct had evolved in Holland since the time of Erasmus. La Court regards virtue, hard work, and prosperity to be characteristics of both a good life and a good society. That his book was widely read suggests this to be true of his readers as well. He argues that prosperity is a joint product of the dispositions of persons living in a society, its form of government, and the public policies adopted by it. These principles and hypotheses provide the basis for his normative analysis of markets and

[20] Belgium and the Netherlands share the delta of the Rhine River, a major outlet for products from central Europe (southern Germany, northern France, and Switzerland). The provinces south of the Rhine remained under Hapsburg rule for the period of the Dutch Republic. This territory became known as Belgium and remained Catholic. Many Protestants left Belgium for the Netherlands in the early days of the republic to avoid discrimination and to be able to more freely practice their religion.

governments. As was true of Grotius, his arguments combine secular and religious reasoning.[21]

> God can give **no greater temporal blessing to a country in our condition than to introduce and preserve a free commonwealth government.** (La Court, *The True Interest and Political Maxims*, [1662] 1746, p. 38)

> Next to a liberty of serving God [religious tolerance], follows the **liberty of gaining a livelihood** without any dear-bought city-freedom, but only by virtue of a fixed habitation to have the common right of other inhabitants. [Such liberties are] very necessary for keeping the people we have, and inviting strangers to come among us. (La Court, *The True Interest and Political Maxims*, [1662] 1746, p. 74)

Notice that La Court does not think it necessary to justify prosperity as an aim in itself. To him, wealth is a blessing, rather than a distraction or sign of moral depravity. Because he expected his readers to find this to be obvious, he spends most of his time writing about where prosperity comes from, and how it can be sustained and extended. The contrast with Erasmus and More could not be greater. Markets and commerce are a natural (God-given) center of life for individuals—essential parts of a good life and good society. Prosperity is a consequence of the openness of Dutch society, the virtues and industry of its residents, and the secure property rights and freedoms associated with republican governance.

> The inhabitants under this free government hope by lawful means to acquire estates, . . . and use their wealth as they please, without dreading that any indigent or wasteful prince—or his courtiers and gentry, who are generally as prodigal, necessitous, and covetous as himself—should on any pretense whatever seize the wealth of the subject. Our inhabitants are therefore much inclined to subsist by the forenamed and other like ways or means, and gain riches for their posterity by frugality and good husbandry. (La Court, *The True Interest and Political Maxims*, [1662] 1746, p. 56)

> It is certainly known that this country cannot prosper, but by means of those that are most industrious and ingenious, and that such patents or grants [monopolies

---

[21] The 1746 Campbell translation from the original Dutch of La Court's *The True Interest and Political Maxims of the Republic of Holland* is used here. An early translation is used because it would not have been influenced by the emergence of economics and before the philosophical and political developments of the eighteenth century. Various digitized versions are available at the Liberty Fund website. As in previous cases, the excerpts are slightly edited. Contemporary rules for punctuation and capitalization are used. A few words in brackets are added to help contemporary readers or provide context for the excerpt used.

and trade privileges] do not produce the ablest merchants. (La Court, *The True Interest and Political Maxims*, [1662] 1746, p. 76)

Moreover, it is apparent that **he who increases his estate by industrious and frugal living** is most burdened [by wealth taxes] and he that by laziness and prodigality diminishes his estate will be less taxed. So that **virtue is unjustly oppressed** and **vice favored**. Whereas on the contrary, the imposts on consumption fall heavy upon the riotous and indulge and encourage the virtuous. (La Court, *The True Interest and Political Maxims*, [1662] 1746, p. 87)

La Court thanks God for providing the circumstances necessary for wealth creation—which include the Dutch form of government and its officials. Echoing Aristotle, he argues that the laws adopted by a good government provide incentives for people to develop virtuous dispositions, rather than undermine them. As far as La Court is concerned, good laws and institutions support both wealth accumulation and ethical behavior. They include the right to choose one's occupation and enter into businesses. They also encourage new residents to work hard and save. Poorly devised public policies, on the other hand, can undermine the virtue of a citizenry by encouraging laziness and drunkenness, rather than encouraging hard work, prudence, and innovation.[22] According to La Court, the Dutch political-economy system is a blessing, and the prosperity associated with it are also blessings rather than temptations to avoid, in contrast with the arguments of More and Erasmus, and to a lesser extent of Aristotle.

By this time, at least in the Netherlands, new virtues have been added to Aristotle's list. La Court's list and those of his readers would include "hard work," "frugality," and "religiosity" in late seventeenth-century Netherlands. Such virtues generate an active life divided between commerce and religious activities. La Court's conception of a good government is similar to that developed by Aristotle. A good government promotes both virtuous behavior and prosperity.

The breadth of La Court's readership suggests that the literate Dutch of this period saw little or no conflict between virtue and prosperity. Many methods of acquiring wealth were moral (those grounded in industry and saving). However, not all methods were moral. Wealth obtained through expropriation and government privileges were not. Moreover, some uses of wealth were virtuous and others not. Saving and investment are good, but gluttony and material gratification (hedonism) are not. He also argues that a republican

---

[22] La Court worries that these beneficial policies were being undermined in the Netherlands, which he expected to reduce the Netherlands' prosperity in the long run.

form of government (a somewhat representative government without a king) is one of the preconditions for prosperity, because kings and other nobles are prone to vice and expropriation.[23]

## Richard Baxter (1615–1691)

We now shift from two Dutch secular writers who occasionally wrote about religious matters to two English theologians who occasionally wrote about secular matters: Richard Baxter, a moderate Presbyterian, and Robert Barclay, one of the most important Quaker theorists of his day and governor of the East New Jersey colony in North America for eight years (1682–1690). Their works remained in print for more than two centuries, and both were widely read by Protestants in the decades after their publication. Insofar as most persons of European descent continued to be very much influenced by religious arguments during the next two centuries, it is likely that their writings and others similar to them were more influential than the secular ones focused on by most contemporary scholars. Such writings played a significant role in Max Weber's analysis of the Protestant work ethic and its significance for the rise of the commercial society.

Baxter's *A Christian Directory* ([1673] 2014) is a collection of recommended practices for all Christians. It is an accessible four-volume work that attempts to provide practical guidance for literate Christians and ministers, rather than theologians, whom he addressed in other work. It remained in print for over two centuries and covers such topics as prayer, conversation, marriage, hiring of servants, performance of contracts, political obligations, and the appropriate time for games and recreation. As a theologian, he naturally relies extensively on religious arguments and motivations, but he argues that one's divine duties include a variety of secular ones.

His *Directory* includes the idea of "a calling," a task or job that God calls on one to do and to do well. And, as true of Aristotle, he suggests that some careers are better than others.

VI. The first and principal thing to be intended in the **choice of a trade or calling for yourselves or children,** is the service of God and the public good; and therefore (ceteris paribus) that calling which most conduceth to the public good is to be preferred. **The callings most useful** to the public good are the **magistrates,**

---

[23] La Court clearly agrees with Weber's argument about the productivity of a work ethic, although he provides greater credit to supporting public policies than Weber does, writing more than two centuries later.

**the pastors, and teachers of the church, schoolmasters, physicians, lawyers,** &c. husbandmen (ploughmen, graziers, and shepherds); and next to them are mariners, clothiers, booksellers, tailors, and **such other that are employed about things most necessary to mankind.** (Baxter, *Christian Directory*, [1673] 2014, KL: 20570–20574)

His discussion of the selection of careers does not stress wealth, but it is clear that most are ones that require some education, and that by the standards of his time, were relatively well paid. Although, like Aristotle, he argues against the accumulation of wealth for its own sake, he goes on to argue that one has a divine duty to maximize profits, when this can be done in an ethical manner.

**If God shows you a way in which you may lawfully get more than in another way** (without wrong to your soul, or to any other) **if you refuse this,** and choose the less gainful way, you cross one of the ends of your calling, and you **refuse to be God's steward,** and to accept his gifts, and use them for him when he requireth it; **you may labor to be rich for God,** though not for the flesh and sin. (Baxter, *Christian Directory*, [1673] 2014, KL: 20600–20602).

Baxter also strongly recommends that individuals develop a work ethic so that they are less tempted to engage in vice.

**Live not in idleness or sloth; but be laborious in your callings,** that you may escape that need or poverty which is the temptation to this sin of theft. **Idleness is a crime** which is not to be tolerated in Christian societies. (Baxter, *Christian Directory*, 1673/2014, KL: 47241–47242)

He argues that secular activities are important to God and will be taken into account, and that one should behave ethically in all one's activities. There is no way to avoid being punished for failing in one's duties.

In contrast to More's *Utopia* ([1516] 1901), productive labor is not a task to be minimized, but rather is an important part of one's duty to God. Indeed, idleness is a sin. Moreover, profits per se are not themselves to be discouraged, as in Erasmus and More, but are also part of God's instruction, as long as one does not use immoral methods to realize them and refrains from using the fruits of one's labors for sinful activities. Indeed, failing to take advantage of profitable opportunities is itself a sin.

Nonetheless, Baxter's ascetic view of the good life implies that most sensual pleasures are sins, including conspicuous consumption, overeating, drinking alcohol, gaming, etc. His perspective on these typifies what to came be known as the Puritanical perspective on a good life. In this he differs from Aristotle, who recommended moderate indulgence in earthly pleasures, rather than the extremes of asceticism or hedonism. Baxter is closer to Aristotle when he suggests that some types of work are more praiseworthy than others. In contrast to Aristotle, he is less concerned about how careers affect one's character than in whether they advance divine interests or the public good. Nonetheless, the occupations listed are nearly all secular ones, and the ranking is broadly similar to that of Aristotle. Only two are religious specialities.

High profits and a frugal, diligent, hard-working lifestyle naturally tend to lift one out of poverty (which was widespread in England and elsewhere at this time). For such persons, one's accumulated wealth provided evidence of industriousness and frugality, both praiseworthy dispositions having God's blessing. As noted in Chapter 3, such traits tend to make markets and team production more productive.[24]

Baxter's justification for all the above activities is that they please God, rather than that they might make one happy or prosperous. One would, however, clearly be better off in one's afterlife if one pleased God; so, self-interest was not entirely absent from his arguments.

VIII. **Remember always that God is present, and none of your secrets** can be hidden from him. What the better are you to deceive your neighbor or your master, and to hide it from their knowledge, as long as **your Maker and Judge seeth all**? (Baxter, *Christian Directory*, [1673] 2014, KL: 47255–47257).

## Robert Barclay (1648–1690)

Robert Barclay wrote on Quaker theology and ethical theory. The latter had a significant influence on English political theory, which made his work more consequential than might be suggested by the extent of his direct readership. His views were influential within Quaker circles and in the American colonies of New Jersey and Pennsylvania, where Quakers were often in government and wrote or contributed to constitutional documents (Congleton 2011, Ch. 18).

Barclay's *An Apology for the True Christian Divinity* (1678) is largely a theological work, but the last two chapters cover topics relevant for everyday life and politics, on which there is much agreement with Baxter. Barclay's

---

[24] In Baxter's work, a strong work ethic and frugal lifestyle have biblical foundations that do not require the assumption of predestination, as Weber suggests. What is important for the emergence of a work ethic for Christians and other theists is the relative importance of the religious norms, rather than fundamental assumptions about supernatural power, knowledge, and intent.

suggested code of conduct for life on earth includes pacifism (except for self-defense), simple dress, not bowing to any man, disuse of titles or other honorifics, and opposition to both laughter and swearing (Ch. 15, part II). As in Baxter, property should not be used for merely superfluous purposes. His conception of the good life is one of hard work and divine duty. His vision of the good society includes central roles for property, voluntary relations, and virtuous behavior.[25]

> Our principle leaves **every man to enjoy that peaceably, which either his own industry or parents have purchased to him**—only he is thereby instructed to use it aright, **both for his own good and that of his brethren**, and all to the glory of God, in which also his **acts are to be voluntary** and **no ways constrained**. And further, we say not hereby that no man may use the creation more or less than another.
> (Barclay, *Apology for the True Christian Divinity*, [1678] 2002, p. 452)

With respect to republican governance, commerce, and their relationship to vice, he points to the experience of the Netherlands.

> God hath often a regard to magistrates and their state as a thing most acceptable to him. But if any can further doubt of this thing, to wit, if without confusion it can be practiced in the commonwealth, **let him consider the state of the United Netherlands, and he shall see the good effect of it,** for there, because of **the great number of merchants, more than in any other place, there is most frequent occasion for this thing** [honesty and promise keeping], and though the number of those that are of this mind be considerable, to whom the [Dutch] States these hundred years have condescended, and yet daily condescend, **yet nevertheless there has nothing of prejudice followed thereupon to the commonwealth, government, or good order, but rather great advantage to trade, and so to the commonwealth.**
> (Barclay, *Apology for the True Christian Divinity*, [1678] 2002, p. 488)

Baxter clearly agrees with La Court when he suggests that the relatively tolerant and open institutions of the Netherlands have divine approval, as evidenced by their prosperity. Moreover, he suggests that a commercial society tends to improve ethics and governance, rather than to degrade them.

Although Grotius, La Court, Barclay, and Baxter were all religious men, as was true of most people during this period, they all favored religious tolerance (freedom of conscience) for reasons similar to those that would be expressed by John Locke the year before Barclay's death. Barclay had some influence

---

[25] Available at Quaker Heritage Press (http://www.qhpress.org/texts/barclay/apology/index.html).

over the 1680 charter of East New Jersey (Thorpe 1909), which includes the following under its title 16:

> **All persons** living in the Province who confess and acknowledge the one Almighty and Eternal God, and holds [sic] themselves obliged in conscience to live peaceably and quietly in a civil society, **shall in no way be molested or prejudged for their religious persuasions and exercise in matters of faith and worship;** nor shall they be compelled to frequent and maintain any religious worship, place or ministry whatsoever. (Thorpe, *The Fundamental Constitutions for the Province of East New Jersey*, 1909, Section XVI)

There was no room for atheists, but in principle, all monotheists were welcome in East New Jersey. It should be kept in mind that most of Europe—including most Protestant domains—had state-supported monopoly religions during Barclay's lifetime.

## John Locke (1632–1704): On the Division between Theological and Secular Law

We conclude Chapter 10 with a short overview of a very influential secular English philosopher and political theorist. John Locke was trained as a physician at Oxford and accepted employment as Baron Anthony Ashley-Cooper's personal physician in 1667. Cooper was a leading English politician, the Earl of Shaftesbury, and founder of the Whig (Liberal) Party in England. Cooper's involvement in high-level and high-stakes English politics naturally encouraged Locke to think and write about the grand issues of his day, although little of it was published until after Cooper's death in 1683. Locke was clearly more than Cooper's resident doctor; he was an assistant, advisor, and dinner companion. Locke helped out on Cooper's colonial Carolina project and coauthored its colonial charter.

Locke spent the 1683–1689 period in the Netherlands to avoid arrest by the British authorities. He used his time there to complete several of his philosophical, political, and religious works. There he would also become more familiar with Dutch ideas about commerce, politics, and religious tolerance, which were very liberal by the standards of the world at that time, and these appear to have influenced his thinking on tolerance and revolution.[26]

---

[26] Cooper had orchestrated a national effort to block James's (the brother of Charles II) accession to the crown. When this failed, fearing for his life, he fled to the Netherlands in 1682, dying the following year. Locke left England in 1683. James II became king in 1685, but was deposed by William and Mary in 1689 (with the support of Parliament and the Dutch army). Locke returned to England shortly afterward.

John Locke wrote about epistemology and ethics, developed a natural law–based contractarian theory of legitimate government, and also wrote about economics and education. Two of his works continue to attract considerable attention: *Two Treatises on Government* (1690) and *An Essay Concerning Human Understanding* (1690). His political theory was sufficiently controversial that his *Two Treatises on Government* were initially published anonymously. Book sales, nonetheless, were sufficient for publishing multiple editions and translations of those volumes. His writings were widely read at the time he wrote them and continue to be so.[27]

For the purposes of this chapter, his work on ethics is of greatest interest. Locke regards ethics to be one of the three main areas of science, which for him encompasses the full range of that which humans can potentially understand.[28]

Science may be divided into three sorts. All that can fall within the compass of human understanding, being either, **First, the nature of things**, as they are in themselves, their relations, and their manner of operation: or, **Secondly, that which man himself ought to do,** as a rational and voluntary agent, for the attainment of any end, especially happiness: or, **Thirdly, the ways and means whereby the knowledge of both the one and the other of these is attained** and communicated. (Locke, *An Essay Concerning Human Understanding*, 2013, p. 538)

His assessment of the aim of ethics is similar to that developed by Aristotle; it concerns rules for life that lead to happiness.

[With regard to the second] Praktike, **the skill of right applying our own powers and actions, for the attainment of things good and useful.** The most considerable under this head is **ethics, which is the seeking out of those rules and measures of human actions, which lead to happiness,** and the means to practice them. The end of this is

---

[27] Locke's work is still widely cited today. His epistemology book, *An Essay Concerning Human Understanding*, has more than 17,000 Google citations (as of June 2017). His books on political theory, *Two Treatises of Government*, also remains widely read and cited, with more than 16,000 Google citations (as of June 2017). In his *Essay Concerning Human Understanding*, Locke argues that the human mind is essentially a blank slate at birth and that learning occurs through the development of ideas stimulated by the data provided the senses developed through reason and intuition. This challenged the ideas of Grotius (whose work he was familiar with and cited) that God wrote natural law directly into the minds of individuals. Given this, education, experience, and one's nature become central to an individual's development. Locke's theory of government was a major contribution to contractarian theories of the state, which is taken up in Part III of this book. He also made contributions to economics. For example, he recognized the effects of supply and demand on prices in the short run, but he argued that labor is the ultimate foundation of both property and value. For a list of the many editions of his texts, see http://www.libraries.psu.edu/tas/locke/bib/early-wk.html.

[28] Quotations are from a digitized collection of his works available from Amazon (John Locke, *The John Locke Collection: 6 Classic Works*, 2013).

not bare speculation and the knowledge of truth; **but right, and a conduct suitable to it.** (Locke, *An Essay Concerning Human Understanding*, 2013, p. 538)

Locke argues that happiness is partly a matter of character, and like Aristotle, that one's character is a consequence of one's judgment and experience. One's experience is, however, only partly a product of one's own making. What one learns from experience is partly determined by the range of opinions that one has been exposed to, which is to say by one's formal and informal education.

But **examples of this kind** [truly self-made men] **are but few**; and I think I may say, that **of all the men we meet with, nine parts of ten are what they are, good or evil, useful or not, by their education.** (Locke, *Some Thoughts Concerning Education*, 2013, p. 540)

Locke also shared Aristotle's belief that ethical propositions are more difficult to characterize precisely than geometry or algebra.

**Another thing that makes the greater difficulty in ethics is that moral ideas are commonly more complex than those of the figures ordinarily considered in mathematics.** From whence these two inconveniences follow. First, that their names are of more uncertain signification, **the precise collection of simple ideas they stand for not being so easily agreed on**; and so the sign that is used for them in communication always, and in thinking often, does not steadily carry with it the same idea. (Locke, *An Essay Concerning Human Understanding*, 2013, p. 452)

Nonetheless, given clear definitions, he argues that the rules of logic apply to ethics as well as to other topics.[29]

Locke goes on to characterize relationships between three general types of laws and associated ideas about good and evil in a community.

**These three laws [determine] the rules of moral good and evil.** These three then, **first**, the law of God; **secondly**, the law of politic societies; **thirdly**, the law of fashion, or private censure, are those to which men variously compare their actions.

[29] For example, he notes that if injustice is taken to mean the violation of rights, then where there are no rights there can be no injustice.

"Where there is no property there is no injustice" is a proposition as certain as any demonstration in Euclid: for the idea of property being a right to anything, and the idea to which the name "injustice" is given being the invasion or violation of that right, it is evident that these ideas, being thus established, and these names annexed to them, I can as certainly know this proposition to be true, as that a triangle has three angles equal to two right ones (*An Essay Concerning Human Understanding*, p. 452).

Locke does not argue in favor of a world without rights. His example simply demonstrates that logic can be applied to clear ethical propositions. Two hundred years later, Pyotr Kropotkin would take this line

And, it is **by their conformity to one of these laws that they take their measures, when they would judge of their moral rectitude,** and denominate their
actions good or bad. **Morality is the relation of voluntary actions to these rules.**
(Locke, *An Essay Concerning Human Understanding*, 2013, p. 452)

Locke's characterization of moral choice is similar to Aristotle, but relies more
heavily on moral maxims and principles (rules). Morally relevant choices
have to be voluntary, but morality itself reflects decisions about how to follow
the rules of one's society. What is radical about his theory of ethics in this especially religious period of European history is his suggestion that not all ethical principles have religious foundations or purposes. Two of the three areas
in which normative rules bind or should bind human behavior do not have
religious foundations.[30]

There are separate religious and civil spheres of morality and law, because the interests advanced by religious and civil activities are distinct. The
former concerns conduct that is likely secure an afterlife, whereas the latter
concerns conduct that creates conditions for a good life on earth. Locke
argues that these distinct interests are best advanced through different types
of organizations.

A church, then, I take to be a voluntary society of men, joining themselves together
of their own accord in order to the **public worshipping** of God in such manner as
they judge acceptable to Him, and effectual to the salvation of their souls. **I say it
is a free and voluntary society. . . . No man by nature is bound unto any particular church or sect, but everyone joins himself voluntarily** to that society in which
he believes he has found that profession and worship which is truly acceptable
to God. **The hope of salvation, as it was the only cause of his entrance into that
communion, so it can be the only reason of his stay there.** (*A Letter Concerning
Toleration*, p. 18)

of argument to heart. He opposed capitalism and favored systems similar to More's *Utopia* ([1651] 1901), in
part because he thought that property is unjust, for example, theft. This and other critiques of capitalism are
beyond the scope of this book, which is focused on the emergence of ethical support for capitalism, rather
than critiques.

[30] His approach to the religious foundation of some ethical rules follows that of Grotius—at least as revealed in his books on governance. "The state of nature has a law of nature to govern it, which obliges every
one: and reason, which is that law, teaches all mankind, who will but consult it, that being all equal and
independent, no one ought to harm another in his life, health, liberty, or possessions: for men being all
the workmanship of one omnipotent, and infinitely wise maker; all the servants of one sovereign master,
sent into the world by his order . . ." (1690, p. 5). "But I moreover affirm, that all men are naturally in that
state, and remain so, till by their own consents they make themselves members of some politic society"
(1690, p. 8).

The purposes advanced by joining or creating a civil society are quite different.

The commonwealth seems to me to be a society of men constituted only for the procuring, preserving, and advancing their own civil interests. **Civil interests I call life, liberty, health, and indolency of body; and the possession of outward things,** such as money, lands, houses, furniture, and the like. **It is the duty of the civil magistrate, by the impartial execution of equal laws,** to secure unto all the people in general and to every one of his subjects **in particular the just possession of these things belonging to this life.** (*A Letter Concerning Toleration*, p. 17)

Locke argues that in areas where there is an overlap, the civil authority should make the relevant policy decisions because its charge involves everyone, not just the members of a particular church.

**The care of all things relating both to one and the other is committed by the society to the civil magistrate.** This is the original, this is the use, and these are the bounds of the legislative (which is the supreme) power in every commonwealth. **I mean that provision may be made for the security of each man's private possessions; for the peace, riches, and public commodities of the whole people; and, as much as possible, for the increase of their inward strength against foreign invasions.** (*A Letter Concerning Toleration*, p. 33)

Commerce is, of course, a voluntary activity within civil society and civil society exists to promote the "peace, riches, and public commodities" of its members. Increasing prosperity (riches) thus is one of the main purposes of a civil society, which implies that the promotion of commerce is one of the main duties of secular governments and a feature of every good society. It is one of the main reasons that individuals join civil societies. Avoiding trespass of those rights is both among an individual's core civic duties and one of the original responsibilities of every government grounded in the consent of those governed.

And thus the common-wealth comes by a power to set down what punishment shall belong to the several transgressions which they think worthy of it, committed amongst the members of that society, (which is the power of making laws) as well as it has the power to punish any injury done unto any of its members, by any one that is not of it, (which is the power of war and peace;) and **all this for the preservation of the property of all the members of that society, as far as is possible.** (Locke, *Two Treatises of Government*, [1690] 2009, p. 30)

Although his philosophical and political arguments were controversial at the time that he wrote, his book sales imply that a substantial subset of literate persons in English and American society were sympathetic with his conclusions. That his impact was greater in the eighteenth than in the seventeenth century suggests that mainstream ethical beliefs were shifting in a direction that made his arguments more and more persuasive over the course of the next century.

## Some Tentative Conclusions: The Enlightenment Diminished Ethical Reservations about Commerce

### Summary

The above writings are not a complete catalog of thoughts on ethics and prosperity from 1500 to 1700, but provide a useful sample of writing by widely read authors who wrote on both economic and ethical issues. The authors are for the most part among those that might be regarded as the vanguard of the liberal movement. That is to say, they often reached conclusions that would in the nineteenth century be regarded as "liberal" concerning most political and economic matters. It is partly for this reason that their work still attracts attention.

There are common elements among all the authors reviewed who wrote between 1600 and 1700. All are theists. They all argue that at least a subset of the grounding principles of their theories have divine origins. All reach similar conclusions about the nature of a good life and good society, at least insofar as economic activities are concerned. Nonetheless, the particular conclusions reached, and the arguments used to reach them, differ.

A significant shift in norms evidently occurred between 1500 and 1700, although not in a great leap, but as a series of refinements. Erasmus asserts that commerce is a corrupting influence on individuals and an institution that should be minimized. More argues that in an ideal society the labors required to produce life's necessities should be minimized to free time for contemplation. Leisure should be maximized. Their Protestant successors agreed that greed could undermine virtue, but disagree with them about the importance of work, and the role of work and commerce in a good life and good society. Grotius and La Court regard trade to be a divine right and prosperity a blessing. Baxter suggests that well-chosen secular careers can be divine callings. La Court, Baxter, and Barkley, in contrast with More, argue that diligent hard work is a virtue and leisure is a vice. In general, moral reservations about commerce diminished and ethical support for an active life in which economic activity plays an important role increased during the two centuries covered.

Nonetheless, the arguments of La Court and Baxter do not provide unbounded support for commerce or for the accumulation and use of wealth. Wealth should be obtained through what might be called ethical or praiseworthy methods. Wealth should be accumulated in a manner that does not harm one's soul—nor should wealth be used extravagantly or squandered on material comforts, but rather passed on to one's children, used to promote their church, or otherwise used to increase the welfare of their communities. Among Protestant religious scholars such as Baxter and Barclay, there is no separation of the religious and worldly spheres of life. Prosperity is desirable because it can reinforce rather than undermine ethical conduct, as in the Netherlands.

Locke, in contrast, argues that there are several distinctions between religious and other spheres of life. He suggests that people differ in their understanding of divine texts and divine duties and so naturally choose to worship in different ways. He also suggests that life in a community has its own ethos and good laws, and that any conflict between those laws and religion-based ethical principles should be resolved by the civil government, rather than by imposing a uniform religious doctrine. This conclusion implies that Locke regarded civil interests to be paramount in a society where persons disagree about the nature of divine duties. It can also be argued that Locke believed that religious societies played a smaller role in securing an afterlife for their members than a civil society plays in securing life, liberty, and property for its members.

Praiseworthy goals within Locke's readership included liberty, leisure, and wealth—or, as he puts it: "life, liberty, health, and indolency of body [leisure]; and the possession of outward things, such as money, lands, houses, furniture." Those goals did not include—at least in Locke's assessment—a moral duty to work hard and prosper. This difference between Locke and La Court may partly account for the greater average income of the Netherlands relative to England at this time insofar as they reflected the prevalence of different ideas about the role of a work ethic in a good life in the late seventeenth century.

## Relationships to Part I

Part I of this book suggests that such trends in a community's ethical dispositions—its ethos—tend to increase the extent of market activity. Greater informal support for commercial activities and the rights that facilitate them would tend to encourage more persons to undertake commercial activities. Support for honest hard work tends to reduce the problem of fraud and increase the effective supply of labor. Diligence and honesty tend to make markets work better, by reducing risks from exchange and the need for monitoring in production. Frugality would tend to increase the supply of capital—the stock of equipment available for production, shipping, and storage. Frugality would also provide funds for loans and reserves for overcoming economic and other shocks.

The effects of such norms are evident in data on the economic standard of living in the period from 1500 through 1800. The GDP calculations of Broadberry, Campbell, Klein, Overton, and Leeuwen (2015) for England from 1270 to 1730 (their figures 4 and 5) show a relatively flat output of agricultural and industrial production until about 1500 and a clear—if modest—acceleration after 1500. A similar figure based on somewhat different data is used in Chapter 13, which shows that the first significant acceleration of commerce began at about the time of La Court and Baxter writings in England.

Many of the ideas of the authors surveyed in this chapter were "in the air" during the time period in which they wrote. Support for hard work was widely shared among Puritans. For example, the Puritan villages and towns of North America often made idleness a crime subject to legal penalties. Separation of church and state and religious tolerance were evident in the Netherlands and also in several English colonies in North America, prior to Locke's highly regarded paper on religious toleration. Social contracts had been proposed in England and had already been signed in several New English colonies in North America before Hobbes ([1651] 2009) and Locke (1690) had worked out their theories of social contract. The *Mayflower Compact* of 1620 is among the most well-known, but there were many others.

What these venerated scholars contributed were overarching, fine-grained, consistent narratives that demonstrated to their readers that what might look like unrelated ideas and maxims were actually grounded in a few general principles and lines of reasoning. Their main innovations are the links in their analytical chains and conclusions, rather than in entirely new maxims or principles—although a few of these were also developed. For example, industry and frugality were added to lists of virtues.

That their reasoning and conclusions resonated with that of their readers is indicated by the success of their books and pamphlets. All the works reviewed in this chapter were widely read at the time of their publication and by many future generations of scholars and students.

# 11
# Classical Liberalism, Ethics, and Commerce

## Setting the Stage: The Deistic Approach to Nature and Society

The Enlightenment of the seventeenth century, together with associated innovations in printing and shipping, had numerous effects on European culture. Censorship diminished somewhat as religious, scientific, and political controversies came to be seen as part of the manner in which new truths come to be understood. These new truths included ideas about virtues that individuals should aspire to accumulate, the appropriate openness of political and economic systems, and the accumulation and dissemination of knowledge about the planet and universe throughout what became known as "the West" in future centuries. Regional languages gradually replaced Latin in most books and pamphlets. Literacy, scientific research, and literature increased.

Censorship did not entirely disappear in the seventeenth century. Laws against blasphemy and sedition continued to inhibit the development and dissemination of ideas about the good life and good society that challenged traditional beliefs about religion and government. This is why many of the works discussed in the previous chapter were initially published anonymously, as with the writings of La Court and Locke, and/or at Dutch presses where there was less censorship, as with the Latin translation of Hobbes's Leviathan. Nonetheless, the rise of Protestantism in the seventeenth century and differences among conclusions reached about divine intent and duties made it clear that even theologies grounded in the same texts can reach quite different conclusions about the best route to salvation. As tolerance in this important sphere of life increased, more critical analyses of religious and political issues were published in pamphlets and books, and it became safer to acknowledge one's authorship of controversial pieces. Secular arguments also became more commonplace, in part because they could engage and persuade a broader readership than those grounded in specific religious doctrines.

Although intellectual progress was evident in the seventeenth century, economic development and political liberalization did not follow quickly,

*Solving Social Dilemmas.* Roger D. Congleton, Oxford University Press. © Oxford University Press 2022.
DOI: 10.1093/oso/9780197642788.003.0011

although a modest acceleration in growth rates was evident. Most of Europe remained under family-based governance—with hereditary kings, dukes, barons, and so forth. Most economic enterprises remained family based, although partnerships were not uncommon. The production of some goods was becoming somewhat more mechanized as wind and waterpower were being used more extensively. Significant censorship remained in many countries, and penalties for criticizing a national church or government were often severe. Formal punishments were often reinforced by informal ones.

England suffered through its civil war, restoration, and glorious revolution in the second half of the seventeenth century, changes which arguably were driven by changes in ideas about religion and the proper scope of monarchical authority, but it nonetheless began the eighteenth century with its long-standing monarchical system with a two-chamber parliament firmly in place—albeit with an increase in parliament's bargaining power. The medieval order was beginning to be replaced with what might be termed the liberal or modern order, but this would be obvious only a century and a half later.[1]

The interest in better understandings of the laws of nature and society led to the founding of numerous scientific clubs and societies.[2] Their members included university scholars, but the majority were simply men and women with sufficient resources, free time, and interest in nature to participate in the various scholarly and scientific enterprises encouraged by those clubs. Experiments and meetings were often conducted in the homes of fellow natural philosophers. The new more analytical and experimental approaches to understanding nature did not reject biblical and classical texts, but they did tend to reduce their importance as explanations for the natural world, as opposed to the spiritual world. To most participants in scientific societies, natural laws were products of divine design, even when not mentioned in religious texts.

---

[1] In the next century (the nineteenth century), the term *liberal* would be applied to policies that supported a written constitution, relatively open and competitive markets, relatively open and democratic politics, religious liberty, and the end of slavery. What might be termed *constitutional liberalism* remains common among all liberals in the twentieth century, although the term *liberal* is used differently now in Europe and the United States. In the United States it refers to what I term *left liberalism*; in most of the rest of the world it refers to what might be called *right liberalism*.

[2] For example, the Royal Society of London was founded in 1660 and attracted eminent philosophers and scientists from throughout the English-speaking world, although initially, members were mostly based in London. Both formal and informal scientific organizations held meetings and published small journals, which allowed critical examination of new results and ideas. Those found useful or interesting would be widely disseminated by members' own research circles. John Locke and Isaac Newton were both members of the Royal Society in the late seventeenth century, and their membership in the Royal Society doubtless increased the impact of their theories. Benjamin Franklin's famous kite experiment was published by the Royal Society. Other local and national societies, such as the French Academy of Sciences, were founded at about the same time. Benjamin Franklin founded the American Philosophical Society in 1743. The appendices of McClellan (1985) provide a complete list of such societies.

Many of the members of the new scientific societies adopted theological perspectives analogous to Aristotle's theory of the first mover or unmoved mover—he who can place things in motion without himself being in motion. From the Deistic perspective, a divine being put the universe in motion and created the natural laws that determined its future path, rather than actively guiding it on a day-to-day basis. From this perspective, the study of nature was simply another method through which one could come to understand the intent of the divine being. This natural law perspective was common among the intelligentsia of Europe and North America, although it was by no means the only theology held by members of scientific clubs. Nor was the Deistic perspective entirely new. Similar perspectives were evident in Aristotle and many other classical scholars. Nonetheless, Deism was a significant shift from late medieval religious views, because it implied that miracles were not commonplace, prayers were rarely directly answered, and divine texts did not provide all that one needed to know about either natural or moral philosophy.

Deists believed that divine laws were not obvious but could be discovered through careful observation, analysis, and experimentation.[3] Galileo's telescope and Van Hookes's microscope, for example, demonstrated that new things could be learned about the universe through careful observation and the use of new instruments. Newton's theory of universal gravitation and three laws of motion (1687) provided an early and powerful example of general natural laws that could be discovered through experimentation and analysis.

The search for natural laws was not limited to astronomy and physics. It included efforts to discover the laws that explained human life, history, and social relationships. Locke's discussion of the science of ethics is an early instance of that approach.

This chapter focuses on widely read scholars of the eighteenth and early nineteenth centuries who wrote on both economic and ethical theory. Three are among the intellectuals most remembered from that century: Montesquieu, Smith, and Kant. Their ideas were ones that literate persons of that century and the next would be familiar with and many later scholars would take for granted. Two other scholars wrote for popular audiences, although they also led distinguished careers and have not been forgotten: Franklin and Bastiat.

---

[3] Such a perspective remained common for centuries. For example, Einstein, who is among the most famous of twentieth-century scientists, once wrote that "[q]uantum mechanics is certainly imposing. But an inner voice tells me that it is not yet the real thing. The theory says a lot but does not really bring us any closer to the secret of the 'old one.' I, at any rate, am convinced that He does not throw dice" (letter to Max Born, December 4, 1926). The deistic approach was completely compatible with theologies predicated on omniscience and predestination, but also the existence of natural laws that were unmentioned in theological texts.

Weber regarded one of these authors as the man whose writings best captured the spirit of capitalism (Franklin). Seventeenth-century developments in ethics, political theory, and economics led to new, broader, and deeper theories in the eighteenth century, as with Montesquieu's theory of law and politics, Smith's theory of market prices and international trade, and Smith's, Bentham's, and Kant's contributions to ethical theory.

All the authors reviewed in this chapter were interested in the foundations of a good life and good society. Most would be regarded today as classical liberals because of their support for relatively open political and economic systems, although the term *liberal* was rarely used to describe such ideas during the eighteenth century. All provided significant moral support for the lifestyles and institutions that tend to support a commercial society, although that support was not always the main motivation for their books, pamphlets, and articles. Again, the main focus is on the relatively small subset of their writings that most directly addressed ethical issues and reached conclusions about the proper role of commerce in a good life and good society.

As before, we take their illustrating examples to be evidence of commonplace ideas in the communities in which they lived—which is to say, we assume that they are products of the scientific approach used in that period. They attempted to discover the underlying natural laws behind the most commonplace moral intuitions and sentiments of their societies. As in the previous chapter, there is evidence of a trend toward somewhat broader and deeper support for commerce. That increase in support was in a sense additive—it added to the panoply of analyses and evidence that tended to accord commercial careers and commerce a larger role in a good life and good society.

## Montesquieu (1689–1755): On Virtue, the State, and Industry

Baron Charles-Louis Secondat obtained the name that he is most associated with through a barony that he inherited from his uncle in 1716 over the territory of Montesquieu. That inheritance, in combination with another barony inherited from his mother, allowed him to withdraw from legal practice and devote himself to managing his baronies and to scholarship. Montesquieu was a member of the local scientific society, the Academy of Bordeaux. And, as true of most of the other authors discussed in this book, Montesquieu was relatively liberal by the standards of his time. This, in combination with the breadth and depth of his analysis of the laws and political institutions governing human societies, attracted the interest of future liberals, including the founding fathers of American constitutional governance. Montesquieu, rather than Locke, is the most mentioned scholar in the *Federalist Papers* (Lutz 1984).

Montesquieu is best known for his 1748 magnus opus, *The Spirit of the Laws*, which includes an analytical history of the emergence of law, a discussion of how climate and culture affect forms of government, and analyses of divided and federal governance. Montesquieu argues that both constitutional and civil laws reflects both causal and accidental factors, including climate, geography, culture, and history. The former implies that political institutions are susceptible to a scientific cause-and-effect-based analysis. The latter implies that the results cannot be as precise as those of astronomy or some parts of physics. Historical accidents, as well as causal forces, affect the course of legal and constitutional developments.[4]

*The Spirit of the Laws* includes both positive and normative theories of governance. It begins with a theory of the natural state analogous to those of Hobbes and Locke, but stresses the formation of groups and relationships among groups. What might be called domestic law emerges within groups. International law emerges between groups. He also discusses constitutional designs. Montesquieu's ideal constitution resembled that of England at the time he wrote. It included a bicameral parliament and a king. In one of the chambers of parliament, positions were determined by heredity or lifetime appointments. Positions in the other were determined by elections. His support for constitutional monarchy and class-based parliaments was shared by most European liberals in the eighteenth and early nineteenth centuries.[5]

The parts of *The Spirit of the Laws* that are most relevant for this chapter are his discussions of the role of ethics in political systems and of the effects of markets on ethical dispositions. As part of his positive analysis of governments, he examined the role of virtue in different forms of government.

---

[4] Excerpts are from the 1752 Thomas Nugent translation of the first edition of *The Spirit of the Laws*. There is also a relatively new and very readable translation of the third edition (published in 1758 shortly after Montesquieu's death) by Cohler, Miller, and Stone (Cambridge 1989). Besides being very readable, it includes some material left out of the Nugent translation, including Montesquieu's analytical history of the emergence of the state and international relations. The older Nugent version has been more influential. It is also widely available on the Web and avoids copyright issues. The Kindle locations refer to the eBooksLib. com version, which is available from Amazon. Boldface has again been added by the author to draw attention to key phrases and ideas.

[5] Montesquieu's support for constitutional monarchy may have been reinforced by laws against sedition and treason. Open support for republican forms of government could still be punished by treason or sedition laws during this period. Thomas Paine's attack on monarchy, the *Rights of Man*, which was written several decades later (1791), caused both him and his publisher to be tried and convicted of sedition in England. Nonetheless, at the time that Montesquieu wrote, constitutional monarchies were clearly among the best governments in Europe, so most supporters were doubtless sincere as well as prudent.

He also discussed positive and negative effects that commerce had on the development of ethical dispositions. Much of this analysis occurs in his analysis of the importance of civic virtues for democratic forms of governance. He argues that the ethical support required for democracies to achieve good results tended to be greater than for other forms of government.

> There is no great share of probity necessary to support a monarchical or despotic government. The force of laws in one, and the prince's arm in the other, are sufficient to direct and maintain the whole. But **in a popular state, one spring more is necessary, namely, virtue.** (Montesquieu, *The Spirit of the Laws*, 1748, KL: 496–498)

The virtue of citizens is important for democracies because public policy is based on popular opinion in that form of government.[6]

He suggests that equality is the normal foundation for democracy, but argues that equality is less necessary for democracy in commercial societies, because commerce reinforces the virtuous dispositions required for democracy.[7]

> True is it that **when a democracy is founded on commerce, private people may acquire vast riches without a corruption of morals.** This is because the spirit of commerce is naturally attended with that of **frugality, economy, moderation, labor, prudence, tranquility, order, and rule.** So long as this spirit subsists, the riches it produces have no bad effect. (Montesquieu, *The Spirit of the Laws*, 1748: 889–94)

A democracy based on commerce tends to be more robust than one based on agriculture and equality because of commerce's support for relevant ethical dispositions. Because inequality tends to emerge in the ordinary course of life, democracies are most likely to be sustained when the spirit of commerce be broadly shared, especially among its most influential citizens. This provides

---

[6] Montesquieu discusses a wide variety of electoral and representative methods and seems to support broad suffrage but class-based representation, giving greater weights to voters who are better educated or accomplished and/or to the representatives that such groups select. The only republics of note in Montesquieu's time were relatively small countries: the Netherlands, Switzerland, and Venice. None of these had a king, but neither were they particularly democratic, except relative to the rest of the world. Other somewhat more democratic republics existed in ancient history, as in Athens and Sparta, which Montesquieu also refers to as republics. So, a reasonable interpretation of what he terms "popular" or "democratic" government is any government in which a variety of interests are well-represented, rather than ones necessarily grounded in elections or equal representation.

[7] Commerce was limited to cities and large towns at the time that Montesquieu wrote. In effect, commerce in free cities was a substitute for the economic equality required to support it in the countryside.

a new political argument in support of commerce for persons who favor democracy, one grounded in the effect of commerce on moral dispositions.

> The mischief is, when excessive wealth destroys the spirit of commerce, then it is that the inconveniences of inequality begin to be felt.
>
> In order to support this spirit, commerce should be carried on by the principal citizens; this should be their sole aim and study; this the chief object of the laws. (Montesquieu, *The Spirit of the Laws*, 1748, KL: 891–897)

Industry and frugality are the civic virtues most necessary to support democratic governance in the long run, because of the need to restrain public expenditures to levels that are compatible with the ability and willingness of voters to pay taxes.

> [I]ndeed, in a well-regulated democracy, where people's expenses should extend only to what is necessary, everyone ought to have it; for how should their wants be otherwise supplied? (Montesquieu, *The Spirit of the Laws*, 1748, KL: 903–905)

As was true of Aristotle and La Court, Montesquieu also believed that laws can support or undermine civic virtues such as industry. An example is inheritance laws.[8]

> It is an excellent law in a trading republic to make an equal division of the paternal estate among the children. The consequence of this is that however great a fortune the father has made, his children, being not so rich as he, are induced to avoid luxury, and to work as he has done. I speak here only of trading republics; as to those that have no commerce, the legislator must pursue quite different measures. (Montesquieu, *The Spirit of the Laws*, 1748, KL: 898–901)

Although commerce supports the virtues most necessary for democracy, he argues that not all virtues are supported by market activities. For example, commerce tends to improve international relations and diminish unfounded prejudices, but also to weaken the virtues of generosity and altruism.

> Commerce is a cure for the most destructive prejudices; for it is almost a general rule that wherever we find agreeable manners, there commerce flourishes; and

---

[8] Another is evidently support for a work ethic. Montesquieu notes, "In [Athens], endeavors were used to inspire them [the people] with the love of industry and labor. Solon made idleness a crime and insisted that each citizen should give an account of his manner of getting a livelihood." (Montesquieu, *The Spirit of the Laws*, 1748, KL: 899–903)

that wherever there is commerce, there we meet with agreeable manners. **Let us not be astonished, then, if our manners are now less savage than formerly.** Commerce has everywhere diffused a knowledge of the manners of all nations: **these are compared one with another, and from this comparison arise the greatest advantages.** (Montesquieu, *The Spirit of the Laws*, 1748, KL: 5120–5123)

If **the spirit of commerce unites nations,** it **does not in the same manner unite individuals.** We see that in countries **where the people move only by the spirit of commerce, they make a traffic of all the humane, all the moral virtues;** the most trifling things, those which humanity would demand, **are there done, or there given, only for money.**

 [T]he **spirit of trade produces in the mind of a man a certain sense of exact justice, opposite,** on the one hand, to robbery, and on the other **to those moral virtues which forbid our always adhering rigidly to the rules of private interest,** and suffer us to neglect this for the advantage of others. (Montesquieu, *The Spirit of the Laws*, 1748, KL: 5127–5132)

Although there is some tension between markets and some aspects of morality, Montesquieu concludes that industry and wealth are blessings for all nations that can be (and should be) encouraged by appropriate laws and taxes.

The **great state is blessed with industry, manufactures, and arts,** and establishes laws by which those several advantages are procured. . . . The **effect of wealth in a country is to inspire every heart with ambition:** that of poverty is to give birth to despair. **The former is excited by labor,** the latter is soothed by indolence. (Montesquieu, *The Spirit of the Laws*, 1748, KL: 3454–3459)

These conclusions suggest that moral support for commerce had become commonplace in France by the mid-eighteenth century. They are similar to La Court's remarks about the Netherlands a half a century earlier, but they differ from La Court's in that they are grounded in a general theory of law and governance, rather than immediate observations and intuition. As a consequence, Montesquieu argues that they are relevant for all nations—not simply for France or the Netherlands.[9]

Montesquieu's analysis implies that the type and relative importance of civil virtues tend to be system-specific. For example, the virtues most important

---

[9] Montesquieu's remarks on taxation also parallel and deepen those of La Court: "Of the Public Revenues. The public revenues are a portion that each subject gives of his property, in order to secure or enjoy the remainder. To fix these revenues in a proper manner, regard should be had both to the necessities of the state and to those of the subject. The real wants of the people ought never to give way to the imaginary wants of the state" (Montesquieu, *The Spirit of the Laws*, 1748, KL: 3442–3445).

for successful open societies (republics with competitive markets) differ from those required to support monarchical and aristocratic systems in which commerce is less central to life. Honesty, industry, and frugality are praiseworthy in private life and underpin the politics of republics. In less open societies, other virtues are relatively more important. Politeness and deference are important to the success and stability of monarchies and moderation for aristocracies.

His reservations about the extent to which commerce provides support for private virtue provide a window into the beliefs of literate Frenchmen in the mid-eighteenth century. If reservations about the ultimate morality of commerce were somewhat greater in eighteenth-century France than in the Netherlands and England, then Parts I and II of this book imply that markets would be more developed in the Netherlands and England than in France at that time, as was evidently the case (Weir 1997).[10]

# Benjamin Franklin (1706–1790) and the Ethos of Capitalism

The English colonies of North America during the eighteenth century were places where ethics and public policies tended to support commerce and democratic government. Indeed, many of the colonies and the largest cities within the colonies had been founded by private commercial companies or partnerships, as with the Virginia Company (1609), the Dutch West Indies Company (1621), and the Massachusetts Bay Company (1630). Norms supportive of civil society and commerce are evident in many colonial and town charters of the seventeenth century. By the eighteenth century, several small cities were flourishing, and a cosmopolitan culture had emerged in the port cities of the Northern and Mid-Atlantic colonies, with a mélange of British, German, and Dutch ideas and customs.

Among the many notable "Americans" of the eighteenth century was a self-made man, printer, scientist, politician, and philosopher by the name of Benjamin Franklin. Benjamin Franklin was the son of an emigrant to Boston. He attended school until the age of 10, learned the printing and newspaper trade from his brother, and taught himself to read, write, and argue well. Franklin read widely as a young man, including works by Aristotle, Plato,

---

[10] This was evidently true in spite of the fact that both the idea and the term *laissez-faire* are of French origin. The term's first known appearance in print was in 1751, a few years after Montesquieu published the first edition of his *The Spirit of the Laws*.

Locke, and Mandeville, among many others. In his late teens, he moved from Boston to Philadelphia, another major city in the territory that a few decades later became the United States. In Philadelphia, Franklin became a successful printer and publisher, a civic leader and politician, an innovative scientist and inventor, and subsequently, a national statesman. His scientific contributions included demonstrating that lightning was electricity (rather than a miracle), and charting and naming the Gulf Stream of the Atlantic Ocean. Later in life, he served as the governor of Pennsylvania, as ambassador to France, and participated in writing the Declaration of Independence and the US Constitution.

What is most relevant for the purposes of this book is his writing. He wrote on a wide variety of topics over his lifetime, including politics, science, and ethics. Much of it was written for the literate public as a means of earning a living, as with his newspapers and almanacs. Other writings were addressed to narrower scientific and philosophical societies. Still others were simply notes to himself or letters to others. His writings were widely read in what became the United States and also, to a lesser extent, in Europe. His analysis of connections between virtue and success in life was well-known among his readers, and it was widely enough known for Max Weber ([1905] 1958) to regard Franklin's pamphlet on *The Way to Wealth* ([1758] 2014) as capturing the essential spirit of capitalism.

Franklin's recommendations for day-to-day ethics provide an excellent window into colonial attitudes toward life, wealth, and markets in the eighteenth-century English colonies along the Atlantic coast of North America. As was true of Baxter, he was a source of maxims that influenced many in his own time and continued to do so into the next century and beyond.

His advice for the most part concerned life on earth, and to be widely read, it had to resonate with ideas already in the minds of his readers.[11]

## Franklin's Deism and Self-Training in Ethics

At the age of 15, Franklin became a Deist in a form that included an extreme form of predestination. He concluded that good and evil were empty words, because all that occurred was set in motion by a benevolent God and so must

---

[11] Franklin's autobiography is still read in many high school and college English and history classes in the United States. His autobiography has more than a thousand Google citations. His persona, as in his day, remains better known outside academia, with many more "hits" on Google than on Google Scholar. His face is on the United States' hundred-dollar bill. Biographies of Franklin continue to be written.

be fundamentally good. In Franklin's mind at least, Deism had essentially eliminated the possibility of biblical foundations for rules of conduct.[12]

Nonetheless, in his early twenties, he changed his mind about the practical value of personal ethics and adopted guidelines for his future behavior. From Franklin's Deistic perspective, there was little that one could do to advance one's likelihood of salvation, but much that one could do to make one's life on earth more pleasant and profitable.[13]

> I grew convinced that **truth, sincerity, and integrity in dealings between man and man were of the utmost importance to the felicity of life;** and I formed written resolutions, which still remain in my journal book, to practice them ever while I lived.
>
> **Revelation had indeed no weight with me, as such;** but I entertained an opinion that, though certain actions might not be bad because they were forbidden by it, or good because it commanded them, **yet probably these actions might be forbidden because they were bad for us, or commanded because they were beneficial to us,** in their own natures, all the circumstances of things considered. (Franklin, *Autobiography of Benjamin Franklin*, [1793] 2012, KL: 829–833)

He suggests, as Aristotle had approximately 2,000 years earlier, that virtuous dispositions are likely to be good for the person developing them. Personal success and satisfaction, Franklin argues, are ultimately based on "virtuous and self-approving conduct." The same virtues tend to contribute to one's economic success.

## Franklin and the Economic Virtues

Franklin's invented character "Poor Richard" plays a role in many of his almanacs and maxims. This was probably not a form of anonymity to avoid

---

[12] Excerpts are from Franklin's *Autobiography* ([1793] 2012), *The Way to Wealth* ([1753] 2012), and *Memoirs of Benjamin Franklin; Written by Himself* ([1839] 2012), a compendium of his letters and notes. "KL" again refers to Kindle locations.

[13] Franklin lists 13 virtues that he attempted to perfect during his youngest days: temperance, silence, order, resolution, frugality, industry, sincerity, justice, moderation, cleanliness, tranquility, chastity, and humility. Each was given a practical definition, and he kept track of his success on each virtue in as notebook. He notes that he was not very good at humility, but that false humility seemed to work nearly as well. (Each of these virtues is given his own definition, which makes some of them a bit easier to follow than they might have been if they had been defined by others, as with chastity.)

censorship, which was relatively light in Pennsylvania during this period, but a marketing device to increase his readership. Poor Richard advocated a life of hard work, enterprise, and frugality.

ADVICE TO A YOUNG WORKER. **Remember that time is money.** He that can earn ten shillings a day by his labor, and **sits idle one half** of that day, though he spends but sixpence during his diversion ought not to reckon that the only expense; **he has really thrown away five shillings besides**. . . .

The **most trifling actions that affect a man's credit are to be regarded carefully. The sound of your hammer at five in the morning or nine at night, heard by a creditor,** makes him easy six months longer. But if he sees you at a billiard table or **hears your voice in a tavern** when you should be at work, he sends for his money the next day. **Creditors are a kind of people that have the sharpest eyes and ears, as well as the best memories of any in the world**. . . .

In short, **the way to wealth,** if you desire it, is as plain as the way to market. It **depends chiefly on two words: industry and frugality.** Waste neither time nor money, but make the best use of both. **He that gets all he can honestly, and saves all he can, will certainly become rich.** (Franklin *The Way to Wealth*, [1758] 2014, KL: 184–200)

INDUSTRY. Friends, said [Poor Richard], **the taxes are indeed very heavy, and if those laid on by the government were the only ones we had to pay we might more easily discharge them;** but we have many others, and much more grievous to some of us. **We are taxed twice as much by our idleness, three times as much by our pride, and four times as much by our folly;** and from these taxes the commissioners cannot ease or deliver us by allowing an abatement. (Franklin, *The Way to Wealth*, [1758] 2014: 54–6)

Most of Franklin's writing takes for granted that the accumulation of wealth through hard work, honest dealings, and frugality is praiseworthy, which implies that this was likely believed by most of his readers, although he may have expressed that sentiment better than they could have. On the other hand, he argues that one should not let one's commercial enterprises rule one's life. Business is important, but not the only matter of importance. Nor is the accumulation of wealth the only goal that young persons should pursue—health and wisdom are also important.

**Drive thy business, let not that drive thee;** and Early to bed, and early to rise, makes a man healthy, wealthy, and wise, Poor Richard says. (Franklin, *The Way to Wealth*, [1758] 2014, KL: 54–58, 70–71)

Franklin has also observed that there is a trade-off between short-term commercial advantages of dishonesty and long-run profits—with honesty being the best strategy for the long run.

> There are a great **many retailers who falsely imagine that being historical (the modern phrase for lying)** is much for their advantage; and some of them have a saying, that it is a pity lying is a sin, it is so useful in trade;
>
> If they would examine into **the reason why a number of shopkeepers raise considerable estates**, while others who have set out with better fortunes have become bankrupts, **they would find that the former made up with truth, diligence, and probity,** what they were deficient of in stock; while the latter have been found guilty of imposing on such customers as they found had no skill in the quality of their goods. (Franklin, "On Truth and Falsehood," [1839] 2011, Vol. II, KL 704–709)

Franklin's observations, here, support the analysis of Part I; consumers tend to support honest and diligent merchants.

In these and other writings, Franklin recommends: a virtuous life centered on work, frugality, honesty, prudence, and the accumulation of wealth—principles that Max Weber writing more than a century later, would refer to as the spirit of capitalism. Commerce was at or near the center of a good life for Franklin and his colonial readers. This is not to claim that such conclusions about the nature of a good life were the only ones present in the colonies at that time, or that necessity played no role in choices with respect to market activities, but it is to suggest that such conclusions were commonplace in the Northern and Mid-Atlantic colonies during Franklin's lifetime.

## Franklin on the Confusion about Ethics as Self-Denial

In other writings for narrower audiences, Franklin analyzes scientific and philosophical issues of his day. For example, Franklin argues that many writers during his time were confused about the relationship between virtue and self-denial. Franklin insists that virtue is not about self-denial, but rather about developing dispositions to behave in accordance with virtue. Once this is done, virtue does not involve sacrifice, a conclusion reminiscent of Aristotle's analysis of self-mastery.

> If to a certain man idle diversions have nothing in them that is tempting, and, therefore, he never relaxes his application to business for their sake, is he not an **industrious man**? Or has he not the **virtue of industry**?

I might in like manner instance in all the rest of the virtues; but, to make the thing short, as it is certain that **the more we strive against the temptation to any vice, and practice the contrary virtue, the weaker will that temptation be,** and the stronger will be that habit, till at length the temptation has no force or entirely vanishes. **Does it follow from thence that, in our endeavours to overcome vice, we grow continually less and less virtuous, till at length we have no virtue at all?** (Franklin *Memoirs of Benjamin Franklin*, [1839] 2011, KL: 401)

This gradual elimination of temptations by developing virtuous habits of thought and action, of course, parallels Aristotle's discussion of self-mastery.

With respect to religion, Franklin evidently remained a Deist, which was fairly common among intellectuals of his day, but he nonetheless believed that virtuous behavior of the sort that he recommends is likely to be rewarded by the deity, which he believed existed, albeit in a somewhat inactive form and not necessarily as revealed in religious texts.

This **my little book had for its motto** these lines from Addison's Cato: "Here will I hold. **If there's a power above us** (and that there is all nature cries aloud through all her works), **He must delight in virtue; and that which He delights in must be happy.**" (Franklin, *The Way to Wealth*, [1758] 2014, KL: 262–264)

## The Ethos of Franklin's America

As with the previous authors reviewed, Franklin is of interest partly for what he says and partly because his writing provides a window into his society at the time that he wrote. The maxims of Poor Richard all take wealth, reputation, and wisdom to be "obvious" central aims of life, rather than salvation or self-denial. There is very little in the way of references to biblical texts in his writings, although also very little criticism of the religious views of others. His focus is on life on earth, rather than an afterlife. He is writing for the literate public rather than a small circle of fellow scholars, as many of today's philosophers and scientists do.

Within Franklin's social circles and readership (both of which were very broad), religion had become less central to life and less important for understanding day-to-day events on earth. Lightning was a product of natural laws, rather than evidence of divine displeasure, and damage from lightning could be better reduced with a well-grounded lightning rod than with prayer. There was an order to nature because of God's will, but the natural order was the product of natural laws, rather than day-to-day divine interventions.

Franklin's support for virtuous conduct is mostly oriented toward life on earth, with a central role reserved for values that tend to be rewarded by markets through their effects on relationships with other people. In his and his reader's view, there is little or no tension between virtue and commercial success. A "virtuous" man or woman can engage in commercial activities without feelings of guilt as long as he or she aims for long-run success rather than short-run profits. His personal success and experience with others provided him with direct evidence about how virtue could enhance one's quality of life. These, together with his genius, allowed him to succeed in a very broad career, although not always on his first try.

Although the themes developed in *The Way to Wealth* continue to reappear in Franklin's other popular writings, it should also be noted that Franklin did not devote his entire life to accumulating wealth. After making his fortune in printing and publishing, he turned to public works, science, and politics for the last third of his life—where the same rules of conduct evidently served him well.

## Adam Smith (1723–1790), the *Moral Sentiments* and the *Wealth of Nations*

We next turn to Adam Smith, who is only our second academic author. Smith grew up in Scotland, attended university at Glasgow and Oxford University. After graduation he taught for 13 years at the University of Glasgow, where he wrote the book that we will spend the most time with, *The Theory of Moral Sentiments* (1759). His is better known for his influential analysis of economic activity, written nearly two decades later, *An Inquiry into the Nature and Causes of the Wealth of Nations* (1776), which is arguably the most important book written in economics, because of its clear characterizations of the returns to specialization, the invisible hand, the advantages of trade, and equilibrium prices. It is his earlier book, however, which provides a psychological explanation for the existence of what he termed "moral sentiments" that is most relevant for this book, although the combination of the two books is more relevant still. *The Theory of Moral Sentiments* provides a new psychological and sociological foundation for ethics.

Smith's intellectual contributions can be used to mark off the end of the period termed the Enlightenment and the beginning of the period often termed the modern or liberal period. When people speak of "classical liberalism," it is often Smith's work that they have in mind. His thinking on economics, ethics, and public policy integrated and extended many of the ideas that were "in the air" during the mid-eighteenth century and his excellent expression of his arguments and conclusions attracted many readers. The subsection on Smith is, thus, for all these reasons a bit longer than that accorded most of the other authors reviewed in this chapter.[14]

In the *Moral Sentiments*, Smith argues that people are not born with ethical knowledge or intuitions, but that each person learns and internalizes virtuous rules of conduct on his or her own. Two factors account for this: the human ability to imagine the joys and sorrows associated with the fortunes and misfortunes of others (an ability he terms "sympathy" or "fellow feeling") and the desire for the approval or praise from the persons about them. One's interest in praise induces individuals to imagine whether their own behavior is likely to elicit approval or disapproval from others and to adopt both principles and actions that tend to produce praise rather than disapproval. Thus, ethical behavior, according to Smith, is in one's self-interest, as in Aristotle and Franklin, but not because it improves one's character, although it does so, but because all humans desire and so benefit from the approval of their family and friends, and also that of strangers.

The idea that virtue is praiseworthy was, of course, not new. It is mentioned in both Aristotle's and Locke's discussion of virtue.[15] What is new is the central role given to it in Smith's theory and its use as a motivation for both praiseworthy behavior and the development of principles of virtue. Smith's account of ethical conduct also provides a new analytical device for discovering ethical rules (the judgement of an "impartial spectator") and a window into what

---

[14] James Buchanan once told me that he invented the term "classical liberalism" to reduce confusion in North America about the term "liberal." In the rest of the world, "liberal" continues to mean support for open politics and markets, as it did in the nineteenth century. In the United States, it refers to a moderate form of social democracy. The latter is often consistent with liberalism, but it is a left of center version that tends to stress redistribution and fairness, rather than rule of law, constitutional governments, and open markets.

[15] Locke (1690) argues that "one of the rules made use of in the world for a ground or measure of a moral relation is that **esteem and reputation** which several sorts of actions find variously in the several societies of men, **according to which they are there called virtues or vices.**" (Locke, *An Essay Concerning Human Understanding*, 2013, KL: 5602–5604).

many of his contemporaries would have regarded to be obvious instances of praiseworthy behavior.[16]

Because his theory of ethical dispositions is explicitly grounded in the reactions of others, his discussion provides many examples of the complex norms internalized by persons in Scotland and England during the mid-eighteenth century.

## Fellow Feeling and the Pursuit of Praise

Smith's analysis of the origins of moral sentiments begins with the observation that members of society are emotionally connected to one another, rather than completely independent from one another. Individuals all have the ability to imagine the pleasure and pains of others, and this ability, together with empathy, causes the imagined joys and sorrows of others to contribute to one's own.

> How selfish soever man may be supposed, there are evidently **some principles in his nature, which interest him in the fortune of others, and render their happiness necessary to him, though he derives nothing from it except the pleasure of seeing it.** (Smith, *Moral Sentiments*, 1759, KL: 12–13)
>
> Mankind, though naturally sympathetic, never conceive [*sic*] for what has befallen another that degree of passion which naturally animates the person principally concerned. That **imaginary change of situation**, upon which their sympathy is founded, is but momentary. (Smith, *Moral Sentiments*, 1759, KL: 256–257)

This empathic connection among men and women is termed "sympathy" or "fellow feeling," and its effects on our own well-being is the reason that we care about the reactions and opinions about us. Insofar as individuals can induce positive reaction in others, they will try to do so within limits. We are all, according to Smith, interested in receiving the approval and avoiding the disapproval of others. Smith argues that this empathic connection, together with the desire for praise, explains all of our "moral sentiments," and his book goes on at great length to demonstrate that this is in fact the case.[17]

---

[16] In his widely read piece on "Adam Smith and Laissez Faire," Viner (1927) makes the same point, but as a criticism of the *Moral Sentiments*.

[17] Excerpts are taken from digitized versions of *The Theory of Moral Sentiments* (1759) and *The Wealth of Nations* (1776). KL refers to Kindle locations in the editions used. Some very modest changes to facilitate

The same ability that allows one to imagine the mental states of others can be used to understand how one's own behavior affects them and their assessment of us.

> We suppose ourselves the spectators of our own behavior, and endeavor to imagine what effect it would, in this light, produce upon us. This is the only looking-glass by which we can, in some measure, **with the eyes of other people, scrutinize the propriety of our own conduct**. . . .
>
> When I endeavor to examine my own conduct, when I endeavor to pass sentence upon it, and either to approve or condemn it, it is evident that, in all such cases, I **divide myself, as it were, into two persons**; and that I, **the examiner and judge,** represent a different character from that **other I**, the person whose conduct is examined into and judged of. The **first is the spectator,** whose sentiments with regard to my own conduct I endeavor to enter into, by placing myself in his situation, and by considering how it would appear to me, when seen from that particular point of view. **The second is the agent, the person whom I properly call myself.** (Smith, *Moral Sentiments*, 1759, KL: 1890–1900)

This two-level characterization of human psychology provides a possible rationale for the virtue and vice payoffs used in Parts I and II to characterize how internalized norms affect an individual's subjective rewards or net benefits associated with alternative actions. Feelings of virtue are generated by behavior that is perceived to be praiseworthy and feelings of guilt by behavior thought likely to be condemned. Smith argues that the most reliable way to attract praise is to act in a manner that is generally praiseworthy.

> [Mankind] **desires, not only praise, but praiseworthiness**; or **to be that thing which, though it should be praised** by nobody, is, however, the natural and proper object of praise. He dreads, not only blame, but blame-worthiness; or to be that thing which, though it should be blamed by nobody, is, however, the natural and proper object of blame. (Smith, *Moral Sentiments*, 1759, KL: 1911–1913)

Praiseworthiness differs somewhat from praise and requires a different level of abstraction to appreciate. One is praiseworthy not only when one's friends approve of one's behavior but when disinterested strangers also approve of

reading have been adopted, as with the use of contemporary spelling and punctuation conventions of the United States.

it—or would if they knew about it. Moreover, one can deserve praise—be praiseworthy—even if one never actually receives praise from others.

> **We are pleased to think that we have rendered ourselves the natural objects of approbation,** though no approbation should ever actually be bestowed upon us....
>
> **When he views [his behavior] in the light in which the impartial spectator would view it,** he thoroughly enters into all the motives which influenced it. He looks back upon every part of it with pleasure and approbation, and though mankind should never be acquainted with what he has done, he regards himself, **not so much according to the light in which they actually regard him, as according to that in which they would regard him if they were better informed.** (Smith, *Moral Sentiments*, 1759, KL: 1947–1954)

Smith argues that people use (and should use) an analytical device, the impartial spectator, to assess the moral worth of both their actions and rules of conduct that they might internalize. The test of the impartial spectator is different from the "golden rule" and also from utilitarian calculation (which is taken up in the next chapter) in that it focuses on praiseworthiness, which is often context specific and may not directly involve tangible benefits or losses for the persons that provide their approval or disapproval.

Smith goes on to discuss two possible measures of praiseworthiness, one that is absolute, and the other, relative.[18]

> [W]hen we are determining the degree of blame or applause which seems due to any action, we very frequently make use of **two different standards. The first is the idea of complete propriety and perfection,** which, in those difficult situations, no human conduct ever did, or ever can come, up to; and in comparison with which the actions of all men must forever appear blameable and imperfect.
>
> **The second is the idea of that degree of proximity or distance from this complete perfection,** which the actions of the greater part of men commonly arrive at. Whatever goes beyond this degree, how far soever it may be removed from absolute perfection, seems to deserve applause; and whatever falls short of it, to deserve blame. (Smith, *Moral Sentiments*, 1759, KL: 337–342)

These standards have implications about the nature of virtue that differ from Aristotle's theory of virtue. According to Smith, perfect virtue is an

---

[18] Some Smith scholars regard the impartial spectator as God, but he clearly states that it is not: "That consolation may be drawn, not only from the complete approbation of the man within the breast [the impartial spectator], but, if possible, from a still nobler and more generous principle, from a firm reliance upon, and a reverential submission to, that benevolent wisdom which directs all the events of human life" (Smith, *The Theory of Moral Sentiments*, 1759, KL: 5115–5117).

unobtainable perfection, a sublime extreme, rather than an entirely feasible intermediate type of behavior. Nonetheless, Smith believes that the pursuit of praise and praiseworthiness tends to produce behavior that is largely consistent with classical ideas about virtuous conduct.[19]

## Smith on Virtue and Success

Smith provides a new psychological theory of virtue, which is surprisingly well aligned with Aristotle's conceptions of virtue in spite of their differences. Smith, for example, also places high regard on self-mastery, prudence, justice, and liberality.

> **The man who acts according to the rules of perfect prudence, of strict justice, and of proper benevolence, may be said to be perfectly virtuous.** But the most perfect knowledge of those rules will not alone enable him to act in this manner....
>
> **The most perfect knowledge, if it is not supported by the most perfect self-command, will not always enable him to do his duty.** (Smith, *Moral Sentiments*, 1759, KL: 4131–4135)

According to Smith, prudence is the most important of the virtues for life on earth.

> **The care of the health, of the fortune, of the rank and reputation of the individual,** the objects upon which his comfort and happiness in this life are supposed principally to depend, is considered as **the proper business of** that virtue which is commonly called **Prudence.** (Smith, *Moral Sentiments*, 1759, KL: 3670–3671)

Smith's notion of prudence is complex. It combines aspects of the Aristotelian virtues of truthfulness, meekness, and self-mastery.

> **The prudent man always** studies seriously and earnestly to understand whatever he professes to understand, and not merely to persuade other people that he understands it; and though his talents may not always be very brilliant, they are always perfectly genuine....

[19] Smith spends considerable time contrasting his ideas with those of Aristotle, mentioning Aristotle 16 times. In this he is unique among the authors reviewed in Part III, although he is clearly not the only scholar familiar with Aristotle's work.

> **He is not ostentatious even of the abilities which he really possesses.** His conversation is simple and modest. . . . But though always sincere, he is not always frank and open; and though he **never tells anything but the truth,** he does not always think himself bound, when not properly called upon, to tell the whole truth.
>
> **As he is cautious in his actions, so he is reserved in his speech**; and never rashly or unnecessarily obtrudes his opinion. (Smith, *Moral Sentiments*, 1759, KL: 3677–3690)

Smith suggests, as did Franklin, that virtue tends to generate appropriate rewards within one's lifetime. In effect, there is an invisible hand that supports virtuous conduct.

> **If we consider the general rules by which external prosperity and adversity are commonly distributed in this life,** we shall find, that notwithstanding the disorder in which all things appear to be in this world, yet even here **every virtue naturally meets with its proper reward, with the recompense which is most fit to encourage and promote it**; and this too so surely, that it requires a very extraordinary concurrence of circumstances entirely to disappoint it.
>
> **What is the reward most proper for encouraging industry, prudence, and circumspection? Success in every sort of business.** (Smith, *Moral Sentiments*, 1759, KL: 2818–2822)

> **Our rank and credit** among our equals, too, **depend very much upon what a virtuous man would wish them to depend** entirely, **our character and conduct,** or upon the confidence, esteem, and good will, which these naturally excite in the people we live with. (Smith, *Moral Sentiments*, 1759, KL: 3668–3669)

Virtues, according to Smith, are rewarded on earth, partly, as Franklin argued, through effects on one's personal prosperity and self-esteem, but also by eliciting the esteem of others. Note that industriousness is on Smith's list, as well as most other such lists in this period, although it was not on Aristotle's list.

With respect to appropriate behavior in markets and politics, Smith argues that the moral sentiments imply that there are both appropriate and inappropriate methods for seeking wealth, honor, and other rewards.

> In the race for wealth, and honors, and preferments, he may run as hard as he can, and strain every nerve and every muscle, in order to outstrip all his competitors. **But if he should jostle, or throw down any of them,** the **indulgence of the spectators** is entirely at an end. **It is the violation of fair play,** which they cannot accept. (Smith, *Moral Sentiments*, 1759, KL: 1331–1334)

Smith notes, as does Franklin, that hard work contributes to the receipt of praise and approbation, although part of that work consists in making others aware of one's excellence.

> He **must cultivate** these therefore: he **must acquire superior knowledge in his profession, and superior industry in the exercise of it.** He must be patient in labor, resolute in danger, and firm in distress.
> **These talents he must bring into public view,** by the difficulty, importance, and, at the same time, good judgment of his undertakings, and **by the severe and unrelenting application** with which he pursues them. **Probity and prudence, generosity and frankness, must characterize his behavior** upon all ordinary occasions. (Smith, *Moral Sentiments*, 1759, KL: 883–887)

These and similar paragraphs indirectly characterize the norms used by others in Smith's time and place. Smith does not argue that a particular pattern of behavior *should* attract praise, but that it actually *does* attract praise and produce success when put into practice.

## Virtue and Life in Society

In a manner consistent with Part I of this book, Smith argues that virtuous conduct makes life in society both more pleasant and more sustainable. Societies do not require altruistic or sympathetic relationships among people, but they do require just ones.

> If there is any society among robbers and murderers, they must at least, according to the trite observation, abstain from robbing and murdering one another. Beneficence, therefore, is less essential to the existence of society than justice. **Society may subsist, though not in the most comfortable state, without beneficence; but the prevalence of injustice must utterly destroy it.** (Smith, *Moral Sentiments*, 1759, KL: 1377–1384)

Perhaps surprisingly, he argues that respect for private property is more important than sympathy or benevolence for life in society. Two decades later, he applies this idea to markets with phrasing that is among the most memorable in the *Wealth of Nations* (1776):

> It is not from the benevolence of the butcher, the brewer, or the baker, that we expect our dinner, but from their regard to their own interest. We address

ourselves, not to their humanity, but to their self-love, and never talk to them of our own necessities, but of their advantages. **Nobody but a beggar chooses to depend chiefly upon the benevolence of his fellow-citizens.** (Smith, *Wealth of Nations*, 1776, pp. 7–8)

Nonetheless, virtuous behavior is commonplace in most societies because virtuous behavior is promoted by the pursuit of praise and avoidance of blame and its associated feelings of virtue and guilt. In the absence of that tendency, the result would be very similar to that postulated by Hobbes.

**Nature has implanted in the human breast** that consciousness of **ill-desert,** those **terrors of merited punishment** which attend upon its violation, as the **great safeguards of the association of mankind, to protect the weak, to curb the violent, and to chastise the guilty.** . . .

**[I]f this principle did not stand up within them in [an individual's] defense, and overawe them into a respect for his innocence, they would, like wild beasts,** be at all times ready to fly upon him; and a man would enter an assembly of men as he enters a den of lions. (Smith, *Moral Sentiments*, 1759, KL: 1390–1396)

## The Pursuit of Praise and Economic Development

The desire for praise from one's fellow men and women also plays a role in the accumulation of wealth because it largely defines how one "betters our condition."

**From whence, then, arises that emulation which runs through all the different ranks of men,** and what are the advantages which we propose by **that great purpose of human life which we call bettering our condition?**

**To be observed,** to be attended to, **to be taken notice of with** sympathy, complacency, and **approbation, are all the advantages which we can propose to derive from it.** (Smith, *Moral Sentiments*, 1759, KL: 794–796)

Smith and his readers consider opulence (prosperity) to be a good and praiseworthy end—a sign of progress—as in Franklin and La Court.

[C]apital has been silently and gradually accumulated by the **private frugality and good conduct of individuals,** by their **universal, continual, and uninterrupted effort to better their own condition.**

It is this effort, protected by law, and allowed by liberty to exert itself in the manner that is most advantageous, **which has maintained the progress of England towards opulence and improvement in almost all former times,** and which, it is to be hoped, will do so in all future times. (Smith, *Wealth of Nations*, 1776, KL: 5178–5182)

Indeed, the accumulation of capital, the quest for profits, and extension of markets that result from frugality, good conduct, and industry is Smith's explanation for economic growth, which is faster in Smith's time than it had been the century before, but slower than it would become in the next century.

[B]y directing that industry in such a manner as its produce may be of the greatest value, [an individual] intends only his own gain, and **he is in this, as in many other cases, led by an invisible hand to promote an end** which was no part of his intention. (Smith, *Wealth of Nations*, 1776, KL: 6709)

[Prosperity] is the necessary, though **very slow and gradual, consequence of a certain propensity in human nature,** which has in view no such extensive utility; **the propensity to truck, barter, and exchange one thing for another.** (Smith, *Wealth of Nations*, 1776, KL: 180)

Nor is it generally worse for society that benevolence is not the main motivation for an individual's industry and frugality.

By pursuing his own interest [within markets], **he frequently promotes that of the society more effectually than when he really intends to promote it.** I have never known much good done by those who affected to trade for the public good. It is an affectation, indeed, not very common among merchants, and very few words need be employed in dissuading them from it. (Smith, *Wealth of Nations*, 1776, KL: 6709)

Although Smith was not himself a "wealth maximizer," it is clear that Smith's readers, like those of Franklin and La Court, generally regard prosperity and the pursuit of personal wealth to be praiseworthy activities, when undertaken properly. Smith thus concludes that most of the individual activities and dispositions that promote general prosperity are praiseworthy—although they are not the only virtuous activities, and not every manner of accumulating wealth is virtuous.

He also notes that markets also directly reward a subset of virtues.

[Managerial] **wages properly express the value** of this labor of inspection and direction. Though in settling them some regard is had commonly, **not only to his** labor and skill, but to the trust which is reposed in him. (Smith, *Wealth of Nations*, 1776, KL: 716–717)

It seldom happens, however, that great fortunes are made, even in great towns, by any one regular, established, and well-known branch of business, **but in consequence of a long life of industry, frugality, and attention.** (Smith, *Wealth of Nations*, 1776, KL: 1717–1719)

Nonetheless, as with Montesquieu and Aristotle, Smith notes that commerce can undermine other virtues. Greed can induce men to abandon virtue.

To attain to this envied situation, **the candidates for fortune too frequently abandon the paths of virtue;** for unhappily, the **road which leads to the one, and that which leads to the other, lie sometimes in very opposite directions.** (Smith, *Moral Sentiments*, 1759, KL: 1027–1029)

In this he seems to disagree with Franklin, who argued that in the long run there is little or no tension between virtuous conduct and wealth accumulation.

## The Good Life and Good Society

Smith does not believe that wealth and power are the main sources of happiness or success; rather, it is the approbation received from others and one's appraisal of their own praiseworthiness.

Power and riches appear then to be, what they are, enormous and operose machines contrived to **produce a few trifling conveniences to the body.** . . . They keep off the summer shower, not the winter storm, **but leave him always as much, and sometimes more exposed than before, to anxiety, to fear, and to sorrow;** to diseases, to danger, and to death. (Smith, *Moral Sentiments*, 1759, KL: 3132–3138)

Regarding governments and conscious efforts to improve society, Smith, like La Court, regards governments and policymakers to be potential sources of problems. This is partly because they fail to take proper account of human nature and partly because they tend to overestimate their ability as reformers.

**The man of system,** on the contrary . . . is often so enamored with the supposed beauty of his own ideal plan of government, that he cannot suffer the smallest deviation from any part of it. He goes on to establish it completely and in all its parts, without any regard either to the great interests, or to the strong prejudices which may oppose it. **He seems to imagine that he can arrange the different members of a great society with as much ease as the hand arranges the different pieces upon a chess-board.**

**He does not consider that the pieces upon the chess-board have no other principle of motion besides that which the hand** impresses upon them; but that, in the great chess-board of human society, every single piece has a principle of motion of its own, altogether different from that which the legislature might choose to impress upon it.

**If those two principles coincide** and act in the same direction, **the game of human society will go on easily and harmoniously,** and is very likely to be happy and successful. **If they are opposite or different, the game will go on miserably, and the society must be at all times in the highest degree of disorder.** (Smith, *Moral Sentiments*, 1759, KL: 4065–4073)

Smith does not argue that all systems of policy are doomed to failure, only those which fail to take account of the motivations of the individual members of society. Smith argues that the "system of natural liberty" is consistent with human nature and accounts for much of England's economic success. The system of natural liberty works well because the pursuit of praise induces virtuous behavior and produces prosperity. Government interventions in markets is largely unnecessary because commerce is largely self-regulating both with respect to prices and virtue.[20]

For Smith, market activities are for the most part morally neutral, motivated by self-interest, rather than a source or test of virtue. Nonetheless, he suggests that commerce is largely motivated by the same impulses that produce ethical conduct, namely the pursuit of praise and praiseworthiness, although much economic activity simply reflects human predispositions to "truck and barter." The accumulation of material comforts generated by specialization, the accumulation of capital, and trade add to the quality of life and so are broadly considered to be praiseworthy—and hence virtuous activities.

[20] Smith also argues that the system of natural liberty is relatively simple to implement: "All systems either of preference or of restraint, therefore, being thus completely taken away, the obvious and simple system of natural liberty establishes itself of its own accord. Every man, as long as he does not violate the laws of justice, is left perfectly free to pursue his own interest his own way, and to bring both his industry and capital into competition with those of any other man, or order of men" (*Wealth of Nations*, 1776, KL: 10486).

# Immanuel Kant (1724–1804): Duty and Universal Law

In the decades after Smith wrote the *Moral Sentiments*, several other philosophers proposed other grounding principles for ethics. Two of these have had profound influence on philosophy and also arguably on the codes of conduct internalized by literate men and women: Immanuel Kant and Jeremy Bentham. Again, the roots of these theories can be found in earlier writers, including Aristotle. Like Adam Smith, these thoughtful men also attempted to create new theories of morality and public policy grounded in one or two overarching principles, an approach that might be considered the Newtonian approach to ethics. Both also had something to say about the role of commerce in a moral life and good society.

We first review Kant's theory and conclusions. Bentham and subsequent utilitarians are taken up in the next chapter.

Kant was raised in a middle-class religious family and showed much talent as a youth and went off to university. Kant, unlike Smith, became a life-long academic. He spent most of his adult life teaching at the University of Köningsberg in what was then in northwestern Prussia, a leading kingdom in the Holy Roman Empire. Kant's philosophical interests were broader and more abstract than those of Smith and had impacts across contemporary philosophy, most of which are neglected in this short overview of his theory of moral action and assessment of commerce. The main focus is again on the intersection of his conclusions about ethics and commerce.

## Kantian Morality

There is a sense in which Kant returns to pre-Enlightenment religious views of ethics in that he argues that moral actions are grounded in duty rather than enlightened self-interest, and that duty is grounded in universal law. Religious deontologists such as Baxter stress duties characterized in divine texts and their implications. Secular deontologists require other methods for determining duties, because one's moral obligations are not always obvious.[21]

---

[21] Excerpts from a digitized collection of translations of Kant's major books are used in this section. The collection used is *The Immanuel Kant Collection: 8 Classic Works* (2013), Waxkeep (Kindle edition). Titles of the individual works are included for those familiar with his work. KL again refers to Kindle locations. As is true of other major works from German, a variety of translations are available for Kant's books. The above collection is used because of its convenience and ready availability, not because it includes exceptional translations. For the purposes of this chapter, it is only the essential features of his theory of morality that are relevant, rather than subtle aspects of the argument that one or another translator might have best captured. (A German philosopher once told me that Kant makes a lot more sense in English than in German, because of the efforts of the individual translators.)

According to Kant, universal law is based partly on moral intuitions similar to Grotius's conceptions of natural law and also, as in Grotius, partly on reason. Kant argues that the rules we have a duty to follow cannot be known perfectly, but that reason helps us to identify such rules and eliminate other rules from consideration.

Kant argues that moral rules are all universal in the sense that if everyone followed them, the results would be good, satisfactory, or appropriate, although he does not himself characterize the best method for assessing the results of appropriately dutiful conduct. This universality principle he terms the "categorical imperative" (*kategorischer imperativ*).

The **categorical imperative** only expresses generally what constitutes **obligation**. It may be rendered by the following formula: "**Act according to a maxim which can be adopted at the same time as a universal law.**" . . . the test, by calling upon the agent to think of himself in connection with it as at the same time laying down a universal law, and **to consider whether his action is so qualified as to be fit for entering into such a universal legislation.** (Kant, "Introduction to the Metaphysic of Morals," 2013, KL: 1098–1103)

The **supreme principle** of the science of morals accordingly is this: "Act according to a maxim which can likewise be valid as a universal law." Every maxim which is not qualified according to this condition is contrary to morality. (Kant, "Introduction to the Metaphysic of Morals," 2013, KL: 1117–1118)

Moral principles must be universal, feasible, and lead to good outcomes when adopted by all persons. Together, these allow rules that one has a duty to follow to be identified and others to be rejected. Like Aristotle, but not Smith, Kant argues that it is feasible for individuals to completely satisfy their moral duties.

[M]orality is in itself practical, being **the totality of unconditionally mandatory laws according to which we ought to act.** It would obviously be absurd, after granting authority to the concept of duty, to pretend that we cannot do our duty. (Kant, *Perpetual Peace*, 2013, KL: 519–521)

Kant, in contrast to Franklin, Smith, and Aristotle, makes a sharp distinction between actions motivated by self-interest and those based on duty.[22] In his view, self-interested actions cannot be moral, although they are not necessarily immoral and can be praiseworthy without being moral. Only actions

---

[22] This is likely to have been a challenge to utilitarian ideas that were taking shape during this period.

taken because of duties associated with universal laws are moral. Kant thus regards the motivation for action to be more important than the actions themselves or their consequences. In this respect, the Kantian perspective clearly differs from that of Aristotle, Smith, and Bentham, for whom it is the nature of the choices or actions and their consequences that jointly determine the morality of a choice, action, or pattern of behavior.

> The **direct opposite of the principle of morality is when the principle of private happiness** is made the determining principle of the will. (Kant, *Critique of Practical Reason*, 2013, KL: 10528–10529)

> [A]ll **the morality of actions may be placed in the necessity of acting from duty** and from respect for the [universal] law, not from love and inclination for that which the actions are to produce. (Kant, *Critique of Practical Reason*, 2013, KL: 11273–11274)

Kant views the natural purpose and aim of reason to be the improvement of one's will—a perspective quite similar to Aristotle's. However, for Kant, perfecting one's will is a consequence of, rather than the purpose of, moral action. Thus, he argues that perfecting one's will or character requires no deeper philosophy than the categorical imperative.

> I do not, therefore, **need any far-reaching penetration to discern what I have to do in order that my will may be morally good.** Inexperienced in the course of the world, incapable of being prepared for all its contingencies, I only ask myself: **Canst thou also will that thy maxim should be a universal law? If not, then it must be rejected,** and that not because of a disadvantage accruing from it to myself or even to others, but **because it cannot enter as a principle into a possible universal legislation,** and reason extorts from me immediate respect for such legislation.
>
> I do not indeed as yet discern on what this respect [for the categorical imperative] is based (this the philosopher may inquire), but at least I understand this, that **it is an estimation of the worth which far outweighs all worth of what is recommended by inclination** [self-interest], and that **the necessity of acting from pure respect for the practical law is what constitutes duty,** to which every other motive must give place, because **it is the condition of a will being good in itself.** (Kant, *Fundamental Principle of the Metaphysics of Morals*, 2013, KL: 13182–13189)

As in other theories of ethics, consequences are not entirely irrelevant. Whether a rule or maxim is suitable as universal law is partly a matter of deduction and imagination and partly how it works in practice. However, the essence of Kantian morality is dutiful rule-following conduct, rather than assessing the consequences of an individual's own conduct—although the rules followed must tend to have good consequences if they are to be part of the body of universal legislation.

## Kant on Ethics, Law, and Markets

Kant observes that although every universal maxim could be incorporated into law, in practice, the domains of law and ethics are different. There are differences in motivation and in the processes through which moral maxims and legislation are adopted. Moral maxims, by definition, all satisfy the categorical imperative. Moral actions are motivated internally by an individual's sense of duty. Lawful actions, in contrast, are determined by governments, and behaving in conformity with them is motivated by external penalties and rewards. Moreover, ethical duties often go beyond those required by law.

For example, Kant argues that one's moral duty may demand the fulfillment of contracts that civil law does not.

> From what has been said, it is evident that **all duties, merely because they are duties, belong to ethics**; and yet the legislation upon which they [legal duties] are founded is not on that account in all cases contained in ethics. On the contrary, the law of many of them lies outside of ethics.
>
> **Thus ethics commands that I must fulfill a promise entered into by contract**, although the other party might not be able to compel me to do so. [The legislature] adopts the law (*pacta sunt servanda*) and the duty corresponding to it, from jurisprudence or **the science of right,** by which they are established. It is not in ethics, therefore, but in jurisprudence, that the principle of the legislation lies. (Kant, "Introduction to the Metaphysic of Morals," 2013, KL 12753–12758)

Kant suggests that the duty of fairness may induce businesspeople to treat their customers better than required by law. However, such behavior is not always motivated by a sense of duty, so it is not always an instance of moral conduct.

> For example, **it is always a matter of duty that a dealer should not overcharge an inexperienced purchaser**; and **wherever there is much commerce the prudent tradesman does not overcharge**, but **keeps a fixed price for everyone**, so that a child buys of him as well as any other. **Men are thus honestly served; but this is not enough** to make us believe that the tradesman has so acted from duty and from principles of honesty. (Kant, "Fundamental Principles of the Metaphysic of Morals," 2013, KL: 13082–13085)

Such economic choice settings illustrate the Kantian difference between conduct and duty. The same conduct may be motivated by duty or self-interest. However, for Kantians, it is not the conduct, but the motivation of the conduct that makes a choice moral or not. Moral action is dutifully following universal laws. One may be honest or fair with one's customers either because it is a duty or because it increases profits. Although the universality of a maxim is based on its consequences, individual actions are moral or not because of their consequences; rather, it is because they are instances of dutiful rule-following behavior, given one's understanding of universal law.

It also bears noting that for Kant the domain of action is not simply divided between moral and immoral actions. There are many actions that are neither moral nor immoral. For example, there are actions that are motivated by self-interest that are praiseworthy, but which are neither moral nor immoral—as in the bargaining example above if the merchant's pricing strategy is motivated by profits rather than internalized duties. When interest rather than duty motivates conduct, Kant regards that conduct to be outside the domain of moral choice as long as it does not conflict with universal law.

Market activities are thus largely outside the domain of Kantian morality because they are largely consequences of self-interest rather than duty.[23]

> [I]n such a case an action of this kind, however proper, however amiable it may be, has nevertheless no true moral worth, but is on a level with other inclinations, e.g., the inclination to honor, which, if it is happily directed to that which is in fact of public utility and accordant with duty and consequently honorable, deserves praise and encouragement, but not esteem. For the maxim lacks the moral import, namely, that such actions be done from duty, not from inclination. (Kant, "Fundamental Principles of the Metaphysic of Morals," 2013, KL: 13095–13098)

Kant notes several praiseworthy effects of markets, including contributions to world peace, but regards these useful and desirable consequences to be outside the domain of morality. He is not a utilitarian.

> The spirit of commerce, which is incompatible with war, sooner or later gains the upper hand in every state. As the power of money is perhaps the most dependable of all the powers (means) included under the state power, states see themselves

---

[23] The use of the terms "praise" and "public utility" above suggests that Kant regards both Smith's and Bentham's theories of moral conduct to be too encompassing. There are praiseworthy and utility-increasing activities that have nothing to do with morality or moral sentiments.

**forced, without any moral urge, to promote honorable peace.** (Kant, *Perpetual Peace*, 2013, KL: 440–442)

Thus, market activities can produce praiseworthy results for reasons that are independent of morality. Market activities are moral only when they are undertaken because of duties that accord with universal law and immoral only when they conflict with duties associated with one's understanding of universal law.

## Overview

Kant created another analytical device for discovering moral rules. It is an alternative to both Smith's impartial spectator and Bentham's aggregate utility-increasing principle (taken up in the next chapter), which were the chief secular rivals during his lifetime. That Kant's theories continue to be taught in virtually every philosophy department in the world suggests that the categorical imperative has been broadly accepted by philosophers as a useful method for evaluating ethical propositions. Indeed, parents often chide their children with comments of the "what if everyone did that" variety, which implicitly uses the categorical imperative to rule out particular kinds of conduct.

Kant's categorical imperative implies that only rules that could be simultaneously adopted by all to good effect necessarily create moral duties. Although candidates for universality require consideration of their consequences, one's duty to follow universal rules does not. It simply requires dutifully following the universal rules that one has internalized. One may mistakenly believe a maxim to be universal, but actions undertaken to dutifully follow such maxims are nonetheless moral—even if mistaken.

Kant evidently regarded such universal maxims to be self-evident, because he does not provide a systematic way of choosing among universal laws that conflict with each other. This aspect of Kant echoes religious and other medieval ideas about duty and honor. The duties mentioned by Kant include promise keeping, abiding by contracts, and honesty. Such norms had long existed, of course, but in Kant's writings were given new universality justifications. They satisfied the categorical imperative.

The categorical imperative clearly allows a variety of maxims to be rejected because they cannot logically be applied universally, as with special privileges in law and rules of conduct that lead to absurd results when applied to everyone and all choice settings. According to Kant, morality is inherently universal and thus moral obligations do not differ by class or region. Kant, like

Aristotle, is not particularly interested in economics, but also uses market transactions to illustrate moral issues. Market activities may be motivated by internalized duties, as with duties to abide by contracts and to be fair toward the less informed, in which case the associated behavior is moral. Other commercial actions and consequences may be praiseworthy, but insofar as they are motivated by profits or gains from trade rather than duty, they are outside the domain of moral theory and action.

It bears noting that both Smith's and Kant's theories reveal that two shifts in ethical theory are taking place in the mid- to late eighteenth century. First, ethical theory begins to look more like Newtonian mechanics in which a few principles are used to both account for and to deduce rules for ethical behavior. Second, the justification for virtuous rules of conduct has shifted. No longer are virtuous habits developed to improve oneself, as in Aristotle or Franklin, or to obtain divine approval, as in theological theories of Baxter and Barclay. Rather, whether conduct is virtuous or not is determined by whether it yields good results for all (satisfies the categorical imperative) or is approved of by all (is deemed praiseworthy by an impartial spectator). Following such rules may also improve one's character or will, but it is their effects on other persons that ultimately make them virtuous, rather than their beneficial effects on an individual's own character or life.

This is not to say that self-improvement does not occur; but that it is no longer the main purpose of ethics. In both Smith and Kant, dutiful behavior contributes to perfecting one's will (or character). According to Smith's theory, one becomes virtuous by systematically engaging in praiseworthy conduct, although the ultimate indicator of virtue is the approval of the impartial spectator, rather than its contribution to virtuous dispositions. In Kant's theory, developing the capacity to recognize and follow universal laws tends to perfect the will, which in turn supports moral actions, but it is the dutiful foundation of behavior that makes an action moral, rather than its effect on character.

The work of deontologist philosophers such as Kant who stress duties rather than consequences, is relevant for the purposes of this book because dutiful behavior often supports market activities. Many of the duties that individuals internalize involve day-to-day life conduct in their private lives and in their occupations. Many of these duties—such as obligations to be honest, keep promises, work with diligence, and follow appropriate rules—tend to increase the productivity of economic organizations and reduce risks associated with market transactions and government policies, as developed in Parts I and II.

Indeed, the words "job" and "duty" can often be used interchangeably. For example, "that's not my job" means "that is not my duty"; I have no moral or contractual obligation to engage in that activity. Such internalized duties tend to extend the possibilities for specialization and the extent of trading networks, as developed in Part I of the book.

## Claude F. Bastiat (1801–1850): On the Harmony among Markets and Ethical Systems

Chapter 11 concludes with an overview of Claude Bastiat's writings. Bastiat wrote in the nineteenth century, but his writings are all in the spirit of classical liberalism and thus he is covered in this chapter rather than the next. Bastiat, like Montesquieu, was from a relatively wealthy French family and inherited great wealth at an early age, although not a noble title. This allowed him to devote himself to writing and politics. Bastiat exemplifies the politically active French liberal of the early nineteenth century. He was not an academic, but rather a businessman and politician who served in local and national offices for much of his life. He was elected to local political offices in the 1830s and to the French National Assembly in 1848. His writing was largely a persuasive exercise aimed to increase his support from French voters and so provides a useful window into French liberalism during the mid-nineteenth century.

His political economy is largely a synthesis of elements from Locke, Rousseau, Say, and Smith, which is why it belongs in this chapter. However, as a popularizer and politician, he sharpens and extends their arguments in much the same manner that Thomas Paine's widely read pamphlets, published at the time of the American and French revolutions, did for Locke and Montesquieu. Many present-day students of economics find his analysis of economic relationships to be clearer and more persuasive than that provided by contemporary textbooks. His writings reveal that reservations about commerce have diminished greatly since the time that Montesquieu wrote— at least among Bastiat's readers.

Most of Bastiat's writings are short pieces written for magazines and newspapers, which were subsequently collected together and turned into books. So, although this section refers to books, the books are actually collections of essays, rather than book-length analyses of particular issues. Nonetheless, because each essay tends to be tightly written, it turns out that longer quotes from his writing are necessary to get his ideas across than for the other writers covered in Part III.

His writings remain of interest to economists because they are laced with clear, early insights on the workings of an open economy. They are important for this book because his analyses take account of the effects that commerce has on morals, and morals on commerce, and also because his stories provide a useful window into the life and ideas of persons in France during the early to mid-nineteenth century. In general, Bastiat argues that commercial systems tend to be moral because of their beneficial effects on everyone who makes use of them. Under a proper civil law, there is a broad harmony between economic and moral interests.

## On the Benefits of Commerce and Specialization

Bastiat is among the first to point out the principle of consumer sovereignty: that markets attempt to please consumers rather than elites, and that this tends to advance general interests.

> [W]e now proceed to consider **the immediate interest of the consumer, we shall find that it is in perfect harmony with the general interest, with all that the welfare of society calls for.** When the purchaser goes to market, he desires to find it well stocked. Let the seasons be propitious for all harvests; let inventions, more and more marvelous, bring within reach a greater and greater number of products and enjoyments.
>
> [L]et time and labor be saved; let distances be effaced by the perfection and rapidity of transit; let the spirit of justice and of peace allow of a diminished weight of taxation; **let barriers of every kind be removed—in all this the interest of the consumer runs parallel with the public interest.** (Bastiat "Economic Sophisms," [1850] 2007, pp. 180–181)

Bastiat often uses parables to get his ideas across to readers, as with the following story illustrating the benefits of specialization. In this short story, Bastiat reminds his readers that specialization and commerce have greatly increased the material comforts and services available to people throughout society, including that of ordinary workmen such as cabinet makers.

> Let us take, by way of illustration, a man in the humble walks of life—a village carpenter, for instance—and observe the various services he renders to society, and receives from it; we shall not fail to be struck with the enormous disproportion that is apparent. This man employs his day's labor in planing boards and making tables and chests of drawers. **He complains of his condition; yet in truth what does he receive from society in exchange for his work?**
>
> First of all, on getting up in the morning, he dresses himself; and he has himself personally made none of the numerous articles of which his clothing consists. Now, in order to put at his disposal this clothing, simple as it is, an enormous

amount of labor, industry, and locomotion, and many ingenious inventions, must have been employed. Americans must have produced cotton, Indians indigo, Frenchmen wool and flax, Brazilians hides; and all these materials must have been transported to various towns where they have been worked up, spun, woven, dyed, etc.

Then he breakfasts. In order to procure him the bread he eats every morning, land must have been cleared, enclosed, labored, manured, sown; the fruits of the soil must have been preserved with care from pillage, and security must have reigned among an innumerable multitude of people. The wheat must have been cut down, ground into flour, kneaded, and prepared; iron, steel, wood, stone, must have been converted by industry into instruments of labor; some men must have employed animal force, others water power, etc.; all matters of which each, taken singly, presupposes a mass of labor, whether we have regard to space or time, of incalculable amount.

In the course of the day this man will have occasion to use sugar, oil, and various other materials and utensils. He sends his son to school, there to receive an education, which, although limited, nevertheless implies anterior study and research, and an extent of knowledge that startles the imagination.

He goes out. He finds the street paved and lighted. A neighbor sues him. He finds advocates to plead his cause, judges to maintain his rights, officers of justice to put the sentence in execution; all which implies acquired knowledge, and, consequently, intelligence and means of subsistence.

He goes to church. It is a stupendous monument, and the book he carries thither is a monument, perhaps still more stupendous, of human intelligence. He is taught morals, he has his mind enlightened, his soul elevated; and in order to do this we must suppose that another man had previously frequented schools and libraries, consulted all the sources of human learning, and while so employed had been able to live without occupying himself directly with the wants of the body.

If our artisan undertakes a journey, he finds that, in order to save him time and exertion, other men have removed and leveled the soil, filled up valleys, hewed down mountains, united the banks of rivers, diminished friction, placed wheeled carriages on blocks of sandstone or bands of iron, and brought the force of animals and the power of steam into subjection to human wants.

It is impossible not to be struck with the measureless disproportion between the enjoyments which this man derives from society and what he could obtain by his own unassisted exertions. **I venture to say that in a single day he consumes more than he could himself produce in ten centuries**.

What renders the phenomenon still more strange is that **all other men are in the same situation**. Every individual member of society has absorbed millions of times more than he could himself produce; yet there is no mutual robbery.

360 History of Ethical Assessments of Commerce

And, if we regard things more nearly, we perceive that the carpenter has paid, in services, for all the services others have rendered to him.

**If we bring the matter to a strict reckoning, we shall be convinced that he has received nothing he has not paid for by means of his modest industry;** and that everyone who, at whatever interval of time or space, has been employed in his service, has received, or will receive, his remuneration.

**The social mechanism, then, must be very ingenious** and very powerful, since it leads to this singular result, that **each man, even he whose lot is cast in the humblest condition, has more enjoyment in one day than he could himself produce in many ages.** (Bastiat, "Harmonies of Political Economy," [1850] 2007, pp. 452–454)

According to Bastiat, well-functioning markets advance a broad range of interests, and so there is little or no reason for public policies to do anything beyond defending individual rights against intrusions (attacks) by others.

## Virtue and Markets

Bastiat also argues that virtues support commerce and that commerce supports virtues, as with the following story showing the value of prudence.[24]

Mondor and his brother Aristus, after dividing the parental inheritance, have each an income of 50,000 francs.

Mondor practices the fashionable philanthropy. **He is what is called a squanderer of money. He renews his furniture several times a year; changes his carriages every month.** People talk of his ingenious contrivances to bring them sooner to an end: in short, he surpasses the extravagant lives of Balzac and Alexander Dumas.

Aristus has adopted a very different plan of life. If he is not an egotist, he is, at any rate, an individualist, for **he considers expense, seeks only moderate and reasonable enjoyments, thinks of his children's prospects, and, in fact, he economizes.**

But things have been so admirably arranged by the Divine inventor of social order that **in this, as in everything else, political economy and morality, far from clashing, agree.**

**The wisdom of Aristus is not only more dignified, but still more profitable,** than the folly of Mondor. And when I say profitable, **I do not mean only profitable to Aristus, or even to society in general, but more profitable to the workmen**

---

[24] Excerpts are taken from a digitized collection of translations of Bastiat's writings assembled by the Ludwig von Mises Institute (Bastiat [1850] 2007). Several translations were consulted, but these seem to be clearer and less bombastic than most others.

**themselves—to the trade of the time.** To prove it, it is only necessary to turn the mind's eye to those **hidden consequences of human actions,** which the bodily eye does not see. (Bastiat, "That Which Is Seen, and That Which Is Not Seen," [1850] 2007, pp. 42–43)

Bastiat goes on to show that Aristus produces more income for more persons over a longer time in his community than does Mondor. Note that Bastiat assumes without hesitation that material comforts, job opportunities, and profits are all praiseworthy consequences of Aristus's approach to life. By the mid-nineteenth century, this perspective evidently could largely be taken for granted in France, although it was not true during Montesquieu's time.

Bastiat also repeatedly argues that there is no tension between markets and morality. In effect, Bastiat argues that the invisible hand is broader than acknowledged by Adam Smith. Markets reward virtuous behavior at the same time that they provide material comforts, and often do so in a manner that is not directly visible. One has to be alert to the invisible benefits of markets and costs of public policies.

However, this natural harmony is not associated with all possible civil laws or public policies. For example, laws protecting private property are important for this harmony of interests.

The French civil code has a chapter entitled, "On the manner of transmitting property." When a man by his labor has made some useful things—in other words, when he has created a value—it **can only pass into the hands of another by one of the following modes:** as a gift, by the right of inheritance, by exchange, loan, or theft. . . .

A gift needs no definition. **It is essentially voluntary and spontaneous.** It depends exclusively upon the giver, and **the receiver cannot be said to have any right to it.** Without a doubt, morality and religion make it a duty for men, especially the rich, to deprive themselves voluntarily of that which they possess in favor of their less fortunate brethren. But this is an entirely moral obligation.

If it were to be asserted on principle, admitted in practice, sanctioned by law, that every man has a right to the property of another, the gift would have no merit—charity and gratitude would be no longer virtues.

Besides, **such a doctrine would suddenly and universally arrest labor and production,** as severe cold congeals water and suspends animation; for **who would work if there was no longer to be any connection between labor and the satisfying of our wants**? (Bastiat, "Harmonies of Political Economy," [1850] 2007, pp. 141–142)

Changes in civil law or policies that force transfers of wealth from the rich to the poor can undermine private virtues and reduce the extent of commerce. His conclusions are similar to Aristotle's with respect to moral choice and private property, to La Court's with respect to income-based taxes and industriousness, to Locke's with respect to religious choice, and to Smith's with respect to the nature of good public policies. Morality cannot be forced, although it can be encouraged, and good public policies have to be compatible with human nature.

Although he strongly argues in favor of open markets, he acknowledges that efforts to accumulate wealth can be good or evil. Whether the accumulations of wealth is good or not depends upon how one goes about it, as in La Court's, Franklin's, and Smith's analyses.

> I willingly grant that **when wealth is acquired by means that are immoral, it has an immoral influence**, as among the Romans. I also allow that when it is developed in a very unequal manner, creating a great gulf between classes, it has an immoral influence, and gives rise to revolutionary passions.
>
> **But does the same thing hold when wealth is the fruit of honest industry and free transactions, and is uniformly distributed over all classes?** That would be a doctrine impossible to maintain. (Bastiat, "Harmonies of Political Economy," [1850] 2007, p. 627)

In a commercial society, wealth is accumulated through honesty, hard work, frugality, and efforts to please consumers, all of which tend to be praiseworthy.

## Bastiat and the Morality of Public Policy

Bastiat repeatedly argues that both private and public interests are advanced through limited government and open markets, an opinion that was not clearly articulated by eighteenth-century philosophers such as Kant and Smith, although both favored such governments. Bastiat suggests that a state that confines itself to ensuring public safety (broadly interpreted) will produce better results than one that undertakes more general responsibilities. This is a perspective shared among "doctrinaire liberals" of the mid-nineteenth century throughout Europe and the United States.

> [U]nder such an administration, everyone would feel that he possessed all the fullness, as well as all the responsibility of his existence. **So long as personal safety was ensured, so long as labor was free, and the fruits of labor secured against all**

**unjust attacks, no one would have any difficulties to contend with in the State.**
(Bastiat, "The Law," [1850] 2007, p. 51)

With respect to other duties that a government may undertake, Bastiat tirelessly reminds his readers to consider both what is seen and what is not seen. The costs of government actions are often less obvious, although no less real, than their benefits. For example, with respect to a proposal to spend 60,000 francs on a new theater in Paris, he notes:

Yes, it is to the workmen of the theaters that a part, at least, of these 60,000 francs will go; a few bribes, perhaps, may be abstracted on the way. Perhaps, if we were to look a little more closely into the matter, we might find that the cake had gone another way, and that those workmen were fortunate who had come in for a few crumbs. But I will allow, for the sake of argument, that the entire sum does go to the painters, decorators, etc.

**But whence does it come?** This is the other side of the question, and quite as important as the former. Where do these 60,000 francs spring from?

[I]t is clear that the taxpayer, who has contributed one franc, will no longer have this franc at his own disposal. It is clear that he will be deprived of some gratification to the amount of one franc; and that the workman, whoever he may be, who would have received it from him, will be deprived of a benefit to that amount.

Let us not, therefore, be led by a childish illusion into believing that the vote of the 60,000 francs may add anything whatever to the well-being of the country, and to national labor. It displaces enjoyments, it **transposes** wages—that is all.

Will it be said that for one kind of gratification, and one kind of labor, it substitutes more urgent, more moral, more reasonable gratifications and labor? I might dispute this; I might say, by taking 60,000 francs from the taxpayers, you diminish the wages of laborers, drainers, carpenters, blacksmiths, and increase in proportion those of the singers. (Bastiat, "That Which Is Seen, and That Which Is Not Seen," [1850] 2007, p. 15)

## Bastiat's Normative Framework

Bastiat's moral or normative assessments rely on "general interests" and emphasize material conveniences, what economists would later refer to as *goods and services*, rather than advancement of private virtue, praiseworthiness, duty, salvation, aggregate utility, or the grandeur of the state. In this, his policy analysis continues the shift in emphasis from private virtue to civic virtue begun in Locke's analysis and continued through Smith, Kant, and Bentham (who is covered in the next chapter). He mentions morals and justice as separate categories, but ones that are not disadvantaged by markets under appropriate civil law.

The benefits of specialization and exchange are nearly all expressed in narrow self-interest terms, as would be done in a contemporary microeconomics class. There are mutual gains from exchange. Markets allow all persons to "enjoy more in one day than he [or she] could himself produce in many ages." The good life in this economic account is material rather than spiritual, social, or ethical—a common conclusion among economists from Smith's *Wealth of Nations* onward.

Bastiat notes that commerce is not a threat, but a means of obtaining a good life. Moreover, although not mentioned in these quotes, it is a means that has gained enormously in its productivity in the period 1700–1850, as ships became larger and safer, canal and road systems expanded, railroads were introduced, and mass production was adopted for more and more products. He argues, as did other liberals in France and elsewhere in the mid-nineteenth century, that commerce should be allowed to play an increasing role in life and society in France and elsewhere.

[O]ne can scarcely conceive anything more easily reduced to practice than this—to **allow men to labor, to exchange, to learn, to associate, to act and react on each other**—for, according to the laws of Providence, **nothing can result from their intelligent spontaneity but order, harmony, progress, good, and better still; better ad infinitum.** (Bastiat, "Harmonies of Political Economy," [1850] 2007, p. 442)

## Bastiat's Intended Audience

As a political activist, rather than an academic philosopher, Bastiat's discussions are more like those of Franklin and La Court than those of the other scholars reviewed. He employs arguments that he believes will resonate with those already in the minds of his readers in order to be persuasive. The simplicity of Bastiat's arguments relative to Smith and Kant and their excited presentation reflects his aim to excite as well as persuade his audience. His relatively straightforward analyses also reflect both advances in economics and the increased material welfare of his readers. These allow relatively simple and direct expressions of sophisticated arguments.

Although Bastiat often demonstrates that material interests are advanced through trade and specialization, he does not rely entirely on self-interest-based arguments. Bastiat is essentially unconcerned about tensions between commerce and the good life, because he believes that commerce promotes a good life both materially and morally. He uses general interests as a norm, but he uses this term in its pre-utilitarian sense, of common or shared interests. He does not assume that it is possible to add up human happiness, but rather suggests that a broad range of persons benefit from commerce. "General interest" is not an aggregate, as it would be for a utilitarian; rather, it is based on whether beneficial effects are realized by most persons in society or not. Indeed, he uses the word "utility" in its older sense of usefulness (or at least his translator does).

That Bastiat was elected to public office while espousing these ideas implies that in his part of France, support for markets (and other liberal principles) had deepened since the time of Montesquieu. Both the wide dissemination of his arguments and his election to parliament suggest that the anti-commerce conservatives of that period had lost the debate with more optimistic liberal assessments of markets espoused in the first half of the nineteenth century. Commerce and prosperity were no longer regarded as placing a good life and good society at risk, but as important features of both.

## New Opponents to Commerce Emerge in the Mid-Nineteenth Century

Bastiat's arguments also provide evidence that a change in French politics was underway in the mid-nineteenth century. His opponents toward the end of his life were not usually cultural conservatives—defenders of the medieval order, as had been the case for the previous generation of liberals. His mid-century political opponents tended to have ideas about the good society that were similar to More's *Utopia* (such as Saint-Simon and Fourier) rather than with conservative defenses of medieval theology, familial privilege, and the divine right of kings.[25] Bastiat is thus the first of the authors reviewed in this volume to address arguments made by nineteenth-century political advocates of communalism or socialism, who gradually replaced defenders of

[25] I refer to Thomas More rather than Karl Marx or other nineteenth-century socialists as the benchmark for arguments from the far left for several reasons. Although Marx had some contact with French intellectuals in the 1840s, his most famous essay, the *Communist Manifesto*, was published in 1848 in German and would not have had a broad impact in France before the time of Bastiat's death in 1850. Marx himself had spent time in France during the 1840s, but partly to study earlier French socialists and communists. Pre-Marxist views of ideal communal societies had been produced by French intellectuals well before Marx, as with Saint-Simon, Fourier, and Proudhon. Many of their ideas arguably were presaged by Catholic theories of ideal monastic societies that would go back at least as far as More's clear statement (in Latin) in his *Utopia*. More's vision of the good society was discussed above in Chapter 3.

the medieval order as the main opponents of doctrinaire liberalism in policy debates during the nineteenth century.

This change in political opponents induced Bastiat to change the kinds of normative arguments made in support of commerce.

[T]hose who tell us that capital is by nature unproductive, ought to know that they are provoking a terrible and immediate struggle.

If, on the contrary, the interest of capital is natural, lawful, consistent with the general good, as favorable to the borrower as to the lender, the economists who deny it, the writers who grieve over this pretended social wound, are leading the workmen into a senseless and unjust effort which can have no other issue than the misfortune of all.

I am convinced [that my argument has awakened] doubts in your minds, and scruples in your conscience. You say to yourselves sometimes: "But to assert that capital ought not to produce interest is to say that he who has created tools, or materials, or provisions of any kind, ought to yield them up without compensation. Is that just?" (Bastiat, "Capital and Interest," [1850] 2007, pp. 139–141)

Less extreme opponents to doctrinaire liberalism (ones that I refer to as "left liberals") had more significant effects on public policy than more radical ones in the mid-to-late nineteenth century. Mainstream debates over policy in the late nineteenth century were largely between doctrinaire and left liberals, who, for the most part, agreed about the merits of an open society and private property, but disagreed about the proper scope of government services and regulation. That debate tended to focus on relatively narrow policy issues such as tariffs, public education, infrastructure, regulation, and suffrage.

However, new arguments made by the far left and right were not ignored and not entirely without influence later in the nineteenth century. Some of these controversies are taken up in the next chapter.

## Conclusions: Eighteenth-Century Innovations in Ethics, Economics, and Political Science

The eighteenth century was a period of progress in our understanding of social systems, the roles that ethics play in them, and in theoretical explanations for the existence of and nature of ethical dispositions. Innovations in political, economic, and ethical theories deepened understandings of the many interdependencies between political, economic, and other social systems. For example, Smith's writings provided a more sophisticated and integrated understanding of ethics, specialization, and commercial competition than previous generations had, in part because markets were becoming more extensive, industrial, and competitive during his lifetime. The logic of the invisible hand overturned centuries of mercantilist arguments that markets needed active regulation to flourish. As advantages of trade and specialization became better understood, consequentialist ethical theories tended to increase their support for commerce. Montesquieu, Smith, and Bastiat all suggest that a nation's laws can simultaneously encourage commercial and ethical development.

Intellectual developments were generating the concept of a "social system." Political, economic, sociological, and ethical systems were increasingly considered to be interdependent phenomena, with ethics affecting politics (Montesquieu), public policy affecting ethics (Montesquieu, Bastiat), ethics affecting economics (Montesquieu, Franklin, Bastiat), economics affecting ethics and politics (Montesquieu, Smith, Bastiat), and political choices of government policies affecting rates of economic development (Montesquieu, Smith, Bastiat). Paradoxically, at the same time that these interdependencies were being noted and analyzed, separate fields of research were beginning to emerge based on the types of choice settings analyzed.[26]

In general, ethical support for markets deepened and reservations diminished during the eighteenth century, in part because of a clearer understanding of the effects of competitive markets and in part because of shifts in ethical theories. Prosperity had become a goal worthy of support, rather than a temptation to avoid.

This is not to say that eighteenth-century classical liberals regarded all pursuits of wealth to be ethical or admirable, but that many—indeed most—such activities were so regarded. Mainstream moral reservations about commerce diminished, although they did not disappear. Montesquieu, for example, was concerned that markets would reduce the strength of ethical dispositions that were not commerce enhancing. Smith noted that not all methods of pursuing wealth were fair, and Bastiat acknowledged that there were immoral as well as moral methods of obtaining wealth. However, in general, reservations were narrower than those raised in previous centuries. The moral failings of markets tended to be considered less important because

---

[26] Ethics, economics, and political science were becoming distinct fields of analysis and writing in part because research and scholarship was becoming more thorough and books were becoming somewhat more narrowly focused. That trend toward greater specialization was reinforced by advantages associated with specialization in intellectual pursuits. It is easier to master and write about one field than about two or more fields. However, philosophy, economics, sociology, and political science did become entirely separate areas of research for another century. Alfred Marshall, for example, held a position in moral philosophy rather than in economics during the first two decades of his distinguished career (until 1885).

commerce was increasingly acknowledged to increase the material wellbeing of most persons in society and this was widely regarded to be a praiseworthy result.

The foundations of ethics also became more secular in the eighteenth century. With respect to character development, more stress was placed on virtues that were market supporting, such as industriousness, frugality, and prudence. Material comfort was increasingly used as an index of general welfare, as in Montesquieu, Smith, and Bastiat. Careers in commerce were considered to be part of a good life and contributed to character development as well as the general welfare (Montesquieu, Franklin, Bastiat), or morally neutral, as in Smith and Kant. Such conclusions, in turn, provided additional support for public policies that reduced legal restrictions on careers in commerce, entry into new markets, and infrastructure projects that tended to expand the extent of commerce. Prosperity and the accumulation of wealth contributed to a nation's stature and power. International trade contributed to both international and domestic peace.

Of course, few of these conclusions were entirely new, but eighteenth-century assessments were more deeply grounded in economics, political science, and human psychology than previous arguments had been. And, although the new theories were largely secular, they were often developed by religious men and women, who regarded their arguments and conclusions to be consistent with their theological beliefs, if not directly grounded in divine texts. One did not have to belong to a particular religion to find the new theories and conclusions persuasive.

Overall, eighteenth-century shifts in both common and elite economic and ethical theories provided stronger support for commercial development than that generated by previous theories and norms. Lifestyles and public policies shifted in response to such changes. The great acceleration had not yet fully taken off, but economic growth in the West was generally faster in 1800 than it had been in 1700 or 1600.

# 12

# Utilitarianism: Commerce and the Good Society

## Setting the Stage for the Nineteenth Century

In 1815, many features of the medieval order were still commonplace in Europe despite significant shifts in ethics, science, economic theory, and political philosophy during the previous century. Government in Europe and elsewhere continued to be largely determined by birthright; kings inherited their thrones, and nobles inherited their positions in the noble chambers of parliament, which were still by and large the most powerful of the chambers. The commoner chambers were largely populated by men from wealthy families (or their employees), most of whom won office in uncontested elections. When elections were contested, only a handful of voters normally voted, generally a small percentage of the wealthiest males in the communities of interest. Senior church officials often held seats in parliament as a right of office. Most high government officials and military leaders were nobles or from noble families.[1]

Most countries and duchies still had monopoly churches, supported by state taxes or tithes collected by their governments. These were mainly Lutheran in northern Europe and Catholic in the south. The Netherlands and England were exceptions to this general rule, although both had state-supported churches and restrictions on Catholic churches and their members.[2]

---

[1] This is not to say that nothing with respect to politics had changed in the West. For example, France's revolutionary or democratic period began in 1789, was replaced with Napoleon's dictatorship in 1804, and by a constitutional monarchy in 1815. Napoleon's military success directly or indirectly ended the republican governments of the Netherlands and Venice, and treaties negotiated after Napoleon was dispatched (at the Vienna Congress) led to significant territorial reforms in the Holy Roman Empire and in Scandinavia. The Dutch Republic became a kingdom. The United States was founded in North America. The ideas of both the French and US revolutions tended to energize both liberals and conservatives in Europe. Slavery had been eliminated in much of Europe and many feudal practices eliminated or curtailed. However, examined with a broad brush, it is fair to say that the monarchical template for European governance appeared to be alive and well in Europe in 1815.

[2] The United States of America is another exception. There was no national church, although a few of the states initially continued to support a particular church. Several states had long had rules for religious tolerance during their colonial periods. The first amendment to the constitution (1791) established religious toleration for the nation as a whole in the sense that no laws were to be adopted in support of a particular religious doctrine. A Catholic national church and aristocratic rule were re-established in France after Napoleon's defeat in the early nineteenth century.

*Solving Social Dilemmas.* Roger D. Congleton, Oxford University Press. © Oxford University Press 2022.
DOI: 10.1093/oso/9780197642788.003.0012

For most persons, religion was as central to life as ever, although miracles were considered a bit less plentiful than in previous periods and the existence of natural laws was more widely accepted. Most persons outside cities remained farmers or employees of farmers, who directly produced most of their own necessities of life.

Urban commercial centers were growing, but major cities were still relatively small, and commerce involved only a small but increasing fraction of the population as a whole. London had grown from a half million to a million persons during the eighteenth century, but would include more than 6 million residents in 1900. Paris had a relatively stable population of about a half million persons during the eighteenth century, but grew to nearly 3 million during the nineteenth century. New York City was a small town in 1700, with a population of about 5,000, reaching 60,000 in 1800, and would reach nearly 3.5 million in 1900. Adam Smith noted that guilds remained strong in British cities in the late eighteenth century and that their members often retained monopoly privileges in production and sales. Imports and exports were often controlled by royal monopolies based in capital cities and major port cities.

Most economic production was accomplished in the old-fashioned way by farmers and farmhands working with fields and animals, and artisans working out of their homes or in small shops nearby. Smith noticed that this was beginning to change in the mid- to late eighteenth century as small factories in England and Scotland began taking greater advantage of in-house specialization and factory production. The cloth industry in particular was expanding rapidly and taking advantage of new wind- and water-powered looms. Nonetheless, highly specialized production was still the exception rather than the rule. Machines had become larger and more sophisticated, as had oceangoing sailing ships, but machines were still mainly constructed of wood and driven by muscle, wind, or water, as they had been for centuries.

Significant technological innovations and institutional reforms were underway. Steam engines had been developed for pumping water out of mines in the late eighteenth century. These were further developed in the early nineteenth century for use in transportation. The old medieval strip farms were being "rationalized" into more or less rectangular fields, enclosed with fences of various kinds during the second half of the eighteenth century through various "enclosure movements." This, together with marketable private titles, made land a more liquid form of wealth than it had been in previous centuries. It also literally changed the landscape in Western

Europe to the patchwork of fields taken for granted outside cities today. Openness to public debates on policy and scientific issues had increased during the eighteenth century, although political censorship increased in many places in the years after the French Revolution. Sumptuary laws had largely disappeared.[3]

The secularization of science continued. More and more phenomena were explained as consequences of natural laws, which were still generally considered to be evidence of divine power and intent. The search for general principles for a "good" life and "good" society continued, as efforts to identify new principles and refine old ones were undertaken by nineteenth-century academics, independent scholars, and others with sufficient time and interest to investigate associated issues and puzzles. Significant progress had been made in the social sciences during the eighteenth century, as with the work of Montesquieu and Smith on law, politics, ethics, and economics, but more could be and would be done in the nineteenth century.

The nineteenth century was a transformational century throughout what came to be called "the West." Together, shifts in normative theories, technological advances, and institutional reforms led to rapid economic development and the emergence of extensive networks of trade during the nineteenth century. The same countries underwent substantial democratization, which was the subject of my previous book (Congleton 2011). The great acceleration had begun.

This chapter focuses on four prominent utilitarians to illustrate both another "new" foundation for ethics and how a single principle-driven theory developed in response to a century of criticism and innovation. For the most part, those changes broadened and deepened utilitarian support for commerce.

## Utilitarianism

At about the same time that Kant was writing, there was another proposal for a single principle that could be used to determine whether an action is ethical or not. Proponents of what came to be called the *utility principle*, in effect, returned to Aristotle's analysis. Their ultimate end, like his, was happiness or utility. As in his analysis of political systems, a good government was

---

[3] Sumptuary laws governed clothing, food, and housing. Restrictions were often class based, as particular colors or type of cloth might be forbidden for one class or sex and mandated for others. Among the most famous in England were the sumptuary laws of Queen Elizabeth in 1574, which had restricted silk and the color purple to the royal family and a subset of nobles.

one that maximized happiness within the community governed. In contrast to Aristotle, but in common with Smith and Kant, utilitarians focused most of their attention on the effects that actions had on others living in their communities, rather than on an individual's character development or salvation. Utilitarians asked (and continue to ask) whether the average person living in a community is likely to be happier after a particular action or policy is undertaken than before. If the members of a community are on balance happier afterward, the action or policy is a good or virtuous one. If not, it is a bad or immoral one. Happiness defines virtue, rather than being a product of it, as in Aristotle.

In contrast to Aristotle, Smith, Kant, and most theologians, utilitarians were almost entirely indifferent to the effect that an action had on character development, except insofar as such effects might increase an individual's own lifetime happiness. It is the consequences of an action, ethical disposition, or public policy on others that matter most—namely, their effects on the total happiness of all persons in the community or society of interest. Private ethics and character development were not irrelevant, because they could contribute to happiness, as argued by Aristotle, Franklin, and Mill, but it was of much less interest and import than in previous approaches.

Ethical rules were means to an end, rather than an ultimate end. And all such rules were subject to a single test—did a rule or rule system increase total human happiness or not? The ultimate aim of all rules was to increase aggregate happiness, rather than that of a single individual. This tended to induce utilitarians to focus on broad public policy issues such as education, infrastructure, economic regulation, and the properties of alternative electoral systems.

Utilitarians are consequentialists, and advances in science that make consequences easier to predict tend to make utilitarian conclusions sharper and more policy-relevant. Most of the most famous English and American economists of the nineteenth century were utilitarians. Together, developments in economic theory and the utilitarian perspective tended to make economic activity more central to a good society, because every voluntary exchange was argued to increase aggregate (and average) utility.

This chapter focuses entirely on utilitarian ideas, which arguably were more important in the Anglo-Saxon domains than in other parts of the West, and within economics than in other social sciences, but which nonetheless influenced all the rest. In some cases, this was through direct effects on the manner in which individual actions were evaluated. In other cases, it was through effects that utilitarians had on our understanding of the effects of markets, politics, and public policies.

# Jeremy Bentham (1748–1832): The Utility Principle as the Foundation for Private and Social Ethics

Jeremy Bentham was born in London and educated at Queens College of Oxford. Bentham, like Montesquieu and Bastiat, was trained in law and subsequently inherited a sufficient fortune to leave that profession at an early age and devote himself to intellectual activities and policy reform. Bentham was the central figure in the group that produced the new moral theory that came to be called utilitarianism, although he preferred the term "felicitarianism."[4]

According to Bentham's utility principle, proper action and good conduct increase the sum of utility in the community of interest (pleasure net of pain). Improper action, conduct, and policies diminish the sum of happiness in a community and thereby make members of that community on average worse off. Bentham argued that this "utility principle" could and should be used to evaluate all actions by all persons and all government policies.

Bentham's utility principle provides universal moral guidance for all personal and government conduct, whereas Smith's and Kant's ethical theories applied only to a subset of an individual's conduct. For a utilitarian every act has moral consequences, in contrast to the theories of Smith, Kant, and Aristotle.

## An Ethics for Life in Society

Bentham begins his justification for the utility principle with the observation that pleasure and pain (broadly understood) are the root source of all human behavior.[5]

**Nature has placed mankind under the governance of two sovereign masters, pain and pleasure.** It is for them alone to point out what we ought to do, as well as to determine what we shall do. On the one hand, the standard of right and wrong, on the other the chain of causes and effects, are fastened to their throne. They

---

[4] A short biography of Bentham appears in the *Annual Biography and Obituary 1833* (London: Longman, Rees, Orme, Brown, Green, and Longman). John Stuart Mill brought the term *utilitarian* into common usage, according to his autobiography. In a somewhat bizarre bequest, Bentham's body was dissected after death, mummified, and reconstructed with a wax head, which sits upright in a glass case in University College London.

[5] Most of the excerpts come from a digitized collection of Bentham's writings assembled by Minerva Classics, *The Collected Works of Jeremy Bentham* (2013), which are taken from the 1843 Bowring collection. Other excerpts are from a digitized version of his *Manual of Political Economy* (2011), available from Amazon. KL again denotes Kindle locations. The entire Bowring collection is available at the Liberty Fund website in various digitized formats. Individual works are cited to aid readers familiar with Bentham's writings or who use other collections or editions. A newer and more complete collection of his works has recently become available from Oxford University Press (2014).

**govern us in all we do, in all we say, in all we think: every effort** we can make to throw off our subjection, will serve but to demonstrate and confirm it. (Bentham, "An Introduction to the Principles of Morals and Legislation," 2013, KL: 3474–3478)

Bentham then shifts to the term "utility," which had been adopted by many others at about the same time, as a term that summarizes the net pleasure gained by a course of action.

**By utility is meant that property in any object, whereby it tends to produce benefit, advantage, pleasure, good, or happiness** (all this in the present case comes to the same thing), or (what comes again to the same thing) **to prevent the happening of mischief, pain, evil, or unhappiness** to the party whose interest is considered. (Bentham, "An Introduction to the Principles of Morals and Legislation," 2013, KL: 3526–3528)

He and other utilitarians emphasized that communities are composed of individuals, and therefore a community's interest or welfare is simply the sum of the individual happiness of its members.

**The community is a fictitious body, composed of the individual persons who are considered as constituting as it** were its members. The **interest of the community** then is, what?— **the sum of the interests of the several members who compose it**. (Bentham, "An Introduction to the Principles of Morals and Legislation," 2013, KL: 3535–3538)

This characterization of communities implies that communities have no interests other than those of their individual members. A community may be said to have interests only insofar as individual members of the community are made happier or not by a given policy or activity. It also implies that every individual counts— not simply the king, members of government, or a privileged subgroup.

**It is in vain to talk of the interest of the community, without understanding what is the interest of the individual.** (Bentham, "An Introduction to the Principles of Morals and Legislation," 2013, KL: 3531–3533)

Having developed the core ideas that grounded his normative theory, Bentham next states what he calls the "utility principle" in a clear way.

**A thing is said to promote the interest, or to be for the interest, of an individual, when it tends to add to the sum total of his pleasures:** or, what comes to the same thing, to diminish the sum total of his pains. (Bentham, "An Introduction to the Principles of Morals and Legislation," 2013, KL: 3545–3548)

**An action then may be said to be conformable to the principle of utility, or, for shortness sake, to utility (meaning with respect to the community at large), when the tendency it has to augment the happiness of the community is greater than any it has to diminish it.** (Bentham, "An Introduction to the Principles of Morals and Legislation," 2013, KL: 3556–3557)

Note that the word "tendency" is used, which implies that an action may have more than one possible outcome because of random or unpredictable effects, but still will tend to promote community utility. (Students of "rational choice"–based contemporary social science will recognize that the above claims provide the foundation for most utility-based models of "rational" choice and also for methodological individualism.)

Bentham argues that all conventional moral terms, such as *duty*, *right and wrong*, and *good and evil*, can be characterized with the utility principle.

**Of an action that is conformable to the principle of utility, one may always say either that it is one that ought to be done, or at least that it is not one that ought not to be done.** One may say also, that **it is right it should be done**; at least that it is **not wrong** it should be done: that it is a right action; at least that it is not a wrong action.

**When thus interpreted, the words ought, and right and wrong, and others of that stamp, have a meaning: when otherwise, they have none.** (Bentham, "An Introduction to the Principles of Morals and Legislation," 2013, KL: 3576–3581)

The utility principle implies that ethics and virtue in the sense of rules of good conduct are not primarily important because they improve one's own character or increase one's prospects for salvation, except insofar as such consequences tend to increase the overall happiness or contentment of a community. A general rule of conduct can be regarded as virtuous only if it tends to advance general interests—which is to say, if it tends to increase total utility. As is true of other principles of morality, the utilitarian principle can be internalized.

A man may be said to be a partisan of the principle of utility, **when** the [internal] approbation or disapprobation he annexes to any action, or to any measure, **is determined, by and proportioned to the tendency which he conceives it to have to augment or to diminish the happiness of the community:** or in other words, to its conformity or unconformity to the laws or dictates of utility. (Bentham, "An Introduction to the Principles of Morals and Legislation," 2013, KL: 3571–3574)

Bentham also suggests that individual actions rarely affect their entire community; thus, in most cases, individuals should simply maximize their own happiness.

[In contrast] **there is no case in which a private man ought not to direct his own conduct to the production of his own happiness, and of that of his fellow-creatures.** (Bentham, "An Introduction to the Principles of Morals and Legislation," 2013, KL: 12047)

Prejudice apart, the game of push-pin is of equal value with the arts and sciences of music and poetry. **If the game of push-pin furnishes more pleasure, it is more valuable than either.** (Bentham, "The Rationale of Reward," 1838–1843, p. 206)

The pursuit of happiness is necessarily a virtuous activity, regardless of how one goes about it, as long as one's actions increase aggregate utility. And in contrast with Aristotle and Locke, Bentham suggests that individuals instinctively know how to advance their happiness.

This rule of thumb does not apply to government officials, however, because their actions tend to affect many others. The policy choices of legislators have broad impacts on their communities and so should be based on a careful analysis of the consequences of their actions.

... the **happiness of the individuals, of whom a community is composed**, that is, their pleasures and their security, **is the end and the sole end which the legislator ought to have in view: the sole standard**, in conformity to which each individual ought, as far as depends upon the legislator, to be made to fashion his behavior. (Bentham, "An Introduction to the Principles of Morals and Legislation," 2013, KL: 4188–4190)

Nonetheless, there are limits to the proper sphere of law and legislation.

**But there are cases in which the legislator ought not** (in a direct way at least, and **by means of punishment** applied immediately to particular individual acts) attempt to direct the conduct of the several other members of the community.

Every act which promises to be beneficial upon the whole to the community (himself included), each individual ought to perform himself, but **it is not every such act that the legislator ought to compel him to perform.**

> Every act which promises to be pernicious upon the whole to the commu-
> nity (himself included), each individual ought to abstain from of himself, but
> it is not every such act that the legislator ought to compel him to abstain from.
> (Bentham, "An Introduction to the Principles of Morals and Legislation," 2013,
> KL: 12048–12053)

In these comments, Bentham is beginning to analyze where "the line" between private and community interests should be placed according to the
utility principle, as opposed to a natural rights or contractarian perspective.
For the most part, individuals should simply attempt to advance their own
interests, while legislators should attempt to increase the total happiness of
their communities. However, not every utility-increasing rule of conduct
should be made a formal law, backed by the sanctions of a judicial system.
There are at least four cases in which the cost of doing so tends to be greater
than the benefits realized.

> Where, then, is the line to be drawn? . . . Now the cases in which punishment,
> meaning the punishment of the political sanction, ought not to be inflicted . . . are
> of four sorts: 1. Where punishment would be groundless. 2. Where it would be
> inefficacious. 3. Where it would be unprofitable. 4. Where it would be needless.
> (Bentham, "An Introduction to the Principles of Morals and Legislation," 2013,
> KL: 12047–12062)

Some punishments do not increase community utility; others will not change
behavior, or do so at a cost (reduction in utility) greater than the benefits
obtained. In many cases, private incentives alone are sufficient to increase aggregate utility, so no formal laws and government sanctions are necessary. All
laws should increase aggregate utility, and this requires taking into account
both the benefits and costs of the rules themselves and their manner of enforcement, which vary with the internalized norms of the persons subject to
the law, as demonstrated in Part II of this book.

## Utilitarian Ethics and Commerce

In contrast to most of the philosophers reviewed to this point, economics is
an interest of Bentham's, and he provides one of the first clear descriptions of
the mutual gains to trade in his *Manual of Political Economy* ([1843] 2011).
Bentham notes that essentially every trade increases the happiness of every

party to an exchange. Although the money value of what is exchanged is the same (as long before noted by Aristotle), each gains utility from the exchange, which increases total utility.[6]

> Some advantage results from every exchange, provided it be made intentionally and without fraud: otherwise such exchange would not be made; there would be no reason for making it.
>
> Under this point of view, the two contracting parties receive an equal benefit [in money terms, but]: **each one of them surrenders what suits him less, that he may acquire what suits him more.** In each transaction of this kind there are **two masses of new enjoyments.**
>
> **But though all trade be advantageous, a particular branch may be more advantageous to one of the parties than to the other.** (Bentham, *A Manual of Political Economy*, [1843] 2011, KL: 2142–2147)

Even though all the parties directly involved benefit from trade, the benefits are not necessarily equally distributed. Since Bentham regards all activities that increase aggregate utility to be "virtuous" ones; trade is inherently "proper," "good," and "moral." All of these terms have essentially the same meaning in Bentham's schema.[7]

The same logic implies that trade between nations should be free and open.

> In commerce, ignorant nations have treated each other as rivals, who could only rise upon the ruins of one another. **The work of Adam Smith is a treatise upon universal benevolence, because it has shown that commerce is equally advantageous for all nations**—each one profiting in a different manner, according to its natural means; **that nations are associates and not rivals in the grand social enterprise.** (Bentham, "Principles of Penal Law," 2013, KL: 25832–25835)

---

[6] Smith (1776), in contrast, does not provide a rational motivation for exchange. "This division of labor, from which so many advantages are derived, is not originally the effect of any human wisdom, which foresees and intends that general opulence to which it gives occasion. It is the necessary, though very slow and gradual, consequence of a certain **propensity in human nature**, which has in view no such extensive utility; the **propensity to truck, barter, and exchange one thing for another**" (Smith 1776, p. 7).

[7] Bentham adds two caveats to this: first, that there should be no fraud, and second, that businessmen be of sound mind. "In recommending freedom of trade, I suppose the minds of merchants in their sound, that is, their ordinary state. But there have been times when they have acted as though they were delirious: such were the periods of the Mississippi scheme in France, and the South Sea scheme in England" (Bentham [1843] 2011, KL: 2172–74). Periods of what Alan Greenspan termed "irrational exuberance" are also exceptions to his broad support for free trade.

Similar logic applies to other areas of markets and life in which net happiness is produced. He argued, for example, that usury (the charging of high interest rates) should not be a crime.

> **Usury,** which, if it must be an offense, is an offense committed with consent, that is, with the consent of the party supposed to be injured. [It] **cannot merit a place in the catalogue of offenses, unless the consent were either unfairly obtained or unfreely.** In the first case, it coincides with defraudment; in the other, with extortion. (Bentham, "Introduction to the Principles of Political Economy," [1843] 2011, KL: 10611–10613)

In this utility-based analysis of markets for loans, Bentham is challenging both Aristotle's assessment of the virtue of careers in finance and Adam Smith's narrower critique of usury.[8]

Bentham suggests that the virtues and honors of the middle ranks of society are most naturally consistent with the principle of utility, and so the middle ranks tend to be the most virtuous segment of society, which is to say that their activities most consistently increase aggregate utility. This is at least in part because they are engaged in commerce where reputation matters.

> **The middle ranks of society are the most virtuous: it is among them that in the greatest number of points the principles of honor coincide with the principles of utility.**
>
> **It is in this class also that the inconveniences arising from the forfeiture of esteem are most sensibly felt,** and that the evil **consequences arising from the loss of reputation produce the most serious ill consequences.** (Bentham, "Principles of Penal Law," 2013, KL: 19665–19668)

The conduct of the middle class is virtuous, however, not necessarily because they have internalized the principle of utility, but because their pursuit of esteem and wealth are well-aligned with the utility principle. They tend to be so because of the nature of their economic circumstances—which during Bentham's time in London tended to be small businesses of various kinds. In

---

[8] Smith is not against the payment of interest, but against high interest rates. He repeatedly comments on the "evil of usury." For example, he notes, "In some countries the interest of money has been prohibited by law. But as something can everywhere be made by the use of money, something ought everywhere to be paid for the use of it. This regulation, instead of preventing, has been found from experience to increase the evil of usury. The debtor being obliged to pay, not only for the use of the money, but for the risk which his creditor runs by accepting a compensation for that use, he is obliged, if one may say so, to insure his creditor from the penalties of usury" (Smith 1776, p. 247).

contrast to Kantian reasoning, it is consequences that matter to utilitarians, rather than motivation.[9]

Bentham is an important historical figure because of the direct and indirect impact his arguments had on normative theory and public policy. The use of benefit–cost analysis, for example, is a direct implication of his line of argument. Bentham did not have the last word on ethics or public policy, but he set in motion a long series of research efforts on utilitarianism that continues today in contemporary philosophy, economics, and policy analysis.

The remainder of this chapter focuses on three influential utilitarians of the nineteenth and early twentieth centuries: John Stuart Mill, Herbert Spencer, and Alfred Pigou. Bentham's utility principle and Smith's classical economics were not simply retaught; instead, their ideas and arguments provided points of departure for newer, more general, and more finely grained arguments, theories, and conclusions.

## John Stuart Mill (1806–1873): Rules of Conduct as Implications of the Utility Principle

John Stuart Mill (1806–1873) is often regarded to be Bentham's successor. His father, James Mill, was a philosopher, early economist, and writer in his own right; and he was closely associated with Bentham's reform and publication efforts. Thus, John Stuart Mill grew up in a utilitarian household, met many prominent liberals and utilitarians, and was encouraged by his father to become an intellectual through a rigorous education at home.[10] With such an upbringing, it is not surprising that John Stuart Mill became a utilitarian and wrote broadly on the policy issues of his day. Mill began writing papers for political magazines and helped Bentham edit his books as a teenager. Relative to young adults in the twenty-first century, he had a head start of 10–15 years on his career as a philosopher and policy analyst.

---

[9] England was sometimes referred to by French critiques as "a nation of shopkeepers," a remark attributed to both Napoleon and Bertrand Barère de Vieuzac in the late eighteenth century. This notion, however, would only apply to the minority living in urban centers at the time.

[10] His father, James Mill (1773–1823), had met Jeremy Bentham in 1808 and took up the utilitarian cause, along with the liberal one that he had already joined. At some points, he was supported by Bentham during his early "writing phase." His father's intellectual and political circles thus brought John Stuart Mill in contact with many other famous liberals of the early nineteenth century, including David Ricardo, Jean-Baptiste Say, and of course, Jeremy Bentham.

He earned his living, however, as a clerk in the London office of the East India Company, rather than as a writer, lobbyist, or academic. He worked for the East India Company from the age of 17, rising from clerk to the rank of chief examiner toward the end of his tenure, as his father had before him.[11] Although Mill earned some income from his writing, it was his "day job" that provided the resources and time for most of his writing. The British government took over the East India Company in 1858, at which point Mill retired on a modest pension at the age of 52 and continued to write, which is the period in which most of the material cited below was written.

Mill wrote on a wide variety of topics, including epistemology, ethics, economics, and political philosophy. As was also the case for most of the other prolific authors reviewed in this book, only a subset of his broad writing is relevant for the purposes of this book. Two books finished in the period after his retirement—*On Liberty* (1859) and *Utilitarianism* (1863)—are especially relevant, as is another book published a decade earlier, *Principles of Political Economy* (1848). The latter was widely used in university courses in economics until it was superseded by Alfred Marshall's textbook (1890) at the turn of the century. The other two books continue to be read in contemporary political theory and philosophy courses.

By the time these books were written, the utilitarian approach to private life and public policy had been refined and criticized for more than half a century. Thus, these two books can be regarded as both responses to the critics of utilitarianism and attempts to better explain its foundations and essential implications.

**The creed which accepts as the foundation of morals, Utility, or the Greatest Happiness Principle, holds that actions are right in proportion as they tend to promote happiness,** wrong as they tend to produce the reverse of happiness.

**By happiness is intended pleasure, and the absence of pain; by unhappiness, pain, and the privation of pleasure.** To give a clear view of the moral standard set up by the theory, much more requires to be said; in particular, what things it includes in the ideas of pain and pleasure; and to what extent this is left an open question. (Mill, "Utilitarianism," 2013, KL: 46372–46376)

---

[11] Mill recounts a period of depression or burnout at about the age of 20, at which time he nonetheless continued to work full-time for the East India Company, participated in a major debate society, and continued to write for the *Westminster Review*, which was struggling financially during this period of his blues. He evidently kept his blues to himself, and it was not clear that anyone but Mill noticed it. See Chapters 4 and 5 of his autobiography.

## Mill on the Utility Principle, Virtue, and Duty

In *Utilitarianism*, Mill argues that general rules of conduct and policy can be deduced from the utility principle, and that such rules imply that utilitarianism is more in alignment with classical theories of virtue and happiness than previously recognized.[12] Against the charge of hedonism, Mill argued that utilitarians have always favored virtue and virtuous pleasures over vices. In this, Mill adopts Aristotle's argument that virtue is an important source of lifetime happiness. The happiness associated with virtue is more permanent and less costly than the "lower" pleasures. Investments in virtue are therefore likely to increase both individual and aggregate utility over the course of a lifetime

> [Utilitarians] **not only place virtue at the very head of the things which are good as means to the ultimate end,** but they also **recognize as a psychological fact the possibility of its being to the individual a good in itself,** without looking to any end beyond it.
>
> And [they] hold that **the mind is not in a right state, not in a state conformable to Utility, not in the state most conducive to the general happiness, unless it does love virtue** in this manner, as a thing desirable in itself. (Mill, "Utilitarianism," 2013, KL: 46917–46922)

Mill, in contrast to Bentham but in a manner similar to Aristotle, emphasizes the relative merits of pleasures that are uniquely human, such as intellectual pleasures and those associated with virtue.[13]

> **It is better to be a human being dissatisfied than a pig satisfied;** better to be Socrates dissatisfied than a fool satisfied. And if the fool, or the pig, are of a different opinion, it is because they only know their own side of the question. **The other party to the comparison knows both sides.** (Mill, "Utilitarianism," 2013, KL: 46429–46431)

---

[12] Excerpts are from a digitized collection of Mills books assembled by Minerva Classics (2016). This collection is an excellent resource for readers who want to explore Mill's writings. Bolding and an occasional bracket are again added by this author and some reformatting and very modest modernization of punctuation has been undertaken. KL again refers to Kindle locations. The individual works from the collection are cited at the end of the excerpts to make it clear which book or paper is associated with the quote.

[13] Spencer mentions in his autobiography ([1904] 2014, KL 6286) that Carlyle (1850, pp. 515–517) had mocked utilitarianism as "pig philosophy," which may account for Mill's use of pigs in his defense of utilitarianism.

Consistent with Bentham's remarks made a half century earlier, Mill argues that utilitarian logic does not usually require all persons to think globally about the effects of their actions, because most actions do not have effects beyond their families and friends.

> **The great majority of good actions are intended not for the benefit of the world, but for that of individuals,** of which the good of the world is made up; and **the thoughts of the most virtuous man need not on these occasions travel beyond the particular persons concerned,** except so far as is necessary to assure himself that in benefiting them he is not violating the rights, that is, the legitimate and authorized expectations, of anyone else.
>
> **The multiplication of happiness is according to the utilitarian ethics the object of virtue.** The occasions on which any person (except one in a thousand) has it in his power to do this on an extended scale, in other words to be a public benefactor, are but exceptional, and **on these occasions alone** is he called on to consider public utility. **In every other case, private utility, the interest or happiness of some few persons, is all he has to attend to.** (Mill, "Utilitarianism," 2013, KL: 46593–46599)

Most individual actions have only effects on a person's own happiness and that of his or her friends and family, and so only these effects need be subjected to the utilitarian calculus.

## Rules of Conduct and Duties That Enhance Life in a Community

Mill attempts to develop principles or rules of conduct that generally increase aggregate utility. For this reason, he is sometimes regarded to be a "rule utilitarian." With respect to life in society, he argues that some rules of conduct are more important than others, because they have larger long-term impacts on aggregate happiness. The rules that make civil society possible are especially important, as previously argued by Hobbes, Locke, and Smith, who of course relied upon different ethical theories to reach their conclusions.

> **The moral rules which forbid mankind to hurt one another** (in which we must never forget to include wrongful interference with each other's freedom) **are more vital to human well-being than any maxims,** however important, which only point out the best mode of managing some department of human affairs. **They have also the peculiarity, that they are the main element in determining the whole of the social feelings of mankind.**

It is **their observance which alone preserves peace** among human beings: if obedience to them were not the rule, and disobedience the exception, everyone would see in everyone else an enemy, against whom he must be perpetually guarding himself. (Mill, "Utilitarianism," 2013, KL: 47364–47368)

Mill (indirectly) suggests that internalized norms solve the Hobbesian dilemma analyzed in Part I of this book. Because life in society advances the utility principle and some rules make life in society possible, individuals have duties to follow those rules.[14] Among the most important rules are those that "forbid mankind to hurt one another" and rules that forbid the breaking of promises. (Note that the harms that Mill has in mind are subjective ones, rather than objective losses or physical damages.)

The important rank among human evils and wrongs of the **disappointment of expectation** is shown in the fact that it constitutes the principal criminality of two such highly immoral acts **as a breach of friendship and a breach of promise. Few hurts which human beings can sustain are greater and none wound more than when that on which they habitually and with full assurance relied fails them in the hour of need.** [A]nd **few wrongs are greater than this mere withholding of good.** [N]one excite more resentment, either in the person suffering, **or in a sympathizing spectator.** (Mill, "Utilitarianism," 2013, KL: 47387–47391)

With respect to markets, Mill notes that the conflict among producers induced by markets—competition—accounts for many of the benefits of markets. Competition tends to increase social utility by increasing the efficiency of production and thereby increasing the quantity and types of products that contribute to human happiness.

It is in the interest of the community, that of the two methods, producers should adopt that which produces the best article at the lowest price. This being also the

---

[14] These civic duties are more clearly stated in *On Liberty*. "Though society is not founded on a contract, and though no good purpose is answered by inventing a contract in order to deduce social obligations from it, everyone who receives the protection of society owes a return for the benefit, and the fact of living in society renders it indispensable that each should be bound to observe a certain line of conduct towards the rest. This conduct consists, first, in not injuring the interests of one another; or rather certain interests, which, either by express legal provision or by tacit understanding, ought to be considered as rights; and secondly, in each person's bearing his share (to be fixed on some equitable principle) of the labors and sacrifices incurred for defending the society or its members from injury and molestation. As soon as any part of a person's conduct affects prejudicially the interests of others, society has jurisdiction over it, and the question whether the general welfare will or will not be promoted by interfering with it, becomes open to discussion. But there is no room for entertaining any such question when a person's conduct affects the interests of no persons besides himself, or needs not affect them unless they like (all the persons concerned being of full age, and the ordinary amount of understanding). In all such cases there should be perfect freedom, legal and social, to do the action and stand the consequences" (Mill, *On Liberty*, [1959] 2013, KL: 41040–41052)

interest of the producers, unless protected against competition and shielded from the penalties of indolence. **[T]he process most advantageous** to the community is that which, **if not interfered with by government,** they ultimately find it to their advantage to adopt. (Mill, *On Liberty*, [1859] 2013, KL: 37158–37161)

Mill's discussion implies that market competition is not only compatible with the utility principle, but is among the prime engines of progress. Progress for utilitarians has a clear meaning. It is characterized by long-run increases in a community's aggregate utility. What is left unstated is whether a life devoted to commerce also tends to be good. Mill's logic implies that such careers are generally good insofar as they advance both self-interest and benefit one's trading partners. However, he does not directly address this issue, most likely because it had disappeared as a source of controversy by the mid-nineteenth century. Utilitarian reasoning implies that one should pursue any career that adds to one's own happiness as long as it does not require harming others.

Similarly, obligations to respect the rights of others, to keep promises, and to pay a fair share of the cost of the state are civic duties, according to Mill. Such rules tend to broadly reduce the disadvantages and increase the advantages of life in communities.

## On the Proper and Limited Role of a Government

Doctrinaire liberals in the mid-nineteenth century, such as Bastiat and Spencer, argued for free trade and a minimal state that focused entirely on the protection of individual rights and security, what some term a *night watchman state*. That perspective was mainstream in the mid- to late nineteenth century, but it was not uncontroversial. The main issue was the proper scope of public policy and the extent to which a government should be active in the sense of producing new rules and regulations. Mill's *On Liberty* attempts to clarify the issues, generalizing Bentham's analysis, and in some cases criticizing points made in Spencer's writing, who is covered in the next subsection of this chapter. Again, one of Mill's aims is to decern general rules of conduct that tend to be consistent with the utility principle.

Mill argues that governments have somewhat broader responsibilities than argued by the doctrinaire liberals of his day, although more limited ones than accorded most twenty-first-century Western governments. Mill again uses the utility principle to support what might be called the *do-no-harm principle*.

The **object of this essay is to assert one very simple principle**, as entitled to govern absolutely the dealings of society with the individual in the way of compulsion and control, whether the means used be physical force in the form of legal penalties or the moral coercion of public opinion.

**That principle is that the sole end for which mankind are warranted, individually or collectively, in interfering with the liberty of action of any of their number is self-protection.** That the only purpose for which power can be rightfully exercised over any member of a civilized community, against his will, **is to prevent harm to others.** (Mill, *On Liberty*, [1959] 2013, KL: 39858–39863)

In all cases in which an individual's actions harm others, the community may legitimately intervene, but in no others. However, because harm is subjective (a reduction in happiness or increase in pain), there is potentially a rather large domain for governments to intervene.

**I regard utility as the ultimate appeal on all ethical questions,** but it must be utility in the largest sense, grounded on the permanent interests of man as a progressive being.

**Those interests, I contend, authorize the subjection of individual spontaneity to external control, only in respect to those actions of each, which concern the interest of other people.** If anyone does an act hurtful to others, there is a prima facie case for punishing him, by law, or, where legal penalties are not safely applicable, by general disapprobation. (Mill, *On Liberty*, [1959] 2013, KL 39883–39889)

Most instances of social interaction have effects on others, by definition, and so according to Mill, a community may intervene in a far broader range of choice settings than the doctrinaire liberals were arguing at this time, because adverse effects on others are commonplace. Nonetheless, a government's domain of legitimate authority is still bounded.[15]

Mill argues that there are many cases in which community interventions should not take place. Some types of laws usually produce more harm than good, even in cases in which there might appear to be a social advantage. The cost and effects of regulation have to be fully taken into account. For example, with respect to commerce, Mill argues:

Independently of all considerations of constitutional liberty, **the best interests of the human race imperatively require that all economical experiments,**

---

[15] In his autobiography, Mill claims to have become a socialist in his thirties, evidently because he was sympathetic with some of the ideas of leading French socialists. The pieces focused on in this chapter were written well after that, during his fifties and sixties, and express very few, if any, socialist views. Rather, his political writings were consistently "left liberal" for his time, as with his support for free trade, emancipation, universal male and female suffrage, proportional representation, public education, and education-weighted voting.

**voluntarily undertaken, should have the fullest license,** and that **force and fraud** should be the only means of attempting to benefit themselves, **which are interdicted** to the less fortunate classes of the community. (Mill, "Principles of Political Economy," 2013, KL: 38890–38892)

This is the so-called **doctrine of Free Trade,** which **rests on grounds different from, though equally solid with, the principle of individual liberty** asserted in this Essay. Restrictions on trade, or on production for purposes of trade, are indeed restraints; and all restraint, qua restraint, is an evil. **[T]he restraints in question affect only that part of conduct which society is competent to restrain, and are wrong solely because they do not really produce the results which it is desired to produce by them.** (Mill, *On Liberty*, [1959] 2013, KL: 41409–41413)

Trade is an example of an area of life in which persons may harm another—for example, a rival may attract all of another merchant's customers—and so is a potentially legitimate area of legislation, according to Mill's reasoning. However, he argues that most economic regulations have consequences that are more harmful than beneficial. Although such laws and regulations cannot be rejected using the liberty principle, most can be rejected by the utility principle.

**Laisse faire, in short, should be the general practice: every departure from it, unless required by some great good, is a certain evil.** (Mill, "Principles of Political Economy," 2013, KL: 39115–39119)

Although Mill was regarded as a radical or left liberal during his lifetime, he favored essentially unrestricted commerce. He did so for reasons that differed somewhat from Smith, Bentham, and Bastiat. He favored open markets partly because the results of exchange usually increase aggregate utility and partly because, *in practice*, the regulation of trade tended to reduce, rather than increase, aggregate utility.[16]

---

[16] During the late nineteenth century, Mill's views gradually became mainstream in Europe, as he and other left liberals gradually won the policy debates of their day. As a doctrinaire liberal, Spencer opposed many of those policies, which he regarded to be paternalistic and unnecessarily coercive. Spencer's work was more widely read than Mill's at the time that they were written and thus provides a more useful window into mainstream liberal views during the second half of the nineteenth century, especially among the upper middle classes of the West. Spencer's philosophical work broke new ground by connecting ethics with human nature, and both biological and social evolution. Nonetheless, it was Mill's line of reasoning that was taken up by Pigou and which dominated twentieth-century policy debates among utilitarians and most economists.

## Virtue, Prosperity, and Progress

Mill uses the term "virtue" repeatedly in his writings, although he generally uses it in a manner that differs somewhat from Aristotle's and Smith's usage. From Mill's perspective, virtue may become an end in itself, one that may be a precondition for happiness.

> Virtue, according to the utilitarian doctrine, is not naturally and originally part of the end, but it is capable of becoming so; and in those who love it disinterestedly it has become so, and is desired and cherished, **not as a means to happiness, but as a part of their happiness.** (Mill, "Utilitarianism," 2013, p. 57).

Mill regards virtuous conduct to be desirable because of positive effects that it tends to have on others. For example, Mill argues that a subset of virtues tends to increase prosperity, which tends to increase aggregate utility. Communities should therefore attempt to promote such virtues.

> What, for example, are the qualities in the citizens individually which conduce most to keep up the amount of good conduct, of good management, of success and prosperity, which already exist in society? **Everybody will agree that those qualities are industry, integrity, justice, and prudence.** But are not these, of all qualities, the most conducive to improvement? **and is not any growth of these virtues in the community in itself the greatest of improvements?**
>
> If so, . . . there is needed more of those qualities to make the society de-cidedly progressive than merely to keep it permanent. (Mill, "Representative Government," 2013, KL: 42095–42100)

These ethical dispositions (integrity, justice, and prudence) tend to increase a community's ability to undertake cooperative enterprises. Increases in such virtues increase the productivity of many human endeavors and produces economic and social progress. Mill also suggests that the widespread internalization of such virtues is relatively new, even in the West.

> **Works of all sorts, impracticable to the savage or the half-civilized, are daily accomplished by civilized nations,** not by any greatness of faculties in the actual agents, but **through the fact that each is able to rely with certainty on the others for the portion of the work which they respectively undertake.**
>
> **The peculiar characteristic,** in short, **of civilized beings is the capacity of cooperation,** and this like other faculties **tends to improve by practice,** and becomes capable of assuming a constantly wider sphere of action.

> Accordingly, there is no more certain incident of the progressive change taking place in society, than the continual growth of the principle and practice of cooperation. (Mill, "Principles of Political Economy," 2013, KL 34678–34684)

To utilitarians, progress is simply an upward trend in aggregate and average utility. Mill suggests such progress is most likely when the normative dispositions that support cooperative enterprises are commonplace. These include industry, integrity, justice, and prudence—virtues very similar to those praised by Smith and La Court, two of which were not on Aristotle's list.

The addition of "industry" to lists of virtues is significant for this book in that it implies that such behavior was widely regarded to be praiseworthy during the period leading up to the great acceleration. Mill adds "integrity" to the list, which suggests that trustworthiness and honesty are increasingly considered to be important virtues. Such virtues increase gains to trade and allow team production to be more effective. Consequently, more such trades and enterprises are undertaken, as developed in Part I. In the language of contemporary economics, an increase in cooperative dispositions reduces free-riding and thereby monitoring costs, which causes both trade and team production to become more productive, and so more broadly used.

By including a role for internalized ethical rules in his explanation for progress, Mill is lending his support to the main hypothesis of this book. Progress, he argues, is partly caused by changes in internalized norms.

## Herbert Spencer (1820–1903): An Evolutionary Perspective on Utilitarian Philosophy

Mill was educated by his father with the intent of producing an intellectual with an interest in utilitarianism and public affairs. His father brought him into Bentham's utilitarian circle and secured a job for him in a major corporation. Herbert Spencer's education and career were far more haphazard. Spencer was born into a middle-class family of teachers who held a more relaxed theory of education than Mill's father did. At the age when Mill was learning Greek and Latin, Spencer was off exploring the forests, streams, and sand pits near his home. Rather than taking rigorous lessons from his father, Spencer was encouraged to figure things out for himself and was given substantial opportunities to do so, although he was also taught by both his father and uncle.

In his late teens and twenties, having shown some talent at geometry and algebra, Spencer pursued various careers in engineering, although none worked out. In contrast, Mill took a single job at age 17, where he worked for most of his adult life. Toward the end of his twenties, Spencer obtained a job at *The Economist* magazine, at which point he began to think seriously about becoming a writer, a career path for which he had little training and had not previously shown very much promise.[17]

Spencer subsequently wrote for the book-buying and magazine-reading public. He sold enough of his books and articles worldwide to make a living off them. Writing and thinking was his "day job" for most of his adult life.[18] Consequently, he was more widely read than Mill in the mid- to late nineteenth century, although somewhat less so in the twentieth century. Although they were both liberals, Spencer was a doctrinaire liberal and Mill a left or radical liberal. They freely criticized each other's philosophical work and policy arguments and occasionally corresponded with one another. Their writing was not a true dialogue, but often included short passages that indicated that the other's arguments were being challenged. Both *On Liberty* (1859) and *Utilitarianism* (1863) were partly responses to Spencer's *Social Statics* (1851).[19]

Spencer regarded himself to be a utilitarian, although he argued that other utilitarians had made several logical errors. In his first book, *Social Statics* (1851), Spencer argues that utilitarians are correct with respect to the best grounding principle for ethics, but they neglected many ambiguities in the utilitarian approach. He also argued that happiness cannot be analyzed without acknowledging an individual's and community's state of evolution. Both individuals and communities tend to change through time.[20]

Neither, if we compare the wishes of the gluttonous schoolboy with those of the earth-scorning transcendentalist into whom he may afterwards grow, do we find any constancy in the individual.

[17] Spencer's autobiography (Spencer, 2014) provides a detailed account of his early life, reconstructed for the most part from letters to and from his father and uncle, and between his father and uncle. His father and uncle were both successful teachers of the children of relatively wealthy families, a few of whom would live in their households at a time. Spencer and Mill knew each other, meeting at academic gatherings and occasionally for supper.

[18] Spencer's writing career was reasonably successful, but it should be acknowledged that it was ultimately made possible by well-timed modest inheritances from his uncles and father.

[19] Spencer's broader readership implies that he had a larger direct impact on mid-nineteenth-century politics and philosophy than Mill's did, although Mill's work was also very influential, especially among academia. Mill's perspective, however, was more influential than Spencer's in the long run. This was partly because politics moved in Mill's direction rather than Spencer's during the late nineteenth and twentieth centuries, and partly because of Mill's more careful mode of thought and expression. Spencer nonetheless made significant contributions to both utilitarianism and social science.

[20] Excerpts are from the digitized collection of Spencer's writings assembled by Amazon (Spencer, 2011). Individual works are cited, bolding is added by this author, and some modernization of punctuation is undertaken to improve readability. KL refers to Kindle locations in the collected works.

> So we may say, not only that every epoch and every people has its peculiar
> conceptions of happiness, but that no two men have like conceptions; and fur-
> ther, that in each man the conception is not the same at any two periods of life.
> (Spencer, "Social Statics," [1851] 2011, KL: 39568)

If individuals change through time in significant ways, obviously, it will be difficult if not impossible to determine the specific practices and rules of conduct
that will maximize long-term total happiness.

Spencer attempted to place utilitarian reasoning on firmer ground by
taking better account of human nature and the potential for individual and
social evolution. His new evolutionary approach to society and utilitarian
ethics were major innovations in both ethics and social theory. Previous work
(and most subsequent work) assumes that human nature is static and that the
goals of life, including ethical ones, are more or less permanent features of
human nature. Spencer regarded human nature—at least as far as aspirations
and interests are concerned—to be evolutionary phenomena and so tend to
improve through time. Ignoring this aspect of humanity, he argued, leads
to significant errors in utilitarian analysis and recommendations for public
policies.

Interest in Spencer's evolutionary approach to society, ethics, the human
mind, and biology greatly increased after Darwin published his famous
book on biological evolution in 1859. Although Spencer's ideas about biological evolution have been put aside as that science improved, his ideas
about the evolution of individuals and society remain important, if under
studied.

## Instinct, Intuition, and Reason in the Development of Ethics

Although Spencer had respect for man's rational ability, he argues that
instincts, rather than reason, often determine our choices, and that the
mechanisms of pleasure and pain have evolved to promote our survival
interests and those of the communities in which we live.

> Quite different [from reason], however, is the method of nature. Answering to each
> of the actions which it is requisite for us to perform, we find in ourselves some
> prompter called a desire. [T]he more essential the action, the more powerful is
> the impulse to its performance, and the more intense the gratification derived

therefrom. **Thus, the longings for food, for sleep, for warmth, are irresistible;** and quite independent of foreseen advantages....

**May we not then reasonably expect to find a like instrumentality** employed in impelling us to that line of conduct, in the due observance of which consists **what we call morality?** (Spencer, "Social Statics," [1851] 2011, KL: 39817–39833)

Spencer goes on to suggest that our natural moral intuitions are imperfect, just as our "geometric sense" tends to be.

[T]he perception of the primary laws of quantity bears the same relationship to mathematics, that this instinct of right bears to a moral system; and that as it is the office of the geometric sense to originate a geometric axiom, from which reason may deduce a scientific geometry, **so it is the office of the moral sense to originate a moral axiom, from which reason may develop a systematic morality.** (Spencer, "Social Statics," [1851] 2011, KL: 40072–40075)

Spencer argues that utilitarian philosophy ultimately rests on a well-evolved moral sense. Nonetheless, Spencer is not an intuitionist. He argues that one's understanding of morality is improved by education, reason, and observation, as is true of most other areas of life. Morality, like geometry, can be reduced to principles that allow us to better understand and use it.

## On the Evolutionary Basis of Happiness and Ethics

Spencer's theory of happiness and right and wrong are grounded in his evolutionary theory of man and society.

**Survival of the fittest insures that the faculties of every species of creature tend to adapt themselves to its mode of life.** It must be so with man. From the earliest times groups of **men whose feelings and conceptions were congruous with the conditions they lived under,** must, other things equal, have spread and **replaced those** whose feelings and conceptions were incongruous with their conditions. (Spencer, "Principles of Ethics," 2011, KL: 17267–17269)

Spencer argued that three types of conduct are relevant for survival: those with respect to (1) one's self, (2) one's children, and (3) fellow members of the same species. Insofar as internalized rules of conduct can be improved for any or all of these types of actions, there are evolutionary pressures that support such revisions.[21]

In keeping with utilitarian ideas, Spencer argues that most conduct that is judged in moral terms tends to be concerned with effects on persons outside the family. It is necessary to praise only a subset of one's actions, because taking care of oneself and one's children is largely compatible with self-interest and is arguably more strongly "hard wired" by evolutionary pressures.

> These ethical judgments we pass on self-regarding acts are ordinarily little emphasized; partly because the promptings of the self-regarding desires, generally strong enough, do not need moral enforcement, and partly because the promptings of the other-regarding desires, less strong, and often overridden, do need moral enforcement. (Spencer, "Principles of Ethics," 2011, KL: 12535–12537)

Spencer also suggests that evolutionary pressures on moral behavior tend to be strongest (and best) during times of peace.

> Recognizing men as the beings whose conduct is most evolved, let us ask under what conditions their conduct, in all three aspects of its evolution, reaches its limit. . . .
>   [T]he limit of evolution can be reached by conduct only in permanently peaceful societies. That perfect adjustment of acts to ends in maintaining individual life and rearing new individuals, which is effected by each without hindering others from effecting like perfect adjustments, is, in its very definition, shown to constitute a kind of conduct that can be approached only as war decreases and dies out. (Spencer, "Principles of Ethics," 2011, KL: 12445–12461)

In the limit, Spencer argues that the coevolution of man and society produces rules of conduct that promote self-development, assure the next generation, and create a society in which prospects for survival are maximized. It also tends to align the human sense of pleasure with conduct that enhances prospects for human survival. Utilitarianism, in this Spencerian characterization of it, has both biological and social evolutionary foundations.

Spencer argues that all viable ethical theories favor life over death and pleasure over pain and so advance utilitarian aims. To do otherwise would be to adopt rules of conduct that are in effect suicidal, and so the persons and

---

[21] "Survival of the fittest" is Spencer's phrase rather than Darwin's, although it was coined well after *On the Origin of the Species* was published (1859 vs. 1879).

communities following such rules are not likely to survive in the long run. He makes this point repeatedly in his writings, arguing from somewhat different perspectives according to the audience that he is attempting to reach, the critics that he is attempting to refute, and the main subject being addressed.

He argues that it is survivorship that accounts for the broad overlap in the ethical theories of communities at similar levels of social evolution.[22]

## The Heterogeneity of Mankind and the Equal Liberty Principle

Although general survival interests and therefore moral instincts are shared among men and women, individuals vary enough that achieving happiness is a bit different in every case, because individuals have different capacities and potentialities.

> **The gratification of a faculty is produced by its exercise.** To be agreeable that exercise must be proportionate to the power of the faculty; if it is insufficient discontent arises, and its excess produces weariness. **Hence, to have complete felicity is to have all the faculties exerted in the ratio of their several developments;** and an ideal arrangement of circumstances calculated to secure this constitutes the standard of "greatest happiness"; **but the minds of no two individuals contain the same combination of elements.** (Spencer, "Social Statics," [1851] 2011, KL 39574–39558)

Given this, there is no single precise guide for life that will work for everyone at a given time or in all times and places.

One might, however, identify a few general rules or maxims that are likely to advance happiness (or survivorship) in most circumstances and communities, regardless of their state of evolution. Spencer argues that the principle of "equal liberty" is one such principle.

> **Thus are we brought by several routes to the same conclusion.** Whether we reason our way from those fixed conditions under which only the Divine Idea—greatest happiness, can be realized—whether we draw our inferences from man's constitution, considering him as a congeries of faculties—or whether we listen to the

---

[22] Spencer is well aware that he was doing so, which gave rise to one of his most enduring quotes: "Hence an amount of repetition which to some will probably appear tedious. I do not, however, much regret this almost unavoidable result; for only by varied iteration can alien conceptions be forced on reluctant minds" (Spencer, "Principles of Ethics," 2011, KL 12213–12216).

monitions of a certain mental agency, which seems to have the function of guiding us in this matter, **we are alike taught as the law of right social relationships, that— Every man has freedom to do all that he wills, provided he infringes not the equal freedom of any other man.** Though further qualifications of the liberty of action thus asserted may be necessary, yet we have seen (p. 89) that **in the just regulation of a community no further qualifications of it can be recognized.** (Spencer, "Social Statics," [1851] 2011, KL: 41393–41399)

Spencer goes on to argue that the equal liberty principle has a number of implications about the proper bounds of law and governance in a community. Among these are:

These are such self-evident corollaries from our first principle as scarcely to need a separate statement. **If every man has freedom to do all that he wills, provided he infringes not the equal freedom of any other man, it is manifest that he has a claim to his life: for without it he can do nothing that he has willed; and to his personal liberty: for the withdrawal of it partially, if not wholly, restrains him from the fulfilment of his will.** It is just as clear, too, that **each man is forbidden to deprive his fellow of life or liberty: inasmuch as he cannot do this without breaking the law,** which, in asserting his freedom, declares that he shall not infringe "the equal freedom of any other." **For he who is killed or enslaved is obviously no longer equally free with his killer or enslaver.** (Spencer, "Social Statics," [1851] 2011, KL: 41550–41556)

Moreover, inequalities based on gender, per se, are not allowed.

Equity knows no difference of sex. In its vocabulary, **the word man must be understood in a generic, and not in a specific sense.** The law of equal freedom manifestly applies to the whole race—female as well as male. (Spencer, "Social Statics," [1851] 2011, KL: 42341–42346)

It bears noting that *Social Statics* was written shortly before slavery was finally overturned throughout the West and well before woman's suffrage had become a great issue.

Spencer goes on to note that many inequalities are consistent with the equal liberty principle. Individuals, for example, may have different capacities, talents, inclinations to industry, good fortune, or aspirations.

If, therefore, out of many starting with like fields of activity, **one obtains, by his greater strength, greater ingenuity, or greater application, more gratifications** and sources of gratification than the rest, and **does this without in any way trenching upon the equal freedom of the rest**, the moral law assigns him an exclusive right to all those extra gratifications and sources of gratification; **nor can the rest take them from him without claiming for themselves greater liberty of action than he claims**, and thereby violating that law. (Spencer, "Social Statics," [1851] 2011, KL: 41940–41944)

## Equal Liberty and Commercial Rights

With respect to commerce, Spencer uses the logic of equal liberty to argue in favor of property and against governmental constraints on exchange, usury, and industry.

[T]he **right of exchange may be asserted as a direct deduction from the law of equal freedom**. For of the two who voluntarily make an exchange, neither assumes greater liberty of action than the other, and fellow men are uninterfered with—remain possessed of just as much liberty of action as before. Though completion of the exchange may shut out sundry of them from advantageous transactions, yet as their abilities to enter into such transactions depended wholly on the assent of another man, they cannot be included in their normal spheres of action (Spencer, "Principles of Ethics," 2011, KL: 24197–241201)

Of course, with **the right of free exchange** goes **the right of free contract**: a postponement, now understood, now specified, in the completion of an exchange, serving to turn the one into the other. (Spencer, "Principles of Ethics," 2011, KL: 24223–24224)

By the **right to free industry** is here meant **the right of each man to carry on his occupation, whatever it may be, after whatever manner he prefers or thinks best, so long as he does not trespass against his neighbors: taking the benefits or the evils of his way, as the case may be. Self-evident as this right now** seems, it seemed by no means self-evident to people in past times. (Spencer, "Principles of Ethics," 2011, KL: 24275–24277)

According to Spencer, commerce is an area of life in which fundamental rights exist. It is not simply a means of earning a living, but a sphere of legitimate activity that is implied by and in accord with both the equal liberty principle and the utility principle. Except for slavery and trade that undermines national defense, trade is a good for individuals, families, and society.

Spencer thus concludes that there is a right to participate in commerce—which implies that individuals should be free to choose whatever occupation that they wish—again with very minor exceptions (no professional robbers, enslavers, or murderers). Spencer also notes that the field of economics as it developed during the nineteenth century reached conclusions about free trade that were broadly similar to those reached through his equal-liberty-based analysis.

> [Economics] teaches that **meddlings with commerce by prohibitions and bounties are detrimental**; and the law of equal freedom excludes them as wrong.
>
> That speculators should be allowed to operate on the food markets as they see well is an inference drawn by political economy; and by the fundamental principle of equity they are justified in doing this.
>
> Penalties upon usury are proved by political economists to be injurious; and by the law of equal freedom they are negated as involving infringements of rights. (Spencer, "Principles of Ethics," 2011, KL: 24595–24598)

Spencer also argues that altruism in its positive and negative forms becomes more common as one shifts from a militaristic to an industrial society, which is to say, from a coercive to a cooperative society.

> But **as civilization advances and status passes into contract**, there comes daily experience of the relation between advantages enjoyed and labor given: the industrial system maintaining, through supply and demand, a due adjustment of the one to the other.
>
> And **this growth of voluntary cooperation—this exchange of services under agreement, has been necessarily accompanied by decrease of aggressions one upon another, and increase of sympathy: leading to exchange of services beyond agreement**. That is to say, the more distinct assertions of individual claims and more rigorous apportioning of personal enjoyments to efforts expended, **has gone hand in hand with growth of that negative altruism shown in equitable conduct and that positive altruism shown in gratuitous aid**. (Spencer, "Principles of Ethics," 2011, KL: 15878–15883)

Commerce thus supports both forms of altruistic behavior and other conduct deemed praiseworthy by contemporary philosophers. In this, Spencer is in agreement with Bastiat, although in Spencer's case, harmony results because ethics and society coevolve.[23]

The coevolution of man, ethics, and society also implies that in the limit, as man and internalized codes of conduct reach perfection, coercion (and government) becomes unnecessary.

It is a mistake to assume that government must necessarily last forever. The institution marks a certain stage of civilization—is natural to a particular phase of human development. It is not essential but incidental. As amongst the Bushmen we find a state antecedent to government; so may there be one in which it shall have become extinct. Already has it lost something of its importance....

Government, however, is an institution originating in man's imperfection; an institution confessedly begotten by necessity out of evil; one which might be dispensed with were the world peopled with the unselfish, the conscientious, the philanthropic; one, in short, inconsistent with this same "highest conceivable perfection." (Spencer, "Social Statics," [1851] 2011, KL: 39713–39763)[24]

## Spencer and "Doctrinaire Liberalism"

Spencer was one of the most widely read and influential writers of nonfiction in the second half of the nineteenth century. He wrote on a broad range of subjects, including psychology, sociology, constitutional theory, and biology. In his mind, all these subjects were linked by the common thread of biological and social evolution. His policy views were well known to sophisticated persons in Europe in the late nineteenth and early twentieth centuries, and they attracted a broad range of critical responses, from Mill to Nietzsche.

Many of his ideas carried forward after his death in 1903. Although less read and cited in the twentieth and twenty-first centuries than Mill, his work in sociology, ethics, and evolutionary psychology continue to attract attention.

---

[23] By negative altruism, Spencer means actions that are not undertaken because they would harm another. By positive altruism, Spencer means actions that are taken—at least partly—because they provide benefits for another.

[24] This idea is part of Spencer's critique of mainstream utilitarianism of the Bentham and Mill variety: "A system of moral philosophy professes to be a code of correct rules for the control of human beings—fitted for the regulation of the best, as well as the worst members of the race—applicable, if true, to the guidance of humanity in its highest conceivable perfection. Government, however, is an institution originating in man's imperfection; an institution confessedly begotten by necessity out of evil; one which might be dispensed with were the world peopled with the unselfish, the conscientious, the philanthropic; one, in short, inconsistent with this same 'highest conceivable perfection.' How, then, can that be a true system of morality which adopts government as one of its premises?" (Spencer, "Social Statics," [1851] 2011, KL: 39759–39763).

That his work was influential in the United States is, for example, suggested by the Holmes dissent to the majority decision of the Supreme Court in the famous 1905 Lockner case. The majority opinion implicitly adopts Spencer's reasoning with respect to freedom to contract, arguing that:

> The **general right to make a contract in relation to his business is part of the liberty protected by the Fourteenth Amendment**, and this includes the right to purchase and sell labor, except as controlled by the State in the legitimate exercise of its police power.

The minority dissent by Oliver Wendell Holmes critiques the majority's reasoning by suggesting that it is grounded in Spencer's arguments with respect to freedom of contract, rather than legal precedent.

> The liberty of the citizen to do as he likes so long as he does not interfere with the liberty of others to do the same, which has been a shibboleth for **some well-known writers**, is interfered with by school laws, by the post office, by every state or municipal institution which takes his money for purposes thought desirable, whether he likes it or not. **The 14th Amendment does not enact Mr. Herbert Spencer's** *Social Statics*.

Although the final Lockner decision was narrower than these excerpts suggest, it is clear that Spencer's positions were both mainstream and taken seriously in the United States and elsewhere at the turn of the century.[25]

With respect to ethics, Spencer provided a new evolution-based interpretation of utilitarianism, which he argued supported a wide range of conventional virtues, including justice, generosity, humanity, veracity, obedience, industry, temperance, chastity, marriage, and parenthood. With respect to commerce, Spencer, like most other nineteenth-century utilitarians, regards voluntary exchange to be a process that increases aggregate happiness. He acknowledges that by praising wealth itself, regardless of how it is acquired, some undermining of morals does occur.[26] However, Spencer is generally

---

[25] Rehnquist (2001, pp. 113–114) provides a short summary of "antiprogressive" Supreme Court decisions.

[26] This is most evident in his essay on "The Morals of Trade" (Spencer 2011). In that piece, Spencer argues that much of the unethical behavior observed in markets (fraud) arises because people in England admire wealth without regard to how it has been obtained, rather than only wealth that has been obtained through industry, honesty, and frugality. He argues that morals are somewhat higher in his own time than in former times, and that further improvements are underway, partly because of the internalization of utilitarian ideas. "And happily the signs of this more moral public opinion are showing themselves. It is becoming a tacitly received doctrine that the rich should not, as in bygone times, spend their lives in personal

more concerned about government restraints on trade than on any corrupting influence that it may have on individuals.

Spencer's grounding of pleasure and pain in the survivorship pressures of evolution was essentially unique at the time of his writing (and remains largely so among contemporary philosophers). Evolutionary pressures, he argued, produced mechanisms for pleasure and pain, and a common moral sense. These, he argued, account for both the overlapping lists of virtues developed by philosophers and for similarities in the maxims adopted by societies at similar stages of development.

The broad appeal of his writing suggests that many of his arguments were grounded on moral intuitions that were commonplace during the second half of the nineteenth century: that industry was virtuous, that commerce was a powerful system through which aggregate utility was being increased, that individuals should be free to pursue any career that advantaged themselves as long as it did not undermine the equal liberties of others.

## Utilitarian Support for Democracy and Commerce in the Nineteenth Century

Bentham, Mill, and Spencer reached many similar conclusions—ones that their readers likely shared—that are of interest for the purposes of this volume. Their conclusions generally provided new support for both commerce and democratic governance. Each provided ethical defenses of careers in commerce and commercial systems that were broader than the religious ones proposed by Baxter and Barclay, and the secular ones of Montesquieu and Smith. Commerce from the utilitarian perspective is not an ethically neutral activity, as it was in Smith's and Kant's accounts, but a morally relevant activity because it increases aggregate utility, understood as the sum of the net happiness of all members in a community. The realization of mutual gains from trade implies that commerce is good—it tends to increase aggregate utility. Thus, to be gainfully and honestly employed in markets was a civic duty—to be industrious—as it had been in Baxter's religion-based theory.

gratification; but should devote them to the general welfare. Year by year is the improvement of the people occupying a larger share of the attention of the upper classes. Year by year are they voluntarily devoting more energy to furthering the material and mental progress of the masses. And those among them who do not join in the discharge of these high functions, are beginning to be looked upon with more or less contempt by their own order. This latest and most hopeful fact in human history—this new and better chivalry—promises to evolve a higher standard of honor, and so to ameliorate many evils: among others those which we have detailed" (Spencer 2011, KL: 76319–76324).

In addition to providing additional support for commerce, nineteenth-century utilitarians provided new support for both democratic governance and constitutional constraints that tend to assure equal protection of the law. For example, Mill and Spencer both supported women's suffrage more than a half century before it became commonplace in the West. Each was interested in voting rules and constitutional reforms that tended to increase the electoral foundations of public policy. And each believed that the proper scope of government action was bounded. Again, these conclusions are mainly of interest for this book because similar—if not quite as well reasoned—conclusions were likely already in the minds of their many readers during this period. Such conclusion were not outliers, but mainstream during the nineteenth century, especially in its second half.

With respect to policies that affected markets, Bentham, Mill, and Spencer were generally more concerned with governmental barriers to exchange and favoritism, than about the commercial society that was emerging around them. Policymakers should take complete account of the effects of their policies on all members of society. With respect to markets, they agreed that governments should adopt more or less "laissez-faire" policies. Society would generally be improved by removing restraints on domestic and international trade (and not imposing new ones), although only Spencer advocated essentially fully laissez-faire policies—albeit he too thought there were a few exceptions to that general rule.

All three agreed that most individuals were, and should be, largely motivated by self-interest. Self-interest was not a problem for society, given appropriate civil laws, because the results of social intercourse under such laws tend to increase utility both for individuals and for society at large. Thus, most people should substantially be left alone to make their own decisions—given well-conceived civil and criminal laws. Commercial development tends to be good both because of increased material comfort and because it tends to support the virtues of industry, frugality, integrity and, to some extent, altruism, which may be direct sources of happiness for the persons internalizing such norms.

There were caveats to their support for commerce, the most serious of which were developed by Mill with respect to the significance of what would later be called externalities—costs borne by third parties not directly involved in the exchanges that produced them. However, even Mill regarded such concerns to be relatively unimportant, concluding that most persons should be free to engage in the activities that added to their and their family's wealth and happiness. Only activities that obviously harm others should be routinely subject to regulation by the state. Other voluntary cooperative relationships were the main engines of progress.

## The Marginalist Revolution, Welfare Economics, and the Monetization of Utility

Although the essential logic of utilitarian analysis was worked out in the nineteenth century, significant developments and extensions of it occurred in the late nineteenth century and throughout the twentieth century. These were partly associated with the new, more complete models of trade and price determination worked out by a group that came to be referred to as neoclassical economists. These "economists" developed models of decision-making and market prices based on ideas previously worked out by utilitarians, but which took account of diminishing marginal utility. The new "marginalist" theories had solved the so-called diamond-water paradox—that diamonds sell at a higher price than water does, although water is necessary for life and diamonds are not.

The neoclassical solution to that paradox was that the extra utility generated by an extra unit of a good (marginal utility) varies with the quantity of the good that one already has. The first unit of a good or service is devoted to its most valuable use, the second to the second most valuable, and so on. Since water was plentiful in the West, the last unit of water tended to produce relatively little extra utility, whereas the last diamond tended to produce relatively large increases in utility (at least for those who admire them) because there were so few diamonds. The price of water was below that of diamonds because the marginal utility of the last drop of water used was lower than that of the last diamond purchased. Prices reflect marginal conditions, rather than total or average conditions.

Diminishing marginal utility also had implications for the distribution of income that tended to reduce support for free markets to some extent—at least among left liberals and social democrats. However, utilitarians (including most Western economists) remained broadly supportive of commerce. Indeed, as the benefits of extended market networks became better understood, overall support tended to increase. By the mid-twentieth century, the extent of markets (gross national product) was routinely used to compare the quality of life across communities, regions, nation-states, and continents.

The last utilitarian scholar reviewed in this chapter is Alfred Pigou, who characterizes the utilitarian perspective of left liberals or moderate social democrats of the late nineteenth and early twentieth centuries—a perspective that had a profound influence on economic thinking during the twentieth century and on public policies insofar as politicians and voters were influenced by economic analyses. It is a perspective that differs in many respects from that of the doctrinaire liberals of the nineteenth century, but which remained broadly supportive of commerce and commercial development.

## Alfred C. Pigou (1877–1959)

Alfred Pigou was raised in an upper middle-class family in England and was educated at Harrow School and Cambridge University. His academic training was in moral philosophy, history, and economics. He became professor of political economy at Cambridge's King's College in 1908, a position that he held until 1943. His most important work is his book *The Economics of Welfare* (1920). It develops a new utilitarian-based economic toolkit for policy analysis that would later be referred to as *welfare economics*. Pigou combined utilitarian reasoning and neoclassical economics in a manner that provided new operational methods for appraising the relative merits of the outcomes of various types of markets and public policies.

Nineteenth-century utilitarians had gradually recognized the difficulty of thinking about all the utility ramifications of individual actions and policies and began attempting to derive rules of conduct that could serve as practical guides for day-to-day decision-making among individuals and governments. Mill's "do no harm" principle and Spencer's "equal liberty principle" are two of the many efforts to contrive such rules. Pigou attempted to make the utility principle quantifiable rather than to develop rules of conduct. Moreover, as an economist, he was more concerned with public policy issues than an individuals' character or moral conduct.

Pigou was more critical of commercial activity than Bentham, Mill, or Spencer, but nonetheless, he begins by arguing that gross national product (the social dividend) can be used as a first approximation or estimate of aggregate utility.

**The one obvious instrument of measurement available in social life is money.**
Hence, the range of our inquiry becomes restricted to that part of social welfare that can be brought directly or indirectly into relation with the measuring-rod of money. This part of welfare may be called economic welfare.
     **It is not, indeed, possible to separate it in any rigid way from other parts, for the part which can be brought into relation with a money measure will be**

different according as we mean by can, "can easily" or "can with mild straining" or "can with violent straining." (Pigou, *Economics of Welfare*, 1920, KL: 295–300)

The preceding discussion makes it plain that any rigid inference from effects on economic welfare to effects on total welfare is out of the question. In some fields the divergence between the two effects will be insignificant, but in others it will be very wide.

Nevertheless, I submit that, in the absence of special knowledge, there is room for a judgment of probability. When we have ascertained the effect of any cause on economic welfare, we may, unless, of course, there is specific evidence to the contrary, regard this effect as probably equivalent in direction, though not in magnitude, to the effect on total welfare. (Pigou, *Economics of Welfare*, 1920, KL: 438–443)

GENERALLY speaking, economic causes act upon the economic welfare of any country, not directly, but through the making and using of that objective counterpart of economic welfare which economists call the national dividend or national income. Just as economic welfare is that part of total welfare which can be brought directly or indirectly into relation with a money measure, so the national dividend [RGNP] is that part of the objective income of the community, including, of course, income derived from abroad, which can be measured in money. (Pigou, *Economics of Welfare*, 1920, KL: 601–604)

Pigou argues that the extent of commerce is correlated with aggregate utility, although it is not a perfect measure of aggregate utility. The greater the extent of commerce, the greater is aggregate utility, other things being equal.

This monetization of utility provided a new measurable utilitarian basis for both supporting and criticizing commercial development. Policies and activities which increased national income were good, and those which diminished it were bad. The money-based index of aggregate utility also had implications for public policy. Other things being equal, governments should strive to maximize the extent of national income, which is simply a measure of the overall extent of commerce.

However, other things were not always equal, for reasons that Pigou explores in his book. Pigou argued that commerce is a good economic system, but it may not be the best system possible. Thus, Pigou argued that governments should do more than simply enforce civil law and provide national defense. After arguing that the extent of commerce could be used as a proxy for social welfare, Pigou shifts his attention to various aspects of commerce that do not tend to maximize aggregate utility. For example, he argues that the distributions of wealth and income generated by commerce do not necessarily maximize aggregate utility.

**Nevertheless, it is evident that any transference of income from a relatively rich man to a relatively poor man of similar temperament, since it enables more intense wants, to be satisfied at the expense of less intense wants, must increase** the aggregate sum of satisfaction.

The old "law of diminishing utility" thus leads securely to the proposition: **Any cause which increases the absolute share of real income in the hands of the poor, provided that it does not lead to a contraction in the size of the national dividend from any point of view, will, in general, increase economic welfare.** (Pigou, *Economics of Welfare*, 1920, KL: 1561–1565)

IT is evident that, provided the dividend accruing to the poor is not diminished, **increases in the size of the aggregate national dividend, if they occur in isolation without anything else whatever happening, must involve increases in economic welfare.** (Pigou, *Economics of Welfare*, 1920, KL: 1468–1470)

The logic of diminishing marginal utility implies that redistribution from the rich to the poor can increase aggregate utility, whenever it can be done without reducing national income.[27]

Some of Pigou's arguments regarding the possibilities for increasing aggregate utility beyond that associated with market outcomes might be classified as socialist. For example, he argues that the government can run some industries as well or better than private entities, as with electricity and telephone companies. However, his argument nearly always aims to maximize the size of the economy, and in this sense takes for granted that commerce is generally both useful and virtuous.

Although policy-orientated utilitarians often neglect the importance of internalized ethical dispositions, Pigou does not entirely do so, noting that what he refers to as the social virtues are imperatives for life in a community. As a utilitarian, he naturally emphasizes those that are most important for utilitarian outcomes: honesty and taking account of how one's behavior affects the entire community.

As a member of a society with interests in common with others, the individual consciously and unconsciously develops the social virtues.

**Honesty becomes imperative** and is enforced by the whole group on the individual, **loyalty to the whole group is made an essential** for the better development

---

[27] The modern term *gross national product* (GNP) is used rather than Pigou's "social dividend," because it is more familiar to readers and has essentially the same meaning. The notion of a social dividend had been introduced by Alfred Marshall. Pigou subsequently played a role in the development of the macro-economic measure that came to be known as GNP. The use of GNP as a proxy for aggregate utility is not perfect, as noted by Pigou. See Chipman and Moore (1976) for a short critique of GNP as a proxy for aggregate utility.

of individual powers. **To cheat the society is to injure a neighbor.** (Pigou, *Economics of Welfare*, 1920, KL: 376–379)

Pigou's analysis shifted the debate from gains-from-trade-based arguments of doctrinaire liberals to the cost-benefit analysis of left liberals. Does a policy increase aggregate benefits (measured in dollars or some other currency) more than it increases aggregate costs? If so, such policies will increase the national dividend (RGNP) and are very likely to increase aggregate utility. When it is acknowledged that significant externality and monopoly problems exist that are not adequately addressed through informal norms or civil law, it may be possible for new regulations or taxes to be adopted that increase rather than reduce aggregate utility. Pigou also argues that aggregate utility can be increased by promoting public education and social virtue.

As a consequence of Pigou's analysis and extensions of it, twentieth-century utilitarians and economists tended to support broader interventions in markets than those advocated by the doctrinaire liberals of the nineteenth-century.

A variety of philosophical and ethical issues are associated with the Pigovian approach to public policies, but most of these are beyond the scope of this book. In addition, there are practical economic questions as well, many of which are empirical in nature. How much redistribution can be undertaken without undermining the social dividend? To what extent can government be expected to pursue utilitarian ends? Such issues were taken up later in the twentieth century. The re-emergence of contractarian approaches to governance was induced partly because of concerns with utilitarianism and welfare economics as a guide to public policy. The appendix to this chapter provides short overviews of two influential late twentieth-century contractarians.

## Conclusion: A Rising and Deepening Tide of Moral Support for Commerce

Part III's review of ethical theories leads to several conclusions that are important for the book and its related research project. First, the survey demonstrates that ethics and economics historically have not been entirely independent subjects. Philosophers who made significant contributions to ethics routinely used choices in markets to illustrate the relevance of their theories. A subset of those philosophers also made significant contributions to economic theory in the period before the great division of the social sciences emerged in the late nineteenth and early twentieth centuries. Adam Smith and Alfred Marshall, for example, both held academic positions in moral philosophy. Jeremy Bentham and John Stuart Mill both wrote economic textbooks as well as philosophical books.

Second, scholars have long differed in both the ethical theories that they applied and their conclusions about the role of commerce in a good life and good society. There is no unique theory of "the good." Although all but two of the scholars reviewed were generally supportive of market activities, their conclusions differed both in the degree of their support and in their reservations about commerce. These variations were partly due to differences in the ethical theories applied and partly due to differences in the commonplace sentiments concerning markets in their lifetimes and places.

Third, in the period between 1600 and 1900, there is evidence of a trend in both support for commerce and the depth of that support. That trend is very likely to be present in their respective communities because the survey has focused for the most part on scholars whose ethical theories had empirical foundations, were widely read, and used what were considered "obvious" illustrations of norms and moral behavior from their respective societies. The empirical grounding of ethical theories allows them to be used as a window into mainstream ideas concerning the good life, good society, and virtue and vice in the societies in which the individual philosophers lived. Table 12.1 summarizes their main conclusions regarding commerce and their reservations about the pursuit of wealth.

Most of the scholars reviewed supported commerce and its associated prosperity. However, that support deepened and broadened in the period covered, while reservations generally narrowed and diminished. Evidence of their more positive assessments about the role of commerce in a good life is provided by their lists of virtues, with industriousness, frugality, and prudence added to the lists of ancient scholars—and others left off. Evidence of their assessments of the proper role of commerce in a good society is provided by their conclusions about appropriateness of regulations for commerce. For example, the regulation of usury (credit markets) was generally supported until the late eighteenth century.

The shift from theologically based assessments to secular ones provides evidence of a broadening of arguments that tended to support commerce. One did not have to be a member of a particular sect or society to be persuaded that commercial progress was generally a property of attractive societies. Arguments that placed greater reliance on reason, observation, and expert opinion could be found persuasive by a wide variety religious men and women during this period.

**Table 12.1** A Short Overview of Conclusions Reached by the Scholars Reviewed in Part I

| Scholar | Ethical Support for the Role of Commerce in a Good Life and/or Society | Reservations |
|---|---|---|
| Erasmus | Very limited if any support. | A corrupting influence on mankind and the church. |
| More | Commerce and production should be minimized in order to free time for contemplation. | Commerce diverts time and attention away from more important activities. |
| Grotius | International trade and trade in general build comity and have divine support. | None mentioned. |
| La Court | Industry and frugality lead to prosperity, which is supported by divine intent. | The manner in which wealth should be obtained is through production and trade rather than expropriation. |
| Baxter | Industry and frugality lead to prosperity, which is supported by divine intent. Secular "Callings" exist. | Wealth should be used primarily for the religious and public interest rather than for material satisfaction. |
| Locke | The protection of life, liberty, and property are the purpose for which governments are created. | None mentioned, but he neither explicitly supports nor criticizes the pursuit of wealth |
| Franklin | A life is made both better and more prosperous through ethical behavior. Commerce is at the center of a productive life. | The pursuit of wealth should not be one's only end. |
| Smith | Prosperity obtained through fair and honest means is praiseworthy in both individuals and nations, although for the most part commercial activities are morally neutral. | The pursuit of wealth can conflict with other ethical norms and the result may be less than praiseworthy. |
| Kant | Ethics concerns behavior motivated by the performance of one's duties, which is rarely the case in commerce. | Commerce may promote praiseworthy behavior without being a moral activity. |
| Bentham | Every trade produces gains for all the parties involved and therefore increases aggregate utility and is moral—or at least not immoral. | As long as trade is not based on fraud or coercion, it is moral. |
| Bastiat | There is a general harmony between ethical and economic interests. | As long as commerce is not based on fraud or coercion, it is moral. |
| Mill | Laissez-faire polices are best, because government restraints on trade tend to reduce rather than increase aggregate utility. | As long as commerce is not based on fraud or coercion, and does not harm others, it is moral. |
| Spencer | The equal liberty principle tends to increase aggregate utility and implies freedom of contract. Trade is both allowed and is to be encouraged. | As long as commerce is not based on fraud or coercion, and does not trespass another's rights, it is moral. |
| Pigou | The extent of commerce (RGNP) is a good approximation for aggregate utility and should be maximized. | Free markets may fail to maximize aggregate utility because of externality, monopoly, and distribution of income problems. |

There is also evidence of a shift away from analyses based on individual "duty" and "character" to ones that focus on the consequences of actions and policies on others within the community of interest. Such an orientation would make it easier for individuals to accept innovations and market outcomes that were not personally beneficial. It would also induce individuals to take greater account of externalities generated by their choices.

The consequences of extended networks of trade, production, and innovation were given increasingly positive assessments, partly because of shifts in ethical theories, partly because of changes in economic theory, but also because those shifts tended to make commercial enterprises a more effective means of increasing human welfare, as was widely recognized by those participating in trading networks. Products improved. Service improved. Income rose while workweeks shrank. Indeed, toward the end of the period covered, income and the associated extent of material comfort became the most widely used metrics for evaluating lifestyles and societies.

Growth rates of commerce also came to be regarded as important indices of a societies merit. The faster commerce grew, the better is a system of government or lifestyle is often deemed to be. Such conclusions could not differ more from the two scholars used to characterize late medieval thinking about markets, both of whom revealed deep skepticism about commerce and the persons who entered commerce. According to Erasmus and More, only corrupt money grubbers would undertake such careers and their associated practices. Leisure was to be maximized rather than minimized.

This three-century increase in support for markets arguably plateaued in the West during the late nineteenth and early twentieth centuries, as the arguments of left liberals such as Pigou became increasingly influential in the twentieth century. However, left liberals also generally supported commerce and a bounded domain for governance. The domain of governance was to be expanded, but not unbounded. Its new responsibilities included externality problems, market concentration, and modest redistribution (those measures that did not reduce the social dividend).

That progress was widely associated with the commercialization of society was indicated by the fact that very few persons in the twentieth century longed for the pastoral lives of subsistence farming, with its hard work with hand tools in farm fields, risks of famine, shorter life spans, and very limited material comforts.[28]

---

[28] It should be acknowledged that most of the scholars covered are proto-liberals or liberals, so would tend to support open market and political systems. That the extent of their support and reasons for that support change through time can be argued to provide even stronger support for a trend in support, because many other things (the scholars' own liberal inclinations) were held constant. However, the authors were not chosen with this in mind. Some were chosen because they were mentioned in Weber's widely read

Shifts in norms also accounted for much of the greater efficiency of markets and market organizations, as noted by many observers of the late nineteenth and early twentieth centuries. Mill and Spencer both noted the increase in cooperative dispositions within the West and contrasted them with their dearth elsewhere. Such observations and remarks were not limited to the English-speaking world. Max Weber ([1905] 1958), for example, also argued that changes in norms both launched and sustained capitalism, by which he means the commercial society that had emerged in the late nineteenth century.

> [I]n general also **an attitude which, at least during working hours, is freed from continual calculations of how the customary wage may be earned with a maximum of comfort and a minimum of exertion. Labor must, on the contrary, be performed as if it were an absolute end in itself, a calling.**
>
> But **such an attitude is by no means a product of nature.** It cannot be evoked by low wages or high ones alone, but can only be the product of a long and arduous **process of education.**
>
> **Today,** capitalism, once in the saddle, **can recruit its laboring force** in all industrial countries with comparative ease. In **the past this was in every case an extremely difficult problem.** (Weber, *Protestant Ethic,* [1905] 1958, KL: 312–316)

By the time Spencer had finished his ethics and Weber began thinking about markets and the origins of capitalism, the great acceleration of commerce and the emergence of nationwide commercial societies was well under way throughout the West. Life in the new more broadly commercial societies was widely regarded to be more attractive than lives in former times by both the persons living in them and those observing them from afar. Migration patterns, for example, were nearly always from less prosperous (less commercial) places to ones characterized by more extended networks of exchange, production, and innovation—which is to say, to more commercial societies.

All this is not to say that Bastiat's or Spencer's perfectly evolved harmony between private actions and social consequences had emerged in 1800, 1900, or in 2000. Nor is it to say that the decrease in the scope of religion typical among scientists and secular philosophers was universal during the nineteenth or

book ([1905] 1958) on the emergence of capitalism. Others were included because their writings remain famous today and were also famous during their lifetimes. Any selection bias present, perhaps paradoxically, provides even stronger evidence of a trend in Western thought during the period covered. It is because the early scholars' ideas are still relevant for today's scholars who reside in commercial societies that they are still read. Without a trend in support for commerce, contemporary interest in their books and conclusions would be far less, and their readerships would not have continued for centuries.

early twentieth centuries. For many, religion and miracles remained important facts of life, and moral duties continued to be largely defined by their preferred divine texts. Secular conclusions about markets, however, were increasingly incorporated into interpretations of divine texts. Nor is it to say that unfettered exchange or efforts to obtain material comforts were universally supported in the late nineteenth century. Critics as well as supporters always existed, but the balance favored supporters during most of this period in most of the West.

The quest for material comforts through careers in commerce had become both praiseworthy and central to life and society throughout the West. The idea that hard work, trade, profit, and innovation were virtuous activities had taken hold and influenced lifestyles, public policies, and rates of economic progress.[29]

The idea of progress had also become increasingly central to Western thought, as noted by Bury ([1921] 2011).[30] Change was increasingly regarded to be the natural state of affairs, and change for the better was regarded to be the rule rather than the exception. The good society was no longer thought of in static terms. Shifts in norms and lifestyles were widely considered to be good on average; as possible improvements, rather than threats or nuisances to be blocked or ameliorated. New theories and products were often better than the old.

A productive creative life had become a good life, and a productive innovative commercial society, a good society.

---

[29] That radical opposition to commerce was a minority viewpoint in the late nineteenth and early twentieth centuries can be deduced from electoral outcomes in northern Europe and in the United States. "Left liberals" were relatively numerous and more influential than right liberals by the early twentieth century, as evident in policies with respect to public education and safety net programs in the United Kingdom and France. Only a handful of relatively moderate Progressive Party candidates were elected to office in the United States during the late nineteenth and early twentieth centuries.

Left liberals did not oppose the commercial society per se; rather they attempted to open society further by equalizing opportunities. Some of the most "radical" argued in favor of shifting the bargaining equilibrium typical in the markets of their time to favor owners of labor, as with proposals for 10-hour days and 6-day work weeks. In Europe, social democratic parties were politically successful after universal male suffrage was adopted in the early twentieth century. However, social democratic governments tended to be left liberals rather than socialists. They did not attempt to reform their commercial societies radically. Rather, they modestly rebalanced labor contracts and created small social insurance programs. They did not nationalize all large industries or undertake massive redistributive programs. Their most radical members abandoned the social democratic parties to form new communist parties after World War I, which tended to be supported by relatively small numbers of voters (5%–10%).

[30] According to Bury, progress had become a measure of the quality of life and society. "For the earthly Progress of humanity is the general test to which social aims and theories are submitted as a matter of course. The phrase CIVILISATION AND PROGRESS [sic] has become stereotyped and illustrates how we have come to judge a civilization good or bad according as it is or is not progressive. The ideals of liberty and democracy, which have their own ancient and independent justifications, have sought a new strength by attaching themselves to Progress" (Bury [1921] 2011, p. vii).

## Appendix for Chapter 12: A Short Overview of Two Contemporary Contractarian Theories of the Good Society

Contractarian normative theory have their roots in Hobbes's ([1651] 2009) and Locke's (1690) theories of legitimate governments, both of whom refer to governments created by consensus as commonwealths. From a contractarian perspective, governments should be grounded in the consent of those governed, and they are formed to advance the shared interests of their citizens. In Hobbes's case, a commonwealth is created to escape from "the war of every man against every other."

> [W]hen **men agree** amongst themselves, to submit to some Man, or Assembly of men, voluntarily, on confidence to be protected by him against all others. This later, may be called a Political Commonwealth, or Commonwealth by Institution. (Hobbes, *Leviathan*, [1651] 2009, p. 96)

Locke's approach is similar but assumes that, rather than a war of every man against every other, individuals create a commonwealth to reinforce natural laws which in the absence of governmental support would provide a less perfect constraint on self-interested behavior. In both cases, the governments of commonwealths are, and should be, grounded in the consent of the governed, rather than conquest by an organization able to impose laws on others.

This line of reasoning preceded utilitarian thought by a century and a half, and also provided a view of the good society in which every person's interests were to be advanced through governance. Contractarian reasoning was subsequently employed by such well-known scholars as Montesquieu (1748), Rousseau (1762), and Blackstone (1765–1770). And it continues to play a role in ideas about legitimate government and the bounds of the authority of many constitutional democracies today.

The twentieth-century revival of contractarian analysis was launched more or less simultaneously by two scholars: John Rawls (1921–2002) and James Buchanan (1919–2013). Rawls's approach was similar in spirit to Locke's, and Buchanan's was similar in the spirit to Hobbes's approach—although each provided significant refinements of contractarian analysis. Rawls's approach is widely regarded to be one of the major innovations in philosophy in the twentieth century. Buchanan won the Nobel Prize in Economics in 1986 for his contributions to constitutional theory, most of which were grounded in his contractarian approach.

Rawls ([1971] 2009) argues that what might be called moral intuitions tend to converge on two principles of justice, an equal liberty principle and a distributional principle, and that these are compatible with many, but not all, institutional designs:

> First: each person is to have an equal right to the most extensive basic liberty compatible with a similar liberty for others. Second: social and economic inequalities are to be arranged so that they are both (a) reasonably expected to be to everyone's advantage, and (b) attached to positions and offices open to all. (Rawls *A Theory of Justice*, (1971] 2009, pp. 60–61)

His analytical device for finding that consensus resembles Smith's impartial spectator, in that it requires individuals to imagine a choice setting in which one is completely ignorant of one's place in society and to choose among societies given that he or she might wind up in any of the positions in that society—he terms this mechanism, *decision-making behind the veil of ignorance*. Such a perspective tends to make one an impartial observer of an entire social order.

Although Rawls begins with an equal liberty position similar to that developed by Spencer, he is by no means a doctrinaire liberal, but rather a left liberal who is very concerned with fairness in the distribution of income (and other advantages), in a manner analogous to Pigou. As also true of Pigou, he generally favors private property and competitive markets—albeit with a role for an even more active government than imagined by Pigou. He favors more redistribution that most utilitarians would, under what he terms the *difference principle* and others have termed the *maximin principle*.

> [H]ow well off men are in this situation plays no essential role in applying the difference principle. **We simply maximize the expectations of the least favored position** subject to the required constraints. (Rawls, *A Theory of Justice*, [1971] 2009, p. 80)

The "required constraints" on this redistributive principle are those required to assure equal liberty. Whether a difference principle would be agreed to from behind a veil of ignorance is not proven, rather it is asserted, and its consequences for institutional design worked out and defended in his *Theory of Justice* and other works.

Buchanan, in contrast, starts from a Hobbesian perspective and is unwilling to make claims about the society that would emerge from consensus at a hypothetical constitutional convention. His work emphasizes the importance of consensus itself. He also emphasizes that the slate is not blank, and that consensus should be the basis of changes from the status quo ante. Unless one is establishing a new community in a new place, one cannot simply assume that no starting point exists. Every individual's interests (as they are understood by him- or herself) must be assessed, and this can most reliably be done by the individuals themselves. Thus, consensus is the only way to determine whether a change is universally believed to be an improvement.

Of course, consensus cannot literally be used for every decision, and so Buchanan argues that in practice consensus should be and would be applied to the choice of institutions for making group decisions. In that respect, his analysis is similar to that of Rawls. The object of a social contract is it framing institutions. However, his approach indirectly criticizes Rawls's willingness to contemplate wholesale reforms of social systems without taking into account the initial conditions or status quo ante.

Buchanan's imaginary ideal is analogous to Spencer's, one in which internalized norms solve most or all social dilemmas and freedom of action is maximized under an equal liberty principle.

> To the individualist, the ideal or utopian world is necessarily anarchistic in some basic philosophical sense. This world is peopled exclusively by persons who respect the minimal set of behavioral norms dictated by mutual tolerance and respect. Individuals remain free to "do their own things" within such limits, and cooperative ventures are exclusively voluntary. Persons retain the freedom to opt out of any sharing arrangements which they might join. . . . Essentially and emphatically, this utopia is not communist even in an idealized meaning of this historically tortured word. (Buchanan 1975, pp. 2–3)

However, as true of Locke, he regards this idealized form of anarchy to be an impossibility for many reasons. There may be, for example, insufficient reciprocity or tolerance or insufficiently strong internalized norms to sustain such a community. One might use such an ideal as a reference point to head toward, but this is not done in Buchanan's work.

Buchanan relies upon what he terms the *veil of ignorance* as the mechanism through which agreement about more or less permanent rules emerges.

> The veil of ignorance and/or uncertainty offers a means of bridging the apparent gap between furtherance of separately identified interests and agreement on the rules that conceptually define the "social contract." Potential contractors must recognize that the basic rules for social order—the ultimate constitutional structure—are explicitly chosen as permanent or quasi-permanent parameters within which social interaction is to take place over a whole sequence of periods. This temporal

feature, in itself, shifts discussion away from that which might take place among fully identified bargainers and toward discussion among participants who are unable to predict either their own positions or how differing rules will affect whatever positions they come to occupy. (Buchanan and Congleton 1998, p. 6)

Although Buchanan's personal opinions are more or less those of a doctrinaire liberal, he argues that whatever emerges from constitutional negotiations grounded in consensus (with full or near unanimity) are legitimate and true improvements over the status quo ante. He regards his own position on constitutional issues to be simply one of many that would be discussed at such an imaginary constitutional convention.

Both these approaches have influenced the analyses of public policies for the past few decades, and both provide new moral or normative insights and justifications. However, both also suffer from weaknesses that the utilitarians noted in their critiques of eighteenth-century contractarians. They provide no justifications for institutions adopted by far less than consensus or based on principles of justice adopted with less than universally agreed upon normative theories in mind. No major polity has adopted its major institutions using unanimous agreement, although there are instances of small towns and villages doing so.

Nonetheless, the quest for consensus generally provides greater support for democratic procedures and for markets than abstract utilitarian analysis tends to, because it begins with individual rights (the ability to propose and reject institutions and other bargains), whereas utilitarians begin with conceptions of utility and simply maximize it regardless of its effects on those harmed by the decisions reached. A utilitarian's only concern is whether the losses of groups of losers are smaller than the gains of groups of winners in the choice settings of interest. In contrast, contemporary contractarians focus on consensus and shared interests.

# 13
# The Arguments Revisited and Summarized

## The Book in a Nutshell

The idea that commercial societies necessarily have ethical foundations may strike most readers as absurd or simply wrong. Business scandals often appear in newspapers. Puffery and worse are typical in most advertising campaigns. Every product is "the finest, new, and improved." Near fraudulent claims are commonplace, as for example, many never-heard-of products are touted to be "world famous." Many "prize-winning products" have won prizes only in contests sponsored by their producers. Negotiations over price and other contract terms often involve withholding useful information or active lying. News accounts of businessmen and women rarely, if ever, mention their ethics or ethical dispositions, but do report instances of fraud, embezzlement, and other forms of criminal behavior. The same is true of most editorial commentaries about commercial societies.

Consistent with these impressions of markets is the usual assumption that economists make about human nature. Economists routinely characterize firm owners as pragmatic profit maximizers—as persons simply out to accumulate as much wealth as possible. Consumers are normally characterized as naive hedonists whose quest for a good life consists largely of the consumption and acquisition of more and more goods and services—the more the better. Economists seem to assert that commerce is most extensive when pragmatists run economic organizations and all consumers are gluttonous materialists. If so, surely market competition must discourage and undermine all manner of ethical conduct, rather than support it.

Yet a subset of economists believe that ethical dispositions matter, as evidenced by the quotes of several Nobel Prize winners in the appendix of Chapter 1. This book has explored the logic and merit of their claims. It demonstrates that such assertions deserve serious attention, because ethical dispositions can potentially increase both the level and the growth of commerce by solving a wide variety of social dilemmas. The illustrating examples

*Solving Social Dilemmas.* Roger D. Congleton, Oxford University Press. © Oxford University Press 2022.
DOI: 10.1093/oso/9780197642788.003.0013

of Part I demonstrate that a subset of ethical dispositions make lives in communities more attractive and can also increase sales, productivity, capital accumulation, and rates of innovation. To the extent that wages reflect productivity, this implies that commerce tends to reward at least a subset of the behavior that is widely deemed ethical. Moreover, even pragmatic consumers tend to prefer merchants and manufacturers with reputations for treating their customers well, and even pragmatic firm owners largely prefer employees who are trustworthy, diligent, industrious, devoted team players. All these conclusions suggest that markets work better when some ethical dispositions are commonplace than when they are not. If so, market activities tend to encourage rather than discourage a variety of ethical behaviors.

This is not to claim that market participants are moral zealots or angels, only that commerce tends to favor persons who have internalized particular subsets of ethical rules over persons who have not.

The reason that ethical dispositions affect economic development is that problematic choice settings are commonplace, rather than rare. If every optimizing decision reached by independent pragmatists produced advantages for all concerned, it is not clear whether internalized rules of conduct would exist, and if they did, whether they could add much to commerce or prosperity. However, the class of choice settings referred to as social dilemmas share the property that the practical interests of the persons whose decisions jointly determine their outcomes tend to generate outcomes that everyone involved would regard to be less than the best possible. Unproductive conflict, excessive use of natural resources, free riding, fraud, shirking, corruption, extractive governance, and many other counterproductive behaviors and outcomes are associated with such settings when critical social dilemmas are not solved or ameliorated.

Solving the myriad of problems confronted is not easy. The first parts of this book show that internalized norms can solve or ameliorate most such problems. The second part of the book shows that internalized norms are often prerequisites for the other political solutions that might be imagined. The third part of the book suggests that the most commonplace ethical dispositions in Northern Europe did in fact gradually become more supportive of commerce and good governance in the period before the great acceleration.

Although the term *social dilemma* is new, the existence of problematic choice settings has been recognized for centuries. Plato and Hobbes, for example, both analyzed dilemmas associated with life in society and political systems. And thousands of playwrights and authors have used problematic choice settings in stories, plays, and books in genres sometimes referred to as tragedies. In tragic circumstances, even thoughtful protagonists may be trapped by circumstances beyond their control.

Although such dilemmas have long been recognized, the precise nature of social dilemmas became clear only after non-cooperative game theory was worked out in the second half of the twentieth century. Simple games in normal form can easily characterize a wide variety of choice settings in which outcomes are produced by many independent decision-makers and in which each decision-maker's interests tend to induce behavior that produces outcomes that are less than the best possible for the persons involved—even when all participants are fully rational and doing the best that they can, given what the other(s) have done. This is not true of all choice settings, as mainstream microeconomics demonstrates, but such settings are sufficiently commonplace that social dilemmas tend to impede or block progress in civil society, politics, and markets.

A few dozen archetypes of such dilemmas were analyzed in Parts I and II of this book to illustrate how they may do so. Each of those archetypes exist in thousands of variations in the real world that we live in. Many of these have passed by unnoticed by most social scientists and philosophers; others are well-known and widely taught in economics and in the rational choice strands of sociology, political science, and philosophy.

The choice settings used to illustrate the dilemmas are the simplest that can be used. Their clarity in two-player, two-strategy games makes social dilemmas appear to be obvious—which is of course the intended purpose of the illustrations. Skeptical readers might be tempted to believe that such problems would solve themselves if they were often repeated. However, repetition alone itself is not sufficient to solve even these simple problems. Although the games are presented as one-shot games, the equilibria are the same ones that tend to emerge in finite repeated versions of the same games—a type of equilibrium referred to as *sub-game perfect equilibria* in game theory. Moreover, the same types of equilibria tend to emerge when there are larger numbers of players and strategies are continuums rather than discrete. The more players involved and the more strategies are possible, the less "obvious" are the problems confronted, and the less likely solutions are to be developed.

Although the cases examined should be crystal clear to readers, the ones faced in the real world are rarely so obvious, nor are solutions always achieved with relatively simple unconditional rules that can be easily internalized. It is for this reason that human progress has been so slow during most of its history. And it is partly for this reason that moral maxims, ethical principles, and laws are often conditional and complex—although once internalized they seem "intuitively obvious" to those who employ them.

Minor, but significant, extensions of rational choice models have been used to demonstrate how internalized rules of conduct—ethical or normative dispositions—can solve all such problems, and why the same rules may not solve other similar problems in which the temptations to violate them are relatively large. The former provides a possible evolutionary rationale for at least a subset of ethical dispositions and also explains why every society exhibits such dispositions—although not identical ones. The latter explains why some problems, even ones similar to those already solved, may remain unsolved.

Perhaps surprisingly—and despite the usual assumptions about the goals of firm owners and consumers—neoclassical economics implicitly assumes that market participants are all dutiful law-abiding citizens, and that a society's law enforcers are all diligent, honest men and women who enforce a civil code that induces even pragmatic firm owners and consumers to behave as if they were such moral agents. The usual models ignore possibilities for fraud, theft, extortion, and rent-seeking as methods of acquiring wealth. As a consequence, the explanatory power of mainstream economic theory diminishes when such problems are commonplace in the societies of interest.

The emergence of civil societies with democratic politics and flourishing markets requires thousands of social dilemmas to be solved or ameliorated. And, unfortunately, the discovery of systems of rules that do so is by no means certain or easy. A variety of rules can often be employed to ameliorate the same problem. And because small changes in rules are usually easier to develop and internalize than larger changes, systems of norms tend to be path dependent. When a system of norms confronts problems that cannot be solved with small reforms, progress may be blocked for centuries.

In many cases, such internalized norms are the only plausible solutions. In others they are complements to or substitutes for other possible solutions. For example, it turns out that most political solutions require ethical support, as demonstrated in Part II's chapters on law and politics. Together the existence of problematic choice settings, the difficulty of recognizing and solving them (especially before game theoretic tools were worked out), and their path dependence provide an explanation for the slowness of social progress.

The same principles also account for the many relatively short periods of progress in human history that were followed by long stable periods (often referred to as periods of stagnation) or periods of retrogression. From the perspective of this book, periods of rapid progress are times following new or better solutions to critical social dilemmas, stable periods are evidence of failures to solve the "next" important social dilemmas associated with continued progress, and retrogressions occur when changes in a community's ethos diminish rather than improve its ability to address significant social dilemmas.

Ethical dispositions solve or ameliorate previously unsolved or new social dilemmas when the preexisting rules of conduct are appropriately refined and internalized by a sufficient subset of individuals in the community of interest. Simply discovering a rule that would solve a dilemma if adopted by everyone is not sufficient to do so, because internalization of such rules is not automatic, and cheating on such rules is often personally advantageous in problematic choice settings. Thus breakthroughs in rules often take considerable time to become part of a community's ethos—which is say, to become part of the systems of rules that most people in a community use to identify their true interests.

The human capacity for internalizing rules—which some term *learning*— is enormous. Humans can internalize very complex conditional systems of rules and apply them without much conscious thought after a few years or decades of practice and study. Perhaps the most obvious example is language, which consists of highly irregular linkages between sounds, symbols, and meanings that most people begin to internalize within a few months of birth, although mastery normally takes decades to achieve. That other complex systems of rules can also be internalized is evident in all the fields of knowledge in which formal education takes place. Many educated persons can easily recognize schematic diagrams of the solar system and atoms, the symbols associated with arithmetic operations, regular geometric figures, the scenes of both expressionist and pointillist paintings, and supply and demand diagrams with just a glance. That most people can quickly learn to drive an automobile in traffic without accidents in complex dynamic circumstances is further evidence.

That these rule systems are nontrivial is indicated by the millions of hours of research undertaken by talented computer programmers to develop software that can do the same things. Versatile and accurate voice-recognition software and safe self-driving automobiles remain out of reach at present, although these tasks are "easy as pie" for most humans. (Of course, few if any contemporary robots can bake a pie using the equipment available in today's Western kitchens.) Complex normative rule systems are simply another instance of complex interconnected conditional rules that can be internalized and applied by humans.

For ethical principles to solve or ameliorate social dilemmas, they must alter perceptions of self-interest in relevant choice settings and thereby make some kinds of decisions more likely than they otherwise would be. For ethical dispositions to play a causal role in social, political, and economic history, they must change through time, yet be sufficiently stable that they do not change rapidly in response to sudden changes in circumstances. To be attributed causal economic roles, changes in the rules systems internalized must occur in the periods just before changes in the level or rate of economic development occur.

Within consequentialist systems of ethical rules, two types of rule changes can induce economically relevant changes in behavior: (1) conditional principles or rules of conduct may be modified; or (2) expectations about the consequences of particular actions may be revised. Evidence of the first change is provided in Part III, which complements the cultural analyses of industrialization by McCloskey (2006) and Mokyr (2016), who reach similar conclusions. Evidence of the second is associated with all histories of scientific and technological progress. Both Smith's reformulation of economic theory and Bentham's utility-based analysis of gains to trade implied that commercial systems need less regulation and tend to be more beneficial than earlier mercantilist theories had concluded.

The evidence developed in Part III suggests that a series of changes in ethical dispositions occurred in the century or two before the great acceleration of commerce in the West in the nineteenth century. These changes were not directly observed but were implied by the examples and implicit assumptions used by widely read authors of that period, which had to be "obvious" for their readers if they were to have their intended effect. For the most part, these changes in norms and normative principles tended to make careers in commerce more attractive and commerce itself more efficient. The various religious, sociological, political, economic, and philosophic arguments in support of commerce and innovation tended to reinforce one another, because they demonstrated that several lines of reasoning led to the same or very similar conclusions. And those conclusions about proper conduct, insofar as they were internalized, would tend to accelerate economic development for reasons developed in Parts I and II.

## Ethics and the Great Acceleration: Some Further Evidence

Figure 13.1 illustrates the great acceleration using data from the 2018 Maddison Data Set for estimated real per capita gross national product (RGNP) in England and Poland between 1275 and 1925—two countries for which long data sets have been worked out by economic historians. (For the years after 1870, Maddison's data for the United Kingdom are used.) Poland

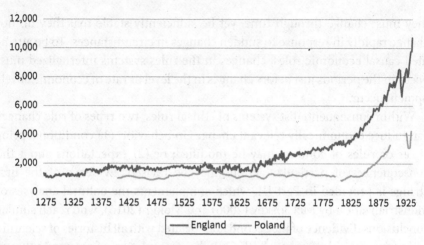

**Figure 13.1.** Real per capita GNP, 1275–1940, England and Poland.

was not part of the same western European culture, nor was it a significant participant in its trading networks or politics. Poland remained Catholic and so was not much affected by the Protestant Reformation, and it is distant enough to have been only weakly connected culturally to Dutch, English, Scottish, and French philosophical and scientific developments—although it was not entirely disconnected from them. Thus, given the theory developed in Parts I and II and the evidence developed in Part III, it is not surprising that the data plots indicate that the great acceleration took place far earlier in the England than in Poland. It is in western Europe and its cultural fellow travelers that the new ethical dispositions first emerged.

Notice that in both cases, initially there was a long stable period on the order of 400 years, with basically similar unchanging and low average incomes. In England, there is a modest acceleration in the late seventeenth century—the period in which La Court, Locke, and Baxter were writing. The growth rate of commerce accelerates in the early nineteenth century, at about the time that liberalism, utilitarian theories, and classical economics were gaining sway. No similar accelerations take place in the Polish data set, although it too begins to accelerate around 1850—by which time the per capita income of England was approximately four times that of Poland.

It bears keeping in mind the Watt's steam engine was developed in 1769, in the middle of the first acceleration and well before the great acceleration took off in England. This and other specific innovations suggest that technology by itself was not the primary source of the acceleration—although it doubtless contributed to it. Technology is portable, and Poland used essentially the same alphabet as England, making technical translations possible at a relatively low cost, yet no acceleration in early nineteenth -century Poland is evident. England's two accelerations occur at the times predicted by our analysis—as a consequence of changes in conclusions reached about the proper role of commerce in a good life and good society. This is not likely to reflect the impact of the theologians, scholars, and philosophers reviewed in Part III, but rather the ethical ideas in the air and their associate dispositions at the times during which the authors reviewed wrote their widely read books and pamphlets.

The ethical dispositions of the persons around them served as data for the theories and analyses undertaken by the authors reviewed. Such unwritten ideas matter, although they are difficult to track.[1]

## Ethical Dispositions as a Prerequisite for Other Explanations of Economic Development

The above discussion is not to suggest that technological developments do not affect the course of economic development. Technological and scientific advances clearly were among the drivers of economic development, as argued by Mokyr (1992). Without the many innovations in agriculture, for example, far fewer persons would have been available for creating, producing, transporting, and selling other products and services. In addition, the changes in political institutions that occurred during approximately the same period doubtless increased governmental support for commerce, because democratization tend to make governments more responsive to the interests of middle-class citizens. However, changes in ethical dispositions clearly facilitated both series of refinements and innovations.

## Ethics and Technological Advance

Technological advance is sometimes characterized as a process of trial and error. If this were literally the case, very little progress would actually take place. Out of the infinite combinations of actions that may be taken—both physical and imaginary—only a tiny handful produce results that enhance

---

[1] For those who attribute the flatness in per capita RGNP in Figure 13.1 to the Malthus effect—that population expands to keep folks at the level of subsistence—which may partly account for the long flat periods, it should be noted that the Malthusian problem can be reduced through suitable changes in norms regarding marriage, the age at which families are begun, subsequent rates of childbirth, and so forth. Again, the problem is fundamentally a social dilemma, in this case one analogous to the commons problem.

prospects for human survival or comfort. Imagine, for example, of all the ways that blades of grass or grains of sand may be combined into different shapes, or all the seeds of plants in a forest or field that might be distributed in a garden and, if any bear fruit, subsequently combined with other materials for eating. Rather than randomly combining things and seeing which works, if-then theories of relationships and causality are worked out and their implications are used to focus attention (trials) on combinations that are deemed likeliest to succeed (non-errors).

Clear hypotheses about natural relationships produce hypotheses about the experiments that are most likely to shed light on the problem at hand—whether it be raising wheat, the building of dams, pumping water out of deep mines, creating an electric light bulb, enhancing networks of trade, or developing a better government. A better characterization than "trial and error" is thus speculate, try, succeed or fail, learn from both one's successes and mistakes, and try again. If every experiment produced only errors, there would be no technological progress. Technological progress requires focused experimentation and trials, rather than completely random ones.

Insightful rules that characterize nature provide a great advantage over simple random explorations of possibilities, because such if-then relationships allow exploration and experiments to be directed at a relatively small subset of the set of all the possible trials that might be imagined. Such focused trials, by affirming or disconfirming hypotheses, may yield results that allow humans to intentionally change the course of nature, as for example when a new dam is built. Mistaken hypotheses tend to produce unintended results, as when a dam breaks and unleashes a torrent that destroys one's village.

Rules of conduct that make trials more likely to be successful thus have survival advantages over those that do not. They reduce the cost of innovations that tend to increase the welfare of individuals and communities. Among the rules that tend to do so are accurate, impartial observation, dispassionate assessments of the data produced (or collected), examining the data to detect systematic if-then relationships that may have passed unnoticed by previous observers, and undertaking replicable trials, so that one has "good" reasons to believe that a particular change generated a particular result, or at least is very likely to have done so.

Speculations about "natural laws" and their associated possibilities and impossibilities are, of course, often wrong, but the data generated by careful tests of such ideas may improve subsequent speculations and produce more successful experiments. Normative rules about the proper way to undertake experiments, record results, and analyze those results increase the extent to which one can learn from both one's mistakes and successes. "Trials" are far more likely to generate useful knowledge when they are guided by "ought to" and "ought not" rules of conduct than when they are not—which is to say when they adhere to specific internalized rules of conduct and ideas about proper and improper experimentation.

This implies that technological advance is ultimately driven by norms and refinements in norms that improve "best" research practices and assessments of results.

## Rules of Conduct and Scientific Advance

The same is true of efforts to distill general principles that describe relationships in nature, among humans, and interactions between humans and nature. Efforts to increase our understandings of possibilities are more likely to be fruitful if the persons undertaking them follow rules of conduct similar to those required for technological advance. Additional normative rules, such as those which call for clarity and logical consistency, have also proven to be productive as well.

The differences between a novel or polemic and a scientific work are sometimes said to be differences in their methods. A novel explores an imaginary setting. A polemic creates arguments that support a particular public policy, theology, or social system. A scientific work attempts to explain the world as it is, has been, or will be. It is not mere description because such descriptions would be infinitely long and not particularly useful. Rather, a scientific work attempts to characterize general if-then relationships among things and phenomena—not all of which are observable or immediately useful.

Systematic speculation, careful fact gathering, statistical and other analysis, and subsequent revised speculations—a process often termed *research*—is said to be characterized by the "scientific method." It turns out, however, that the scientific method is ultimately a system of internalized norms, rather than specific procedures. Those norms describe the manner in which a "good" or "proper" scientist should undertake his or her research and report his or her results. Individual scientists should be truth-seekers, not in the sense of mediation or transcendentalism, but in the sense of attempting to carefully observe and explain the world as it is, has been, or will be.

A proper scientist often makes up his or her theories, and although he or she may assemble or generate data (via experimentation or simulations) with particular problems and expectations in mind, he or she never falsifies the evidence assembled or the results from various tests of the theories of interest.

Temptations to cheat on these rules are, of course, always present, but must be resisted if the results are to be trustworthy.

Scientific progress is accelerated when the data and conclusions shared are deemed trustworthy by others interested in the same phenomena, which allows the conclusions reached by others to be used as a point of departure for subsequent research. The same norms also promote and facilitate specialization—a focus on subsets of possible problems and relationships—which, as in other endeavors, tends to increase rates of progress.

It is the ethos of science that ultimately characterizes the methodology of science, rather than education, laboratories, or specific conclusions about the world. (Indeed, every conclusion reached according to the ethos of science is subject to refutation and improvement by other scientists—although they too must follow the rules of scientific inquiry.) All this suggests that the acceleration of scientific progress that produced the paradigm shifts that emerged after 1600 were arguably caused by changes in the norms of research as argued by Mokyr (2016).

## Ethical Dispositions and the Reform and Productivity of Governance

Another factor associated with the great acceleration was the transformation of governance in most of the West. Hereditary determination of a nation's most powerful policymakers was gradually replaced with electoral determination of officeholders during the nineteenth and early twentieth centuries. The new electoral foundations of governance shifted the center of gravity of policymaking by making the interests of middle-class citizens more important to policymakers and those of nobles and royals less important. The result in the West was a series policy reforms that tended to increase education, urbanization, economic competition, and rates of innovation. These policy changes also tended to increase both the extent and rate of commercialization. Many, perhaps most, of these policy changes reflected norms that were already widely internalized by middle-class and upper middle-class voters of that period (McCloskey 2006; Congleton 2011).

Governance that advances broad interests is no more natural than a "good" society or "good" life as shown in Part II. It also has normative foundations. Mercantilist policies that benefited the aristocracy and families of those holding positions of authority in government were historically commonplace.

They typically reduced economic competition and rates of innovation, while enriching the already wealthy and well connected—which of course was their intended purpose—but also slowed economic development.

One might be tempted to insist that elections alone are sufficient to avoid the dilemmas of mercantilist public policies, but that is not true, for reasons explored in Part II. Ruling majorities are also tempted to use governmental authority to take from their opponents and give to their supporters, and also to lock in their authority by biasing electoral procedures in their favor, as developed in Chapter 7. Holding routine elections requires normative support. Assembling a bureaucracy that implements policies without significant favoritism requires both rules that promote neutrality and internalized norms that encourage diligent dutiful behavior by government employees. Avoiding excessively extractive policies and corruption requires moral support.

However, prosperity requires more than non-extractive governance. It requires policies that do not undermine the potential advantages of market transaction and innovation. Such policies require support from voters and government officials. Both voters and government officials must generally believe that commerce is for the most part a moral activity, worthy of modest support through public policies that make markets better instruments for advancing general interests—as Western civil law of the eighteenth and nineteenth centuries tended to. Other governmental support for innovation, such as mass education and short-term patents, can also help to improve the production and distribution of goods and services sold in the long run by encouraging improvements in products, production, and lifestyles.

Evidence of a shift in the norms of governance was provided by my previous book (Congleton 2011). The rise of liberalism—with its associated systems of normative principles and maxims—in the eighteenth and nineteenth centuries produced governmental reforms and policies that dismantled mercantilist policies, reduced class distinctions, encouraged mass education, reformed the bureaucracy, and supported technological innovation. Without liberal reforms, it is doubtful that competition or scientific and technological advance would have generated the increasingly prosperous societies of the twentieth and twenty-first centuries.

Although several authoritarian regimes of the twentieth century promoted industrialization, they did not, with rare exceptions, produce commercial societies or achieve widespread prosperity.

## On the Usefulness of the Theory Proposed

It could be argued that all the above observations are analogous to an astronomy of social life, a theoretical sketch that explains how communities and markets emerge and develop, analogous to theories of the Big Bang and gravity. And there is some truth in that conclusion. According to the theory proposed, social progress occurs as a long series of punctuated equilibria, as an endless series of important social dilemmas are gradually solved or ameliorated through normative innovations.

A critic might suggest that the theory proposed provides an internally consistent organizing principle that accounts for much of human history, but it fails to provide any obvious practical insights or opportunities. Achieving the former is itself a worthy accomplishment, yet the theory also provides several useful implications about how to encourage and sustain a prosperous society.

First, do not take prosperity or progress for granted. Both are rare events in human history. Even today, there are many places where lives are far from prosperous. Prior to 1700, very few if any regions of the world were prosperous judged by today's standards. This book offers a possible explanation for both. The theory proposed also accounts for the lack of significant prosperity and commercial development over most of the course of human history. Prosperity and economic progress require supportive systems of norms which ameliorate thousands of social dilemmas that otherwise tend to inhibit capital accumulations and innovation. A commercial society is not simply a matter of getting off to a "good" start. New dilemmas emerge, and without a bit of luck in the evolution of normative systems, a society normally hits a roadblock and progress is blocked. With a bit of bad luck in the evolution of norms, a society may retrogress rather than stagnate or progress. Few people in Egypt are as wealthy as the average person living in Sweden or California today, although the reverse was true four thousand years ago.

Second, although the normative systems that support prosperity share many features, they are not identical. Contemporary Western systems of norms all regard hard work and diligence to be virtues but differ in many other respects. Thus, in principle, prosperity is not the product of a single unique system of norms. Not all systems of norms promote commerce, but the subset of normative systems that do is not vanishingly small.

Third, continued prosperity and growth require continued support for the virtuous dispositions that have solved or ameliorated older social dilemmas as well as newer ones that tend to enhance prosperity and encourage capital accumulation and innovation. This implies that some degree of cultural conservatism is appropriate in societies in which flourishing commercial societies have emerged.

However, history does not imply that a prosperous society should strive for complete social conservatism. New dilemmas are always confronted as progress takes place, which implies that some innovations in norms will be required to sustain progress. The degree of cultural conservatism that is appropriate is analogous to an Aristotelian mean—strong enough to encourage transmission of the values that have worked in the past, but open enough at the margin to allow the new norms to emerge that address the next social dilemmas confronted.

Fourth, together, cultural conservatism and the positive and normative rule-bases of commerce imply that commercial societies are difficult to export, although probably easier to export than liberal democratic political institutions, which are even more dependent on ethical support for their productivity. Thus, we should not be surprised that all the "foreign aid" given to countries with less than thriving commercial societies or reasonably productive governments has failed to generate flourishing commercial societies. Such transformations require normative shifts as well as more physical and human capital.

Fifth, after commercial societies emerge, cultural conservatism implies that markets are more robust than one might imagine. The durability of supportive norms in the medium term allows commercial societies to recover from natural and political shocks more rapidly than one might expect. This is, for example, suggested by the rapid rebirth of commercial societies in eastern Europe after the so-called Iron Curtain fell in 1990, following several decades of centrally planned economic systems and efforts to inculcate other anti-commerce norms.

However, while quite robust, commercial societies are not completely resilient. Disruptions in trading networks and the emergence of unsupportive normative systems can induce gradual shifts in norms that undermine commercial societies both directly through effects on behavior and indirectly through effects on public policies and governing institutions—although such changes normally take decades to become obvious. This arguably occurred in western Europe's major and minor cities after the collapse of the Roman Empire and the spread of anti-market strands of Christian theology. Many previously flourishing cities disintegrated as a consequence, and many technological accomplishments were forgotten from both disuse and lack of interest.[2]

---

[2] This is not to deny the importance of geopolitical events on European history. For example, trading networks tended to shrink throughout the former Western Roman Empire both within the Mediterranean Sea and with respect to the far East as the main trading routes fell under Islamic and subsequently Turkish control after the much longer-lived Eastern Roman Empire gradually expired. But it is to suggest that a major change in norms regarding the most important focus of life have significant effects as well—many of which were associated with the normative changes associated with such changes in governance.

All the above demonstrates that the theory has at least a few practical implications for public policy. It provides insights about what is feasible, what is destructive, and what is constructive—at least if the aim is to achieve social systems in which relatively high levels of material comfort are commonplace.

## What This Book Is Not Saying

The assertion that prosperity is at root an ethical phenomenon is not to claim that the persons in a more prosperous community are more ethical than those in a less prosperous community—although from the perspective of the norms internalized by members of a commercial society, it may appear to be so. It is, rather, a claim that some systems of rules and their associated ethical dispositions are significantly more supportive of commerce and economic development than others.

The most general of the conclusions of this book are (1) all societies have an ethos and a collection of customary laws that mitigate a wide variety of social dilemmas, (2) some ethical systems ameliorate or solve a broader array of dilemmas than others, and (3) some internalized systems of ethical and normative rules provide more support for commerce than others. Persons living in impoverished societies may be just as devoted (or more devoted) to their ethical systems than those living in wealthier countries.

Nor does the analysis of the book imply that focusing on technological advance or using economic theories that implicitly assume that normative dispositions are stable during the period analyzed is always mistaken or a waste of time. Norms change more slowly than technology (at least they have for the past two or three centuries) and so tend to be stable for decades at a time. Thus, for many short-term analytical and empirical projects, ignoring differences in normative systems will not undermine the main conclusions reached. However, ignoring the role of economically relevant ethical dispositions is mistaken when undertaking comparative studies or long-term analyses of economic development. In those cases, both differences and changes in ethical dispositions tend to be important causal factors that should not be ignored.

Nor is the book claiming that the European path to commercial societies is the only one that is possible. Asian countries such as Japan and Korea have made similar transitions that were also at least partly driven by refinements in the most commonplace normative systems in those societies. In some cases, the importance of norms for economic development were also well recognized. For example, the importance of moral development for prosperity was explicitly acknowledged in Japan's educational reforms of 1871:

> The only way in which an individual can raise himself, manage his property and prosper in his business and so accomplish his career is by cultivating his morals, improving his intellect, and becoming proficient in the arts. The cultivation of morals, the improvement of the intellect, and proficiency in the arts cannot be attained except through learning. This is the reason why schools are established.... It is intended that henceforth universally (without any distinction of class or sex) in a village there shall be no house without learning and in a house no individual without learning. (quoted in Pittau 1967, p. 24)

Shibusawa Eiichi (1840–1931), a very influential statesman and entrepreneur during Japan's transition from a medieval society to a commercial one, argued that the ethics necessary for economic development in Japan could all be found in Confucian thought if one adopted a somewhat broader perspective of the meaning of "family" than the traditional one.[3]

Rather, the main point of the book is that subtle changes in norms can induce changes in behavior and rates of innovation that have significant economic effects. From this perspective, it is not very surprising that the extent of commerce and its growth have varied greatly through time within specific regions and also varies among regions at specific moments in time. Not all markets are equally efficient because ethical systems vary in the extent of their direct and indirect support for commerce. Such historical facts would be more surprising if technological advance was the main driver. Technological advances tend to be more portable and exportable than a community's ethos, because technological refinements usually require smaller adjustments to preexisting systems of internalized rules.

Major changes in lifestyles, as with shifts from a hunter-gatherer society to an agricultural one, or from an agricultural to a commercial lifestyle, or from authoritarian to liberal forms of government, are unlikely unless they are supported by preexisting ethical systems—although all three transitions were possible and were fruitful when so supported. The ethical systems that

---

[3] For more on the role of moral developments in Japanese industrialization and commercialization, see Sager (2018). For more on Shibusawa's ideas and the norms that he regarded to be most important for business and political leaders, see Fridenson and Takeo (2017). However, it should also be noted that Shibusawa's reinterpretation of Confucian thought was influenced by his experiences in Europe, familiarity with translations of many books from Europe, and the penetration of liberal ideas into Japanese society during the second half of the nineteenth century. It was a different line of thought, but not entirely independent of European developments.

provide the necessary support are, however, evidently rare, complex, and not very portable.

Moreover, the existence of an endless series of social dilemmas implies that prosperity and progress are not the natural condition of humankind and that it is not inevitable that the future will be more prosperous than today—although the progress of the past two centuries suggests that there is a good chance that it will be.

## Appendix I to Chapter 13: Place of This Book in the Contemporary Academic Literature

This appendix discusses relations between this book and other research undertaken in the past few decades. This book, for example, has much in common with Elinor Ostrom's ([1990] 2015) pioneering research on institutional solutions to commons problems, Fukuyama's ([1992] 2019) influential overview of cultural innovations that gradually produced liberal systems of governance and markets, and Bicchieri's (2006) cultural explanation for many of the results of experimental economics. It also has an obvious resonance with recent books by Deidre McCloskey (2006, 2016), David Rose (2011), Ian Morris (2010), Philip Kitcher (2011), David Schmidtz and Jason Brennan (2011), Joel Mokyr (2016), and Steven Pinker (2018).

Although this book shares much with these and other works, it also differs in significant ways. McCloskey's books focus for the most part on the nineteenth century and are more literary than analytical exercises. Rose's book attempts to identify a particular morality—one that resembles McCloskey's *Bourgeoisie Virtues*—that tends to make markets work more efficiently. This book shares McCloskey's evolutionary thrust and entirely agrees with her analysis of the importance of normative shifts in the nineteenth century. It shares Rose's emphasis on the importance of ethics for market efficiency. It differs from McCloskey and Rose in both its use of elementary rational choice models to characterize the effects of alternative ethical dispositions on the extent of trade, production, and innovation and its analyses of the role of ethical dispositions in supportive legal and political institutions—subjects neglected in their books.

It differs from Fukuyama's, Morris's, Schmitz and Brennan's, and Pinker's well-written and far-reaching analyses of human progress by (1) its focus on ethical theories and dispositions, as opposed to advances in the organization of warfare, technology, institutions, or humanism per se; (2) its narrow focus on social dilemmas as impediments to social, political, and economic development; and (3) its use of models to illustrate both commonplace social, economic, and political dilemmas and the manner in which internalized rules of conduct can ameliorate those dilemmas. Mokyr also emphasizes culture as a source of support for the technologies of commerce, but he neglects the main reason why normative theories affect growth—not by facilitating science per se, but by ameliorating social dilemmas that would otherwise impede social, scientific, technological, and economic progress.

No previous book brings social dilemmas to the center of analysis and demonstrates that ethical dispositions can solve or ameliorate dilemmas associated with thousands of economic, political, and social choice settings, and thereby can contribute to both periods of stagnation and human progress. Shifts in ethical dispositions can account for the existence of and the timing of the great acceleration that created the commercial societies in western Europe, North America, and several places in Asia.

Ostrom's and Bicchieri's influential books also focus on social dilemmas, use game theory, and mention the role of norms as possible solutions to those dilemmas, but they focus for the most part on other social dilemmas. Ostrom's research focuses mainly on commons problems. She does not ignore other dilemmas, but her analysis mainly concerns how formal and informal institutions can solve important commons problems. Bicchieri focuses most of her attention on games that have captured the attention of experimental economists, such as the dictator game. This book places greater emphasis on social dilemmas resembling the one identified by Thomas Hobbes ([1651] 2009), although commons problems are also analyzed and are also likely to have been first solved through internalized norms. It shares their interest in the evolutionary tendencies of normative systems that can ameliorate social dilemmas. This book extends and generalizes their analyses by shifting social dilemmas to center stage and including social, economic, and political dilemmas. One cannot simply assume that firms or governments will solve all social dilemmas, because such organizations are all riddled with their own social dilemmas.

Kitcher's (2011) book, the *Ethical Project*, was recommended to me by one of the reviewers for Oxford University Press. I had not read his book before completing the previous draft of the book, and so it did not influence its development. However, as the reviewer noted, his approach is quite similar in spirit to mine in that he regards ethical rules and principles to be both useful and evolutionary phenomenon. Although his book is more focused on philosophical issues than those of greatest interest to social science, there are themes in his book that resonate with this one—although also a variety of differences. First, he regards ethical rules to be solutions to what he terms failures of a particular type of altruism—the altruism of the familial variety postulated by evolutionary psychology—rather than solutions to social dilemmas that block progress, as progress is understood by the persons in a given society and context. He too finds the biological roots of ethics to be thin, and also argues that social evolution and ethical innovation are central to human progress, as argued in this book. However, no series of dilemmas are explored to make this point; rather, it is taken to be intuitively obvious that solutions to social dilemmas (a term not used) tend to be useful. Many of his conclusions, however, are similar in spirit to that developed herein: ethical systems are (at least partially) systems of useful rules for living in societies.

My entry point into this literature was quite different from theirs, as noted in the next appendix. It emerged from a political economy perspective rather than the political science, economic history, environmental science, experimental economics, or philosophical perspectives. And, it was more influenced by James Buchanan's and Gordon Tullock's many contributions which, incidentally, are not mentioned in the Fukuyama, Pinker, Bichieri, and Kitcher books, although they are mentioned in the Ostrom, McCloskey, and Schmidtz and Brennan books.

As is often the case, overlaps and simularities do not necessarily imply inspirational or causal connections, but rather indicate that some problems and some solutions are "in the air," and that persons interested in particular puzzles at a given time often reach complementary or similar conclusions even when their efforts are entirely independent of one another.

I have argued elsewhere that shifts in ideology played an important role in the emergence of Western democracy (Congleton 2011). This book suggests that complementary shifts in ethical dispositions played an important role in the emergence of commercial societies in the West during roughly the same period, the latter being a point not made or emphasized, except by McCloskey—although she neglects the importance of politics and policy reforms in this process. Together, my two books suggest that changes in ideas about the good life and good society were central to the emergence of the new patterns of life and politics that emerged in the West during the mid- to late nineteenth century and which still largely characterize contemporary Western societies. Figure 13.2 illustrates the logic behind one of the main conclusions of the analyses undertaken in these two books with a Venn diagram.

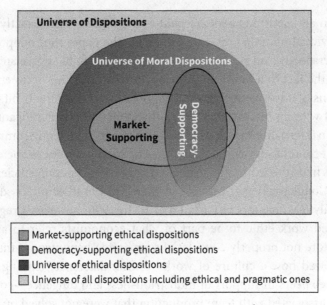

Figure 13.2.  Venn diagram of types of dispositions.

## Appendix II to Chapter 13: Some Notes on the Background of This Book Project and Thanks to Many Colleagues

The present project can be said to have begun shortly after a seminar that James Buchanan presented in the Center for Study of Public Choice's weekly seminar during the spring of 1990 (if I remember correctly). In the draft paper presented, he argued that a work ethic is an important determinant of economic development. His analysis was greeted with much skepticism by most of the audience, which consisted mainly of economist members of the Center and graduate students. Why would you need a work ethic to encourage work beyond that elicited by a competitive wage rate equal to marginal revenue product? I was among two or three attending who were sympathetic to his argument, and he and I joined forces for a month or two to write a joint paper on the economic consequences of a work ethic. At some point, Buchanan lost interest in the argument as I had developed it, and our joint paper became two separate papers. My part was published in the *Journal of Economic Behavior and Organization* (1991a) and Jim's in one of his many books a few years later (Buchanan and Yong 1994b).

The idea developed in my paper was that an external work ethic—a culture of work—could solve problems associated with team production that exist even when all team members are paid a competitive wage exactly equal to their individual marginal revenue products. The paper thus adopted Adam Smith's perspective on norms, although I did not fully appreciate it at the time, nor the fact that Smith's argument provided a bridge between our two conceptions of a work ethic. Social support can generate the habits of mind associated with an internalized work ethic; and without significant cultural support, an internalized work ethic is unlikely to be sufficiently commonplace to impact economic development within a firm, community, or society.

Insights from the work-ethic paper and an earlier paper on efficient status-seeking (Congleton 1989) influenced many of the illustrations developed in the analytical chapters of Parts I and II. In 1990, however, I regarded an internalized work ethic to be part of what economists refer to as "tastes" and therefore not properly considered a separate phenomenon. Instead, my paper showed how a culture of work—praise, deference, chiding, and the like by one's peers in support of industriousness and diligence—could solve problems associated with team production that were not solved by competitive wage rates. This was not the first time that I had thought or written about normative theories and behavior, but it was the first time that I focused on the relationship between a specific norm and prosperity. Buchanan had, of course, previously written much on the roles of ethics in economic systems and politics and on ethics itself. As one of his students and colleagues, I had done a bit of writing on such topics as well, but it was not a major focus of my research—the first of which was Blewett and Congleton (1983).

After my work-ethic paper and a paper on the evolution of norms to solve prisoner's dilemmas (Vanberg and Congleton 1992) were completed, I shifted to other projects in part because connections between ethics and economics were not easy to publish at that time and in part because my wife was killed in a car accident in 1994, which disrupted my life in many dimensions for several years. Raising a family on my own naturally reduced my time for writing, research, and academic travel. If there was a theme to my research during the next decade or so, it was on the effects of formal institutions, especially political institutions, and how they might be improved as instruments for advancing broadly shared interests. One project completed in that period was a book coauthored with James Buchanan (1998).

My return to thinking about the economic effects of ethical dispositions began in 2005 when I was invited to do a bit of summer teaching in the excellent philosophy and economics program at the Universitet Bayreuth in Germany. One of my responsibilities was teaching game theory to philosophy students, and to do so, I developed a series of one-shot games in normal form to illustrate philosophical concepts. It was an approach I had used off and on in other research and teaching, but that was the first time that I had applied it to philosophical and ethical issues. Those summer courses also induced me to read more philosophy than I had in the past. Although that reading informed my teaching in Bayreuth and subsequent work, it led only to one rather obscure publication on what I termed the "moral voter hypothesis" (Congleton 2007).

In general, I continued working on constitutional theory and history during this period, along with other public choice research. Some of that research turned out to be relevant for the present project. For example, in the course of attempting to determine the key causal determinants of the rise of democracy in the West, it became evident that ideology—specifically the rising tide of liberalism—played a central role in that transition and also in the transition to industrial society (Congleton 2011). No country that industrialized during the nineteenth century did not democratize its political systems (or vice versa), although full democracies were not reached in western Europe until the early twentieth century in most cases. Shifts in ideology (what would be termed ideas about "the good society" in the present volume) largely accounted for the reforms of parliaments in Europe and Japan that produced what we now refer to as Western or liberal democracy.

A year or two before I left George Mason University for West Virginia University, Diedre McCloskey presented a seminar on the role of bourgeois virtues in a commercial society. It was a largely intuitive exercise, but I found her argument entirely convincing and compatible with my project on Western democracy, which I was finishing up after nearly a decade of work. I filed her idea away in the back of my mind, as I do with all grand ideas that I find of interest, and when I was asked a few years later to teach a course on the moral foundations of capitalism at West Virginia University, I dug out her trilogy with the idea of using it for the course. However, it was not sufficiently analytical for my purposes, so I began this writing this book.

The first draft or two were aimed at producing a textbook for upper-level undergraduates in economics, philosophy, and political science programs (often abbreviated as PPE). However, while on sabbatical in 2017, I changed my mind about both the book's best organization and its targeted audience. In the early drafts, the philosophical material came first—and I have returned to teaching it that way. However, after presenting chapters at various seminars in Europe and the United States, I decided that the analytical material should go first. At roughly the same time, I also came to believe that a broader and deeper book aimed at academic audiences would be a useful addition to the literature, which induced further reorganization, refinement, and generalization.

These conclusions required a major reorganization and rewrite of the book and a few more years of writing, reading, and thinking.

A variety of books and papers read as part of my background reading affected the ideas and focus of my more or less biennial major revisions of the book. Toward the end of the project, I listened to a fine book by Steven Pinker (2018) while driving from the West Coast to the East Coast in the spring of 2018 during the second half of a sabbatical year spent mostly on the third major revision of this book. One more complete rewrite would follow. Pinker's book was not on the same topic, although his title made it sound like it would be, but its sweep was inspiring and led me to generalize and extend the book at various edges. It also encouraged me to write a few interdisciplinary articles for publication that deepened and clarified several of the grounding ideas and models used in the present book (Congleton 2018a, 2020a, 2020b, 2021).

The writing of *Solving Social Dilemmas* proved once again the value of what I call "author's illusion." A book that I initially thought would take a couple of years to complete has taken more than a half dozen. I believe it to have been worth the time, and I hope that readers will agree.

## Acknowledgments and Thanks

Although a solo book project mainly involves many solitary hours spent reading, thinking, and writing, such a book is not entirely a product of data collection, introspection, puzzle solving, and synthesis. Conversations, opportunities to present one's emerging ideas, and comments received are important inputs into the final result. In this concluding section, I wish to acknowledge and thank several friends and colleagues for helpful suggestions, comments, and opportunities.

A variety of helpful comments, reactions, and suggestions during the course of this project were provided by Toke Aidt, Thomas Apolte, Christian Bjørnskov, Peter Boettke, Geoffrey Brennan, James Buchanan, Andrew Cohen, Lars Feld, Ami Glazer, Bernard Grofman, Rainer Hegselmann, Arye Hillman, Randall Holcombe, Hartmut Kliemt, David Levy, Bryan McCannon, Peter Nannestad, Martin Paldam, Stergios Skaperdas, Thomas Stratmann, Gert Svensen, Nicolaus Tideman, Robert Tollison, George Tridimas, Gordon Tullock, Viktor Vanberg, Stefan Voigt, Richard Wagner, Andrew Young, and Akira Yokoyama. Nicolaus Tideman deserves special thanks for reading a near final draft of the book and providing numerous comments and suggestions for improvement. Akira Yokoyama also read through an early draft and caught several typos in the more mathematical parts of the book, which surely would otherwise have been missed. He also suggested that I take a look at recent work in English on Eiichi Shibusawa.

In addition to many conversations with colleagues, I benefited from opportunities to present parts of the book at seminars and academic meetings where many helpful comments were received. Among these were talks given at Aarhus University, University of California-Irvine, Cambridge University, George Mason University, University of Hamburg, Kings College of London, and West Virginia University. Insightful comments were also received after presentations and during conversations at the annual meetings of the Public Choice Society, the European Public Choice Society, the BB&T Conferences at Clemson University, the Silva Plana Conference, and the PEDD conference at the University of Muenster.

The book has also been enriched by many student reactions and questions on the ideas and parts of the book used in classes taught at the University of Bayreuth, Muenster University, and especially at West Virginia University. Financial support for summer research and some of my travels were provided by the BB&T foundation, whose support is gratefully acknowledged. Many helpful comments and editorial suggestions were also provided by Pamela S. Cubberly and also by the reviewers of this book.

Thanks are due to all of the above, and doubtless to others whom I am forgetting, for helping to clarify my thinking and inducing refinements, although none can be blamed for the use to which I put their fine comments and advice.

# References

Aguiar, M., and Hurst, E. (2007). Measuring trends in leisure: The allocation of time over five decades. *The Quarterly Journal of Economics, 122*(3), 969–1006.

Aidt, T. S. (2003). Economic analysis of corruption: A survey. *Economic Journal, 113*(491), F632–F652.

Aidt, T. S. (2009). Corruption, institutions, and economic development. *Oxford Review of Economic Policy, 25*(2), 271–291.

Aidt, T. S. (2016). Rent seeking and the economics of corruption. *Constitutional Political Economy, 27*(2), 142–157.

Akerlof, G. A. (1970). The market division of labor is limited by the extent of the market for lemons: Quality uncertainty and the market mechanism. *Quarterly Journal of Economics, 84*(3), 488–500.

Alchian, A. A., and Demsetz, H. (1972). Production, information costs, and economic organization. *The American Economic Review, 62*(5), 777–795.

Aristotle. (1897). *The Nicomachean ethics.* Translated by D. P. Chase. London: MacMillan.

Aristotle. *The politics.* (1992). Translated by T. A. Sinclair. London: Penguin Books.

Aristotle (1995). *Politics.* (Translated by E. Barker). Oxford: Oxford University Press.

Arrow, K. J. ([1951] 2012). *Social choice and individual values.* New Haven, CT: Yale University Press.

Arrow, K. J. (1972). Gifts and exchanges. *Philosophy and Public Affairs, 1*(4), 343–362.

Bak, P., and Sneppen, K. (1993). Punctuated equilibrium and criticality in a simple model of evolution. *Physical Review Letters, 71*(24), 4083–4086.

Barclay, R. ([1678] 2002). *An apology for the true Christian divinity.* Glenside, PA: Quaker Heritage Press.

Barnett, S. A. (1968). The "instinct to teach." *Nature, 220*(5169), 747–749.

Bastiat, F. ([1850] 2007). *The Bastiat collection* (2nd ed.). Auburn, AL: Ludwig von Mises Institute.

Baxter, R. ([1673] 2014). *A Christian directory: A sum of practical theology and cases of conscience.* (Vols. 1–4). Retrieved from Amazon.com. Kindle edition.

Baye, M. R., and Harbaugh, R. (2021). Good, better, best: Comparative price signaling. Kelley School of Business working paper, Indiana University.

Becker, G. S. (1968). Crime and punishment: An economic approach. *Journal of Political Economy, 76*(2), 169–217.

Becker, G. S., and Stigler, G. J. (1974). Law enforcement, malfeasance, and compensation of enforcers. *The Journal of Legal Studies, 3*(1), 1–18.

Becker, G. S., and Stigler, G. J. (1977). De gustibus non est disputandum. *American Economic Review, 67*(2), 76–90.

Bentham, J. ([1843] 2011). *A manual of political economy.* Retrieved from Amazon.com. Kindle edition.

Bentham, J. (2013). *Collected works of Jeremy Bentham.* Minerva Classics. Retrieved from Amazon.com. Kindle Edition.

Bentham, J. (1838–1843). *The rationale of reward. The Works of Jeremy Bentham.* Vol. 2. Edinburgh: William Tait, 253–254.

Bento, P. (2014). Competition as a discovery procedure: Schumpeter meets Hayek in a model of innovation. *American Economic Journal: Macroeconomics, 6*(3), 124–152.

Beugelsdijk, S., and Van Schaik, T. (2005). Social capital and growth in European regions: An empirical test. *European Journal of Political Economy, 21*, 301–324.

Bicchieri, C. (2006). *The grammar of society: The nature and dynamics of social norms.* Cambridge, UK: Cambridge University Press.

Bienen, H., and Van De Walle, N. (1989). Time and power in Africa. *American Political Science Review, 83*(1), 19–34.

Bjørnskov, C., and Méon, P. G. (2013). Is trust the missing root of institutions, education, and development?. *Public Choice, 157*(3–4), 641–669.

Black, D. (1948). On the rationale of group decision-making. *Journal of Political Economy, 56*(1), 23–34.

Blackstone, W. ([1765–1769] 2016). *Commentaries on the laws of England.* Oxford: Oxford University Press.

Blanco, L., and Ruiz, I. (2013). The impact of crime and insecurity on trust in democracy and institutions. *American Economic Review, 103*(3), 284–288.

Blewett, R. A., and Congleton, R. D. (1983). Non-global social contracts: A note on inefficient social institutions. *Public Choice, 41*(3), 441–448.

Blitz, R. C., and Long, M. F. (1965). The economics of usury regulation. *Journal of Political Economy, 73*(6), 608–619.

Boettke, P. J. (2002). *Calculation and coordination: Essays on socialism and transitional political economy.* London: Routledge.

Boyd, R., and Richerson, P. J. (1988). *Culture and the evolutionary process.* Chicago: University of Chicago Press.

Boyd, R., and Richerson, P. J. (2002). Group beneficial norms can spread rapidly in a structured population. *Journal of Theoretical Biology, 215*(3), 287–296.

Brennan, G., and Buchanan, J. M. (1980). *The power to tax: Analytic foundations of a fiscal constitution.* Cambridge, UK: Cambridge University Press.

Brennan, G., and Hamlin, A. (1998). Expressive voting and electoral equilibrium. *Public Choice, 95*(1–2), 149–175.

Brennan, G., and Lomasky, L. (1997). *Democracy and decision: The pure theory of electoral preference.* Cambridge, UK: Cambridge University Press.

Brennan, G., and Pettit, P. (2004). *The economy of esteem: An essay on civil and political society.* Oxford: Oxford University Press.

Broadberry, S., Campbell, B. M. S., Klein, A., Overton, M., and van Leeuwen, B. (2015). *British economic growth 1270–1870.* Cambridge, UK: Cambridge University Press.

Broman, B., and Vanberg, G. (2021). Feuding, arbitration, and the emergence of an independent judiciary. *Constitutional Political Economy.* https://doi.org/10.1007/s10602-021-09341-x.

Brosnan, S. F., Parrish, A., Beran, M. J., Flemming, T., Heimbauer, L., Talbot, C. F., Lambeth, S. P., Schapiro, S. J., and Wilson, B. J. (2011). Responses to the assurance game in monkeys, apes, and humans using equivalent procedures. *Proceedings of the National Academy of Sciences, 108*(8), 3442–3447.

Buchanan, A. (1985). *Ethics, efficiency, and the market.* Totowa, NJ: Rowman and Allanheld.

Buchanan, J. M. (1965). Ethical rules, expected values, and large numbers. *Ethics, 76*(1), 1–13.

Buchanan, J. M. (1968). *The demand and supply of public goods* (Vol. 5). Chicago: Rand McNally.

Buchanan, J. M. (1975). *The limits of liberty: Between anarchy and leviathan.* Chicago: University of Chicago Press.

Buchanan, J. M. (1978). Markets, states, and the extent of morals. *American Economic Review, 68*(2), 364–368.

Buchanan, J. M. (1984). Politics without romance: A sketch of positive public choice theory and its normative implications. In J. M. Buchanan and R. D. Tollison (Eds.), *Theory of public choice II* (pp. 11–22). Ann Arbor: University of Michigan Press.

Buchanan, J. M. (2005). *Why I too am not a conservative.* Cheltenham, UK: Edward Elgar.

Buchanan, J. M., and Congleton, R. D. ([1998] 2006). *Politics by principle, not interest: Towards nondiscriminatory democracy.* Cambridge, UK: Cambridge University Press.

Buchanan, J. M., and Stubblebine, W. C. (1962). Externality. *Economica, 29*(116), 371–384.

Buchanan, J. M., and Tollison, R. D. (Eds.) (1984). *The theory of public choice II.* Ann Arbor: University of Michigan Press.

Buchanan, J. M., and Tullock, G. (1962). *The calculus of consent: Logical foundations of constitutional democracy.* Ann Arbor: University of Michigan Press.

Buchanan, J. M., and Vanberg, V. J. (1991). The market as a creative process. *Economics and Philosophy, 7,* 167–186.

Buchanan, J. M., and Yoon, Y. J. (1994a). Increasing returns, parametric work-supply adjustment, and the work ethic. In J. M. Buchanan and Y. J. Yoon (Eds.), *The return to increasing returns* (pp. 343–356). Ann Arbor: University of Michigan Press.

Buchanan, J. M., and Yoon, Y. J. (Eds.). (1994b). *The return to increasing returns.* Ann Arbor: University of Michigan Press.

Burke, J. (1978). *Connections: An alternative view of change.* New York: Little Brown.

Bury, J. B. ([1921] 2011). *The idea of progress: An inquiry into its origin and growth.* London: Macmillan. Retrieved from Amazon.com. Kindle edition.

Bush, W. C., and Mayer, L. S. (1974). Some implications of anarchy for the distribution of property. *Journal of Economic Theory, 8*(4), 401–412.

Card, D., Heining, J., and Kline, P. (2013). Workplace heterogeneity and the rise of West German wage inequality. *The Quarterly Journal of Economics, 128*(3), 967–1015.

Carlyle, T. ([1850] 1898). *Latter Day pamphlets.* London: Chapman and Hall.

Carnes, Lord. (2013). *Aristotle's Politics* (2nd ed.). Chicago: University of Chicago Press.

Chipman, J. S., and Moore, J. C. (1976). Why an increase in GNP need not imply an improvement in potential welfare. *Kyklos, 29*(3), 391–418.

Coase, R. H. (1937). The nature of the firm. *Economica, 4*(16), 386–405.

Congleton, R. D. (1980). Competitive process, competitive waste, and institutions. In J. M. Buchanan, G. Tullock, and R. D. Tollison (Eds.), *Toward a theory of the rent-seeking society* (pp. 153–179). College Station: Texas A&M Press.

Congleton, R. (1982). A model of asymmetric bureaucratic inertia and bias. *Public Choice, 39*(3), 421–425.

Congleton, R. D. (1986). Rent-seeking aspects of political advertising. *Public Choice,* 249–263.

Congleton, R. D. (1989). Efficient status seeking: Externalities, and the evolution of status games. *Journal of Economic Behavior & Organization, 11*(2), 175–190.

Congleton, R. D. (1991a). The economic role of a work ethic. *Journal of Economic Behavior & Organization, 15*(3), 365–385.

Congleton, R. D. (1991b). Ideological conviction and persuasion in the rent-seeking society. *Journal of Public Economics, 44*(1), 65–86.

Congleton, R. D. (1997). Political efficiency and equal protection of the law. *Kyklos, 50*(4), 485–505.

Congleton, R. D. (2001). Rational ignorance, rational voter expectations, and public policy: A discrete informational foundation for fiscal illusion. *Public Choice, 107*(1), 35–64.

Congleton, R. D. (2003). Economic and cultural prerequisites for democracy. In A. Breton, G. Galeotti, P. Salmon, and R. Wintrobe (Eds.), *Rational foundations of democratic politics* (pp. 44–67). New York: Cambridge University Press.

Congleton, R. D. (2004). The median voter model. In C. K. Rowley and F. Schneider (Eds.), *The encyclopedia of public choice* (pp. 707–712). Boston: Springer.

Congleton, R. D. (2007a). Informational limits to democratic public policy: The jury theorem, yardstick competition, and ignorance. *Public Choice, 132*(3–4), 333–352.

Congleton, R. D. (2007b). On the feasibility of a liberal welfare state: Agency and exit costs in income security clubs. *Constitutional Political Economy, 18,* 145–159.

Congleton, R. D. (2007). The moral voter hypothesis: Economic and normative aspects of public policy and law within democracies. *Journal of Public Finance and Public Choice,* *25*(1), 3–30.

Congleton, R. D. (2011). *Perfecting parliament: Constitutional reform, liberalism, and the rise of Western Democracy.* Cambridge, UK: Cambridge University Press.

Congleton, R. D. (2013). On the inevitability of divided government and improbability of a complete separation of powers. *Constitutional Political Economy,* *24*(3), 177–198.

Congleton, R. D. (2015a). The logic of collective action and beyond. *Public Choice,* *164*(3–4), 217–234.

Congleton, R. D. (2015b). Rent seeking and organizational governance: Limiting losses from intra-organizational conflict. In R. D. Congleton and A. L. Hillman (Eds.), *Companion to the political economy of rent seeking.* Cheltenham, UK: Edgar Elgar, 488–508.

Congleton, R. D. (2018a). Toward a rule-based model of human choice: On the nature of homo constitutionalus. In R. E. Wagner (Ed.), *James M. Buchanan* (pp. 769–805). New York: Palgrave Macmillan.

Congleton, R. D. (2018b) A short history of constitutional liberalism in America. *Constitutional Political Economy,* *29*(2), 137–170.

Congleton, R. D. (2019). Toward a rule-based model of human choice: On the nature of *Homo Constitutionalus.* In R. E. Wagner (Ed.), *James M. Buchanan: A theorist of political economy and social philosophy.* Volume III of the series *Remaking Economics: Eminent Post-War Economists.* New York: Palgrave Macmillan, 769–805.

Congleton, R. D. (2020a). Ethics and good government. *Public Choice,* *84*(3), 379–398.

Congleton, R. D. (2020b). Governance by true believers: Supreme duties with and without totalitarianism. *Constitutional Political Economy,* *31*(1), 111–141.

Congleton, R. D. (2020c). The institutions of international treaty organizations as evidence for social contract theory. *European Journal of Political Economy,* *63*(June), article 101891.

Congleton, R. D. (2021, forthcoming). Behavioral economics and the Virginia school of political economy: Overlaps and complementarities. *Public Choice.*

Congleton, R. D., and Bose, F. (2010). The rise of the modern welfare state, ideology, institutions, and income security: Analysis and evidence. *Public Choice,* *144*(3–4), 535–555.

Congleton, R. D., Grofman, B. N., and Voigt, S. (Eds.). (2018). *The Oxford handbook of public choice,* Volume 1. Oxford: Oxford University Press.

Congleton, R. D., and Hillman, A. L. (Eds.) (2015). *Companion to the political economy of rent seeking.* Cheltenham, UK: Edgar Elgar.

Congleton, R. D., Hillman, A. L., and Konrad, K. A. (Eds.). (2008). *40 years of research on rent seeking.* Heidelberg: Springer Science and Business Media.

Congleton, R. D., and Vanberg, V. J. (2001). Help, harm or avoid? On the personal advantage of dispositions to cooperate and punish in multilateral PD games with exit. *Journal of Economic Behavior and Organization,* *44*(2), 145–167.

Cowen, T. (2011). *The great stagnation: How America ate all the low-hanging fruit of modern history, got sick, and will (eventually) feel better.* New York: Penguin Group.

Cowen, T., and Fink, R. (1985). Inconsistent equilibrium constructs: The evenly rotating economy of Mises and Rothbard. *American Economic Review,* *75*(4), 866–869.

Cox, G. W., North, D. C., and Weingast, B. R. (2012). The violence trap: A political-economic approach to the problems of development. SSRN Working Paper.

Crisp, R. (2014). *Aristotle, Nicomachean ethics.* Cambridge, UK: Cambridge University Press.

Crook, T. R., Todd, S. Y., Combs, J. G., Woehr, D. J., and Ketchen Jr, D. J. (2011). Does human capital matter? A meta-analysis of the relationship between human capital and firm performance. *Journal of Applied Psychology,* *96*(3), 443–456.

Davies, G. (2010). *History of money.* Cardiff, UK: University of Wales Press.

De Haan, J., and Sturm, J. E. (2003). Does more democracy lead to greater economic freedom? New evidence for developing countries. *European Journal of Political Economy*, *19*(3), 547–563.

De Mesquita, B. B., Smith, A., Siverson, R. M., and Morrow, J. D. (2003). *The logic of political survival.* Cambridge, MA: MIT Press.

Debreu, G. (1959). *Theory of value: An axiomatic analysis of economic equilibrium.* New York: John Wiley & Sons (Cowles Foundation Monograph Series).

Diamond, J. (2005). *Collapse: How societies choose to fail or succeed.* New York: Penguin.

Downs, A. (1957). *An economic theory of democracy.* New York: Harper and Row.

Durose, M., Harlow, C. W., Langan, P. A., Motivans, M., Rantala, R. R., and Smith, E. L. (2005). *Family violence statistics: Including statistics on strangers and acquaintances.* Washington, DC: Bureau of Justice Statistics.

Eckel, C., and Holt, C. A. (1989). Strategic voting in agenda-controlled committee experiments. *The American Economic Review*, *79*(4), 763–773.

Edens, J. F., and Cox, J. (2012). Examining the prevalence, role and impact of evidence regarding antisocial personality, sociopathy and psychopathy in capital cases: A survey of defense team members. *Behavioral Sciences & the Law*, *30*(3), 239–255.

Einzig, P. (2014). *Primitive money: In its ethnological, historical and economic aspects.* Amsterdam: Elsevier.

Eldredge, N., and Gould, S. J. (1972). Punctuated equilibria: An alternative to phyletic gradualism. In F. J. Ayala and J. C. Avise (Eds.), *Essential readings in evolutionary biology.* Baltimore, MD: JHU Press.

Emsley, C. (2021). *A short history of police and policing.* Oxford UK: Oxford University Press.

Erasmus, D. ([1532] 1993). *Praise of folly and letter to Maarten Van Dorp 1515.* Translated by B. Radice. New York: Penguin Press.

Farquharson, R. (1969). *Theory of voting.* New Haven, CT: Yale University Press.

Feddersen, T., Gailmard, S., and Sandroni, A. (2009). Moral bias in large elections: Theory and experimental evidence. *American Political Science Review*, *103*(2), 175–192.

Feld, L. P., and Frey, B. S. (2002). Trust breeds trust: How taxpayers are treated. *Economics of Governance*, *3*, 87–99.

Feld, L. P., and Tyran, J. R. (2002). Tax evasion and voting: An experimental analysis. *Kyklos*, *55*(2), 197–221.

Festinger, L. (1962). Cognitive dissonance. *Scientific American*, *207*(4), 93–106.

Fiorina, M. P., and Plott, C. R. (1978). Committee decisions under majority rule: An experimental study. *American Political Science Review*, *72*(2), 575–598.

Fischer, D. H. (1989). *Albion's seed: Four British folkways in America*, Volume 1: *America: A cultural history.* Oxford: Oxford University Press.

Fitzgerald, M. P., Lamberton, C. P., and Walsh, M. F. (2016). Will I pay for your pleasure? Consumers' perceptions of negative externalities and responses to Pigovian taxes. *Journal of the Association for Consumer Research*, *1*(3), 355–377.

Fitzgerald, P. (1995). Word-of-mouth effects on short-term and long-term product judgment. *Journal of Business Research*, *32*, 213–223.

Frank, R. H. (1988). *Passions within reason: The strategic role of the emotions.* New York: W. W. Norton.

Franklin, B. ([1758] 2014). *The Way to Wealth.* Best Success Books. Retrieved from Amazon. com. Kindle edition.

Franklin, B. ([1793] 2012). *The autobiography of Benjamin Franklin.* Amazon Digital Services, 25–27.

Franklin, B. ([1839] 2011). *Memoirs of Benjamin Franklin; Written by himself.* New York: Harper and Brothers. Amazon Digital Services. Retrieved from Amazon.com. Kindle edition.

Franklin, B. ([1860] 2012). *Self-denial is not the essence of virtue.* Volume II of *Memoirs of Benjamin Franklin; Written by himself.* Retrieved from Amazon.com. Kindle edition.

Frey, B. S., and Bohnet, I. (1995). Institutions affect fairness: Experimental investigations. *Journal of Institutional and Theoretical Economics* (JITE)/*Zeitschrift für die gesamte Staatswissenschaft, 151*(2), 286–303.

Fridenson, P., and Takeo, K. (Eds.). (2017). *Ethical capitalism: Shibusawa Eiichi and business leadership in global perspective.* Toronto: University of Toronto Press.

Fukuyama, F. ([1992] 2006). *The end of history and the last man.* New York: Simon and Schuster.

Fukuyama, F. (2011). *The origins of political order: From prehuman times to the French Revolution.* New York: Farrar, Straus and Giroux.

Garfinkel, M. R., and Skaperdas, S. (2008). *The political economy of conflict and appropriation.* Cambridge, UK: Cambridge University Press.

Gillies, J. (1797). *Aristotle's Ethics and Politics.* London: Cadell and Davies [1813 edition].

Glaeser, E. L., and Scheinkman, J. (1998). Neither a borrower nor a lender be: An economic analysis of interest restrictions and usury. *Journal of Law and Economics, 41*(1), 1–36.

Gordon, R. J. (2016). *The rise and fall of American growth: The U.S. standard of living since the Civil War.* Princeton, NJ: Princeton University Press.

Gordon, S. (2009). *Controlling the state: Constitutionalism from ancient Athens to today.* Cambridge, MA: Harvard University Press.

Gotwalt, E. (2002). *Moral determinants of rational behavior with an application to state abortion restrictions.* Dissertation. Fairfax, VA: George Mason University.

Gourevitch, V. (1997). *"The Social Contract" and other later political writings.* Cambridge Texts in the History of Political Thought. Cambridge, UK: Cambridge University Press.

Greenwood, J., Hercowitz, Z., and Huffman, G. W. (1988). Investment, capacity utilization, and the real business cycle. *American Economic Review, 78*, 402–417.

Grofman, B., Owen, G., and Feld, S. L. (1983). Thirteen theorems in search of the truth. *Theory and Decision, 15*(3), 261–278.

Grossman, G. M., and Helpman, E. (1991). Quality ladders in the theory of growth, *Review of Economic Studies, 58*, 43–61.

Grotius, H. ([1609] 2004). *The free sea, with William Welwood's critique and Grotius's reply.* Translated by R. Hakluyt. David Armitage (Ed.). Indianapolis, IN: Liberty Fund.

Güth, W., and Kliemt, H. (1994). Competition of cooperation: On the evolutionary economics of trust, exploitation, and moral attitudes. *Metroeconomica, 45*(2), 155–187.

Gwartney, J. D., Lawson, R. A., and Holcombe, R. G. (1999). Economic freedom and the environment for economic growth. *Journal of Institutional and Theoretical Economics, 155*(4), 643–663.

Hanusch, H., and Pyke, A. (Eds.) (2007). *Elgar companion to neo-Schumpeterian economics.* Cheltenham, UK: Edward Elgar.

Hardin, G. (1968). The tragedy of the commons. *Science, 162*(3859), 1243–1248.

Harmon-Jones, E., and Mills, J. (2019). An introduction to cognitive dissonance theory and an overview of current perspectives on the theory. In E. Harmon-Jones (Ed.), *Cognitive dissonance: Reexamining a pivotal theory in psychology* (pp. 3–24). Washington, DC: American Psychological Association.

Hayek, F. A. (1945). The use of knowledge in society. *American Economic Review, 35*(4), 519–530.

Hayek, F. A. ([1968] 2002). Competition as a discovery process. *Quarterly Journal of Austrian Economics, 5*(3), 9–23.

Hayek, F. A. ([1979] 2011). *Law, legislation, and liberty* (Volume 3). Chicago: University of Chicago Press. Retrieved from Amazon.com. Kindle edition.

Hayek, F. A. (Ed.) [(1935) 2009]. *Collectivist economic planning: Critical studies of the possibilities of socialism.* Auburn, AL: Ludwig von Mises Institute.

Hillman, A. L., and Katz, E. (1984). Risk-averse rent seekers and the social cost of monopoly power. *Economic Journal, 94*(373), 104–110.

Hillman, A. L., and Katz, E. (1987). Hierarchical structure and the social costs of bribes and transfers. *Journal of Public Economics, 34*, 129–142.

Hobbes, T. ([1651] 2009). *Leviathan.* Overland Park, KS: Digireads.com (Neeland Media LLC). Retrieved from Amazon.com. Kindle edition.

Holcombe, R. G. (1989). The median voter model in public choice theory. *Public Choice, 61*(2), 115–125.

Holt, C. A. (1999). Teaching economics with classroom experiments: A symposium. *Southern Economic Journal, 65*(3), 603–610.

Hunt, G. (Ed.) (1910). *The writings of James Madison,* Volume 9: *1819–1836.* New York: G. P. Putnam's Sons.

Inglehart, R. (1997). *Modernization and postmodernization: Cultural, economic, and political change in 43 societies.* Princeton, NJ: Princeton University Press.

Irwin, T. (1999). *Aristotle, Nicomachean ethics* (2nd ed.). Indianapolis, IN: Hackett.

Jowett, B. (1885). *The politics of Aristotle.* Oxford: Clarendon Press.

Kant, I. (2013). *The Immanuel Kant collection: 8 classic works.* Waxkeep. Retrieved from Amazon.com. Kindle edition.

Keeley, L. H. (1997). *War before civilization.* Oxford: Oxford University Press.

Kirzner, I. (1973). *Competition and entrepreneurship.* Chicago: University of Chicago Press.

Kitcher, P. (2011). *The ethical project.* Cambridge, MA: Harvard University Press.

Kliemt, H. (1986). The veil of insignificance. *European Journal of Political Economy, 2*(3), 333–344.

Knack, S., and Keefer, P. (1997). Does social capital have an economic payoff? Across-country investigation. *Quarterly Journal of Economics, 112*(4), 1251–1288.

Knight, F. H. (1921). *Risk, uncertainty and profit.* New York: Houghton Mifflin.

Konrad, K. A. (2009). *Strategy and dynamics in contests.* Oxford: Oxford University Press.

Krueger, A. O. (1974). The political economy of the rent-seeking society. *The American Economic Review, 64*(3), 291–303.

Kuhn, T. (1957). *The Copernican revolution: Planetary astronomy in the development of Western thought.* Cambridge, MA: Harvard University Press.

Kuhn, T. (1962). *The structure of scientific revolutions.* Chicago: University of Chicago Press.

Kuran, T. (2004). *Islam and Mammon: The economic predicaments of Islamism.* Oxford: Oxford University Press.

La Court, P. ([1662] 1746). *The true interest and political maxims of the Republic of Holland.* Translated by J. Campbell. London: J. Nourse.

Landa, J. (1994). *Trust, ethnicity, and identity: Beyond the new institutional economics of ethnic trading networks, contract law, and gift-exchange.* Ann Arbor: University of Michigan Press.

Lavoie, D. (1985). *Rivalry and central planning: The socialist calculation debate reconsidered.* Cambridge, UK: Cambridge University Press.

Levy, F., and Murnane, R. J. (1992). US earnings levels and earnings inequality: A review of recent trends and proposed explanations. *Journal of Economic Literature, 30*(3), 1333–1381.

Locke, J. ([1690] 2009). *Two treatises of government.* Retrieved from Amazon.com.

Locke, J. (2013). *The John Locke collection: 6 classic works.* Retrieved from Amazon.com. Waxkeep. Retrieved from Amazon.com. Kindle edition.

Lott, J. R., and Bronars, S. G. (1993). Time series evidence on shirking in the US House of Representatives. *Public Choice, 76*(1–2), 125–149.

Luce, D., and Raiffa, H. (1957). *Games and decisions, introduction and critical survey.* New York: John Wiley & Sons.

Lutz, D. S. (1984). The relative influence of European writers on late eighteenth-century American political thought. *American Political Science Review, 78*(1), 189–197.

Maddison, A. (2007). *The world economy*. Washington, DC: OECD.

Marshall, A. ([1890] 2012). *Principles of economics*. Digireads.com. Retrieved from Amazon.com.

Martinez-Vazquez, J., and Winer, S. (Eds.) (2014). *Coercion and social welfare in public finance*. Cambridge, UK: Cambridge University Press.

Mauro, P. (1995). Corruption and growth. *The Quarterly Journal of Economics, 110*(3), 681–712.

McCallum, B. T. (1988). Real business cycle models. *NBER Working Paper*, No. 2480.

McChesney, F. (1987). Rent extraction and rent creation in the economic theory of regulation. *The Journal of Legal Studies, 16*(1), 101–118.

McClellan, J. (1985). *Science reorganized*. New York: Columbia University Press.

McCloskey, D. N. (2006). *The bourgeois virtues: Ethics for an age of commerce*. Chicago: University of Chicago Press.

McCloskey, D. N. (2016). *Bourgeois equality: How ideas, not capital or institutions, enriched the world*. Chicago: University of Chicago Press.

Melosi, M. V. (2005). *Garbage in the cities: Refuse reform and the environment*. Pittsburgh, PA: University of Pittsburgh Press.

Meltzer, A. H., and Richard, S. F. (1981). A rational theory of the size of government. *Journal of Political Economy, 89*(5), 914–927.

Menger, K. (1892). On the origin of money. *The Economic Journal, 2*(6), 239–255.

Mesquita, B. B. de, Smith, A., Siverson, R. M., and Morrow, J. D. (2003). *The logic of political survival*. Cambridge, MA: MIT Press.

Mill, J. S. ([1859] 1901). *On liberty. London1*Mill, J. S. ([1859] 2013). *On liberty*. Walter Scott Publishing. Retrieved from Amazon.com Kindle edition.

Mill, J. S. (2013). *Complete works of John Stuart Mill*. Minerva Classics. Retrieved from Amazon.com. Kindle edition.

Miller, A. H. (1974). Political issues and trust in government: 1964–1970. *American Political Science Review, 68*(3), 951–972.

Mokyr, J. (1992). *The lever of riches: Technological creativity and economic progress*. Oxford: Oxford University Press.

Mokyr, J. (2016). *A culture of growth: The origins of the modern economy*. Princeton, NJ: Princeton University Press.

Montesquieu, C. ([1748] 1989). *The spirit of the laws*. Translated by A. M. Cohler, B. C. Miller, and H. Stone. Cambridge, UK: Cambridge University Press.

Montesquieu, C. ([1748] 2008). *The spirit of the laws*. Translated by T. Nugent. Dublin Ireland: G. Faulkner, Kindle edition, Retrieved from Amazon.com. Digitized by BooksLib.com.

More, T. ([1516] 1901). *Utopia*. D. Price (Ed.). London: Cassell. Retrieved from Amazon.com. Kindle edition.

Morris, I. (2010). *Why the West rules for now: The patterns of history and what they reveal about the future*. New York: Farrar, Straus, and Giroux.

Mueller, D. C. (2003). *Public choice III*. Cambridge, UK: Cambridge University Press.

Mueller, D. C. (Ed.) (2005). *The dynamics of company profits: An international comparison*. Cambridge, UK: Cambridge University Press.

Murtaza, G., Abbas, M., Raja, U., Roques, O., Khalid, A., and Mushtaq, R. (2016). Impact of Islamic work ethics on organizational citizenship behaviors and knowledge-sharing behaviors. *Journal of Business Ethics, 133*(2), 325–333.

Nelson, P. (1974). Advertising as information. *Journal of Political Economy, 82*, 729–754.

North, D. C. (1981). *Structure and change in economic history*. New York: W. W. Norton.

North, D. C. (1990). *Institutions, institutional change and economic performance*. Cambridge, UK; New York: Cambridge University Press.

North, D. C. (1992). *Transaction costs, institutions, and economic performance*. San Francisco, CA: ICS Press.

Nozick, R. ([1974] 2013). *Anarchy, state, and utopia*. New York: Basic Books.

Olson, M. (1965). *The logic of collective action*. Cambridge, MA: Harvard University Press.

Olson, M. (1993). Dictatorship, democracy, and development. *American Political Science Review, 87*(3), 567–576.

Olson, M. (2000). *Power and prosperity: Outgrowing communist and capitalist dictatorships*. New York: Basic Books.

Ostrom, E. ([1990] 2015). *Governing the commons: The evolution of institutions for collective action*. Cambridge, UK: Cambridge University Press.

Paine, T. ([1776] 2003). *Common sense*. New York: New American Library (Penguin Group).

Paine, T. ([1791] 1894). The *writings of Thomas Paine*, Volume II: *1779–1792*. M. D. Conway, Ed. New York: G. P. Putnam's Sons.

Paldam, M., and Gundlach, E. (2008). Two views on institutions and development: The grand transition vs the primacy of institutions. *Kyklos, 61*(1), 65–100.

Paldam, M., and Gundlach, E. (2018). Jumps into democracy: Integrating the short and long run in the democratic transition. *Kyklos, 71*(3), 456–481.

Palfrey, T. R. (2016). Experiments in political economy. In J. Kagel, and A. E. Roth (Eds.), *The handbook of experimental economics*, Volume 2 (pp. 347–434). Princeton, NJ: Princeton University Press.

Pareto, V. (1927). *Manual of political economy* (Translated by Ann S. Schwier). London: Macmillan.

Pigou, A. C. (1920). *The economics of welfare*. London: MacMillan.

Pinker, S. (1995). *The language instinct: The new science of language and mind*. London: Penguin.

Pinker, S. (2011). *The better angels of our nature: The decline of violence in history and its causes*. New York: Penguin.

Pinker, S. (2018). *Enlightenment now: The case for reason, science, humanism, and progress*. New York: Penguin.

Pittau, J. S. J. (1967). *Political thought in early Meiji Japan*. Cambridge, MA: Harvard University Press.

Plato. ([360 BCE] 1894). *The republic*. Translated by B. Jowett. Oxford: Clarendon Press.

Pollitt, M. (2002). The economics of trust, norms, and networks. *Business Ethics, 11*(2), 119–128.

Posner, R. A. (1972). *Economic analysis of law*. Boston: Little Brown.

Potts, J. (2019). *Innovation commons: The origin of economic growth*. Oxford: Oxford University Press.

Rawls, J. ([1971] 2009). *A theory of justice*. Cambridge, MA: Harvard University Press.

Reeves, C. D. C. (1998). *Politics*. Indianapolis, IN: Hackett.

Rehnquist, W. H. (2001). *The Supreme Court* (revised edition). New York: Random House.

Romer, P. M. (1990). Human capital and growth: Theory and evidence. *Carnegie-Rochester Conference Series on Public Policy, 32*(1), 251–286.

Rose, D. C. (2011). *The moral foundations of ethical behavior*. Oxford: Oxford University Press.

Ross, W. D. (1925). *Ethica Nicomachea*. Oxford: Clarendon Press.

Rousseau, Jean-Jacques. ([1762] 1999). *Discourse on political economy and the social contract*. Translated by C. Betts. Oxford: Oxford University Press. Kindle edition.

Routledge, B. R., and von Amsberg, J. (2003). Social capital and growth. *Journal of Monetary Economics, 50*(1), 167–193.

Sagers, J. H. (2018). *Confucian capitalism, Shibusawa Eiichi, business ethics, and economic development in Meiji Japan*. New York: Palgrave Macmillan.

Sally, D. (1995). Conversation and cooperation in social dilemmas: A meta-analysis of experiments from 1958 to 1992. *Rationality and Society, 7*(1), 58–92.

Schmidtz, D., and Brennan, J. (2011). *A brief history of liberty*. New York: John Wiley & Sons.

Schultz, B., and Varouxakis, G. (Eds.). (2005). *Utilitarianism and empire*. Lanham, MD: Lexington Books.

Schumpeter, J. A. ([1912] 1934). *The theory of economic development: An inquiry into profits, capital, credit, interest, and the business cycle.* Cambridge, MA: Harvard University Press. Translation. Digitized by Transaction Publishers.

Schumpeter, J. ([1942] 2012). *Capitalism, socialism, and democracy* (2nd ed.). New York: Harper Row. (Kindle version from Start Publishing.)

Sen, A. (1999). *Development as freedom.* New York: Alfred A. Knopf.

Shackle, G. L. S. (1969). *Decision, order, and time in human affairs.* Cambridge, UK: Cambridge University Press.

Shepsle, K. A., and Weingast, B. R. (1981). Structure-induced equilibrium and legislative choice. *Public Choice, 37*(3), 503–519.

Sherman, N. (2007). *Stoic warriors: The ancient philosophy behind the military mind.* Oxford: Oxford University Press.

Shiller, R. J. (2012). *Finance and the good society.* Princeton, NJ: Princeton University Press.

Skaperdas, S. (1992). Cooperation, conflict, and power in the absence of property rights. *The American Economic Review, 82*(4), 720–739.

Skyrms, B. (2001, November). The stag hunt. *Proceedings and Addresses of the American Philosophical Association, 75*(2), 31–41.

Smith, A. (1759). *The theory of moral sentiments.* Retrieved from Amazon.com. Kindle edition.

Smith, A. (1776). *An inquiry into the nature and causes of the wealth of nations.* Retrieved from Amazon.com. Kindle edition.

Smith, V. L. (1962). An experimental study of competitive market behavior. *Journal of Political Economy, 70*(2), 111–137.

Solow, R. M. (1970). *Growth theory: An exposition.* Oxford: Oxford University Press.

Sowell, T. (2009). *Black rednecks and white liberals: Hope, mercy, justice and autonomy in the American health care system.* New York: Encounter Books.

Spencer, H. ([1851] 2011). *Social statics, or The conditions essential to human happiness specified and the first of them developed.* London: Chapman. Kindle version. Digitized and distributed by Amazon.com.

Spencer, H. ([1904] 2014). *An autobiography: Volume 1 and 2.* New York: D. Appleton. Retrieved from Amazon.com.

Spencer, H. (2011). *The complete works of Herbert Spencer.* Kindle edition. Retrieved from Amazon.com.

Stigler, G. J. (1951). The division of labor is limited by the extent of the market. *Journal of Political Economy, 59*(3), 185–193.

Tabellini, G. (2010). Culture and institutions: Economic development in the regions of Europe. *Journal of the European Economic Association, 8*(4), 877–716.

Tayler, T. (1811). *The politics and ethics of Aristotle.* London: Wilks.

Taylor, F. (1913). *The principles of scientific management.* New York: Harper and Brothers.

Temple, J., and Johnson, P. A. (1998). Social capability and economic growth. *Quarterly Journal of Economics, 113*(3), 965–990.

Thorpe, F. N. (Ed.) (1909). *The federal and state constitutions, colonial charters, and other organic laws of the states, territories, and colonies now or heretofore forming the United States of America.* Washington, DC: Government Printing Office.

Tinbergen, J. (1964). *Central planning.* New Haven, CT: Yale University Press.

Tullock, G. (1967). The welfare costs of tariffs, monopolies, and theft. *Economic Inquiry, 5*(3), 224–232.

Tullock, G. (1972a). *Explorations in the theory of anarchy.* Blacksburg, VA: University Publications.

Tullock, G. (1972b). The edge of the jungle. In G. Tullock (Ed.), *Explorations of the theory of anarchy* (pp. 65–75). Blacksburg, VA: Center for Study of Public Choice.

Tullock, G. (1977). *The logic of the law.* New York: Basic Books.

Tullock, G. (1980). Efficient rent seeking. In J. M. Buchanan, R. D. Tollison, and G. Tullock (Eds.). *Towards a theory of the rent seeking society* (pp. 97–112). College Station: Texas A&M Press. (Reprinted in R. D. Congleton, A. L. Hillman, and K. A. Konrad [2008], *40 years of research on rent seeking.* Heidelberg, Germany: Springer.)

Usher, D. (1981). *The economic prerequisite to democracy.* New York: Columbia University Press.

Vanberg, V. J., and Congleton, R. D. (1992). Rationality, morality, and exit. *American Political Science Review,* 86(2), 418–431.

Van den Berg, H., and Lewer, J. J. (2007). *International trade and economic growth.* New York: Taylor and Francis.

Viner, J. (1927). Adam Smith and Laissez Faire. *The Journal of Political Economy,* 198–232.

Von Mises, L. ([1927] 2002). *Liberalism in the classical tradition.* San Francisco, CA: Foundation for Economic Education.

Von Neumann, J., and Morgenstern, O. (1944). *Theory of games and economic behavior.* Princeton, NJ: Princeton University Press.

Wärneryd, K. (2019). The structure of contests and the extent of dissipation. In R. D. Congleton, B. Grofman, and S. Voigt (Eds.), *The Oxford Handbook of Public Choice,* Volume 1. Oxford: Oxford University Press, 519–532.

Weber, M. ([1905] 1958). *The Protestant ethic and the spirit of capitalism.* Translated by R. Parsons. New York: Scribner.

Weber, M. (1947). *The theory of economic and social organization.* Translated by R. Parsons. New York: Scribner.

Weir, D. (1997). Economic welfare and physical well-being in France, 1750–1990. In R. H. Steckel and R. Floud (Eds.), *Health and welfare during industrialization* (pp. 161–200). Chicago: University of Chicago Press.

Whiten, A. (1999). Parental encouragement in gorilla in comparative perspective: Implications for social cognition and the evolution of teaching. In S. Parker, R. Mitchell, and H. Miles (Eds.), *The mentalities of gorillas and orangutans: Comparative perspectives* (pp. 342–366). Cambridge, UK: Cambridge University Press.

Western canon. (2021, April 24). In *Wikipedia.* https://en.wikipedia.org/wiki/Western_canon. Subsection on "Ancient Greece."

Wilson, E. O. (2014). *The meaning of human existence.* New York: W. W. Norton.

# Index

Figures, and notes are indicated by *f* and n following the page number